WITHDRAWN

SURVEY DESIGN AND ANALYSIS
Principles, Cases and Procedures

301.8
H997s

SURVEY DESIGN
AND ANALYSIS

PRINCIPLES, CASES AND PROCEDURES

By *Herbert Hyman* COLUMBIA UNIVERSITY

With a Foreword by Paul F. Lazarsfeld

THE FREE PRESS, PUBLISHERS, GLENCOE, ILLINOIS

COPYRIGHT 1955 BY THE FREE PRESS, A CORPORATION

PRINTED IN THE UNITED STATES OF AMERICA

AMERICAN BOOK–STRATFORD PRESS, INC., NEW YORK

DESIGNED BY SIDNEY SOLOMON

LIBRARY OF CONGRESS CATALOG CARD NO.: 55-10996

To Helen

CATMay10'56

117553

To Helen

Preface

THIS BOOK is the product of twelve years of survey research experience. As the writer groped to apply his training to surveys of many types in a number of different countries, he faced many problems for which he did not have the answers and learned through hard experience some of the analytic principles which he has here presented. Whatever merit the book may have is the product of these years of experience and of the stimulation and guidance of colleagues in a number of agencies. My debt is great to the Program Surveys Division of the Department of Agriculture and the Morale Divisions of the German and Japanese Strategic Bombing Surveys, within which I worked, and to Rensis Likert, head of these agencies, and among others to such close friends and colleagues in these agencies as Richard Crutchfield, Daniel Katz and David Krech. Similarly, my experience in the Surveys Division of the Office of War Information has been invaluable to me and I wish to specially acknowledge my association with Elmo Wilson, chief of that Division and, again, Daniel Katz. My long connection with the National Opinion Research Center of the University of Chicago has been the source of much of my professional training and I especially appreciate the association with Clyde W. Hart, Director, and Paul B. Sheatsley and Herbert Stember, my co-workers in that organization. Opportunities to practice the trade or profession of a survey analyst also came my way in the course of other research undertaken in Norway, Austria, the United States and Japan and to the friends and colleagues in these undertakings I owe a debt of gratitude. To other friends and colleagues of those years, too many to be named, I am also greatly indebted.

My obligations to my teachers in Psychology and Social Psychology are great. More particularly, my training under F. S. Keller, Otto Klineberg, Gardner Murphy and John Volkmann must be acknowledged.

These constitute the intellectual *sources* from which this work stems. However, it was Paul F. Lazarsfeld who provided the inspiration for this actual work and the support for the undertaking. In addition, his sensitivity to the unsolved training problems of students and his imagination as to the direction a solution must take was a fruitful source of guidance in the writing of this work. For all these reasons, I owe him a special debt of gratitude. To Patricia Kendall, I also have a special indebtedness. A manuscript which she had prepared on problems of survey analysis was made available to the writer and was the basis for a number of sections now incorporated in the present work, notably in Part III and Appendix D. Her contribution to this volume is so considerable that it is specially acknowledged in the text. While Paul Lazarsfeld and Patricia Kendall are thus responsible for much in this volume, the writer must bear the sole burden for whatever defects remain.

I should also acknowledge aid from Henry Cooperstock in the early phases of the work, and the conscientious labors and assistance of Richard S. Halpern as a research assistant and Mrs. Michael McGarry who did the tedious work of typing the manuscript. I also benefited from the careful reading and criticisms of various drafts of the manuscript by Clyde W. Hart, I. L. Kandel, Daniel Katz, Charles Wright and Hans Zetterberg.

The text makes extensive use of unpublished studies from the National Opinion Research Center. Clyde W. Hart was most generous in making his complete files available to me, and again I must express my appreciation to him. I am indebted to Professor Sir Ronald A. Fisher, Cambridge, and to Messrs. Oliver and Boyd Ltd. Edinburgh, for permission to quote from their book *The Design of Experiments.*

HERBERT HYMAN

June, 1954
Columbia University

Foreword

BY PAUL F. LAZARSFELD

IN HIS OWN introductory pages Professor Hyman has clearly described the organization of his book, uses to which students and teachers can put it, and the principles by which he was guided in writing it. There is left for me the task of explaining the relationship of this text to the larger unit of which it is a part—the Columbia University Planning Project for Advanced Training in Social Research. The social sciences today find themselves in a situation which is often characteristic of a rapidly developing science. At the present time there is a wide gap between work being done by pioneers in the field and the resources available to students, even those on the graduate level, which would help them to keep in touch with the advancing frontier. One of the main tasks of the Columbia Project is to experiment with various means by which this gap can be filled. And the publication of Professor Hyman's book offers a welcome occasion to sketch this plan in some detail.

The Language
of Social Research

The success of any scientific endeavor depends on three elements: a clear identification of the objects to be investigated, an imaginative theory as to how they hang together, and clear insight into the specific problems of evidence and proof most adequate to the subject matter at hand. The Columbia Project, for the time being, is concerned mainly with the first and the third of these elements, and even with these in a rather specific way. We have assumed the task of clarifying for ourselves and for others the following sequence of problems:

(a.) How do we recognize and classify complex social objects? What is common in an effort to order workers by the degree of their industrial morale and underdeveloped countries by the degree of their industrialization? The problem can be restated in a variety of ways. Can the concepts of the social sciences be translated into indices amenable to empirical research? Or, more appropriate in the present context, how does one form the variables which are the building blocks of any systematic discourse on sociological subject matters?

(b.) How are these variables related to each other on their various levels of complexity? What do we mean if we inquire whether television programs make for juvenile delinquency or when we discuss the relations of a person's opinion to his position in the economic system? How do the century-old speculations on causality look when they are applied to concrete data about human behavior and social events? What can we say about the relation between the group and the individual when both are represented for us in sets of empirically ascertained properties?

(c.) We thus describe the social world by a set of variables and we study the interrelations between them. But the social world does not stay at rest and we do not want it to do so. As a result, changes over time become a third crucial area for investigation and clarification. Sometimes we want to predict from the past to the future; at other times we want to know what effect a specific interference has had either upon individual people or upon a whole social system. Finally we are interested in the whole dynamic interplay of variables which change over time for whatever reason. In its broadest meaning this is a question which history raises. Within the reach of today's empirical research it becomes a question of short range social and psychological change. Its methodological foundation is the study of repeated observations on the same individuals and collective units along a given set of variables.

(d.) The creation of variables, their interrelation and their interrelated change over time form the core of what one might call the language of empirical social research.* But it is not claimed that this language can express all the concerns of social scientists. It requires concrete investigations to decide, even in principle, whether we can express certain ideas of totality or "gestalt," or whether certain notions of striving towards goals or performing certain functions can be profitably studied in such variable-language. The way to find out is to take the writings of social scientists who have used a less atomistic and more qualitative approach. Do we gain in clarity by translating the statements into a variable-language or do we lose some essential aspect of their work if we make this effort? The border lines, the common ground and the possible distinctive realms of empirical social research and the more qualitative ways of analysis form an important part of the whole problem.

Professor Hyman's text is mainly dedicated to the second in this set of problems, the study of the interrelation between variables. But it is also the first example of the way in which the Columbia Project deals with all of the topics with which it is concerned, and therefore the character of this book as a training and teaching device deserves some programmatic comment. As the author himself explains in considerable detail, a great part of his discussion is centered upon a number of "cases." He has selected some of the most representative re-

---

* A rather detailed outline of this whole program together with a large number of research examples can be found in the first major publication of the Columbia Project, *The Language of Social Research*, eds. Lazarsfeld and Rosenberg (Glencoe: The Fress Press, 1955).

search publications and has come back to them every time he could use them to illustrate a point in his systematic presentation. This technique has been discussed in a year-long seminar held by the staff of the Project, and it will be followed in all future volumes. We are grateful to Professor Hyman for having caught the spirit of the common intent, and for providing us with a fine example to emulate. But the broader context of this effort deserves some additional comments.

Research Commentaries as Case Material for Advanced Training

The Columbia Project is working on educational designs for graduate education in the social sciences. This is likely to be watched with skepticism because it seems to contradict the spirit in which graduate work was introduced into American universities. The men who, toward the end of the 19th century, fought to establish graduate centers in this country stressed that graduate students should have complete freedom to choose what they wanted to learn and how they wanted to learn it. As a carry-over from these pioneering days the accent of many a discussion is still on the *differences* between graduate and college education. But they are both education after all. And wherever we want to transmit experience and to develop skills in the most efficient way there is a corresponding need for educational procedures. We should not let the terminology of 60 years ago obscure the reality of the present. At that time there were about 300 graduate students in the entire country, whereas today there are approximately 30,000. In 1890 one could hope that with a small and highly selected group each of the few graduate teachers would by intuition hit on an efficient way to transmit his knowledge. Today this is too great a chance to take, especially since the amount of material which students might, and perhaps should, learn has vastly increased both in volume and complexity. Can there be serious doubt that some element of rationalization has to be introduced in graduate education? Even after the general principle is conceded, there still remains the problem for each specific discipline: what are on the graduate level the appropriate tools to implement concretely its general educational program?

The medical school has its natural educational tool in the hospital and its patients. Law schools find theirs in court decisions.* But what of the social scientist? For a while it was thought that field work would provide the solution. First it was the social case type of field work—the 1892 catalogue of Colum-

---

* These references threaten to evoke another controversy: the distinction between professions and liberal arts on the graduate level. But this again is a hangover from an older period rather than a real issue in the contemporary academic policy. Consider the economists and the psychologists today. They have outlets in a broad variety of jobs, ranging from teaching and basic research to clinical (consulting) practice and service in private and public bureaucracies. That we don't have Schools of Economics and Psychology similar to our Law and Medical Schools is merely a result of historical circumstances: the institutional structure of our universities became set at a time when some of the "professions" already existed while others were not fully developed and their study was therefore first depreciated and then, in a compensatory mood, glorified as "liberal arts." Today both professional and liberal graduate education suffer equally from this lag between social function and institutional structure.

bia University emphasized that a major advantage of pursuing social studies in New York was that the city contained so much vice and poverty. Later on came the development of research bureaus, like the social research center at the University of North Carolina, the Bureau of Applied Social Research at Columbia and the National Opinion Research Center at the University of Chicago. But it soon became clear that mere participation in studies was not the solution. This kind of experience did not give the student a clear understanding of the logic which lay behind his work, and without such understanding he was unable to see the implications of what he was doing. Most of all, mere participation in studies could not help the student connect his empirical work with the store of theoretical and speculative thinking which was presented to him in systematic classroom lectures.

The solution with which the Columbia Project is experimenting is to prepare detailed commentaries on studies which have actually been carried out and are available in published form. This is what we mean here by "cases" of social research. Sometimes these commentaries pay particular attention to the techniques which researchers have used to solve a problem. At other times they lay greater emphasis on how an investigator's general concern led to the specific problem he undertook to study. In still other instances, emphasis is placed on the alternative ways in which an investigator might have proceeded, in an effort to weigh the merits and demerits of such decisions.

Such analytical commentaries are difficult to prepare and even more difficult to describe. Subsequent volumes from our Project will show the great variety which they can take and will, if possible, offer general rules for a general program documenting the logic and procedures of social research, an effort which we usually refer to as our "documentation program." For the present we shall publish them separately for each of the problem areas outlined above. As they come out we shall renew our efforts to explain their material and their purpose. The few remarks just made will, we hope, induce our colleagues to look at the present selections not only in terms of immediate utility but also as a first example of a basic position.

But from the beginning a possible misunderstanding has to be met. These social research cases should not be confused with another kind of educational idea which has long been described as the case study *method* in professional training. In its extreme form it was to provide a kind of educational self-service: from the cases the student could get whatever he needed by himself, and guidance or instruction by a teacher would not be required. This is not at all the philosophy behind our work. The study of case materials and systematic teaching can be combined in any number of ways. For example, one can conceive of a series of formal lectures organized around commentaries of the kind exemplified in Professor Hyman's book. Certainly, on the basis of our experience in preliminary trials, we would be tempted to de-emphasize the notion of self-service, and to assign the teacher a very strong role. As a matter of fact, toward the final stages of such training, the preparation, under proper guidance, of new analytical documents might itself be an important educational device, and, at the same time, a test as to the success of the whole program.

With some hesitation we might suggest an additional use of these commentaries on social research cases. An advanced graduate student must review a great deal of literature; he usually reads with haste to obtain the general flavor of the writers with whom he is expected to be familiar. Many graduate teachers know how badly their students assimilate what they read. Of course, a brilliant candidate, or one deeply involved in a specific topic, will probably acquire the ability to scrutinize a piece of writing closely so as to apprehend its structure and to relate it to other statements on the same subject which he has read. But here again there have been no provisions for systematic training in the art of incorporating a serious communication into one's own thinking. This is perhaps due to the emphasis on spontaneity which, as we said earlier, has been the guiding philosophy for graduate training. Those who endorse this philosophy in a superficial way only are likely to disdain any suggestion that young scholars, about to receive their doctor's degrees, should be provided with training material which helps them "learn how to read." But one could make the point that spontaneity and freedom of intellectual choice would be increased if graduate students had better and speedier command of the research material available to them. In this connection, teachers who use Professor Hyman's book might want to test, more or less informally, what effect his case materials and the connected problems he has worked out so carefully have on the ability of their students to understand the essential elements of other scientific writing more successfully.

Now to the specific part of the whole project which Professor Hyman has undertaken to develop—the study of the interrelation between social variables, sketched above briefly under point b.

The Idea
of Variable Language

Much of the discourse in the social sciences—even that which occurs on an abstract and qualitative level—can be clarified by finding answers to the following three questions: How many variables are involved in any particular sequence of thought? What is the specific nature of these variables? In what way are they supposed to be interrelated? These three questions clarify the *meanings* of propositions; they have no necessary connection with problems of quantitative evidence; they are related to empirical research only in an indirect way. In carrying out a particular piece of empirical research one is necessarily forced to answer these questions; one must therefore acquire some facility in dealing with them.

It is at this point that the importance of survey analysis comes in. There is no need here to define precisely what is meant by a survey, for its main features are easily recognized. The investigator decides what information he wants to collect and from which population; once he has collected the information he transforms it into some form of code, usually transferred to a mechanical punch card; he is then free to interrelate the various elements of his code with any degree of complexity which he chooses. Under this loose definition, the United States Census would be called a survey, and many of the data which an economist uses are probably not very different. It is true that much of the material now easily available to social scientists comes from attitude and opinion surveys. But this is quite accidental, and due only to the rapid development of this kind of work. From our point of view, the essence of a survey is that it is confined to, but can completely exhaust, all the possibilities inherent in a variable language.*

The central problem of Professor Hyman's book is thus the following: How does one translate ideas on social matters into variables, and how does one analyze the interrelations between these variables so that new ideas can be derived from them? It is not claimed, of course, that the procedures of variable language or the concrete procedures analyzed in Professor Hyman's book cover all that the social scientist has to say or wants to say. It is not even clear whether all empirical research, let alone more general reflections, can be carried on in this kind of discourse. What additional "languages" are needed for well-rounded social science must be left to future methodological investigations. But such efforts will undoubtedly be helped if at least one such system has been clarified as far as possible.

How far can such clarification be carried at any one specific moment? The methodologist is the first to assert that this is an ongoing effort which is never quite completed, and where the work of one scholar builds on the endeavors of his predecessors and awaits the achievements of his successors. Perhaps one way to exemplify this is to single out one line of continuity in social research from the Columbia Project. As Professor Hyman mentions, Part III of his book is built on previous work done by some of his associates at Columbia. Their central concern was to study the extent to which survey analysis permits statements on causal relationships. There is great danger, in discussing such a problem, that one gets immersed in discussions, where haziness in terminology and biases unconnected with the problem at hand can make any real progress difficult. The merit of the solution upon which Professor Hyman built and which he presents in his Chapter VII lies in the following idea.

We can define a research operation called "elaboration," consisting of the following three steps: Two attributes are cross-tabulated; then a third attribute, called a test attribute, is introduced. As a result of giving the test attribute different values, there develop certain partial relations between the original two attributes. This procedure of elaboration can lead to two main types of configurations between the three attributes, depending on the nature of the partial relationships. Next we can make certain assumptions as to the time sequence of the three attributes. Again, there are two main possibilities, according to whether the test attribute is assumed to intervene between, or to precede the two original attributes. The two statistical configurations and the two time orders thus result in four combinations, which, up to this point, have been defined in completely formal terms, without reference to any established terminology. If one then inspects these four main types, a good case can be made that they correspond to four modes of analysis for which a variety of descriptive terms is available. For easy communication, one might say that the four modes represent the uncovering of conditions, of contingencies, of spurious factors, and of interpretations. If we find that city size is positively correlated with the size of the crime rate, the following four elaborations are easily conceivable. The type of finding is only true for cities with specific ethnical composition (condition); it is not true

---

* It has sometimes been suggested that the kind of problem with which we are concerned here is better referred to as "multi-variate analysis" rather than as "survey analysis," because the latter term has so often been used in the restricted sense of opinion polling. But there was a time when this same term was used to describe all kinds of social inquiry, including vivid qualitative descriptions of social conditions within a specific group of people. Because it has had these varied, and extreme meanings, we feel justified in using it in the way which we specified.

if a managerial type of city government is set up (contingency); it is the result of previous criminal elements being more attracted to the larger cities (spurious factor); it occurs because the larger the city the greater the social isolation of people which, in turn, is followed by corrosion of moral standards (interpretation). The rich material of Chapter VII will leave no doubt as to what these four empirical modes are. For the present it is enough to focus on one point. The distinction between the four types cannot be controversial: they are developed in a completely formal way. Disagreement is possible only at a later stage where a specific analytical mode might be called explanation by one writer and interpretation by another. Even which one of them should be labeled as a causal relation becomes a secondary decision. The real importance of the formalization lies in the fact that we can clearly separate substantive distinctions and terminological disagreements.*

And yet this earlier effort in no way exhausted what could be done with this approach. It left especially two matters unsettled. For one, the notion of the time sequence of variables was discussed quite loosely. The four types of elaboration were developed under the assumption that the time sequence had been established somehow. In Chapter VII Professor Hyman discusses in great detail the problem of the time ordering of variables which can be carried out. He points out the difficulties in arriving at such an ordering, and offers illuminating examples as to procedures by which the research student can obtain the best possible answer.

On this point, then, the present text carried the original analysis forward. A second problem was raised and left unanswered in the early effort. The four major types of elaboration do not depend on having the three variables ordered in time. Any other ordering principle would also lead to four formal types. But their substantive meanings might change considerably. The two main ordering principles which were suggested for further investigation are of special importance for social psychologists and sociologists. One is the order of *generality* which would apply, for instance, if we were dealing with three variables like patriotism, honesty in dealing with the government, and saluting the American flag. The other ordering principle might be called one of *structural level*, exemplified by a set of variables like membership in an occupational group, employment in a specific factory, and membership in a special clique within the shop. In Chapter VI, Professor Hyman has given a large number of examples of the kinds of problems which such distinctions create. But it has not yet been possible to develop for this material a systematic formalization of the kind worked out for variables ordered in time; thus, the task of connecting the rich materials of Chapter VI with the more rigid procedures of Chapter VII still remains. It would have been a mistake to delay publication of the present volume until this difficult task is accomplished. It is to be hoped that the two chapters mentioned will stimulate other students to try their hands at this problem. By providing this opportunity Professor Hyman contributes to an ongoing effort to clarify long-standing philosophical problems in the light of modern procedures of social research.

---

* It was gratifying to note recently that this analysis was also found useful in the treatment of economic data. See Herbert A. Simon, "Spurious Correlation: A Causal Interpretation," *Journal of the American Statistical Association*, 49 (1934), pp. 467-479.

Some Additional Contributions

At one point the present book unavoidably overlaps with another unit in preparation by the Columbia Project, the first one listed above on the translation of concepts into systems of empirical indices. We have remarked in passing that coding is a typical phase in any survey work. Sometimes this term is used just to indicate the technical task of preparing collected information for quantitative analysis. But the term also has a deeper meaning, closely connected with the notion of a variable language. The concepts we use in our general thinking have many shades of meaning; these come into the foreground or recede according to the general context in which they are used. But when the same concepts are represented by the use of a relatively small number of variables, we commit ourselves to take into account certain sectors of a broad conceptual spectrum and to omit others. The concept of morale is an excellent example because it appears in many contexts when we study a factory, an army, or any other institution. Professor Hyman participated in a post-war study of morale among the Japanese population under various degrees of exposure to American bombing expeditions. He describes how the notion of morale first had to be broken down in its various dimensions of belief in the purpose of the war and in ultimate victory, confidence in leadership and fellow Japanese, psychological vitality, and so on. Then specific questions had to be devised which would permit the grading of each respondent along the various dimensions. Finally all the information had to be combined into one overall index of civilian morale.

Chapter III of the present book provides several other examples of this empirical complexity of conceptualization. They are included so that, from the beginning, students could be aware of how many problems lie behind the variables they manipulate in the analysis of a survey. But it was not the purpose of the present book to provide all the detail which would be necessary to clarify the whole road from a general intellectual imagery to an analysis of its main dimensions, from there to the choice of empirical indicators, and then finally to the formation of measurements, typologies, and other classificatory devices needed in empirical social research. In *The Language of Social Research* the first and the fourth sections are devoted to a programmatic discussion of this whole field of conceptualization. A subsequent publication of the Columbia Project will provide detailed case studies, prepared by other staff members over the last few years.

Special mention is due to two contributions which Professor Hyman has made, and which go beyond the original assignment he undertook. In Chapter I of his book he discusses in detail some problems which have resulted from the rapid growth of empirical social research since the first world war. The universities were not prepared for this swift development, and consequently social research has not yet been fully integrated into the general scheme of higher education. Most improvisations took the form of special bureaus, institutes and laboratories which were financed on a day-to-day basis by foundation grants, contracts with business organizations, and government subsidies. In many respects this had bad consequences. The scholars responsible for these institutes had to overemphasize their importance, and, as a result, came in conflict with the traditional humanistic interests of their colleagues in other sectors of the universities. The hierarchical organization necessary to carry out a research project, in some ways a healthy experience for graduate students, conflicted with an older tradition in which students, for better or for worse, were left to beat their own path through the academic forest. The role of the sponsor who provided money for projects was looked on with suspicion. The issue between basic and applied research became exaggerated. All of this is reminiscent of the period during the first half of the 19th century when the study of natural sciences was slowly integrated into the work of European and American universities. But this problem developed much more quickly in the case of social research, much larger budgets were involved, and the private universities, in particular, had to meet the issue under the strain of greatly decreased financial reserves. Professor Hyman has had firsthand contact with all of these problems at several universities and in several government agencies. His judicious presentation of some of the factors involved will help greatly to lift the discussion to a more rational level.*

Finally, in Part IV, Professor Hyman has put on the agenda a topic which will undoubtedly have to remain there for quite some time. What are the substantive contributions which survey work makes to social theory as well as to practical affairs? This is a vast topic and, for elucidation, will require help from many men who are involved in the three-cornered relation between social theory, empirical research and practical affairs. For the time being the Columbia Project is not equipped to give it full attention; but we appreciate the challenging examples which Professor Hyman has provided.

This Introduction was mainly concerned with the use of Professor Hyman's book in academic teaching. But it will certainly also find its place in the workshop of the commercial survey expert. The numerous specific instances and concrete problems which are included will stimulate his thinking and will often give him new ideas even if he will not always wish to follow up all theoretical details. Many of our commercial colleagues have the problem of training and of keeping alert a staff of assistants; a task which is not so different from training on the campus.

Finally it should be stressed how much the whole Columbia Project owes to its supervisory faculty committee, Professors Otto Klineberg, Robert Lynd, Robert Merton, Frederick Mills, Schuyler Wallace, for their time consuming and often difficult task of coordinating our specific enterprise with the general goals of Columbia's Faculty of Political Science. They acquitted their task with wisdom, tact, and often added helpful professional advice on specific subject matter. We hope that as the list of our documents grows they will feel that their efforts were not wasted.

---

* The institutional problems which survey centers create for the universities, and the matters of training and documentation mentioned above, can be understood only in a broad historical context. There have been quite a number of similar turning points in higher education over the past few hundred years. A careful study of past experiences—successes and failures—is part of the program of the Columbia Project. Professor Bernhard Stern has prepared an annotated collection entitled, "Historical Materials on Innovations in Higher Education." His work, carried out from the point of view of a sociologist, is now being discussed and extended by a group of historians of higher education. The final product will be published as part of the present series.

Contents

xix

Tables

Illustrative Materials
for Training

Part I

Part II

Part III

Part IV

A Guide to the Use of the Book

THE PRESENT WORK, intended as a manual for the training of students in survey analysis, is one of a series undertaken under the direction of Paul F. Lazarsfeld. The series is oriented to critical problems in the training of professional research workers in the social sciences and makes extensive use of case study and other training devices in addition to the usual textbook presentations of principles. While the general philosophy of the series has been well described by Professor Lazarsfeld in his Foreword it also seems desirable for the writer to describe his specific approach and to suggest features of the work which may be exploited. The ultimate value of the book will depend on skill and ingenuity in its use.

The training of a survey analyst requires first the imparting of technical knowledge. But technical knowledge is hardly sufficient. The student may be well schooled in principles of research but he must somehow be converted into the experienced and wise professional. While this can be achieved through slow maturing on the job, it is our hope that some approximation to this slow process may be achieved in the course of training itself. Actual experience in research provides at least three opportunities, and this work will attempt to simulate these opportunities.

First, there is the opportunity to practice the procedures of analysis in the course of concrete research studies. Confronted by a wide range of substantive and technical problems and immersed in the actual research process, the student ultimately develops sound judgment and skill plus efficiency in the way he applies technical principles.

In addition, technical principles of research are normally studied piecemeal. They become a list of separate fragments. By contrast, the actual research problem binds the principles into a unity. On the job, the student sees how the fragments fit, how organic is the total research process.

Second, he works in the context of practical reality. He must perforce

1

accommodate to the necessities imposed by the research operation. Deadlines, limited resources, pressures of various sorts call for compromises. The compromises must be made—but yet without severe sacrifice of ideals. Compensating for these hard aspects of reality are the gains that may come from working in large-scale research organizations, and the student must also learn how to exploit the good features of reality.

Third, there is opportunity to see the disparity between the academic finding and one that is useful either for practical or for theoretical purposes and ultimately to reduce the disparity through effective planning for the utilization of findings.

The book is written in such fashion as to simulate or provide analogies to these opportunities. More specifically, the writing is organized into four major parts. Part II and III provide the technical principles for analysis of surveys. Part I, a treatment of the institutional setting within which the analyst works and the problems which are the starting point for his inquiries, provides the initial setting within which these principles are taught. Part IV, a preliminary treatment of selected problems in the utilization of survey findings, provides a final setting for the learning of the technical principles. These two parts of the work should give the student vicariously some of the essential experiences of normal professional life.

Institutions do change and it may well be that some of the features described in Part I will not be present in the research situation of future generations of survey analysts. Thus Part I only outlines certain elements which are especially changeable and does not give specific data on costs and personnel requirements even though the analyst should be familiar with such details. The mature reader may feel Part I presents too harsh and critical a picture of the difficulties imposed on the researcher working within a particular institutional setting. The bias is there, but it is a conscious one. We saw no need to present an objective appraisal of all the good and bad features of large-scale survey research. The good features will automatically yield their benefits. It is the difficulties to which the analyst must be sensitive!

The technical principles of Survey Analysis have been separated into two major sections, Part II on Descriptive Survey Analysis and Part III on Explanatory Survey Analysis. The distinction is real, but not always operative. Many surveys as noted in the text combine features of description and explanation and require the integration of the technical principles which we have here separated. However, it seems an effective didactic approach to separate these Parts and present *simpler* analytic principles first. When these are effectively learned, it is easier for the student to embark on the especially complicated principles. Moreover in our judgment, a lamentable state of affairs exists which may be remedied by devoting special attention to Descriptive Survey Analysis. Students tend to disparage the descriptive survey as below them and thereby incapacitate themselves for a wide range of problems for which surveys are undertaken. In addition, they wish to appear sophisticated by accomplishing tricky and difficult explanatory analyses, and in the process forget the base upon which all these tricks rest. The treatment in Part II is intended to reinstate the dignity which the descriptive survey deserves, and to emphasize the essential workmanship which *all* analyses must exhibit.

Throughout all four parts of the work heavy emphasis is placed upon concrete cases. Illustrations, charts, figures, narrative accounts of surveys have been used. The emphasis on the concrete survey is intended to give the student the intimate feeling of a research undertaking, so that the formal principles are seen in operation. While there is nothing new in the use of examples, as such, we should like to point out certain special ways in which we have employed concrete cases.

First, we have relied on a *small number* of cases, which carry the running thread of the presentation in many places in the text. This, it was felt, would give the student greater sense of the unity of the research process than he would get if fragmentary and independent illustrations from a host of different surveys had been used. In addition, there is an advantage in *sheer* length of treatment of a given case. No student can be expected to understand the decisions made in the analysis of a survey or to grasp the complexity of the research process from a short illustration. The detail, the narrative, the flow of the total survey is needed, and the use of a small number of surveys, carefully chosen for their richness of content, is a desirable feature. To convey the quality of these surveys, we have incorporated an appendix which reproduces many of the documents employed in the original surveys. These documents are the concrete embodiments of the inquiries and increase the verisimilitude of the case studies. In addition, they may be studied directly for their value with respect to the pre-analytic stages of survey research. Supplementing the documents on our particular cases, we have presented in a separate appendix an assortment of other more general materials to illustrate the many details of survey research operations.

Our treatment of a given survey is broken frequently in the text by the discussion of abstract principles, thereby destroying the unity of the case; a word of explanation appears desirable. The historic discussions of case study as a method of teaching have pointed to the dilemma: Concrete case studies leave out the abstract principles which the student must learn. The exposition of abstract principles leaves out the exemplification of the principle in the concrete instance. We sought a compromise—articulate presentation of principles plus the concrete case. The integrity of the case perhaps can be restored, assuming it is lost by the frequent interruptions in the text, through reference to the *"Name and Study Index."* From this index, the student can recapture the biographical thread of a given study, by noting the different pages where the study is treated.

The cases used have been chosen with the goal of wide coverage of substantive problems, technical procedures, and research sites and to represent the endeavors of many different agencies and scholars. Thus, we hope to broaden the vista of the student by showing the many different situations possible, and to show that analytic skill is not the monopoly of any one scholar, or discipline, or country. Any writer is limited by his own experience, and certain of the cases used come naturally to mind because of past association with the actual research undertaking. The one failing in this respect which may be apparent in the work is the heavy emphasis on social psychological surveys rather than those from traditional subject matters in the field of commercial market research, labor force or economic research, or sociological research. This limitation is, we hope, not too serious. At least the analytic *principles* illuminated by our examples should be general for the wider range of surveys, and in many instances, the institutional setting will be the same no matter what subject matter. But, the restriction was not imposed merely by the writer's background. Despite attempts to broaden the range of disciplines covered in the cases, we were forced often into the social psychological realm in order to find illustrations of particular analytic problems.

Another feature characterizes most of the major cases used. They have been selected because they are *published* and available to the student, and their publication has been accompanied by much critical literature. We see a number of advantages. It is our belief that additional valuable training exercises can be invented *by the instructor* or the conscientious reader through the study of the original surveys and the published critiques. For example, the student can read portions of the original survey prior to the assignment of a particular portion of this text. From the comparison of the student's criticisms with the subsequent treatment in the text, he can observe what aspects he has missed, and just as well what aspects he may feel we have neglected. The disagreements and differences can then be the subject of classroom discussion.

Readings in the published critiques may yield still other gains. The critiques illustrate a number of central features of research. For one thing, they convey an essential feature of science as a human endeavor, the *tentativeness* with which discrete research is conducted and the attempt to achieve definitiveness through the *continuity* or cumulative efforts of many scientists. Each research worker is fallible, but in the interplay or opposition among scientists, improvement is effected. Consequently, published appraisals of another's research convey directly this feature of science. Moreover, by the study of such materials the student will understand the standards that will be applied by his professional colleagues, the requirements they will impose before accepting his research as at least approximating to the ideal, the crucial technical elements of a project upon which they focus and even the larger values they bring into play in evaluating research. And granted that reviews may on occasion be prejudiced, or replications tendentious in purpose, the student nevertheless, can sharpen his own judgment by considering the relevance of certain considerations that the most prejudiced critic may invoke. In addition, the diversity of published criticisms helps convey to the student the wide variety of standards applied to survey methodology and constitutes therefore an ideal antidote to orthodoxy or rigidity about research. Nor should we forget the sheer value of the dramatic in stimulating or electrifying the student. When one of our case studies, the first Kinsey Report, is greeted by one critic with the remark that: "It seems to me that the inadequacies in the statistics are such that it is impossible to say that the book has much value beyond its role in opening a broad field," while another comment contains the statement, "I am convinced that it is substantially sound," we think we have a dramatic issue for the student which leads him to profitable examination of the study.

Among the case studies of surveys that have been used, much controversy has attended four of our major examples: *The American Soldier, The Authoritarian Personality, The Kinsey Report, The Psychology of Social Classes.* All but the last have been subject to criticism of such elaborate character that it has even required monographic publication.[1] The remaining major cases, while not rich in controversy, have other values. For example, the Japanese Bombing Survey yielded a unique, lengthy published narrative account of the original research undertaking which presents the stops and starts, errors and revisions of plans, and the like.[2] *The People Look at Radio* has a companion volume representing a second or follow-up study which gives the student a sense of the changes that were made in research plans, design, objectives and analyses between the first and second inquiry.[3] Also, an appendix on the development of the questionnaire instrument is a unique narrative document capturing some of the thoughts of the analysts as they planned the undertaking. Similarly, the comparison of the first and second volumes of Kinsey's inquiry provides opportunity to observe the changes in methods and to evaluate the analysis in the light of the published critiques of the first report.

Detailed attention has been given to a number of other surveys. Durkheim's *Suicide* as an illustration of certain methodological problems of pri-

---

1. R. K. Merton and P. F. Lazarsfeld, Continuities in Social Research: *Studies in the Scope and Method of the American Soldier* (Glencoe: The Free Press, 1950); M. Jahoda and R. Christie, *Studies in the Scope and Method of the Authoritarian Personality* (Glencoe: The Free Press, 1954). The Kinsey Report produced a critical literature too vast to cite in entirety. For a distinguished methodological treatment, the reader is referred to the official Committee Report of the American Statistical Association. See: W. G. Cochran, F. Mosteller, J. Tukey, *Statistical Problems of the Kinsey Report* (Washington: The American Statistical Association, 1954).

2. D. Krech and E. Ballachey, *A Case Study of a Social Survey,* Japanese Survey, United States Bombing Survey, University of California Syllabus Series, Syllabus T.G. (University of California Press, 1948).

3. P. F. Lazarsfeld, and P. Kendall, *Radio Listening in America* (New York: Prentice-Hall, 1948).

mary and secondary analysis is almost unparalleled. Moreover, it shows that the solution to many survey problems is not so much at the procedural level as at the logical level and perhaps by example will stimulate the speculative or creative powers of the student. Perhaps, too, it will give the student some sense of the long history of the analytic problems in surveys, and correct any tendency to think of all this as new and modern. Among the other major cases used, those on the atom bomb and bond redemption have lengthy original treatments in book form. In addition, the atom bomb inquiry provides a rare instance of two parallel surveys and analyses bearing on the same problem and undertaken by different methodologies. The comparison of the two surveys may be made into an effective exercise. The remaining major case, industrial morale, has had detailed discussion in a number of sources.

All of the case study materials, however, are narrative. The student is exposed to them and may or may not read the passages—let alone absorb the lesson. Consequently, the text plus appendices contain a series of exercises, which the student must complete. These aim to provide actual practice for him, and are so constructed in many instances as to pose a particular problem to which he must himself find the solution.

Among other aids to training, we might remark on the extensive citations to other methodological works, many of them not discussed in the text. Our intention was to provide suggestions for collateral reading wherever the student is interested or the instructor deems it desirable.

A final word about the text. We have tried to be comprehensive in our treatment of all the major analytic problems. There may well be omissions. A limitation for the *beginning* student may be the restriction of the work to survey *design* and *analysis*. It is our assumption that the reader has some familiarity with the non-analytic aspects of survey research: interviewing, coding, sampling, pre-testing, etc. No analyst can function effectively without knowledge of the total research operation, but since the task of treating survey analysis is itself a major one, we must leave to other courses, more general works, and to experience itself the fundamental task of imparting these essentials. However, the omissions are a lesser concern to us than the danger that the work may be uneven in the level of treatment. We have kept in mind as the reader the relatively advanced student in Social Psychology and Sociology. Perhaps certain portions may be too difficult for given students and classes; other portions may be superfluous and already in the student's repertory. The text has been broken into frequent sections and chapters within the major parts and perhaps discrete readings can be so fashioned as to meet special needs.

Part I

THE ORIENTATION
OF THE SURVEY ANALYST

Introduction

THE TRAINED SURVEY ANALYST has a body of general knowledge as to the principles and procedures to be followed in the treatment of quantitative data. But skill in the practice of survey analysis requires much more than merely such knowledge. The formal features of survey analysis are no different at an *abstract* level from the procedures of more traditional scientific work. They were derived from general traditions of science and aimed at the same basic problems. Survey research, like other forms of research, involves appropriate techniques of observation or measurement of phenomena, the detection of regularities or uniformities in these phenomena, the formulation of hypotheses and larger bodies of theory, and the accumulation of reliable knowledge of the phenomena and evidence in relation to the hypotheses. Like other forms of research, it is dedicated to objectivity and concerned with accuracy; each individual inquiry is provisional, but the totality of inquiries are cumulative. Like some forms of research, it makes considerable use of technical apparatus and statistical methods. But awareness of these universals will not make a skilled survey analyst. All these aspects take on a *specialized form* suited to the peculiar operating circumstances of survey research.

It is the *knowledge* of effective application of general principles of scientific methods; of the peculiar modifications of procedures within the framework of general principles, that must be learned. To be an effective survey analyst one must know how to relate general methodological principles to the particular operating context of a survey. Now the skilled practitioner of survey analysis has the feel of this context through long experience, for which there is no real substitute. How then shall we achieve the same objective? We aim to approximate such experience for the student first through the use of many examples from past surveys which reproduce certain essential features and circumstances of survey research operations and convey the variety of problems which initiate inquiries. In so doing, we hope that the student will gain an understanding of the technical decisions and special modifications of more general scientific method that occur in a survey.

In this portion of the text, these same examples are so used as to convey the general social setting of survey research and to develop an institutional analysis of survey operations. Our goal here is to enlarge the analyst's vision beyond the sheer technical realm. Thus, we hope that he will anticipate the professional role in which he will function and the pressures that will affect him so that ultimately he will be able to combine technical competence with professional responsibility for the proper application of his techniques.

8

The General Context of Survey Research and the Proper Orientation of the Analyst

WE PRESENT first brief descriptions of seven well known published surveys. These case studies do not adequately represent the great variety and number of inquiries that have been conducted by survey methods. Nor do we present a complete description of each survey. But even this brief treatment of a small number of surveys will be revealing of the conditions of survey research.

We shall not discuss the implications of any of the cases at this point. These cases will be alluded to at various places in the text and treated for their relevance to particular topics. The reader, however, might note what he regards as salient features of the methodology and keep in mind certain questions which we shall raise about these cases. For example, in this section we shall ask ourselves what is there to be noted about the size of inquiry in survey research? What are the consequences of this factor for the analyst? We shall ask about the degree to which survey research occurs in an organizational context, and what are the consequences of the organizational setting for the analyst? We shall ask about the forms of sponsorship of inquiry. What are some of the varied implications of different sources of sponsorship, and financial support for the analyst?

Survey #1—Industrial Absenteeism: [1] An inquiry was initiated in 1943 by the Surveys Division of the Office of War Information of the United States Government to establish certain facts about the nature and extent of industrial absenteeism in war industry and to determine some of the factors leading to such absence. The social atmosphere in which the research was conducted was emotional and partisan. Absenteeism was often identified as sheer malingering on the part of labor and as a national evil reaching such magnitude as to endanger the war effort. Some discussion of punitive legislation against absent workers as a remedial procedure had started. As the original analysts remark "the average discussion failed to distinguish between involuntary absence and actual truancy, and the elementary question as to whether there was really any problem of absenteeism was not voiced above a whisper."

A total of 1800 respondents representing samples of 100 workers systematically drawn from the rolls of each of 18 different plants were interviewed. The 18 plants were selected to represent both good and bad community living conditions in the following industries: shipbuilding, electrical equipment, non-electrical machinery, aircraft, ordnance, and non-ferrous metals. The rates of absence for each plant as a unit were computed and the individual rates of absence for each worker were determined from the plant records. The phenomenon of variation in absenteeism rates at both the plant and individual level was related to the factual characteristics of the workers involved, to their individual conditions of work and to a variety of attitudes of satisfaction with the plant and the community. Such factors were determined in the course of interview. Other hypothesized correlates of absenteeism such as the objective in-plant and community conditions were determined through observation and the use of informants. In addition, approximately 150 workers known to have been recently absent were interviewed intensively for a detailed account of their behavior.

Survey #2—Public Opinion and the Atom Bomb: [2] In 1946, the Committee on Social Aspects of Atomic Energy of the Social Science Research Council planned an inquiry into the thinking of Americans about the atomic bomb and international affairs. Grants of approximately $48,000

---

1. This study is described most elaborately in D. Katz and H. Hyman, "Industrial Morale and Public Opinion Methods," *Int. J. Opin. Attit. Res.*, Vol. 1, #3, 13-30. Reference is also made to particular aspects of the analysis in: Morale and Motivation in Industry by Katz in *Current Trends in Industrial Psychology* (Pittsburgh: University of Pittsburgh Press, 1949). A copy of the questionnaire used in the study of industrial absenteeism appears in Appendix A.

2. For a summary treatment of the inquiry, the reader is referred to L. S. Cottrell and S. Eberhart, *American Opinion on World Affairs* (Princeton, Princeton University Press, 1948). For a detailed report the reader is referred to *Public Reaction to the Atomic Bomb and World Affairs* (Cornell University, April, 1947). (litho) This description applies to the first of two inquiries. The design in actuality involved parallel surveys both before and after the Bikini Atom-Bomb Test. However, the before and after measurements to determine the impact of the Bikini Test on public sentiments do not concern us here. A copy of the questionnaire used in the study of public opinion and the atomic bomb appears in Appendix A.

were made by the Rockefeller Foundation and the Carnegie Corporation and an elaborate program of surveys was initiated. Approximately 3000 respondents representing the national population were interviewed by the American Institute of Public Opinion and a parallel inquiry was conducted by the Survey Research Center of the University of Michigan on a national sample of about 600 respondents.

Only a few months prior to the inquiry the Atomic Energy Commission of the UN had been established. Deliberations as to international control of the atomic bomb were under way, and disputes among the nations as to the type of controls to be required and the order of procedures for establishing international control occurred within the next two year period. As a general background to policy formulation, factual information on the public's views was desired. Moreover, it was felt that the average citizen "confronted by the necessity of participating in decisions of incalculable importance" would be more effectively guided if he had at his disposal factual information on the public's thinking.

To describe American opinion in this realm, the analysts inquired into the public's awareness of the existence of the atomic bomb, their knowledge of such specific facts as the mode of construction, the government officials who were responsible for atomic bomb policy, which countries possessed the bomb, etc., their degree of concern about the bomb and their attitudes towards international control of the bomb. The opinions that prevailed were described for the public as a whole and separately for major segments of the population.

In addition to the questions specifically on the atomic bomb, the analysts inquired into opinions as to international affairs generally. The extent of support for the UN as an organization, support for American loans to other countries, and attitudes towards Russia, for example, were determined. Similarly, in addition to specific knowledge about the atomic bomb, the analysts inquired into the person's general awareness and knowledge about a variety of international events.

Survey #3—American Opinion on Commercial Radio: [3] In the winter of 1945, the National Association of Broadcasters commissioned "a national survey of the public's understanding and acceptance of radio in the United States. The object was to assess the strengths and weaknesses of the radio industry, to ascertain where radio stands with the public, in order to blueprint a sound plan of action for the future of broadcasting." [4]

The NAB commissioned the National Opinion Research Center to con-

---

3. A copy of the questionnaire used in the study of American opinion of commercial radio appears in Appendix C.

4. The detailed report of the study is presented in P. F. Lazarsfeld and H. Field, *The People Look at Radio* (Chapel Hill: University of North Carolina Press, 1946). The quotation used appears on p. vii and is quoted by permission of the publisher.

duct the investigation and the nationwide inquiry was carried out at an approximate cost of $10,000. Following the collection of data, the Bureau of Applied Social Research, Columbia University, was asked to cooperate in the analysis and interpretation of the findings.

The social context in which the inquiry was undertaken is noted in the published report as involving a concern on the part of the radio industry to "mold a constructive program of action from the great variety of forces which impinge upon it" and if we elaborate upon some of these forces we note that this was a period of considerable criticism on the part of certain individuals and groups of the commercial character of American radio and its presumed neglect of its public responsibility for providing more enlightenment in its programming.[5] Such critics were asserting their views with the hope of some redress being achieved through the regulatory powers of the Federal Communications Commission.[6]

Approximately 2500 respondents were queried by personal interview.[7] Satisfaction with the radio industry as an institution, with specific types of programs, with radio advertising, etc., were determined and attitudes towards government regulation of stations were investigated. In addition, satisfaction with other media and community institutions, satisfaction with forms of advertising other than radio commercials and attitudes towards government control of industries other than radio were also determined.

Such opinions were related to personal characteristics of the respondent such as the extent of his radio listening and established for such sub-groups in the population as the educated and uneducated, men and women, young vs. old, and small town vs. big city dwellers.

Survey #4—Prejudice & Personality: The American Jewish Committee in 1944 invited a group of scholars to a conference at which a research program on the problem of prejudice was outlined. Ultimately out of this conference grew an organized department of Research which planned a series of inquiries into the problem. Among these inquiries was an elaborate study oriented to the basic proposition that certain factors in the personality of modern man predispose him to hostility to racial and religious groups.

---

5. Klapper refers to such vivid examples of criticisms of radio as the remark of DeForest, inventor of the audion tube, to the National Association of Broadcasters that they "have debased this child (radio was his invention or child), you have sent him out on the street in rags of ragtime, tatters of jive and boogie-woogie, to collect money from all and sundry for hubba hubba and audio jitterbug. . . ." For this and other demonstrations by critics, the reader is referred to *The Effects of Mass Media* (Columbia University: Bureau of Applied Social Research, 1950) (mimeo), Memorandum I, pp. 3-5.

6. For a description of the regulatory powers of the Federal Communications Commission and the character of official criticism of the radio industry the reader is referred to the report of the Commission, *Public Service Responsibility of Broadcast Licensees,* reprinted in B. Berelson and M. Janowitz, *Reader in Public Opinion and Communication* (Glencoe: The Free Press, 1950), 252-262.

7. This is a minimal statement of the size of inquiry. It is noted that two supplementary inquiries were made to refine some of the problems inadequately treated in the first inquiry. These additional inquiries involved another 1500 respondents.

This inquiry ultimately was published in the volume *The Authoritarian Personality,* and was intended as a long-range contribution to the work of the agency.[8] The aim was not immediate implementation of the findings in a defense program against anti-Semitism, but rather to contribute to fundamental knowledge as to the sources of anti-Semitism and as an empirical test of a series of basic scientific hypotheses as to the correlates of the phenomenon of prejudice. Nevertheless, it should be noted that the context of the research was not the quiet atmosphere that might accompany a purely scientific inquiry. Note the relatively recent persecution of Jews in Nazi-Germany, a concern about continuing, if latent, anti-Semitism, and considerable confusion among scholars of various disciplines and ordinary but articulate individuals as to the extent and nature of prejudice.

Between the years of 1945–46 the inquiry was conducted under the joint sponsorship of the Berkeley Public Opinion Study and the Institute of Social Research by a team of social scientists including T. W. Adorno, Else Frenkel-Brunswik, Daniel J. Levinson, and R. Nevitt Sanford, in collaboration with Betty Aron, Maria Hertz Levinson, and William Morrow. Grants of considerable magnitude were made available by the American Jewish Committee and supplementary grants were made by the Social Science Research Council, the Rosenberg Foundation, the Research Board of the University of California, the Institute of Social Sciences of the University of California, and the Graduate Division of Western Reserve University.

The theoretical orientation of the investigators led to the view that anti-Semitism was part of a pattern of more generalized sentiments of prejudice, and that these were in turn part of a broad coherent pattern of political and social convictions. The individual characterized by such a pattern of authoritarian sentiments was believed to have derived these sentiments from a more basic personality syndrome which in turn had its roots in certain child and infantile experience. Consequently, the analysts measured by means of written questionnaires such variables in the sample of approximately 2000 respondents as anti-Semitism, more generalized ethnocentrism, politico-economic ideology, and more basic personality traits. A smaller sample of respondents who exhibited particular patterns of attitudes as revealed by the questionnaires were subsequently interviewed in order to establish in detail their personality traits and developmental histories so as to test the major hypotheses.

Survey #5—American Sexual Behavior: Beginning in 1938, Alfred C. Kinsey and his associates began conducting interviews on the sexual behavior of Americans. Their concern was to collect sufficient information to describe American sexual behavior, and to establish what factors account for individual differences in sexual behavior and for group differences

8. T. W. Adorno, *et al., The Authoritarian Personality* (New York: Harpers, 1950).

among the various major segments of the population. The findings based on approximately 5300 interviews with American white males represent the substance of what has been known as "The Kinsey Report." [9]

The National Research Council's Committee for Research on Problems of Sex administered the necessary funds which were granted by the Rockefeller Foundation in support of the inquiry. Additional support was obtained from Indiana University.

While the investigation was an objective factual one, the auspices academic and the purposes scientific, it should again be noted that the atmosphere of the inquiry was far from serene. As the writers note "the failure to learn more about human sexual activity is the outcome of the influence which the custom and the law have had upon scientists as individuals, and of the not immaterial restrictions which have been imposed upon scientific investigations in this field." Further, they declare that it was necessary to assume deliberately an orientation towards their work in which "no preconception of what is rare or what is common, what is moral or socially significant, or what is normal and what is abnormal has entered into the choice of the histories or into the selection of the items recorded on them." The writers also note during the first two years of their investigation that "there were attempts by the medical association in one city to bring suit on the ground that we were practicing medicine without a license, police interference in two or three cities, investigations by a sheriff in one rural area."

Through personal interviews, a detailed history of the sexual behavior of each respondent was obtained, and data were collected on the person's personal characteristics. Sexual behavior was described essentially in terms of orgasm, and the incidence and frequency of orgasm via different sources, i.e., masturbation, nocturnal emission, homosexual outlet, intercourse of a pre-marital or extra-marital or marital nature, etc., were determined. Total outlet, the sum of sexual behavior from all sources, was related to such factors as age, education, religion, place of residence, and the like. Specific modes of outlet were also related to such characteristics.

Survey #6—Class Consciousness: [10] In 1945, Richard Centers planned a survey to collect data which would provide a factual basis for testing past theories about the problem of class consciousness. The facilities of the Office of Public Opinion Research of Princeton University were made avail-

9. A. C. Kinsey, W. B. Pomeroy and C. E. Martin, *Sexual Behavior in the Human Male* (Philadelphia, Saunders, 1948). The publication of the second volume in the series, on female sexual behavior, creates some confusion in terminology. Unless otherwise noted all later references are to the first volume. The number of interviews is taken as 5300 on the basis of Kinsey's statement. For a discussion of inadequate reporting of the correct number of observations for given findings, see W. A. Wallis, "Statistics of the Kinsey Report," *J. Amer. Stat. Assoc.,* 44, 1949, 463-484.
10. The study is described in detail in Richard Centers, *The Psychology of Social Classes* (Princeton: Princeton University Press, 1949). A copy of the questionnaire used by Centers in his study of class-consciousness may be found in Appendix A.

able and through the offices of Hadley Cantril, funds for conducting the research were obtained. The theory to be tested stated that "a person's status and role with respect to the economic processes of society imposes upon him certain attitudes, values and interests relating to his role and status in the political and economic sphere . . . further that the status and role of the individual in relation to the means of production and exchange of goods and services gives rise in him to a consciousness of membership in some social class which shares those attitudes, values and interests."

The aim of research was theoretical, to provide an objective test of specific hypotheses growing out of this general "interest group theory of social classes." The mode of testing these hypotheses will be clear shortly, but the larger significance of the problem was always in the scene. Centers was concerned with class conflict as "the most serious and central social problem of our era," with the contribution that social scientists could make to understanding upheavals, crisis, social change. He quotes in support of the need for such research the remarks of Robert Lynd: "Current social science plays down the omnipresent fact of class antagonisms and conflicts. . . . Social science does this because the concepts of 'class' and 'class struggle' lead straight into highly inflammable issues. . . . The body of fact and theory around the highly dynamic situation of class conflict will have to be much more realistically and centrally considered if social science is to deal adequately with current institutions. The issue here does not call for the lining up of social scientists on either side of this conflict situation. The need is rather to analyze closely and realistically this stubborn and pervasive complex of factors." [11] Twelve hundred respondents representative of the national adult white male population were assigned for interview.[12] To test the theory a

---

11. R. Lynd, *Knowledge for What* (Princeton: Princeton University Press, 1939). By permission of the author and publisher. T. H. Pear, the British social psychologist, discussing at about the same time as Lynd the social status of the *psychologist* and its effect on his work makes a somewhat similar point to Lynd. He remarks: "At present, British and perhaps most American psychologists are explicitly middle-class in their attitude. They aim at a 'middle of the road' treatment and a classless outlook. This however is apt to result merely in a middle-class account of the middle-class mind. . . . For the latter part of his life and almost until his last days, Freud was rich. Moreover during the whole of his professional career he was a consistently individualistic piece-worker, for he held no public appointment. If these facts had not influenced his general outlook Freud would not have been human. Professor C. G. Jung has mixed with rich people for many years and has spent most of his life in a beautiful, wealthy town in a fortunate country. Adler lost money by having to begin again after his split with Freud, and died while fulfilling the heavy demands of a lecture tour. It seems certain that he understood poor people, and he is naturally the father of the inferiority-complex." See "The Social Status of the Psychologist and Its Effect upon His Work," *The Sociol. Rev.* (England), 34, 1942.

12. While the sample size was initially 1200, Centers notes that due to "unforeseen circumstances of various kinds" only approximately 1100 of the assigned respondents were interviewed. This fact emphasizes a distinction too frequently neglected between the sample as it is *designed initially* and the *obtained sample*. The discrepancy between these two is a function of operating conditions of a variety of sorts; some respondents refuse, others are not available, given types are hard to find, interviewers depart from their instructions, etc. Such departures from the original design must be considered in relation to the dangers of bias, and can be forgotten when the distinction between *plan* and the *execution of a plan* is not borne in mind.

questionnaire was developed which covered the following three areas: a. Basic politico-economic orientation was measured by a battery of six questions, covering the belief that America is a land of opportunity, the belief that greater political power for workers would lead to greater good for everybody, the belief that government control of industries would have favorable economic consequences, endorsement of the view that government's primary responsibility is to guarantee the individual's economic security, support of labor in labor-management conflicts, and the belief that employers take advantage of workers.[13]

A number of other questions dealt with the general ideological area but were not part of this battery, e.g., vote in 1944 presidential election, union membership, belief that gains derive from union membership.

Outside of this ideological domain, there were some other attitude and opinion questions asked which were designed to cover the more diffuse value systems and psychological tendencies of the respondent.

b. Class consciousness was measured by a question on the respondent's subjective class identification, and a number of questions on what might be labelled the phenomenology of class.

c. Measures of the person's objective position included an interviewer's rating of standard of living, and two indices derived from his occupation: the degree to which he had power or control over others by virtue of his occupation and the general hierarchical position of his occupation.

The test of the theory involved correlating the various stratification indices with the measures of class consciousness and politico-economic ideology. Correlations were determined between the *individual* measures or questions and between two *indices* obtained by pooling the six ideological questions into an over-all measure and the three stratification measures into an over-all measure.

Survey #7—War Bond Redemption: [14] From the beginning of World War II the Treasury Department of the United States Government sponsored a series of surveys which were conducted by the Division of Program Surveys of the Bureau of Agricultural Economics of the Department of Agriculture. The general purpose of these surveys was to guide policy and action related to problems of inflation control. At the end of 1945 the Treasury requested a study which would provide "information permitting a prediction of the course of war bond redemptions during the following year. The end of the war in August had resulted in a marked increase in redemptions and Treas-

---

13. We have presented only one aspect of the question, generally the "radical" aspect. For the exact wording and the opposing alternatives provided for the respondents, see Centers, *op. cit.*, pp. 39-40.

14. The description of this survey is taken from a summary account by D. Cartwright, Survey Research: Psychological Economics, in J. G. Miller, ed., *Experiments in Social Process* (New York: McGraw Hill, 1950). Reprinted by permission of the publishers. A comprehensive treatment of this study in book form by Cartwright is now in press.

ury officials now wanted to know what effects on redemptions there would be as a result of reconversion and the appearance of consumer goods on the market."

A decision to conduct a survey of a sample of family units representing the national population emphasizing certain areas of inquiry was made, and the theoretical orientation underlying the decision is clearly noted. The analysts believed that one of the major difficulties in predicting economic trends was the "absence of direct empirical evidence concerning the operation of the causal determinants" of such trends. This absence in their judgment was a function of the lack of data on sub-groups and individuals, since these predictions in the past were made from such aggregate indexes as national income, national employment, etc. "Such indexes shed no light on the differential effect that these factors have on different segments of the population, nor do they make provision for differential motivation among different segments of the population." These hypothesized defects were remedied in the planning of this survey. Required information for the prediction was to be obtained from the analysis of: A: objective economic data on distribution of bond ownership among various segments of the population and corollary data on the family's economic vulnerability in terms of such facts as other forms of savings and employment status, and B: of psychological data on the cognitive and motivational factors underlying buying and keeping or redeeming bonds examined in relation to various anticipated economic developments in the country.[15] Thus, the analysts asked questions in each family as to the size of the bond holdings, amount and type of other savings held, occupation, and type of industry (e.g., war industry), presence of children, and questions as to the conception of bond holdings as a "nest-egg" or as a source of money for routine purchases, on the existence of particular plans for future spending, etc. and in the light of these findings could estimate the consequences of various events. Thus, for example the occupations of the large bond holders were found to be such that they would be least affected by reconversion unemployment. Similarly, the return of consumer goods to the market would not be too significant because bond holders were planning to keep their bonds till maturity and their circumstances were such that they seemed capable of carrying out the intentions.

What common features has the student noted about these seven surveys that he must be aware of and skilled to treat if he is to be an effective analyst? We shall discuss these below. While in practice they are interconnected, we shall describe each one separately for purposes of clarity.

---

15. For a short general treatment of the formal problems of design and analysis of opinion surveys intended for prediction purposes the reader is referred to H. Hyman and P. B. Sheatsley, "The Use of Surveys to Predict Behavior," *International Social Science Bulletin*, 1953, 5, 474-481. For a treatment of prediction surveys in the economic realm, see L. Moss, "Sample Surveys and the Administrative Process, *ibid.*, 482-494.

Size of Inquiry
and Its Consequences

First we may note a common feature of all of the inquiries described that
characterizes survey research. All such inquiries are massive in size. We
note such numbers of cases as 2000, 5300, 1800, and the like. Generally, the
number of observations that must be treated or manipulated far exceeds
this total number of cases since it is characteristic of these inquiries that
many factors are measured simultaneously in each case. Moreover in these
surveys the results are generally tabulated not merely for the entire number
of cases but tabulated separately for many sub-groups within the study in
order to provide more precise descriptions and by revealing variations in
the phenomenon to demonstrate its relation to other factors. Consequently,
the amount of processing and tabulating of data is great.

Contrary to usual belief, large size inquiry has been a persistent feature
of social research and is not merely characteristic of modern work although
its frequency may have increased. For example, in early work in Social Psychology, we find inquiries involving thousands of observations. Murphy,
Murphy and Newcomb in what is the best summary of empirical research
in the attitude measurement field prior to World War II note inquiries
such as the following: As early as 1928 Bogardus conducted an inquiry into
social distance toward ethnic groups involving 1725 cases; Katz and Allport
in 1931 conducted a study of social attitudes among college students involving 1406 respondents; in 1932 L. D. White's inquiry into attitudes toward
public employment involved approximately 7000 observations.[16] If we go
back to the classic origins of the social survey in Europe, we also find inquiries of almost a century ago involving thousands of observations.[17]

It is this feature of survey research which gives the findings stature, for,
if other features of the methodology are up to high standard, the increase
in size gives us greater confidence in the stability of the findings, permits of
generalizations, and provides enough play for the analyst to engage in descriptions of sub-groups within the total inquiry. But, it is also this feature
of survey research which makes it imperative that the analyst have *consid-*

---

16. All of these early social psychological inquiries of a survey nature are reported in Chap. XIII
of Murphy, Murphy and Newcomb, *Experimental Social Psychology* (New York: Harpers, 1937).
For an earlier summary see R. Bain, "Theory and Measurement of Attitudes and Opinions,"
Psychol. Bull., 27, 1930, 357-379.

17. For a concise history of the origins of survey research, the reader is referred to Chapter I
of M. Parten, *Surveys, Polls, and Samples* (New York: Harpers, 1950). For a more detailed history
the reader is referred to D. D. Caradog-Jones, *Social Surveys* (London: Hutchinson, 1949).

For a historical treatment with special reference to the origins of sampling methods in survey
research, the reader is referred to F. F. Stephan, "History of the Uses of Modern Sampling Procedures," *J. Amer. Stat. Assoc.*, 1948, 43, 12-39.

erable skill in the manipulation of quantitative data, for the normal pro-cedures of case study, qualitative analysis, or immersion in the data are inadequate *by themselves* to the task of ordering or comprehending such a volume of data or processing it efficiently and expeditiously. But while this has been always the fact, a revolution in the mode of treatment of such data, arising out of technological change, has more recently occurred. It is almost universal in current survey research that automatic or machine methods of processing data are used. It is therefore a further demand upon the survey analyst that he have *considerable familiarity with machine methods.*

The very history of the origins of the International Business Machines Corporation demonstrates the need: [18] While Dr. Herman Hollerith was working on the compilation of the 10th Census of the United States (1880), he became aware of the enormous problems involved in the reduction of great quantities of data into usable form. The Census Bureau was still com-piling data in 1885 that had been collected five years earlier. It was obvious that if the country's rate of growth continued, the time would not be far off before a new census would have to be undertaken before the previous one had been published. Dr. Hollerith therefore devoted himself to developing a mechanical tabulating method.

By 1887, when the 10th Census was processed, he had worked out the major features of his recording, compiling, and tabulating system. Accord-ing to a prearranged code, data were transferred by means of punched holes to paper strips (Hollerith soon found cards more efficient), and, using a simple electromagnetic principle, the holes in the paper actuated an auto-matic tabulating machine. The census description of each individual was punched on a single strip or card and the holes functioned as counting or adding devices. Dr. Hollerith's method was then applied to the United States Census of 1890.

It was only at a later date that the private corporate structures which produced and marketed these machine services were established. In other words, the very technological development of such equipment arose in re-sponse to the need of the scientist involved in survey research to process quantitative data efficiently.[19]

While the origins of the application of such methods go back to 1890 in

---

18. From "Inventor's Shop to International Corporation," *American Machinist,* Vol. 81, No. 12, June 16, 1937, p. 481; "Development of International Business Machines Corporation" (pam-phlet, No. AM–1-2), 1936, International Business Machines, p. 1 f.

19. An example of the overwhelming character of the problem of data reduction is afforded by the field of current history in the instance of the official United States history of the Army and Air Forces in World War II, planned as a series of 96 volumes. From a reported interview with the chief military historian, Harvey Breit of the New York Times Book Review Staff notes that the recorded data from which the histories are to be written amounts in bulk to 17,120 tons, and "in filing cases set end to end, 188 miles." In the absence of technologies and methodologies for manipulating such a body of data, the student can readily see the opportunities for inadequate and incomplete analyses. See, New York Times, Book Review, July 5, 1953, p. 8.

the Census Bureau and the corporate structure to market such equipment dates from about 1914, it is only in recent years that the applications have become almost universal and a revolution in scientific procedure has occurred. The flavor of this revolution is provided by the contrast of the Census Bureau's operations in 1880 with a recent news report of its operations. "The United States will number 160,000,000 persons sometime before noon Monday (August 10, 1953). The figure will appear at about 11 o'clock with a flash of lights and a clang of bells on an automatic census calculator in the lobby of the Commerce Department. . . . The calculator is a map of the nation standing ten feet high, topped by an over-sized gadget that registers population. It records a new resident every twelve seconds as a net result of the following approximate calculations: a birth every eight seconds, a death every twenty-one seconds, the arrival of an immigrant every two minutes and an exit by someone leaving the country every seventeen minutes. . . . The Census Bureau changes the machine's speed frequently. Two months ago it stepped up the birth calculation from one every nine seconds to one every eight." [20]

One can also note this revolution from the coverage by textbooks in the field. For example, one of the most widely used early textbooks in survey research in its first edition as recently as 1939 makes absolutely no reference to machine methods for the reduction and processing of data. In the second edition in 1949, there is still no reference to machine methods.[21] Lundberg's textbook in social research, a widely used source, devotes in 1942 in its second edition only one-half page to the topic.[22]

Today this revolution has brought with it a new vocabulary of research. Such words as "code," "run," "clean," "verify," "transfer," "101," "selector," "wiring," "cross-tab" have a special meaning and the analyst is lost who does not know their connotations. We find, of course, specialists and technicians in the operation of such machines involved in the organization of survey research, but nevertheless the analyst must have some insight into the techniques and problems. Otherwise, he cannot gain the benefits in efficiency, speed, and accuracy that accompany the innovation.[23] This fact is even given official credence in *The Clapham Report,* an official British inquiry sponsored by Parliament into governmental provisions for social and economic research.[24] The Committee reports: "For extensive researches, calculating machines (i.e., machine equipment) which are also very expen-

20. N. Y. Times, August 9, 1953.

21. P. V. Young, *Scientific Social Surveys and Research* (New York, Prentice-Hall, first edition, 1939, second edition, 1949).

22. G. Lundberg, *Social Research* (New York: Longmans, 1942).

23. For a most objective treatment of the pros and cons of hand vs. machine tabulation the reader is referred to Parten, Chap. XV, *op. cit.*

24. *Report of the Committee on the Provision for Social and Economic Research* (London: Her Majesty's Stationery Office, July, 1946, CMd. 6868). By permission of Her Brittanic Majesty's Stationery Office.

sive, are indispensable. For small undertakings, they are great economizers of time; it is really not a sensible use of resources, that those engaged on such work should have to spend months doing themselves, by laborious and often inaccurate methods, computation and manipulation which could be done in as many weeks or perhaps days, by mechanical methods of complete precision in a properly organized office." It might be commented that the recommendations for governmental funds and for various provisions for research in the Committee's report were passed in Parliament with no difficulty. The revolution has been so vast that the most recent technical bibliography specifically on one method of machine processing, the use of IBM equipment, as it applies to scientific, statistical or educational research, numbers over 500 titles.[25]

A series of exercises in the fundamentals of machine processing of social research data appear in Appendix C, and the essential materials for the exercises are available from the instructor. A general understanding of machine processing can be derived from Figure I below. The flow from raw data into coded data, then the transformation into punch card form is shown. Understanding of the way in which the punch card data in turn are manipulated by machines so as to provide statistical results useful to the analyst can also be derived from the figure. Illustrative materials from the processing phases of a survey are presented in Appendix B.

Vannevar Bush gives us the vision of the new horizons in science attendant on the revolutionary use of technical aids to handling of data:

> The investigator is staggered by the findings and conclusions of thousands of other workers—many of which he cannot find time to grasp. . . . Professionally our methods of transmitting and reviewing the results are generations old and by now are totally inadequate for their purpose. . . . But there are signs of a change as new and powerful instrumentalities come into use.
>
> [The scientific investigator of the future] wears on his forehead a lump little larger than a walnut. It takes pictures 3 millimeters square. . . . As the scientist of the future moves about the laboratory or the field, every time he looks at something worthy of the record, he trips the shutter and in it goes, without even an audible click.
>
> [The machines of the future] will have enormous appetites. One of them will take instructions and data from a whole roomful of girls armed with simple keyboard punches, and will deliver sheets of computed results every few minutes. . . . Relief must be secured from laborious detailed manipulation of higher mathematics. . . . , if the users of it are to free their brains for something more than repetitive detailed transformations in accordance with established rules.

Bush notes finally the possibilities for consulting the accumulated findings of past scientists in relation to a current investigation.

---

25. *Bibliography on the Use of IBM Machines in Science, Statistics, and Education,* compiled by A. D. Franklin and E. V. Hankam, International Business Machines Corporation, January, 1952.

FIGURE I.—The Processing of Survey Data by Machine Methods

PHASE A—CODING

QUESTION

Q.8: How would you feel about this country belonging to a world organization where we would have to follow the decisions of the majority of the nations?

ANSWER

"No, American people don't want laws from someone else. We want to make our own and live by them. We do pretty well by ourselves. It's fine to have an organization to settle fighting and war—but leave America out of everything else. We've got it pretty good here, and we don't want to change. You said the majority of the nations. What if they gang up on us? Then we're liable to have to do pretty near anything. Look at how Europe followed Hitler—he'd have lots of votes. We don't want any messing with our government. Anyway, that kind of organization wouldn't work. You couldn't get the nations to follow what was decided. They'd walk out on what they didn't like, just the way Russia's been doing."

CODE

Column 19   Attitude toward U.S. Belonging to a world organization which would involve following majority rule.

→1–disapproval
2–disapproval with qualifications
3–undecided
4–approval
5–approval with qualifications
0–attitude not ascertained

Column 20   Reasons for Disapproval
1–U.S. should have chief power in a world organization
2–Small nations should not have equal vote with large
3–U.S. would suffer economically
→4–U.S. should not yield sovereignty over internal affairs
→5–Such an organization would not be practicable
6–Would cause greater rather than less international friction
7–Russia would attempt to control the organization
8–Miscellaneous
9–Reason for disapproval not ascertained
0–Attitude not ascertained, or code inapplicable

PHASE B—PUNCHING

CARD PUNCHING is the basic method of converting source data, in this case coded data, into IBM punched cards. The operator reads the source document into punched holes. Normally, the operator need not be concerned with the card since the machine feeds, positions, and ejects the card automatically. The operator's primary concern is to depress the proper keys in the correct sequence. On the next page (in the upper half) an IBM card punched with the appropriate information in Columns 19 and 20 is reproduced.

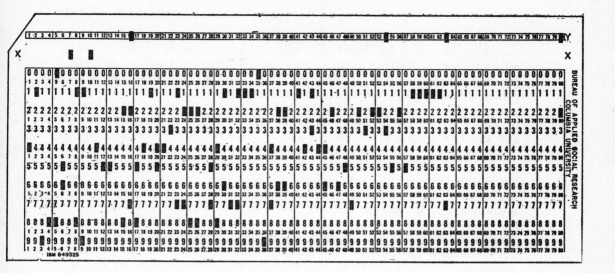

PHASE C—MACHINE RUNNING

SORTING is the process of grouping cards in numerical sequence according to any classification punched in them. For example, in order to group cards by the information punched into column 19, the column indicator, or sorting brush on the sorter is set to 19 and the cards "run." Each card will automatically fall into the pocket whose number corresponds to the number punched into the card.

The first portion of the figure is reproduced by permission from *Theory and Problems of Social Psychology* by D. Krech and R. Crutchfield, 1948, McGraw-Hill Book Company, Inc., p. 301. Photographs used in the other portions of the figure by courtesy of The International Business Machines Corporation and William Price.

Selection devices . . . will soon be speeded up from their present rate of reviewing data at a few hundred a minute. By the use of photocells and microfilm they will survey items at the rate of a thousand a second, and will print out duplicates of those selected. . . . Consider a future device for individual use, which is a sort of mechanized private file and library. It needs a name, and to coin one at random, "memex" will do. A memex is a device in which an individual stores all his books, records and communications, and which is mechanized so that it may be consulted with exceeding speed and flexibility. . . . It consists of a desk. . . . On the top are slanting translucent screens, on which material can be projected for convenient reading. There is a keyboard and sets of buttons and levers. . . . In one end is the stored material. The matter of bulk is well taken care of by improved microfilm. . . . If the user inserted 5,000 pages of material a day it would take him hundreds of years to fill the repository, so he can be profligate and enter material freely. . . . Most of the memex contents are purchased on microfilm ready for insertion. Books of all sorts, pictures, current periodicals, newspapers, are thus obtained and dropped into place. And there is provision for direct entry . . . longhand notes, photographs, memoranda, all sorts of things. . . . If the user wishes to consult a certain book, he taps its code on the keyboard, and the title page of the book promptly appears before him. . . . On deflecting one of these levers to the right he runs through the book before him. . . . A special button transfers him immediately to the first page of the index. . . . He can leave one item in position while he calls up another. He can add marginal notes and comments, taking advantage of one possible type of dry photography. . . . All this is conventional, except for the projection forward of present-day mechanisms and gadgetry.[26]

While the virtues of the machines should be apparent to all, there are evils that are less frequently recognized. Just as some critics of the larger social scene have regarded the age of the machine as ominous, so too among social scientists a number have explicitly cautioned us against certain unanticipated consequences for social research of the advent of machine methods for processing large scale quantitative investigations. Thus Glazer, in the context of a review of *The American Soldier*, one of the largest survey research undertakings ever reported, remarks: [27]

The questionnaires supply . . . fodder for The Machines. . . . The machines in question—and we must understand them before we can understand *The American Soldier*—are IBM or Hollerith machines, which take punched cards. . . . There will be one or more cards for each respondent. . . . The original questionnaire is transferred by the operator of the punch machine to the cards, according to a system devised for this questionnaire by the social scientist, who tries to arrange the punches so as to permit the maximum amount of manipulation of the data in search of significant correlations. . . .

This whole process reaches its apotheosis when the cards are 'run'—that is fed into the machine, with whatever punch one wishes counted at some

26. Vannevar Bush, *Endless Horizons* (Washington, D.C.: Public Affairs Press, 1946). All the above is from Chapter II, pp. 16 ff., by permission of the author and publisher.
27. N. Glazer, "The American Soldier as Science," *Commentary*, Vol. 8, 487-496, 1949.

superhuman speed by electrical impulses. Without such a technical process, *The American Soldier* would not have been possible. With it, we can discover in no time at all—to take a hypothetical example—how many men prefer oatmeal to farina, how many of these have been in the army one, two, or three years, how many of each of these categories are married, and of these how many have completed college, and thus we may know how many unmarried college men who have been in the army one year prefer farina. In short, *questions that would otherwise never have come to trouble the human mind can now be asked and answered by the machines.*[28]

The utilization of the reckoning devices of modern technology requires the production of numbers; and questionnaires, along with the way in which they are analyzed, can supply us with a vast number of numbers. The question, however, now arises *whether they are important numbers,* whether they are numbers which tell us about the real world of social behavior, and permit us safely to go on to higher steps of the scientific process.

Glazer underscores his argument in a specific discussion of the treatment of the problem of "personal adjustment" in *The American Soldier,* in which he is critical of the use of questionnaire data on opinions rather than a smaller number of indexes of an objective nature as the measure of adjustment. We are not here concerned with this theoretical problem of index construction, but with the extension of the remarks in relation to machine processing of data.

The relatively few objective indexes one can use mean technological unemployment for the machines, while the instrument for measuring personal adjustment involves no less than twenty-three questions, divided into four areas. And we can run the machines far into the night correlating scores on the total index with scores in each area, even on each question, and then correlating these with our background information on age, marital status, rank, and so on. A good part of this book is filled with just such information. And the clicking of these intricate machines so impressively resembles the cold, hard rhythm of *real* science.

Glazer is warning us that the efficiency of the machines makes things too easy. The analyst may fall victim to a tendency to excessive empiricism, may sacrifice focus in the analysis because he can examine so many things in so short a time, and the magic of the technology may delude him as to the significance of his analysis. These consequences are of course *not intrinsic* to machine methods of research, but the analyst may easily fall prey to them.

Another criticism of the combination of machine methods with large scale inquiry is so fundamental that we must concern ourselves with it. We have noted in passing that the survey analyst cannot keep his work manageable if he merely applies traditional qualitative modes of analysis appropriate to small scale inquiries to the massive data of a survey. And yet, the insights the scientist gains when he is immersed in the direct observation of social phenomena or treats an original body of data prior to its re-

---

28. Italics ours to emphasize the points of Glazer's argument of most relevance to our discussion.

duction to the abstract form of punch cards must not be sacrificed. Edwin G. Boring, the famous historian of Psychology, notes that in the *stretching out of the process* of research, the contact of the scientist with the original data becomes remote—and in the *enlargement* of the inquiry his contact with the human setting of the phenomena becomes indirect through the necessary use of subordinates. Boring describes the danger in the course of reviewing a paper by Likert in a symposium on *Current Trends in Psychology*, in which Likert summarizes the Department of Agriculture's National Survey of Liquid Assets made for the Federal Reserve System.[29]

In these inquiries approximately 3000 family units were sampled and queried as to their savings. Boring remarks:

> Is everything to be bigger, more numerous, more expensive, many peopled, cooperative, with researchers congregated into huge metazoic projects, *with the individual scientist as far away from the ultimate discovery as one of Likert's interviewers leaving the specified sixth house from the corner of 20th and Green Streets in Philadelphia? Is nature now to reveal itself first to the IBM tabulator, and only later to man?* Or may the personal insights of Maxwell, Mendel and Pasteur come in style again? . . . Men of imagination and insight are needed even more at the top of mass research. If Mendel needed 3000 grains of corn to get a ratio, why should not Likert have 3000 dwellings? In such ways the trend is toward the large project. Bigness is a direction in which a trend can move. But let us keep clear. The increase in the frequency of big units in psychology is not likely to mean a diminution in the frequency of small units. The psychological population is increasing and we are likely to have more of all sizes of undertakings.[30]

In a similar vein, Tom Harrison comments on the dangers. Harrison, founder of *Mass-Observation,* a unique British survey agency emphasizing techniques of covert observation, qualitative data, and quasi-ethnological procedures in its surveys, is concerned with the superficiality attendant on gross inquiries of large numbers and with the loss of insight into the human phenomena studied. He notes with respect to a recent British Survey that it "contains 330 pages of principally statistical information about houses, shops, business, etc. in an English county town . . . without a word or sign anywhere from the people who make the trade, use the shops, live in the houses. *Among many thousands of numerical figures, there nowhere appears the figure of a man.*" Commenting on the Clapham Committee's report he notes that their orientation is towards "elaborate and obsessive statistics. . . . A random sample of statistics about miners' lavatories is no more realistic than the anthropological study of a mining community. Numbers are no more 'real' than narks. 'Computers and sorters' cannot become 'investiga-

---

29. W. Dennis, ed., *Current Trends in Psychology* (Pittsburgh: University of Pittsburgh Press, 1947). Chapter by R. Likert, The Sample Interview Survey.

30. E. G. Boring, "Current Trends in Psychology, a Special Review," *Psychol. Bull.*, 45, 1948, 75-84. Italics ours to emphasize the problem that concerns us. Quoted by permission of The American Psychological Association.

tors'." Later he comments on the excessive emphasis on sampling and statistical inquiry with the remark: "You cannot, yet, take a census of love in Liverpool, or random sample the effect that fear of the future has on the total pattern of contemporary life in Leeds." [31]

Neither Boring nor Harrison is rejecting quantitative survey inquiries. They point to a proper balance in methods. Thus Harrison summarizes his position, "in most sociological research we require an adequate admixture of words and numbers, of penetration and tabulation, representation and interpretation, understood situations and unimpeachable correlations, the raw material of life with the authentic statistic of validity." But granting the desirability of such a compound, here the dilemma cannot be so easily solved as in the case of the problem that Glazer poses. There one must simply watch against excessive empiricism not guided by theory, and one merely exhorts the analyst to maintain the proper orientation. But Boring is pointing to a feature of survey research which cannot be resolved simply by exhorting the analyst. It is inevitable that he is physically remote from the original data—that he operates through a farflung network of agents—field workers, clerks, coders, computers—and that he deals with such abstractions as punches on cards. These adjuncts are essential to large scale inquiries, and one must invent substitute or new forms for the gaining of insights, since the character and size of the inquiry precludes exclusive use of traditional methods. It is this dilemma that has led to the *supplementation* of quantitative forms of survey analysis by a variety of qualitative *adjuncts incorporated at the proper place* in the survey process.

Thus, it is the case that the survey analyst *marshals his associates to act as informants* and to report to him on the subtle flavoring of the data and to communicate unique concrete but strategic observations to him. And this has led to the development of *interviewer report forms* on which the human situation within which the data were collected is described systematically for the analyst's benefit, to *interviewer's ratings* of the respondent or to *"thumbnail sketches"* of the respondent which are second hand but nevertheless evaluations of the respondent based on someone's direct observation, to *coder "flagging"* or noting of particular responses for the analyst's attention which convey the character of a response subsumed under some more abstract classification.[32]

Thus it is the case that the analyst makes up for the inevitably segmental character of the mass of processed data by *supplementary classification and analytic procedures which convey the structural or molar features of the phenomena.* The segmentalization is introduced in the course of the coding

31. T. Harrison, "The Future of British Sociology," *Int. J. Opin. Attit. Res.,* 1, 1947, #1, 47-62. Italics ours.

32. For a detailed treatment of interviewer report forms, the reader is referred to P. B. Sheatsley, "Some Uses of Interviewer Report Forms," *Publ. Opin. Quart.,* 11, 1947–48, 601-611.

of *discrete* responses, and is compensated for by subsequent *over-all coding* of total interviews, by *typological or multi-dimensional classification* of respondents, and by *index-construction* or pooling of data from a series of related answers into a more comprehensive description of the respondents.[33]

There is the realization that the standardization of inquiry in large scale survey research, while making for efficiency and necessary to insure comparability among field workers, at the same time may impose some artificiality on the phenomenon studied, particularly when the analyst does his planning far away from the live events. Consequently the analyst engages in a *series of prior planning procedures to insure that the standardized procedure will nevertheless be adapted to the natural frame of reference of most of the subjects under study.* This had led to such procedures as the *pilot or exploratory study,* prior to a major inquiry, the use of *pre-testing* of the questionnaire instrument, *community background inquiry and quasi-ethnological inquiry* in conjunction with a survey in order to formulate the inquiry in terms most meaningful to respondents.[34]

With the realization that statistical analysis of the usual standardized data of a large scale inquiry may tend to reveal the gross and perhaps superficial aspects of the phenomenon, there have developed supplementary forms of data and analysis. The use of *projective questions* is intended to reveal subtle or hidden aspects of the phenomenon. *Deviant case analysis* supplements the gross modal findings with evidence on the less frequent results and their dynamics. The use of *open-ended questions* increases the likelihood that the final form of the inquiry will not distort the phenomenon and will provide a richer context of data by which the analyst senses the meaning of what is otherwise rather abstract statistical results.[35]

---

33. For examples of over-all coding or treatment of data the reader is referred to Helen Peak, *Some Observations On the Characteristics and Distribution of German Nazis.* Psychol. Mon., 276, 1948. D. Riesman and N. Glazer, "Social Structure, Character Structure, Opinion." *Internat. J. Opin. Attit. Res.,* 2, 1948, 512-527, or Babette Samelson, "Mrs. Jones' Ethnic Attitudes," *J. Abnorm. Soc. Psychol.,* 1945, 40, 205-214. For treatment of typologies, indexes, and multi-dimensional systems, see P. Lazarsfeld and Alan Barton, Qualitative Measurement in the Social Sciences; Classification, Typologies, and Indices, in Lasswell, H. and D. Lerner, ed., *The Policy Sciences* (Stanford: Stanford University Press, 1951), or H. Zeisel, *Say It With Figures* (New York: Harpers, 1947), especially Chapters VI-VII. For the development of a specialized network of informants used in conjunction with survey findings, see E. Herzog, "Pending Perfection: A qualitative complement to quantitative methods," *Internat. J. Opin. Attit. Res.,* I, #3, 1947, 31-48.

34. For a discussion of community background as an adjunct to planning and analysis of surveys, see H. Hyman, "Community Background in Public Opinion Research," *J. Abnorm. Soc. Psychol.,* 40, 1945, pp. 411-413. For a discussion of ethnological adjuncts to surveys see J. B. Holland, "The Utility of Social Anthropology as an adjunct of a Social Survey," *Internat. J. Opin. Attit. Res.,* 5, 1951-52, pp. 455-464. For discussions of pre-testing and pilot studies see such standard texts as M. Jahoda, M. Deutsch and S. Cook, *Research Methods in Social Relations* (New York: Dryden Press, 1951).

35. For a discussion of open-ended questions the student is referred to R. Likert, The Sample Interview Survey as a tool of Research and Policy Formation, in Lasswell and Lerner, *The Policy Sciences, op. cit.*
M. Haire, "Projective Techniques in Marketing Research," *J. Market.,* 14, 1950, pp. 649-656.
P. Kendall and K. Wolff, The Analysis of Deviant Cases, in P. Lazarsfeld and F. Stanton, ed., *Communications Research,* 1948–49 (New York: Harpers, 1949).

These specialized adjuncts to the analyst's quantitative work represent only a partial listing of procedures that have been developed in relation to the dilemma that Boring posed. But a detailed treatment of even this listing is beyond the scope of this work. It is assumed that the student will familiarize himself with the papers cited and that he will obtain training in these supplementary analytical skills. Otherwise his skill in the more quantitative aspects of survey analysis will be insufficient to the job.

Organizational Form
and Its Consequences

We note a second feature of the case studies presented. With one exception, the research was conducted not by an individual scholar, but by a research organization, comprised of many people.[36] We note such established agencies involved as the Surveys Division of the Office of War Information, the American Institute of Public Opinion (Gallup Poll), the Survey Research Center of the University of Michigan, the National Opinion Research Center of the University of Chicago, the Bureau of Applied Social Research of Columbia University, the Institute of Social Research (Frankfurt), the Office of Public Opinion Research of Princeton University, the Division of Program Surveys of the Department of Agriculture and the team of scholars labelled the Berkeley Public Opinion Study.

That survey research generally has taken on this organized form is clearly seen from the inventories of survey research published annually by the American Association for Public Opinion Research, the professional body most closely identified with survey research.[37] For example, in their inventory of research in progress in 1952, some 56 substantive survey research projects are abstracted. As well as can be determined, only 13 of these, less than one-quarter of the projects, represent research conducted by a single individual scholar, the remainder being conducted by research organizations of either a commercial or academic nature. But these inventories do not provide an adequate picture of the extent of organized survey research, since direct reports by government agencies are not well represented. Alpert reports, for example, that in the years 1950–51, no less than 29 surveys of the opinion and attitude type were conducted *directly* by federal research agencies, and this total does not include reports from par-

For a concise treatment of the use of qualitative materials in conjunction with quantitative analysis, the reader is referred to Jahoda, Deutsch, and Cook, *op. cit.*, pp. 295-304.

36. For a treatment of the organizational form of science in the United States, see, B. Barber, *Science and the Social Order* (Glencoe: The Free Press, 1952), Chap. V.

37. American Association for Public Opinion Research, Inventory of Research-in-Progress, June, 1952 (mimeo).

ticular types of agencies, e.g., those where the survey involves a security classification, surveys overseas, etc.[38]

The feature of survey research of large size inquiry already described necessitates this pattern of employment of more than the single scholar. Otherwise, a project is never ending. Glock in a paper devoted to the analysis of organizations of research remarks on the *collection* of data problems, "It's all very well for a single observer to work in an alleged society of 50 to 100 families, but surely no individual can alone obtain the data necessary for the study of large complex societies." [39]

Lippitt describes the *analytic* difficulties that the individual scholar must surmount.

> As the social researcher gets more and more into the study of complex problems of group life, he also gets more and more into problems of having a mountain of data to analyze. All too often there are active and energetic first steps toward analysis which grow feebler and feebler as it becomes evident that little progress is being made with the very limited analysis personnel, often part-time students. The project may well end up with only one or two small quantitative analyses using one percent of the data. The rest remain in the files for 'further analysis' until finally the desperate need for file space pushes the interview and observation records into a box which can more easily be hidden and forgotten.[40]

A sense of the personnel requirements of large scale survey research is provided by the table of organization of the Morale Division of the United States Strategic Bombing Survey of Japan. This was an official inquiry of the Military Establishment into the effect of bombing on the morale of the people of Japan and their consequent will to resist and prosecute the war. The inquiry represented one of the most ambitious and adequately financed survey researches ever undertaken. There were also the peculiar and difficult operating conditions of war and a foreign language requiring personnel for translation of documents and interviews and special administrative personnel. However, because of the detailed narrative account of the inquiry, almost unique in survey literature, it gives us a detailed record of personnel requirements. These requirements were established in relation to a sample design calling for approximately 4000 interviews and a time schedule calling for the survey to be carried out and completed within approximately a five month period. The research organization was to involve a total of 122 personnel, exclusive of the machine tabulation unit. The interviewing staff was to total 50, the professional staff for planning, analysis and supervision

38. H. Alpert, "Opinion and Attitude Surveys in the U.S. Government," *Publ. Opin. Quart.*, 16, 1952, 33-41.

39. Charles Y. Glock, "Some Implications of Organization for Social Research," *Social Forces*, 30, 1951, 129-134.

40. R. Lippitt, "Techniques for Research in Group Living," *J. Soc. Issues*, 2, 1946, 55-61. By permission of the publisher.

to involve 12 individuals, coding and clerical staff about 30 personnel depending on the stage of inquiry.[41]

The one survey earlier described which departs from an organizational form and approximates closest to the pattern of work of the individual scholar is *The Kinsey Report*. But even in this case Kinsey had two major associates plus three other interviewers. And the time schedule of that study underscores our point. It was some *ten years* after the initiation of the inquiry that the first volume of the findings appeared, and the field work or collection of the required volume of data (approximately 5000 cases) by such a small number of interviewers took approximately $5\frac{1}{2}$ years.[42]

Consideration of several of the other surveys is also revealing. In the instance cited in which an individual investigator initiated an inquiry, *The Psychology of Social Classes,* Centers availed himself of the agency of the Princeton Institute of Public Opinion for the staffing of the field inquiry, so as to expedite the research. In the instance of the Berkeley inquiry, which involved a team of investigators, the requirements of a large field staff from an established survey agency were obviated by the decision to use a research design which involved written questionnaires self-administered to the total sample. Since interviewing was conducted on only a small sub-sample of approximately 80 respondents selected from the extremes, the field staff requirements could be met informally out of the small group of investigators involved in the planning.[43]

In addition to the large staff required for conducting a survey, there is the problem of specialized resources such as machine equipment. When the rental of a relatively simple IBM installation may cost conservatively $800 a month, it is the rare individual scholar who can avail himself of equip-

---

41. These data are taken from the narrative account by D. Krech and E. Ballachey, *A Case Study of a Social Survey,* Japanese Survey, United States Bombing Survey, U. of California Press, Syllabus T G, 1948, p. 10. The remainder of the personnel not accounted for in the breakdown above were stenographic and administrative. For other examples of personnel requirements see Jahoda, Deutsch and Cook, *op. cit.,* 344-349; Parten, *op. cit.,* Chap. V.

42. This figure of $5\frac{1}{2}$ years must be qualified in the light of the fact that the investigation was novel, and a considerable amount of the time in the first phase was expended in the *development of techniques* rather than on routine collection of data. Nevertheless even in the most productive periods of the inquiry, long after the investigation was stabilized, the maximum productivity achieved by this small staff was about 2700 interviews in one year. Kinsey, *op. cit.,* p. 10.

43. Such a design solves one practical operating problem in survey research which is one central desideratum in planning. However, the problem that is foreshadowed to which we shall return later is the complex of factors which operate and must be taken into account by the analyst in deciding upon a research design. For example, practical considerations enter—time, money and such resources as staff, but these may oppose theoretical considerations of accuracy and appropriateness of procedure, and the like. It is the balancing of all these factors and arriving at an optimal solution that makes research design complex and requires great skill. Thus, for example, the written questionnaire while economical is by definition unsuited to the study of illiterates. The study of extremes reduced the magnitude of the interviewing but raised problems of what inferences could be made from the sub-sample of extreme cases to the larger total sample. The written questionnaire may be defective for certain types of subject matter and certain formal types of question construction. For a discussion of the pros and cons of the written questionnaire vs. the personal interviewer the student is referred to H. Hyman, *et al., Interviewing in Social Research* (Chicago: University of Chicago Press, 1954), Chap. IV.

ment without the aid of an agency. Moreover, there is the need for *specialized skills* required to operate the total survey *research process* effectively. The development of complex sample designs is a technical specialty all its own; the administration of a field staff ranging from perhaps a minimum of 60 interviewers in a small national sample survey to perhaps 150,000 enumerators in the 1950 Decennial Census of the United States becomes a full time responsibility; [44] the operation of a large machine tabulation section requires a trained supervisor; the administration of the staff of clerks who do the editing and checking and coding of the collected data similarly requires special personnel.

Glock notes the gains to be derived from the hierarchy of personnel and the specialization at different levels—"in field research, for example: specialists in sampling, in the supervision of field interviewing, in the analysis of qualitative materials, and so on." He remarks on the essential "research administration" provided by an organizational form.[45]

> The administration of research is often a misleading term to refer to what are essentials of any field work investigation. Providing for initial and sustained contacts with informants, preparing the groundwork for effective rapport and then, allocating research resources to their most strategic use, seeing to it that the proposed sampling design is followed in practice, preparing for and checking on the reliability of data—these and other similar activities intrinsic to any social research based on field work have been often tagged as "mere" administrative details. . . . They are, in fact an integral part of the research process in sociology and psychology.

Again, if we refer back to our case studies of past surveys the point is underscored. While Kinsey ran his studies without apparent benefit of research organizations, he notes in his introduction the cooperation and consultation of a considerable number of specialists, for example, statisticians to advise on such problems as sample design and the estimation of error and the aid of at least four other persons as research assistants.[46]

These are the skills needed on the technical or methodological side, but consider the *substantive problems* for which surveys are undertaken. They are frequently not the theoretical problems exclusive to a given scientific discipline. Instead they are often inquiries into complex and critical situations which need illumination and solution through the aid of factual knowledge. Thus, the study of absenteeism might well have been the proper province of experts in industrial or labor relations, industrial sociology, industrial psychology, labor economics, and social psychology. The inquiry

---

44. For a detailed narrative account conveying the complexity of the problems of field administration in a single large scale survey in a difficult operating situation, the reader is referred to Huey's discussion of the United States Strategic Bombing Survey of Morale in Japan. See, H. Huey, "Some Principles of Field Administration in Large-Scale Surveys," *Publ. Opin. Quart.,* 1947, 11, 254-263.

45. *Op. cit.* By permission of the publisher.

46. *Op. cit.,* pp. VII-VIII.

into bond redemptions called for knowledge of economics and psychology at least; Kinsey's inquiry involved biologists or taxonomists, the aid of two psychologists, and one anthropologist.[47] The subject matter is a meeting ground for all humanity and for such other professional disciplines as psychiatry, medicine, sociology, and law. Alan Gregg, former director of the medical sciences of the Rockefeller Foundation, the sponsors of the investigation, conveys how multi-form the phenomena of survey research may be in his introduction to *The Kinsey Report* by the metaphor, "Seen from the four points of the compass a great mountain may present aspects that are very different one from the other—so different that bitter disagreements can arise between those who have watched the mountain, truly and well, through all the seasons, but each from a different quarter."[48]

Organizations or collectivities involve by definition some interaction. When the contact involves individuals of varied skills or substantive backgrounds there are desirable consequences for research into complex problem areas. As Glock notes,

A research organization affords an opportunity for continuing interaction between staff members on problems of common concern and focus. In this respect, it furnishes a stronger impetus to the advancement of interdisciplinary consideration of problems than does the university organization itself. Because they often work with different methods on relatively unrelated problems, the occasion seldom arises for the members of the various social science departments on the university campus to work together in any continuing way on matters of common intellectual concern. . . . Potentially, research organizations have the ability to bring a wide range of varied skills and specialists to bear on any research problem.[49]

But this interaction may produce still another benefit neither of a substantive nor of a technical sort. Beyond the skills or knowledge or energies of the researcher as these affect the conduct of a survey, there is the possibility that an individual's own biases will intrude and affect his work. It is well known to the student of the sociology of knowledge that seemingly irrelevant values held by researchers will enter into their work.[50] Benne and Swanson note that such biases intrude at least into: the choice of problem, the methods, the interpretations put upon the data, the place, time and manner of publication, the relationships drawn between the current findings and earlier findings by colleagues, the kind of professional discipline or ethics by which the scientist will be bound and will enforce on other scien-

---

47. *Ibid.*, pp. VII-VIII.
48. Kinsey, *ibid.*, p. V.
49. *Op. cit.*
50. For a general account the student is referred to R. K. Merton, *Social Theory and Social Structure* (Glencoe: The Free Press, 1949), Chap. VIII. For an explicit discussion of bias in survey research, see H. Hyman, *et al.*, *Interviewing in Social Research* (Chicago: University of Chicago Press, 1954).

tists and the relationships he will establish with colleagues as members of a research team.[51]

Hart mentions a number of additional ways in which such values intrude, for example, in the kind of generalization that the researcher would regard as a satisfactory solution to the problem, and in the basic orientation or concepts by which the researcher schematizes the problem.[52]

Such biases jeopardize the ideal of science. Feigel remarks, for example, that characteristic features of science are "the possibility of removing disagreements concerning matters of fact" and "objectivity (better perhaps 'intersubjectivity') of the scientific method." [53] To make the practice of science conform to this stated ideal it is usually recommended that science as a social enterprise involve the cross-checking of one investigator by scholars with different points of view and that the individual scientist in conformity with his professional duties be sensitive to and explicit about his own values.

But Hart points out that these tendencies "are so subtle, so implicit, so deeply rooted that it is difficult for us to discern them in ourselves or, when they are called to attention, to avoid rationalizing them instead of examining them objectively." [54] And therefore the individual checks suggested may be inadequate. Moreover, Benne and Swanson in their analysis of the problem point out that the very social checks to bias are themselves matters of *volition*, and therefore may be inoperative. They state that the scientist must *choose* the professional discipline by which he will be bound, and must *choose* the relationship he will establish with his colleagues, and therein lies the difficulty. It is an interesting feature of research organization that the very conditions of work, the occurrence of interaction whether the individual wills it or not, *insures* that the scholar becomes aware of his bias. The presence of others *enforces* upon him some discipline.[55] Merton brings this interpretation to our attention in contrasting the situation of the individual scholar and the member of a research organization both working in the field of communications. Of course, his remarks have a more general import:

The lone scholar is not constrained *by the very structure of his work situation,* to deal systematically with reliability as a technical problem. It is a remote and unlikely possibility that some other scholar, off at some other

51. K. Benne and G. Swanson, "The Problem of Values and the Social Scientist," in Values and the Social Scientist, A Symposium, *J. Soc. Issues,* VI, 1950, 2-7. The student is also referred to other papers in this symposium for a general treatment of the problem.

52. C. W. Hart, "Some Factors Affecting the Organization and Prosecution of Given Research Projects," *Amer. Sociol. Rev.,* XII, 1947, 514-519.

53. Herbert Feigel, a paper delivered in the above symposium, *op. cit.*

54. C. W. Hart, *op. cit.*

55. We are neglecting in this discussion, research biases which are *cultural* rather than *idiosyncratic.* It is conceivable that all the scholars of a given era or within a given society have certain fundamental orientations which cannot be attenuated by any organizational form. For a contemporary discussion of such biases, see, R. Ackoff, "Scientific Method and Social Science— East and West," *Scient. Month.,* LXXV, 1952, 155-160.

place in the academic community, would independently hit upon precisely the same collection of empirical materials, utilizing the same categories, the same criteria for these categories and conducting the same intellectual operations. . . . Empirical studies in mass communications ordinarily require the systematic coverage of large amounts of data. The magnitude of the data is such that it is usually far beyond the capacity of the lone scholar to assemble, and the routine operations so prodigally expensive of time that they are ordinarily beyond his means to pay. If these inquiries are to be made at all, they require the collaboration of numbers of research workers organized into teams. . . . With such research organization, the problem of reliability becomes so compelling that it cannot be neglected or scantily regarded. The need for reliability of observation and analysis which, of course, exists in the field of research at large, becomes the more visible and the more insistent in the miniature confines of the research team. Different researchers at work on the same empirical materials and performing the same operations must presumably reach the same results (within tolerable limits). Thus, the very structure of the immediate work group with its several and diverse collaborators reinforces the perennial concern of science, including social science, with objectivity: the interpersonal and intergroup reliability of data.[56]

The analyst has much to gain from these and other attributes of organized research, *providing he is properly oriented to these potential advantages of a research organization, has the skill to mobilize them effectively, and is simultaneously oriented to the possible dangers arising in practice from the organizational form.* The basic skill and orientation demanded is effective direction of the organizational structure as it bears on his project, and here the greatest danger arises when the analyst considers his responsibility to be merely that of stepping in at the *terminal phase* of the survey.

And it is so easy to assume this view. Analysis, of course, implies the treatment of the data and is therefore terminal in the research process. Moreover, when the earlier phases are *institutionalized* as someone else's job, it is easy to think of it as *exclusively* the other fellow's responsibility. It is interesting to note in this connection that the analyst in a research organization is rarely called an "analyst." In the hierarchical structure he is generally labelled a "study director," "project director," "assistant study director," "research associate," "research executive," or "program director." The title is significant of the analyst's responsibility to direct or control the *total* process—to mobilize it, for only then will the terminal phase, the analysis *per se* be successful.

An historic example of the complexities in mobilizing staff in large scale surveys is afforded by the first British Census conducted in 1801. Jones describes the process:

The responsibility for making the count of the population was laid upon the overseers of the poor or, in default of them, "some substantial house-

---

56. R. K. Merton, *Social Theory and Social Structure* (Glencoe: The Free Press, 1950), p. 214.

holder in each parish, township, or place." But the task of collecting the returns was given to the Justices of the Peace. They delivered them to the High Constables, who were to pass them on by a certain date to the Clerks of the Peace or Town Clerks, and they in turn forwarded them to the Home Secretary. . . . But this count was only half the matter. The other half concerned the increase or diminution of the population, which was also to be measured. This duty was entrusted to the clergy and ministers of each parish, who transmitted the particulars they collected to their Bishops, and they sent them on to the Archbishops.[57]

The elaborate administrative structure that is required becomes evident if we inspect the organization of a modern census. In Chart I we reproduce the table of organization of the U.S. decennial census of 1950.

For the analyst to guide and mobilize and control the sampling, the interviewing, the processing via the steps of coding, editing, and tabulation, he must obviously have intimate knowledge of these procedures. Then, operating within the framework of these research phases, he must provide for his analytic requirements. He does this either by written materials where the organization is large or by direct face-to-face guidance. Therefore, while these phases are not intrinsically part of *analysis,* they are part of the analyst's training. It is outside the scope of the later sections of this work to treat these phases, and the student is referred to more general sources on the total research process.[58] However, we present in Appendix A and B some illustrative materials from particular surveys showing how detailed is the guidance of the personnel involved in these phases and to familiarize the potential analyst with these problems.

In the effective direction of the total process, the analyst must also reckon with peculiarities of the given organization which create difficulty. Size of staff provides resources, but at the same time makes communication to the analyst of significant information from the early phases of research unwieldy. Hierarchical structure, a necessity for effective functioning and for study direction, may similarly impede communication from subordinates to superiors and produce problems of opposition and strain within the total agency.

It is in this context that we must note a strange problem that burdens large scale survey operations, a problem unknown in the research undertakings of individual scholars. There has been much discussion of the "Cheater Problem" or the "Cheater Interviewer" who fashions the answers out of his own head but presents them to the analyst as the genuine opin-

---

57. D. Caradog Jones, *op. cit.,* p. 25. Reprinted by permission of the publishers.

58. For example, Jahoda, Deutsch and Cook, *Research Methods in Social Relations* (New York: Dryden Press, Vols. I and II, 1951). W. Goode and P. Hatt, *Methods in Social Research* (New York: McGraw-Hill, 1952). M. Parten, *Surveys, Polls and Samples: Practical Procedures* (New York: Harpers, 1950); L. Festinger and D. Katz, *Research Methods in the Behavioral Sciences* (New York: Dryden Press, 1953).

For a concise coverage of the major steps of the survey process, see: E. Maccoby and R. Holt, "How Surveys Are Made," *J. Soc. Issues,* 2, #2, 45-57.

Chart I

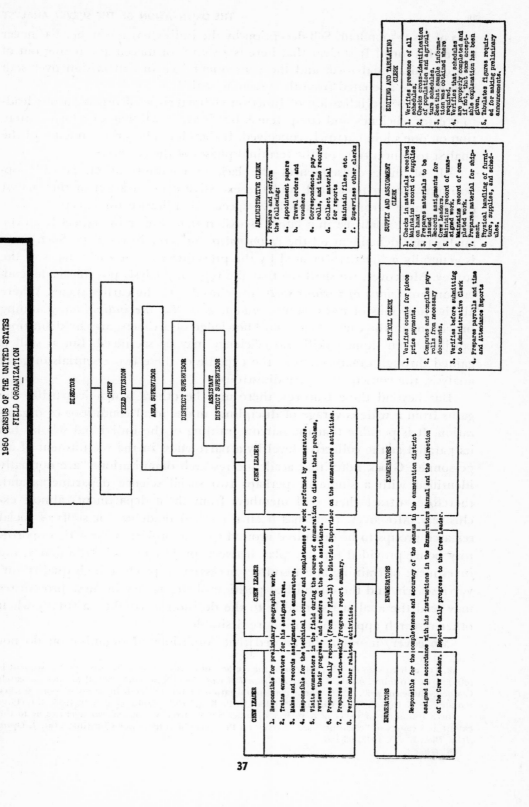

1950 CENSUS OF THE UNITED STATES
FIELD ORGANIZATION

DIRECTOR

CHIEF
FIELD DIVISION

AREA SUPERVISOR

DISTRICT SUPERVISOR

ASSISTANT
DISTRICT SUPERVISOR

ADMINISTRATIVE CLERK

1. Prepare and perform
the following:
   a. Appointment papers
   b. Travel orders and
   vouchers
   c. Correspondence, payrolls, and time records
   d. Collect material
   for reports
   e. Maintain files, etc.
   f. Supervises other clerks

**EDITING AND TABULATING
CLERK**

1. Verifies presence of all
schedules.
2. Checks cross-identification
of population and agriculture schedules.
3. Sees that each information was obtained where
required.
4. Verifies that schedules
are properly completed and
if not, that some accept-
able explanation has been
given.
5. Tabulates figures required for making preliminary
announcements.

**SUPPLY AND ASSIGNMENT
CLERK**

1. Checks in materials received
2. Maintains record of supplies
on hand
3. Prepares materials to be
issued
4. Records assignments for
Crew Leaders.
5. Maintains record of unas-
signed work.
6. Maintains record of completed work.
7. Prepares material for ship-
ment.
8. Physical handling of furni-
ture, supplies, and schedules.

PAYROLL CLERK

1. Verifies counts for piece
price payments.
2. Computes and compiles payrolls from necessary
documents.
3. Verifies before submitting
to Administrative Clerk.
4. Prepares payrolls and time
and Attendance Reports

CREW LEADER

1. Responsible for preliminary geographic work.
2. Trains enumerators for his assigned area.
3. Makes and records assignments to enumerators.
4. Responsible for the technical accuracy and completeness of work performed by enumerators.
5. Visits enumerators in the field during the course of enumeration to discuss their problems,
reviews their progress, and renders on the spot assistance.
6. Prepares a daily report (Form 17 Pld-13) to District Supervisor on the enumerators activities.
7. Prepares a twice-weekly progress report summary.
8. Performs other related activities.

CREW LEADER

CREW LEADER

ENUMERATORS

Responsible for the completeness and accuracy of the census in the enumeration district
assigned in accordance with his instructions in the Enumerators Manual and the direction
of the Crew Leader. Reports daily progress to the Crew Leader.

ENUMERATORS

ENUMERATORS

37

ions of his respondent. Self-deception by the individual researcher has never taken this form! It is clear that here is a source of inaccuracy arising out of the organizational form and the consequent lack of supervision over staff who may be alienated from the research goal.[59]

The very specialization of function characteristic of organizations leads to greater efficiency and competence, but it also encourages exclusive attention on one's job, narrowly conceived. It therefore abets the tendency of the analyst to concentrate on the terminal phases of the research.

All of these consequences—the lack of communication, possible oppositions among personnel, and the excessive concentration of the analyst on the mere terminal phases have special significance for effective survey research. We shall see in a later discussion that proper inferences from the analysis are dependent on the *examination of error* in the data. Such error is generally *artifactual*—created by the procedures in the early stages of the survey. Moreover, we shall see that the type of analysis possible is dependent on *provisions of various sorts* introduced into the earlier stages. Where all the functions of research are *embodied in the one individual,* planning provisions in the early stages and knowledge of artifacts, are, by definition, possible, even though skill and efficiency may be sacrificed. But if skill is gained through organization at the expense of these two essentials of good analysis, the consequences are disastrous.

But beyond these features, there may be others which jeopardize the gains from a wide coverage of disciplines under ideal conditions of organization. It is possible that the narrow training of the individual scholar has its parallel at the collective level by a narrowness in the recruitment of all personnel. Glock notes that academic research organizations "are normally identified with a single or perhaps two social science departments and, therefore, attract their staff members from these departments almost exclusively. Moreover, there has been a marked tendency for staffs of social research groups to be organized around specific projects with little opportunity being provided for interplay between project teams." [60] Similarly, the investment of training and resources necessary to produce high quality survey research, and the established position of the agency in these procedures may lead the analyst too readily to the decision to conduct a survey when other research approaches are more desirable.

Moreover, it might be argued that conditions of organization do not

---

59. For a discussion of this problem in the context of election prediction surveys, the student is referred to Mosteller, *et al., The Pre-Election Polls of 1948* (New York: Social Science Research Council, Bulletin #60, 1949). For a conceptualization of the problem in terms of poor worker morale, see L. Crespi, "The Cheater Problem in Polling," *Publ. Opin. Quart.,* 9, 1946, 431-445.

For a round-up of views of a variety of practitioners from various survey agencies as to the extent and causes of "cheating," see "Survey on Problems of Interviewer Cheating," *Int. J. Opin. Attit. Res.,* I, #3, 1947, 93-106.

60. *Op. cit.*

provide the fertile medium for novel discoveries in science—the existence of leisure, freedom to work in an undisciplined way on whatever tack the scientist deems worthwhile. Thus, Oppenheimer in the course of Congressional Hearings on a National Science Foundation recognizes that "many of the undertakings of current science involve the cooperation of relatively large numbers of people, and the use of relatively expensive equipment." But he comments that "this pattern must not be imposed except insofar as the technical requirements of the problems demand it." Elsewhere he argues that "gigantic concentrations of scientific talent into highly organized projects while appropriate for development in fields involving no fundamental difficulties and no fundamental novelty, would almost certainly retard progress and the real understanding of nature, and the opening up of those avenues of insight upon which the whole future of science depends." He also states that "too-strict organization is liable to stifle the imagination, especially in the *junior* members of the research groups to the extent that several of the young men no longer consider it their responsibility and duty to think out problems for themselves but expect problems to be handed out to them by their superiors." [61]

The attenuation of the bias of the individual scholar through interaction with opposing minds in the organization presupposes that the personnel have varied viewpoints. But where recruitment is within a narrow range, no such good effect will occur, and like minds may even reinforce each other. We may substitute for the bias of the individual the bias or fanaticism of a sect! [62]

Research organizations might also be more prone to biases involving accommodations to the prevailing point of view of the general public or of strategic publics. Organizations are more visible than individuals; they are subject to a variety of legal regulations (e.g. via tax exemptions) and to governing boards. The heavy investment of resources may make them conservative about risky projects. Moreover, for reasons to be elaborated shortly they may be more responsive to outside pressures both because of the necessity of subsidization, and the fear of attack because the substantive problems for which surveys are initiated are potentially controversial. The outside professional pressures that might lead to *reduction* of bias, namely the operation of established codes of ethical practices and technical standards, are ill-suited to control of organizations, since such codes have usually been promulgated by professional bodies whose memberships are *individuals*. Hence while there is governance of individual personnel, the behavior of the *organization* per se is not covered.

---

61. Testimony of Dr. J. R. Oppenheimer, Hearings on Science Legislation, Part 2, *op. cit.*
62. For a discussion of biases that might particularly afflict research organizations, see C. W. Hart, *op. cit.*, especially pp. 517-518.

Sponsorship of Inquiry and Subsidization—Consequences for the Analyst

A feature of the case studies to be noted is the fact of sponsorship and sub-sidization. In some instances the problem under study does *not* represent the individual choice of a research worker, but grows out of the needs of some other party which acts as the sponsor and supporter of the research. In other instances, the research represents an initial choice of the scholar or organi-zation, but subsidization must then be sought from some outside source. Thus, in the instance of the surveys on absenteeism and war bond redemp-tion the work was initiated directly by *government* agencies and subsidized through government appropriations, because the problems were deemed to be of public significance. In the case of the inquiry into radio, the outside party initiating the inquiry and providing contract funds was a quasi-*commercial* entity, the National Association of Broadcasters. In the case of the inquiry into the atom bomb, the sponsor was a *non-commercial entity,* a *foundation,* which provided grants of money to the research organization. The inquiry into prejudice and personality represents a mixture of spon-sors. A *social agency* provided initial impetus for the inquiry and some financial support and this was supplemented by foundation grants. The final pattern of support is evidenced in the case of Kinsey and Centers, in-dividual scholars who ostensibly initiated the choice of problem, but who then approached outside bodies and foundations for the necessary sub-sidization.[63]

There is no alternative to one or another form of sponsorship or sub-sidization. Some idea of the magnitude of the costs of large scale surveys was available from the descriptions of the surveys described earlier. The radio inquiry involved an outlay of $10,205.65 and this figure is exclusive of the analytic costs. Further, this figure gives a very conservative picture of the outlays needed for survey research since, in the years from 1947, costs have risen conservatively by 25%. Further, this inquiry involved the method of quota sampling, a cheaper form of sampling design than probability sampling, and the questions were essentially pre-coded reducing editing, coding and related processing costs. The program of research into opinions about the atom bomb involved an expenditure of about $50,000 for the 4 specific surveys involved and here again at current prices for research services the approximate costs in 1954 would easily run $65,000.

---

63. A type of sponsor not available in the case studies but occasionally found is that of the "interest group," i.e., a political party, a union, etc. Such sponsors are difficult to place on the continuum of commercial to non-commercial sponsors, but their purposes are clearly private rather than public.

Such costs are beyond the resources of individual scholars, and the financial structure of research organizations is such that they do not have *continuous* or routine sources of funds for initiating and conducting their own research. The Clapham report remarks on the paradox in Britain that:

> the idea that provision for research in these fields (the social sciences) by way of libraries, calculating machines, computers and research assistants, is as important as provision for laboratories and experimental stations seems still to present an appearance of novelty. . . . It is regarded as natural that the maintenance and equipment of laboratories should be a standing charge on regular university funds. But the number of universities in which there exists *continuous provision* for research in social questions is still extremely small.[64]

The point holds equally well for the United States. In the absence of such provisions, the intervention of sponsors is, of course, desirable for it at least insures that social research will occur. However, the existence of such patterns of support makes it clear that the *individual analyst or the research agency operates in relation to some network of obligations, pressures, forces, or controls arising out of the relation to sponsor, client, or supporter.* How these controls operate, whether they are desirable or not, we shall elaborate upon shortly. The important point, however, is that the analyst be oriented to the existence of this pattern in survey research.[65]

Government sponsorship of research represents perhaps the most frequent pattern in the recent scene. For example, as noted earlier, 29 opinion and attitude surveys were conducted directly by government agencies during 1950–51.[66] This pattern is part of a larger current pattern of government stimulation of a wide array of scientific activities, which has early historical antecedents,[67] and it grows out of the administrative needs of governments to collect exact information on a vast range of matters. Statistics of populations, data on employment and unemployment, figures on the cost of living, evidence on public health are all essential for practical purposes, but indirectly provide a basic archive of information for further scientific analysis. From early times this has been the case. The first British Census was conducted in 1801; and the first United States Census of pop-

---

64. *Op. cit.* Italics ours. By permission of Her Britannic Majesty's Stationery Office.

65. This problem is, of course, not peculiar to survey research. In other fields, subsidization has occurred and there has been much discussion of its good and bad consequences. See for example, the papers which were originally delivered as part of a symposium on the problem which appeared in the *American Psychologist*, 1952, 7, 707-721.

66. H. Alpert, *op. cit.*

67. Kaempffert reminds us that the Federal government's interest in science is very old. He notes that the Constitution specifically calls for the cultivation of science, that the National Academy of Sciences was founded by Congress in 1863 at Lincoln's request to assist the government in utilizing research in the public interest, that Wilson established the National Research Council in World War I. See, *Should the Government Support Science*, Public Affairs Pamphlet #119. For another treatment of the historical growth of government research see B. Barber, *op. cit.*, Chap. VIII.

ulation in 1790; the first U.S. Census of Agriculture in 1840. However, beginning about 1933 in the United States, a great many governmental surveys were conducted. These arose out of the need for information in relation to the emergencies of the depression, and were made possible through the relief funds and personnel available.[68] However, with the second World War there was a further expansion of governmentally supported social research and the establishment of many government agencies directly engaged in the conduct of surveys. These activities were part of a much larger mobilization of science in prosecution of the war. Research expenditures by the Federal government increased from approximately 70 million dollars in 1940 to approximately 700 millions in 1944 giving some indication of the effect of the war on the growth of governmentally sponsored and supported scientific activities.[69]

Surveys which are the basis for fundamental public policy require that the information be beyond criticism and therefore that the research operations not be in the hands of private parties.[70] Moreover, the costs involved become so vast in particular instances as to preclude any other form of sponsorship. When we note that a Census costs millions, it is clear that no private agency can provide support.

In many instances, the activities of the government as a sponsor of social research go beyond the use of direct government research organizations. By means of grants or contracts, the government sponsors surveys undertaken by private research organizations. In this manner the government can draw on knowledge and experience and facilities in particular types of research which it would not be economical to provide for on a continuing basis within its own agencies. Such support, incidentally encourages the growth of social science agencies in a diversity of institutions and provides training opportunities for personnel. Moreover, it has been pointed out that "research institutions free of governmental commitments and administrative responsibilities, and under responsibility to exercise their own judgment with respect to techniques and standards of work, have been and will continue to be an outstanding source of contributions of a basic character

68. F. Stephan, *op. cit.*

69. Report on Science Legislation from the subcommittee on war mobilization to the Committee on Military Affairs, United States Senate, 79th Congress, Washington, Government Printing Office, February 27, 1946. Presumably only a small fraction of this total budget represents social science research funds.

For an analytic treatment of the relation of the American social scientist to government and its historical development the student is referred to R. K. Merton and D. Lerner, Social Scientists and Research Policy, in H. Lasswell and D. Lerner, *The Policy Sciences* (Stanford: Stanford University Press, 1951). For another treatment of the rise of survey research under governmental sponsorship, with special emphasis on comparative cultural differences in the official use of surveys in different countries, see: W. Nielsen, "Attitude Research and Government," *J. Soc. Issues*, 2, #2, 1946, 2-13.

70. For a general description of the statistical activities of U.S. Government Agencies the student is referred to P. Hauser and W. Leonard, eds., *Government Statistics For Business Use* (New York: Wiley, 1946).

and of types which less frequently develop within the governmental service itself."[71]

This pattern of government subsidization via contract is an exceedingly common one familiar to the survey analyst. Thus, Alpert shows in 1950–51 that 20 surveys were conducted by non-government research organizations under grant or contract with the Federal government.[72] The inventory of research in progress in 1952, of the American Association for Public Opinion Research indicates that some 27 of the total 56 projects abstracted were supported by government agencies.

The pattern of commercial sponsorship is also exceedingly widespread in survey research, with many research groups or organizations specializing in surveys of consumer preferences and wants, analysis of markets, surveys of the public for purposes of public relations of commercial companies, and surveys of the labor force for purposes of better industrial relations. It is difficult to estimate the magnitude of this pattern of subsidization of surveys, but one estimate of the annual income accruing to organizations from these sources ran as high as 30 million dollars.[73]

The extent of foundation support of survey research is unknown. While it is large in absolute terms, it is in all probability smaller than government and commercial sources, and there seems some evidence that it is declining in magnitude.[74]

There are obvious gains from the institutional pattern of subsidization. It provides for the continuation of survey research and maintains the expensive established facilities. It provides opportunities for training of new analysts. It even eases the difficult decision as to which among the myriad subjects for research should be chosen for immediate study. It insures for the action-oriented researcher that his findings will be applied to some extent by the sponsor or will at least find some receptive audience in the sponsor. It increases the efficiency of the researcher's skills since he must confront the practical realities of deadlines, cost factors, etc. It provides access to research sites and problems from which the social scientist is otherwise barred, since the sponsor's permission is essential to entry into such settings as a plant, a housing project, a government agency, or an army. Finally, it provides some prestige and social position for social scientists in the society and insures social support for the discipline, for only as research serves in some measure the larger society will it be maintained.

---

71. Memorandum of the Social Science Research Council on the Federal Government and Research on the Social Sciences, Hearings on Science Legislation, Part IV, October, 1945, 79th Congress, Washington, Government Printing Office, 1946.

72. *Op. cit.*

73. Newsweek Magazine, Nov. 15, 1948, cited from R. Myers, "Whose Business is Opinion Polling," *Int. J. Opin. Attit. Res.*, 2, 1948, 543-549.

74. If we compare the sponsorship of the research in progress reported in the inventory of 1952 of the Amer. Assoc. for Public Opinion Research, we note that 27 projects were sponsored by government, 9 by commercial groups, and 5 projects were foundation supported, *op. cit.*

We need not elaborate on the gains from subsidization. They create no problems for the analyst. However, the difficulties created by subsidization do need to be stressed at length for it is the *problems* of subsidization to which the analyst must be oriented.

In instances of subsidization where the sponsor specifies the initial problem, the analyst is involved in difficulties of communication and discussion and accommodation attendant on a definition of the problem that will satisfy the sponsor's needs as well as the analyst's requirements. Only insofar as the sponsor's needs are met will the research be applied in action. Only insofar as the analyst's requirements are in the picture will the research be satisfactory. This point expands the earlier discussion of the analyst's problems of communication and direction of the phases of the research as it flows through the parts of the research organization. He must also concern himself at beginning and conclusion of a survey with relations with a sponsor, and there are formidable difficulties in this relationship. With respect to the drawing of conclusions from the research findings and the effective communication of these to the action person, the policy maker or the sponsor, we shall defer any detailed treatment till Part IV, which deals with the utilization of survey findings. However, with respect to the influence of sponsors on the definition and design of surveys, we shall consider some of the problems.

Ackoff and Pritzker present a diagram which conveys an idea of the complexities of communication in the course of survey research, and the problems this creates for the analyst.[75] (See Figure II.) It should be noted that the diagram even simplifies the situation, since the sub-parts of the research *organization* which must be in communication are merely represented as a *unitary* "agency." Further simplification occurs in that the *sponsor* is identified as *unitary*. It may often be that the sponsor is an agency or collectivity with many personnel and sub-parts, each requiring research with a slightly different orientation. Merton remarks on the "hazards of competing research demands" from different practitioners and notes that "one practitioner's relevance is another's irrelevance." [76]

Merton and Lerner analyze some of these *specific technical* difficulties attendant on communication between analyst or research organization and sponsor of the research. They note, for example, that the sponsor often does not formulate his problem in terms translatable into a research design, and consequently there must be a clarification of the initial formula-

---

75. R. Ackoff and L. Pritzker, The Methodology of Survey Research, *Int. J. Opin. Attit. Res.*, 5, 1951, 313-334. With minor variations the diagram is reproduced, and the discussion elaborated in Ackoff's recent book, *The Design of Social Research* (Chicago: University of Chicago Press, 1953). Reproduced by permission of the publishers.

76. R. K. Merton, The Social Psychology of Housing, in W. Dennis, ed., *Current Trends in Social Psychology* (Pittsburgh: University of Pittsburgh Press, 1948). Specific examples of such competing demands in the field of housing research are noted on pp. 169-171.

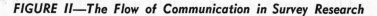

FIGURE II—The Flow of Communication in Survey Research

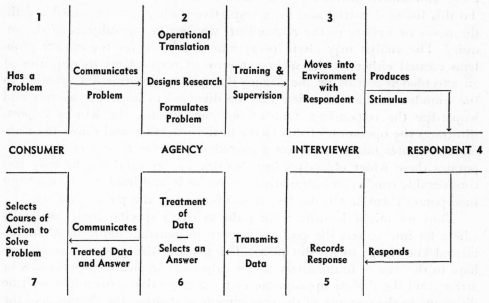

tion. They also note that the sponsor may often formulate his problem in ways which are not even appropriate for his *own* action needs. They further note a series of orientations or basic assumptions which both sponsor and analyst bring into the research situation which may impede the most desirable research formulation.[77]

But apart from the *technical* difficulties in such communication as these affect the design of the research, there are also *conflicts of interest* which affect the definition of the problem and the design of the research. Ackoff and Pritzker note that there is a series of objectives which may conflict one with another and have effects on the research formulation. They identify these at a *formal* level as including not merely the immediate objectives of the sponsor and the researcher but also the larger objectives of science in

77. R. K. Merton and D. Lerner, *op. cit.* For one case study of the way in which the orientation of social scientists narrowed the types of research needed for improvement of the situation in Puerto Rico, see, F. S. Cohen, "Science and Politics in Plans for Puerto Rico," *J. Soc. Issues*, 3, 1947, #4, 6-17. For another case study of the way in which the orientation of both the sponsors and analysts narrowed the research formulation, the reader is referred to the general field of industrial sociology. For example, Daniel Bell, in a critique of a variety of such studies, notes that such studies have rested generally on the "assumption that better face-to-face relations between management and union, and management and worker would lead to peace. Few attempts have been made to study how differences in social role in the factory give rise to differences of ideology and create conflicts between worker and management that are more basic than any question of defective or unintelligent management. . . . Another unstated assumption underlies the persistent tendency to pose the problem of industrial harmony in terms of the difficulties of *communication* . . . industrial relations . . . happen to be much less a problem of setting up a smoothly functioning organization than a problem of accommodating diverse and conflicting *interests.*" See: D. Bell, "Adjusting Men to Machines," *Commentary*, 1947.

general and the interests of other potential users of the research results or
those who will be affected by the action taken on the basis of the results.[78]
To this list of 4 parties and their respective goals might be added a fifth,
the needs or welfare of the *respondents* who act as the subjects in the inquiry. The analyst may often incorporate a concern for the *ethical* problems created either by the sheer exposure of respondents to inquiries of
an affect-laden sort or by the danger that private information revealed in
the confidence of an interview may be divulged to improper sources and
jeopardize the respondent. One of our case studies, the Kinsey Report,
illustrates the operation of this factor in the planning, and shows the elaborate measures taken to protect anonymity.[79] Insofar as the analyst incorporates these wider objectives into his day to day thinking, he may feel
considerable conflict in formulating the research, and insofar as he does not
incorporate them at all, the loss is to science and the public welfare.

Thus we might identify among the analyst's specific goals, especially
where he internalizes the goals of science in general, additions of fundamental knowledge to his discipline. The goals of the sponsor, except perhaps in the case of foundations, might emphasize immediate application or
action, and the designs appropriate to these respective goals might well be
different. In the instance of the government as sponsor, the character of the
findings sought would probably be somewhere between the respective poles
of findings of narrow but immediate practical value and findings of a more
general or abstract nature.[80] In the case of commercial sponsors and social
agencies, the goals would be knowledge of a more immediate, applied sort.
Glock, with experience as a director of a research organization within an
academic institution, notes this fact. He remarks that the research organization's "opportunity to do basic research is restricted since these sponsors,
for the most part, are interested in practical rather than scientific problems." [81]

The analyst will no doubt feel some pressure as a result of this potential
conflict with sponsor. In addition, insofar as he is also action-research oriented, he will incorporate some of this conflict within himself. Consequently, he must balance the gains from findings that have more immediate
application but less theoretical value against the gains of findings with less
immediate applicability to action or policy but with more relevance to the
growth of fundamental knowledge. In this decision he must weigh the pos-

---

78. Ackoff and Pritzker, *op. cit.*
79. For a treatment of these ethical problems, see Jahoda, Deutsch and Cook, *op. cit.*, 351-55.
80. It should be noted that short-range goals are not *intrinsic* to governmental support of
survey research. Such goals are characteristic of the specific government agencies which have
administrative responsibilities and which buy research services as an aid to their administrative
needs. One of the major arguments on behalf of a National Science Foundation was that while
it was a government agency, it was free of administrative responsibilities and would therefore be
dedicated to furthering long-range contributions to knowledge through its subsidies.
81. *Op. cit.*

sibility of alienating sources of funds. As illustrative of this problem, we may turn to a review of a survey research program under government sponsorship. Eysenck mirrors all these forces in his reaction to the publication of *The American Soldier,* one of the largest survey undertakings ever reported, based on the social research conducted under the auspices of the U.S. Army to provide factual information as a guide to military administration and policy.[82] Eysenck notes that the work incorporated in the volumes represents a "tremendous success" and demonstrates the "benefit of the wholesale application of science to human needs." He even notes that the findings have general significance in many instances beyond their immediate practical military value, and that they enable us "to check up on theory and hypotheses in various fields on the basis of mass data not previously available." He emphasizes the technical quality of the inquiries. Yet he also notes that "a great deal of what is reported is of importance only to those interested in the specific situation, i.e., an Army at war . . . and that much of the work reported is piece-meal and ad hoc; each investigation described has a given practical aim and is often of little general importance and does not lead to any general scientific knowledge of the subject."

We are not concerned here with the validity of Eysenck's contention, nor with the frequency with which such criticisms occurred in the reviews of these studies.[83] The review illustrates the conflict a given analyst might feel in the situation in which the sponsor or subsidizer's needs differ from the research worker. Insofar as accommodation to the sponsor's need for immediately applicable findings is the price the analyst must pay for the sponsor's subsidization, it might appear that there is no satisfactory resolution for the analyst. One avenue to such a solution however lies in *"secondary analysis,"* a body of procedures and modes of analysis designed to extract more fundamental by-products from survey investigations which were designed initially and primarily for more immediate practical purposes. Consequently, throughout this volume reference will be made to the principles of secondary analysis and detailed case study of one major secondary analysis will be presented.[84]

The sponsor's pressure towards immediate, practical survey research generates not merely conflicts over the *conceptualization* of the problem.

---

82. H. J. Eysenck, Review of The American Soldier, *Brit. J. Sociol.,* 1, 1950, 358-361.

83. For a discussion of a variety of reviews of these studies, the student is referred to D. Lerner, The American Soldier and the Public, in *Continuities in Social Research:* Studies in the Scope and Method of the American Soldier, R. K. Merton and P. F. Lazarsfeld, eds. (Glencoe, The Free Press, 1950).

84. For illustrations of secondary analysis and for further discussion of the general approach, the student is referred to P. L. Kendall and P. F. Lazarsfeld, Problems of Survey Analysis in *Continuities, op. cit.;* H. Hyman, "The Value Systems of Different Classes," J. Greenblum and L. Pearlin, "Vertical Mobility and Prejudice: A Socio-Psychological Analysis," in R. Bendix and S. M. Lipset, *Class, Status and Power* (Glencoe: The Free Press, 1953).

It may also generate effects during the *technical phases* of the analysis. Usually the sponsor's demand for practical findings is coupled with a sense of *urgency*—a desire for the findings to be available quickly. Merton notes that the analyst in the field of housing research, for example, is subject to "unyielding pressure, from all sides, to produce results, long before he is in a position to have warranted, adequately grounded results." [85] The analyst must be especially attuned therefore to the dangers of inaccuracy arising from excessive demands for speedy findings.

Apart from the question of conflict arising out of the concern for long-range vs. immediately applicable findings, there may well be ideological conflicts between sponsor and analyst. Thus the government as sponsor of surveys has naturally the view that the findings shall work in the service of existing policies or institutional arrangements which may conflict with the values or ideology of the analyst.

Robert Lynd expresses such an ideological conflict in his review of *The American Soldier*.[86] Lynd, also praises the *technical* quality of the analyses and remarks on the exciting *substantive* findings. He alludes to the impetus to the social sciences given by wartime research. Yet, he titles his review "The Science of Inhuman Relations" and remarks:

> These volumes carry magnificent promise and serious threat. On the one hand, social science is seen at work on the urgent affairs of contemporary man. . . . But, on the other hand, these volumes depict science being used with great skill to sort out and to control men for purposes not of their own willing. It is a significant measure of the impotence of liberal democracy that it must increasingly use its social sciences not directly on democracy's own problems, but tangentially and indirectly; it must pick up the crumbs from private business research on such problems as to how to gauge audience reaction so as to put together profitable synthetic radio programs and movies or, as in the present case, from Army research on how to turn frightened draftees into tough soldiers who will fight a war whose purposes they

---

85. R. K. Merton, Housing, *op. cit.* This is not to counsel slow-up of research for its own sake. That urgency must not be ignored, and that the pace of social science may be too slow for certain tastes is suggested by a review of one of our case studies, intended for policy making purposes. Hornell Hart in his review of the inquiry into the atomic bomb, remarks on the: "ponderous slowness with which our social science processes operate, as compared with the almost lightning swiftness of developments in the atomic crisis itself. The atomic bomb was dropped in the summer of 1945. The present report was published in April, 1947. A complimentary copy of the report reached the present writer on August 12, 1947. The request to write the present review was embodied in a letter dated December 6, 1947. The review is being dictated on January 6, 1948. These delays are to be charged, not to the culpability of any individual, but to the fact that social science has not yet accelerated its processes to any degree of speed even remotely adequate to grapple with the accelerated developments of modern destructive technologies. If we are to do any more than merely watch the atomic age shatter our ivory tower to hopeless fragments, we shall have to plan deliberately to speed up and improve our social science, with a radical thoroughness and courage comparable to that which has been applied, for example, in atomic research, in the development of military air forces, and in other developments on the destructive side." Review of Public Reaction to the Atomic Bomb and World Affairs, *Int. J. Opin. Attit. Res.*, 2, 1948, pp. 109-110.

86. *The New Republic*, August 29, 1949, 22-25.

do not understand. With such socially extraneous purposes controlling the use of social science, each advance in its use tends to make it an instrument of mass control, and thereby a further threat to democracy.

A labor spokesman, Solomon Barkin, the Research Director for the Textile Workers Union of America, indicates the ideological conflict that may attend the use of surveys in labor-management relations. He remarks on the partisan use of such surveys by management and argues that they serve distinctive functions which would be in opposition to the goals of organized labor. While he praises certain contributions of such surveys, he argues that *even where there is no bias in the techniques* employed, such surveys may work detrimentally to the interests of organized labor. He notes that such surveys, by determining sources of discontent which management may in turn correct, may be intended to counteract the strength of the union. He further notes that the data may provide management with an independent check on unions demands and proposals and thereby undermine a union function. He states: "the union is clubbed through all channels of communication with the results of supposedly objective surveys of worker opinion, and its position and right to speak for its members strongly challenged." [87]

Apart from the conflicts that may arise because of ideological differences and because of differences in concerns for long-range findings, there may well be conflicts for the analyst arising out of the pressures on the part of the sponsor toward *non-objectivity* in the research. Such a pressure would be especially prominent in commercially subsidized survey research, and might on occasion occur in governmentally sponsored research because of bureaucratic factors. For example, C. W. Hart notes that government research agencies may be prohibited from collecting certain types of data for fear of Congressional criticism.[88]

Under such conditions, the analyst's proper function is debased and the survey ceases to be science. Such pressures towards non-objectivity most readily operate in the phase of utilization of the ultimate findings of a survey, through suppression of findings and partial or slanted reporting. In many instances, the analyst's official responsibility is discharged when he presents a report to the sponsor, and he may have little control over dissemination or publication or use of the findings which may rest with the sponsor. This would be true not only of commercial sponsors but also of

---

87. Solomon Barkin, Opinion Surveys in Labor-Management Relations, Address delivered before American Association for Public Opinion Research, Annual Meeting, Vassar College, June, 1952.

88. *Op. cit.*

It is interesting to note, however, in this context that the agency traditionally regarded as conservative and bureaucratic, the army, made the basic data available which insured the publication of the volumes *The American Soldier*. The data were given to the Social Science Research Council in order to insure frank and impartial analysis. The army exercised no control over the published interpretations or conclusions.

social and action agencies and interest groups seeking to use the findings for purposes of public persuasion. Where private auspices and funds for research are not diversified, there is the danger of one-sided sponsorship and one-sided reporting. But these mechanisms of non-objectivity are not irremediable, and do not affect the analyst's intrinsic activities.[89]

What concerns us more is the danger that even in the *technical* phases of research design and analysis, pressures towards non-objectivity or bias may operate upon the analyst. For example, Kornhauser presents evidence that the accumulated research of the major public opinion survey organizations has been biased in an anti-labor direction, and that the mechanisms involved include not merely biased interpretation or reporting and slanted questions, but also the more subtle mechanisms of choice of phenomena around which the issues are posed, etc.[90]

Kornhauser in a later and more general treatment of this problem of "top-level bias" emphasizes the fact that the *technical skill* of the analyst is not crucial. "Problems of inadequate knowledge and skill and problems of conscious or unconscious slanting of procedures need to be perceived and tackled *separately*." [91] In this paper he notes a number of additional mechanisms by which the analyst consciously or unconsciously may bias the results to accommodate to the pressures of the sponsor. For example, he notes that the choice of *universe,* and mode of *sampling* may be the mechanism and illustrates this possibility with the hypothetical example of "a survey on infringements of civil rights conducted among white people only." Another mechanism may involve the *choice of particular dimensions* of a complex variable or *particular modes of index-construction,* as illustrated by his hypothetical example of magazine readership surveys, in which a mass magazine might be described by total readership figures, but a less popular magazine could be made to appear just as desirable through emphasizing the social status or purchasing power of its readers.

Kornhauser notes that such pressures are rarely exerted overtly by the sponsor but that the analyst or organization, dependent on continued support, may voluntarily accommodate to what is *believed* to be the sponsor's desires. And Lee remarks on the same phenomenon: "Sociologists . . . are now finding their usefulness appreciated by corporation and trade associations which underwrite their opinion and attitude studies under conditions

89. For example, in relation to pressures towards non-objectivity working through this mechanism, many research organizations have written into their contracts clauses with respect to publication policies. In the instance of survey findings of a public opinion poll nature, disseminated through syndication via newspapers, additional problems arise because of the inherent inadequacy of the medium for scientific and comprehensive reporting, but these can also be ameliorated through proper contractual arrangements. See, on this score, Chap. IV, *The Pre-Election Polls, op. cit.*

90. A. W. Kornhauser, "Are Public Opinion Polls Fair to Organized Labor," *Publ. Opin. Quart.,* 1946–47, 484-500.

91. A. W. Kornhauser, "The Problem of Bias in Opinion Research," *Int. J. Opin. Attit. Res.,* 1947, 1, #4, 1-16. Italics ours.

said to protect the freedom, objectivity and general academic respectability of the researchers . . . A perfectly open mind . . . is a . . . difficult accomplishment . . . especially when the situation is complicated by the fact of a donor's grant renewal always around the corner. At the least it requires a patient, understanding, or deceased donor." [92]

Kornhauser's claim with respect to surveys on labor has been disputed and his evidence questioned by members of a number of the well known opinion research organizations, who were the targets of his criticisms.[93] But disputing his evidence does not detract from our fundamental point. The proof of bias, rather than sheer error, on the part of the research agency or analyst always involves some estimate of the hidden motives of the researcher and/or the subsidizer, and is therefore difficult to establish and easy to contest. However, whether the case of Kornhauser vs. Organized Pollers is decided one way or another, it illustrates the likelihood that *imputations of bias* will be made simply because the existence of subsidization by interested parties leads other parties to question the objectivity of the research. *Bias* may not be frequent under such conditions, but *claims* and counter-claims about bias are bound to arise.

The danger of actual bias with consequent discrediting of the findings cannot be ignored by the analyst. Nor can imputations of bias, irrespective of proof, be ignored for they cast doubt on the findings. This point can be documented dramatically by the "code" or "Criteria for Marketing and Advertising Research" promulgated by the Advertising Research Foundation.[94] This code, originally formulated by the American Association of Advertising Agencies in 1938 as a guide for appraising market and advertising research, after a revision was reviewed and approved by the Advertising Research Foundation. It is intended primarily for determining the validity of surveys of consumers by the inspection of the crucial phases of the survey process. In the revision of the original code, a changed point of view is made explicit—"that it is the duty of *those conducting the survey* to prove that no bias exists, rather than *caveat emptor.*" And in the list of specific criteria, while such technical areas as questionnaire and sample design are covered, it is first noted that the report of the findings should include a statement of *the conditions under which the study was made,* and the statement should note *who financed the study.* In other words, knowledge of the subsidizer of the study is regarded as necessary to enable readers to appraise the quality of the research and presumably establishes

92. A. M. Lee, "Sociological Theory in Public Opinion and Attitude Studies," *Amer. Sociol. Rev.,* 12, 1947, 312-323.

93. H. C. Link, A. Freiberg, *et al.,* "Is Dr. Kornhauser Fair to Organized Pollers," *Publ. Opin. Quart.,* 11, 1947, 198-212.

94. *Criteria for Marketing and Advertising Research* (New York: Advertising Research Foundation, 1953), (pamphlet).

at least the basis for the "shadow of a doubt" about the purity of the research.

One of the surveys described earlier, on public opinion about American radio, is illustrative of the problem of imputations of bias. As noted earlier, the survey was conducted by the National Opinion Research Center, then of the University of Denver, a research organization, prohibited by its charter from conducting surveys for profit and by its very academic nature less likely to be pro-commercial or to need the continued good will of *commercial* sponsors. The study was analyzed by the Bureau of Applied Social Research of Columbia University, also a non-profit and non-commercial agency. The final report contains many statements which put the problem of evaluation of radio as an institution in a larger context than merely that of "mass tastes" and incorporates a detailed treatment of the public's criticisms as expressed in the survey. Thus in the preface, it is remarked that "while public satisfaction is a very important criterion, it is only one of several which should be applied to the evaluation of radio's performance. The *intrinsic merit* of programs and the social implication of their development . . . must also be considered." Later it is noted that "a study of the social structure and social implications of the radio industry would seem to be a second necessary element in an overall evaluation." And it is further noted that *"public opinion is only one* of several pillars upon which the final evaluation of radio should be based." There is a thirteen page detailed treatment of criticisms of radio advertising, and a twenty-five page chapter on the "critic" in a total text of 90 pages.[95]

Yet, despite the widely accepted image of the integrity of the two research organizations and the balanced coverage in the text, the auspices of the investigation create an aura of doubt, and the presence of interested parties leads to imputations of bias. Thus the reviewer in the New York *Times* comments as follows:

> The criticism of this one-third minority is aired, *not thoroughly as the authors claim,* but in a manner which comes close to being a *skilful apologia for the broadcast industry's* product. For although the authors are aware that such a "minority" does exist, their salute to the remaining "majority" as . . . "the people who do not write letters to the editors and who do not participate in discussions in women's clubs" *scarcely indicates a truly scientific, unbiased approach* to the minority's grievances about radio.
>
> On the question of artistic standards, in a medium which is sadly deficient in same, the authors *equivocate* with statements such as . . . "it is quite inevitable that as the market for the fine arts expands, its product becomes less subtle." The minority will perhaps question that there ever was a time when radio was "subtle," and will perhaps feel let down by such *appeasement of the status quo.* Certainly it is true that "radio shares this problem with all commercialized arts and crafts" but just as certainly,

---

95. *Op. cit.* Italics ours.

those who purvey programs to the 90% of American homes having radios are under an enormous cultural responsibility, which even an overwhelming "yes" vote of 82% cannot obviate.[96]

The comment of the reviewer that the original analysts were not unbiased because of their "salute" to the majority as "people who do not write letters to editors and who do not participate in discussions in women's clubs" is especially relevant to our point on the imputation of bias because of the social context of survey inquiries. This remark by the analysts appears in the preface of their book.[97] The reader is referred to the exact text to evaluate for himself the implications of the statement. Reading of this passage will suggest that the statement was not intended to disparage the sentiments of the minority but simply to stress the well-established technical feature of sample surveys in distinguishing opinion based on the activities of vocal and articulate individuals or pressure groups from mass opinion which is normally not channeled politically.[98] Yet, the critic who is involved in the controversy created by the findings does not see the surveys in a neutral or indifferent light and regards the remark as evidence of bias.

It should be noted that the original research organizations and analysts involved did not ignore disputes on the findings and the imputation of bias. In the case of this inquiry it was intended as the first survey in a series which would provide periodic information on the American public's feelings about radio. Consequently, a second nation-wide inquiry was conducted two years later which provided trend data on some of the original areas and new data on problems not previously examined. In planning the second inquiry, considerable attention was given to the criticisms that had been levelled at the first report. It is noted, for example, that "after the final questionnaire had been developed, it was submitted to a group of social scientists who had previously criticized the first report. They made a number of improvements which were incorporated into the questionnaire on which the present report is based." In the text of the new report, the qualifications expressed in the first volume as to the use of popular satisfaction as a criterion for evaluating an institution are repeated verbatim. In addition, there is a detailed appendix describing the development of the new questionnaire and the reasons for modifying or omitting questions that had been used in the first inquiry. Certainly, one of the reasons for this appendix, incidentally an almost unique and excellent source for learning of the technical problems of questionnaire design and the welter of decisions the analyst confronts in developing a questionnaire, must go deeper than the

---

96. N. Y. Times, November 17, 1946, reviewed by Peter Irving. Italics ours. By permission of the author and publisher.

97. p. VIII.

98. See, for example, Rowena Wyant, "Voting Via the Senate Mailbag," Part I, *Publ. Opin. Quart.*, 1941, 3, 359-382.

mere gain to the student. It serves as evidence with respect to the possible charge that bias was introduced into the second inquiry through the omission of questions on areas which had previously shown radio in public disfavor.[99]

The moral for the analyst of survey research, operating under conditions of sponsorship, is clear. Despite attempts at objectivity or unbiased research his analysis will be subject to criticism on grounds of bias arising from subsidization. He must be especially concerned to prevent any biases that could *actually* arise from felt pressures on the part of his sponsor and he must be especially effective in marshalling evidence in support of the objectivity of his findings in relation to his audience.

However, the problem in given instances can become even more acute. While the reception of a research may be hostile, the issue of bias often remains at the level of speculation. But the condition of subsidization of research may mean not merely the subsidization of *one* analyst's study, but the subsidization of *several* studies on the same issue by opposing parties. Where a multiplicity of sponsors report opposing findings, it of necessity leads to questions about the objectivity of the analysis. That this is not academic can be documented in a number of well known cases. In one instance, opposing survey findings were reported on the degree of public support of governmental programs of medical care.[100] The later examination of the respective surveys revealed the *technical mechanisms* within the research process which led to the different findings, but, of course, leaves unanswered the question of *why* the different techniques were employed by the respective research organizations. When the questions of motives for the employment of particular procedures is raised, the factor of "bias" in relation to the vested interests of the respective sponsors and the ideologies of the researchers must inevitably be considered.

In another instance opposing findings were reported with respect to the influence of television viewing on sports attendance.[101] Here again, the detailed analysis of the respective procedures reveals the technical grounds for the findings, but leaves unanswered the question as to why particular, and often misleading procedures were employed. In the latter instance, the deterioration in the public image of social science as "objective" following such disparate results can be documented. John Crosby, the well-known

99. P. F. Lazarsfeld and P. Kendall, *Radio Listening in America* (New York: Prentice-Hall, 1948).

100. S. Payne, "Some Opinion Research Principles developed through studies of social Medicine," *Publ. Opin. Quart.*, 10, 1946, 93-98.

101. The study reporting no permanent deleterious effects on sports attendance as a result of television was: J. N. Jordan, *The Long Range Effect of Television and other Factors on Sports Attendance*, Washington, D.C., 1950, Radio Television Manufacturers Association, (privately printed). The study in which losses in attendance were demonstrated as a result of television viewing was *The Effects of Television on College Football Attendance*, Report #3, National Opinion Research Center, University of Chicago, 1952, (privately printed).

radio columnist of the *Herald Tribune,* devoted an entire column to the discussion of the disparate findings, titling it "You Can Prove Anything." And instead of presenting a factual treatment of the respective surveys, he damned the entire institution of social research, as representing merely services that can be bought by any client who wishes to have any type of findings documented. We quote relevant portions of his column, and parallel it with the facts of the matter.

One of the wonderful things about this age of electronics is the research business, which can prove anything you like with absolute dependability and a magnificent flow of statistics. The more money you spend on your survey, the more positive is the conclusion and, of course, the more beautiful the pamphlet embodying your research.

It has always seemed to me that the fundamental purpose of any survey is to prove what you set out to prove—not, for heaven's sake, to discover what the facts are. Now you take the football situation. Does television affect football attendance? Or doesn't it? The National Collegiate Athletic Association, which rather wanted to prove that TV does hurt football attendance, hired the National Opinion Research Center of the University of Chicago for $50,000 to survey the situation. They spent the $50,000 and proved exactly what the N.C.A.A. wanted proved. "Television does definite damage to college football attendance."

Let's leave it at that for a moment and turn to another survey. The National Association of Radio and Television Broadcasters paid the bills for this one. The conclusion sought—and I mean just that—was exactly opposite to that of the N.C.A.A. The broadcasters wanted to prove that TV didn't hurt the gate—and damned if they didn't prove just that. In fact this survey proved—and I use the word "proved" with some misgiving—that football attendance was better in television areas than in non-television areas, leading to the suspicion that TV helped the gate rather than hurt it.

What are we to make of those diametrically opposite conclusions from two research outfits dealing in the same situation? My feeling is that we ought to switch them around, that the broadcasters ought to hire the National Opinion Research Center and the football association ought to hire the other outfit, each of them to disprove conclusively what they have already proved conclusively. For $50,000 this shouldn't be hard.

This doesn't mean that the researchers are not adequate to their tasks; it means, instead, that they are entirely too adequate. They can, as I say, prove anything with any set of facts.[102]

Crosby neglected a significant fact. The NORC report he discussed was: "No. 3 in a series, and . . . the first two surveys were paid for *jointly* by the NCAA and the four television networks—NBC, CBS, ABC and Dumont— on an equal basis. We were approached by the two groups—the colleges and the networks—precisely because they both were confused by differing opinions and contradictory 'surveys,' they wanted a systematic investigation of

---

102. New York *Herald Tribune,* May 28, 1952. By permission of the publishers.

the problem, and they recognized NORC as an impartial, non-profit, academic research agency." [103]

Controversial Subject Matter
and Its Consequences

In the instance of the radio inquiry, it can be recalled from the initial description of the survey that the social context of the inquiry was one of strong conflict, and competing demands by a variety of interests for a policy decision by the FCC congenial to their interests. In such a situation it is, of course, likely that rival parties will try to contest findings that are detrimental to their cause. In this process, it is most common that imputations of bias are made so as to discredit the results. Insofar as the analyst has a responsibility to his sponsor who wishes to see the results applied, and insofar as the analyst himself is action-oriented, it is essential that he be able to defend the objectivity of the research as well as possible. Moreover, in the larger context, the perpetuation of social research as an institution requires that the image of such research be that of objective procedures and findings. Otherwise, support will not long continue.

But this problem is not an occasional one for the analyst. Surveys *generally* deal with subject matters that are controversial. The social setting within which they are undertaken and a solution presented is *generally* loaded with conflict. The reader need only re-examine the case studies presented initially to see how frequently this is the case—even where the inquiry appears academic or theoretical in its character.

The emphasis on the controversial dates back to the major beginnings of social surveys. While early surveys differ methodologically and their focus is more diffuse, the growth of the survey movement occurred in the 19th century in the context of presenting facts leading to social reform. The early inquiries centered on poverty, drinking, delinquency, crime, industrial accidents, charity, child welfare, etc. [104]

As already noted, where the research is subsidized, there is often an interested party eager to use the findings as scientific evidence which supports a particular position in a controversy, or planning to apply the findings so as to make more likely the achievement of a prior goal. Naturally, opponents are eager to see different goals achieved or different policies set and argue the findings. However, even where there is *no specific issue* to be resolved at a policy level, and the sponsor is *disinterested*, there may well be conflict and controversy. The sheer contents of most surveys when published en-

---

103. Cited from an official reply to John Crosby by NORC.
104. See Parten, *op. cit.,* or Caradog-Jones, *op. cit.*

gender controversy. This occurs either because some *diffuse* social consequence is envisioned as a result of popular exposure to the findings and rival interests become concerned or simply because the findings offend individuals or groups with particular ideologies.[105]

In either instance, the question of the objectivity of the survey may arise. Particularly where such diffuse social consequences *actually* can follow from the publication of findings, the analyst has a heavy obligation to protect the research from bias.

We can illustrate the problem from one of our case studies. Kinsey's inquiry had no explicit propagandistic or manipulative purpose; its sponsorship was academic and from foundation sources. Yet it is obvious that its implications were relevant to a variety of interest groups. Crespi and Stanley report a variety of public reactions to the book noting for example the influential *Reader's Digest* commenting "Because of newly published polls and *'cold, detached, scientific' surveys,* many people have come to fear that old anchors are now being swept away . . ." [106]

The point can also be documented from the history of election prediction surveys. Generally, these inquiries have been subsidized by newspapers, whose interest is essentially in news features that will appeal to the readership. No specific action or decision is to grow out of such inquiries, and the data are not intended to persuade any specific policy maker to accept some position. Nevertheless, there is a belief that the publication of such results have social consequences of a *diffuse* sort. In the case of the election polls this has involved the notion of "bandwagon effect" with large numbers of voters being swayed in their ultimate voting behavior, by the mere knowledge from the published surveys of who is the popular candidate.[107] And the adherents of one party fearing such consequences may well contest the

---

105. A recent newspaper item provides a perfect illustration. Louis B. Heller, Democratic Congressman from New York requested the Postmaster General to bar the second volume of the Kinsey Report from the mails on grounds of obscenity. Heller made the request in advance of actual publication and on the basis of the advance publicity. He remarked "it appears to me that Dr. Kinsey, who is accusing the bulk of American womanhood of having sinned before or after marriage, is actually himself committing the greatest sin against the women of America. Under the pretext of making a great contribution to scientific research and to social progress, he is hurling the insult of the century against our mothers, wives, daughters and sisters." Rep. Heller called Dr. Kinsey's conclusions about women's sex lives "highly questionable, if not downright ridiculous." He said Dr. Kinsey "is contributing to the depravity of a whole generation, to the loss of faith in human dignity and human decency, to the spread of juvenile delinquency, to the misunderstanding and the confusion about sex. He is helping to undermine the institutions of marriage and family life which are the mainstay of our civilization. Those weak in mind and weak in spirit will surely be misled by the so-called facts and conclusions of the Kinsey report based on the experiences of less than 6,000 women, many of them frustrated, neurotic and outcasts of society." N. Y. Herald Tribune, August 30, 1953.

106. The quotation is reported in L. Crespi and E. Stanley, "Youth Looks at the Kinsey Report," *Publ. Opin. Quart.,* 12, 1948, 687-696. It is taken from a longer article, Must We Change Our Sex Standards, *Reader's Digest,* June, 1948. Italics ours.

107. For discussion of the bandwagon effect, the student is referred to Wm. Albig, *Public Opinion* (New York: McGraw-Hill, 1939), p. 233.

findings which show their candidate as defeated while the adherents of the other party—believing in such consequences might have motives to bias the original results or their presentation.[108] Thus the apparent pastime of seeing into the future takes on social significance, and engenders such controversy that official Congressional Inquiries into such polls were made in 1945.[109] Gallup further informs us that the question of government regulation of polls has come up in nearly every Congress over a recent 20 year period.[110]

Considering the controversial subject matter of many surveys, the relevance of the findings to matters of public welfare, and the opportunities for the interests, prejudices and bias of individual and organized researchers or clients to distort the results, Edward Bernays has even adopted the extreme position that "pollsters ought to be required to pass state examinations as to their character and skills, and ought not to be allowed to practice without a license issued by government." [111]

Merton describes this atmosphere in which the analyst works for the field of housing research, but his remarks apply equally to most of the other topics of survey research. He remarks on the "hazard of institutional crossfire" and notes that around various alternative policies,

> are ranged large and important groups, more concerned with satisfying their interests than with having research establish the sociological, economic, and psychological consequences of alternative policies. The social psychologist bent upon entering into housing research, therefore, must know that he is forsaking the relative calm and peace of his academic laboratory for the strife and embroilments of the institutional battlefield. What is more, belonging to neither army, the social psychologist must be prepared to be caught in the heavy cross-fire. Little if any of his research work will be taken for what he intends it to be: scientific analyses of the social-psychological consequences of alternative policies in housing. Instead, each research finding will be taken as a sign of abiding allegiance or of desertion from one army or the other. . . . In the arena of large decisions, some social-psychological findings are tagged as 'dangerous thoughts' irrespective of the objectivity of the research. . . . The social psychologist . . . may believe that he is merely engaging in socially relevant research, that, attuned to current changes in the institutional structure of housing, he is gearing his scientific inquiries to problems having both scientific and practical pertinence. In actual fact he is doing much more. He is volunteering for a hazardous reconnaissance in a sociological no-man's land, where he will be exposed to pitiless cross fire from all camps. . . . Yet the social psychologist must be . . . stoic.

108. For discussion of the public reporting of results of election surveys and possible biasing or misleading treatments of the results see, D. Katz, "The Polls and the 1944 Election," *Publ. Opin. Quart.*, 8, 1944–45, 468-482, or Chap. IV, Pre-election Polls of 1948, *op. cit.*
    109. The inquiry under the direction of Clinton P. Anderson as Chairman of the House of Representatives Committee to Investigate Campaign Expenditures, 1945.
    110. G. Gallup, "On the Regulation of Polling," *Publ. Opin. Quart.*, 12, 1948, 733-735.
    111. E. L. Bernays, "Should Pollsters be Licensed," *Int. J. Opin. Attit. Res.*, 3, 1949, 6-12.

When research bears on large and important decisions, it has none of the privileges of neutrality. When his research is socially relevant, the social psychologist must expect to be alternately praised and damned, as his findings seemingly lend support to one or another interest group.[112]

112. R. K. Merton, in Dennis, *Current Trends in Social Psychology, op. cit.* The material quoted is from pages 165-169 by permission of the publisher.

CHAPTER II

Variations in Technical Context
and the Proper Orientation
of the Analyst

THUS far we have discussed certain general features of the broad *social* setting within which survey research occurs. The case studies we described have certain features in common and the analyst must be aware of the consequences for his work. These features since they are not specifically technical in character and since they are pervasive are often taken for granted or neglected. The analyst often overlooks their existence. But while survey research must perforce operate within a particular *social* setting, it is not restricted to certain narrow *technical* or *substantive* realms. The seven case studies cited were intended to convey the wide variety of substantive contents and formal problems and the correspondingly different procedures used within the general common framework. They were intended to broaden the image that the student has of survey research, because that image usually involves a rather rigid or narrow conception of the technical aspects of a survey. The growth of established organizations to conduct surveys of particular types and the continuing demands of sponsors has generally led to particular practices becoming stabilized. These practices may be appropriate for particular problems that have been studied, but their prominence should not mislead the analyst into thinking that they are appropriate for *all* types of problems.[1]

---

1. For a treatment of this problem of the institutionalization of certain procedures to the detriment of effective survey research, see: D. Katz, "Survey Techniques and Polling Procedures as Methods in Social Science," *J. Soc. Issues*, 2, 1946, 62-66.

Thus modern survey research received much encouragement and both popular and strategic support from the rise of public opinion polls as forecasters of elections and arbiters on specific political issues. In the service of this problem, emphasis naturally was placed on the *sampling of the electorate*. For many problems, however, the national cross-section of voters may not be the most relevant universe. Moreover, the problem of voting preference relates to an apparently *unitary phenomenon*—whether one is for or against a candidate. For many problems, however, a single question of preference cannot comprehend the complexity of the phenomenon. The unit of description here is that of the *individual* since the outcome under study, voting, is apparently the product of the acts of many separate individuals. But for many problems the more appropriate unit of study may be a family or some other collectivity.

Public opinion polls have traditionally supported themselves by selling news services to the mass media. Consequently, the phenomena studied have often tended towards the hot but *transient issues* of the moment rather than towards more general persistent phenomena. In addition, the space requirements of a news release have strengthened the tendency to study a limited number of aspects of the problem. But such practices may be inappropriate to other conditions of survey research.

Modern survey research also received much impetus from commercial sources whose concern was to establish consumer preferences or purchasing behavior. Here, too, emphasis was naturally placed on simple questions, few in number, and the examination of the results by *characteristics relevant to the distribution problems or markets* of the sponsor. For many other types of problems, however, the classification of data by region, area, or economic status of the respondent is not the most appropriate procedure.

Encouragement of survey research often came from the fact that the results were applicable to the immediate problems of commercial and governmental sponsors, and here the emphasis is upon phenomena and variables at a *concrete* level, rather than on variables stated at a relatively abstract level. But for many theoretical purposes, more abstract variables may be appropriate.

These and many other *historical accidents* in the growth of survey research have tended to institutionalize certain practices and thereby narrow the vision of the analyst in planning the survey that is most appropriate to his given problem. Actually, the analyst in any established organization must deal over time with a wide variety of assignments. A sense of this variety of contents, formal problems, and correspondingly, of research designs can be obtained from the index of the studies undertaken by any major established survey organization. We reproduce in Chart II two examples of such an index. Because of its availability and admirable detail we choose first the *official descriptions* of a small number of the total number of inquiries conducted by the British Social Survey, an official government agency in charge of survey research.[2] Of course, this example will not give the full diversity of survey research because the British Social Survey must naturally work in the service of the administrative needs of government. By contrast, the index of the research of an academic or commercial research organization would emphasize other substantive problems. We therefore reproduce for comparative purposes an index of selected studies by the National Opinion Research Center of the University of Chicago, a non-profit survey organization affiliated with an academic institution.

Chart II

Selected Examples of the Research of the British Social Survey

Heating of Dwellings
A study for the Building Research Station of space and water heating in domestic buildings, in conjunction with an expert committee of the Ministry of Works.

Lighting of Dwellings
A study for the Building Research Station of the efficiency of domestic lighting, in conjunction with an expert committee of the Ministry of Works.

Cooking Habits
Study made for the Ministry of Health of methods used for cooking vegetables.

Scottish Housing
A study for the Department of Health for Scotland of the Social Factors relevant to the location of new housing.

Venereal Disease
A study for the Ministry of Health of the impact of its campaign against venereal disease.

Stoke and Salford Dietary Survey
Special studies of the diets of school children in these towns in connection with Ministry of Health experiments with vitamin supplements.

Middlesborough
A survey for the Ministry of Town and Country Planning designed to indicate the social factors involved in town planning.

The Employment of Older Persons
This inquiry was carried out for the Industrial Research Board of the Medical Research Council to determine the proportion of persons over 60 still in employment in 1945. The survey discussed the possibility of a continuing decline in the employment of old people and the reasons why they continue to work. The circumstances in which old people live are also considered.

Diphtheria Immunisation [3]
A second inquiry made for the Ministry of Health to find out how their im-

---

2. List of Reports published since 1941, The Social Survey, Home Ministry, Great Britain (mimeo).

3. Because these are the official descriptions in the original index, we follow the English spelling rather than the American.

munisation scheme was working and to assess the effect of their publicity campaign.

Recruitment to Civil Service

A survey for the Treasury of attitudes to employment in the executive and clerical grades of the Civil Service.

Carpets

A survey for the Carpet Working Party of the Board of Trade to determine the future demand for carpets and the extent to which working class homes are now carpeted.

Willesden and the New Towns

An inquiry carried out for the Ministry of Town and Country Planning and designed to show the social facts related to movements of population to New Towns and in particular to provide guidance on the dovetailing of the movements of population and industry.

Survey of Deafness

An inquiry made for the Medical Research Council's Committee on Medical and Surgical Problems of Deafness to provide estimates of the incidence of different degrees of deafness and the probable demand for hearing aids.

Attitudes to Road Safety and the Road Safety Campaign

An inquiry designed to measure some basic trends in attitude towards, and opinion of, road safety problems made for the Ministry of Transport.

Women and Industry

An inquiry carried out for the Ministry of Labor to find out the social facts related to the willingness of women to take up employment with a view to developing a recruitment campaign for this purpose.

Public Opinion and Colonial Affairs

An inquiry carried out for the Colonial Office into public knowledge about the colonies designed to provide a basis for an information campaign aimed at giving information about colonial territories and creating an interest in their affairs.

Betting in Britain

A report on Betting Habits and spending in 1949/50 prepared for the Central Statistical Office in consultation with the Royal Commission on Betting, Lotteries, and Gaming.

Food Supplements

An investigation made for the Ministry of Food to discover the extent to which mothers made use of the fruit juices and cod liver oil supplied by the Ministry of Food.

Audience Reaction to the Film—"The Undefeated"

A survey, made at the request of Films Division of the Central Office of Information, on public reaction to a film called "The Undefeated" which is concerned with disabled ex-Servicemen.

Children out of School

An inquiry made for the Ministry of Education into the Interests and Pursuits of school children out of school hours and the provision made for them. The results were used to help the Ministry's Advisory Council for Education in its consideration of the extent to which school work and activities could and should be related to and develop those interests.

Selected Examples of the Research of The National Opinion Research Center

Leisure Time
Inquiry into the leisure time activities of adults in New York City.

Political Attitudes
A Study using a probability sample of the population of New York, Illinois and California, designed to elicit attitudes toward national and international affairs.

Cincinnati Looks at the United Nations
A survey of Cincinnati residents designed to evaluate the effects of an information campaign on attitudes toward the U.N. Interviews were held both before and after the campaign.

Dual Study of Foreign Affairs and Religious Prejudices
Study combining questions for both the U. S. Government and the American Jewish Committee utilizing a national sample. Questions on both foreign affairs and sentiments towards Jews were included, along with some items from the California F scale.

Interviewer Effects
A five year program of research on interviewing as a method of data collection in the social science field, with particular reference to sources of error in the interview and means of controlling these sources.

Disaster Effects
A series of studies designed to isolate the factors related to the maintenance or rapid re-establishment of effective social organization and morale in community disasters.

Attitudes toward International Affairs
Survey of a national sample designed to elicit attitudes toward selected international issues.

Mental Health
Large scale national survey designed to study the state of popular knowledge, belief and practice with respect to mental health.

Chronic Illness
An inquiry in Hunterdon County, New Jersey, into the physically and socially disabling effects of chronic illness and of methods of estimating the rehabilitative potential and needs for care of various types of chronically ill persons. Study was co-sponsored by the National Commission on Chronic Illness and Hunterdon County Medical Center.

Aircraft Noise
Research into factors underlying public annoyance with aircraft noise and into community reactions to airport location and operation. The introducing of control groups by means of a complex sample design made it possible to test the differential effects of various airport locations, flight paths, and local neighborhood noise levels on experienced annoyance.

Costs of Medical Care
National survey based on a probability sample of 3000 households, and two local studies based on samples of 2000 households in Boston and 1500 in Bir-

mingham, of consumer expenditures for health care and of the mediating effects of pre-paid medical insurance with respect to these expenditures. Study was sponsored by the Health Information Foundation.

Election Study

Panel study based on a national sample designed to compare pre-election attitudes and vote intentions, with post-election attitudes and vote behavior. Respondents were interviewed just before, and immediately after the 1944 presidential election.

Effect of Television on Football Game Attendance

Inquiry made for the National Collegiate Athletic Association and the television networks based on a national sample of football fans, designed to determine the effects of the televising of football games on actual paid attendance at the stadiums.

Businessmen's Attitudes toward Foreign Trade

An inquiry conducted for The Center for International Studies, Mass. Inst. of Technology into attitudes of business leaders toward various aspects of foreign trade with particular emphasis on reciprocal trade treaties, tariff questions, and international currency arrangements. Patterns of communication behavior are examined in relation to the formation of such attitudes.

Alcoholism

Inquiry of a national sample into public knowledge and attitudes about alcohol and its effects, plus factual data concerning consumption.

Recruitment of Doctors into Medical Corps

Samples of medical personnel at various stages of a medical career: medical students, internes, practicing physicians, were used for a comparative study of attitudes toward recruitment into the medical corps.

We shall not discuss in detail these inquiries by the British Social Survey or the National Opinion Research Center, Our seven case studies will constitute the major illustrations of the different formal problems for which surveys might be undertaken and the research designs appropriate to these problems. However, the student might now inspect this Chart and the earlier cases in the light of some of the future questions we shall raise. For example, what kinds of populations seem to be required for particular surveys? What are the advantages of a particular decision about a choice of population? What should be noted about the range of substantive contents? Are the contents under study objective characteristics or subjective phenomena? Are the contents complex or unitary? Are the formal problems calling for solution of such a nature that an estimate or description is involved, a prediction of the future, or a test of an hypothesis? If any hypothesis is involved, what kinds of independent variables are emphasized? In later chapters we shall take up in detail each of these problems as they arise in particular types of survey analysis. In this chapter we shall use our case materials to outline the major types of formal problems and corresponding designs that occur in survey research.

The Major Types of Surveys

Several of the case studies cited earlier illustrate the use of surveys for the *sheer description of some phenomenon*. Kinsey's inquiry was concerned with the description of the sexual behavior of the American male; The Radio inquiry with the description of the American public's general feelings about radio; the investigation under the auspices of the Social Science Research Council with the description of American opinion on the atom bomb. While the specific contents under investigation varied, all three inquiries have this common purpose and a methodology that is parallel.

By contrast, the inquiries into Absenteeism, Class Consciousness, and The Authoritarian Personality have a different formal problem for study. All these are concerned not with sheer description of a phenomenon, but rather with seeking an *explanation*. In the instance of the latter two inquiries, this mainly takes the form of a test of some *specific hypothesis* growing out of some larger theory as to a particular determinant of the phenomenon. Such explanatory surveys we will label, for want of a better term, *theoretical or experimental* surveys. By contrast, many explanatory surveys are concerned with testing the *contribution of a number of factors* to the causation of a phenomenon. In some instances, such surveys are *evaluative* or *programmatic* where factors that respectively *have been or can be manipulated by some action agency* are studied for their contribution to the determination of the phenomenon. Here the immediate objective is application, modification or change of some state of affairs or phenomenon on the basis of proven knowledge as to the factors which are involved. Such was the case with the Absenteeism inquiry, for its auspices were governmental and the findings were to lead to recommendations for remedial action through the manipulation of the in-plant or larger environment. This is not to imply that theoretical considerations are not involved in the basic planning of such inquiry, but merely that the specific determinants that are ultimately the focus of the analysis are manipulable entities. In certain other explanatory surveys, not exemplified by any of our cases, the concern is also with the contribution of a number of factors to the determination of some phenomenon, but the survey is *diagnostic*. It involves a *search* for possible causes in a relatively *unknown* realm.

In all these types of explanatory surveys, there is a common methodology, establishing reliably the nature of the *relationship between one or more phenomena, or dependent variables, and one or more causes or independent variables*. But the specific way in which this task is elaborated varies with the type of explanatory survey involved. We shall see later in the text that the programmatic or evaluative survey emphasizes the analytic modes labelled *specification and explanation*. The specific concrete conditions under which the causative factor will operate to affect the phenomenon must be elaborated, so that action will be more effective. The theoretical survey, in addition, emphasizes the analytic mode later labelled interpretation. That is, intervening variables are incorporated into the analysis so as to show the process underlying an empirical relationship between some *initiating* condition and some *end* product. The programmatic and theoretical surveys emphasize *rigorous safeguards on the trustworthiness of the findings* whereas the diagnostic survey can commit less resources to such safeguards and must spread itself to achieve understanding or *suggestive evidence* on a broad realm. The conceptual structure of the theoretical survey will naturally be more *abstract* whereas the programmatic or evaluative survey will use more *concrete* variables and the diagnostic will partake of both levels of conceptualization.

One of our cases, the inquiry into bond redemptions, fits none of these types of surveys. It belongs to the special class of *prediction surveys* where the ultimate objective is not to describe nor explain a *current* situation but to estimate some *future* state of affairs.

All seven case studies have *one* feature in common. The primary purpose of the investigation was known in advance, and the survey was specifically designed to meet this express purpose. Apart from human fallibility, the research design had built-in properties essential for an effective analysis. However, none of these case studies illustrates a fairly common class of survey analyses, *secondary analysis,* in which the analyst makes use of material from surveys previously conducted for other purposes to illuminate his problem. Secondary analysis involves whatever general methodology corresponds to the type of problem under study, for example, the description of a phenomenon, the explanation of a phenomenon, but emphasizes one new requirement. The design of the survey is not likely to contain all the properties desirable for the analysis; the various expedients or approximations must be invented after-the-fact.[4] The omission of such a case will soon be remedied. We shall present one elaborate example of secondary analysis in subsequent portions of the text, using Durkheim's classic work, *Suicide,* for this purpose. Durkheim, as the reader may recall, analyzed previously collected records of suicides and was most ingenious in the invention of the approximations necessary in secondary analysis.

The detailed requirements for effective analysis of a descriptive survey will be treated in Part II; the detailed requirements for effective analysis of explanatory surveys will be treated in Part III. The requirements for effective analysis of prediction surveys will *not* be treated in the text because

---

4. For a discussion of secondary analysis, see P. F. Lazarsfeld and P. Kendall, Problems of Survey Analysis, in R. K. Merton and P. F. Lazarsfeld, *Continuities, op. cit.*

the literature is vast and the problems very specialized.[5] Secondary analysis will not receive systematic treatment at any one place in the text, because the approximations are too diverse to be readily codified into a short statement. Moreover, the analytic principles may either correspond to the problems of descriptive surveys or to the problems of explanatory surveys and thus are better treated in the corresponding chapters.

Before treating descriptive and explanatory analyses in detail, we will discuss in this chapter certain general problems that are not normally treated under the techniques of analysis. We will discuss the *relation* between these two major types of surveys and analyses, placing considerable emphasis on the descriptive survey since it is normally relegated to an inferior position and is regarded as having a purely empirical and applied value. There will be little need to emphasize the value of explanatory surveys, since their role in social science is so accepted.

1. Descriptive Surveys

The focus of such an analysis is essentially precise measurement of one or more dependent variables in some defined population or sample of that population.

Such inquiries may appear pedestrian and the technical problems of analysis too simple to warrant further treatment but the research design and subsequent analysis must have certain essential properties which are often neglected and which reduce the effectiveness of the survey. In brief, the *proper conceptualization* of a phenomenon is a pre-requisite to precise measurement. And while this is not difficult for phenomena of a unitary sort in certain sciences, most of the phenomena of descriptive surveys are complex in character and so ambiguous in nature that they are subject to a variety of possible definitions and conceptualizations. In the case of the inquiry into radio, for example, one notes that attitudes about radio is not a narrow problem—it is a wide domain. Shall the analyst describe attitudes towards the programming, and if so, towards what type of programs? Shall he describe attitudes towards advertising and if so towards what kinds of advertising? Shall he describe attitudes towards such institutional aspects of the American radio industry as commercial sponsorship?

Kinsey's inquiry represents an even more dramatic illustration of this very point. One can readily see that the object of inquiry in the radio survey was of a manifold nature—but sexual behavior appears to be a unitary phenomenon, perhaps presenting serious *technical* difficulties in the process of

---

5. The student is referred in the case of election prediction surveys to Mosteller, *et al., op. cit.,* or the symposium on the 1948 election surveys in the *International Journal of Opinion and Attitude Research,* throughout Vol. II. For elaborate examples of several such surveys in other content fields, see Stouffer, *et al., The American Soldier,* Vol. 1V., Chaps. XV, XVI, or the forthcoming book by D. Cartwright. For brief treatments of the theoretical problems in prediction surveys, see, J. Dollard, "Under What Conditions do Opinions Predict Behavior," *Publ. Opin. Quart.,* 12, 1948, 623-632, or H. Hyman and P. B. Sheatsley, *op. cit.*

inquiry but certainly simple to define. But as Kinsey finally conceptualized the problem, it included description of behaviors that might normally be disregarded in the initial thinking about sexual behavior, for example, any behavior that led to orgasm even though it involved less modal patterns such as animal or homosexual contacts. To cover comprehensively the domain of sexual behavior Kinsey had conservatively no less than 300 items of information to cover in the interview, indicating the degree of complexity of the phenomenon.[6]

For a classic sociological example of the problem of definition and conceptualization of the phenomenon in a descriptive survey, we can refer to Durkheim's *Suicide*.[7] We have here a phenomenon apparently unambiguous in meaning and unitary in character. Durkheim himself insists that "the sociologist must take as the object of his research groups of facts clearly circumscribed, capable of ready definition, with definite limits, and adhere strictly to them." He then notes that one of the reasons for his choice of the problem of suicide was that "among the various subjects that we have had occasion to study in our teaching career few are more accurately to be defined." Yet a few pages later, there is a detailed treatment of the difficulties of defining the phenomenon appropriately in which it takes Durkheim approximately 5 pages to examine alternative methods of defining his problem for study and to arrive at a definition that he regards as satisfactory.

Ackoff and Pritzker provide another illustration of how deceptive is the apparent simplicity of the dependent variables that might be the subject of a factual descriptive survey. They cite the hypothetical survey in which the problem is "to determine how many chairs people have in their living rooms. To make such a determination we have to define 'chair.' . . . If we define chair in terms of physical properties, such as size, shape, weight, etc., we can always find a chair which does not satisfy these conditions. For example, if 'one or more legs' is taken as a necessary property of chairs, we could point to a chair built into a wall, or built on a solid base, and hence having no legs. A 'chair' is, of course, a functional concept; its essence is its use, not its structure." [8]

Deming makes this point in most general terms by noting that *"no distribution is an intrinsic property of a universe,* but is the result of doing something to it," and what is done in the operations of a survey is dependent on the original conceptualization of the phenomenon. Deming illustrates this with the apparently simple concept of a *dwelling place* in a hypo-

---

6. Kinsey reports that the maximum history for any respondent involved 521 items of information, but our figure does not include those items of inquiry which were intended for classificatory purposes, rather than for description of the actual phenomenon of sexual behavior.

7. E. Durkheim, *Suicide* (English translation) (Glencoe: The Free Press, 1951). We shall return again and again to Durkheim's work and present a detailed analysis of its other methodological features as illustrations of some of the problems of descriptive and explanatory surveys.

8. Ackoff and Pritzker, *op. cit.*

thetical survey with central objective of describing the distribution of inhabitants per dwelling place in a city. The findings would be dependent, for example, on the fact that the definition of a dwelling *place* might have been "an address appearing to the lister to contain not more than three dwelling *units*." [9]

In virtually every descriptive survey, there is considerable theoretical difficulty in the conceptualization of the very phenomenon that shall be described. Moreover, there is considerable problem in *defining the nature of the population* that is most desirable to describe with respect to the phenomenon.

Generally, in descriptive surveys, the aim is to study a population which is *large and heterogeneous*. For what surveys offer through the application of sampling is the opportunity to determine with relative efficiency the state of affairs for a very large number of people. It is easy with other methods or through casual observation to determine the state of affairs for a small number of people or for a homogeneous group, but the need of government administrators or heads of large industrial work forces or huge consumer businesses is to have reliable knowledge of great masses of people. This fact alone has encouraged the growth of survey research of a descriptive sort, for the sample survey is uniquely geared to these requirements.

There will be rare occasions in applied research of a descriptive sort where the population to be studied is very limited in scope. Such would occur purely where the administrative need is for *very concrete* information for example, on a local or community level, or on a specific type of consumer or occupational group. However, such cases apart, the applied descriptive survey usually tends towards the choice of the large and diverse population. Where the goal of a descriptive survey is of a more academic or theoretical character, the choice similarly will be in the direction of the large and heterogeneous population for this means that the findings have more generality. But granted this usual direction of the decision there is still considerable difficulty in defining the type of population. One can attempt to study everybody in America or limit oneself in some way, for example, to males, to adults, to voters, city dwellers, industrial workers, etc. While there is some restriction on the variability within such groups as compared with the total population of a society, they could still be regarded as relatively heterogeneous. For example, instead of studying industrial workers in one specific type of industry in one community, one might draw a sample of such workers from a variety of areas and industries. Instead of

---

9. W. E. Deming, "On Training in Sampling," *J. Amer. Stat. Assoc.*, 40, 1945, 307-316. Italics ours. For another example of an apparently simple phenomenon subject to great complexity in conceptualization, the reader might examine the history of the surveys concerned with measuring "unemployment" or membership in the labor force. See for example, *Labor Force Definition and Measurement* (New York: Social Science Research Council Bulletin #56, 1947).

urban dwellers in small cities, one can include cities of all sizes in all parts of the country. The decision as to where to make the choice and still have a rather heterogeneous population is vital, and the basic principle to be followed is that the population have some especial *relevance* to the problem under study.

With respect to one of our cases, the American public's views of radio, for example, are adults the relevant universe, or shall we include children, a sizable part of the radio audience? Shall we limit ourselves to those who own radios and therefore have some experiential basis for their attitudes? Shall we limit ourselves to those who have been exposed to radically other forms of radio programming and therefore have an informed basis for criticism? [10]

The same problem of definition of the population arises in the case of the inquiry on the atom bomb and similar inquiries into political issues.[11] Shall the universe include all adults or be restricted to voters, since they are the individuals whose opinions are backed up by some minimum sense of political responsibility or shall it be those who have still a further political qualification such as high information, habitual voting activity, or some type of influence on the political process?

There are the two major *theoretical* problems in a descriptive survey, the conceptualization of the phenomenon and the decision as to the relevant population. But there are serious *technical* problems which then arise. The conceptualization must then be translated into a *series of operations* which yield data which will ultimately provide accurate measurements or indices of the phenomenon to be described. And here there is much difficulty and perhaps compromise for the concepts may be difficult to translate into operations which are feasible. Moreover, all measurements are subject to some error and there must either be methods developed for the *reduction of errors* or at least for their *estimation* so that the results may be qualified in the light of known error. Effective analysis of a descriptive survey is therefore far from simple and requires considerable training.

By way of illustrating the difficulties in translating a simple problem into research operations, we quote what is, luckily, a *fictional* account of an interview from *Punch,* the British comic magazine.[12]

---

10. It is not necessary that the decision to restrict the universe of study be followed out in the actual respondents who are enumerated. In some instances it is more desirable or at least more practicable to ask a series of questions which permit the irrelevant groups to be sorted out after-the-fact. On the general problem of relevant populations for study and the procedures for treating this problem, before or after-the-fact, see D. Katz, "The Interpretation of Survey Findings," *J. Soc. Issues,* 2, #2, 35-36.

11. For a treatment of this general problem in relation to the concept of the public in public opinion research surveys see, D. Cahalan, "On the Concepts of Public and Public Opinion," *Int. J. Opin. Attit. Res.,* 1, 1947, #4, 99-102.

12. Cole, W., *The Best Humor From Punch* (Cleveland: World, 1953), pp. 31-34. Reproduced by permission of the Proprietors of *PUNCH.*

AN ORGAN OF PUBLIC OPINION

"Excuse me, sir," said the man in the belted raincoat and beret, "would you mind telling me how you would vote if the General Election were being held to-day?" He licked the point of his pencil and looked up into the eyes of the Regular Customer.

The regular customer took a pull at his tankard and several shorter tugs at his right ear before replying. "Why," he said, "by puttin' a cross side of the name of the chap I . . . I was goin' to say like *best,* but there's such a thing as the ballot-box, isn't there? By putting a cross side of the name of *one* of the chaps. How's that?"

"Yes, yes, of course," said the investigator, smiling benignly. "I mean which political *party* would you vote for?"

"Today, eh?" said the regular customer as he rubbed his left eye slowly with his knuckle.

"That's right—to-day," said the investigator.

"Bit late though, isn't it," said the regular customer, drawing his watch from a waistcoat pocket and studying it at arm's length. "Booths would be closed up by now, wouldn't they?"

"Well, suppose you'd voted this morning, bright and early," said the investigator.

"Ah, then you mean, 'ow 'ave I *voted,* not 'ow *shall* I vote," said the regular customer.

"All right—how should you have voted?" said the investigator. He licked his pencil again.

"What kind of a choice did I 'ave?"

"Look, sir, I'm sorry I troubled you," said the investigator. "It isn't really fair to take up so much of your spare time. I'll be—"

"No trouble at *all,*" said the regular customer. "In fact it's all very interestin'. Carry on."

"Well, let's say there are three candidates—Liberal, Socialist and Tory. Which would you vote for?"

"Which would you?"

"I'm asking you, sir."

"An' I'm asking you. Fair's fair."

"I'm independent, neutral."

"'Aven't the courage of your confections, eh?"

"It's not that. Now, sir, *how would you vote?*"

"Well, I should 'ave to think, shouldn't I?"

"That's right—Liberal, Socialist, Tory?" said the investigator in a voice entirely devoid of enthusiasm.

"Who's the Socialist chap?"

"What chap?"

"The chap puttin' up, 'course!"

"Does that matter? Can't you give me a rough idea of your preference?"

"I can't very well vote for a chap I don't know nothin' about; now can I?"

"I mean which *party* would you support?"

"Not knowin' what they're proposin' to do, I can't say."

"But you know what they've *done,* their general principles—"

"I knows what they *'aven't* done," said the regular customer.

"Thank you, sir. I'll put you down as 'Don't know.' Thank you very much. Good night!"

"Hey, come back! Don't know what?"

"Which party to vote for," said the investigator wearily.

"Who don't?"

"Well, sir, you said yourself—"

"I said nothin' of the sort. I knows 'ow to use me 'ard-earned vote, me lad. You'll scratch that 'Don't know' out."

"With pleasure, sir, if you'll give me a definite answer."

"Ask me a def'nite question and you'll get a def'nite answer," said the regular customer, tapping the investigator on the chest with his pint.

"Would you vote for the Tories, the Conservatives?"

"Not much choice there, is there? But if I've got to take me pick I'll 'ave the Conservatives."

The investigator's eyes rolled in anguish. He flicked a tick at his pad. "Thank you, sir," he said. "I'm much obliged. Good night."

" 'Arf a sec.," said the regular customer, grabbing at the investigator's raincoat. "You 'aven't asked me yet about the Liberals."

"Some other time, sir. That's quite enough for the moment. I must be pushing." He broke free and walked rapidly out of the saloon.

"Sim'lar, Charlie," said the regular customer.

When the barman returned with the beer he found the regular customer chuckling softly, shaking his head slowly to and fro an inch or two above the counter. "What's the big joke, Bert?" he said.

"That young chap in 'ere just now," said the regular customer. " 'E's gone away with me vote, an' 'e's forgotten to take me name. 'E won't 'arf be kickin' 'isself. I reckon 'e'll be back in a bit."

Analytic ability in descriptive surveys is of importance in its own right. Much of applied social research sponsored by government or commercial or action agencies is of this character—for factual knowledge provides a sound basis for administrative actions. Moreover, such descriptive data is central to certain academic disciplines. For example, Lazarsfeld clearly conveys the value that descriptive survey data on the social scene would have for the historian.[13] And on the basis of an inquiry among historians working in the field of modern American history, Parry presents actual data showing the considerable value that historians attach to such current and possible future survey data as an historical source.[14]

But the analytic skills associated with purely descriptive surveys have profound value for the development of skill in treating more explanatory surveys intended to test various kinds of hypotheses. For the essence of such analysis is the establishment of the relationship between some phenomenon or dependent variable and some hypothesized cause or independent variable. In analyzing such surveys, all the sophistication in the manipulation of independent variables, in the invention of fruitful hypotheses as to causes

13. P. F. Lazarsfeld, "The Obligations of the 1950 Pollster to the 1984 Historian," *Publ. Opin. Quart.*, 14, 1950, 617-638.

14. H. J. Parry, "Historians and Opinion Research," *Int. J. Opin. Attit. Res.*, 2, 1948, 40-53.

of phenomena, in the techniques of controlling extraneous independent variables, and the like, will be of no avail if the *dependent* variable is not effectively conceptualized. The superstructure of determinants in an explanatory survey must rest on a firm base. Thus, skill in the analysis of descriptive surveys is a prerequisite for effective analysis of explanatory surveys. It is not sufficient to the task, but it is essential. One can, it is true, learn skill in descriptive analysis in the course of more explanatory surveys, for such skill is a component part of such an analysis. But here the complexity is great and many things must be learned at once. The descriptive survey, in other words, permits the learning of a part of the ultimate total array of skills under relatively simplified conditions.

We turn again to the authoritative example of Durkheim's work, *Suicide,* to illustrate the point. We have previously noted the care with which Durkheim conceptualizes the phenomenon of suicide, the dependent variable under study as must be done in any descriptive survey. But Durkheim ultimately was concerned with explanation, with the testing of a general theory, with the determination of causes of suicide. Yet he takes all the pains of elaborate prior conceptualization of his phenomenon, engages in the most careful descriptive research, for, as he remarks in his introduction, lack of care in conceptualizing the phenomenon creates the risk that "categories of very different sorts of facts are indistinctly combined under the same heading, or similar realities are differently named. . . . We risk distinguishing what should be combined, or combining what should be distinguished, thus mistaking the real affinities of things, and accordingly misapprehending their nature. . . . A scientific investigation can . . . be achieved only if it deals with comparable facts, and it is the more likely to succeed the more certainly it has combined all those that can be usefully compared. . . . Our first task then must be to determine the order of facts to be studied under the name of suicides." [15]

Clarity in the definition and conceptualization of the phenomenon is thus one requirement for effective explanatory analyses. Otherwise the relationship to the independent variable will be obscured. But the descriptive survey involves still another element which is essential to effective explanation in surveys. Clarity in *conceptualization* is no insurance that a relationship can be established—that a theory can be put to test. The later measurements and *operations* may obscure the initial clarity! Any relationship will then be blurred. And as we have noted consideration of procedures for the reduction and estimation of error are central to descriptive surveys, for the sole purpose of such surveys is to provide an *accurate* representation of the phenomenon.

Here again we turn to Durkheim's work to note the persistent emphasis upon the examination of error in the description of the phenomenon when

---

15. E. Durkheim, English Translation, *op. cit.,* pp. 41-42.

he considers and evaluates and accepts any demonstration of a relationship.[16] We shall note only a small number of the total instances of this recurrent procedure in the work italicizing the argument about errors.

Durkheim's "Suicide"—A Case Study of Recurrent Attention to Error:

In establishing the relationship of Age to suicide in various societies, he notes the general finding that it increases regularly with age. Yet he remarks that there are slight exceptions. He considers these and rejects their importance to his theory on the ground that they are "due perhaps to errors of tabulation." (p. 101)

In establishing the relationship to seasonal variations in temperature, he notes that a prior investigator reported one striking exception to the general finding of a maximum incidence in summer. This maximum was demonstrated only once in the autumn season in a series based on data from 18 countries and 34 different time periods. Durkheim evaluates the implication of this inversion and remarks: "This last irregularity, observed only in the Grand-Duchy of Baden and at a single moment of its history, is *valueless,* for it results from a calculation bearing on too brief a period; besides, it never recurred." In three other exceptional instances the maximum occurred in springtime. Durkheim remarks "The other three exceptions are *scarcely more significant.* They occur in Holland, Ireland and Sweden. For the first two countries the available figures which were the base for the seasonal averages are too uncertain for anything positive to be concluded; there are only 387 cases for Holland and 755 for Ireland. In general, the statistics for these two peoples are *not wholly authoritative.* . . . If we consider only the states concerning which there are authentic figures, the law may be held to be absolute and universal." (p. 107)

The student might well raise the question here as to when such considerations as to error factors are applied in an arbitrary manner. An investigator can of course invoke the concept of error to reject any finding he doesn't like. It is a requirement that there be some formal method or logical canon for deciding what is an error-producing procedure and what is not, and that the consideration be applied in an unbiased fashion.[17]

Later, in a parallel treatment of the phenomenon of insanity as a function of seasonal variations in temperature, in an attempt to see whether *morbidity in general* is related to temperature, Durkheim remarks on the inadequacy of the primary source data. "The distribution of the cases of insanity

---

16. Durkheim's study represents survey research method based on *previously collected data* rather than data collected specially for the purpose of the investigation. In such instances, actual procedures for the *reduction* of error are not possible, and instead *estimation and allowance* for error which is in actuality present is the only possibility. One might perhaps advance the general principle that secondary analyses require *extra* attention to error factors. In the case of primary analyses the investigator at least *knows* what cautions were applied in the collection and manipulation of data, if any, but in secondary analyses the original errors may be insidious, since one has little knowledge of the earlier stages of the survey process.

17. This is one reason why so much attention is given in the later text to discussion of the major error factors and to early phases of the survey process, during which phases the errors are generally created, i.e., are artifactual.

among the seasons can be estimated only by the number of admissions to the asylums. Such a standard is very *inadequate;* for families intern invalids not immediately but some time after the outbreak of the disease." [18] (p. 109, footnote)

Later in a treatment of the relationship of the phenomenon of suicide to month of the year, rather than season, Durkheim notes certain irregularities in the general findings. He rejects these on the ground that "the greatest irregularities, moreover, usually appear in series too small to be very significant." (p. 111)

Later in a general discussion of the relation of religion to suicide, manipulated through the procedure of examining suicide rates for nations of different religious compositions, Durkheim notes that England has a low rate among Protestant countries. He remarks, however, that "to be sure, the statistics of English suicides are not very exact. Because of the penalties attached to suicide, many cases are reported as accidental death. However, this inexactitude is not enough to explain the extent of the difference between this country and Germany." (p. 160, footnote)

This particular example strikes home the observation made above about the problem of arbitrariness in evaluating error. Why does Durkheim regard the presence of error in one instance as sufficient to *completely invalidate* the empirical finding, and in the other instance, an *insufficient basis* for rejecting the finding. The thorny problem of *accuracy requirements* is again posed. In the absence of a logical procedure for knowing when something shall be regarded accurate or inaccurate, and how crucial the level of inaccuracy is, there inevitably is some arbitrariness.

Later in establishing the relation of the phenomenon of suicide to sex, Durkheim notes the general finding of a much greater incidence among men with the exception of the Spanish statistics. And he remarks "but not only is the accuracy of Spanish statistics open to doubt, but Spain cannot compare with the great nations of Central and Northern Europe." (p. 166, footnote)

Here again one underscores the problem of arbitrariness in evaluating error components, for the addendum that Spain cannot compare with the great nations seems strangely out of place. Yet, Durkheim may simply not be explicit on the logical grounds for drawing this conclusion about Spanish sources. Elsewhere, his comments are a model of objectivity and care, and he elaborates the exact reason for regarding a datum as artifactual.[19]

Thus far, it might appear that the evaluation of error is introduced as a procedure only in relation to slight irregularities or exceptions or inver-

---

18. It might be noted that here the error component is an artifact having to do with the *independent* variable, season of onset of disease, rather than the dependent variable, insanity per se. In the explanatory survey error components must, of course, be evaluated in both these realms. However, the quotation illustrates the general problem of attention to error problems.

19. See, for example the detailed analysis on pp. 175-176 by which he buttresses his categorical statement that certain Swedish statistics are "useless."

sions in the general findings, and as a basis for deciding what qualifications must be put upon the general conclusions. But Durkheim in many places considers whether an artifact, an error, is responsible for a very *general* finding. This is of course just as essential a procedure. We cite merely one such instance.

> Thus in noting the general negative relation between suicide and wartime conditions, he remarks on the possibility that the finding might be completely artifactual. "It might perhaps be considered due to the drafting of a part of the civilian population in war-time and the fact that it is very hard to keep track of suicides in an army in the field." (p. 205) He is able to reject this possibility on the basis of a particular and ingenious analytic procedure, but he then entertains the possibility that there is still a second artifactual basis for the finding. He speculates as to whether the cause "might not be that the record of suicides was less exactly kept because of the paralysis of (civil) administrative authority." (p. 206) Here again, he derives a logical model of the way other data would have to distribute if this artifact were involved and is enabled to reject the argument.

We have already noted no less than 7 specific instances in which Durkheim makes reference to a possible error factor in the findings. There are at least 13 other instances which we have not reported, which establish the prominence that Durkheim gave to this methodological aspect of survey analysis. Instead of reporting some of these instances, we shall now use them for a problem exercise the answers to which appear in Appendix E.

PROBLEM EXERCISE II
Durkheim's "Suicide" as an Exercise in the Evaluation of Findings in Relation to Artifacts

Find five other instances in Durkheim's *Suicide* where consideration of error factors is introduced in the evaluation of the findings.

Discuss whether there appears to be arbitrariness in the way in which the concept of error is invoked, or whether there is an explicit basis for the decision as to the existence of error and its consequences.

Note whether there is a logical or empirical procedure developed to test the possibility that the finding can be invalidated on the ground of the hypothesized error factor.

Note whether the error applies to the measurement of the dependent or the independent variable.

The descriptive survey is thus a training ground for the development of skill in conceptualization of the phenomenon and in the treatment of the findings in relation to error factors, both essential to effective analysis of explanatory surveys. But there is still another feature of the descriptive survey which is especially valuable for ultimate work in the design and analysis of explanatory surveys. Out of the findings of such surveys often comes the basis for the formulation of fruitful hypotheses about phenomena, or at least for some reduction in confusion in theorizing about a phenomenon.

The usual image of the explanatory survey is that there is a hypothesis always waiting to be put to the test, but oftentimes one faces novel problems and phenomena for study and one has little sense of what are the possible determinants. This has always been recognized as a problem and leads to the usual practice of consulting the literature and other informants directly. For example, Ackoff and Pritzker remark with respect to explanatory surveys that "no individual can be aware of *all* the facts, laws, and theories that are potentially useful to him in selecting pertinent variables. There are usually so many things of which we are not aware. . . . Here what we need is the maximum of cooperative effort, for no one person chosen from one scientific discipline is ever in a position to think of all the pertinent aspects of a situation. There should be a realization that the solution to this problem can come about only through the broadest type of social (not individual) experience, and hence it is essential to have wide consultation with people from all sorts of *diverse* fields and backgrounds." [20]

But this solution imputes too much wisdom to our colleagues, past and present, particularly when the survey deals with a novel problem. The alternative is the exploration of the phenomenon directly with the hope that in the experience, one will glean some insight. Thus, Jahoda, Deutsch and Cook remark on the value of an "experience survey," and illustrate various informal or exploratory types of study of the phenomenon leading to the formulation of hypotheses.[21] The descriptive survey, in one sense, represents a more formalized and more elaborate type of exploratory study. But its value in the initial stage of formulating an explanatory survey goes beyond this.

Oftentimes, one faces an apparently significant phenomenon and imposes a huge structure of hypothetical determinants upon this without a second thought as to whether there is sufficient clarity or stability and regularity involved so that a key or explanation can be found. We are addicted to determinism, and find the notion of the ephemeral or unsolvable abhorrent. But it may well be that some of the problems we commit to explanatory surveys should never be undertaken for they are so elusive. The descriptive survey because of its wide sampling can be conceived of as an inquiry into the *uniformity or regularity* of some phenomenon. It permits a better decision as to the wisdom of undertaking any explanatory inquiry at all. Further the descriptive survey by providing data on the *rarity* or *universality* of some phenomenon and its *distribution socially* gives guidance as to what type of determinants might lead to the most fruitful hypotheses. There is, of course, still no assurance that we will pick phenomena that are fruitful to study or invent fruitful hypotheses, but the likelihood is greater.

---

20. Ackoff and Pritzker, *op. cit.*
21. *Op. cit.*

We may again turn to Durkheim's work to note the way in which these benefits of the descriptive survey are used as a prelude to the more experimental phases of his analysis. Thus early in his work, Durkheim examines the descriptive data on suicide rates for different nations and over a series of years. He notes a *stability* to those data, or even, as he remarks, that they are almost *invariable* for each nation over time. He is thus led to affirm the fact that the phenomenon of national differences is a fact with "its own unity, individuality and consequently its own nature." Because of its regularity over time for each nation, he sees its nature as "dominantly social." (p. 46) [22] In other words, the examination of data such as would be treated in a descriptive survey for their stability and social distribution leads him to support further experimental study and to seek the causes in certain directions.[23] We use his own words to show the conclusion he arrives at:

> The suicide rate is therefore a factual order, unified and definite, as is shown by both its permanence and its variability. For this permanence would be inexplicable if it were not the result of a group of distinct characteristics . . . and this variability proves the concrete and individual quality of these same characteristics, since they vary with the individual character of society itself. . . . Each society is predisposed to contribute a definite quota of voluntary deaths. This predisposition may therefore be the subject of a special study belonging to sociology. This is the study we are going to undertake. (p. 51)

He goes on to argue that a phenomenon which has been demonstrated to be so lawful or regular for such a huge entity as a nation "can depend only on extra-social causes of broad generality or on causes expressly social" and thus is guided as to the hypotheses he should test. (p. 52) [24]

The point becomes clearer if we take as a contrasting example, one of our case studies, *The Authoritarian Personality*. We have here an explanatory survey designed to test certain hypotheses as to the causes of a particular ideology. But whereas Durkheim had at his disposal descriptive data on a national level to lead him to the realization that his phenomenon had a regularity at a very macroscopic social level and then to search for this

22. It should be noted that Durkheim had descriptive data for successive periods of time. A phenomenon may be widespread, but if it is *temporary,* its cause would naturally be sought in the *situational* rather than in some *persistent* social fact. Descriptive surveys *on a trend basis* thus permit the location of determinants more effectively since the transient social can be differentiated from the more permanent social.

23. Of course, one may well argue that this was Durkheim's theoretical orientation to the problem *before* he ever examined these descriptive data. But this does not change the point. He nevertheless examined the data and thereby gained confidence in the direction that more experimental research should take.

24. This same use of descriptive surveys as a basis for the inference as to determinants is, of course, widespread in certain disciplines, although it is not necessarily formulated as an example of descriptive survey method. Thus support for the concept of "culture" as a determinant of behavior derives from descriptive work in Ethnology through the sheer demonstration of uniformities within a society, and differences as between societies.

social determinant, *The Authoritarian Personality* study had a relatively homogeneous, although large, sample and could not gain the benefit of knowledge as to whether a phenomenon was frequent or rare in the society. Therefore, on occasion a phenomenon that independent descriptive research shows to be well nigh universal is imputed to an idiosyncratic cause. Hyman and Sheatsley in a long critique of this study make this point under the heading of "the value of national norms." [25]

> If the researcher, because of his sampling design, cannot tell whether the given attitude is normative for the general population, he may seek the explanation in the wrong place. We are suggesting that a sample of the heterogeneous total population illuminates the direction for analysis and makes less likely the drawing of broad conclusions which may be unwarranted. We . . . will merely illustrate it . . . with one example.
> In discussing the political ideology of ethnocentric individuals, the authors note that such persons are distinguished by an emphasis on the "inevitability of war." The interpretation is then given in individualistic psychodynamic terms: the high scorer has much "psychological passivity," "and underlying sympathy for war-making." . . . When this same question is put to representative samples of the population, one notes that the expectation of war is characteristic of a great many people and not a deviant few; that it fluctuates in a rather orderly fashion according to the objective facts; and that it shows a high negative correlation with education. If one had at his disposal the data from such samples, one might have interpreted the meaning of this sentiment quite differently.

2. Explanatory Surveys

We have now outlined the central theoretical and technical problems that the analyst will face in the descriptive survey and have pointed to the many values such surveys have. Among these values there is the great benefit in training that the analyst gains for ultimate work in what we have labelled explanatory surveys. The findings of descriptive surveys are a guide to theorizing in explanatory surveys; the skill in conceptualizing a phenomenon, so central to the descriptive survey, is as crucial in the explanatory survey. Here the same power of conceptualization must be extended to the problem of independent variables as well. Technical skill in reducing errors in the procedures or estimating them is required. Otherwise the findings cannot be trusted. But we have not as yet outlined the unique analytic requirements of the explanatory survey. To insure that the obtained relationship of a phenomenon to some particular hypothesized cause is meaningful, one must have confidence that factors operative in the situation other than the hypothesized one are not responsible. This has been a classic problem with which laboratory experimentation has been concerned and methods for ruling out these extraneous factors have been developed which

---

25. H. Hyman and P. B. Sheatsley, The Authoritarian Personality—A Methodological Critique, in M. Jahoda and R. Christie, ed., *Continuities in Social Research*—Studies in the Scope and Method of the Authoritarian Personality (Glencoe: The Free Press, 1954), pp. 50-122.

are dependent on the manipulation of the laboratory setting and the initial selection, matching and arrangement of subjects.[26] For example, any differences between laboratory subjects exposed to different values of the independent variable canot be allocated to other extraneous characteristics since the initial matching or selection and subsequent arrangement of subjects for exposure insures that such is not the case. Moreover, since the independent variable is created and applied at will by the experimentor, it can be separated from other stimulus conditions which might otherwise accompany its operation.

The explanatory survey follows the model of the laboratory experiment with the fundamental difference that it attempts to represent this design in a *natural setting*. Instead of *creating* and manipulating the independent variables whose effect is to be traced the survey analyst must find in the natural setting instances of these factors. By measuring their presence and magnitude, their relationship to the phenomenon can be established in the course of the analysis. But since these variables are not created, but merely found in the natural setting, there is the great danger that a variety of other factors accompany them, and that respondents characterized by particular attributes may vary in other important respects. The influence of these other sources of variability must somehow be reduced. Otherwise any inference about the hypothesized cause may be shaky. *The restriction of the universe which is covered and the design of the sample in the explanatory survey provides the basic technique by which other sources of variation in the phenomenon are excluded.*[27] It is in relation to this problem that the descriptive and explanatory surveys lead to opposing designs. In the descriptive survey, generality is achieved through the study of the heterogeneous universe. But this generality permits the total array of determinants to operate.

In the explanatory survey confidence in the inference as to causality is achieved through restricting the heterogeneity of the universe. We can illustrate the way in which such restriction of the universe is the formal equivalent of the matching in the laboratory experiment by one of our cases and by other examples of explanatory surveys. In the inquiry into the causes of absenteeism, instead of taking the universe of workers throughout the United States, and running the danger that any correlation between some independent variable and absenteeism might be due to almost an infinite number of other operative factors, the universe was restricted.

---

26. We shall discuss experimental methods in Part III. The student is referred to the general sources there cited.

27. See D. Katz, "Survey Techniques," *op. cit.* It is vital, however, to distinguish restrictions of the universe which reduce *extraneous* sources of variation from restrictions which reduce the variation in the phenomenon under study. It is well known that a reduction in the range within which a phenomenon can vary affects the magnitude of any correlations that are established, and obviously one wishes to study the phenomenon at all levels. Therefore, one must not impose the latter type of restriction.

Workers from only 18 plants were studied. Only six industries were represented. By definition, any findings as to the causes of absenteeism could not be invalidated on grounds of the contribution of factors in the wider industrial complex that were excluded. But further, the analysts located workers in such types of plants in two classes of communities, those with good and those with bad community conditions again reducing the sources of variation in the out-plant complex.

We can take as another example of this principle a study from the literature which makes the methodological principle exceedingly explicit. We shall later treat in detail an inquiry by Sewell in which certain hypotheses from psychoanalytic theory about the effect of infantile experience on later personality patterns were tested. We have here a set of independent variables such as whether weaning was abrupt or not, bowel training early or later, feeding by bottle or breast, which obviously cannot be treated in the laboratory setting. Subjects cannot be arbitrarily chosen because they are matched in particular respects and then instructed to rear their children in particular fashions. We can only find subjects who happen to be contrasted with respect to the way in which they were or are being reared and examine the consequences in the personality patterns. But it is obvious that parents who rear their children in contrasted ways may also differ in many other respects, e.g., class, education, ethnicity, which might account for the personality consequences. Sewell attempts to control these sources of variation by the restriction of the universe.

> In the design of the study an attempt was made to approximate experimental conditions by the prior control of several factors believed to be associated with personality adjustment. Thus diverse cultural influences were eliminated by selecting only children of old American cultural backgrounds in a predominantly old American community. By selecting children from a single occupational group (farm children), occupational and socioeconomic influences were roughly controlled. Age was held constant by selecting only children in the age group five to six. Personal-social experiences were in some measure controlled by the selection of children who had not yet been subject to the socializing effects of school. Only the children of unbroken and never broken unions were selected; consequently, disrupted family situations could not affect the findings.[28]

In both these examples, the absenteeism inquiry and the Sewell study, there remains of course, the possibility that the findings are due to residual factors whose variability has not been controlled by the initial restrictions on the universe and the design of the sample. The natural conditions characteristic of the survey method make for a *very wide* array of factors to be operative, and this fact requires that further protection against the influence of extraneous factors be applied after-the-fact, in the terminal stage

---

28. W. H. Sewell, "Infant Training and the Personality of the Child," *Amer. J. Sociol,* Vol. 58, 1952, pp. 150-159.

of the analysis, by statistical techniques. Such techniques are described in detail in Part III. However, the greater the approximation to the model of an experiment by the initial restriction of the universe, the less is the need for such laborious manipulation and the greater is the confidence in the validity of the obtained explanation. While the restriction of the universe and consequent control of extraneous factors produces these gains, the gain is accompanied by a loss in generality. The reader can see that the explanatory findings naturally only apply under the original restricted conditions. This foreshadows the many conflicts the analyst may experience in the course of designing his survey.

Conflicting Goals and Compromises in Research Design

Thus far it would appear that survey research is relatively simple. The analyst merely decides on the basis of his problem which orthodox type of design to follow and executes it as effectively as his resources will permit. The analysis follows routinely from the design since the properties built-in at the planning stage insure success. However, the complication that frequently arises is that the goals of a survey are various and the analyst wishes to accomplish a variety of objectives. Under such conditions, he inevitably must compromise and pick a design that is not ideally suited to any single purpose, but perhaps the optimal design considering the multi-purpose character of his research.

The problem has been foreshadowed in Chapter I. Compromises are required by the conflicts in the social setting of the research. Sponsor and analyst may be in opposition about the goals of the survey. The larger controversial aspects of the study exert pressure. Research personnel within the organization may disagree. Practical goals such as economy, speed, and the like militate against the introduction of certain technical safeguards. However, here the analyst's dilemma is clear and while a decision may be unpleasant, it can be made.

The problem is self-evident in the instance of surveys which cover a variety of *content* areas. The high cost of surveys often leads the analyst or research organization to include in one questionnaire a battery of questions on one problem, and other batteries of questions on other problems. Since the overhead costs of field investigation do not change markedly with the length of the questionnaire, each problem is treated at a relatively low expenditure or each client only pays a small portion of the total costs. The gains in economy from such multi-content surveys is considerable, but the loss in quality of research may also be considerable. Where each problem is complex, it may be impossible to treat it comprehensively with a limited number of questions and corresponding measurements. But here again the dilemma is obvious and the choice usually a conscious one.

Quite frequently, however, the analyst experiences no conflict over the content aspects of a survey. Only one content area is to be covered. However, conflict may still arise because there is a desire to study more than one *formal* problem within the content area. Thus, the analyst may be interested in a *descriptive* inquiry—estimating as precisely and comprehensively as possible some state of affairs—and at the same time interested in an *explanatory* inquiry of a theoretical type—testing some particular hypothesis about the determinants of that state of affairs. These respective formal problems might call for opposing features of the research design, and the analyst inevitably compromises.

We can illustrate this very effectively by reference to one of our cases, Centers' inquiry into Class-Consciousness. As noted earlier the main purpose of the inquiry was such as to call for a theoretical and explanatory survey, a test by empirical means of the validity of the theory that certain attitudes arise from a person's economic position. Such an inquiry logically calls for a design of the type we have previously noted as analogous to laboratory experiment. Ideally, groups should have been sampled who varied with respect to their position in the society and attempts should have been made to match these groups initially with respect to other variables so that any obtained differences in attitude could have been allocated to the independent variables with confidence. Such matching would have been achieved as well as possible in advance of the analysis by the principle previously noted of restriction of the universe. Thus, the design for the explanatory survey would have represented the best approximation to the controlled laboratory experiment that was possible under natural field conditions apart from the crudity of measurement and curtailment of the scope of the observations that might accompany the natural setting. However, Centers was interested in a *descriptive* inquiry into class consciousness in addition to his interest in testing a particular hypothesis. From the point of view of a descriptive inquiry, one would seek the most comprehensive and accurate measurement of the phenomenon for some defined large population or sample of that population. To restrict the study to a few contrasted groups within a relatively homogeneous universe would have defeated the purpose since no generalized description of the phenomenon for the entire population would have been possible. And to sample all groups in adequate numbers within the total population apart from prohibitive costs would complicate the inquiry since the description of the state of class consciousness in the aggregate would involve specialized computations. To match the contrasted economic groups *in advance* with respect to other independent variables by restricting the universe severely would have been a mistake for this would not permit any description of the phenomenon as it operated in the natural

American setting. This would provide only a description under relatively artificial or restricted conditions. Thus, the better the initial approximation to the laboratory experiment in a survey research design, the less effective is the inquiry as a descriptive one, and this choice is irreversible and ir-remediable. To use the design of a descriptive inquiry, however, is flexible. One can approximate to the matching of cases after the fact by selecting sub-groups from the original larger number studied who happen to be alike in other respects, and one can hope to find in the mass of the cases a suffi-cient number of individuals contrasted with respect to the major variable under study. If one is successful in this procedure, one achieves his explan-atory findings under conditions where more generality attaches to them because of the wider coverage of the sample. However, it is fortuitous whether the ideal conditions for testing the hypothesis will be present, since the procedure is after-the-fact, and there is much laborious work involved in the manipulation of the constellation of many variables.

In summary, the *choice of a descriptive design permits the later test of a hypothesis by an approximation after the fact to an explanatory design, but the initial choice of an explanatory design precludes any later approx-imation to the design needed for a descriptive inquiry.* We can now illus-trate this from Centers' text.

Centers' Psychology of Social Classes—A Case Study in Conflicting Goals: [29]

He chose a *descriptive design:*

> The method decided upon for the present study was that of a public atti-tude survey of a *representative cross-section* of the adult white population. Such a method is peculiarly designed to give *macroscopic, over-all results* rather than the kind that might be obtained by *studies of specific popula-tions in limited areas under conditions allowing rigid control of variables.* (p. 34)

The reason is explicit. While earlier, he stated his theory and indicated his plan to engage in an empirical verification, he now remarks:

> The over-all picture (of class consciousness) is still so vague and indistinct that clarification of it is an imperious necessity and certainly logically prior to studies of this latter type. The problem is of such a nature as to demand that great masses of people of every adult age group, of every section of the country, of rural, small town, large town and city residence, and of every socio-economic stratum be represented. (p. 35)

Yet he imposes certain restrictions on the population to be sampled, because of the complications otherwise created for an experimental or explanatory type design.

---

29. Italics ours to emphasize the central points. All quotations are from Centers, *op. cit.* See Appendix A for a copy of the ballot used in the study.

> Because Negroes constitute such a small minority of the population and
> have in addition a caste-like relationship to the white majority to complicate
> matters, their class psychology could reasonably be regarded as a problem
> for later separate study, and hence no Negroes were included in the survey.
> Women were not included because in a research where stratification is the
> basic variable, it is important to get definitely placed persons as far as occu-
> pation is concerned, and women do not universally have occupations other
> than that of housewife. (p. 35)

Such restrictions of a universe occasionally occur in a *purely* descriptive
inquiry for *practical* reasons of economy or facilitating the research process.
But here it is clear that the restrictions are intended to *simplify,* to *make
unambiguous,* the comparisons of the ideology of given groups, a purpose
compatible with an explanatory survey, but certainly not appropriate in relation to the purposes in the earlier quotation cited above of a description
of class-consciousness for groups of *all* types. Moreover, if the inquiry had
been purely descriptive there would have been no problem of classifying
Negroes or women according to their objective economic position, since
one would have been merely interested in the phenomenon of class-consciousness rather than its correlates.

He makes his decision but later he expresses the limitations the descriptive design imposed on his ability to analyze the data effectively for
a test of his hypothesis:

> The nature of the data obtained in this cross-sectional study imposes limits
> upon the analytical possibilities. . . . Causal relationships between two given
> variables can be unequivocally asserted, if they can be asserted at all, only
> when by rigorous experimental techniques all variables but that to which
> causal efficacy is to be attributed are held constant—and such control of
> variables is most difficult to achieve. It is an obvious impossibility in an
> *exploratory study* of the present type which deals with an entire cross-section
> of a population that *varies in an almost inexhaustible* fashion. To hold
> constant everything but occupation, for example, would require a sample
> several hundred times as large as the present one. Before groups large
> enough for statistically reliable comparisons and matched for all possibly
> relevant characteristics save occupation were obtained, such a sample might
> have to contain fifty or one hundred thousand persons. (p. 162)

Admittedly, the logical problems that Centers imposes in such extreme
form could not be solved by any explanatory design. It is of the nature of
humans that they vary "in almost inexhaustible fashion" and that holding
constant everything is impossible, but certainly some of the variation in
extraneous respects could have been reduced by deliberate methods in advance. Centers actually did this in part by excluding women and Negroes,
thus implicitly matching respondents of the contrasted classes in sex and
color. Moreover, certain groups could have been expanded in size to en-
hance particular experimental comparisons at the price of dropping out
less essential groups.

All this is not intended to imply that Centers should have pursued a *pure* explanatory type of design. Both goals seemed important, and the limitations of each design are made articulate. He made a compromise between these goals, chose a slightly modified design of a descriptive sort and approximated the controls and other properties of the experimental design after the fact by laborious methods of partial correlation, and higher order breakdowns. These procedures were an essential under such conditions and are elaborated in Part III. Moreover, some gain does occur by such a decision. Whatever experimental findings are possible are made under conditions of greater generality and less artificiality. The case is merely intended to show the conflicts that the analyst faces frequently and the problems of resolving these conflicts.

Another source of conflict often occurs where *diagnosis* and *testing* are simultaneous goals of an explanatory survey. Testing an hypothesis might call for restriction of the universe. Where the explanatory survey tends towards the *diagnostic,* where the emphasis is less on the test of one specific hypothesis and more on the search for fruitful determinants plus an *ultimate* test, the point earlier noted about the guidance that descriptive data provide for theorizing would lead to the choice of a descriptive design and the attempt to approximate experimental conditions after-the-fact.

Where the explanatory survey is of a *programmatic* or *evaluative* nature, there may also be practical constraints upon the restriction of the universe for study. The universe that might be most desirable for clarifying the operation of an independent variable and providing the most unambiguous experimental test might not be the one that approximates best to the requirements of the action agency. We can illustrate this from the history of the *United States Strategic Bombing Survey,* a case we shall use repeatedly. In this instance, a presidential directive from Franklin D. Roosevelt led to the formation of a special research organization within the military establishment. The explicit directive was that there "be an impartial and expert study of the effects of . . . aerial attack . . . including effects upon the morale and will of the enemy to resist." [30] It is clear by implication that the test of the influence of bombing on morale and will to resist had to provide evidence on the *total* problem, for one specialized finding on the effect of bombing in one city or on a limited group of people would not provide adequate information for the military establishment. Yet, by considering the morale in the total Japanese or German society, and attempting to determine the specific contribution of bombing, one brings into the

---

30. This and all later references are taken from a detailed case study of the Japanese Bombing Survey, an almost unique narrative account of the entire history of the inquiry. See, D. Krech and E. Ballachey, *A Case Study of a Social Survey,* Japanese Survey, United States Bombing Survey, University of California Syllabus Series, Syllabus T G, University of California Press, 1948. The ballot used in the Strategic Bombing Survey of Germany appears in Appendix A.

picture not only the operation of the variables of bombing but also the effect of all other forms of military action as they impinged on the population, and the whole gamut of environmental factors that impinged on the civilian population. But, there was no alternative and the survey had to treat the universe that approximated the total population, and try to abstract during the analysis from the total complex of determinants of morale in wartime the influence of bombing.

The Bombing Survey illustrates one other difficulty in setting up an experimental model for the explanatory inquiry when it is of the evaluative type. Even if the sponsor's needs would have been met by limited findings applicable to the artificially restricted conditions of a few cities or a specialized human population, it would have been *impossible* to locate these ideal conditions anywhere in the society. For example, the analyst in designing such an inquiry might desire to restrict the universe to cities of a certain size and compare the morale changes accompanying different levels of bombing. The populations of cities of different sizes had suffered different degrees of deprivation in wartime, were provided with different degrees of air raid protection and the like and these sources of variation in morale could thus be ruled out. But the original needs of the military establishment were such that bombing was not meted out in accordance with an experimental design, and one could not find zero degrees of bombing within the class of cities that were of large size. For example, among the six largest cities of Japan—Tokyo, Yokohama, Nagoya, Osaka, Kobe, and Kyoto—only one, Kyoto, did not receive a very heavy weight of bombs. For all cities with populations over 100,000 there was only one sub-group of such cities in Japan which were unbombed or lightly bombed and *all* of these were confined to one geographical area, Northeastern Japan.[31] In the programmatic or evaluative survey the needs of the analyst are overriden by the requirements of the action agency and it would be absurd to expect that heavy bombing would occur in unimportant isolated rural areas or that a large and strategically important city would be unscathed.

The frequency of such dual or conflicting purposes—desires to accomplish both a general description and an explanation, to achieve a test but to aim towards generality, to gain diagnostic power from the descriptive data as a prelude to sharpened theory and an ultimate test, to implement an experimental design in the face of the programmatic goals of the sponsor—lead often to the more flexible choice of a descriptive design with some price paid in terms of the laboriousness of the terminal stages of the analysis. The emphasis in Part III on statistical manipulation and after-the-fact approximations of controlled experiments grows in part out of this dilemma.

We shall now turn in Part II to the technical problems with which the

---

31. D. Krech and E. L. Ballachey, *ibid*.

analyst deals in particular types of surveys. For purposes of clarity of presentation and ease of training, the analytic requirements of descriptive surveys will be separated from those of explanatory surveys. Moreover, some of the practical operating difficulties in translating these requirements into practice, and the conflicts of purposes already discussed will be neglected. However, the student should keep this larger context for his ultimate work in mind.

Part II

DESCRIPTIVE SURVEYS AND
THE FUNCTIONS OF THE ANALYST

Introduction

Part II

WE HAVE already noted that the central theoretical problem for the analyst of a descriptive survey is the *effective conceptualization* of the phenomenon to be studied. Otherwise, any description actually obtained following the interpretation of the data may be incomplete or may distort the nature of the phenomenon. It is the *complexity* of the phenomena the survey analyst is usually called upon to describe that makes for this difficulty in conceptualization.

In addition to conceptualization, the analyst must decide what *population* is the most appropriate group within which to study the phenomenon, and then he must develop a series of techniques or procedures which ultimately produce *data and then indices* of the phenomenon as conceptualized. Usually, he seeks for the most *generalized* description that is possible, but at the same time provides for considerable *detail* in the description. Both the uniformities and the irregularities, the statistical findings and the subtle qualitative nuances should be reported. Among the procedures, he must provide for the *reduction or estimation of errors* whose presence inevitably mars the accuracy of any description.

We shall take up in some length these major features of the descriptive survey as well as a number of supplementary specialized features which the analyst must handle in order to conduct an effective descriptive survey.

The exact nature of these phases of a descriptive survey analysis will naturally vary with the particular survey. Some phenomena are more complex than others. Some are more difficult to translate into operations which are feasible under field conditions. The likely error factors will depend on the quality of the interviewers, coders, and other research personnel; on the degree to which reports from respondents are affected by such social forces as fear, embarrassment and the like; and on the degree to which the population under study shows certain stable characteristics, e.g. is articulate. The entire process is dependent on the nature of the resources provided in terms of money and time allotments. All the general principles now to be advanced must be qualified in the light of such factors in the concrete survey situation.

CHAPTER III

Theoretical Problems
in the Descriptive Survey

Complexity of Conceptualization

Before embarking on any elaboration of principles, we shall illustrate the complexity of translating the initial crude statement of the phenomenon into a more elaborate set of concepts and in turn into a set of operations in the descriptive survey.

The Japanese Bombing Survey—A Case Study of Complexity of Conceptualization: We turn to the detailed narrative account of the United States Strategic Bombing Survey of Japan. As we have already noted, the phenomenon to be described was the morale and will of the Japanese people to resist. But as the director of the planning staff of analysts notes, this directive as to the nature of the survey was not adequate. He writes in his report at the end of the planning phase:

> The first step in the actual planning of the survey consisted in laying out as specifically and clearly as possible the conceptual system that was to guide the survey. A survey without an adequate set of concepts . . . can at best only collect a set of "interesting" but unrelated facts which would not be amenable to a systematic analysis and which would not permit the unequivocal answering of the basic questions the USSBS would want answered. Before going into the field to collect interviews one must have clearly formulated

what kind of facts are to be sought; one must know how to find these facts; and one must have a good idea of why those facts are wanted. (p. 103) [1]

Consequently, the planning staff before leaving for Japan analyzed the concept of morale and will and capacity to resist, and listed seven major psychological factors which were regarded as the major components for study. These seven components were:

1. Confidence in the purpose of the war.
2. Confidence in the leadership.
3. Confidence in other Japanese—that is, in each other.
4. Confidence in the organizational and institutional efficiency of the nation at war.
5. The psycho-biological status of the individual.
6. Confidence in a Japanese victory.
7. Sense of orientation—confidence in the news and information provided by Japanese authorities.

But these seven components were still too broad and somewhat abstract. Consequently, they were further analyzed into a series of sub-areas which would ultimately be the subject of measurement. The first six components were broken down into 37 sub-areas which are listed below.

I. *Confidence in Purpose of the War.*
  1. Belief that Japan had to fight in order to avoid economic enslavement.
  2. Belief that Japan fought a rightful war to secure world domination.
  3. Japan fought to bring a better way of life to the world.
  4. Japan fought a holy war on the behalf of the Asiatics.
  5. Japan fought to preserve self from actual extinction or enslavement at the hands of the Allies.

II. *Confidence in Leadership.*
  6. Faith in the Imperial institution.
  7. Faith in the Emperor as an individual.
  8. Faith in the government leaders—cabinet ministers, vice ministers, privy councillors, cabinet advisors, and others of similar rank.
  9. Faith in the administrators of government bureaus and sub-divisions.
  10. Faith in business and industrial leaders.
  11. Faith in the leaders of the local group of which respondent is a member.

---

1. D. Krech and E. Ballachey, *op. cit.* All quotations to follow are taken from this monograph and represent the actual work notes from the original survey. Quoted by permission of the publishers.

    12. Faith in the leaders of the class of which respondent is a member.

    13. Faith in the news and information issued from official sources.

    14. Faith in the military leaders at home and in combat areas.

III. *Confidence in other Japanese.*

    15. Faith in immediate associates—those with whom respondent has face-to-face contacts.

    16. Faith in the local community (village, town, or city) of which respondent is a member.

    17. Faith in the home front in general.

    18. Faith in the military forces.

    19. Faith in Japan's Allies.

    20. Attitudes toward Koreans, Chinese and other minority groups in Japan.

IV. *Confidence in the organizational and institutional efficiency of the nation at war.*

    21. Faith in industrial and production capacity.

    22. Faith in the transportation and supplies system.

    23. Faith in the economic system.

    24. Faith in the organizational efficiency of the armed forces.

    25. Faith in the training and discipline of the people.

    26. Faith in the manpower.

    27. Faith in the adequacy of war equipment.

    28. Faith in the adequacy of food, shelter, and medical facilities.

    29. Faith in the adequacy of evacuation measures.

    30. Faith in the adequacy of air-raid protection facilities.

V. *The Psycho-biological Status of the Respondent.*

    31. The history of the respondent's health during the war.

    32. The history of the respondent's diet.

    33. The history of the respondent's housing and clothing experiences.

    34. The history of the respondent's emotional status during the war. (fears, hopes, susceptibility to rumors, depression, apathy, determination)

VI. *Confidence in Japanese Victory.*

    35. Attitude toward victory at the beginning of the war.

    36. The time and circumstances at which doubt first appear.

    37. The time and circumstances at which respondent became convinced that Japan was or would be defeated.

But it was then noted that these 37 components of the gross phenomenon, morale, with the possible exception of the area labelled "psycho-biological status of the respondent," relate only to certain psychological processes. While they might be regarded as the dependent variables under study, the level at which they truly operate is as *intervening variables*—internal states of the individual presumably leading to behavioral consequences. Since the objective of the survey was to inquire into *will* and *capacity* of the Japanese to resist, it would be begging the ultimate question to assume that changes in such internal states of the individual of *necessity* had behavioral consequences for the conduct of the war.[2] Even if the systematic connections of such internal states to behavior had been established under *ordinary* conditions, the severe social controls of wartime might well attenuate the normal behavioral consequences of any such conditions of demoralization. Consequently, the analysts added to the conceptual system a series of eight other areas, all behavioral in character, which presumably constituted indicators of capacity to resist. These behavioral indicators included, for example, disruptive behavior, such as looting, hoarding, sabotage, panic, crimes, etc., work behavior, like absenteeism and subversive behavior.

These 45 components of the phenomenon under study were then translated into a series of items or questions which presumably elicited data appropriate for indices of morale. To illustrate the difficulty of this translation process it may be pointed out that in the planning stage, prior to any empirical inquiry in Japan, there were three revisions of the initial instruments. The first instrument, an interview schedule, contained 93 major questions, exclusive of factual and classificatory data. In a first revision, the schedule was felt to be excessively long for actual field use and was cut to 61 questions. Two further revisions occurred in which, while the length of the instrument was stabilized at approximately 60 basic questions, there were modifications of wording, order, and minor features of the conceptualization. However, all this process of translation occurred in the planning prior to any experience with the reality of the field situation. The analysts upon arriving in Japan and after preliminary work and conferencing report:

> Early in the pre-test it became evident that . . . the Steering Committee would have to adjust its research aspirations . . . to the realities of the interviewing personnel available. . . . A further consideration naturally was the length of the schedule. (p. 136)

The basic instrument was therefore reduced following such experience to 40 items or questions. Further experience with this instrument led to two more revisions because of operating difficulties and minor improvements in conceptualization.

---

2. For a systematic discussion of the two levels—will vs. capacity to resist, internal states vs. behavior, see H. Speier, Psychological Warfare Reconsidered, in Lasswell and Lerner, *op. cit.*

The case of the Bombing Survey admittedly had unusual complexities.[3] The operating conditions involved a strange country. Unavoidably, there was no opportunity to plan the investigation in contact with the actual field setting. However, the oscillation between the theoretically adequate plan and the operationally feasible plan is characteristic of surveys in general, and the multiplicity of components that enter into the gross phenomenon is also characteristic. Consider such common subjects for survey inquiries as prejudice, political apathy, internationalism, knowledge of some elaborate political entity such as the UN, attitude toward some complex object such as American radio, an organization of sentiments or an ideology such as class consciousness. All of these gross phenomena permit of analysis into many component parts. But if such complexity is characteristic, what principles can be advanced to aid the analyst in solving the problem?

1. Distinctions Between Different Psychological Dimensions

Many descriptive surveys deal with phenomena that are ultimately psychological. By this we do not mean the fact that there is a verbal report by the respondent, for that may be merely the *procedural avenue* to the revelation of some datum which is essentially *non*-psychological such as bond holding, medical history, job status, number of children, etc. Such surveys are not concerned with psychological phenomena. However, where the survey's objectives involve psychological variables, it is most essential that the conceptualization consider different psychological dimensions as a pre-requisite to comprehensive coverage in the survey or to a rational choice of that level which is most appropriate for study. Otherwise, there is the great danger that the findings will be partial and misleading as a description, or that findings meaningful only at one level of psychological functioning will be arbitrarily extended to other levels. Psychological systematists who have been associated with survey research emphasize this point. Thus, Krech, makes this point a fundamental criticism of public opinion research. He writes:

How many of our public opinion agencies have actually concerned themselves with *a basic study of the nature, characteristics and dynamics* of be-

---

3. The complexity of the conceptual system has not been adequately treated even by the discussion of the 45 components. The Bombing Survey as an *explanatory* survey involved problems in the conceptualization of the independent variable, bombing, which also might be regarded as complex in character. For example such different dimensions as weight of bombs, type of bombs, night or day bombing, area or precision bombing, etc., may have different consequences. In addition a whole series of other variables having to do with the specific institutional setting were incorporated so as to specify the social conditions under which bombing has different consequences. A parallel series of intervening variables having to do with the respondent's ideology and background were incorporated to test the factors which sustain the individual in the face of the bombing. But all this merely underscores our point that the basic training in conceptualization for descriptive survey analysis is a pre-requisite to effective analysis of explanatory surveys. One of the forthcoming publications of this project treats exclusively of the problems of concept and index formulation in the social sciences and will constitute a basic source on these problems.

liefs, attitudes, judgments, opinions? How many of our most skilled and renowned surveyers and pollsters can make theoretically meaningful distinc· tions among verbal reactions, beliefs, attitudes, judgments, and opinions . . . Our journals are replete with studies, both empirical and theoretical, of question construction, interviewing, sampling, coding, training, etc., but it is only very rarely (if at all) that one finds in these journals any discussion of the basic nature of the "things" which all these interviewers, question-constructors and coders are presumably measuring, weighing, counting, and reporting.[4]

Krech's comments are appropriate to one of our case studies. In his critique he argues that distinctions must be made between attitudes and such other concepts as beliefs, judgments and opinions, and if we enlarge upon this suggestion in the light of his more general writings we must distinguish between essentially *cognitive structures* or dimensions and *motivational* dimensions.[5] This distinction might be applied profitably to Centers' inquiry into class consciousness, neglecting for the moment the explanatory goals of the study and concentrating on Centers' other purpose, to describe ideology. It will be recalled from the earlier description that the basic index of this dependent variable was a battery of six questions designed to measure politico-economic orientation. We earlier presented the essence of each of these six questions and re-examination of these will now reveal that they implicitly relate to *purely cognitive* structures. Thus one of the questions reads in entirety: "Do you think working people are usually fairly and squarely treated by their employers, or that employers take advantage of them?" Inspection of the content of this question shows that it involves the respondent's judgment or appraisal. An honest employer might conceivably appraise the relations of labor and management as involving exploitation, might at the same time possibly have the desire to continue such exploitation and therefore approve of it. We are not being pedantic about the matter, nor ignoring the possibility that such a desire might not be accompanied by such intellectual honesty in admitting the situation. Nor are we denying that *empirically* one might find that the cognitive indicator correlates with a more direct measure of motivation in this area. But these are empirical questions and one should not beg them by assuming such a correlation initially.[6] Similarly the question as to whether

---

4. D. Krech, "Public Opinion and Psychological Theory," *Int. J. Opin. Attit. Res.,* 2, 1948, 85-88.

5. D. Krech and R. Crutchfield, *Theory and Problems of Social Psychology* (New York: McGraw-Hill, 1947). See especially Chapter V.

6. Centers actually presents data on the inter-item correlations for all these questions, results of an item analysis, and correlation with a "behavioral criterion." These statistical findings support the fact that the cognitive items function fairly well as predictors of these other levels. However, in a more rigorous test of the unidimensionality of Centers' battery, Case reports contrary empirical findings which do support our psychological analysis. He administered the battery to a sample of respondents in the State of Washington in 1950 and did a Guttman Scale Analysis. At least for this sample at this time period, Case concludes: "It is safe to assume that Centers' C-R battery, as it stands, is looking primarily at an attitude variable of dominant

government ownership of industry would lead in general to fairer wages, steadier employment and less unemployment involves an appraisal of the future but does not indicate that the respondent *favors* government ownership. What might be regarded as the public good would not necessarily lead to the private advantage of the respondent and might actually be opposed. So, too, the item on the consequences of an increase in labor's power in government is essentially cognitive. Only two of the six items relate at a *conceptual* level to attitudinal orientations, that is, to the respondent's support for or motivation to achieve a certain end and the findings should be interpreted in this light.

Sometimes this distinction between the cognitive and attitudinal, while conceptually correct, might appear to be academic. Such seems to be the case, for example, where the respondent is asked about his awareness or knowledge of a certain practice, or his judgment as to whether a given party is engaged in one practice or another. Where the practice has a seemingly well-established culturally determined value, e.g. negative, the analyst may reason that merely to be aware of its existence is to reject it or to judge a party as engaged in such a practice is to oppose or dislike him. And on this basis he may skip the attitudinal area. But this is to impute *too much* cultural uniformity to the attitudes of a sample of respondents, or to assume too readily the validity of the apparent cultural valuation. We can illustrate this problem from a survey conducted among East German Youth with respect to attitudes about East vs. West German conflict. In the course of this inquiry a series of questions were asked about propaganda practices by the "West" and "East." The analysts remark: "The term 'propaganda' was specifically employed. In the understanding that the term might convey *odious implications* . . . it was used advisedly." A question in the *cognitive* realm was asked, "So far, have you had the impression that the West is making propaganda?", and 52% of the sample said "No" and the remaining 48% said "Yes." [7]

One might have taken these respective figures as indicative of the *attitude* towards the West for as the analysts noted initially the practice of "propaganda" is usually regarded as "odious" and the belief of 48% of the sample in the occurrence of this practice might be thought to signify their criticism of the West.

---

proportions, plus one or more of lesser proportions." However, the empirical findings on scalability by Case vs. Centers, whichever are accepted, do *not* alter our basic point. Centers might well have used *six cognitive* items as a result of initially ignoring the conceptual distinction we have made. Under such conditions, neither he nor Case nor anyone else would have had any empirical data available for testing whether or not the distinction was operationally unimportant. For Centers' data, see Chapter IV, *op. cit.* For Case, see "Guttman Scaling applied to Centers' Conservatism-Radicalism Battery," *Amer. Journ. Sociol.*, LVIII, 1953, 556-563.

7. Office of the U.S. High Commissioner for Germany, Office of Public Affairs, Reactions Analysis Staff., *Reactions to Eastern vs. Western Propaganda*, Series #2, Report #108, 1951, (mimeo), italics ours.

Similarly, the belief of the 52% of the sample that the West was *not* engaged in propaganda might have been thought to signify their approval of Western practices. However, the analysts did not make this assumption and asked a series of additional attitudinal questions. Those who had stated that the West was engaged in propaganda were asked about their endorsement of the practice with a question on whether the West should make "more or less or about the same amount of propaganda." Only one-eighth of this group said that the West should make less propaganda, thus indicating that the apparent odious implications of propaganda practices do not hold for the great majority of this group. Those who had stated that the West was *not* engaged in propaganda were asked whether they would favor the practice. Approximately half of this group said "Yes," thus indicating that the apparently desirable implications of *not* propagandizing do not hold for large numbers of this group.

Sometimes this distinction between the attitudinal and cognitive may appear academic to the analyst for reasons which are parallel but just the reverse of the example just presented. This occurs in the instance where the attitude toward some object or practice is determined, which has a seemingly *well established cultural meaning*. The assumption in this instance might be that the attitude being empirically determined, the cognitive structure underlying the respondents' attitude can be inferred from the apparent objective or culturally defined content. On this basis questions on cognition are skipped. But this procedure imputes too much cultural uniformity to the cognitions of the respondents, or assumes too readily the validity of the apparent cultural content. The point can be documented from the study just cited. The connotations of the term propaganda usually involve notions of persuasion, manipulation, lies and certainly a pattern of procedures somewhat contrasted with fact or truth. When the large proportion of this sample of German Youth expressed attitudes of approval for the West engaging in propaganda, the analyst might have inferred that this represented endorsement of any of these practices. But this turns out not to be the case. For example, from questions asked on the difference between Western and Eastern propaganda, one notes that the essential image or cognitive structure of the propaganda the West should practice is that of communication of truth, objective information, fact. To know the referent of the attitude that was elicited required specific questions on the cognitive structure of the term propaganda.

Another survey conducted by the Reactions Analysis Staff in Germany illustrates this same problem even more dramatically. A general question on attitudes toward a European Union was asked and indicated that a large majority of the sample of West Germany endorsed such a union. The analysts in deciding what particular political form was being endorsed by these respondents asked a direct question to explore the cognitive content of the term "a union of Europe" rather than make any assumptions about this content from the objective nature of proposals that had been discussed. Among this sample, there was tremendous variability in the conception of such a union and no single feature of such a union elicited more than 15% of the total number of answers to the question on respondent's personal conceptions.[8] The general principle of the distinction between these respective psychological levels and its translation into practice in descriptive surveys goes far to prevent false inferences being made by the analyst.

Thus far we have suggested the need for the analyst to distinguish between the broad psychological realms of cognition and motivation as a basis for effective conceptualization of a descriptive survey. But both these realms operate in the form of intervening variables. It is therefore most desirable in certain surveys for the analyst to distinguish these two *taken together* from a more *behavioral* or *action* level. Where the survey is concerned with the description of the extent of past or current behavior or with intended future actions, or with support for some possible course of action, or where a survey is concerned with the causes of some behavioral outcome, emphasis should not merely be placed on intervening variables of a cognitive or motivational type. The Bombing Survey example is a case in point. From the point of view of the sponsors of the survey, the success of bombing in altering such psychological processes as emotions, motivations, cognitions depended on such states being translated into behavior that was politically or militarily relevant. Consequently, the conceptual structure of the survey incorporated this level as well as that of the intervening variables.[9] Especially under conditions of severe governmental controls and a variety of counter measures, the normal voluntary translation of sentiments into actions will be attenuated and the distinction must be emphasized. Janowitz notes this same problem in connection with attitude surveys among German military personnel, where he remarks that studies of the morale of Wehrmacht prisoners were prefaced with the proviso "it has become a commonplace among those involved in psychological warfare against the Ger-

8. Reactions Analysis Staff, *West German Thinking on a Federation of Europe*, Series #2, Report #111, 1951 (mimeo).

9. We shall not discuss the many theoretical aspects of this problem. There are many examples of this type of conceptual problem in surveys, and a variety of procedures for treating it. For a discussion of this same problem in election prediction surveys where the inference from the person's *preference* for a candidate to his *action* in voting for him on election day may be questionable, the reader is referred to Mosteller *et al., op. cit.*

For a general treatment of the factors responsible for so-called inconsistencies between attitude and behavior and modes of treating the problem in surveys, see *J. Soc. Issues, Vol. 3,* 1949. This same problem has also been treated in classic discussions of the validity of attitude measurement where behavior has been taken as the criterion of validity. Our discussion makes no assumption that a lack of correspondence between these levels is a demonstration of invalidity. For an especially interesting treatment of this traditional notion of validity and a stimulating theoretical discussion of the significant implications that are glossed over by associating validity with the prediction of behavior see pp. 21-22 of R. K. Merton, "Fact and Factitiousness in Ethnic Opinionnaires," *Amer. Sociol. Rev.,* 1940, 5, 13-28.

mans, that attitudes encountered before or after capture bore only a limited relationship to fighting behavior under combat conditions," for, as he notes, there are powerful controls and rewards and punishments which attenuated the relationship between attitude and behavior.[10]

Centers' inquiry is also illustrative of this problem of psychological levels ranging from intervening variables to behavioral variables. Apart from the questions on voting behavior and union membership all the measures of the phenomenon of class consciousness and radicalism were of a cognitive or attitudinal sort. Granted the findings of class cleavages and of radical ideology at this level, there is the ultimate question of whether these processes are being translated into *behavior* of a radical sort or behavior corresponding to the class interest expressed. Centers makes no categorical inferences about possible behavioral outcomes, but in his conclusions he wishes to treat the political implications of his findings and one notes the difficulties he faces because of the lack of data at a behavioral level.

> Class cleavage . . . *as yet exists only as a sort of non-support* and dissent of a class, and as an organized protest and struggle for many immediate and tangible goals by a militant minority of that class . . . Organized labor, as the vanguard of the working class . . . is *as yet apparently not determined to take over control,* but bent mainly upon wringing concessions and privileges and at most merely a share in control . . . *Nor has there yet arisen* in America, of course, any nationally significant political party with a working class program . . . So far *there are only stirrings and precursors of such political phenomena* . . . But there has been found in this exploration the kind of crude and *elemental class consciousness out of which* time and events and the exhortations of agitators *might make these things.* (pp. 218-219) [11]

We shall turn shortly to another problem of conceptualization which Centers alludes to in these conclusions. He remarks on the *temporal development* of these beliefs in America, and admittedly, cannot predict the course of future development of the *sentiments* he studied. But aside from this problem, it is clear that any inferences as to *behavior* that he might wish to make rest on shaky ground, for *Centers only knows the elemental psychological processes out of which such behavior might or might not flow,* and has no direct indicators of any behavioral sort. And he is aware of factors that might attenuate the relation between sentiments and action, for he remarks in this same conclusion on forces in the social situation which might prevent the formation of behavior of a class conscious sort.[12]

---

10. M. Janowitz, A review of two surveys conducted in Germany, *Publ. Opin. Quart.,* 13, 1949, pp. 343-345.

11. Italics ours to emphasize the problem.

12. In a replication of Centers' study, Case also alludes to this formal problem by noting that Centers' findings, generally confirmed in the second study, can lead to "alternative non-Marxian predictions . . . with much sounder roots in American social structure." He cites as example the response to a social reform movement and he notes that his study in 1950 suggests

Within each of these two psychological realms, the conceptualization should often involve further distinctions. Discussions in the literature of such *abstract dimensions* of cognitive structures as their *clarity, differentiation,* and the like and such dimensions of attitudes as their *saliency, intensity, strength, organization,* and the like guide the analyst in making these distinctions.[13]

Such distinctions permit better inferences from the descriptive survey for attitudes can be lightly or strongly held, easily activated or not, knowledge can be vague or clear. Such differences in characteristics of people with *nominally* the same views have consequences which should not be neglected.

It has always been the objection of theorists in the clinical fields, in depth psychology, in case study methods, in the field of politics, that these distinctions are ignored and that the descriptive findings of surveys are therefore superficial and misleading. For example, Erich Fromm, the psychoanalyst, remarks with respect to opinion polls that "they are not the tool for understanding the forces operating underneath the surface of opinion . . . every opinion is worth only as much as the emotional matrix in which it is rooted." [14] Psychoanalytically oriented authors of one of our illustrative examples, *The Authoritarian Personality,* also object to usual poll data on ground of superficiality. Goldhamer summarizes and interprets the criticisms of public opinion surveys made by Lindsay Rogers, a political scientist, as follows:

> The polling agencies ignore or minimize in their work the relation, to expressed "opinions" of numerous factors: the highly variable degree of information on which opinions are based, the variations in affect intensity, conviction and interest associated with expressed judgment, the existence of ambivalence and various complicated qualifications of opinion, the discrepancy between announced opinion and private thought (which is by no means simply a matter of concealment or deceit), the stability of expressed opinion, the conative component of opinion. . . . Mr. Rogers' contention is very simply and very soundly that expressions of opinion where these matters are ignored are generally of little or no value except as a form of journalism, and are positively dangerous and lay their publicizers open to accusations of fraud when they are passed off as meaningful expressions of what the people "think" or "want." [15]

---

that these interest-groups are "behaving non-militantly and non-violently within a framework of capitalism." See H. M. Case, "An Independent Test of the Interest-Group Theory of Social Class," *Amer. Sociol. Rev.,* 17, 1952, 751-755.

13. For an elaborate general treatment of such dimensions, see D. Krech and R. Crutchfield, *op. cit.* For a very useful discussion of certain of these dimensions, see D. Katz, "Three Criteria for Evaluating Polls: Knowledge, Conviction, and Significance," *Publ. Opin. Quart.,* 4, 1940, 277-284. For a most interesting treatment of rather unusual dimensions, e.g., the time perspective of opinions, and examples of their fruitfulness see, M. B. Smith, "The Personal Setting of Public Opinions," *Publ. Opin. Quart.,* 11, 1947, 507-523.

14. Erich Fromm, Sex and Character, in D. P. Geddes and E. Curie, eds., *About the Kinsey Report* (New York: New American Library, 1948).

15. H. Goldhamer, Review of Lindsay Rogers, *The Pollsters, Publ. Opin. Quart.,* 13, 1949, 131-134. Reprinted by permission of the publishers.

Arthur Schlesinger, Jr., the historian, makes similar comments in evaluating the volume by Strunk and Cantril which provides an encyclopedic compilation of thousands of survey results over a decade of public opinion research. He raises the question of the usefulness of such data to political historians and remarks: "A response to a public opinion poll, one would think, is essentially an *irresponsible* expression of opinion—irresponsible because no action is intended to follow. The expression of opinion is not burdened, in other words, by a sense of accountability for consequences." [16]

Such criticisms can be too narrow and extreme at times and neglect the primary purposes of surveys as instruments for mass description rather than for deep case study. Also they may neglect the attention given to these very problems by sophisticated analysts in survey research. But it would be a mistake to reject their general import for survey research. Proper distinctions between different dimensions of these phenomena will allay legitimate criticisms of these types and insure more meaningful findings.

With respect to dimensions having to do with *content* of attitudes or beliefs, a number of distinctions have been found very useful in the concrete operations of descriptive surveys. Many descriptive surveys deal with the area of knowledge or ignorance of some complex entity, e.g., knowledge about the UN, about Russia, about ethnic groups, etc. In many of the same surveys, inferences are drawn from the pattern of ignorance or information or misinformation as to the attitudes or behavior that will follow. In such surveys, it is well to distinguish between *knowledge with possible instrumental significance and knowledge that is academic.* For example attitudes towards the UN might show no particular relation to the knowledge of the way the annual budget is determined but might relate to knowledge of the UN's actions on behalf of "Human Rights." In a survey during World War II it was found that compliance with the OPA was related to knowledge that special dispensations were made in case of hardship but unrelated to knowledge of the legal process by which price regulations were established.[17]

It is also very desirable in the cognitive realm to examine in detail the *content or cognitive structure* of some entity or object or institution about which an initial gross cognitive question is asked. Quite often, the analyst may assume that an object with an apparently well-defined cultural *meaning* is regarded in that light by the respondents, and simply to be aware of this total object is to be aware of or familiar with the detailed culturally defined sub-properties. Instead the fact may be that there is wide variation in the understanding of the entity and only through inquiry into these aspects or properties can the description of the cognitive level be reliable. An illustration of this problem is provided by a survey conducted in Western

16. A. Schlesinger, Jr., Review of M. Strunk and H. Cantril, *Public Opinion, 1935–1946*, in *Publ. Opin. Quart.*, 15, 1951, 147-150. Reprinted by permission of the publishers.

17. Unpublished survey conducted by the Division of Surveys, Office of War Information for the Office of Price Administration, 1943.

Austria shortly after World War II in which one of the purposes was to describe the degree of understanding of the operations of Democratic government.[18]

A series of questions as to the modes of operation of particular democratic institutions was asked. These revealed that the respondent's conceptions of these institutions often did not correspond with the usual American conception or textbook conception, and, incidentally, that attitudes in favor of democracy did not represent endorsement of specific institutional patterns normally comprehended by the term democracy. Illustrative material from a variety of questions asked in this survey is presented in Table I below.

TABLE I—Variations in the Cognitive Structure of the Concept of Democracy Among Proponents of a Democratic Regime

	Percent of Those Favoring Democratic Regime [19]
Good aspects of a democratic regime are: freedom, political decisions reached by group process	56%
Democratic regime would function according to the usual parliamentary principle	65
Party conflicts to be mediated by debate or compromise rather than by imposition of authority	68
Approval of popular discussion of politics	52
Number of minority parties allowed to function should be subject to restriction	33

Similarly, in the case of surveys dealing with motivational or attitudinal and behavioral variables, it is well to distinguish between a general orientation or an *attitude toward a more general institution or object and attitudes toward more specific and concrete objects* within the general class. There is vast documentation of the fact that people endorse a general principle often without corresponding endorsement of instances of that principle.[20]

2. Wide Coverage of the Objects of An Attitude or Opinion

Apart from variations in the psychological level dealt with, for example, cognitive or motivational, deep or superficial, general or particular, a particular orientation can be manifested towards a wide array of objects. Thus, the orientation in Centers' battery implies so to speak a concept of radicalism—conservatism, a desire to see certain types of changes in the social order

---

18. Unpublished survey conducted by a staff from the United States Strategic Bombing Survey, Morale Division, 1945.

19. The percentages are based on 208 cases who constituted the sub-group who favored a democratic regime. The original total sample was restricted to the population of selected cities and villages in that area of Western Austria under Allied Occupation Control.

20. For an interesting example of this see H. Hyman, "Inconsistencies," in *J. Soc. Issues*, 5, #3, 38-42. For a recent treatment of this problem with most interesting empirical data on the confusion created by lack of such a distinction in past public opinion research see, G. Wiebe, "Some Implications of Separating Opinions from Attitudes." *Publ. Opin. Quart*, 1953, 328-352.

or to be critical of certain current social practices. But there is a wide range in the features of the social order towards which the individual could manifest his opposition. Centers labels his battery, "politico-economic orientation," but all six of the items relate purely to the economic sphere.

This does not deny the value of his description of the extent of this particular orientation in the sample of the American public, but merely limits the findings to a description of a given sub-area. This problem of conceptualization, however, has important consequences also for the explanatory aspects of the survey. In the test of the influence of objective economic position on ideology as measured by this battery, Centers finds that those in lower positions are more radical, and this constitutes a verification of his theory. But, in actuality the verification is only for economic aspects of the social scene, and results might be otherwise if different aspects of the phenomenon were covered. For example, some readers might plausibly argue that opposition to women being relegated to the conventional role of housewife and lack of prejudice towards Negroes, while not economic, is indicative of radicalism towards certain current institutional arrangements. Centers in the course of his inquiry did actually include two questions on these respective areas. Here his findings were by contrast that the working class was *more "conservative."* [21]

If an investigator had picked the latter area for study, the theory would have been disproved! The same point can be documented by another one of Centers' explanatory findings. In the course of his analysis, Centers tests the influence of formal religion on ideology and finds that *Catholics are more radical* than Protestants.

The finding seems somewhat anomalous since Centers remarks that the Catholic Church has been "the traditional foe of all leftist ideologies" (p. 185). Now, granted that the paradox can be resolved to some extent by distinguishing *élite* from mass opinion, there is also the theoretical problem as to what is the conception of radical ideology. Suppose that instead of using the *economic orientation* battery the dependent variable had been defined in terms of American policy toward Russia or Spain. Public Opinion Polls show here a consistent tendency for Catholics to be more pro-Franco and anti-Russian and in this sense the findings might be interpreted as supporting the hypothesis that Catholic church membership leads to *greater conservatism.*[22]

Conceivably one might have found that conservatism was a highly generalized pattern or even a unity, but to have assumed this in the first place would have been to beg the question. The distinction conceptually between orientations towards a wide array of objects insures more comprehensive

21. See Chapter IX, Other Psychological Differences.
22. For such findings, see for example, H. Cantril and M. Strunk, *Public Opinion* (Princeton: Princeton University Press, 1951), p. 808, No. 8, where the difference between Catholics and Protestants in support of Franco was + 41%.

description, or at least a rational choice as to that sphere of objects that is most desirable to describe. With respect to any tests of an hypothesis in an explanatory survey it insures a more comprehensive test or proper qualifications on the conclusions reported.

One of the other case studies exemplifies the same general problem of conceptualization and its consequences for *explanatory* surveys. In the inquiry into absenteeism, it will be recalled that worker morale was studied by a variety of questions on satisfaction with plant and community conditions. Morale was regarded from the view point of this study not as a dependent variable, not as a phenomenon to be described, but as an independent variable whose effect on absenteeism was to be determined or as an intervening variable mediating the relationship between objective working conditions and ultimate absenteeism.[23] Here too, there is the problem of what aspects of the worker's environment should be considered in order to decide that he was satisfied or not, demoralized or not. At least six separate aspects of the in-plant setting were the object of questions, and it can be noted from the published results that the findings on the relation of morale to absenteeism vary with the area used as the measure of morale. For example, dissatisfaction with promotional policy in the plant increased the rate of absence by 6 percentage points, but dislike of the plant as a place of work increased the rate by 13 percentage points.[24]

In other words, depending on what the specific object of satisfaction or dissatisfaction may have been, the findings on effects of morale on some other phenomenon varied. In a later program of research in the industrial morale field, Katz presents even more elaborate evidence that the component of morale that is studied affects the findings. The components have different consequences on productivity treated as the phenomenon to be explained, and in turn the determinants of these different components of morale vary. Katz writes:

> The results from this study . . . suggest that morale is not a strictly unitary concept but that it consists of a number of dimensions. The dimensions investigated were (1) intrinsic job satisfaction—that is, the satisfaction that derives from the content of the work itself; (2) pride in work group; (3) satisfaction with wages and with promotional opportunities; and (4) identification with the company. Of special interest was the finding that of these four morale dimensions the only one significantly related positively to productivity was pride in work group. In fact, some of the attitudes usually regarded as indicative of high morale were negatively related to productivity.

23. Depending on where the explanatory sequence starts from, morale could be regarded either as the independent variable whose effects are to be traced or as a mediating link. However, from the point of view of the status of such a concept in psychology it would always function as an intervening variable, that is an internal state of the organism.

24. D. Katz and H. Hyman, *op. cit.,* p. 21.

> In general, the causal determinants of the various dimensions of morale were not the same. Intrinsic job satisfaction was primarily a function of the type of work performed. . . . The main determinants of satisfaction with salary and status were not so much the actual salary and position . . . rather they were salary and status in relation to experience and training and expectation of advancement. . . . The groups who showed a feeling of pride were the groups who enjoyed the better supervisory practices.[25]

Another example from the morale area, but in this case from military rather than industrial surveys, documents in the most elaborate way the fact that a given attitudinal domain may turn out not to be unitary in character. If an analyst picked one sub-realm to cover rather than another, an hypothesis in an explanatory survey as to the determinants of morale can be confirmed or denied. To prevent such "capriciousness" in survey research one must conceptualize a given phenomenon as relating to a constellation of objects and provide a whole array of tests of the influence of a determinant. The example is provided by the detailed surveys of the Research Branch of the United States Army on the phenomenon of the personal adjustment of soldiers.[26]

In these inquiries, the analysts defined personal adjustment as covering the four broad areas of "personal esprit," "personal commitment," "satisfaction with status and job" and "approval or criticism of the army." They note in their analysis that *the four areas do not constitute a single dimension of attitude*. Rather they constitute a *profile of attitudes,*" by which they mean that a particular characteristic of the soldier treated as a determinant of adjustment has different consequences depending on which of these four areas is studied. Thus, they show that the better educated had *better* adjustment if defined in terms of "personal esprit" or "personal commitment," but *worse* adjustment, if defined in terms of satisfaction with status or job or in terms of approval or criticism of the Army. Similar variation in the influence of other independent variables on adjustment occurs depending on which of the four sub-areas of adjustment is used for the empirical test.

We have tried to convey thus far the complexity in the conceptualization of the phenomenon to be studied in a descriptive and, by extension, an explanatory survey. We have suggested certain distinctions as a guide to the analyst. Cognitive, motivational, and behavioral levels may enter. Within each of these levels, more refinements can be introduced by conceptualizing other abstract or formal dimensions of the phenomenon. A variety of content dimensions can then be considered, and there is a wide domain of pos-

---

25. D. Katz, Morale and Motivation in Industry, in W. Dennis, ed., *Current Trends in Industrial Psychology* (Pittsburgh: U. of Pittsburgh Press, 1949), pp. 160-163. Reprinted by permission of the publishers.

26. S. Stouffer, *et al., The American Soldier* (Princeton: Princeton University Press, 1949), Vol. I, Chap. III.

sible objects towards which the person can manifest a given orientation. We are not suggesting, however, that the analyst in every investigation engage in a broad coverage of all of these aspects of a phenomenon. There are many instances in which the survey's objective is better met by a specific focus on a narrow problem. There are instances where given dimensions are irrelevant. And there are other instances where comprehensiveness must be sacrificed because limited resources must be applied to one relatively crucial aspect. But these choices can be best made if all the alternative conceptions of the problem are in view, and it is in this light that we presented our detailed discussion.

Decisions about the Location of the Phenomenon

Thus far we have discussed the problems the analyst must deal with in theorizing about the nature of the phenomenon he plans to study. But the nature of the phenomenon does not have any reality apart from its location in *some defined population,* living within some defined *boundaries,* at some *point in time.* In the theorizing prior to the descriptive survey, decisions as to these problems are of great importance. The analysis must ultimately state the boundaries within which the description applies.[27] And if the description is sophisticated, but refers to an irrelevant time period, or a population that does not concern the sponsor, the findings are wasted. And there are instances, as we shall see, where a bad decision may not only be wasteful, but actually be misleading, for a phenomenon may take on a very atypical pattern at given moments in time and in specialized populations, and under such conditions inferences about the more general picture are dangerous. These decisions are also inextricably bound up with the conceptualization of the phenomenon. The specific features of a phenomenon vary with the setting within which it is studied and therefore affect theorizing. Moreover, careful decisions as to location in time and space and in a human population are essential to efficient field operations.

While there is much, and well deserved, attention to problems of sampling design and theory in survey research, there is considerable neglect of these *prior* questions of the location within which the phenomenon ought to be studied.[28] It is only after this decision is made that the sampling prob-

---

27. We are not referring here to questions of sampling design and inferences made in the light of sampling errors. Even if a complete census of a given population were taken, and there were no question of sampling error, there would still be the problem of whether the description of *that* population is crucial to the problem under study.

28. For a concise statement of sampling considerations which includes the temporal location of the phenomenon, see M. B. Parten, *op. cit.,* 116-117.

lems arise, and the most unbiased sample of a given population cannot rectify the mistake that might be made in choosing that population to sample.

1. Temporal Location

Since the *temporal* location of a study is perhaps least frequently considered, let us examine this problem first. Centers' inquiry into class consciousness provides a useful illustration of many of these problems of decisions and their consequences for the analyst. We shall defer for the moment the explanatory aspect of his study and emphasize merely the fact that one part attempted an empirical description of class consciousness and ideology in a sample of American white males and was conducted in the year 1945. Of course, these same issues of the location of a phenomenon will have obvious consequences for explanatory surveys as well. We have here a phenomenon that all theorists agree is dynamic in character, in process of change. Centers recognizes this essential feature of his problem. Scattered through the text are comments emphasizing the temporal: *"long enduring* contest," "this conflict *has now reached* a critical phase"; "the data present a picture of *incipient* cleavage . . . *beginning* as far back as a generation ago and *becoming* increasingly wider with time"; "Americans have *become* class conscious, and a part of them, calling themselves the working class, have *begun* to have attitudes and beliefs at variance with traditional acceptances and practices."; "class consciousness . . . is *as yet confined* to a fairly narrow politico-economic compass and is even there only in the *incipient* stage." [29]

It is clear that the time period at which Centers conducted his inquiry is central to the proper interpretation of the findings obtained as a description of American class consciousness, for as he and other theorists note, this is a phenomenon in process, related to specific events and long term currents. Therefore, if the inquiry were conducted in 1955 rather than 1945 this might change the specific results. However, the *inherent* limitation of survey research as a method should be noted. It is research conducted essentially over a *narrow range of time*. The range of time for *total* field work can be extended from one week to a few weeks or perhaps from one month to a maximum of several months, so that the *aggregate* description has some quality of duration even though the observation on *each* respondent is generally for a finite point in time. Questions can be asked which historically refer to wide ranges in time, but here problems in distortion of memory limit the procedure.[30] Consequently, description is quite circumscribed as to

---

29. The quotations are taken from scattered places throughout the text, *op. cit.* (italics ours).

30. An unusual example of this approach is provided by a survey of the job history of a sample of respondents in which questions on the entire pattern of jobs that each respondent held over many years were asked. However, such rarities in survey research pose very serious technical problems in the need to reduce or estimate memory errors. See S. Lipset and R. Bendix, "Social Mobility and Occupational Career Patterns. I. Stability of Job Holding," *Amer. J. Sociol.*, LVII, 1952, 366-374.

its temporal location, and the survey as such does not represent a method characterized by protracted observation.

With respect to this inherent limitation, the most the analyst can do is to specify the time period covered in the *collection of the data*,[31] so that the temporal boundaries of the description are at least known, and any inferences can be drawn with this context in mind.[32]

In his planning the analyst should consider what would be the most appropriate time period if any for initiating his inquiry. If the phenomenon appears to be exceedingly dynamic in character, if events are in flux, the analyst may decide that an ordinary descriptive survey is not adequate to the problem. Since the goals of such a survey are usually in the direction of *generality* of findings, findings so circumscribed by too narrow time boundaries would be inconsequential. Under such conditions, one might decide upon a series of surveys over time to establish the *trend* and to characterize the more stable aspects of the phenomenon. Or one might decide upon a panel design in which the same *individuals* are studied repeatedly over time. Both of these designs extend the observations, although they are expensive, complex procedurally, and have intrinsic limitations for *exceedingly* protracted observation. Perhaps the longest *social* research panel on record does not extend over more than a span of a few years, and trend data based on sample surveys cannot to date have exceeded a 20 year period because of the recent historic origins of the modern large scale sample survey.[33]

Where such designs are not feasible, various expedients might be introduced. If the period for collection of data over the *entire sample* is lengthened, one at least has *aggregate* descriptive data which is somewhat more generalized in its significance, but such a mode of operation is somewhat inefficient. Such a decision again points up the differences in desirable procedure for explanatory vs. descriptive surveys and the possible conflicts for the analyst. By extending the duration of the survey, one protects the description against the dangers of being too narrow in time. But one also by this same device exposes different respondents within the sample to variations in events and environment corresponding to the time at which each

---

31. The relevant time period is of course that period within which the data were collected and not the period corresponding to the publication of the report or the analysis which may be long afterwards.

32. For another example of inferences about the effect of the time period on the conclusions, see: L. Cottrell and S. Eberhart, *op. cit.*, pp. 12-14, 16, 49.

33. For two very long-term panels of a social research sort, see T. M. Newcomb, *Personality and Social Change* (New York: Dryden Press, 1943), and G. Murphy and R. Likert, *Public Opinion and the Individual* (New York: Harpers, 1938). For more formal treatment of panel designs see M. Rosenberg, W. Thielens, and P. F. Lazarsfeld. The Panel Study, in Jahoda, Deutsch and Cook, *op. cit.* It is noteworthy that these two very extended panels both involved academic students as populations making it easier to maintain the observations over so long a period. By contrast the more usual panel of a less selected population is shorter in duration because of the operating difficulties. For an example of trend designs see H. Cantril, "Opinion Trends in World War II: Some Guides to Interpretation," *Public Opin. Quart.*, 12, 1948, 30-40.

person was studied. Since the explanatory survey must cope with the problem of uncontrolled factors which might account for differences between respondents contrasted on some independent variable, the extending of the time creates another sources of variation and is unwise.[34]

Even where the time period is relatively short, a sudden major event may intervene and produce incomparability between respondents studied early and late in the sequence. Centers' inquiry provides a very interesting empirical example of this problem. The period in which his data were collected extended from July 20th to August 3rd, 1945. On July 26, 1945, the announcement of the British Labor Party's victory occurred and Centers realized that this event might well strengthen the convictions of respondents who had incipient, but weak, identification with the working class. It would thus alter the descriptive findings on class consciousness, and with respect to comparisons between groups contrasted in their objective position might introduce a source of incomparability, depending on the date at which they had been studied. He presents empirical data suggestive of the temporary influence of this event by comparing groups interviewed prior to the event, and those interviewed on the day. The increase in working or lower class identification was 16 percentage points.[35]

Where a single survey is chosen and the description will apply to a relatively narrow time period, the analyst must decide whether the period is *unrepresentative* and if so, whether the inferences he wishes to draw will be seriously affected.[36] We can illustrate some of these problems with Centers' study. In July 1945, the United States was at war, and Centers remarks that one might assume "that national solidarity at such a time was a maximum" and peace-time class cleavages would be in abeyance. One might conceivably use this assumption as a basis either for postponing such an inquiry to a later date, or as Centers does, draw the inference that whatever level of class consciousness was demonstrated in the survey would be a *conservative*

---

34. In theory, there would be a formal solution to this problem in the random assignment of different classes of respondents to dates for interview. But such a formal solution to the problem is academic, for it is impossible under normal field operations to maintain such a scheme. A storm in the North postpones the date of interviewing; impassable roads in another region change the time table; an interviewer takes ill suddenly. All such contingencies defeat the procedure.

35. *Op. cit.*, p. 139. The illustration provides a demonstration that the pedestrian item in most surveys of date of interview can be of crucial methodological significance. In this same example, and his discussion of it, Centers also provides an illustration of the exploitation of accidental findings. For the empirical demonstration of the influence of the Labor Party victory leads Centers to elaborate a conception of classes as psycho-social groups that are supra-national in character.

36. For a very dramatic example of the influence of the time period on the descriptive findings, the student is referred to the field of labor force measurement. It is obvious that temporal factors affect the magnitude of employment that is demonstrated. For example, agricultural employment changes by as much as 3 million from winter to summer. Employment as measured by current activity status will vary depending on whether the period for observation includes holidays, weekends, etc. For a discussion of this problem see Chap. II, *Labor Force Definition and Measurement* (New York: Social Science Research Council, Bulletin #56, 1947).

statement of the general phenomenon.[37] Since Centers was concerned to demonstrate that class consciousness *did* exist, the time period chosen, even though not a "typical" period was perhaps a desirable one, because the positive findings become peculiarly *compelling*. Class consciousness was demonstrated, so to speak, under experimental conditions making it especially difficult to achieve such a demonstration. However, for the sake of our methodological argument, if the time period were such as to understate the general phenomenon and little or no class consciousness were demonstrated, the investigator would have been faced with the dilemma of deciding whether the finding was generally true or merely an artifact of the temporary state of war.

In addition, Centers' reasoning that wartime conditions would reduce normal class cleavages, while plausible, must remain at the level of *speculation* as long as the empirical data apply at only *one* point in time. Insofar as the survey method is characterized usually by the lack of trend data, the problem is insurmountable. However, in this instance Centers does report a follow-up survey conducted in February 1946 under peacetime conditions.[38] And in 1949, the National Opinion Research Center independently inquired into the class identification of a national sample to establish the longer trend.[39] This was also a peacetime period, but one characterized by more unemployment than the earlier two periods and therefore would provide a more appropriate context for evaluating the growth of class consciousness over the 1945 level. In point of fact the trend data do support the original assumption made by Centers. However, the instance does indicate the problem attendant on the temporal location of the phenomenon and the desirability of trend data.

The data on this trend are presented below in Table II.

It is in the light of this same problem of temporal location of the findings that one of our other examples of a descriptive inquiry, the National Association of Broadcaster's Study of American opinions about radio, planned explicitly at the time of the original inquiry for a *periodic* evaluation of the problem, and did actually conduct a second national study. Thus for example, a reader of the original findings which indicated a certain pattern of preferences for given types of programs on the part of the American public might have speculated that these preferences were due to incidental temporary factors in the 1945 situation. For example, the finding of striking interest in news broadcasts might have been taken to be a temporary consequence of war-time interest; the lack of interest in classical

---

37. *Op. cit.*, p. 77.
38. *Ibid.*, p. 77.
39. National Opinion Research Center, University of Chicago (unpublished survey results, September, 1949). For another replication in 1950 of the study, on a more limited population, the reader is referred to H. Case, "An Independent Test of the Interest-Group Theory of Social Class," *Amer. Sociol. Rev.*, 17, 1952, 751-755.

TABLE II—Variations in Subjective Class Identification as Related to the Time Period of the Survey

(An illustration of the problem of temporal location of a phenomenon.)

	Percent Identifying With Each Class In		
	July 1945	Feb. 1946	Sept. 1949
Upper class	3%	4%	1%
Middle class	43	36	32
Working class	51	52	65
Lower class	1	5	1
Don't know	1	3	1
Don't believe in classes [40]	1		
N =	1097	1337	559

music and serious programs to be an aftermath of the escapism of a wartime situation. However, when we examine the stability of preferences from 1945 to 1947 we note that such speculations are not tenable. Partial data from the published report are presented below:

TABLE III—The Consistency of Radio Program Preferences [41]

(An illustration of the problem of the temporal location of phenomena.)

	Percent of Total Samples	
	1945	1947
Preference for:		
News Broadcasts	76%	74%
Comedy Programs	54	59
Popular and Dance Music	42	49
Talks or Discussions about Public Issues	40	44
Classical Music	32	30
Religious Broadcasts	20	21

The comments by the analysts of this inquiry about such trend data on program preferences underscore our point made earlier in connection with Durkheim's work. We noted there that descriptive inquiries which established *uniformities over long periods of time* and over large aggregations of population guide us through the complexity of such theoretical alternatives as situational determinants, individual determinants, and major social determinants. Lazarsfeld and Kendall note the guidance received from these trend data:

General tastes apparently remain relatively unchanged over a two-year period. This fact . . . is important to bear in mind. For we occasionally hear that a particular program type has gained in popularity, or that the ratings for a specific program have suddenly become higher. Such events are, of course important for the broadcasters and sponsors involved, but they seem largely due to incidental circumstances. The basic attitudes of lis-

---

40. This category is not reported in Centers' second survey, and was not coded in the NORC survey, making for some minor non-comparability in the trend data.

41. P. F. Lazarsfeld and P. Kendall, *Radio Listening in America* (New York: Prentice Hall, 1948), p. 21. The subsequent quotation is reprinted by permission of the publishers.

ceners, uncovered in such a study of preferences, seem to change very slowly.[42]

In extreme instances, the problem of temporal influences on the findings cannot be solved by any of the expedients thus far described—use of short-term panels or long-term trend studies or the selection of particularly appropriate dates for the research. The only solution is caution. A most dramatic demonstration of the problem is provided by Durkheim's *Suicide*. In this particular instance, the problem arises in connection with an explanatory aspect of the survey rather than with a descriptive aspect, but its import is general for all types of surveys.

From our previous discussion, the reader will recall that Durkheim sought the explanation of Suicide in social factors. In the subsequent analysis of specific social causes, he established that in periods of crisis such as great national wars the suicide rate *drops* markedly. The interpretation given was that war rouses the collective sentiments of the population and increases the integration of society with consequent salutary effects on the suicide rate. It should be noted that Durkheim established this finding not on the basis of a limited coverage of time, but for a variety of time periods and wars, e.g., a war between Austria and Italy in 1866, between Denmark and Saxony in 1864, between France and Germany in 1870.[43] Other investigators who followed Durkheim established the same regularity over still wider ranges of time: e.g. for Germany and other European nations in World War I, for the United States in the Civil War and World War I. Certainly there is good reason why scholars and investigators have raised this *persistent empirical* finding almost to the level of an invariant scientific *law*.

Yet the temporal coverage of all these inquiries while great has one particular limiting feature. The inquiries we have discussed, Durkheim's and others, refer—yes—to a variety of wars, but not to a *modern* war in which civilian populations are now exposed to a variety of threatening and possibly isolating experiences such as mass bombing. Perhaps under these new conditions, the integrative and morale building functions of war for the civilian, which Durkheim stressed, are offset by the disruptive effects. Perhaps, a new temporal location of the problem might establish that in the balancing of such factors the rate does not drop and conceivably even rises.

---

42. P. F. Lazarsfeld and P. Kendall, *Radio Listening in America* (copyright, 1948, by Prentice-Hall, Inc.), pp. 22-23. Reprinted by permission of the publisher. Elsewhere, Lazarsfeld shows that the temporal location of this survey may be equally relevant for analyses of a more explanatory sort involving cross-tabulations. Thus, in the radio inquiry, it was found that program preferences varied with age and education. Conceivably the patterns among these subgroups also might be due to some temporary situational factor. However, when these same analyses are made in the second radio inquiry, it becomes clear that the differentiated preferences among population groups are stable phenomena. See, P. F. Lazarsfeld, Communication Research and the Social Psychologist, in W. Dennis, ed., *Current Trends in Social Psychology* (Pittsburgh: University of Pittsburgh Press, 1948), 237-239.

43. *Op. cit.*, pp. 205-208.

It was this reasoning that led Loomis in connection with the United States Strategic Bombing Survey of Germany, one of our later case studies, to examine the suicide rate for a large number of German cities over the years of World War II.[44] These data like Durkheim's own data must be analyzed with special care because of a variety of artifacts in the statistical records. Nevertheless, they indicate that the rate shows *no consistent drop* as would be expected if Durkheim's past empirical generalization still held. Neither does there appear to be any pattern of a rising rate. Thus, we have an instance in which even extensive coverage of time is no guarantee that the findings may be extended and generalized to an extreme degree.[45]

2. Location in Some Human Population

Thus far we have considered the problems raised by a decision about the temporal location of the phenomenon, but we must still consider the location of the phenomenon in some defined *human population*. As we noted in earlier chapters, the usual goals of a descriptive survey lead to the choice of a large and heterogeneous population. However, this choice still leaves great latitude to the analyst in deciding what type of large, heterogeneous population is the most *relevant* for his inquiry. Here the only general principle to guide the analyst is that the *relevance of a given type of population varies with the nature of the inquiry, and even with the time at which a particular type of inquiry is conducted*. This latter point is well illustrated by the field of labor force measurement.[46] The aim of United States government surveys in this field is to describe the current activity, e.g., employed, unemployed, etc., of the general population. Obviously, the relevant population must subsume the entire country, but just as obviously, certain exclusions from the total population seem appropriate. By definition inmates of prisons and certain other types of institutions were excluded in the past. Even though many inmates engage in productive work, they are regarded as irrelevant to the problem of describing the labor force picture in the country since they are not in the competitive labor market. Individuals under 14 years of age have traditionally been excluded, on the ground that for a variety of reasons such individuals are normally not part of the total population that might be engaged in productive work. The figure of age 14 is somewhat arbitrary but appeared for the era in question to define the age boundary of the relevant population, because of the average school leaving age and the age at which economic dependency on parents is still

---

44. *The Effects of Strategic Bombing on German Morale,* Vol. II (Government Printing Office, December 1946), Chap. IV; reprinted in Charles Loomis, *Studies in Applied and Theoretical Social Science* (East Lansing: Michigan State College Press, 1950), Chapter 21.

45. These are the manifest findings. It should be noted that Loomis on the basis of estimating various biases in the crude data argues that the manifest pattern implies a drop in the actual suicide rate. The reader is referred to the original report where the argument is elaborated.

46. The discussion that follows and the data are taken from S.S.R.C. Bull. #56, *op. cit.*

likely to hold in the U.S.[47] That the choice was meaningful is indicated by the empirical fact that only a negligible number of 14 and 15 year olds and younger individuals were actually in the labor force in the peace-time era. However, other empirical data do indicate that such a boundary for the relevant population is time-bound, for during the years of World War II many children under 14 engaged in work. The exclusion of such groups from the relevant population provided a somewhat incomplete picture of the wartime extent of American employment. So, too, as legal and educational practices change in the future, this age boundary for what might be regarded as the relevant population for the description of the American labor force would be likely to rise.

One of the surveys that we have used as a frequent illustration provides another interesting example of a decision as to the relevant population. In the Strategic Bombing Survey of Japan the problem of the morale effects of bombing was determined for a cross-section of the entire Japanese civilian population, but there was an exclusion from study of individuals under 16 or over 70.[48] Obviously such very young and very old individuals represent fairly sizable numbers of people and were certainly susceptible to psychological effects from bombing. Perhaps, in planning one might even have conjectured that these groups would be especially vulnerable. But at the same time, the implicit principle that the objective was to determine morale effects that jeopardized the prosecution of the war led to their exclusion, for it seemed plausible that the very old or very young were not of particular military or strategic significance.

One can readily see from these several examples that there is always some uncertainty and difficulty in deciding on the relevant population for an inquiry. Moreover, as was noted in passing, a particular decision may commend itself on logical grounds, but it may create considerable operating difficulties to screen out *in advance* those sub-groups who are not needed for the inquiry. Such would be the case where the criterion of relevance for inclusion of individuals in the population sometimes cannot be known at all in advance and must be determined empirically in the course of the inquiry.[49]

---

47. For a treatment of the variations in school leaving age in different countries, states, and different areas, see, I. L. Kandel, *Raising the School Leaving Age* (Paris: UNESCO, 1951), Chap. VII (pamphlet). The data herein presented show that the age boundary of 14 might well not be relevant in given situations.

48. D. Krech and E. Ballachey, *op. cit.*, p. 14. The inmates of institutions were also excluded from the population to be sampled.

49. The case of election prediction surveys presents a most interesting example of the problems at various levels. What is classically labelled the problem of turnout—i.e., estimating the results in the light of the fact that some of the sample who have expressed preferences may not vote, is clearly an instance of knowing intellectually what is the relevant population to sample but being unable to locate such a population in advance of inquiry. The relevant population is those who will vote on election day, but the population that is usually sampled represents all adults with certain minor restrictions, such as those under 21, those who are not citizens, those who are disfranchised, e.g., inmates, those who are ineligible for various local reasons such as lack of residence. However, these restrictions only define the *potential* elector-

For example, such is the case in an inquiry in which one wished to determine the sentiments of those with some *experiential basis* for the development of these sentiments. It is clear that both of these considerations lead the analyst to the practical decision to subsume a larger population than is necessary. Groups can then always be removed from the calculations in the course of the analysis and the findings presented for differentiated populations within the total population, but groups that have not initially been included permit of no appraisal whatsoever.

We can illustrate this decision and the operating procedure of later *breakdowns* of the total number studied from one of our other case studies, the national inquiry into radio. As we commented earlier, the description of the American public's feelings about radio was determined for a sample of the adult population. One might well argue that data predicated on such a population base provides a misleading picture of the situation, for there is some small number of individuals who do not own radios, and there certainly is a larger number who do not listen to the radio. Any lack of criticism found might arise because of a lack of experience with the product to be evaluated. One would like, so to speak, to describe the sentiments of those who have some knowledgeability. However, there is no easy method for separating such individuals in advance of inquiry. Moreover, one might speculate that those who do not listen should *not* be excluded. Perhaps these are the very individuals with such past experience that they have rejected the institution of radio and voluntarily excluded themselves from the audience. Consequently, the analysts took a sample of the general population, but present the data separately for those with various degrees of exposure to radio. The method involves procedurally what is known as a *cross-tabulation* or *breakdown*. It will be elaborated in Part III and exercises will be provided there for the student, since the procedure is crucial to the analysis of the explanatory survey. However, while the procedures are the same, it will be noted that the purpose is radically different in the case of descriptive inquiry. To return to our example, a general question on attitude toward American radio elicited the finding that 28% of the total sample said radio was doing an excellent job. However, this finding includes the views of people with all degrees of exposure to the radio. Consequently, the opinions were tabulated separately for those varying in degree of exposure to radio as indicated by amount of evening listening. In this instance, it turns out that among those who listen not at all, 14% give the rating "excellent"

---

ate, and include many who do not exercise their privilege to vote. Some attempt can be made to screen some of this remaining group out of the population to be studied by the *advance* method of undersampling groups who have been found on the basis of past empirical evidence to vote in small numbers, e.g., Southerners. This still leaves within the population to be sampled those who may not vote for adventitious reasons, e.g., sickness, and those who are not motivated to vote in the *particular* election. Consequently, in the course of analysis one must eliminate these from the estimate by reference to data collected in the course of the inquiry on interest in the particular election, intention to vote, etc.

whereas among those who listen four or more hours a night, 41% appraise radio as excellent. In this instance, to have initially excluded those with no current experiential basis for the attitude would have resulted in a description of much greater public satisfaction with the institution. It is evident that the tendency to exposure is either a dynamic consequence of a prior sentiment or that with the accident of increased experience one appreciates the product more. However, other breakdowns in this same work by the experiential basis for the person's sentiments show reverse findings—with increased experience, one becomes more critical.[50] The complexity of the problem clearly indicates in this instance the desirability of a more inclusive population for initial study and the necessity for elaborate breakdowns by various criteria of relevance.

In these instances, the intention of the analyst is *not to explain* the phenomenon of satisfaction with radio by demonstrating the variations that correspond to different degrees of exposure. If it were so, one would raise all the problems of what other uncontrolled factors associated with the degree of exposure might account for the different patterns of sentiments. Here, no such refinements of controlled experimental methods are introduced. One merely uses the cross-tabulation to present the *differentiated description* of the situation that corresponds so-to-speak to various possible definitions of the relevant population.

3. Relevant Units

One other factor of great importance remains to be discussed that must be considered in determining the relevant population to be studied in a descriptive survey. Thus far all our examples of populations that are relevant to given kinds of inquiries have been couched in terms of *individual persons*. In some instances the persons that constitute the relevant population were men; in other instances white; in other instances adults, etc. However, all of these different types of relevant populations are nevertheless populations of separate individuals. In considering the relevant population, the analyst must also decide whether it is more appropriate to his needs ultimately to describe characteristics of a population of *individuals* or of a population of *collectivities*. There are many instances where this problem may not arise until the terminal stage of analysis and a description of a collectivity, e.g., a work force, a military unit, can be obtained by the later manipulation of data originally collected on a *sample of the individual members* of that collectivity.[51] However, our concern here is with those instances where the lack of such a decision *in advance* of inquiry affects the

---

50. *Op. cit.*, Chap. I.

51. For a formal treatment of the relation between individual data and indices of a collectivity, see P. F. Lazarsfeld and P. Kendall, Problems of Survey Research, *op. cit.*, especially pp. 182-196. For a treatment of the appropriate units for sampling, see M. B. Parten, *op. cit.*, 117-121.

subsequent analysis and prevents the analyst from obtaining a description of the collectivity.

It is an almost universal rule in sample surveys which deal with populations of individuals that no more than *one* member of a household or family is sampled. This restriction on the sampling is usually invoked because of the technical difficulty of preventing interaction between the individual first interviewed within a family and other members of the family who might be interviewed subsequently. Such interaction naturally distorts the determination of the separate *individual* sentiments of the people who constitute the sample and the objective of the survey is regarded as jeopardized. However, there are instances where the objective of the survey is better met by the study of the family as a *unit,* for determination of characteristics in some social context may be required for special purposes.[52] Such would be the case where the behavior of the *individuals* to be ultimately described is strongly affected by characteristics of other members of their family or where the actual functioning entity which is significant for the study is the family. The inquiry into bond redemptions illustrates the latter instance very clearly. In this instance the population to be studied, in contrast with the other six surveys described, was a population of family units. To understand the likelihood of bond redemptions occurring, the analysts felt that one must regard the economic status of the *family* as the relevant characteristic rather than the pure economic status of individuals. The likelihood of any bond redemptions depended not only on the personal savings of individuals but on the total assets of the family, for the reasonable assumption is that resources within a family are pooled.

The former instance arises implicitly in a great many opinion surveys where the relevant population for study is a population of individuals. While the sentiments of *individuals* are the phenomena, it is almost universal that the economic status of the individual, regarded as a possible determinant of his opinions, is conceived to be a function of the status he derives from family. Thus, in most surveys the occupation of the *breadwinner* is determined,[53] and the interviewer rates the standard of living of the *household.* In these instances, we have, so to speak, a mixed decision as to the size of the unit that is the relevant population to be studied. The sentiments under study are sentiments of individuals but some of the de-

---

52. We are not discussing here the *technical* questions of whether several members of a family are each *queried.* One may decide to obtain data on a family unit by interviewing only one individual and using him as an informant on the entire family. Or one may decide on the technical procedure of interviewing each household member. In either case, the goal of the procedure is the same—namely, to establish certain characteristics of the family as a unit.

53. Here again one sees the distinction between a *technical* procedure to treat the problem and the *conceptual* aspect of the problem. One usually determines the occupation of the breadwinner by asking the respondent to act as an informant, but one could also interview the breadwinner directly on his occupation.

terminants of these individual sentiments are regarded as characteristics of the family unit rather than characteristics of that individual as such.

In all of these instances, where it is relevant to the inquiry to know certain characteristics of a family unit, either for ultimate purposes of understanding an *individual's* sentiments or for their own value to the inquiry, one must make this decision as to the size of the unit to be studied in advance. No manipulation of information about *separate, unrelated* individuals at the terminal stage of analysis can provide the necessary data on the family in the absence of a prior decision.

We shall not elaborate further on this general problem. The student is referred to other sources.[54]

4. Differentiation of the Description

In the descriptive survey, all decisions as to the nature of the relevant population do not change the fact that whatever population is described is usually very large and heterogeneous. The findings with respect to any phenomenon are therefore highly general and while this is desirable, it leads to one complication. As the population described becomes larger and more heterogeneous, the description takes on a very *abstract* and global character. If we consider our case studies, we note this quality in the findings. It is certainly meaningful and important to know that only 30% of the American public in 1946 showed any knowledge of the materials in an atomic bomb, or that 30% of the public believed that the United States alone had the secret, or that Kinsey's data permitted the estimate that about one-third of American males have had homosexual experience in their adult life, or that two-thirds of the American public had felt like criticizing American radio during the course of their listening.[55] Such findings give us a sense of the whole; they are in striking contrast to findings that have only limited application to a tiny deviant group. However, they are somehow disembodied. They apply to so vast a mass that the analyst or the reader or the theorist or the action agency does not know what to do about it. For action, one must locate more concretely where those findings apply. For theory, one immediately asks who are the people who have this characteristic for only by knowing the specific location of a finding is one given much understanding. Consequently, in all descriptive surveys where the population is large and heterogeneous, the analyst plans not only to describe the whole, but also to present differentiated descriptions for sub-groups within

54. P. F. Lazarsfeld and P. Kendall, *op. cit.*; M. Riley, *et al*, *Sociological Studies in Scale Construction* (New Brunswick: Rutgers University Press, 1954), especially pp. 193-196; H. Hyman, Inconsistencies, *op. cit.*; R. Lippitt, "Techniques for Research in Group Living," *J. Soc. Issues*, 2, 1946, 55-61; especially pp. 58-59; C. W. Hart, *op. cit.*, especially pp. 516-517.

55. Cottrell and Eberhart, *op. cit.*, pp. 15-16. A. C. Kinsey, *op. cit.*, p. 623, Lazarsfeld and Field, *op. cit.* p. 15.

the total population under study. Only in this way do the findings take on any concrete character.

The technical procedure involved is simple. It is the same as discussed earlier and will be discussed later in the analysis of explanatory surveys. It is the procedure of *cross-tabulation or breakdown* of the data. The description in the *aggregate* for the entire population or sample of a population is matched by a series of descriptions for *sub-groups,* for example, the characteristics of women, of men, of Northerners, Southerners, city people, farmers, etc. We earlier noted that such breakdowns occur sometimes in the descriptive survey to compensate for the analyst's uncertainty in the original decision as to which is the most relevant population. However, even where there is no such uncertainty, the analyst will engage in such breakdowns in order to differentiate a description that is initially too abstract. Again, it should be noted that such breakdowns in the descriptive survey are *radically different* in purpose from the same procedure when employed in the explanatory survey. Here they do not constitute procedures to determine the *causes* of the phenomenon. In the explanatory survey, for example, if men are compared with women or farmers with city people and the analyst finds *no differences* between the contrasted groups, usually he has a vague sense of disappointment. He feels that he has not yet found a clue to the phenomenon for it does *not* vary with characteristics he may have hypothesized to be independent variables. But properly no such disappointment should occur in the case of the descriptive survey. For example, it is just as relevant to know that action should be taken in all groups, in all parts of the country, as it is to know that action must be focussed in only one region. The breakdown is not intended to find relationships. It is merely intended to make the descriptions precise and useful for understanding or action purposes. In addition, in the explanatory survey, if a difference in the phenomenon is found for different sub-groups, the analyst usually feels that he *must continue* to examine the relationship. Such characteristics as Southern or Northern, Negro or White, rural or urban, denote *complexes of many factors,* and the analyst in the explanatory survey feels that he must dissect the complex and determine precisely which is the causative agent within the complex. But in the descriptive survey, no such feeling should occur. The analyst is not required to dissect such complexes. If anything, he should be prohibited from such analysis! His intent, here, is merely to provide a more concretized description—to locate the phenomenon and not to explain it. And it may be *positively misleading* for purposes of action to provide a differentiated description of the phenomenon, for sub-groups that are made artificial by techniques of control, e.g., Southerners as compared with Northerners, who are equated by refined procedures in their level of education. This is to present a differtiated description not for the South as a functioning complex, but for an abstraction which is not the real South. The meaning of a procedure is thus relative to the type of analysis undertaken.[56]

Also, the analyst confronting such breakdowns in the explanatory survey has additional resources which permit him to trace the processes underlying the empirically obtained relationship and he is concerned with these processes. He has measured a series of intervening variables which presumably emerge from such complexes. The breakdown in the descriptive survey usually does not permit such tracing of the process for auxiliary data on intervening variables are generally not available. And they need not be available since this was not the intent of the study. Consequently, when the analyst indulges himself in attempts to trace out the causal process, rather than regarding these breakdowns as a basis merely for differentiated descriptions, he usually ends up in a series of sheer speculations. This is clearly demonstrated in one of our case studies, *the Kinsey Report*. Hyman and Sheatsley in their analysis of the methodology note that Kinsey's "plan of analysis is to break down the statistical data for various population groups," a perfectly appropriate procedure for a *descriptive* survey. But they note that Kinsey then seeks to explain and interpret such findings on sexual behavior among different groups in the absence of data on psychological factors. They remark on the conjectures into which he is forced by virtue of a lack of auxiliary data and cite such passages as:

> Homosexual relations, both among single and married males are sometimes a substitute for less readily available heterosexual contacts. On the other hand, it must be recognized that the homosexual is in many instances, among both single and married males, deliberately chosen as the preferred source of outlet; and it is simply accepted as a different kind of sexual outlet by a fair number of persons, whatever their marital status, who embrace both heterosexual and homosexual experiences in the same age period. Consequently, the high incidence of the homosexual among single males is not wholly chargeable to the unavailability of heterosexual contacts. The increased incidence and frequency among older single males are, as previously noted, partly dependent upon the freer acceptance of a socially taboo activity as the individual becomes more experienced and more certain of himself. The very high incidence among the still older males may depend upon the fact that those persons who are not exclusively or primarily homosexual are ordinarily married when younger and those who have no interest in heterosexual contacts are left in higher proportion in the older, unmarried populations.

Hyman and Sheatsley then refer to the breakdowns and differences by education and occupation, and note that "Kinsey provides us with a variety of remarks about the reasons—with no supporting data":

---

56. For a very clear formulation of this analytic problem see Cochran, Mosteller and Tukey's discussion of whether or not *standardized rates* should have been used by Kinsey in describing sexual behavior, *op. cit.*, Section A-43, pp. 129-131. Also see Cantril's distinction between "descriptive" and "analytical" breakdowns, H. Cantril, *Gauging Public Opinion* (Princeton: Princeton University Press, 1944), Chapter XIII.

We do not yet understand all the factors which may account for the fact that with advancing age there is a steady decline and finally a near disappearance of extra marital intercourse from lower level marital histories; differences which exist in the incidences and frequencies of the homosexual in the three educational levels, would seem to indicate basic differences in attitudes toward such activity, but we are not sure that we yet understand what these differences are.[57]

Now, it is certainly legitimate when striking differences occur following such breakdowns in a descriptive survey for an analyst to conjecture about the differences. But such *casual* attempts at interpretation should be distinguished from interpretations in an explanatory survey, where the analyst has *resources* to trace the process with some confidence. The sheer breakdown by various classificatory characteristics cannot serve this latter purpose effectively, and should be limited in its function to providing more effective description. We thus see that the same procedures take on different functions relative to the type of survey analysis.

The provision for differentiated descriptions is relatively simple. The techniques for making such breakdowns are usually automatic machine operations. Practice Exercises of this type are presented in Appendix C and will give the student some training in the procedures. The planning for such descriptions is also relatively simple. The questionnaire or interview schedule or instrument for the collection of data on the phenomenon incorporates a "face-sheet," or "factual data sheet," which permits the total sample to be classified in a variety of ways.[58] There is, however, one danger in the planning for such breakdowns which arises from the fact, earlier alluded to, of certain practices in survey research becoming institutionalized. Traditionally, the face-sheet has contained a small number of *standard items*—sex, age, an index of economic position such as occupation or income, place of residence (permitting the determination of region and size of place) and color. Moreover, the *categories* by which such information is usually recorded are generally stabilized.[59] Thus, there are the four main geographical sectors corresponding to the compass points to record region; occupation will usually be recorded in terms of seven or nine hierarchically arranged categories such as professional, business, skilled, semi-skilled, etc.

---

57. H. Hyman and P. Sheatsley, *op. cit.* The passages from *Sexual Behavior in the Human Male* are reprinted by permission of the author and publisher.

58. For an example of a "face sheet" on which appears factual data relating to a respondent's personal characteristics, see the last page of the ballot used in the study of American opinion of commercial radio located in Appendix C.

59. See C. W. Hart, *op. cit.* for a discussion of this.

Here again we are not discussing *technical procedures,* but the conceptual side of the problem. Thus, the analyst might decide to collect exact information on place of residence and employ the procedure of office coding to subsequently classify the respondents into four regions. Alternatively he might pre-code the four regions and have the interviewer merely check which region applies. These respective procedures must be evaluated carefully in relation to questions of efficiency and error, but both lead to the same number of categories for ultimate classification of the respondents.

The analyst tends to employ what is common practice and may neglect the fact that the specific needs of the survey call for descriptions being differentiated in other terms. For example, in certain descriptive studies conducted during the war for the Office of Price Administration, the extent of total public compliance was determined. The level of compliance for different geographical areas was also reported. The analyst might have easily reported data for the four standard regions. However, since the administrative structure of the agency was organized in terms of special regions which did not correspond to the usual geographical divisions of the country, the classification of place of residence was in terms relevant to the OPA administrative areas.[60]

In surveys dealing with opinions toward Russia and Spain, the analyst often adds the additional classificatory item, religion, a relatively uncommon factual item, but appropriate because of the official Catholic position with respect to these governments. In surveys dealing with presidential elections, states with large numbers of electoral votes may be reported separately from other states within the same region. There are innumerable examples of modes of classifying the phenomena of a descriptive survey in unusual ways that are especially relevant to specific actions or to the understanding of the phenomenon. We shall also see that these more unusual modes of classifying descriptive data have great significance for the problems we shall consider in Chapter VIII of appraising the policy or political implications of public opinion surveys.

Ackoff and Pritzker remark on both these aspects of the problems and cite various alternative modes of classification of usual face-sheet variables which illustrate the need for careful planning in the light of the specific inquiry. For example, they note that typically survey data are broken down by size of community, but they remark that "a nearby large industrial city and a distant small industrial community may be more alike in their influence on public opinion than two nearby large cities, one industrial, the other governmental." In other words, the variable that might be more illuminating than the size of place or the geographical region for a particular survey would be the economic base. They also illustrate the problem of the categories for classifying respondents with respect to a given variable by reference to the concept of time. "Consider the way 'time' is usually classified; we use a clock and break the day into periods of time defined by clock readings, 9:00 A.M. to 11:00 A.M., 11:00 A.M. to 1:00 P.M., etc. Yet these hours may mean entirely different things to different people. Conducting interviews in the morning will be effective in some areas, but not in others, depending on what activity is interrupted by the interviewer. It is the ac-

---

60. Unpublished survey conducted by the Office of War Information, Surveys Division for the OPA, 1943.

tivity indulged in at the time of the interview-interruption that influences the responses, not the reading on the clock." [61]

The Inclusion
of Related Phenomena

In the descriptive surveys that were included among our case studies we can note a feature of the conceptualization which at first might appear incongruous. In the inquiry into public opinion about the atomic bomb, the analysts collected information not only on knowledge and attitude in that realm but also determined public knowledge and attitude about a variety of other international and political entities. Such phenomena certainly are of interest but strictly considered are not part of the phenomenon under study. So, too, in the inquiry into American thinking about radio, the analysts collected information not only on satisfaction with radio advertising but on satisfaction with advertising in other mass media; not only on attitudes towards government control of radio but also on attitudes towards government control of other industries; not only on satisfaction with radio as an institution but on satisfaction with other institutions. We have already discussed the need for the analyst to regard his phenomenon as complex— as involving many component beliefs and attitudes—but the inclusion of such additional areas for inquiry cannot be predicated on this principle. These areas are not part of the phenomenon under study, even if the phenomenon is regarded in a very broad sense. And yet these additional areas are not completely unrelated phenomena. There is a certain parallelism between the phenomenon under study and the additional phenomena that are included. The study of such related or parallel phenomena serves two very important functions for the analyst of the descriptive survey, and if we turn to our case studies and examine the use to which such data were put in these instances, we shall soon sense the value of such additional data.

1. Norms for the Evaluation of a Descriptive Finding

In the radio inquiry the analysts present findings bearing on the American public's over-all appraisal of radio as an institution. They report that 82% of their sample of the nation believe that the radio stations are doing an "excellent" or "good" job.[62] How shall the analysts appraise the implication of this finding? Does this represent *overwhelming* public satisfaction? Shall the analyst remark on the fact that *as many* as 18% were not satisfied, or shall he stress the fact that *only* 18% did not show satisfaction?

---

61. *Op. cit.*
62. *Op. cit.*, p. 6.

Certainly there are the logical extremes of zero vs. universal satisfaction which are perhaps easy to evaluate, but here the analyst faces a statistic, a figure, which is intermediate and which could be appraised in a variety of ways. Similarly, there are occasionally guides to evaluation of a descriptive finding provided by the sponsor who has specific norms as to what is a good or bad, large or small, finding. But, generally, indeterminacy surrounds the evaluation of a descriptive finding on some phenomenon and it is quite arbitrary what terms the analyst employs in his findings.[63] The same inquiry provides many illustrations of these difficulties for the analyst.

In a chapter on attitudes towards advertising on the radio, about one-third of the public is found to be opposed to radio commercials.[64] This is the bare finding, but what is its implication? Does this represent serious criticism of the current pattern of American radio, or is this to be expected and regarded as innocuous from the point of view of change in the institution?

In a later chapter, the public is queried on the issue of radio's degree of impartiality in handling controversial issues. 81% regard radio stations as being fair to both sides in general.[65] Shall we regard this as a high praise of the radio industry, or should the analyst and reader stress the fact that *as many as* 19% did not explicitly express the view that radio was fair?

Again at a later point the analysts report that 70% of the sample believe that it would be better for radio to be in private business hands rather than under government control.[66] Does this represent overwhelming opposition to government control? Is this unusual as a finding?

In all these instances, the analyst can report the bare facts. Or he can use such neutral terms as "a majority," a "minority," and the like. But this is after all not the point of a descriptive survey. Such facts must be evaluated to be of some use, and they are bound to be evaluated by others and even by the analyst. The evaluations are bound to be capricious in the absence of norms for deciding whether such findings are large or small, frequent or rare.

To illustrate the way in which findings, apparently clear in their implications, can be misinterpreted in the absence of some standard of comparison, we might present one example of a descriptive finding from the National Opinion Research Center along with data on parallel phenomena.[67]

---

63. We are not referring here to indeterminacy in such evaluations created by technical problems of *error*. The analyst always faces the question of whether a given statistical finding is artifactually inflated or deflated because of sampling biases, question wording, etc. But beyond all these considerations, there is still the question of what standards of judgment to apply to the descriptions obtained. What are their implications? It is this latter problem that we are concerned with in this section.

64. *Op. cit.*, p. 17.

65. *Ibid.*, p. 78.

66. *Ibid.*, p. 86.

67. Unpublished data in the files of NORC.

In a survey conducted in 1947, 37% of a national sample indicated that they had a favorable feeling towards the English government. Only a minority of the public had favorable feelings. Should the analyst regard this finding as indicative of serious hostility to England? Upon examination of parallel data for a variety of other foreign countries, it is revealed that, while 37% is not a very high figure in terms of absolute magnitude, if anything, it represented unusual favorability on the part of the American public, for the only country towards which a larger proportion of the public indicated a favorable feeling was Canada.

To safeguard the interpretations, the analyst usually provides norms for himself by collecting data on parallel phenomena from the same individuals.[68] We shall turn back to the radio inquiry, and note how in the instances already cited, the evaluation of a descriptive finding takes on clarity through the juxtaposition of norms on parallel phenomena.

Thus with respect to appraisal of radio as an institution, where the finding was that 82% of the sample were well satisfied, the analysts juxtapose the finding that parallel questions on satisfaction with the churches, newspapers, schools, and local government never yielded a figure as high as for the institution of radio. Radio is therefore seen to stand in *unusual* public favor. This particular example illustrates one problem in the use of norms and a method for treating it. It is obvious that there can be considerable arbitrariness exercised by the analyst in choosing the parallel phenomena that are juxtaposed against the specific finding. For example, one might pick only institutions towards which it is known that there is great public dissatisfaction and thereby present a misleading picture of relative satisfaction with radio. The analyst must therefore pick a series of parallel phenomena ranging over the probable spectrum of one extreme to the other. In this particular instance, it is clear that the institution of the "church" is chosen for the very purpose of providing a *compelling* norm for comparison. It would be reasonable to assume that the church as an institution is in relative favor in America, and if the radio industry stands up to such a yardstick, the evaluation is even clearer. As the analysts remark, *"Even the churches* do not rank as high as radio." [69]

With respect to the finding that 81% regarded radio as providing fair play for both sides in controversial issues, the analysts juxtapose the findings that 45% of the same sample regard magazines as giving fair play to both sides, and 39% regard newspapers as giving fair play to both sides. The parallel data on other media provide a norm for evaluation of the original

---

68. Sometimes, it is unnecessary for the analyst to collect such data for purposes of norms. There may already exist for other samples of the same population data on parallel phenomena. For example, national samples are queried periodically by all the major survey agencies on a host of issues. Examination of the archive of existing data from such prior research may reveal that norms already exist for evaluating the findings of the new survey.

69. *Op. cit.*, p. 6, italics ours.

finding. This example also illuminates one problem in the interpretation of such norms. An individual might well feel that in certain instances there are absolute standards of a unique sort that govern the evaluation of a finding on a particular phenomenon. For example, the radio industry is governed by a series of *legal* conventions as to impartiality, and other media are not required to conform to the same legal standards. Similarly, custom or tradition sanctions the expression of particular editorial positions on the part of newspapers. Thus, in some instances norms that are inappropriate might be juxtaposed in a misleading way. The example we have cited indicated that the analysts tempered their handling of this procedure in the light of such considerations. "The figures pertaining to the other two media should not be used for invidious comparisons. Newspapers, after all, . . . are entitled to editorial opinion and they do not claim to present both sides of every argument." [70]

With respect to the finding that 70% of the public favored private business control of the radio industry, the analysts present data on attitudes towards government control in four other industries: coal mining, banking, utilities, and newspapers. The analysts then note that a plurality of the public favor private control in each of the five instances. We thus see that this sentiment about American radio is not unique or unusual. However, it is also noted when these norms are available that government control is less favored for the radio industry than for the other industries, with the exception of newspapers.

Thus far all our examples of the inclusion of related phenomena for purposes of providing norms have been examples for the *total group* under study. We have already noted that it is the general practice of the analyst to provide differentiated descriptions of the phenomenon for sub-groups in his population or sample. Here again the evaluation of the findings for a sub-group often gains in clarity from the use of norms. The procedure for obtaining such sub-group norms to correspond to any differentiated descriptive finding is simple. Equivalent breakdowns are made for the phenomenon under study and for the related phenomena that were included in the inquiry.

A recent survey provides an unusually good illustration of the use of *sub-group norms* as a basis for interpretation and a dramatic example of the *necessity* of total sample norms for making proper inferences from a descriptive survey. The survey was conducted by Elmo Roper and directed by Julian Woodward and dealt with the attitudes of residents of a number of counties in Florida. Prior to the survey, four Negroes had been accused of raping a white woman, had been tried in Lake County, Florida, and convicted. An appeal was made to the Supreme Court of the United States and a retrial was ordered. One of the grounds for the retrial was that conditions

---

70. *Op. cit.*, p. 79.

in the county in which the trial had occurred were such that the issue was prejudged by the jurors. The retrial was therefore scheduled in an adjoining county, Marion County, which the defense also argued was so prejudiced as to preclude a fair trial. The survey was then commissioned by the Defense in order to determine the extent of pre-judgment of guilt or innocence of the defendant Walter Irvin, by the citizens of Marion County, as a basis for requesting a Change of Venue. Among the results of the survey were the following: 43% of the sample of white residents of Marion County answered, "I feel sure the men are guilty." 1% of the Negro residents gave the same reply. On a question which inquired as to whether the respondent felt that "something might happen" to a juror who voted "not guilty," 84% of the Negro residents of the county said "yes." Woodward remarks about the first findings that they are exceedingly difficult to evaluate: "The scientific research man has to be very careful about interpreting the absolute meaning of these percentages: in other words he cannot tell as a scientist whether *43% for Marion County is such a degree of pre-judgment as to preclude the possibility of a fair trial or not.*" With respect to the 84% finding, Woodward again remarks: "The scientist is in no position to interpret the exact significance of this 84% figure, except to point out that a percentage that high—in other words a measure of agreement that great—is very unusual in the annals of public opinion research and occurs very infrequently." [71] We might interrupt Woodward's statement for the moment to note that implicit in this last conclusion is an *informal use of norms* based on general experience with past survey literature. Woodward continues: "The decision as to whether a fair trial can be had in a situation where 17 out of 20 Negroes express fears to what might happen to them if they voted one way on the guilt or innocence of the accused is technically a matter for the court."

However, the analyst had in this instance anticipated the problem of interpretation and availed himself of the use of related phenomena to provide norms for an interpretation. These were of a number of types. Two parallel questions were asked of the residents of Marion County. The case of Sheriff Sullivan who had been removed from office in Miami on grounds of corruption was described, and the respondents were asked whether they "were sure Sullivan was guilty" and whether a juror sitting in that case would feel safe from reprisal by gangsters if he voted the Sheriff guilty. As Woodward comments, these questions were intended as "a sort of rough parallel" and the comparison of the results in the Irvin case with the Sullivan case would provide norms. The analyst would then be able to establish whether the prejudgment in the Irvin case was unusually great or merely the residual prejudgment characteristic of all publicized cases and whether

---

71. J. E. Woodward, "A Scientific Attempt to Provide Evidence for a Decision on Change of Venue," *Amer. Sociol. Rev.*, 17, 1952, 447-452, italics ours.

the fears of reprisals among Negro residents was unusually great or merely the residual fear characteristic of Negro Life generally in the South. The comparisons were striking. Only 14% of White residents had prejudged Sullivan (as against 43% prejudgment of Irvin) and only 59% of Negro residents were fearful of reprisal in the Sullivan case (as against 84% in the Irvin case).

This survey also provides an illustration of another type of norm to which we have not alluded, although its analytic function is of the same order as we have already described. In addition to the survey conducted in Marion County, the potential seat of the new trial, parallel surveys were conducted in Lake County, the seat of the original trial, and in two other counties in remote Northern Florida. Woodward makes explicit the fact that these supplementary surveys were intended to provide norms for interpretation. He remarks: "They would provide a baseline against which to measure the degree of pre-judgment" in Marion County.

2. Intercorrelations to Establish the Generality or Specificity of the Phenomenon

By the *juxtaposition* of data on related phenomena for a given *aggregation* of respondents, one establishes whether in *some defined population* a specific phenomenon is unusual or is part of a more general constellation —but the fact that a given *group* shows a consistent pattern in a number of different phenomenal areas does not establish that the same *individuals* within the group show consistent tendencies over a number of areas. The inclusion of data on related phenomena serves the additional function of permitting one to establish the intercorrelations between phenomena for individuals within the given group, and thereby to establish whether the phenomenon under study is discrete in character or part of a more general constellation. Such information is exceedingly useful to the analyst in interpreting the findings from descriptive surveys.

Where the descriptive survey has the *applied* objective of providing guidance for some action agency, the problem often arises as to whether the findings demonstrated constitute a discrete problem calling for *specific remedial* action, or whether the findings are part of some larger, more general problem calling for measures of a more global sort. The analyst must decide between these alternative interpretations of his findings and can only do so if he can determine the intercorrelations with related phenomena. We can illustrate this problem from a wartime survey conducted to provide guidance to the Office of War Information in setting policy on the amount of wartime information that should be released to the public over the radio.[72]

---

72. Surfeit with War on the Radio, Surveys Division, OWI, Memorandum #47, 1943. (mimeo).

In the course of this inquiry, 15% of the sample stated that there was too much about the war on the radio. The finding might have led the analysts to conclude that *radio programming* had shown a slightly excessive emphasis on war news, and that the solution to such "surfeit" was to change radio policy with respect to programming. However, there was the alternative possibility that this surfeit was simply expressive of the fact that those individuals with a generalized sensitivity to war news constituted this 15%. If so, the problem was not to remedy the programming on radio alone, but either to remedy the flow of war news throughout the *total* environment or to assume that this sensitivity represented a type of anxiety which would be unresponsive to any alteration in the objective amount of war news disseminated. In either of these latter instances, the action agency would know that the solution did not lie in specific attention to the radio industry. The analysts anticipating this problem of interpreting their data had asked parallel questions on surfeit with war contents in newspapers and in movies. It was found that those individuals who felt there was too much war news on the radio were also the ones inclined to say that there was too much war material in the papers and in movies. The analysts therefore were enabled to draw the conclusion that "apparently surfeit with war content is a generalized attitude toward all media and not a special problem for radio alone."

This same inquiry illustrates an interesting and helpful extension of the method of including related phenomena for purposes of demonstrating the generality or specificity of a phenomenon. The interpretation of this generalized tendency to report that there was too much war news in all media was still open to some doubt. It might represent an objective reaction to the total stimulation of the general wartime environment; it might represent a more irrational kind of criticism. The analysts therefore asked an additional question as to whether there was too much popular music on the radio. Insofar as the same individuals who were surfeited with war news reported surfeit with the amount of popular music, this would suggest that the problem lay simply in a kind of temperamental or consistent grouchiness and readiness to criticize. Instead the analysts found little relationship between surfeit with war news in all media and surfeit with popular music suggesting that the findings were not indicative of a general temperamental or personality trait of criticism or grouchiness.

A study by Hyman and Sheatsley provides another illustration of the analysis of related phenomena to establish whether or not there is a generalized pattern underlying some specific finding.[73] Shortly after World War II there had been many proposals for massive information campaigns to reduce areas of public ignorance in the political realm; such campaigns being predicated on the theory that the ignorance was a function of the lack

---

73. H. Hyman and P. Sheatsley, "Some Reasons Why Information Campaigns Fail," *Publ. Opin. Quar.* (1947–48), 11, 412-423, esp. 413-414.

of publicity. Sheatsley and Hyman therefore raised the question as to whether ignorance was mainly a product of the objective lack of information or whether it was due to a persistent trait of certain individuals to avoid exposure to knowledge. To determine which of these alternatives was correct, they analyzed a survey conducted by the National Opinion Research Center in 1946 in which a series of questions on related areas of information about current events had been asked. One of these questions asked whether the subjects had heard about the report of the Anglo-American Committee on Palestine, issued in May, 1946, and recommending that 100,-000 Jews be admitted to Palestine. Of the nearly 1300 persons included in the survey, nearly three-quarters answered that they did not know anything about this report. As the authors point out, this lack of information might mean only that the report of the Committee was not widely publicized in the United States, and that, had more attention been paid to it in the press and on the radio, a significantly larger proportion of persons would have been able to answer the question. If this interpretation is correct, then there should be no relationship between a "Don't know" response to the question about the Palestine report and "Don't know" responses to other questions of public information.

But, the authors continue, lack of knowledge about the work of the Anglo-American Committee may be indicative of general apathy on all public issues. If this is the correct interpretation of the original "Don't know" answers, then there *should* be a relationship between lack of knowledge on this count and on others.

The next step was to determine which interpretation seemed more likely. To do this, Hyman and Sheatsley cross-tabulated knowledge of the Palestine report with knowledge, or lack of it, of other matters then in the public eye. Specifically, they studied how knowledge of the Palestine report was related to knowledge of the Acheson-Lilienthal report on atomic energy, to awareness of the Spring, 1946 meeting of the Foreign Ministers in Paris, and to knowledge that a proposed loan to Great Britain was then under discussion. Their results are presented in Table IV.

TABLE IV—Relationship Between "Don't Know" Responses on Palestine Report and "Don't Know" Responses on Other Public Issues

	Not aware of Palestine report	Aware of Palestine report
Per cent aware of Acheson-Lilienthal report on atomic energy	32%	64%
Per cent aware of Spring, 1946, meeting of Foreign Ministers	39	85
Per cent aware of proposed loan to Great Britain	73	96
Total cases	931	358

There is a definite, quite strong relationship between lack of knowledge of the Palestine report and lack of information on other national and international events. The authors therefore conclude that lack of knowledge in the specific realm is not due to inadequate publicity on the specific issues. Remedial action lay in another more general direction.

The value of descriptive surveys as a prelude to explanatory inquiries of a *theoretical* sort has already been discussed. The descriptive findings constitute a valuable guide to theorizing about determinants. In this connection the decision whether or not a particular phenomenon is part of a larger constellation is most helpful, for according to the finding it may lead the analyst to seek the relationships in independent variables of a specific or general sort. Durkheim's *Suicide* has already been cited as an ideal example of the way in which effective description is a guide to effective explanation. Durkheim devoted an entire chapter to *Relations of Suicide with Other Social Phenomena* and the logic of the procedure of examining related phenomena is made explicit.[74] Thus he remarks "In order to decide to what extent suicide partakes of immorality, let us examine first its relation with other immoral acts, especially crimes and misdemeanors."[75] He then presents various data on the correlations between crime rates and suicide rates, and attempts to draw various inferences as to the direction of the causation of suicide. We shall not abstract the argument or evidence but merely present illustrations of conjectures and hypotheses to show how the examination of related phenomena is a guide to theory. Thus he asks, with respect to data on the correlation between homicide and suicide, "are the psychological conditions of crime and suicide the same? Is there a polarity between the social conditions on which they depend?" Later he considers the "psychological unity of the two phenomena."[76]

One of our case studies of an explanatory survey illustrates the way in which the study of related phenomena may even be a *central* feature of the analysis. In *The Authoritarian Personality,* the analysts took as the initial focus for their study the phenomenon of Anti-Semitism. However, they wish to establish whether Anti-Semitism is part of a larger pattern of prejudice and whether prejudice is in turn part of a still larger pattern of sentiments. Thus they state at the very beginning of the book the hypothesis that "the political, economic and social convictions of an individual often form a broad and coherent pattern."[77] They then establish the extent of this generalized pattern by questioning individuals in a variety of related ideological areas and determining the intercorrelations. The implication of such findings on generality for remedial action in the realm of Anti-Semitism is obvious. If Anti-Semitism is part of some larger pattern, the key to its explanation and in turn its manipulation does not lie in *specific* actions or programs having to do purely with Anti-Semitism. The key must be sought in some larger determinant. The analysts hypothesize that "this pattern is

74. *Op. cit.,* Book III, Chapter II, pp. 326-360.
75. *Ibid.,* p. 338.
76. *Ibid.,* p. 341.
77. *Op. cit.,* p. 1.

an expression of deep-lying trends in . . . personality." [78] Their research design and analysis so-to-speak involves these two stages; the establishing of the extent of generality of the phenomenon and then the determination of the relation of the general phenomenon to trends in the personality. The pursuit of the latter problem is guided by the initial findings on generality.

It is very important to note one limitation of the use of evidence about related phenomena for explanatory surveys. In the examples cited it is clear that the *determinant* of a generalized pattern in the individual is *not* established. The analyst can draw the inference that the determinant is not of a narrow or specific sort. However, the determinant may lie in some persistent, general factor in the *environment* or may represent some general *intrapsychic* process or some combination of these.

The mere demonstration of generality does *not* answer the question as to the exact content of the determinant. It merely locates the level at which the determinant should be sought, and the analysis must then proceed to an empirical demonstration of the determinant.[79] Thus in the study of information campaigns, Hyman and Sheatsley suggest the possibility that the "chronic know-nothings" might be individuals living in an environment in which they are *generally deprived* of information sources; alternatively they might be individuals with some general personality pattern of apathy. They seek then to test which of these alternative general factors is the explanation. Thus as an index of the general impoverishment of the information sources in the environment, the analysts classify respondents in terms of the size of community in which they live and establish that there is very little relationship to the general level of ignorance of the respondent. As an index of a personality pattern of apathy, respondents are classified by reference to a battery of questions on interest in world affairs and it is then found that this shows a strong relationship to the phenomenon of ignorance.

Similarly, in the *Authoritarian Personality,* direct measures of the personality of the respondent are obtained and these are related to the kind of ideology he expresses. However, in a critique of this work, Hyman and Sheatsley note that at times the sheer demonstration of generality of the phenomenon is used as if it were adequate evidence in itself that the determinant lies in the personality patterns of the individual.[80] The passage is

---

78. *Ibid.,* p. 1.

79. Again, Durkheim's *Suicide* constitutes an interesting example of the way in which proper limitations are applied to analyses of general phenomena. We alluded in Chapter II to the fact that Durkheim establishes the fact that Suicide is not a transient phenomenon, but is regular over time and for given societies. He thus is led to seek the determinant in some general factor, rather than in some temporary situational or local factor. But, he notes that such a general factor might either be *social* or some *extra*-social factor with a very wide and stable distribution. Such a factor, for example, could be climatic or cosmic. Durkheim cannot choose between these respective general determinants until he has tested empirically the relationship of suicide to extra-social factors. He proceeds to such analyses.

80. *Op. cit.,* pp. 111-112.

cited below in detail to show the dangers of such inferences, and the strict use to which evidence on generality should properly be put.

It is often noted that a person who holds one certain prejudice also holds another, and from this finding it is argued that, since such generality of sentiment cannot be explained in terms of specific factors relating to the particular objects of prejudice, the explanation must consequently lie in some personality factor. Let us look again at the quotation we cited earlier in this section: "It would appear that the more a person's thinking is dominated by such general tendencies as those found in Mack, the less will his attitude toward a particular group depend upon any objective characteristics of that group, or upon any real experience in which members of that group were involved." In other words, a generalized attitude can be explained only in terms of some general factor. Then the inference is immediately drawn: "It is this observation that draws attention to the importance of personality as a determinant of ideology." An even clearer example occurs a little later: ". . . the conception of personality would be forced upon us by observation of the *consistency* with which the same ideas and the same modes of thought recur as the discussion turns from one ideological area to another. Since no such consistency could conceivably exist as a matter of sociological fact, we are bound to conceive of central tendencies *in the person* which express themselves in various areas. The concept of a dynamic factor of personality is made to order for explaining the common trend in diverse surface manifestations." Again: ". . . we have seen that anti-Semitism or anti-Negroism, for example, are not isolated attitudes but parts of a relatively unified ethnocentric ideology. The present chapter suggests that ethnocentrism itself is but one aspect of a broader pattern of social thinking and group functioning. Trends similar to those underlying ethnocentric ideology are found in the same individual's politico-economic idealogy. In short, ideology regarding each social area must be regarded as a facet of the total person and an expression of more central ('subideological') psychological dispositions." And finally: "This does not mean, however, that those high scorers whose prejudiced statements show a certain rationality *per se* are exempt from the psychological mechanisms of the fascist character. Thus the example we offer is high not only on the F scale but on all scales. She has the *generality* of prejudiced outlook which we have taken as evidence that underlying personality trends were the ultimate determinants."

One may accept without question, of course, the existence of generality, not only in the field of prejudice but over a wider domain as well. Obviously, there is some organizing principle in social attitudes, and such patterns suggest that the source is not to be found in the specific features of any particular object of prejudice. But whence does it necessarily follow that the organizing principle is a deeper psychological disposition, and that "no such consistency could conceivably exist as a matter of sociological fact"? Societies and groups do not necessarily indoctrinate the individual piecemeal. We find the extreme of this in the *Weltanschaung* sought by the totalitarian society, and we find patterns of sentiments expressed in the programs of almost every organized group. That the degree of patterning itself, and not just the content of specific attitudes, varies with different groups was noted earlier in our discussion of the sampling methodology, and such variation supports the fact that social factors affect generality. Certainly, consistency must be explained, not in terms of the specific objects of prejudice, but as a generalized disposition within the person—but the organizing factor behind this generalized disposition may very well be societal. We are far from being inevitably thrown back on deep personality factors.

We have now seen the value of inquiring into related phenomena in the descriptive survey. It provides norms for interpretation and it permits the establishment of the generality of the phenomenon under study. The gains are many. The steps the analyst must take are relatively simple. In the planning of the inquiry, the mere inclusion of questions on related phenomena permits both the determination of norms for evaluation and the determination of the degree of specificity of the phenomenon. Procedurally, however, the technical operations are different. In the first instance, the descriptive findings or marginals for the series of phenomena are merely juxtaposed. In the latter instance, cross-tabulations are performed. In the one instance the machine operation is merely that of automatic counting of the sets of results for the total group whereas in the second instance the machine must engage in a somewhat more complex tabulation, determining the frequency with which individuals classified in particular ways on one variable fall into parallel categories on the second variable. Practice exercises in such cross-tabulations are provided for the student in Appendix C.

CHAPTER IV

Technical Aspects of the Analysis
of the Descriptive Survey

W E HAVE treated the analyst's problems of planning the descriptive survey in great detail for it is only through such careful planning that the effectiveness of the actual analysis is insured. The manipulation of data in the terminal stages of analysis cannot insure an adequate description of the phenomenon if there is a fundamental omission in the original planning. If there are no relevant data to manipulate, if the data represent descriptions of the wrong population or correspond to a point in time that is unimportant or unrepresentative, if the implications of the findings are ambiguous because of a lack of collateral data; if the descriptions are gross because of inability to differentiate the data in meaningful terms, the analyst can only fumble. He can and must engage in various approximations some of which we have noted earlier, but his success is always limited. On the other hand, while the analyst is always fallible and his planning never perfect, planning of the type we have described increases the likelihood of success.

In the terminal stage of analysis the analyst engages in a series of relatively routine procedures: 1) The data corresponding to each aspect of the phenomenon that have been conceptualized are tabulated for the aggregate group and provide a general statistical or quantitative description. 2) The data are similarly tabulated for each sub-group that is regarded as significant and provide the differentiated quantitative descriptions desired as well as descriptions for any redefined population that is regarded as especially relevant to the problem. 3) Various modes of consolidating data for the many separate aspects of the phenomenon are employed to provide statistical descriptions of a *molar* sort. Here such technical operations as index-construction, scaling, construction of typologies, profiles, etc., are employed. Molar descriptions may be presented either for the aggregate or for appropriate sub-groups. 4) All these data are then examined in the context of data on related phenomena so as to improve the evaluation of the findings. 5) A variety of qualitative, non-statistical materials are examined and used to supplement the quantitative descriptions. Comments from individual respondents, long verbatim answers to open end questions, interviewers' reports, background materials, etc. all reduce the inevitable abstractness of the statistical reporting, illustrate the meanings and point up the variety underlying the categories used in the statistical analysis. The same procedures will naturally constitute the preliminary phases of the analysis of an explanatory survey, for as noted effective description of the phenomenon—of the dependent variables—is the base upon which effective explanation is built.

None of these procedures is easy to accomplish, and the analyst can handle them inefficiently and even improperly. Skill and care are needed. But these procedures will not be discussed for they are relatively *routine* and covered in a variety of sources such as those alluded to in Chapter I. When they are executed properly and in relation to elaborate planning they provide the core of the analysis and yield the descriptions which led to the survey being initiated. However, they are only the *core* of the analysis. There is one additional phase of the analysis which we shall treat in considerable detail. It is too often neglected although it is crucial to success in the descriptive survey as well as in the explanatory survey.

The steps we have discussed thus far in planning and in actual analysis are intended to yield conclusions about the nature of the phenomenon under study. But survey findings are not strictly a description of reality; they represent in actual fact the product of a series of operations or procedures. The apparent properties of the phenomenon that the analyst describes may be a very misleading representation of the reality depending on the degree to which *errors* have occurred throughout the procedures used. Even where errors have not been frequent, nevertheless, the conclusions drawn, the description obtained, must always be seen as a product of some specific series of procedures. As Katz remarks in discussing the interpretation of surveys,

The results of scientific research are sometimes regarded as pure objective statements of absolute truth devoid of interpretation. But if research findings are to have even scientific meaning, they must be interpreted in terms of the conditions and assumptions of the investigation of which they are the outcome. . . . In fact the failure to make explicit the assumptions and conditions of the research investigation creates the impression of a finding more universal than the facts justify. Scientific findings must always be considered . . . in the framework of the particular research study. . . . The . . . interpretation of scientific results imposes the task of criteria and precautions for the evaluation of data.[1]

Similarly, Deming remarks: "One must be concerned chiefly with the procedures by which the statistics were collected and processed. It is necessary to look to the sample design, the devices by which the universe was listed, the effect of non-response or failure to cover certain segments of the universe, the questionnaire, the training of the field force, the instructions, the auspices, the office processing, the coding errors, and all else in the machinery that finally puts the figures into the tables."[2]

It is in the light of this fundamental that the analyst functions not merely as planner and analyst at the *initial* and *terminal* stages of a survey, but must act as the study director *throughout* the total process. At the very least this gives him *knowledge* of the operations in relation to which he must draw his conclusions. But knowledge is only a small blessing if the analyst must conclude that the description is inaccurate because of major errors created by faulty procedure. Thus, he exercises great pains to develop the best possible sampling plan, questionnaire and related instruments, scheme for supervision and control of interviewers, plan for coding, tabulating and processing of data. This leads to a reduction in error. And in addition a considerable part of the actual analysis is then devoted not to analyzing the phenomenon as such, but to the analysis of the actual magnitude of the residual error still present that may attend the conclusions.

We shall not discuss the actual operations of the survey that intervene between planning and analysis and reduce error but the terminal phases of the treatment of error and the qualification of conclusions will be dealt with. There is no simple way for the analyst to treat this problem, for errors are manifold in number and subtle in their operation. However, some guides can be provided.

Presentation of the Procedures

Since survey research is generally conducted for some outside sponsor and is intended to serve some larger objective, the report and the statement of the findings naturally must contain a statement of the procedures employed. While the analyst can *implicitly* evaluate his own findings in relation to his

---

1. D. Katz, "Interpretation of Survey Findings," *op. cit.,* reprinted by permission of the publishers.
2. W. E. Deming, "On Training in Sampling," *J. Amer. Stat. Assoc.,* 40, 1945, 307-316. Reprinted by permission of the publishers.

procedures, this provides no standard for another reader, a sponsor, a policy maker, independently to evaluate the correctness of the findings and make a wise decision. Moreover, even where research is academic in nature, a critic or colleague must be provided with sufficient information as to the procedures employed so that he can evaluate the validity of the conclusions and determine their relativity to the operations used. Deming in a classic paper, *On Errors in Surveys,* remarks that "in the presentation of data the omission of an adequate discussion of all the errors present and the difficulties encountered constitutes a serious defect in the data and is sure to lead to misinterpretation and misuse." [3]

If we examine our case studies we note how large a proportion of effort is expended by the analyst not in analyzing or discussing the substantive findings on the phenomenon, but merely in discussing the procedures used and errors involved in obtaining the data on the phenomenon. Thus, in Kinsey's inquiry a section of approximately 125 pages is devoted purely to the exposition of the procedures and an analysis of the errors attendant on the conclusions. In *The Authoritarian Personality,* while such methodological aspects of the analysis are not consolidated in the textual report, there are scattered throughout the text many pages describing the procedures employed and specific sections on validity of the data, reliability of coding, etc. In the Radio inquiry, there are specific appendices describing the sampling, presenting the exact questionnaire, and data bearing on the methodological questions of error. In the inquiry into absenteeism, about three pages of the short 17 page paper are devoted to an exposition of the design and procedures and another page reports empirical data on the magnitude of errors present. The implication is clear—*a large portion of the analyst's resources must be devoted to methodological questions of the quality of the data.* To illustrate how far this principle might be carried, and legitimately, one might repeat the comment of one of the critics of Kinsey's report. Wallis, in a detailed discussion of the problems attendant on sampling for such an inquiry remarks: "I should judge that *nearly half of the total cost* of analysis for a project such as this would be in checking on the population-sample relationship; but it is worth it, for the validity and usefulness of the research depends fully as much on this as on the soundness of the actual measurements." [4]

And if we examine the criticisms of particular descriptive or other types of surveys, we can again note that the critic gives prominence often to the methodological questions of what information on procedures is presented and what evidence there is on the quality of such procedures. Oftentimes, questions of conceptualization, of the analysis of the substantive data

---

3. W. E. Deming, "On Errors in Surveys," *Amer. Sociol. Rev.,* 9, 1944, 359-369.
4. W. Allen Wallis, *op. cit.,* p. 469, italics ours.

even become secondary and the survey stands or falls by reference to the quality of the methodological treatment.

The sheer *presentation* of the procedures by which the data were collected could have no significance and be no help to the analyst or reader if it were not for the fact that there are *fairly well established standards* as to which aspects of procedure are the essential context for evaluating survey findings and what constitutes good practices for these procedural aspects. Otherwise, no analyst would know how to treat this problem and any presentation would be wasteful. That such standards exist is readily documented for example by illustrative criticisms of one of our case studies, *The Kinsey Report*. We take three specific reviews of this survey to illustrate the unusual unanimity with which the critics fasten on crucial omissions in the presentation despite Kinsey's lengthy methodological account.[5] Thus, with respect to certain aspects of the *sampling,* it is noted that there is an omission with respect to certain critical information.

> *Wallis:* How many refusals are encountered? How does the refusal rate vary among segments? What are the determinable characteristics of refusers in the various segments? . . . future reports should show the actual number of histories involved and how they are distributed with respect to all the controls—age, education, occupation, religion, etc.
>
> *Hyman and Sheatsley:* Nowhere for example, is there a description of the characteristics of the 5300 respondents actually interviewed, the number of cases in all the major cells, or the number of refusers in the groups from which the volunteers came.
>
> *Terman:* The report is open to criticism, however, for not giving us the information needed to judge the representativeness of either the volunteers or the hundred-per-cent samples. The Ns of contributing groups are almost never stated . . .

On the Interviewing Technique the critics remark:

> *Terman:* Unfortunately, the author tells us almost nothing about the wording of questions asked, a matter which the professional pollsters have found to be extremely important. The reason given for this omission is lack of space, but since the wording of questions vitally affects the interpretation of almost every statistic in this 800 page book, the omission is regrettable. What the author does say about the questions is not always reassuring. In the first place, we are told that they have never been standardized; instead, the manner of wording them varies. . . . The necessity of alternative forms of wording will be granted, but without knowledge of the forms deemed permissible, no other investigator can repeat the Kinsey experiment with any assurance that he is getting comparable results.
>
> *Hyman and Sheatsley:* No questionnaire is presented in the book. While the definition of each item in the survey was standard, the wording of the

---

5. W. A. Wallis, *ibid.*, by permission of the publishers; H. Hyman and P. Sheatsley, *op. cit.*; L. Terman, *op. cit.*, by permission of The American Psychological Association. For a comprehensive demonstration of the agreement among critics on matters of standards, see Cochran, Mosteller, and Tukey, *op. cit.*

questions and the order of the questions were not standardized, being varied in the most meaningful manner for each respondent. Kinsey sought on the one hand, the ideal setting for each individual interview, and on the other a real or functional equivalence in the interviews administered to all respondents. Experimental studies have shown that the standardization of poll questions in public opinion research sometimes gives a spurious picture of attitudes, owing to the varying reactions of different individuals to the identically worded question. But the dilemma of Kinsey's method is that when the objective conditions of the interview are not uniform, any differences between individuals and groups may be due to differences in question wording and order, even though one may have achieved a more valid clinical picture of the given individual.

Wallis: I hope that the next volume (or at least a mimeographed supplement to it) will give an account of the actual questions used. There are admittedly difficulties in doing this, for the questions are numerous and "have never been standardized" (p. 51) because "the form of each question has varied for the various social levels and for the various types of persons with whom the study has dealt." For example, "sexual vernaculars must be used in interviewing lower level individuals" and "such vernaculars vary considerably among different groups" (p. 52). Nevertheless, the point which each question covers is said to be "strictly defined" (p. 51) and terms such as "petting" and "prostitute" are precisely explained to the subjects. The interpretation of nearly everything in a study like this depends upon the questions, and their absence makes it impossible for other workers independently to test or to supplement Kinsey's data.

What the illustrations demonstrate is the weight given to specific procedural information in the evaluation of the quality of research findings and the striking agreement as to what is proper operating procedure in given areas.

The codification of principles as to what is essential presentation of procedure has reached such a point of development that there are a number of published lists of the aspects that shall be reported. For example, The Advertising Research Foundation lists eight areas in which there should be a statement of methods used, including information on the questionnaire, interviewing, sampling, control of editing, coding, and tabulating, and statistical analysis. Each of these general areas is then treated in detail.[6] Deming in his paper *On Errors in Surveys* lists 13 factors which affect the quality of research findings, and on which information should be available. These are reproduced below in Chart III.

Chart III
Factors Affecting the Quality of Findings
1. Variability in response;
2. Differences between different kinds and degrees of canvass;
   (a) Mail, telephone, telegraph, direct interview;
   (b) Intensive vs. extensive interviews;

---

6. Advertising Research Foundation, *op. cit.*

(c) Long vs. short schedules;

(d) Check block plan vs. response;

(e) Correspondence panel and key reporters;

3. Bias and variation arising from the interviewer;

4. Bias of the auspices;

5. Imperfections in the design of the questionnaire and tabulation plans;

   (a) Lack of clarity in definitions; ambiguity; varying meanings of same word to different groups of people; eliciting an answer liable to misinterpretation;

   (b) Omitting questions that would be illuminating to the interpretation of other questions;

   (c) Emotionally toned words; leading questions; limiting response to a pattern;

   (d) Failing to perceive what tabulations would be most significant;

   (e) Encouraging nonresponse through formidable appearance;

6. Changes that take place in the universe before tabulations are available;

7. Bias arising from nonresponse (including omissions);

8. Bias arising from late reports;

9. Bias arising from an unrepresentative selection of date for the survey, or of the period covered;

10. Bias arising from an unrepresentative selection of respondents;

11. Sampling errors and biases;

12. Processing errors (coding, editing, calculating, tabulating, tallying, posting and consolidating);

13. Errors in interpretation;

   (a) Bias arising from bad curve fitting; wrong weighting; incorrect adjusting;

   (b) Misunderstanding the questionnaire; failure to take account of the respondents' difficulties (often through inadequate presentation of data); misunderstanding the method of collection and the nature of the data;

   (c) Personal bias in interpretation.

The Standards Committee of the American Association for Public Opinion Research has presented a similar list, and the Bureau of the Budget of the U.S. Government has a list of criteria. In the presence of such elaborate codification of principles, neglect on the part of the analyst in proper presentation of analytic findings is deserving of serious criticism.

In our examples thus far, it might appear that lengthy accounts of procedure were required. *Coverage,* not length, is of course the important consideration. By way of illustration, we cite a passage from Deming's paper in which he reproduces a statement of procedure attached to a government survey. Despite its brevity it will be seen how many procedural details are treated.

These statistics are based on a mail canvass supplemented by a field enumeration conducted by the U. S. Forest Service and the Tennessee Valley Authority. In the field enumeration Forest Service and TVA representatives interviewed mills that did not respond to the mail canvass, and, in addition conducted an intensive search for mills . . . Among the smaller mills, book-keeping is generally inadequate. Even the total cut for a mill may be an estimate, and the species breakdown for such a mill, particularly in areas of diversified growth, must frequently be estimated by the mill operator or by the enumerator . . . Difficulties in enumeration because of lack of ade-quate mill records were overcome in many cases where the mill disposed of its total cut through a concentration yard. In such instances enumerators were able to obtain information for individual mills from the yard operator, particularly in the South and Southeast where concentration yards are an important factor in the distribution of lumber. This approach was not sat-isfactory, however, when an operator sold his lumber to several different yards in the course of the year, and where the records at the concentration yard did not indicate clearly whether the cut was for 1942 or 1941. . . . Mills engaged solely in remanufacturing, finishing, or otherwise processing lumber were excluded. . . . In a number of cases, the mill reports were in terms of dressed or processed lumber, since many integrated mills, i.e., those both sawing and dressing, were able to report only on a finished basis. The discrepancy, which is of unknown magnitude, is equivalent to the amount of waste in processing. In canvassing integrated mills, however, the cut was counted at only one point in the processing operation, so that no duplication occurred. . . . An ever-present complicating factor in the canvass was the extreme mobility of the smaller mills . . .[7]

PROBLEM EXERCISE III
Presentation of Procedures and Error Factors

As an exercise in sensitizing the student to consideration of conclusions in the light of procedures and error factors, he should now re-examine this passage in the light of Deming's list of criteria, noting what portions of the text explicitly treat or implicitly allude to one or more of the specific factors Deming presents as significant in evaluating the accuracy of survey findings. The student should not necessarily expect to find all of the factors from the list, since the text is only a small excerpt from the original survey report. Moreover, as Deming notes, these factors vary in their relative importance depending on the nature of the original inquiry, and some may even be completely irrelevant in given surveys. Break the text into fragments, and label each portion to correspond to the factors listed by Deming. Then, the student should compare his work with the answer provided in Appendix E.

The Qualification
of Specific Conclusions

The presentation of the *general procedures* used in the survey while an essential is not sufficient. Such information does provide a sense of

7. *Production of Lumber, by States and by Species;* 1942 (Bureau of the Census, November 1943).

the operations which constitute a context for evaluating the accuracy of the description of the phenomenon. Because of accepted methodological standards it does provide either a sense of confidence or suspicion of the total findings. However such information is *not focussed enough* to provide proper qualification of *specific conclusions*. It is not presented in the context of a particular finding. Moreover, the general procedures may not apply uniformly to each finding, and the presentation may omit reference to a procedure which occurred rarely in the total survey but which affects a given finding. Therefore, any conclusion should be qualified by reference to those aspects of procedure which are relevant to the specific data. One of our case studies of a descriptive survey illustrates the care with which specific findings are placed in proper methodological context so that their accuracy and their implications can be evaluated. We shall use the inquiry into the atomic bomb to show how the analysts handle their data.[8]

Thus in relation to a finding that the majority of the public believed other countries had the secret of manufacture of the bomb, the analysts remark: "One caution must be inserted here, however. People can voice acceptance of a fact without incorporating it into their thinking—that is, without bringing it to bear upon their opinions." (p. 17) [9]

In relation to certain findings on the expectation of future atomic attacks, the analysts again qualify a conclusion in terms of *the limited aspect of the problem that was being measured*. They remark: "the danger may nevertheless appear simply hypothetical." (p. 25)

In relation to finding that a large majority think the U.S. should retain the secret rather than have international control, the analysts qualify the finding as *a function of the type of question put:* "Our 'secrets' question undoubtedly posed the control issue in its most 'unfavorable' light." (p. 32)

Later in relation to another finding on the same problem, the analysts note that *the datum is predicated on only a portion of the sample* with consequent effects: "If the question had been asked of the entire sample—including the most poorly informed one third—the results would probably have been less favorable." (pp. 35-36)

In relation to a finding on support for U.S. participation in a world organization, a variety of methodological considerations lead the analysts to remark: "The issue is obviously uncrystallized, at least so far as public familiarity with it is concerned, and the reactions found in surveys are heavily dependent upon how the questions are phrased." (p. 41)

Later in a detailed treatment of data on international actions the U.S. might take, the analysts specifically *limit the findings in terms of the type*

---

8. All quotations and page references are from Cottrell and Eberhart, *op. cit.*

9. It might be noted here that the context which qualifies a conclusion includes not merely a procedure, such as the interviewing or coding, but the conceptualization. Cottrell and Eberhart are remarking that this finding bears purely on a cognitive aspect of the phenomenon and may have no relevance to other aspects of the phenomenon.

of open-end question construction used. "The proportions of the people who offer each of these suggestions are undoubtedly much smaller than would be the proportions who would agree to them if they were specifically proposed." (p. 121)

Later in a treatment of findings based on questions about world organization, the analysts qualify the conclusions in the light of the *context of the questionnaire and the order of the questions.* "The formulation of the first question probably influenced some people's answers to the second." (p. 126)

There are many other examples scattered throughout the report of this survey illustrative of the way in which the analysts qualify specific conclusions in the light of the procedures employed. They demonstrate the degree to which the analyst must expend considerable effort and resources not on the sheer examination of substantive findings but on the problem of error factors and the examination of findings in relation to procedures. By contrast, another one of our case studies illustrates inadequate attention to the specific procedural context within which the conclusions are demonstrated despite the fact that the general procedures are reported in great length. The fact that it is an explanatory survey only underscores our previous point that the skills of treating a phenomenon in a descriptive survey are valuable in any explanatory survey. In their detailed critique of *The Authoritarian Personality,* Hyman and Sheatsley remark that "an inherent feature of any standardized measuring instrument is the element of artificiality. The nature of the phenomenon under investigation is inevitably affected by the design and technical features of the measuring instrument. The decision as to the content of the questionnaire, the number and types of answer categories and the formulation of items—all these technical, and often minor, features of the instrument influence and may even determine the results achieved. This fact is recognized as a virtual truism in all empirical research, and allowances are made for it in the course of the analysis." Hyman and Sheatsley then examine many of the conclusions reported in the inquiry and note that this proper context is ignored: "In the treatment of the data the limitations of the responses are periodically ignored, the answers are accepted at face value and the statistics manipulated in an unimaginative way." [10] Thus, for example, the conclusion that Anti-Semites engage in stereotypy is not qualified in the light of the fact that the mode of question construction required a categorical answer. Therefore, any stereotypy demonstrated may be an artifact of the questionnaire and cannot be regarded as evidence on the problem. The interrelations between various kinds of sentiments may be an artifact created by the presence of almost identical items in scales which presumably measure different variables. The observed relation between authoritarianism and prejudice may constitute no test of the hypothesis as to the relationship between these senti-

10. *Op. cit.,* p. 70.

ments, since in the development of successive forms of the authoritarianism scale, items which did not correlate with Anti-Semitism were dropped from the instrument. The conclusion about the validity of the questionnaire instruments on the basis of their agreement with the interview data neglects the fact that the interviewers were aware of the questionnaire results when they conducted their interviews and therefore any consistency may be spurious.

These constitute only a summary of this portion of the critique but should suffice to demonstrate that inadequate attention to the methodological limitations of specific conclusions can jeopardize the analysis.

With respect to qualifying specific conclusions in the light of the procedures employed, it is important to emphasize *minor conventions* attached to the procedures or *departures* from the original procedures. The proper context within which a conclusion is reported is not so much the *formal* procedure of sampling, question wording, code categories, and the like. These formalized procedures represent initial prescriptions of aspects of the survey, but in the execution of the survey, minor decisions are deliberately or accidentally introduced which alter the initial prescription or truly define the nature of the procedure. It is the ultimate practice of the procedure rather than the theory of it to which the analyst must be sensitive. There are many instances of this significant distinction. For example, in generalizing about a conclusion based on a sample, one must consider not merely that the original sample *design* was such as to yield an unbiased estimate of the characteristics of the population but whether or not the interviewers departed from the requirements of the design in the field situation. We might illustrate the way in which minor conventions in the course of the process should qualify the conclusions by reference to an NORC survey on attitudes toward the United States Foreign Service.[11]

At one point a statistic describing the extent of public knowledge of the foreign service is reported. It is then noted that the finding probably represents a "maximum estimate of the extent of public awareness," because, with respect to the answers as to knowledge elicited by an open-ended question, the *"coders were instructed to be liberal* in classifying answers as correct."

Similarly, with respect to a finding on degree of personal contact with the Foreign Service, it is noted that the estimate is probably a maximum because the *instructions given to interviewers with respect to defining the category of contact were "even the slightest contact is sufficient basis for circling 'yes.'"*

11. Unpublished report, National Opinion Research Center, 1947.

Empirical Estimates of Errors

The presentation of conclusions in relation to general or specific procedures, while essential, does not yet exhaust the analyst's task in evaluating his conclusions. The problem of treatment of error is more complex. While there is considerable agreement as to what aspects of the survey process shall be reported and agreement as to the adequacy of certain procedures, there remain in *each specific investigation uncertainties as to the magnitude of error that has been introduced by a given procedure.*

Quite often one can make reasonable assumptions about the effect of a given procedure, and it is plausible in the light of past experience that a certain error may be present, but this nevertheless remains speculation. Therefore, wherever possible, the analyst must introduce *empirical data* on the actual error factors so as to reduce the speculative element that otherwise attaches to his conclusions. Most of these methods for obtaining empirical evidence on error or on the limitations of the conclusions require that the analyst *plan initially* to collect specific types of information. In our earlier discussion of conceptualization of the survey, we omitted reference to these considerations, and the student should now supplement that section in the light of what follows. This point is emphasized, for example, by Lazarsfeld and Kendall who remark that "sophisticated research technicians . . . look for procedures through which survey findings can be safeguarded against pitfalls . . . and work continuously to build these necessary checks and controls into their study designs." [12]

The distinction between *empirical data* on the quality of procedures and their effect on the findings as compared with the mere *juxtaposition* of conclusions and procedures is easily illustrated. For example, survey findings are dependent on the quality of interviewing, for no manipulation during analysis can remedy errors in the collection of the original data. The presentation of certain facts about the interviewing staff and the method is helpful in evaluation of the findings. The interviewers' past experience, the degree of supervision exercised, the way in which they were originally trained, method of compensation, whether they are employed on a full or part-time basis, their group-membership characteristics, e.g., class, ethnicity, sex, etc., are all relevant and the experienced research worker appraises these facts as *plausible* grounds for deciding whether or not the data were collected adequately. However, in the absence of evidence on actual magnitude of cheating, bias, or interviewer effect, the question of error in the collection of data must always remain a speculation. However, the analyst could provide for estimates of interviewer error by a planned series of pro-

---

12. Lazarsfeld and Kendall, *Survey Analysis, op. cit.,* p. 169.

cedures which might include—cheater trap questions, interpenetrating sample design, spot checks, office rating of a sample of interviews, etc. Only if these procedures were included would it be possible to appraise the conclusions with any degree of precision.[13]

Such empirical estimates of error can be introduced into the survey for all the major phases of the process. With respect to sampling, systematic report forms on refusals and non-availability of respondents and checking of findings from the sample against control figures on the same characteristics obtained from independent sources are some of the methods used. With respect to coding, independent re-coding of a sample of responses is normally employed as a measure of reliability. With respect to errors in punching, verification is employed on a sample of questionnaires. The net quality of both punching and coding is normally determined by consistency checks or "cleaning" of the cards.

Perhaps the most subtle type of error and consequently the most difficult to appraise is normally labelled "response error." Apart from all other sources of error, the accuracy of the description of a phenomenon in a survey is dependent on the quality of the verbal reports that the respondent gives in answer to the questions asked. These reports ultimately yield indices of the many variables that were conceptualized by the analyst. But these reports may be inaccurate for a variety of reasons. *Questions always elicit data that are meaningful but the problem for the analyst is to read the right meaning!* The data may not represent the phenomenon that the analyst intended because the questions are *too difficult to understand,* or because the respondent *does not give a serious reply,* or because the respondent *interprets an ambiguous question to refer to an entity other than the one the analyst* intended. In certain content areas other difficulties enter— the respondent *may be honest but unable to recall the information* or *may be competent but evasive and dishonest in his reply.*

These problems are particularly acute in the *descriptive* survey where the aim is to provide an *aggregate* description. The analyst must interpret the meaning of the statistical findings and his inference is wrong insofar as he cannot estimate the presence of these response errors. In the explanatory survey, where the concern is with the relation of the phenomenon to some independent variable, the analyst *sometimes* can advance the assumption that such response errors are distributed equally throughout all the groups contrasted for study. Consequently the response error may be present but will not obscure the differences between the contrasted groups and the inference as to the influence of the independent variable. However, even here,

---

13. For a comprehensive discussion of errors in the interview and methods for reducing, controlling and estimating such error, see H. Hyman, *et al., Interviewing in Social Research, op. cit.,* Chap. VII.

the assumption as to the error being constant may be unwarranted and empirical evidence on response error is desirable.[14]

The accumulation of past experience is of course the ideal basis for *reducing such errors at the source.* Thus, through many surveys, the analyst may know that respondents falsify reports of income when the question is asked in one way and will give more reliable replies when the question takes another tack. He may know that respondents tend to inflate their formal education in their replies and are constrained from this when the question is prefaced by a certain prior question. Sometimes, past experience provides *no solution* to the problem, but at least permits an empirical *estimate of the magnitude* of such response error. Thus, while the reasons are unclear it is well known that reports of voting in past presidential elections inflate the vote for the candidate who has been victorious. More people claim to have voted for the winner than could possibly be the case in the light of the official voting statistics. While no solution has been invented, the order of inflation is known and this factor can be employed in the analysis.[15]

But each inquiry is *novel* in some respect and a *pre-test* of the specific instrument is therefore employed on the assumption that prior experience is an insufficient guide to the analyst. Skilled interviewers try out the instruments and an appraisal of the preliminary findings permits the analyst to revise the instrument—reduce the ambiguities that were observed, shorten the instrument, add or modify questions, etc. However, some estimation of residual errors that remain despite all pretesting is required, and there are two general classes of methods available for treating this problem, methods involving internal or external checks.[16]

1. Internal Checks

Internal checks on the meaning of answers and the response errors present require that in the planning of the instrument specific methodological data be collected.[17] *The internal check is predicated on the logic that the meaning and quality of a given reply can be inferred from its relation to some other datum or reply.*

The logic becomes clearer, and the limitations of the procedure evident

---

14. One empirical study provides a demonstration that such response errors are not distributed as a constant. Invalid reports of bond redemptions, as determined by checking official Treasury reports, were found to be more characteristic of upper income groups; reports of absenteeism, as determined by checking official plant records, were found to be more invalid in certain plants than in others. Correlations would therefore be in error. See: H. Hyman, "Do They Tell the Truth," *Publ. Opin. Quart.*, 8, 1944, 557-559.

15. For a discussion of this problem, see Mosteller, *et. al., op. cit.*, pp. 212-213.

16. For a discussion of both types of checks and findings based on the application of such checks, see M. B. Parten, *op. cit.*, 485-498.

17. For a discussion of such internal checks as used in the survey research of the U.S. Army, see Lazarsfeld and Kendall, Survey Analysis, *op. cit.*, pp. 169-179. For a discussion of such internal checks upon "don't know" answers, see H. Zeisel, *op. cit.*, pp. 53-65.

if we take a very simple example. Respondents are known on occasion to falsify their age in reply to the usual question. Consequently, the analyst might determine the characteristic of age twice during the interview—once, by asking the person "how old he was" and the other time by asking for his "birthdate." If the ages of respondents as calculated from the results of the two questions do not agree, the analyst knows that some error attaches to the findings on age. One of the two replies cannot mean what it is intended to mean; otherwise it must show a perfect relationship to the other reply.

The technical procedure for manipulating the data from such internal checks is self-evident. Either the over-all findings from the parallel items are *juxtaposed and compared for some defined group* to determine the *net* consistency, or a *cross-tabulation* is performed generally with the aid of machine equipment. The latter procedure permits one to determine for *each individual* whether his replies are consistent.

The value of the procedure should now be self-evident, but its limitations are also evident. If the two replies are consistent, the analyst is still not sure that the findings are an accurate description of the objective ages of the respondents. Since the check is *internal* in the questionnaire, a clever but dishonest respondent could falsify the report in both instances, and the analyst would be unable to detect the error. This limitation of internal checks may create a kind of continual warfare on the part of the analyst in which he improves and dissembles his strategy.[18] If the analyst is wise enough to dissemble the requirement that given answers must be consistent, he may catch the respondent. But any errors in reporting due to a persistently dishonest respondent or to one whose memory is consistently vague, or to a consistently dishonest interviewer or to a consistently biased mode of questioning, or the like, cannot be detected. If the checks *are not independent* of one another, and internal checks within the same instrument or within the same interview, by definition, are not independent, some consistent error remains undetected. The internal check is therefore a *minimal* measure of response error. This limitation leads to the development of checks of an *external* or independent sort to which we shall refer later.

A second limitation is that any inconsistency that is reasonable to regard as arising from some type of *error* confronts the analyst with the dilemma of deciding what conclusions to draw—which datum shall he use, if any;

---

18. In one of our case studies, the *Kinsey Report,* one notes such a grand strategy. Kinsey describes all the methods invented to foil the respondent's cover-up of his true pattern of sexual behavior. While Kinsey does employ methods of rapport and stresses the anonymity of the respondent, he also uses more "aggressive" methods—placing the burden of denial on the subject, rapid-fire of questions, cross-check questions, the use of language which if recognized is a give-away that the subject has had certain experiences, denunciation of the apparently dishonest respondent, "looking the subject squarely in the eye," etc. Despite all these internal checks, there is of course the rare possibility that an occasional respondent can *consistently* dissemble the facts.

what qualification shall he attach to his conclusions. This dilemma of interpretation is inescapable and there is no formal solution available.

A final limitation upon the internal check arises from the very logic of the procedure. In the instance of our example, the assumption of the procedure is warranted. The report of age is intended to refer to *a unique, objective fact* and the two reports from the two different questions must be in perfect agreement or something is wrong. But in many instances, the question of what the determinate relation between the two different measurements should be is difficult to state. The meaning of something is hard to define if the thing to which it is related is itself unclear in its meaning or if the relationship of the two entities is obscure.[19] This problem is especially frequent in internal checks on social-psychological phenomena, since a variety of *bizarre but legitimate* connections between psychological phenomena are possible.

Provided these cautions are kept in mind, the analyst can employ a variety of built-in internal checks on response error. These aid him in interpreting the true context of meaning underlying the respondent's reply and the presence of flagrant distortion if any. The most direct internal check involves *the use of questions which require the respondent to elaborate an initial reply*. This elaboration can be secured in a number of ways. *A series of specific interlocking polling questions* can be constructed, or *probing procedures* can be employed, or *broad open-ended questions* can be used initially. All of these procedures provide a richness of material which gives the analyst a well-defined context for interpreting the initial replies. From an elaboration, one can infer whether or not the referent of the answer is the one the analyst intended and inserted in the original question. One can infer the subtle qualifications and peculiarities of the sentiments initially expressed. The consistency or confusion of the total answer permits some estimate of vagueness of memory and competence of the respondent. The limitation that the response is an artifact of specific procedures employed in the initial question is reduced because the many sub-questions approach the issue by different techniques and the open-ended questions are nondirective in their structure. The approach, however, is not too effective in

---

19. A story attributed to John Dewey, and recounted to us by Clyde W. Hart, illustrates the dilemma of interpretation through such internal checks. The story goes that "A Columbia psychologist called several of his colleagues together to discuss his first venture in the development of a scale for measuring some psychological variable. After he had described his new scaling method, the meeting was thrown open to general discussion in the course of which John Dewey is said to have remarked about as follows: "Mr. ———'s interesting and ingenious scaling device reminds me of an experience during my boyhood days on a farm in Michigan. We had no scales, yet we frequently wanted to weigh things we were taking to market—steers, for instance. What we did was to find a huge boulder with a fairly sharp ridge on top to use as a fulcrum. Then we cut and trimmed a sturdy, straight young sapling for the beam of a balance, and rigged up a sling for each end of the beam. One of these slings was put under the belly of the steer; into the other sling was piled small stones until the feet of the steer were barely lifted off the ground. Then, all we had to do was guess the weight of the small stones and we knew the weight of the steer!"

relation to *motivated* response errors, since it is *not covert* and the respondent can infer the analyst's purposes and foil them if he wishes.

Internal checks for response errors of a more devious sort follow the same general logic, but simply are more subtle and dissembled in their purpose. The most immediate extension of the devices already described is to *separate* the *check items in the questionnaire,* but still leave each item fairly direct in its intent.

An internal check following the same logical pattern but exceedingly expensive to employ involves the traditional concept of *"repeat reliability."* The same item is repeated, not within the same unit interview, but after an interval of time in a second interview. Insofar as the replies are different, one questions the reliability of observations. The data are then regarded as capricious and subject to the accident of the transitory circumstances (e.g., the interviewer used, the mood of the respondent, etc.) or to the incompetence of the respondent. Such procedures cannot be evaluated as unequivocal in their meaning except for phenomena of a *factual* nature which by definition, are unchanging. In the case of opinion items, change may either be indicative of unreliability of report or of systematic changes in the respondent over time and there is no precise way of deciding between these alternative interpretations.

One of our case illustrates the application of this internal check. In Kinsey's inquiry a sub-sample of respondents were re-interviewed after an average interval of 38 months and the consistency of their reports on sexual behavior was examined. The example is helpful in pointing out one problem in the procedure. Normally a respondent who wishes to conceal himself can consistently lie in both initial and repeat interviews. However, here the interval of 38 months is so long that any pseudo-consistency due to memory of the original reply that was given is probably negligible. The procedure can be employed routinely with negligible expense in *panel* studies where the subjects are repeatedly interviewed. However, other than this, it is prohibitively expensive.[20]

Further extensions of the method of internal checks involve construction of items whose connections or relationships are not apparent to the respondent. In this practice, of course, there is a kind of calculation the analyst makes—the less apparent the connection to the respondent, the more the possibility that the expected relationship between replies is truly indeterminate or tenuous. If the clever respondent cannot sense that he ought to be consistent or he will be caught, perhaps it is because there is no necessary consistency between the items. We shall illustrate some examples of such internal checks as they were employed in various surveys.

20. For a treatment of the internal check of repeat reliability measures in panels, see P. Kendall, *Conflict and Mood, Factors Affecting Stability of Response* (Glencoe: The Free Press, 1954). For an analysis of such check data and a technique for allocating the unreliability to the interviewer, see H. Hyman, *Interviewing, op. cit.,* Chap. VI.

A study of personal influence and opinion leadership provides an illustration of a relatively direct check with a logic that is reasonably indisputable. Movie going behavior was selected as one of the areas of interest.[21] Each of the respondents was asked two questions about the personal influences she experienced or exerted in regard to recent movie going experiences. One of these asked whether anyone had *advised* her to attend the last movie she saw; the other asked whether she had proffered such *advice*. On the basis of answers to these two questions, it was possible to construct a typology of the movie-goers. One type consisted of those who gave and received advice about what movie to see; a second type was made up of those women who only sought but did not give advice; a third type included those who gave but did not receive any advice. There then remained a fourth group who, according to their answers to these two questions, neither gave nor received personal advice regarding what movie they should see. According to their responses, they were outside of the "influence market." These women, it turned out, made up a large number of the respondents—about 40 percent. To the analysts, this seemed an excessively large number, in view of their common-sense knowledge of movie-going behavior. They therefore began to question whether these women had understood the two queries put to them as the schedule designers had intended them to be understood. It was possible, by a very simple cross-tabulation, to determine that the meaning attached to these questions by many of the respondents was not the same as that attached to them by the analysts. The subjects had been asked whether, when they last went to the movies, they had gone alone or in the company of someone else. It then developed that nearly all of those who apparently were outside the influence market with regard to the last movie they saw had actually attended this movie with someone else. The analysts reasoned that if two or more people visit a movie theatre together, there must be some give and take of "advice" as to which movie to see. That is, one of the movie-goers must have given advice, and the other or others must take it. The fact that so many of the women who had experienced this give and take nonetheless reported in the interview that they had not was taken by the analysts as an indication that the notion of "advice-giving" does not adequately describe the kind of interpersonal exchanges which take place in connection with movie-going behavior and that the original replies could not be interpreted as intended.

In this particular case, the cross-tabulation of the respondents' initial answers was with check items on their relevant experiences. The inconsistencies could only mean that the questions had been understood differently than the analysts intended.

The type of check used here is clear in its meaning but at the same time

---

21. (Unpublished survey, Bureau of Applied Social Research.) The sample was confined to women residents of a particular mid-Western community.

would not be proof against *motivated* errors. Insofar as the original replies were obscured by *honest confusions,* this would be revealed, but insofar as a respondent would wish to appear free from someone else's influence, he might sense the import of the check question on experience and give a false but consistent reply to both items.

Another survey provides an illustration of a somewhat more covert internal check less prone to detection by the respondent, but perhaps more tenuous in its interpretation.[22] In a survey among medical internes, a question was asked which was intended to reveal the primary motive of the individual in becoming a physician. The replies indicated that there were two classes of motives—those involving relatively selfish gain, e.g., status, money, and those involving more altruistic or idealistic motives, e.g., service to humanity. The analysts had entertained the possibility that respondents would not wish to appear crass and selfish and would either deliberately understate the frequency of selfish motives or would rationalize their motives to themselves. An internal check on the meaning of the original findings was provided by another question which asked the interne's income aspirations in the next five years. On this question respondents could be sorted into two general classes—those who aspired to relatively high incomes and those who aspired to modest or low incomes. Cross-tabulation of the replies indicated that the "idealists" as defined by the original datum on motives did not differ in their average income aspiration from the "materialists." If anything the observed difference was in the "wrong" direction. The analysts therefore questioned the validity of the original datum insofar as it be interpreted as an accurate measure of the distribution of genuine motives of the respondents.

We have here a check which is somewhat more devious than the original one reported, although still detectable by a respondent who wishes to conceal his motives. The logical connection to be expected between replies to these items seems relatively indisputable. Yet, to show the complexity of interpreting such checks, it should be noted that another survey research analyst disputed the inference of invalidity from this check and argued that it was perfectly reasonable for the "idealists" to want to earn more money. The ground on which this argument was predicated was that the idealists in all probability were upper income people and would consequently have higher standards of living which were expressed in their income aspirations.[23]

---

22. The survey was conducted by the National Opinion Research Center. The specific Internal check and its logic was reported by the major analyst, P. B. Sheatsley. See, "How Cross-Tabs Can Question Validity," *Publ. Opin. Quart.,* 11, 1947, p. 612.

23. H. B. Durant, *Publ. Opin. Quart.,* 12, 1948, pp. 127-128. The student can see that this alternative interpretation of the internal check could be tested by repeating the cross-tabulation, controlling socio-economic status of the respondents. However, this does not alter the point in the text about the complexity of interpretation of such checks.

Surveys conducted in 1948 for purposes of making election predictions provide another example of covert internal checks against deliberately evasive replies. It will be recalled that a third party, the Progressive Party with Henry Wallace as candidate for president, was running on the ballot. The climate of opinion was such that many analysts reasoned that some individuals would be afraid to reveal their support of Wallace and would falsely report their preferences. It was reasonable that such individuals would be more likely to reply "don't know" rather than state that they favored Dewey or Truman. Depending on the magnitude of this concealed Wallace vote, it could affect the conclusions drawn. A method that commended itself as a basis for deciding what was the meaning of the overt "don't know" answers involved examining the replies of the don't know respondents to a variety of other questions on ideology. Insofar as the group showed a profile of radical sentiments this would suggest to the analysts that the question on presidential preference was subject to considerable response error.[24]

One notes in this example that the check is likely to be effective against evasion. It is covert in character, and the respondent is not likely to realize that his ideology is a give away of his presidential preference. Especially is this the case since the stigma was in relation to the commitment to the third party rather than in relation to one's opinions. However, one sees that the connection between a true Wallace preference and the check questions on ideology to be expected is somewhat in doubt since the correlation between ideology and political partisanship is certainly far from unity.

In the examples cited thus far the check questions are questions whose contents are opinions, attitudes, reports of experiences or of past behavior which the analyst has reason to expect should correlate in some defined way with the reply whose validity is being gauged. Another type of internal check which is quite common involves *the examination of the reply under study for sub-groups differing on some factual characteristic.*[25] This type of check where possible is exceedingly desirable because it is not vulnerable to some of the criticisms of the other type of internal checks. First of all, in the other internal checks some *unreliability* in the enumeration of the *check* items (e.g., clerical error) may be responsible for discrepancy between the two replies, and therefore the apparent invalidity of the original data is misleading. Presumably, although it is not always the case, unreliability in

24. For a presentation of this method and the conclusions possible, see Mosteller, *et al, op. cit.* Chap. XI, especially pp. 284-289. In this same chapter other internal checks on other possible interpretations of the "don't know" reply are presented, for in election predictions there is also the problem of allocating "don't knows" that are not evasive but represent individuals not as yet decided in their preference. The problem for the analyst is to infer what the future preference of these undecided individuals will be.

25. This check in survey research constitutes the closest approximation to the usual validation procedure in psychological test construction where two contrasted groups are compared with respect to their responses on the new test. Independent knowledge about the nature of the contrasted groups leads the psychologist to expect a certain distribution of the replies for each of the groups, if the test is a valid measure of the variable under study.

enumerating simple factual data would be less. Secondly, we have already commented on the fact that unless the purpose of the check item is dissembled it will not be effective against evasion by clever respondents. But, there is no apparent connection between a factual characteristic of the respondent and a reply to a question. Sometimes the factual item is not even asked of the respondent and is merely appraised by the interviewer. Similarly, consistency between the check item and the suspect item cannot generally be regarded as pseudo-consistency due to such constant errors as general mode of questioning, chronic interviewer errors, etc., because the enumeration of factual data is somewhat independent of the rest of the interviewing procedure. In this sense, factual items used as check data are checks which approximate to external checks, to which we shall come shortly.

The factual characteristic used as a check item, however, is predicated on a logic which limits its applicability to special instances. It requires that the analyst have some fairly good, independent basis for knowing how the several sub-groups contrasted on the factual item shall array themselves on some variable akin to the suspect item. The logic and the procedure as well as its limitations will become clearer if we present a number of brief examples.

Shortly after World War II, Japan saw the sudden growth of a large number of public opinion research agencies. The possibility was entertained that Japanese respondents, at that time, would have great fears about giving honest replies and would conceal their true opinions by replying "don't know." The don't know then would not be indicative of ignorance, lack of crystallized opinion, and the like but would conceal individuals with crystallized ideologies. A check on this was instituted by tabulating the size of the don't know groups for various factual categories—e.g., rural vs. urban respondents, men vs. women. The analysts had an independent basis for assuming that lack of opinion was in truth more characteristic of the rural and female segments of the society. Therefore, when specific tabulations turned out in accordance with this general expectation, the inference was drawn that the "don't know" truly had the meaning of lack of opinion rather than representing evasion.[26]

Another example is available from a special study conducted during the course of the United States Strategic Bombing Survey on the morale of Germans. We shall allude to this example again, but it involved survey analyses of several thousand letters written by Germans during the war and captured by the Allied Forces prior to official German censorship. The relationship between deterioration of the writer's morale and indices of his exposure to bombing was determined by reference to passages in the letters.

---

26. For a report of this test and other checks on the validity of early Japanese social research, see H. Hyman, "World Surveys—The Japanese Angle," *Int. J. Opin. Attit. Res.*, Vol. I, #2, 18-29.

However, the finding might not be accurate. Even though no overt official censorship had yet been exercised, Germans were aware of the likelihood that censorship would be imposed. Perhaps they distorted their feelings to avoid danger of reprisal. Perhaps other types of distortion occurred. A wife writing to her husband at the front may not have wanted to increase his anxiety. Other writers from the home front may have wished to overdramatize the sufferings they too were experiencing. All these considerations may have led to errors in the reports in the letters and falsified the finding as to the true relationship between bombing and morale. The analysts were able to employ a check through the use of factual data. The letters were subdivided according to the town or region from which they originated. Official data on the magnitude of bombing for these corresponding areas were available. Insofar as the letters were not affected by distortion, the descriptions of certain experiences by the letter writers from different regions should increase in magnitude with the severity of the actual bombing in their regions. A whole series of such correlations supported the inference that the letter writers were reporting their experiences in a *relatively* truthful way.[27]

One other example from a survey of medical students will be presented.[28] In this inquiry, the subjects were asked at one point to pass a judgment on their faculty. The question that was used was as follows: "Everyone recognizes that it is difficult to generalize about 'the faculty.' But, in your own experience, how much *interest*—on the average—do members of the following groups at ———— Medical College take in their students? The house staff? The basic science faculty? The full-time clinical faculty? Practitioners who teach part-time?" This is the kind of question which typically calls forth evasive answers. No amount of assurance can fully convince the subjects that their anonymity will be maintained or that their frank answers will not lead to punishment at the hands of institutional authorities. We are therefore likely to find a large number of evasive "Don't knows" in answer to a question of this kind. In this particular instance, however, it was possible to ascertain that there was a minimum of evasion in the responses of the students. While there were a number of students who reported that they had no opinion about the interest which different groups of the faculty took in their students, a check by the use of factual data permitted the conclusion that these replies were not evasive in character. The replies were compared for sub-groups of respondents at different stages of formal training. In the medical college where this survey was carried out, as in most, medical training follows a rigid pattern. The first two years are given over

27. See *The Effects of Strategic Bombing on German Morale*, Vol. II, The United States Strategic Bombing Survey, Morale Division (Washington: Government Printing Office, 1946), Appendix A, 43-45.

28. Unpublished survey, Bureau of Applied Social Research, Columbia University.

almost entirely to training in the basic sciences—anatomy, biochemistry, parasitology, and so on. These courses are conducted, by and large, in the lecture-hall and laboratory, rather than in clinics or hospital wards. As a result, the beginning students—those in their first two years of training— have only accidental contacts with the house staff of the teaching hospital connected with the medical college, with the clinical teaching staff, or with the practitioners who supervise the clinical work of the more advanced students. The finding that students in their first two years of training said that they do not know how much interest such faculty members have suggests that the answer is not an evasion but, rather, an indication of their *relative* lack of experience.

The check involving factual data is of course limited in applicability to a relatively narrow class of situations in which some independent knowledge is available on the way in which factual sub-groups array themselves. Where such knowledge is available, it is also generally the case that it is knowledge *not* with respect to the exact variable which is under suspicion but is knowledge about some related phenomenon or variable. If prior knowledge were completely appropriate to the problem under study, it is unlikely that the new survey would be initiated. Consequently, some apparent inconsistency should be expected on grounds of the attenuation of the relationship between the variable that is suspect and the related variable that was the basis for ordering the factual groups. However, there is one crucial limitation to this check which makes it *applicable basically to problems of response error in explanatory surveys.* It has no strict value for estimating response errors in descriptive surveys. The student should have noted in two of the examples cited above, that the analysts drew the conclusion that the responses were *relatively* valid. In the Bombing Survey example, if letter writers from *every region* distorted their reports in the *same* direction and to the same *extent,* the correlation between reports of bombing experience by region and independent official data would still have been unity. In the Medical School example, if freshman and senior students distort their replies in equal amounts, the correlation between magnitude of Don't know reports and Year of Study would still come out just as expected on grounds of the independent evidence. In other words, the test *does not reveal any constant errors* over the sub-groups. This constitutes no limitation with respect to the explanatory survey since the presence of such constant errors will not jeopardize the purpose of the inquiry— namely a test of the relationship between variables. However, for descriptive surveys where the aim is to provide an accurate estimate of the magnitude of some phenomenon in the population, such constant errors are harmful. They yield a biased description. The employment of such checks therefore has little strict value for descriptive surveys. That value, such as it is, is predicated on the rather loose assumption that if sub-group findings are accurate representations of the relative state of affairs, it is unlikely that the constant errors have occurred.

There is one final type of internal check in common use which is somewhat unique in character. It is a check not so much on the meaning or validity of a *given reply* as it is on the *general trustworthiness* of the respondent. The most characteristic example of it is the *"confusion control"* in media research.[29] However, modifications for other types of surveys are easily invented. The item that is used to check on the trustworthiness of the respondent is an item so designed that a particular type of reply *by definition* must represent an invalid answer. The answer can be invalid either because of deception or because of legitimate confusion in the respondent's mind. However, in either case the competence of the respondent is rendered questionable. In media research such an item is constructed by asking whether the respondent has been exposed to some content which has never yet existed. Thus, he might be shown in the course of an interview a page from a magazine which will not reach the news stand for some months to come and asked if he had seen or read it. If his reply is "yes," he is rendered suspect. The same procedure can be employed for example in opinion polls where a person might be asked if he had heard or read about a series of international events one of which had never occurred; or he might be asked to indicate his familiarity with a series of public personages, one of whom is fictitious, or he can be asked whether he has an opinion about a fictitious piece of legislation, or if he has discussed it with friends in the last week.[30]

The problem posed for the analyst by such confusion controls or "sleeper" items, as they are sometimes called, is complex. He can be relatively conservative and discard all untrustworthy respondents before examining the survey. Or he can apply various kinds of manipulations to the data from different classes of respondents. The question that the analyst ponders, of course, is whether confusion or evasion as revealed by the sleeper item is a *general character trait*. Perhaps the confusion does not carry over to particular replies under study. On this problem, there is no final answer.

Sometimes checks are employed which constitute approximations to the "sleeper" item. In the instance of such items, a certain type of answer constitutes *proof* of untrustworthiness. However, there are other internal checks which raise *reasonable doubt* about the trustworthiness of given respondents. Such items are invented in specific inquiries by the analyst reflecting

29. For a general treatment, see D. B. Lucas, "A Rigid Technique for Measuring the Impression Values of Specific Magazine Advertisements," *J. Appl. Psych.*, 24, 1940, 778.

30. When the sleeper item involves an attitude or opinion question, it no longer functions as a test of accuracy. Instead it is indicative of the fact that attitudes constitute generalized patterns and are not the product of actual specific experience with any real entity. For an example of the ingenious use of sleeper items of this type, see E. L. Hartley, *Problems of Prejudice* (New York: Kings Crown Press, 1946).

on *the conditions which would be likely to lead to untrustworthiness, and then constructing questions in which the respondent reports on the presence of such conditions.* We label such internal checks *approximate* for the analyst may be fallible in his analysis of what conditions will lead to response errors. The most simple and defensible example of such an approximate check occurs in survey inquiries about the *past.* The analyst can make the reasonable assumption that the more remote the experience is from a given respondent, the less is his memory to be trusted. Consequently, respondents would be classified into sub-groups varying in remoteness from the event on the basis of some item in the questionnaire, and their responses would be given differential weight in the conclusions. Terman in his critique of one of our case studies, the *Kinsey Report,* remarks on the absence of such an internal check. He notes that Kinsey:

> gives the same weight to reports based upon remote recall as he gives to reports of current activities. In the computation of mean frequency of masturbation at age 15, for example, the memory report of a 50 year-old counts as heavily as the report of a 15 year-old. . . . It would have been helpful if he had shown in the tables what proportion of the N at any given age level was accounted for by subjects at or near that age . . . for all we know . . . the data for the lower ages in the tables may all be based on the memory reports of older subjects, many of them 20, 30, or 40 years older.[31]

A variety of checks of this type can be constructed. In surveys, where the respondents act as *informants* on some feature of the environment rather than as reporters of their own feelings, the analyst can invent an approximate check based on the assumption that *those with greater access to or ability to discriminate that part of the environment can make more reliable reports.* Thus, those who have been there longer, or are in a more central place within the environment are probably more to be trusted. An example of this type of check on trustworthiness can be cited from the Bombing Survey on German Morale. For reasons to be elaborated shortly, in addition to the sample of Germans who were studied, samples of French, Italian and Russian displaced persons were interviewed. In addition to questions on their own reactions to raids, they answered in the role of informants on the general reactions to bombing they observed among the Germans. But as the analysts point out,

> Some of the respondents were in a better position to report on certain specific questions than others. This fact must be remembered throughout this analysis and on *a priori* grounds more weight given to some respondents than to others. Thus, for example, it is reasonable to expect that the French would be in a better position to report on the radio-listening habits of the Germans, or the personal reaction of the Germans to the evacuation of members of their families, etc., than would either the Italians or the Rus-

---

31. *Op. cit.,* p. 446, reprinted by permission of the American Psychological Association.

sians, because the French were more accepted by the Germans as fellow-creatures than were either the Russians or the Italians. Similarly, the French probably were in a better position to report on the distribution of Allied leaflets addressed to foreign workers, because they could more easily distinguish between a leaflet written in French and in German than could the Russians, to whom both types of leaflets would appear pretty much the same, a Latin-script tongue. Again the more educated and literate person was probably in a better position to report on such subjects as the operations of the "black market" than the less educated worker. Throughout the analysis an attempt will be made to call attention to this differential validity.[32]

2. External Checks

The one limitation of *all* the checks presented thus far is that the check data and the datum under scrutiny are not collected independently. Findings of consistency may only involve a pseudo-validity due to all the constant elements in the situation applicable to both the check and the original data. True, certain internal checks are less vulnerable by such criticism, but the possibility is always present. For reasons of historical accident, survey research, especially the opinion poll variety, has tended to regard its domain as limited to the opinions of the respondent. Consequently, only data of one type have been employed, namely verbal responses of the respondents. This has prevented the growth of external checks. But as Katz points out, in actuality, "the survey method while utilizing the verbal responses of the subject often seeks to obtain data from all available sources. Field workers are not only interviewers. They may be asked to make behavioral observations, to give ratings or evaluations of the respondent's attitudes and personality, or to check available records for objective data." [33] Consequently, external checks can and should be employed by the analyst. There are a variety of these varying in their appropriateness to given response error problems and also varying in their ease of application.

The most obvious external check and one that is simple and exceedingly valuable is the *comparison of the datum under study with findings on the same or related problems collected by other agencies or individuals,* on equivalent samples of the same population. One of our case studies, the inquiry into the atomic bomb, provides an excellent illustration of the systematic use of this external check on the quality of the findings. It will be recalled that this inquiry involved parallel surveys on the same problem

---

32. U. S. Strategic Bombing Survey, Vol. II, *op. cit.*, pp. 17-18. In this same chapter a variety of other internal checks are employed as indicators of the relative validity of the replies of the three national groups. By way of showing the complexity of interpretation of certain of these checks the student is referred to Ansbacher's critique of the chapter, in which it is argued that the interpretation of Russian replies as less valid is not warranted and represented a personal bias on the part of the original analysts. See, H. Ansbacher, "The Problem of Interpreting Attitude Survey Data," *Publ. Opin. Quart.,* 1950, pp. 126-138.

33. D. Katz, Survey Techniques, *op. cit.*, p. 64.

conducted by two different research organizations. These respective surveys used different methods of sampling and questioning and were analyzed by different analysts. Thus the "poll-type inquiry" was conducted by the American Institute of Public Opinion and was analyzed by Richard Crutchfield. The intensive survey was conducted by the Survey Research Center of the University of Michigan and was analyzed by A. A. Campbell, S. Eberhart and P. Woodward. In other words, external checks were not employed after the fact by comparing the findings of the inquiry with incidental available data collected by other agencies. The comparison with the work of independent agencies was insured by commissioning two parallel studies using different approaches. Any findings characteristic of both inquiries could therefore not be regarded as limited by the method of sampling, mode of questioning or bias of the particular analyst. Admittedly, very few analysts are in a position to afford the luxury of studying a problem twice. However, this inquiry also illustrates effective use of data that were accidentally available from the past work of other survey agencies. Insofar as there was agreement, the analysts could conclude that their findings were not an artifact of the specific procedures employed in the new inquiry. Insofar as there was disagreement the analysts could qualify the conclusions or clarify the implications of the respective findings. We cite some illustrations of the way in which data from other agencies were used.[34]

Thus in reporting on findings on public awareness of the atomic bomb, the analysts are able to argue that their conclusions are not limited by the specific procedures they employed. They cite an independent and confirmatory study by the Iowa Poll. (p. 20)

With respect to a finding on American opinion that the secret of the atomic bomb should be kept by the U.S., the analysts raise the question of whether the replies only refer to the question posed in a relatively biased light. The analysts check this by independent data on the problem, involving different modes of questioning, collected by the Iowa Poll and the National Opinion Research Center. (pp. 32-33)

With respect to findings on support for American participation in a world organization, the analysts compare their findings with those obtained by Roper, the Gallup Poll, and the National Opinion Research Center and thereby realize that the findings are "heavily dependent on how the questions are phrased." (p. 41)

With respect to findings on attitudes towards cooperation with other nations, the meaning of the findings is illuminated by comparison with findings from Gallup, and from another inquiry by the Survey Research Center. The analysts are able to conclude that the attitudes expressed are indicative of a highly generalized attitude. (p. 51)

---

34. All quotations are from Cottrell and Eberhart, *op. cit.*

A second type of external check, already indicated in the comments by Katz, involves the use of *interviewers' reports on the survey or ratings of the respondents and of specific replies*. The replies of all respondents are evaluated in the light of the interviewers' systematic reports that a question was difficult to understand, led to evasion, was uninteresting, etc.[35] Specific respondents are evaluated in the light of ratings of their honesty, the circumstances attendant on the specific interview, and by reference to marginal comments the interviewers are instructed to make.

Both of the external checks described thus far can be routinely applied in any survey with negligible expense. The remaining three types of checks to be presented are limited in their application by factors of considerable expense or their inappropriateness to a wide range of surveys. The first of these limited in its application to one specific problem is the *use of split ballots*. Where the analyst is concerned to evaluate the effect on the replies of the specific wordings of the questions used, or the specific order in which questions are put, the total sample will be split into two equivalent groups and each will be interviewed with a different type of instrument. Comparison of the split ballot results indicates the degree to which the findings are an artifact of the specific procedure used or are relatively general and independent of the mode of questioning.[36]

The second type of such external check is exceedingly rare in social research. It is very expensive and only occurs for a very narrow range of phenomena. It involves the *collection of data from a second respondent to check on the quality or meaning of the report of the first respondent, under conditions where there is some complementarity between the two respondents*. The example to follow will convey the logic more clearly, but the procedure is to be distinguished from the use of a second person as *informant* or rater of the original respondent. Here, the second person reports about *himself*. One of our case studies, the *Kinsey Report*, provides an example of this method. In a sub-sample of married couples, both husband and wife were interviewed with respect to their sexual behavior. Presumably the interviews were conducted independently. Since the reports of both partners about their sexual experiences *in marriage* had to coincide, any discrepancies were an indication of invalidity in the data.[37]

---

35. For a systematic discussion of the use of interviewer report forms, see P. B. Sheatsley, "Some Uses of Interviewer Report Forms," *Publ. Opin. Quart.*, 1947, 11, 601-611.

36. For a discussion of the use of this check, see Lazarsfeld and Kendall, Survey Analysis, *op. cit.*, pp. 176-179.

37. It is interesting that the same type of external check has been employed to test the validity of macroscopic data in economics. Just as the report of sexual relations of a husband must find its parallel in the report by the wife, so, Morgenstern notes that the validity of data on international monetary transactions requires that the sale by one country and aggregate sales by all countries must find a balance in the purchase by one country or all countries in the aggregate. By examining such complementary sets of figures, Morgenstern infers the presence of error in international economic data. See *On the Accuracy of Economic Observations* (Princeton: Princeton University Press, 1950). We can report one instance in the literature of an ingenious

The final type of external check is the *use of criterion data against which the survey data can be compared*. There is a variety of such criterion data, and the procedure can be employed in a number of different ways which we shall elaborate. The method appears to commend itself as the ideal check on response error. If the analyst wants to know whether his respondents get confused, falsified their reports, answered in terms other than intended, the procedure to check on them is to compare what they said with some gilt-edge data on the same phenomenon whose validity is established and accepted by everyone. What is more direct and obvious and acceptable as a check! Since the logic of the approach cannot be denied, it appears paradoxical at first that the method has been rarely employed in survey research, and the instances where it has been employed are very specialized in character.[38]

It is clear first of all that the method can be expensive since the criterion data that are desirable may not be readily available or may not even exist in collected form. Secondly, the method is not as perfect as it might seem. Criterion data are never infallible. Official records of election returns, purchases, past behavior, etc., can be somewhat in error, just as survey research can involve response error. Thirdly, it is clear that such direct criteria can only exist for *overt actions or objective entities* and not for intervening variables such as opinions, beliefs or attitudes which, by definition, are not behavioral. Where criterion data on behavior are used to check or validate opinion data, any discrepancy found may be difficult to interpret for the correlation properly to be expected is unknown.

Even where the survey deals directly with some behavioral or objective entity, the relationship of the phenomenon to the criterion in a *descriptive* survey is generally indeterminate and not easy to interpret. The criterion data rarely exist for the very phenomenon under study. More generally they bear on behavior that is similar in character. If they existed for the very entity under study, there would be no point in undertaking the de-

---

use of the complementarity check upon *psychological data* other than behavioral entities. Deutsch and Collins in a study of interracial housing projects obtained reports from *white* respondents as to their relations with Negro people within the same housing projects. In independent interviews with the *Negro* occupants, they were asked about their relations with white people in the projects. By definition, if the whites are reporting validly on the state of social relations within the project, there must be equivalent reports from the Negro respondents. The agreement of these reports was very satisfactory. However, if these replies are regarded as measures of psychological processes rather than as measures of objective events, it may well be that different reports from Negroes and Whites would constitute simply different frames of reference or scales of judgment for the evaluation of friendly relations rather than evidence of response errors. The larger question posed by this example is whether the complementarity check can ever be used *unambiguously* for surveys into *non-behavioral* entities. See M. Deutsch and M. Collins, *Interracial Housing* (Minneapolis: University of Minnesota Press, 1951), 79-80.

38. For a comprehensive summary of such validation procedures in past survey research, see, H. J. Parry and H. Crossley, "Validity of Responses to Survey Questions," *Publ. Opin. Quart.*, 14, 1950, 61-80.

scriptive survey.[39] These limitations account for the rarity of the procedure and the way in which it is generally applied.

The most common variety of this external check involves the comparison of the aggregate findings from the survey with some official record about the same entity for the *population* as a whole. To compare the response of *each individual* with a criterion on each individual is much more laborious. The records must be manipulated much more elaborately—the two sets of data must be keyed to each other. Moreover, criterion records generally do not exist in this fashion. Election returns are available for collectivities, and not for the individual voter. Total sales of a commodity may be known by a given distributor, but it is very unlikely that the company knows which people in the area purchased the product. The interpretation of checks against aggregate data should be very strict. The agreement in the aggregate can be perfect even though many individual respondents gave invalid replies, so long as invalidity operated in opposing directions in equal magnitude. Consequently, such an external check is not crucial evidence for *explanatory* surveys. The correct relations between variables can still be obscured by errors that might not operate on the aggregate results but would operate on sub-groups who are contrasted for study.

Occasionally, criterion data are available for each individual in a study. Such data permit a computation of the net error in the aggregate, valuable for a descriptive survey, and also the computation of error for any subgroups or individuals isolated for an explanatory study. Because of the laboriousness and expense of this procedure, the analyst might well make such a check only on a *sub-sample* of all the respondents. From the subsample check inferences could still be drawn for *all* the error problems that might apply to the total inquiry.

One of our case studies, the inquiry into absenteeism, illustrates the latter type of check against criterion data. Respondents were queried as to their past absences. Official plant records were also available and constituted a criterion against which the responses could be compared. The existence of these records on the very phenomenon under study, incidentally, did not obviate the necessity of the inquiry because only the survey could provide a test of the effect of certain determinants of absenteeism.[40]

There is one type of check on error which partakes of elements from the different checks we have thus far reported. It has some similarities to the internal check. Thus, it is difficult to classify. It is called a *"quality*

---

39. The point would not apply to the explanatory survey. Criterion records might exist in the aggregate on the very phenomenon to be studied and an explanatory survey might still be undertaken, because the determinants of the phenomenon are unknown and the distribution of the phenomenon in given sub-groups or individuals might not be revealed in the existing records.

40. *Op. cit.*, pp. 29-30. Various other checks on error are also reported here and illustrate some of the other methods we have described earlier.

check" and is best exemplified by work of the Bureau of the Census which employed it on a very large scale in the 1950 Census.[41] Such importance attaches to the results of a decennial census that a strong concern for error and the expenditure of considerable funds is warranted. Consequently, on a very large sample of the general population, a quality check was instituted in 1950. This sample had already been enumerated by the ordinary Census Enumerator and were then re-visited by interviewers who were of *superior* quality. An interview was conducted which was longer in duration than the original interview and which presumably involved more elaborate and detailed methods of questioning. The data from this quality check were then taken as a criterion of the correct results and comparison with the original enumeration data yielded an empirical estimate of the errors that attached to the findings of the Census. The procedure is straightforward although expensive for routine survey research. It provides a minimum estimate of the error because the re-interview data may also be in error either because the enumeration procedure is not perfect or because the respondent persists in the original error. The reader will see that this method has some of the features of an internal check involving repeat reliability procedures, although it differs in that the re-interview is not like the original one.

We have described the major types of internal and external checks on response error at considerable length. There are many specific variations within these general types, and the imaginative analyst can improvise new checks of his own as the survey requires it. Each of these checks has some limitations, but each at least brings the analyst closer to accurate conclusions, and the combination of checks is likely to be a very effective guide. The analyst's decision as to how elaborately he should treat the problem of response error is dependent on his resources; on the degree of importance that may attach to the findings and the seriousness of the consequences if his conclusions are misleading; and on some assumption as to the vulnerability of the inquiry to response errors. We can illustrate this operating context and the decision to deal with response error in a comprehensive fashion from one of our case studies, the Bombing Survey on German Morale.

The German Bombing Survey—A Case Study in the Treatment of Response Error: First, let us examine the practical context. The analysts in this inquiry had lavish resources available to them so that no practical limitations other than urgency affected their plans. Moreover, in an applied sense, great importance attached to the inquiry and mistaken conclusions could lead to exceedingly serious consequences. The results of the German Bombing Survey were presumably to guide military strategy with respect

---

41. See, for example, P. M. Hauser, "Some Aspects of Methodological Research in the 1950 Census," *Publ. Opin. Quart.*, 14, 1950, 5-13.

to the war with Japan and longer term strategy in the military establishment.

At a theoretical level, the analysts felt that the problem was of such a character that response errors were of unknown magnitude but potentially large in magnitude and that no prior empirical basis existed for dealing with the problem. For example, since the inquiry had to be conducted after the cessation of hostilities and yet dealt with the effects of bombing raids which had occurred several years before, the likelihood of vagueness of memory was considerable. Or possibly the traumatic effect of such raids originally was such as to cause distortions in memory. But, in addition there were all sorts of other grounds for the assumption that distortion in the reports was likely to occur. The German respondents would be speaking to representatives of the American Army and might either be hostile or wish to curry favor with the victorious power. In either case, deception in reporting might occur. There was speculation that the societal background of totalitarianism was not conducive to the individual feeling free and easy in an interview and reporting his genuine opinions, even when these dealt with innocuous subjects.

None of these speculations could be ignored, for there was no past experience on which the analyst could predicate a judgment. Consequently, a whole series of checks were instituted, some of which have already been mentioned in passing. The limitations of a given check were compensated for by other checks. The cumulative evidence from all these checks permitted great confidence in the data. It is significant in this connection that the parallel Japanese inquiry—involving the same possible sources of error —did not incorporate many checks on response error. By then the analysts had the prior experience of the German Survey and the empirical data from the checks therein instituted; so that some of the speculations could be rejected.

The series of major checks used and their specific functions is outlined herewith: [42]

EXTERNAL CHECKS

1. *Interviewer Ratings:*
   These constituted general checks on the trustworthiness of the interview, and in addition were employed in special instances to check on specific variables important in the conceptualization which appeared susceptible to falsification, e.g., Nazi identification.
2. *Criterion Data from Official Records:*
   Records of Nazi party membership and destruction and casualties follow-

---

42. For a treatment of these checks see, U. S. Bombing Survey, *op. cit.;* H. Peak, *op. cit.;* and D. Katz, Survey Techniques in the Evaluation of Morale, in J. G. Miller, *Experiments in Social Process* (New York: McGraw-Hill, 1950).

ing bombing were available. Projections from the interview data were compared with these official records to provide an *aggregate* check on these specific variables. By extension, the validity of other characteristics not subject to such criterion checks was supported on the ground that admission of Nazi party membership was probably a response more dangerous in its consequences than most other responses. Therefore this check gave a *maximum* picture of error in the aggregate.

3. *Use of Other Samples as Informants:*

The replies of the German sample were compared with the information given by the *displaced persons* who presumably did not have the same motives of hostility and consequent error in their reports.

Interrogations of a small sample of local officials as to the consequences of bombing in their cities were compared with the findings from the cross-section.

4. *Split Ballot Procedures:*

Two different interview schedules were used on equivalent samples. One involved a fairly *direct* approach in which the respondent reconstructed his experiences under the reactions to bombing. The other schedule never raised the issue of the study directly. A series of opinion and attitude questions were asked and the impact of bombing on morale was ascertained indirectly by correlating the results with official records of the magnitude of bombing of the respondent's place of residence. In the indirect approach, the assumption seemed reasonable that any errors in report of morale due to retrospection or duplicity would be distributed equally among the residents of the cities that were contrasted as to bombing exposure. The measurement of the independent variable, bombing, was, by definition, accurate. Consequently the relationships demonstrated should have been accurate. In addition, the more covert approach could be used to check on the overt approach, and general problems of indeterminacy due to question formulation could be checked.

5. *Comparison with Earlier Survey Data:*

Two pilot studies were conducted in two occupied German Cities prior to the armistice. While these involved the same personnel and procedures, they constituted a quasi-external check in that these procedures were not subject to the conditions characterizing the major survey. Retrospection was not as remote in time and the German respondents were not in the situation of being officially defeated as a nation and occupied.

6. *Captured Mail Check:*

Since *all* the interview data were retrospective and subject to possible errors of memory, the findings from the survey were compared with findings on the same problem as revealed by letters written at the very moments of bombing.

INTERNAL CHECKS

1. *Dependent Variables Arrayed for Given Factual Categories:*
   By way of illustration, Nazi identification as revealed in the interview data for different religious groups was compared with the hypothetical array to be expected, e.g., Catholics would be less identified.
2. *Consistency Checks through Elaboration of Initial Answers:*
   The general method of questionnaire construction and interviewing involved the use of open-ended questions and supplementary probes. Consequently, the elaboration of the replies provided a context for interpreting the data.

These eight major types of checks provided an elaborate basis for the analysts to estimate the existence of response errors. However, as the reader will have noted on the basis of earlier discussion, the treatment of error creates a kind of spiralling analytic process. Some of the check data may themselves be suspect, and before they can constitute a standard their limitations must be investigated. Thus, we described earlier the fact that the letters might have been subject to distortion through self-censorship. This possible response error had to be evaluated before the letters in turn could constitute a check on memory error in the interviews. Similarly, the data from displaced persons acting as informants had to be weighed in the light of limitations on their opportunity and ability to observe, before such information could constitute a standard for the German interview data. The interviewers might have been fallible in their appraisals of the respondents. Consequently, their field ratings were first compared with new ratings made by the analysts themselves on the basis of careful over-all reading of the interviews.

We have completed the discussion of specific techniques the analyst can employ in treating response errors and errors in other phases of the survey process. When the analyst has employed these techniques and evaluated the substantive conclusions obtained from the prior analytic procedures, he has completed all the steps of the analysis of the descriptive survey.

However, there is one complexity attendant on the treatment of error which we have not yet noted. It should be clear that there is a *system of component errors* which affect the conclusions. There are, for example, a variety of response errors operating and not just one such error. In addition, there are component errors introduced by the sampling, interviewing, coding, and tabulation. All of these converge to affect the conclusions. If these errors were simply *independent and additive,* our earlier discussion would be adequate. The analyst on the basis of the specific procedures for treatment of error would assess his conclusions. However, these errors may in given instances not be additive, but may oppose each other or distribute themselves in such a way that it is difficult for the analyst to assess their total impact on his conclusions. Sometimes, the analyst may depreciate his data more than is necessary, for there are occasions where the *net* effect of a series of errors in such that the findings are unimpaired. There are even occasions where this accidental possibility is deliberately converted into an asset. Such is the case where the analyst deliberately uses a biased method of questioning to compensate for the tendency of respondents to conceal behavior in their replies. Two of our case studies, the *Authoritarian Personality* and the *Kinsey Report* employed just such a method of questioning for the reduction of error. However it should be pointed out that the assumption that such sets of errors balance generally remains a speculation, and where there is such a balancing process, the balance can be quite precarious and unstable.[43] On the other hand, there are instances where a series of component errors, each small in magnitude and unimportant in itself, so accumulate as to create serious error in the net results. Such, for example, is the interpretation put upon the procedures used in the *Authoritarian Personality* by two critics.[44] Here the sampling, coding, and interviewing all appear to have conspired to give a spurious support to the original theory. We can provide no simple solution to this problem for the analyst, and merely present this problem so that he will be as alert as he can in each particular survey to the examination of all the component errors and their combined effects.

---

43. For an example of such a system of errors which balanced so as to yield no *net* error in one set of surveys, but did not in a later set of surveys, the reader is referred to national election predictions. Roper's inquiries up to 1948 involved a balancing of errors due to an oversampling of Southern respondents operating in an opposing direction to an oversampling of the educated segments in the country at large. See, Mosteller, *et al.*, *op. cit.*, for a detailed treatment.

44. H. Hyman and P. B. Sheatsley, *op. cit.*

The Transfer of Training

Wᴇ ʜᴀᴠᴇ ɴᴏᴡ completed our discussion of the analyst's functions in the descriptive survey, and we shall turn in Part III to the special analytic features of the explanatory survey. But the lessons of Part II should be retained. The training in descriptive survey analysis must be transferred to the new context. Only as the analyst employs the knowledge and skill he has gained in descriptive surveys will he achieve effective explanatory analyses.

In earlier chapters we argued and documented the relevance and great value of descriptive survey analysis for ultimate success in analyzing explanatory surveys. For example, we pointed out the way in which thorough descriptive data on the phenomenon can be a guide to fruitful theory as to its explanation. Obviously, one can execute properly all the procedures for testing hypothesized explanations of a phenomenon and *never* achieve any confirmation if the hypothesis were chosen unwisely. We also pointed out the complexities in the stage of defining, conceptualizing, and locating a phenomenon that precedes the descriptive survey. Obviously, all explanations are limited by the way in which the thing to be explained, the phenomenon is treated. In addition, errors were shown to arise in translating the original conceptualization into the operations which yield the actual data that are manipulated by the analyst. Any explanation derived through the demonstration of a relationship between variables is obviously vulnerable to the errors in the original measurements of each of the variables. Unless the essential skills from descriptive survey analysis are incorporated into any explanatory survey analysis, the new procedures to be described below will not be sufficient for the analyst's needs.

There is always the danger in the exclusive concentration on the difficult and *specialized* problems of the explanatory survey that the analyst neglects the preliminary, more simple problems. And yet such problems may well obscure or invalidate his explanation. Thus it is as one reads explanatory surveys that are most sophisticated analytically that one often notes a lessened attention to the more simple problems. The analyst funnels all his energies and concerns into one area like a military strategist allocating limited resources. But he then runs the risk of leaving himself weak at another point. We refer again to one of our case studies of an explanatory survey, *The Authoritarian Personality*, as an illustration because a detailed critique is available.[45] We are not concerned here with the validity of the particular criticisms, but merely with showing that the critics mainly rest their argument not on the *intrinsic* aspects of the explanatory analysis but rather on the very problems which would be present even in a *descriptive* survey analysis. A rudimentary content analysis of the critique will make the point. Paradoxically, out of 85 pages of detailed criticism, some 51 pages are devoted to stages of the research which will *not* be discussed in the next Part. The detailed count is as follows:

Chart IV

A Content Analysis of a Critique of the Authoritarian Personality—An Illustration of the Centrality of Descriptive Survey Analysis for Explanatory Surveys

Pages

Discussion of the *sampling* features of the inquiry. Hyman and Sheatsley speculate and present evidence that the particular population chosen and the method of sampling may affect the explanatory findings 20

Discussion of the nature of the *instruments* used to measure the variables under examination. The critics speculate and present evidence that the relationships may in part be artifactual 12

Discussion of *collection and processing* of data where again it is argued that some of the explanatory findings may be artifactual 12

Brief discussion of problems of *response error* due to method of retrospective reporting. The critics argue that the conclusions are not qualified sufficiently in the light of this source of error 3

Brief discussion of method employed for constructing a *typology of cases* from the data on a number of dependent variables. The critics argue that the findings may be specific to the specific typology used 2

---

45. Hyman and Sheatsley, *op. cit.*

To convey to the student the way in which these specific problems—apparently unrelated to problems of explanatory analysis—combine to affect the explanatory findings, we quote from the summary in the original critique: [46]

> The mistakes and limitations—no one of them perhaps crucial—uniformly operate *in favor* of the authors' assumptions, and cumulatively they build up a confirmation of the theory which, upon examination, proves to be spurious. Even in their choice of past research for reference purposes, they have largely ignored contrary findings or hypotheses. Their theory itself may yet be correct and provable, but the methodological weaknesses of the present study prevent its demonstration on the basis of these data.

But the reader may feel that the example cited is a rare one. Again, we can illustrate the same problem by reference to another one of our case studies of an explanatory survey, the *Psychology of Social Classes,* and the comments of one critic. Angell in his review of this work devotes his main attention to the problem of *conceptualization* of the variables which enter into the ultimate empirical test. He remarks:

> Of the three main variables dealt with, two seem to be appropriate and to have been measured adequately. . . . It is class identification as Centers employs it that, to a sociologist, seems inadequate as a principal variable. . . . Surely the term "class consciousness" refers to a consciousness of something external to the mind! But for Centers it does not. The mental patient who thinks himself Mr. Rockefeller is an upper-class person . . . Centers' analysis has omitted completely the rating given by others to a person. This is the essence of social class to most sociologists. The class identification which the person himself makes is a reflection, more or less accurate, of this external rating. It is awareness of being a part of such an externally classified category of persons that constitutes class consciousness.
> Now, Centers had no means of determining how others rated an individual. But he could at least have recognized that such a rating is the heart of social class and that the person's own identification is a derivative of it. Then class identification could have been used operationally as a rough index of class position. That he himself vaguely sensed that something was wrong is evidenced by the fact that he slips over from the phrase "class identification" to the phrase "class affiliation" about halfway through the book. The latter is the important datum, but is one on which he has no information. This book, then, is an object lesson in the pitfalls of approaching matters

---

46. *Ibid.*, p. 121.

of social structure from the point of view of the individual alone. One simply cannot obtain all the crucial data that way.[47]

And Angell is joined by another sociologist. Vance in his review concentrates on the very same problem of conceptualization, and like Angell makes favorable remarks on procedure. But he notes that Centers':

> book is subtitled a Study of Class Consciousness and he does well to focus on that baffling phenomenon. But Centers' group is given no idea of how they are rated by others. The class consciousness they have is that of their own class identification. . . . Centers' criteria and the crux of his analysis are the self-identification of class position. . . . Certainly Centers' greatest need is to check his sample's self-identification with an objective rating like Warner's. . . . In this reviewer's mind he leaves untested and unproved the validity of his main thesis—that class position can be self-defined.[48]

Similarly, Bower in what is generally a favorable review remarks:

> In the statement of the theory, the author burdens himself with the added task of proving that class affiliation really means class consciousness in the sense of feelings of group belongingness and common purpose. In establishing this he is less successful. . . . We can forgive Centers for an overinterpretation in regard to class consciousness . . . and for his intolerance of any but a "subjective" definition of class, for there is enough in this book to justify a general ebullience.[49]

Our purpose in presenting these comments is not to take sides. There is no need to answer the question posed by these critics. Other critics might well prefer to side with Centers in his definition and conceptualization of class. Apart from the answer given, the *question* points to the fact that the central problem of the explanatory survey may often reside not in the special technical analytic procedures that are employed, but rather in realms already treated for descriptive surveys, for example, conceptualization.

One basic point is implicit in both of these examples of explanatory surveys. While the explanation obtained in *The Authoritarian Personality* is jeopardized by problems of procedure and the findings of *The Psychology of Social Classes* by problems of conceptualization, both inquiries are questioned in the light of problems common to descriptive survey analysis. These problems have been treated in detail in the previous chapters. Thus, whatever training may have been gained already must now be transferred by the student to the new context of explanatory survey analysis.

---

47. R. C. Angell, Review of the Psychology of Social Classes, *Amer. J. Sociol.*, 55, 1949–50, pp. 208-210. Reprinted by permission of the publishers.
48. R. Vance, Review of the Psychology of Social Classes, *Soc. Forces*, 28, 1949–50, p. 333. Reprinted by permission of the publishers.
49. R. Bower, Review of the Psychology of Social Classes, *Publ. Opin. Quart.*, 1949, 13, 338-340. Reprinted by permission of the publishers.

Part III

EXPLANATORY SURVEYS AND
THE FUNCTIONS OF THE ANALYST

Introduction

IN CHAPTER II, we classified surveys into two major types, descriptive and explanatory. We now turn to the explanatory survey and the skills the analyst requires to function effectively. Earlier, we also noted that there are a number of different kinds of explanatory surveys. Correspondingly there will be variations in the specific analytic procedures employed or emphasized to which we shall allude later. However, all such surveys will have in common certain *core* procedures in which the analyst must be skilled. These procedures are intended to yield a solution to the general problem underlying *every* explanatory survey. *They should yield reliable evidence on the relationship of the phenomenon to one or more independent variables or causes, and thereby provide the solution to the analyst's general problem of finding an explanation.*

To *execute* the analytic procedures well is difficult but to *understand* them is even more difficult. To have the sense of when a particular procedure shall be applied—to draw the proper inference from the obtained result—to see the appropriate modifications for the particular survey—all these refinements of understanding must be studied. We shall treat the basic principles in detail in this part and attempt to provide skill and understanding through a variety of illustrations and exercises. First we shall treat *a series of problems* arising in the treatment of simple relationships between a phenomenon or *one* dependent variable and *one* independent variable or cause. The demonstration of such simple relationships between two variables is, of course, the basic unit of explanatory survey analysis, and while it may appear uncomplicated, there are special problems which the analyst must be able to solve.

In addition, the analyst must have *skill in the sheer technical operations* associated with the demonstration of such relationships. Such technical operations involve the use of *machine methods* for obtaining the actual empirical relationships in the data, and the subsequent *manipulation and evaluation of quantitative data* in tabular form. We shall not treat these skills in detail in the discussion to follow, but we shall present a series of exercises which will give the student practice and ultimately skill. Some of the machine operations involved have already been mentioned in the earlier discussion of "differentiated descriptions," since these operations are *identical mechanically* with those involved in the demonstration of simple relationships for purposes of explanation. The additional machine operations are treated in Problem Exercise IV, Appendix C, and the handling of quantitative data is treated in Practice Exercise I, Appendix D and Problem Exercise V, p. 327 and will be assigned to the student in due course.

CHAPTER V

Problems in Treating Simple Relationships Between Two Variables

Emergent Error Arising from Contamination

We have emphasized that a problem crucial to surveys of *all types* is the treatment and control of error. Errors arising in the stages of a survey *prior* to analysis, such as response errors, must ideally be controlled, for validity cannot be conferred on invalid data by any feat of analytic magic. So the analyst seeks the best possible measures of both his independent and dependent variables, and knows the various methods for achieving this ideal. The guides presented in previous chapters are appropriate to control of error in the explanatory survey. There is, however, an additional type of error, arising from the prior stages of the survey, which often can be ignored in descriptive surveys, but which must be taken into account in explanatory surveys. Moreover, we now confront "a most ingenious paradox." There even arise *peculiar* instances in which the *best possible and most valid* measurement of a particular single variable when treated in isolation, as in the descriptive survey, may lead to the *worst possible* consequences when that same variable is to be used in the demonstration of a relationship in an explanatory analysis. There, is, so-to-speak, an *emergent* error, which

179

takes on the status of "error" only as a consequence of the analytic process of demonstration of relationships.[1]

This potentiality for error arises from the occurrence of what we shall call *Contamination* in the pre-analytic stages of the survey. The term is chosen, because its general classical connotation of something *being rendered impure by contact or mixture* is quite revealing of the problem.

Contamination in the survey similarly involves a mixing or contact and consequent impurity. What occurs is that, either through accident or design, a *procedure* is introduced in some pre-analytic stage which leads the measurement recorded for one variable to be *dependent* on the measurement obtained on some other variable. A variety of procedures can lead to this occurrence and it is quite commonly the case in surveys that contamination is present. But we must emphasize that contamination does *not in and of itself* always produce error. As implied earlier, there are many instances where contamination is a legitimate procedure and leads to increased efficiency and even more valid measurement and description of a particular variable.[2] The error only emerges when such contamination distorts the *conclusions* that are to be drawn. And such distortion is especially the case in explanatory surveys for reasons which will soon be clear.[3]

In the explanatory survey, the analyst seeks to prove that some phenomenon is *truly* related to, or dependent upon, some other factor. He claims to prove this when he establishes such a relationship *empirically*. But if in the process of establishing such an empirical relationship the measurement of one of the variables has been made to be affected by the measurement of the other variable under study, the analyst has *no* way of knowing whether the relationship obtained is *genuine,* or simply an *artificial* creation of his measurement procedures. The one variable or rather measurement has contaminated the other, so that the relationship is not pure.

We shall now return for a moment to our paradox and resolve it. It is obvious that the more information one has about some variable the more valid is the measurement going to be. Thus, it is often the case that analysts will deliberately institute a variety of procedures by which auxiliary information on certain characteristics is used to illuminate some particular other feature of the respondents in the survey. Presumably, there is a gain in the validity of the *description of that feature*.[4] But the analysts cannot then re-

1. This discussion will again illustrate the dilemma posed generally in Chapter II that the simultaneous goals of description and explanation in one survey often create problems of conflict, for the procedures best suited to one goal may be undesirable in relation to the other goal.

2. There are occasional instances where contamination distorts the description of a phenomenon, but the problem is especially acute and pernicious in explanatory surveys.

3. See the remarks by Daniel Katz in his paper on "Survey Techniques in Evaluation of Morale," in Miller, *op. cit.,* p. 70.

4. For example, the student is referred to our earlier discussion in Chapter IV of internal checks on response error, where auxiliary data elsewhere in a questionnaire are used as a check on the validity of some other datum.

late the other characteristics to the particular feature as a basis for some conclusion about an hypothesized explanation. The relationship was pre-determined by the introduction of contamination. Both options—to contaminate or not to contaminate the measurements—are initially available, but the gain in possible validity by contamination is achieved at the price of losing the opportunity to determine the true relationship.

The problem will become clearer if we examine some of the procedures and conclusions in one of our major case studies, *The Authoritarian Personality*, in the light of the detailed criticisms by Hyman and Sheatsley.[5] In this survey the phenomenon of ideology was hypothesized to be determined by independent variables of a personality nature. Various procedures and measuring instruments were applied to a large number of respondents and positive relationships between these variables were demonstrated leading the analysts to conclude that their hypotheses were verified. Hyman and Sheatsley in examining these findings and the conclusions argue that the procedures were so designed that the measurements of the variables frequently were contaminated and that the empirical relationships therefore do not provide valid evidence as to the true nature of the relationships between these variables.

Thus, for example, one finding adduced in support of the hypothesis was a positive relationship between scores on a scale designed to measure the phenomenon of politico-economic orientation and scores on a scale designed to measure personality trends of a "fascist" nature. Hyman and Sheatsley question the relevance of the finding to the conclusion on grounds that contamination was introduced in the procedures of scale construction.

> It would seem that a major finding . . . the demonstration of a syndrome of attitudes of political conservatism and authoritarianism, as revealed by the formal statistics of a correlation between the numerical scores—could instead reflect the mere fact that the PEC scale and the F scale both contain questions which are basically similar in content. . . . Indeed no less than eight of the sixteen items in the initial PEC scale suggest to us a closer relation to the dimension of fundamental values tapped in the F scale than to what is normally conceived of as the politico-economic dimension . . . The authors take early note of this difficulty and even move some of the items from one scale to another because of their contents, but when they later demonstrate a positive correlation between authoritarian personality trends and politico-economic conservatism, there is no hint of the possibility that the relationship may be a *spurious* one owing to the overlapping content of the scales . . . Many of the items seem almost interchangeable on the two scales, and it is therefore not surprising that a correlation is found (pp. 73-74).[6]

---

5. *Op. cit.*

6. *Op. cit.*, italics ours. Later in our text we restrict the term "spurious" to a very special meaning other than the one implicit in this quotation. Here, of course, the term is used in its general sense of *falsity*.

Here contamination arises out of procedures of instrument construction in which the contents of the instruments are not independent of one another, and the consequent empirical relationship and conclusion therefrom may be distorted. Hyman and Sheatsley suggest that contamination may have occurred elsewhere in the study, through interviewer bias with serious consequences for the general conclusions. In the original work, two groups of respondents extremely contrasted in ideology, on their *questionnaires*, were found to differ in their personality, as revealed by *interview* data, in a direction consonant with the hypotheses. Hyman and Sheatsley note that:

> In each case the interview was preceded by the study, on the part of the interviewer, of the information gathered previously, especially a detailed study of the questionnaire responses." . . . It cannot be gainsaid that the interview achieves greater focus and penetration when it follows the leads of the questionnaire. . . . But one cannot achieve these advantages and simultaneously point to the resultant responses for purposes of validation. There is abundant evidence, even from surveys in which the freedom of the interviewer is deliberately and maximally restricted that . . . interviewers are inevitably guided . . . by whatever clues they may have as to the natural or expected response. Especially, in this case, in which the interviewers were deliberately urged to use the prior scale scores as leads . . . one would naturally expect a high motivation on their part to make the interview data conform to what they already knew about the respondent on the basis of his questionnaires. . . . There is no evidence whatever in the text of the volume to support the authors' implicit assumption that the interviewers' awareness did not systematically enhance the correlations in the direction of proving the original hypothesis (pp. 77-81).

Elsewhere, Hyman and Sheatsley argue that still another relationship established, that between prejudice, as revealed by scores on one scale, and personality, as revealed by the F or "Fascist" scale, is not good evidence because of a contamination in the measurements arising from a certain feature of the construction of the F scale. They also note that the interview was coded in an *over-all fashion,* with the entire interview being read by the coder before deciding on specific codes. They suggest that this might have well have produced contamination in the measurements of pairs of variables treated within the interview and possibly also have contaminated the relations between ideology and personality. We shall not discuss these examples any further since the general problem should be clear.[7] Contamination in measurements, arising from a wide variety of pre-analytic procedures such as the method of instrument construction, method of interviewing, or coding, becomes a dangerous source of emergent error when the conclusions refer to the variables which have been contaminated.

Another one of our major cases, Centers' *Psychology of Social Classes,*

---

7. The reader is referred to pp. 74-76, 85-86 of the critique for the detailed discussions.

illustrates the possibility of contamination which may distort a rather different type of conclusion and one which is periodically drawn in explanatory surveys. In the examples used thus far, contamination in the measurement of *dependent and independent* variable may distort the conclusions as to some relationship. Now, it is quite frequent in surveys for analysts to *replicate* the test of some relationship, by using several different measures of an independent variable. Each of these measures, in turn, is related to the phenomenon under study, and agreement in the findings on these separate tests is used often by the analyst as stronger confirmation of his hypothesis than one test alone. Such an analytic procedure is highly desirable. If properly conducted, it precludes the possibility that the finding is an accident of some peculiarity in the procedure underlying the particular relationship. However, insofar as the different measurements of the one independent variable are contaminated, the additional tests can hardly be regarded as contributing any massive additional confirmation to the finding. One single test has so-to-speak been given double weight. While this type of contamination has hardly been a basis for complete distortion of certain of Centers' conclusions, it does weaken one of his assertions about the relation between ideology or class consciousness and the independent variable of stratification. Thus, early in the work, Centers describes three different measures of stratification that will be employed, an index of the hierarchical position of the occupation, an index of the dominance-subordination aspect of the occupation, and an interviewers' rating of the respondent's standard of living. He makes explicit the fact that these three different indices are "not entirely independent" since the rating by the interviewer is based on observation and therefore implicitly on occupational and other economic information.[8] Thus, even though the three indices may refer *conceptually* to different aspects of that complex, *operationally,* the actual measurements of occupation may well contaminate the rating of standard of living. Thus, it seems an overstatement when Centers in a later chapter neglects this consideration, and uses the agreement between the two tests of the relationship between ideology and stratification, as based on these respective indices, as additional confirmation. "If one *doubts* that these . . . relationships are general manifestations of socio-economic stratification, then scrutiny of the relationships to other stratification indices *will be certain to reassure him,* for there . . . the same patterns of relationship are manifested as those shown between these variables (ideology) and occupation."[9]

The reader should by now be sufficiently cautioned about the dangers of contamination arising in many stages of the survey. Therefore, let us turn to the next major problem affecting the treatment of simple relationships.

---

8. *Op. cit.,* Chap. III.
9. *Ibid.,* p. 109, italics ours.

The Use of Many Refined Values of the Independent Variable in Establishing a Relationship

As indicated, the analyst seeks the explanation of a phenomenon in its relationship to one or more independent variables. Depending on the outcome of such analyses some inference is drawn as to causation. In making such inferences, the analyst must be confident that a variety of problems have been resolved. Thus, he must concern himself with errors in measurement, with contamination leading to pseudo-findings, with problems of the time sequence implicit in the obtained relationship. Only as these problems are resolved can he be confident about his conclusions. But there is another problem which must be treated if the analyst is to make proper inferences as to the explanation of the phenomenon.

Let us insinuate ourselves into the middle of the analysis of one of our major case studies, the Bombing Survey of Germany, recasting the actual historical process for purposes of presentation, where we shall find a dramatic example of the new difficulty. The analysts sought to test the effect of the independent variables of strategic bombing on the phenomenon of morale. Various measures of component aspects of morale were obtained and these were related to the magnitude of bombing of the place of residence of the respondents. We shall examine certain *partial* findings, which *according to all the principles* thus far advanced appear to constitute a legitimate explanatory analysis. Individuals living in communities which had histories of moderate bombing, as indicated by an average total tonnage of *6000 tons* of bombs dropped were compared with individuals who had been exposed to very heavy bombing, approximately *30,000 tons* of bombs dropped. Selected results on only a number of the indices of morale as a mode of explaining the effects of bombing are presented below.[10]

TABLE V—*Selected Findings from the United States Strategic Bombing Survey of Germany Bearing on the Relationship Between Morale and Exposure to Bombing*

Percent of each group exhibiting following indices of morale	Moderate Bombing (6000 tons)	Heavy Bombing (30,000 tons)
Expressing anxiety	12%	12%
Showing increased fear	36	33
Showing war weariness	62	62
Listening to Allied broadcasts	35	36
Change in opinion that Germany could win the war	47	47
Showing willingness to surrender	59	59
Belief that leaders had best interests of people at heart	44	48

10. *Op. cit.*, Vol. I, Chapter 3. The data are taken directly from the chart on p. 23, Vol. I.

Having protected these relationships from sources of response error, and the like, the analysts on the basis of such unequivocal findings might well have drawn the conclusion that losses in morale bear *no* relation to intensity of bombing, as measured by tonnage dropped. There appears to be no difficulty whatsoever in evaluating the above data in these terms. Yet there is one conclusion other than this negative one which the analysts might well entertain. They might feel that while the procedure employed to make the test of the hypothesis was impeccable technically, while the findings on the series of indices were unequivocal, that they had not manipulated the independent variable of bombing intensity properly. The logic implicit in any test of a relationship is obviously that some change will be produced as the magnitude of the independent variable is changed. Perhaps the change in exposure from 6000 tons to 30,000 tons, while it constitutes in *arithmetical* terms a big change, is *psychologically* not much of a change. If the analysts had compared individuals or groups who differed in their experience by a still *greater* amount, some change in morale would be reflected in the data. Pursuing this line of speculation, let us examine a third group of respondents who on the average had been exposed to only about *500 tons* of bombs. The data are presented below and the reader should juxtapose them against the previous table.[11]

Percent exhibiting following indices of morale	Light Bombing (500 tons)
Expressing anxiety	9%
Showing increased fear	18
Showing war weariness	48
Listening to Allied broadcasts	38
Change in opinion that Germany could win the war	45
Showing willingness to surrender	54
Belief that leaders had best interests of people at heart	52

Examining the changes across the three groups, the analysts observe some loss in morale as bombing intensity increases, but the differences are at best moderate and somewhat inconsistent. The analysts might well still conclude that bombing intensity has an unimportant effect on morale, but again, they might ponder the same logic as previously presented. Perhaps the change in the value of the independent variable from 500 tons to 30,000 tons is still not marked enough. Consequently, the analysts introduced a fourth group, contrasted with the others by being exposed to *zero bombing*. It then became evident that the unbombed were *quite different* in their morale, and that the three groups of "bombed respondents," while not differing much among *themselves,* showed, so-to-speak, considerable losses in their morale whether or not they had experienced light, or moderate, or heavy bombing, so long as they were exposed to bombing.

The lesson of the Morale analysis is clear. The examination of such a

---

11. The data are taken from the same original chart appearing on p. 23, Vol. I.

relationship ideally calls for the independent variable to be treated in terms of *many refined values*. Only then can the analyst resolve the *indeterminacy* in his findings, and decide whether negative findings are definitive or simply the artifact of the particular narrow contrasts accidentally employed in the comparisons of groups.

The reader may feel, however, that the case of the Bombing Survey is bizarre, and that the finding there reported is uncommon. If this is a rare instance, certainly the tedium of many cross-tabulations can be obviated, and the analyst might take the risk of merely comparing two adjacent groups, without fear that the contrast in values is too small to produce a change in the phenomenon. However, another one of our major cases exhibits the same feature, showing that the problem is certainly not unique to the Bombing Inquiry. In the Survey into American Opinion on the Atom Bomb, the reader will recall that one of the major explanatory variables used to account for opinions was the level of information about international affairs and atomic energy of the respondent. Seven refined groupings were made on the independent variable, ranging from extreme *low* information to extreme *high* information. Here again, if the reader examines the detailed cross-tabulations, he will observe that *often* the progression of changes in opinion as one moves from moderate information to extremely high level of information is *small*. Thus it would appear, if only these few groups had been contrasted in the analysis, that information has only small effect on expectation of war, on support of UN control of the atom bomb, on belief that the United States could work out an effective defense against the bomb, and on another issue having to do with the United States continuing its manufacture of the bombs.[12]

If, by happenstance, just as in the case of the Bombing Survey, the analysts had only compared adjacent groups they might well have concluded that information has little or no effect on opinions. However, the same problem of indeterminacy would have attended this conclusion. Perhaps, if greater contrasts in level of information had been examined, greater effects would have been observed making any previous negative conclusion false. And in actual fact when one examines the difference between extremely uninformed and extremely informed, the differences in opinion on the above issues become quite marked.

The reader may feel, however, that the *argument* advanced on the basis of these two examples is still not sound, and the analytic principle of comparing many refined groups is *not* required. Certainly, the reader might be ingenious and argue that all that is proven thus far is that the analysts should have contrasted *two extreme* groups, *unbombed* people with *bombed* people, ignoramuses with sophisticates. This would have simplified the

_____
12. The detailed tables are presented in Appendix B, Cottrell and Eberhart, *op. cit.*, pp. 105, 107, 113, 115.

amount of cross-tabulation and analysis and have yielded positive findings. Also the general use of many refined groups requires prior refinements in the initial instruments of measurement and such refinement may be impossible or excessively expensive. We shall soon examine this principle, the contrasting of *two extreme* groups and evaluate the relative merit of this approach vs. the use of many refined values as a *test* of an explanation. However, there is one immediate practical argument against it. From the point of view of a *programmatic or evaluative* inquiry, it makes quite a difference to establish that 500 tons of bombs produces almost the same results as 30,000 tons of bombs. A practical man is not only concerned with producing an effect and having evidence that his efforts are generally worthwhile, but also with knowing that goals can be achieved with a certain economy of effort. Thus, the use of the *intermediate* groups in the analysis, even if *not* required to demonstrate *a* relationship, establishes precisely the *nature* of the relationship, and permits more effective practical decisions.

But the use of two extreme groups may also be *positively misleading* as a principle. It *just so happens* that in the Bombing Survey the extreme groups differed while the intermediate groups approximated towards one extreme. However, this occurrence may be far from general. The changes in the phenomenon with variations in the value of an independent variable may take on all possible forms. If extreme contrasted groups were alike with respect to some phenomenon while the intermediate groups differed from *both* extremes, any conclusions by the analyst from the comparison of two extremes would be false. In such instances, he would draw the inference that the independent variable is not explanatory, when, in fact, it is. That this argument is not academic, and that curvilinear functions of this shape do occur is demonstrated by another of our cases. Thus, for example in the Industrial Absenteeism inquiry, the analysts sought one explanation of individual proneness to absence in the variable of *recency of employment,* initially hypothesizing that those who would be novel in industry would have difficulties in adjustment which might issue into absence. Fortunately, in demonstrating this relationship, they used *three* values of the independent variable, long term, short term, and intermediate length of employment. Let us, for the moment assume that only the *two* extreme groups had been used. The analysts might have then concluded that proneness to absence showed little relation to the independent variable of recency of employment for the percentage point difference between the extremes was only 6%. However, by having the intermediate group available, they then observed the peculiarity that those with moderate lengths of employment were *most* prone to absence, differing in proneness to absence from either extreme by a large amount; in one instance 19%.[13] Such curvilinear relationships, in

---

13. The table in question is reproduced on p. 328 of this text as part of a training exercise for the student.

which the extremes approximate to one another will force the analyst into erroneous negative conclusions when only two extreme groups are contrasted.

The Authoritarian Personality, one of our other major case studies, employed the analytic principle of comparisons between *two extreme* groups as a basis for drawing conclusions about the personality determinants of ideology. Hyman and Sheatsley in their critique of this inquiry suggest that the conclusions may well be indeterminate, and present some other illustrations of curvilinearity from the literature.

> Intensive investigation was made of eighty individuals who showed extreme scores on the ethnocentrism questionnaire. These eighty were drawn in approximately equal numbers from both extremes, and were used as contrasted groups to isolate the personality correlates of social attitudes. . . . Insofar as any generalizations drawn from the intensive study are limited to such extreme individuals, there is no problem. But insofar as inferences are drawn from these extreme cases about the dynamic processes underlying attitude formation *in general,* the question must be raised as to whether the sampling of extremes permits any inference as to the processes of similar but less extreme individuals. This question involves some assumption as to the linearity of the regression between any attitude measure and some specific other variable such as a personality trait. The writers raise this question explicitly, but do not resolve it. . . . Research studies have frequently revealed a curvilinear relation between social attitudes and various determinants of those attitudes, and a number of investigations have indicated that extreme individuals differ from others in the degree of organization of their sentiments and in the relation of such sentiments to personality factors. For example, Vetter, in a very early study of the personality correlates of social attitudes, compared groups arrayed along the reactionary-radical continuum on the basis of their questionnaire answers. The design is rather similar to the current study, except that Vetter also examined the intermediate groups, and he noted curvilinear functions on a number of variables. Thus, while radicals had an average income of $7,100 and reactionaries of $7,700, the "conservative" group, contrary to what one would expect on the assumption of linearity, had a mean income of $10,500. Similarly, the mean score on the Allport Ascendance-Submission scale for reactionary men was .2, for radicals 1.2—but for conservatives it was 9.3. On the Laird Personal Inventory, an index of introversion, reactionary men scored 16.1 and radicals 18.5, but conservatives scored only 14.8. In this instance a mere study of the extremes would have provided no adequate estimate of the middle group.[14]

It should be clear to the reader that for any or all of the reasons indicated, the use of many refined values of the independent variable in the demonstration of relationships is an analytic principle to be highly recom-

---

14. *Op. cit.,* pp. 65-66.

mended.[15] This, of course, poses prior problems of the refinement of the measuring instruments and increases the extent of machine processing, but the benefits far outweigh the disadvantages.

The Evaluation of a Relationship Through the Use of Norms from the Study of Other Determinants

In our discussion of the descriptive survey we referred to the inclusion of related phenomena. We noted that the analyst often engages in a rather strange procedure. He is concerned with a description of a *particular* phenomenon in some defined population, yet he often goes to the extra trouble to describe other parallel phenomena in the same population. The reader will recall, for example, the radio inquiry, in which the analysts not only described satisfaction with Radio as an institution, but also satisfaction with newspapers. Such data provided a standard of comparison—a norm—for the analyst to use in evaluating the meaning of the descriptive data on the phenomenon under study. Otherwise, there is great indeterminacy in appraising a descriptive finding as "large" or "small," "good" or "bad," "critical" or "satisfied."

In explanatory surveys we often note a similar procedure that, at first sight, appears strange. The analyst may be concerned with testing empirically the influence of a *particular* independent variable on some phenomenon. Yet he will often include in the plan of the study a series of *other* parallel determinants, in which he may have no intrinsic interest, and he will later establish empirically their influence on the phenomenon under study.[16] Again, this apparently incongruous procedure will be seen as a solution to the problem of *ambiguity* in evaluating explanatory survey findings. Just as the inclusion of related phenomena aids in the evaluation of descriptive data; so, too does the inclusion of related determinants aid in the evaluation of a relationship that has been demonstrated between a phenomenon and a particular determinant. By way of emphasizing the prob-

---

15. We have throughout this discussion talked of many refined *values,* as if the explanatory factors used were continuous measurable variables. Where the explanatory factors are *attributes,* the principle is nevertheless to be recommended, and the only modification involved is that the *classification* of such factors be on a refined basis.

16. We are not referring here to explanatory surveys of a programmatic type in which the analysis of a series of programmatic factors may permit the choice as to which one is most likely to produce some desired change or consequence. Even in the theoretically oriented survey the parallel determinants may well be included for a special purpose to be discussed. Nor are we referring to the procedure of playing-*off* findings derived from one theory against findings derived from another theory for polemic purposes which we discuss later. While the procedure appears the same, the purpose will be seen to be quite different. Here there is no intent to reject a theory.

lem, let us turn to a general criticism advanced by McNemar in his classic discussion of survey research.

> It should be recognized that the analysis of relationships via percentages is none too precise. Since practically all relationships so studied do and will show varying degrees of association, it would be far better to use, if possible, a measure which reflects the degree of correlation. That verbal description of percentage tables may be subjective and misleading is well illustrated by two examples culled from reports of a government polling agency. One relationship is described as 'intimate'; had the analyst or reporter realized that the underlying correlation was only .60, it is extremely doubtful whether that misleading term would have been employed. The phrase "closely related" is used to describe a relationship which is a mere .40 on the product moment scale, and this same phrase is applied to various degrees of relationship. At another place a percentage table which leads to a correlation of .12 is referred to as showing a relationship. It is of course, possible for such a correlation to be statistically significant if based on a sufficient number of cases, but its practical significance is nil. In regard to difficulties encountered in substituting verbal descriptions for more precise statements of correlation, it might be pointed out that statisticians have long stressed fallacies which are inherent in interpreting relationships from percentage tables.[17]

McNemar is emphasizing the very problem. When groups are contrasted with respect to some independent variable and the variations in the phenomenon are examined as a function of that variable, an empirical finding of some difference is observed. But shall the analyst call it a "large" difference, a "small" difference, and correspondingly shall he say that this is a "major" determinant, an "important" determinant, or what shall he call it? Obviously some standard must be applied by the analyst which is *external* to the finding itself. The finding can provide no guidance. That this problem is real is attested by the general verbal form into which most survey cross-tabulations are translated. Usually, the analyst remarks that a certain *large* proportion of Group A exhibit a particular attribute, but *only* a certain *small* proportion of Group B exhibit that attribute. By what standard does he apply the word "only"? Is the difference between groups, the demonstration of the influence of the independent variable, really a large one? True, the analyst can be neutral in his evaluation and remark that one group shows "more" or "less" of the phenomenon, or report the mere arithmetic fact of the size of the difference. But this merely leaves the evaluation implicit, or puts the burden on the reader or client.

   How shall the analyst solve this problem? McNemar provides one *formal* solution which implicitly involves a standard or norm for comparison. He suggests that the empirical data from the cross-tabulation be converted into a correlational term, and that zero or one, the maximum or minimum value

---

17. *Op. cit.*, p. 340. Reprinted by permission of The American Psychological Association.

the correlation coefficient can take theoretically, be used by the analyst as the standard in deciding whether the obtained relationship is large or small. True it is that this provides some solution for *crude* instances of the problem and is of some help. One is not likely to call a correlation coefficient of .2 large or one of .9 small, but the skilled analyst would be unlikely to make *wild* judgments even from the raw difference in percent which also has the implicit formal limits of 100% or zero as a norm for evaluation. Moreover, the limits suggested of the correlation coefficient are formal in nature, and what the analyst needs is some more *intimate* feel for the problem of whether or not he has gotten close to the *best available explanation* of the phenomenon. He can express the relationship in terms of a variety of coefficients, but he still faces the problem.

A vivid demonstration that McNemar's suggestion does not provide a final solution for the problem is available for one of our case studies of an explanatory survey, Centers' *Psychology of Social Classes*. The reader will recall that the theory was tested by examining the relationship between the independent variable, objective position or stratification score, and two dependent variables, ideology and subjective class identification. Centers expresses these findings not only in tabular form. He also computes the correlation coefficients. That the interpretation on this basis is still not unambiguous is attested by Angell's remarks.[18]

> The relationship between this stratification index and the class with which each person identifies himself is then established. The tetrachoric correlation is .67. The next step is the demonstration that the stratification index is related to answers in six questions that reflect conservatism-radicalism and to political behavior. The tetrachoric correlation between stratification and conservatism-radicalism is .61, and that between stratification and voting or not voting Republican in the 1944 presidential election is .43. *Centers regards these correlations as high enough to prove that both class identification and attitudes and behavior are strongly related to the person's objective position in terms of stratification.* When he relates these two sorts of derivatives from stratification to each other, however, the correlations are only .49 for class identification with conservatism-radicalism and .36 for class identification with political behavior. Centers seems to believe these relationships close enough to validate a concept of class consciousness, of which class identification is one aspect and economic-political attitudes and behavior the other. He thus concludes that the interest-group theory of classes is in large measure confirmed. Despite further tests which he devises to prove this, *this reviewer remains unimpressed by the degree of covariation demonstrated.*

An alternative solution is to study the influence of a variety of related factors. Their effects on the phenomenon can then be used as norms in appraising whether the original determinant under study has a "large" or

18. *Op. cit.*, italics ours. Reprinted by permission of the publishers.

"small" effect, is of "primary" importance or not. Let us illustrate this with a few examples. In connection with programs of American relief and economic aid to Europe after World War II, a survey was conducted on public support for these governmental measures. Among the independent variables that affected attitudes of approval toward these programs was a *belief* as to the impact of the situation in Europe on American economic life.

For example, a belief having to do with economic or self-interest was found to correlate highly. Thus among those who believed that American business would suffer as a result of *not* aiding Europe, 72% approved of the programs, but among those who did not see any bad economic consequence to the U.S. if Europe did not recover, 51% approved. The difference of 19% in percentage points is of a rather large order of magnitude for opinion research, and might have led the analysts to appraise this belief as a highly significant determinant and one to be emphasized in any program of information or propaganda to the American people. However, the analysts also included a series of questions on other beliefs. For example, it was found that those who believed that suffering would occur in Europe if the program was not implemented were more in favor of it than those with the contrary belief by 38% percentage points. Against this standard, it becomes clear that the anticipated consequence of an economic sort is not a determinant of great significance, and the analysts appraised it accordingly.[19]

Let us take as an illustration a similar survey, in which the findings are available in *correlational* terms, so that our comments on McNemar's solution to the problem take on additional clarity. This was an inquiry in 1947 into public support for President Truman's program of American military aid to Greece. From the political setting of the phenomenon, it was clear that one of the possible determinants of favorable attitudes would be the belief that Greece might be in danger of becoming Communist. The presence of this belief was, indeed, found to be a determinant of the attitude. It increased support by 29 percentage points. Yet expressed in correlational terms the relationship was of the order of magnitude of .44. Against the formal limits of 1.00, this is moderate in magnitude, but against the run of experience with opinion phenomena, the finding is quite striking and unusual. What evaluation shall be given? The analysts had also incorporated into the inquiry a question on a related belief as to whether such military aid increased the likelihood of a general war. The absence of this belief increased support by 68 percentage points. By contrast with the former finding, this latter relationship expressed in correlational terms had a value of .91, leading the analysts to appraise the relative importance of the former determinant as of considerably lesser significance.[20]

---

19. Unpublished NORC survey, Public Attitudes toward Aid to Europe, November 21, 1947.
20. Unpublished NORC survey, Public Attitudes toward Aid to Greece and Turkey, May 8, 1947

The Problem of
the Time Order of Variables

In the explanatory survey, the analyst seeks the explanation of a phenomenon in its relation to one or more independent variables. In demonstrating such relationships, there are a variety of technical problems, some of which have already been treated; others are to be treated below. But granted that all such problems are solved, and the relationship found can be regarded as valid, one central problem still remains. Generally, the analyst's purpose in demonstrating a relationship is to make some inference as to *causality*. He wishes to argue that one variable is a cause of the other. For this inference to be made, not only must the other problems be solved. In addition, the variables must stand in a determinate time relationship, with the assumed cause *preceding* the assumed effect.[21]

In classic *experimentation* an inference as to causality from the empirical relationship presents no difficulty. By definition, the independent variable precedes the phenomenon, because it is *created* at will by the experimenter, *imposed* arbitrarily on the captive subjects, and the subsequent effects on the dependent variable are observed or measured. Similarly, in certain methods of a *natural sort under field conditions,* no problem attends this inference. Such is the case in protracted field studies in which a process is observed over a *long* time period and the temporal location and ordering of variables is patent simply from observation. Similarly, in panel studies, inquiry is *initiated* under field conditions and carried on over a *small time period.* The use of repeated measurements insures the temporal location of variables that have *emerged* within the time period of the inquiry or of recent changes in the *values* of variables which are long-standing in origin. However, the survey method has none of these built-in safeguards. It is characterized by measurement conducted in a field setting at only *one point in time,* and does not routinely provide evidence on the time order of variables. Consequently, in particular instances, the inference as to causality from the empirical relationship must be safeguarded by special procedures.

Sometimes no special safeguards are required. A basic logical distinction must be made between the temporal location of the *measurements* of the variables and the temporal location of *the variables themselves* to which the

---

21. We shall not refer again to these other problems in the remainder of this section. Thus, it may appear to the reader as if the solution of the problem of time order were sufficient for the inference as to causality. Merely for the sake of convenience we shall not introduce the qualification that the other problems must also be solved before any such inference can be made, and the reader should always keep this in mind.

measurements refer. Granted that the measurements are made at one point in time, nevertheless, particular variables are implicitly dated as having occurred in the life of the respondent at some earlier point in time. For example, it is quite obvious that when a respondent 70 years of age is queried in a survey in 1954 as to how much formal education he has, the location implicitly is the turn of the century and not the moment of measurement. What is crucial to the problem therefore is the temporal location of the *variable,* and the fact that survey research measures entities at one point in time is only a limitation *in principle* because this logical distinction is obscured.

Since most survey research involves *verbal* procedures rather than observational methods, the respondent often reports on the future, or the past in addition to the present. He *symbolically* creates or re-creates events thus locating the variables in the span of time rather than at the mere moment of measurement. As Vernon once put it: "Words are actions in miniature" and thus the moment of measurement may compress within it a huge span of time. This basic feature of the survey can be deliberately exploited as a special technique for treating time order and we shall return to this discussion later.

Consequently, when the relationship demonstrated is between variables each of which has a defined and distinctive temporal location, the decision as to which is the independent or causative factor is no more a problem in the survey method than in any other method. Merely on the basis of sheer *inspection,* the analyst can infer the time order. For example, there is no apparent difficulty in interpreting a survey finding of a relationship between length of engagement and marital happiness. The first variable, *by definition,* preceded the second one in time. Even where the order is not absolutely clear by definition, the analyst, along with other reasonable men, can often make a safe guess. Consider the relationship between educational level and preference for different radio programs; it is almost sure that education precedes radio tastes. Consider the finding that persons on a low income level are less likely than those on a higher level to belong to formal organizations. Even though a few individuals may have lost their money after joining organizations, by and large we can assume that present economic status is acquired prior to organizational affiliations. Similar assumptions can be made in studies which, for example, relate fairly permanent personality traits to performance in school or on the job.

Yet there are many instances where guesses on the basis of inspection of the nature of the variables are dangerous. The complexities of behavior are such that bizarre time orders are possible. Naturally, the more knowledge the analyst has, the more he is aware of such possibilities, and thus it is often the *naive* analyst who is less likely to see a problem of inferring the correct time order. Similarly, the analyst who is prejudiced towards one systematic point of view rather than another will often see no problem, whereas the more neutral analyst will see alternative possible time orders. For example, the relationship between economic status and political attitude might mean to one sociologically oriented analyst that class membership generates some process which leads to ideological changes. To a more psychologically oriented analyst, the inference might be plausible that individuals with a particular ideology are more likely to be successful occupationally and thus rise into a certain class. The latter possibility may appear somewhat academic, but both time orders are at least possible in principle, and the more neutral analyst will see the problem.

In addition, inspection as procedure is fraught with danger in situations of four types. First, *variables are not always as simple as they appear to be.* A variable when measured may often be merely the culmination of some *process.* No variable could appear to have a greater *finality* than committing *suicide.* It is by definition the final point in the entire life sequence of the individual. Thus, any relationship of suicide as a phenomenon to individual characteristics such as marital status, occupation, military experience, class, etc. would appear to have a determinate time order. The other variables *must have preceded* the act of suicide. Yet, this is only true if suicide be seen as a unitary act. If one introduces the notion of process, of tendency, of predisposition, of incipient suicide, it becomes perfectly possible to see the time order as the reverse. Let us use Durkheim's work again to emphasize that the conception of *a variable in terms of process* inevitably makes inspection for the determination of time order a dangerous procedure.

Durkheim establishes generally that married persons have greater immunity from suicide. He considers the possibility that the time order of this empirical relationship might obviously be "due to the influence of the domestic environment. It would then be the influence of the family which neutralized the suicidal *tendency* or prevented its outburst." But he also entertains the possibility that "this immunity is due to what may be called matrimonial selection. Marriage in fact does make for some sort of selection among the population at large. Not everyone who wants to, gets married; one has little chance of founding a family successfully without certain qualities of health, fortune and morality. . . . Hence, if this part of the population is so far inferior to the other, it naturally proves this inferiority by a higher mortality, a greater criminality, and finally by a stronger *suicidal tendency.* According to this hypothesis, it would not be the family which was a protection against suicide, crime or sickness; the privileged position of married persons would be theirs simply because only those are admitted to family life who already provide considerable guarantees of physical and moral health." (180-181) [22]

The quotation is intended to stress not the phenomenon of matrimonial

22. Durkheim, *op. cit.,* italics ours to stress the concept of process underlying a variable.

selection which is only incidental to the present discussion, but Durkheim's treatment of suicide as *a tendency,* a process. Given this conception, the *act* of suicide itself may be final in the total life sequence and therefore follow marital status. However, since the act is only part of a long-term process, the tendency to suicide might precede the decision as to marriage. Ideally, one would need measures of the presence or absence of the suicidal tendency prior to marriage plus the follow-up of all individuals till the moment of death—perhaps many years later. The survey method obviously provides Durkheim with no *ready* solution. Nor would a panel inquiry work in practice because it is not extended enough in time to provide the necessary measurements. Durkheim thus must cope with the problem of deciding between the alternative time orders, and is forced into a variety of analytic devices *within the framework of survey method* which we shall discuss below. That this constitutes the *unique* solution for such research problems should be obvious to the reader, and commends all the more the study of such survey devices.

There is a second class of variables, in which inspection does not provide assurances about the time order. Some measured variables conceived not as long run processes or tendencies, are nevertheless *complex* and therefore *ambiguous* as to time. They may be indices of more than one phenomenon, so that the time order, rather than being fixed, is determined by the particular problem being considered. Age is perhaps the most typical example of such "ambiguous variables." People who are 60 years of age are characterized by certain physical handicaps as compared to 20 year olds. But they are also characterized by the fact that they were born and grew up in the 19th century rather than after the first World War. Therefore, the timing of the variable depends upon the context in which it figures. When we point to the fact that older people are less well educated than younger people, what matters obviously is the period during which the individuals grew up. Therefore age, as the indicator of time of birth, is prior to education. If, on the other hand, we relate the age at which people die to the kind of climate they live in, then age is subsequent to climate. Similar distinctions can be made in connection with other attributes concerned with time. The "pioneer" status of community residents can be significant either as an indication of the length of time they have lived in the community, or as an indication of the specific time when they first arrived.

Actually, these "ambiguous variables" are more common than might generally be supposed. We encounter similar problems when we compare married and single people. Being married can either mean the ability to have acquired a spouse, or it can mean living together as a family unit. The time order of marital status, as well as of the other examples which we have considered, depends therefore on the meaning which is assigned to it in a given case. Once the ambiguity were resolved, there would be no difficulty.

One variable would be of long prior standing and have a particular time location, but the problem for the analyst is to decide what is actually operating under the heading of these various measured indices.

There is a third type of situation in which problems arise. Here the variables are unambiguous, of long standing and apparently clear temporal location, but the *independent* variable is subject to *response errors* in the process of measurement. Therefore, the inference as to time order may be difficult. We earlier pointed out that *logically* there is a distinction between the time of measurement of the variable and the time location of the variable itself. The survey answers may refer to a remote point, years earlier in time. While this has obvious advantages which we have still to elaborate, it occasionally creates problems. Since one *variable* is unequivocally earlier in its location, it therefore must be independent and the cause of the other. However, since the measurement is, of necessity, retrospective, the status of the respondent on the later variable may have colored his *report* of the independent variable. The obtained relationship may thus involve the order that is just the reverse of what it ought to be logically. The dependent and later variable is the cause of the *reported values* of the earlier variable. We take as an example one basic finding from one of our major cases, *The Authoritarian Personality*. The analysts obtain a relationship between *adult* attitudes and pattern of *childhood* experience in the family. Logically, the time location of the two variables is indisputable. The attitudes must derive from the childhood experience of years before. But childhood experience was *reconstructed* in the course of the survey. As Hyman and Sheatsley remark:

> The work aimed at providing a test of the relation of ideology to personality, and . . . implicitly the personality structure was regarded as a product of *actual familial experience*. In the interview data, which provided the measures of personality, were subjective reports by each respondent of his childhood attitudes, behavior and relations with the family group . . . In view of the elaborate evidence which the authors bring to bear showing that the prejudiced are characterized by irrationality and distortions of objective reality, and that they tend either to glorify their parents or to report victimization by them, it appears inconsistent to accept their retrospective reports of distant events as factual accounts. In the absence of any validating data, one is compelled to qualify very seriously any conclusions which relate to the influence of *actual* childhood upon prejudice. It may well be that the individual who is characterized by the prejudiced, authoritarian outlook in adult life is simply generalizing his *Anschauung* back upon his childhood, and that the non-prejudiced, non-authoritarian similarly distorts his experience (pp. 99-100).[23]

We are not suggesting that the analyst should regard this as a *routine* problem with all variables of long standing. One would properly invoke

---

23. *Op. cit.*

this consideration only in relation to variables remote in time which are likely to be subject to autistic perception or memory. In these instances, sheer inspection of the apparent time order is inadequate, and neither a survey nor even a panel, since its extension in time is short, would solve the problem. Checks on response error of the type described in Part II are the only safeguards.

Finally, there is a fourth type of situation in which the inference as to time order from the obtained relationship is a problem. Here we deal with two variables that have no necessary time location or ordering in the life of the individual. Both may be of recent origin, and their order is *truly indeterminate* from mere inspection. Typically this is the case when we study the relation between information and attitude, or between exposure to media and attitude, for it has been well established that exposure to information may be *voluntary* and *selective* on the basis of pre-existing attitude.[24] Such indeterminacy is troublesome to the analyst because he would like to make statements about short-run effects and the survey data provide no answer as to which is cause and which is effect. Here, a panel would provide a definitive solution but in the absence of such a procedure, specialized survey devices must be used.

The same kind of difficulty is met when the survey materials reveal a relationship between two attitudes. One of the War Department Research Branch studies, for example, uncovered a relationship between attitudes toward officers and willingness for combat.[25] Which of these attitudes developed or was acquired first? Does a soldier reluctant to go into combat "rationalize" his feelings by saying that his officers are not good? Or does a soldier with favorable attitudes toward his officers develop a feeling of confidence which makes him willing for combat? Because of our inability to answer these questions, because we do not know and cannot know which of the attitudes developed first, we cannot decide which is the causal sequence. Similarly, if we find that Democrats are more likely than Republicans to favor government interference in business matters, we cannot establish definitely the time sequence of party affiliation and opinion.

In all the instances of the above four types, some solution to the interpretation of the time sequence of the relationship must be obtained by the introduction of specialized devices within the survey framework. All of these devices are approximations, and each is subject to some difficulty. However, despite their limitations they are to be highly recommended. In many instances, they constitute the unique solution to the problem, because no other method provides an appropriate solution. Even where another method, such as a panel or long term study, would be preferable, it may

---

24. For example, see P. F. Lazarsfeld, *Radio and the Printed Page* (New York: Duell, Sloan and Pearce, 1940).

25. *Op. cit.*, II, p. 126, Table 7.

not be practicable, and again recourse to these approximations is necessary. Moreover, by employing several such approximations simultaneously, their individual limitations are overcome, and great confidence can be placed in the inference as to time sequence. We shall describe and illustrate a series of such approximations, without any claim to exhaustiveness. Those we present were invented by clever analysts under the spur of necessity, and we hope such inventiveness is not now at an end.[26]

1. Comparisons by Length of Exposure to Some Independent Variable of an Experiential Nature

We have earlier noted that one definitive solution to the problem of time order is provided by *panel* study in which short term effects are traced over a period of time. By observing whether or not a respondent alters his characteristics, e.g., attitudes at some point or points *subsequent* to an earlier experience, the time order of a relationship is established unequivocally. In such instances, procedural questions apart, one infers that some process originally generated by an experience unfolds or develops. Such a *developmental theory* leads various investigators naturally to an approximate solution, even when a panel design is not possible. Each individual is studied only at *one* point in time, but the total group is divided according to the length of the exposure to the experience that is presumably the independent variable. If the experience was actually selected on the basis of initial attitude or trait, one would expect no difference in attitude between respondents no matter what length of exposure. They would have had the attitude to start with! Only if the attitude were a developmental product of experience, would it change with the magnitude of experience. The reader should note that this latter finding does not preclude the possibility of *both* sequences being operative. It cannot, however, be interpreted as *solely* the product of selection, for then no further changes would occur with increased exposure.

Certain difficulties accompany this approximation. While time is a vehicle for prolonged exposure and corresponding development, it is also punctuated periodically by new events, by radical changes in institutions. Consequently, individuals who have contrasted lengths of exposure may have been initiated into experiences which are not identical in certain crucial respects, and at the time of their initiation differing patterns of selectivity may have operated. Under such conditions, a relationship with length of exposure may not prove the influence of experience, but merely the differing nature of selective processes at different points of the calendar. There is no substitute for knowledge, and the analyst should examine this

---

26. For an excellent systematic treatment of such approximations for interpreting whether different personality traits among the followers of different occupations can be due to selectivity, see H. Menzel, *The Social Psychology of Occupations: A Synthetic Review*. Unpublished M.A. Thesis, Indiana University, 1950, pp. 76-83.

possibility in the light of generally available information. In addition, the comparisons by length of exposure should be in terms of *many refined categories of time*. If adjacent groups differ in the apparent dependent variable, the possibility of radical changes in the experiential entity is less plausible. The use of refined categories also solves one other difficulty to which we shall now turn.

If when this procedure is introduced there are *no* variations in the apparent dependent variable by length of exposure, one must entertain one inference other than selection. It may be that the attitude has developed but required only a *brief* exposure. Thereafter additional increments of experience create no further change. The solution is, of course, to use many refined categories of time.

A third difficulty accompanying this procedure is the possibility that longer periods of experience simply mean that the person is *older* chronologically. Thus the variations in the attitude may simply reflect the biosocial factor of age as such, rather than the effect of experience. For example, a person exposed to a newspaper for 30 years may obviously be much older than a person exposed to it for only 1 year. Again, a solution is to use many refined categories of time, and also to control age or make independent analyses by age.

Let us illustrate this general procedure with a number of classic studies. We first turn to one of our major cases, Durkheim's *Suicide*.

As the reader will recall, Durkheim devotes considerable attention to a variety of suicide which he labels *altruistic*. He cites such instances in primitive societies where the act is "expressly imposed by society." Durkheim notes that such conditions are generally rare in modern society but that "even today there exists among us a special environment where altruistic suicide is chronic: namely, the army." He then reports various statistical data which establish for "all European countries that the suicidal aptitude of soldiers is much higher than that of the civilian population of the same age." But before Durkheim can use these data as proof of the phenomenon of *altruistic* suicide, he must establish a certain military morality which the soldier *develops* which in turn leads him to abnegate life. Otherwise, these data might well mean to the critical reader that individuals predisposed to suicide for "non-altruistic" reasons select to join the army.[27]

Durkheim's data strongly contradict this possibility of selection. By a

---

27. It is interesting that Durkheim *himself* does not dwell on this alternative of selection in explaining the military statistics, although he is especially sensitive to the problem in other places, e.g., the relation of suicide and marital status. However, the material *intrinsically* is highly relevant and we present it as an especially illuminating example of the procedure of time comparisons. The data might also be interpreted as due to uncontrolled factors accompanying military life, other than the moral constellation leading to altruism. Durkheim treats this problem elaborately, e.g., he examines whether the increase in suicide might be due to the non-marital status characteristic of the military and is able to reject such alternatives. The interested reader is referred to the original discussion on pp. 228-239, *op. cit.*

comparison of suicide rates for groups with varying lengths of military service, he shows that "In France, in less than 10 years of military service, the suicide-rate almost triples. . . . In the English armies of India, it becomes eight times as high in 20 years." Moreover, the length of experience groups are relatively refined and the comparisons are among 4-5 groups. For both of these countries the regression is fairly regular and progressive.

Such increases in suicide with increased exposure argue that the phenomenon develops as a consequence of military life. However, there is the danger that the increase reflects simply chronological age, rather than cumulative experience. We have previously mentioned this problem in such comparisons, and it is especially tenable in the light of Durkheim's earlier demonstration of the increase of suicide with age.[28] Durkheim solves this difficulty in the ways reported above. The changes between *refined* categories argue against it. He also has independent data on the change in *civilian* suicide rate with age. Since this change is much smaller than the change with increased military service, chronological age is ruled out. The inference is warranted that suicide is the product of military life.[29]

We shall present two other studies in which the approximate solution of time comparisons is employed.

In classic work on Negro intelligence, it had been established that Northern Negroes measure higher and approximate more closely to the scores of whites than Southern Negroes. The interpretation of these results naturally was quite crucial to theories of innate or racial differences in intelligence. Various writers argued that the superiority of Northern Negroes was due to the environment they experienced—for example, an environment of greater educational opportunity—by extension that traditional tests of intelligence are responsive to such environmental factors and therefore that the generally lower scores of Negroes does not constitute evidence for a theory of innate white superiority. By contrast, other writers have argued for racial differences and explain the higher scores of Northern Negroes in terms of a doctrine of selective migration, i.e., "in migrations of Negroes from South to North definite selective factors have been at work,

---

28. The argument appears even more tenable initially. Durkheim has French data divided by length of military service. However, the limitations of secondary analysis are such that he does not have the English Army data by length of service. He is forced to compare suicide rates for English soldiers varying in chronological age, presumably using this as the best equivalent of actual length of service. *Ibid.*, p. 232.

29. The reader may wonder at the paradox that this analysis is carried out in detail despite the fact that we have stated that Durkheim does not entertain the theory that selection is involved. Actually, his purpose in presenting such comparisons is to test an alternative explanation of the data other than that of altruistic processes, but the data also are appropriate to a test of selection. His alternative involves the notion of time and developmental processes, but interestingly enough the theory calls for a curvilinear relationship with length of service. It is that the military life is the cause, but the process is one of disgust with the hardships. Durkheim suggests that if this were operative, the rate should go down with increased service because of adaptation.

causing the more intelligent stocks to leave and the less intelligent to re-main behind. In that case the Negroes now in the North would not repre-sent an average group obtaining high scores because of the better environ-ment but a group that was superior to start with." [30]

Klineberg in an attempt to obtain objective evidence on this important issue of interpretation made use of time comparisons. The "method was to give intelligence tests to Southern born Negro children now living in New York City, but differing in the number of years of residence there, in order to determine whether there is any noticeable change in their scores pro-portionate to the length of time they have been in New York. If the differ-ence between northern and southern Negroes is entirely due to selective factors, length of residence should make no appreciable difference; if the environmental factors are important, there should be an improvement in direct relation to the length of time such factors have been operative." [31]

A whole series of such comparisons were made. In general, they estab-lished a progressively higher level of measured verbal intelligence with increased length of residence in New York City, leading Klineberg to re-ject the interpretation that selective migration was the explanation of the usual differences reported. Detailed discussion of the procedure will show how Klineberg solved some of the special difficulties associated with such time comparisons. We earlier indicated that one dilemma is that increased experience may be confounded with chronological age. Here by definition the problem was controlled since all the children were 12 years old, and differed merely in being residents of New York for periods from one to eleven years. In relation to the technical problem earlier mentioned that the effect of experience may occur abruptly after initial short exposure, it should be noted that the categories used were many and refined, starting with one year of residence, permitting Klineberg to observe that the changes were generally regular and progressive. Klineberg notes the other difficulty associated with such time comparisons. The pattern of selection may itself change over time and the groups differing in length of experience may therefore differ in other important respects. "It may be that the quality of the more recent migrants is inferior to that of the earlier arrivals. The su-periority of the six-year over the two-year group may be due, not to environ-mental influences, but to the fact that each year the northward migrants are inferior to those who preceded them." One solution Klineberg provides involves, as earlier indicated, the refined categories used. "It is not very probable that such a difference would appear in successive years; one year or even two or three would hardly suffice to alter the conditions of migra-tion sufficiently, although when migrants are compared after, let us say, a

30. O. Klineberg, *Negro Intelligence and Selective Migration* (New York: Columbia University Press, 1938), p. 4. Reprinted by permission of the publishers.
31. *Ibid.*, p. 13.

ten-year interval, such a difference in selective factors might possibly show an effect." (p. 37) [32]

In addition, Klineberg invents an interesting empirical solution to this difficulty which in generalized form is very valuable. He conducts several studies, each involving comparisons by length of residence, but the *studies vary in the calendar year in which they are conducted.* Thus one study was conducted in 1931 and another in 1932. The subjects "in the 1931 study who have been in New York four years, for example, arrived in 1927; those in the 1932 study who have been in New York for a similar period arrived in 1928. If the migrants are becoming inferior as time goes on, the four-year group in the later study ought to be inferior to the corresponding group in the earlier one." (p. 38) To state the solution generally, if length of experience findings are dependent on some innovation or critical change in selection processes in given years, replication of the comparisons by length of experience, *but in another time period,* should produce some corresponding systematic change in the results. On the contrary, in Klineberg's study, the findings from the replication in a different year strengthened the original interpretation.

Another well known study making use of comparisons by length of experience, constitutes an ideal companion piece to the Klineberg inquiry. Klineberg made use of such comparisons in a study of the intelligence of Negro migrants to the North. In Sims and Patrick's study, the prejudice of whites towards Negroes was studied among white migrants to the South.[33]

In this inquiry, Southern students at the University of Alabama were found to score higher in prejudice against the Negro than Northern students enrolled at a Northern institution. In addition, a third and critically important group was studied. These were students from Northern homes who had also enrolled at the University of Alabama and their prejudice scores fell between the other two groups. The position of this group leads one to the conclusion that a certain constellation of experiences in the South

---

32. Elsewhere, Klineberg uses another method to establish whether or not selective migration could account for the higher measured intelligence of Northern Negroes. He compares the school records of migrants and non-migrant children in several Southern cities for the period 1915–1930, the very years during which the migrant children studied by intelligence tests were recruited from the South. This more direct test *confirms* the indirect evidence based on comparisons by length of residence. There is no evidence that the children recruited into the North had higher abilities initially, as evidenced by their school grades. These same school records also provide evidence that the higher intelligence scores with longer residence in the North *cannot* be due to decreasingly severe selection out of the South during the time period of the investigation. If anything, the *more recent* arrivals in the North had higher average school marks than the earlier migrants. Thus, his findings on the higher intelligence of the groups with longer Northern residence is demonstrated despite the handicap of a possibly lower starting point in terms of ability. This makes the comparisons all the more compelling. See Chap. III, *ibid.*

33. V. Sims and J. Patrick, "Attitude Toward the Negro of Northern and Southern College Students," *J. Soc. Psychol.*, 1936, 7, 192-204. Reprinted in T. M. Newcomb and E. L. Hartley, ed., *Readings in Social Psychology* (New York: Holt, 1947), 358-365.

leads towards prejudice, since the Northern students who are exposed to a Southern atmosphere are significantly different from their Northern counterparts who remain in the North and begin to approach their Southern classmates in attitude. However, there is the alternative possibility that those Northerners who enter a Southern college selectively migrate on the basis of a predisposition towards prejudice. Sims and Patrick therefore break this group down by year in school. This is "taken as a measure of the length of time that these students have been exposed to the Southern environment and to the Southern Negro, and should therefore tell us whether the North-in-South students score low (prejudice) due to their being negatively selected or due to contact with the Southern environment."

This analysis reveals that in "the North-in-South group there was a consistent drop (increase in prejudice) from year to year. . . . As time goes on their attitude approaches that of the typical Southern student, until in the Junior and Senior years there is not a significant difference between the two groups." Thus the argument of selective migration is rejected. Again, the reader will recognize one difficulty inherent in these data. Conceivably the change with year in college might simply represent the influence of chronological age and corresponding development of such attitudes. That this is not relevant is demonstrated in much the same way as in the Durkheim analysis described earlier. Sims and Patrick also divide the other two groups, North in North and South in South by year in school. For these groups there is no systematic change with increased college residence. Consequently, this cannot be the explanation of the data for the group that has migrated.

2. Exploitation of the Verbal Feature of Survey Research to Locate in Time a Variable or Changes in Its Value

We earlier commented on one feature of survey research which leads to a variety of approximate solutions of the problem of time order. We noted that while the measurements occur at a given moment of time, it is the capacity of humans to symbolically re-create the past through memory and to verbalize such memories. The reports of respondents within the unit moment of a survey may thus range implicitly over wide spans of time. It is only one step from this natural occurrence to introduce deliberately the dimension of time into the questioning, and trust to the fundamental human capacities of respondents to report either the exact *location* of events and variables in time or *changes* in experiences and characteristics over time.

By way of illustration of the former procedure we cite a finding in *The American Soldier*. The analysts were interested in the relationship between marital status and rank. They found that married men were more likely to have higher rank, even when age and length of service in the Army were controlled.[34] But which came first, marriage or promotion? Is it that married

---

34. *Op. cit.*, I, pp. 118-120, especially Chart V.

men are more likely to be promoted, or that promotion encourages the soldier to marry? With knowledge only of marital status and rank, very little can be said in answer to this question. But fortunately, Research Branch analysts obtained one other bit of information which provided some clue to the time sequence: They knew whether the soldier had been married prior to his entrance into the Army or whether he had married after becoming a soldier. These data enabled them to make the following observations. They noted that there was very little relationship between rank and having been married prior to entering the Army. On the other hand, there was some relationship between rank and marriage taking place after induction. This leads the authors to suggest that "marriage was even more likely to be a *resultant* of promotion or of expected promotion than to be a factor *predisposing to promotion.*[35] The clue to the sequence of the variables was the fact that where the time location was known, only one kind of relationship was seen to exist; where it was unknown, another relationship, involving the reverse time sequence might conceivably have prevailed.

We earlier noted that for studying short-run cause and effect sequences, panel study provides a definitive solution for the problem of the time sequence of the two variables. Since the same respondents are interviewed successively over a period of time, any *changes* in the value of some variable between successive interviews can be located and allocated to the other variable.

This feature of a panel can be represented diagrammatically showing the analogy of a panel to one type of experimental design. In the diagram, the value of the variable at each of the time points is denoted by the symbol (x).

	"Experimental" group
Time 1	x_1
	"Exposure" to stimulus
Time 2	x_2

The "effect" of whatever stimulus or independent variable is being considered is indicated by the difference, $(x_2 - x_1)$.

However, panel methods have their practical limitations. They are more expensive to conduct. Operating difficulties arise: respondents move, be-

---

35. *Ibid.,* I, p. 120, authors' italics.

come ill, and unable to participate further in the study, become bored and refuse further participation, etc.[36]

The analyst may therefore have made the calculated decision not to undertake a panel. However, even where no such considerations enter, he may not have been fortunate enough to have undertaken a panel. His judgment may have been poor, or he may have come into the situation only after the occurrence of the event whose effect he would like to study. In such instances, he has no choice but a survey. However, he may exploit the fundamental memory capacities of humans by asking *retrospective questions*. By asking the respondents to recall what their attitudes were at some earlier period, generally prior to a crucial experience whose effect we are trying to study, we attempt to reconstruct symbolically what would have been observed had there been a previous interview. We ask, "How did you feel about *B* before *A* took place?" In this way we attempt to place variables in their proper time sequence without encountering the difficulties faced in the application of panel procedures. Retrospective questions too find their representation in a diagram similar to that used for a panel.

	"Experimental" group
(Time 0)	(x_0)
	"Exposure" to stimulus
(Time 1)	x_1

The measure of "effect" is once more the difference, $(x_1 - x_0)$. We have bracketed the upper measures in this scheme to indicate that they are not actual observations which we have made, but rather retrospections of our subjects. This suggests a limitation of the method which we shall consider presently.

Current survey literature yields varied examples in which retrospective variables have been used in order to facilitate the study of changes. The reader may recall that the War Department Research Branch used a question of this kind in checking the relationship between service in bi-racial companies and the willingness of whites to serve with Negroes. In addition to stating their present willingness to serve in mixed companies, the respondents were asked to recall what their attitudes had been before Negro platoons were put in their companies.

In their study of Puerto Rican migrants to New York City, Mills and his

36. Detailed treatment of panel research methods is presented in a forthcoming monograph in the same series as the present volume.

colleagues made use of retrospective questions in investigating whether there had been any change in intentions to remain in New York.[37] One of the first questions they asked their subjects was, "When you came to New York, did you intend to visit or to settle down permanently, or something else?" Later on in the interview, the subjects were again asked, "Now that you are here, do you intend to visit or to settle down permanently, or something else?" Comparison of the answers to these two questions yielded the following cross-tabulation:

TABLE VI—Original and Present Intentions of Puerto Rican Migrants to Stay in New York

		Original Intention		
Present Intention	Stay	Stay, With Reservations	Undecided *	Visit
Stay	89%	63%	(67%)	57%
Stay, with reservations	4	9	(—)	5
Undecided	5	19	(11)	15
Visit	2	9	(22)	23
Total cases	786	101	9	111

* Parentheses indicate that base for percentages is very small.

Whatever their original intentions, most of the migrants now plan to remain in New York. In fact, more than half of those who originally planned only to visit indicated at the time they were interviewed that they then wanted to settle down permanently. This is very much the kind of result—and the kind of table—which is obtained when panel techniques have been used, but it is obtained here through the approximation of retrospective questions.

Other questions enabled Mills and his associates to study the upward and downward occupational mobility of their subjects. In addition to asking the respondents about their present work, they asked them to trace their job histories from the time just before they left Puerto Rico, through the early stages of their residence in New York, up to the time they were interviewed. By appropriate classification, the analysis could trace the upward or downward trend in occupational status between any successive stages in the migrants' careers. It was then possible for them to make the observations, presented in Table VII below, which deals with the status of the migrants as related to sex and time of migration.[38]

The table illustrates the usefulness of retrospective questions in revealing shifts which cannot normally be observed in a survey.

There are a number of difficulties associated with the use of retrospective questions as an approximation to panel techniques. We noted earlier that the report of variables which are very *remote* in time may be distorted

---

37. C. Wright Mills, C. Senior and R. Goldsen, *Puerto Rican Journey* (New York: Harpers, 1950). See especially p. 47,

38. *Op. cit.*, p. 70.

TABLE VII—Occupational Mobility of Puerto Rican Migrants According to Time of Arrival and Sex

| | Men | | Women | |
Direction of Mobility	Early Arrival	Late Arrival	Early Arrival	Late Arrival
Upward	42%	15%	11%	12%
Stable	38	63	75	73
Downward	20	22	14	15
Total cases	144	167	122	143

and colored by subsequent experiences and characteristics of the respondent. Consequently it is difficult to know whether respondents are accurate in their answers to retrospective questions deliberately introduced into a survey. Do they tend to remember selectively? Do they discount the extent to which they have actually changed their attitudes or habits? [39] That such errors may occur is demonstrated in one classic empirical study, which provided a direct test of the validity of retrospective questions on change. In Murphy and Likert's early panel study, students had been given a series of opinion tests in 1929. Five years later a sub-sample of these students were constituted into a panel and re-tested to determine the extent of actual change. Approximately 130 students replied. At that time, a series of questions were also asked to which the respondent reported his own appraisal of the way in which his views had changed and, the factors responsible for change. Comparisons of these two measures of change—the retrospection and the panel—were then made. Murphy and Likert remark on the basis of their analysis that "a large number of individuals *do not know* in which direction they have shifted on on these issues." [40]

The careful analyst will therefore introduce checks to try to detect gross inaccuracies in the retrospections of his subjects. [41] Much of West's study of college graduates, for example, was based on retrospective questions. [42] All of the questions dealing with the experiences of the graduates in college necessarily rested on the ability of the subjects to remember what their experiences had been. Some of these questions did not call for difficult feats of memory—what college one went to or what subject one majored in are experiences which are not easily forgotten. But how many extra-curricular activities one participated in, and exactly what these were, are details which may tax the memory of someone who has been out of college for 30 or 40

39. There is also the problem of specifying the exact time period to which the subjects should retrospect. "Before *A* took place" covers a wide time span.

40. G. Murphy and R. Likert, *Public Opinion and the Individual* (New York: Harpers, 1938). The materials are presented in Chap. VII, but the quotation used in the text is from p. 251. Italics ours.

41. The reader is referred to the detailed discussion of checks on response error in Part II. Errors of retrospection are simply one variety of response errors, and many of the checks described are appropriate.

42. *Op. cit.*

years. And what grades one received in college may call on the graduate to report information which he perhaps wanted to forget even at the time he was attending college and which, perhaps, he has succeeded in forgetting during the intervening years. Since it was essential to the purposes of her study to have some measure of the performance of the graduates while in college, however, West was forced to rely on the retrospections of her subjects. She took the precaution of applying a check, however. Reasoning that gross distortions—intentional or through forgetfulness—would have resulted in a distribution of grades skewed to the upper—or "A"—side, she examined the distribution reported in the schedules. Since this distribution reflected the "normal curve" of performance, she felt justified in concluding that there were not gross inaccuracies in the retrospections of her subjects.

A somewhat more elaborate check was applied by Stouffer and his associates in one of their studies. In investigating the effects of combat on the incidence of psychosomatic symptoms, the researchers used a number of procedures. First of all, they cross-tabulated such variables as nearness to combat and length of time in combat with questions about psychosomatic symptoms.[43] In one study of combat veterans, however, they included a retrospective question. In addition to asking, "Since you have been on active combat duty, are you ever bothered by (hand tremors, stomach disturbances, fainting spells, shortness of breath, and pressure in the head)?" They also asked, "During your civilian and military life, but before you went on active combat duty, were you ever bothered by . . . ?" Comparison of the retrospective form of the question with the post-combat form revealed a marked increase in the proportion of men experiencing many anxiety symptoms.[44]

But how accurate were these retrospections? As a check, the analysts compared the pre-combat answers of the veterans with those given by Infantrymen in training in the United States. The close correspondence of the answers provided some assurance that the combat veterans did not distort their answers, either consciously or unconsciously, to any extent.[45]

---

43. See Appendix D of the present work for the relationship between nearness to combat and the incidence of psychosomatic symptoms.

44. *Op. cit.*, Vol. II, p. 448, Table 17.

45. *Ibid.*, Vol. II, p. 448, Table 16. There is one caution to be noted in connection with this kind of check on the accuracy of retrospections. At Time II we ask respondents to recall their attitudes of Time I. If these retrospections are checked, it should be with data collected at Time I. In a highly dynamic situation, checks based on data obtained at Time II may introduce a distortion. Let us consider what this distortion might have been in the Research Branch study. The authors note that the Army adopted a permissive attitude toward fear and anxiety symptoms among the troops. (*Ibid.*, Vol. II, pp. 196ff.) But this attitude might have been more apparent at later stages of the war, so that soldiers were more willing to express their anxiety at Time II, let us say, than they were at Time I. If this were the case, and if the checks had been based on data obtained only at Time II, then the actual extent of increase in anxiety symptoms would have been underestimated. (Actually the checks were based on material collected at "Time I" and at "Time II.")

3. Quasi-Experiments Through Manipulation of the Questionnaire Design

The deliberate introduction of retrospective questions provides an analogy to a panel design and therefore constitutes one approximate solution. Other manipulations of the questionnaire can be employed to simulate experimental situations. In the classic experiment, a stimulus variable is created in the laboratory setting, subjects are exposed, and the effects observed or measured. By analogy, the questionnaire can be regarded not merely as an instrument to obtain answers, but as a method of exposing respondents to experimental, albeit verbal, stimuli.[46] An illustration of this solution to certain instances of the problem of time sequence is provided by Hyman and Sheatsley.[47] They are concerned with a problem mentioned earlier, that of establishing a time order between information and attitude. They anticipated, at the time the survey was designed, that if they simply had their subjects indicate their level of information and express their attitudes, that time order would remain indeterminate. Consequently, they introduced an interesting variation on the usual survey procedure. They started out by gauging the level of information possessed by their respondents on certain specific issues; on the basis of this questioning they were able to divide their subjects into those who were initially informed and those who were not. Once this classification was made, *all* respondents—those who had indicated their awareness of the issue as well as those who had not—were given a brief summary of the information originally called for.[48] Thus all had a common base of knowledge. All of them were then asked a related opinion question. Despite the fact that they now had a common base of information, on all issues, where this technique was employed, the initially informed respondents manifested quite different attitudes than did the initially uninformed. From this the analysts conclude that attitudes lead to the acquisition of knowledge, rather than knowledge leading to the development of specific attitudes. For the attitudes of the two groups differed, even when their level of information was *made* the same by the researchers.

Hyman and Sheatsley in essence created a particular time order between information and attitude in a quasi-experimental way. Because they still observed differences in the attitudes of the initially informed and the initially uninformed groups, they infer that the actual time sequence governing the behavior of most of their subjects was the opposite of that which they created.

---

46. Of course, these experimental manipulations can employ aspects of the measurement situation other than the questionnaire. For example, the type of interviewer can be systematically varied and the effects traced. For a discussion of such experimental analogies within survey research, see H. Hyman, "Inconsistencies," *op. cit.*

47. Information Campaigns, *op. cit.*, pp. 417-418.

48. Those who had shown themselves to be informed were told, "As you may recall . . ." with a summary of the relevant information following.

4. Checks Upon the Volitional Basis for the Phenomenon of Self-Selection

Self-selection of an experience, selective exposure or behavior, upon analysis can be conceptualized in terms of two factors. Since *self*-selection is, by definition, *voluntary* behavior on the part of the individual, there is first, an assumption that there is *motivation* to engage in selective behavior, the motivation being in some way related to an attitude, predisposition, or characteristic, and second, a set of *conditions insuring or permitting the individual's engagement in the particular act of self-selection.* These conditions are several. In the instance of a single act, the individual must have some *prior knowledge, or at least belief,* that one choice or option or pattern of behavior will lead to his desired end. In the instance of repetitive behavior, the individual does not need foreknowledge, but then the assumption is necessary that *he can and does revise his initial decision* on the basis of subsequent knowledge. Another condition for the *act* of self-selection is that *other motives or external restraints are not operative* which block the consummation of the original desire for self-selection. Sometimes, the concept of self-selection implies not the positive choice of something so much as the avoidance of a class of entities. In such instances, a condition that must be operative is that *external pressures or accidental factors do not lead the individual into the acts* he wishes to avoid.

Consequently, the analyst by adducing evidence on the presence or absence of the conditions required for the voluntary act of self-selection can make a reasonable decision as to which time sequence is involved in his data. This evidence can be obtained either from collateral sources or by the introduction of special questions into the survey.

Such a model of self-selection as an *individual voluntary* process is of course not appropriate to selective behavior that is *socially* determined. However, a corresponding model can be elaborated for the social case, and the presence or absence of these necessary conditions can be used, as an approximate solution by the analyst. Thus, in these instances, the external agent who engages in selection must have the motive to recruit respondents of the particular type into the particular experience, must have some basis in knowledge or belief in order to make the judgment, and must not face counter-pressures or counter-motives which block the initial motive.

The approximation will become clearer if we turn to some examples.

Klineberg's inquiry provides an illustration of this procedure. He uses a variety of collateral source materials to see in what degree the conditions for the operations of self-selection were present.

Thus the historical data establish that migration was not purely a *self-initiated voluntary* act, but was determined by various factors *external* to the individual. Klineberg notes that "various social and economic causes . . . contributed . . . the need for unskilled labor in the North . . . the boll-weevil plague . . . which added to an industrial depression already very marked." He notes "the sending of labor organizers to the South who recruited Negro laborers." (p. 7) In other words, voluntary selective migration by the intelligent Negroes appears less plausible when one considers the massive external pressures towards migration and the external factors of recruitment.[49]

Similarly, Klineberg shows that the migration of Negroes to the North was part of a mass movement of Negroes. "In 1920, 19.9 percent of Negroes born in the United States were living in a state other than that of their birth. Most of this migration was into a relatively small number of large Northern cities. Between 1910 and 1920 the Negro population of Detroit, for example, increased 611 percent." (p. 7) The implication is that the movement was too massive in numbers to warrant the notion of the selective migration merely of the intelligent.

More precise evidence is cited by Klineberg from a study by King which involved direct inquiry among 110 migrants of the conditions which led to their leaving the South. The reasons given emphasized *external pressures:* "no employment at home," escape "because of misdemeanors they had committed," "taken North by a labor agent," "got married and accompanied their husbands." King also observed that "most of those who left had definite connections with someone who had previously migrated to the city or to the North . . . and in almost every case it was a suggestion or an invitation . . . that prompted the migration. This being the case, 'the energy and initiative' which has so often been regarded as a prerequisite to migration need hardly play an important role." (p. 11)

A variety of such sources argue that the conditions for selective migration, free or voluntary behavior by the more intelligent, were not present generally and strengthen Klineberg's conclusion that the reverse time sequence is operative.

Sometimes, the conditions appropriate to voluntary behavior and in turn self-selection are present in *some degree.* Then, this approximation becomes somewhat more involved. The analyst must separate those for whom the conditions are operative from the remainder of the group and compare the findings. Self-selection and the corresponding time sequence require that the finding be more powerful in the group where the conditions are present.

Durkheim's treatment of altruistic suicide, as manifested by the high rates of suicide among the military, provides an excellent illustration of this

---

49. It is, of course, possible that selective migration can either be *socially* or *self*-determined. Thus those recruiting or impressing a group into some experience can selectively choose a particular group, e.g., the intelligent. However, in this instance the recruitment was massive and for a variety of unskilled positions making it less likely that the recruiters were discriminating as to the intelligence of the group selected. Klineberg documents this last point from historical analyses.

approximation. As we earlier noted, this high rate could be interpreted in "altruistic terms," as the product of military life; or as due to selection into the army of those with incipient tendencies toward suicide. If selection is at work, one would expect, therefore, that the rate would be differentially higher among those who join the army on a *voluntary* basis, since the argument of selection often implies an individualistic act of volition. Durkheim provides us with just the data appropriate for this approximation. He presents the rate for *volunteers,* and it is seen to be "exceptionally high." By juxtaposition with other tables, the rate seems to be at least *twice as great* as it is in the total soldier population taken without regard to volunteer status. (p. 233) [50]

But Durkheim presents yet another datum which is appropriate to this approximation procedure, and which is even more compelling. As we shall have occasion to illustrate later, self-selection as a voluntary act may be based on *false* premises, false knowledge of the situation which is being selected. To take some literary license, one may have married the army in haste, and repented at leisure. While such selections on *false* premises are legitimate instances of self-selection and should be included in any tests of the process, we shall see that it is more *compelling* a test to examine volitional behavior based on good knowledge.

Durkheim provides such a demonstration. He presents the suicide rate for those soldiers who have *re-enlisted*. These are also volunteers, but of a special kind. They have had full opportunity to reconsider their initial selection of the army. If they regretted it, they could have escaped the military situation. If they had selected it initially on some false premise, they now have sufficient basis of experience to correct their knowledge. This group nevertheless decided to rejoin. Certainly, this is a group in which self-selection is extreme. The rate of suicide in this group is found to be exceedingly high; almost twice as high as the relatively high rate for "volunteers" of all types.[51] (p. 233)

These tests unfortunately work out in such fashion that it is *not* possible to reject the hypothesis that self-selection was at work. The very group in whom selection could have operated show the phenomenon of suicide in greater magnitude. However, the earlier test by length of military service argued against the hypothesis of self-selection. Thus the total results are

---

50. Strangely enough Durkheim's model precision in handling quantitative data seems absent from this table. No caption in the table or discussion in the text makes clear which army in which country at which time is the basis for the statistics. Nor is the corresponding statistic for non-volunteer soldiers presented. Based on clues in the text, the best reconstruction to the writer is that it is the French Army 1875–1890, and conclusion above is based on comparison with the total French Military statistics for about that period, which Durkheim presents earlier in his text.

51. We earlier noted that Durkheim was not sensitive to the interpretation of the military findings in terms of self-selection. Yet, here again he presents a test appropriate to the problem. Again, the paradox is resolved by the fact that the analysis in question was used by him to test a totally different hypothesis. However, it functions ideally for our purposes.

somewhat indeterminate and therefore Durkheim's conclusion is mixed. He explains the high military rate "by the sum total of states, *acquired* habits, or *natural* dispositions making up the military spirit (p. 234),[52] thus giving credence to both time sequences.

5. Properties the Phenomenon Would Exhibit for Self-Selection vs. Experience Are Derived Logically and the Findings Are Examined for Congruence

The previous approximations have in common the fact that they require highly specialized data. Corresponding methods have to be incorporated into the survey at the planning stage so as to insure that such data are available, for it is rarely the case that *by sheer accident* an analyst will be lucky enough to ask a retrospective question, or manipulate the questionnaire experimentally, or have a basis for dividing the group by length of experience, or insert checks on the volitional aspect of the behavior. In the absence of such planning, the problem of time sequence appears impossible of solution. Especially, in a secondary analysis the problem seems insurmountable, for the analyst must take what data he can find, and it appears very unlikely that the available materials will be appropriate to these special approximations. Yet, there is, in principle, a solution which can be employed, and its only requirement is considerable ingenuity on the part of the analyst. Not that such a procedure is to be recommended routinely. However, if the problem of time sequence were not anticipated in the planning of a primary analysis, or if the inquiry involves secondary analysis, it should be tried.

The starting point for such a solution is the recognition that what is under study is not an "all-or-nothing" phenomenon. The same general phenomenon can exhibit a variety of properties; some of these to be expected under conditions where selection occurred; others to be expected under conditions where the phenomenon is the product of experience—of the hypothesized independent variable. If the analyst can speculate and develop such a conception or model of the phenomenon, of the varied properties it will exhibit, he can then examine the findings to see whether they are congruent with one interpretation or the other. The *construction* of such a model is, of course, dependent on considerable knowledge of the background theory and literature as well as on powers of speculation. Naturally, its *applicability* to our problem is dependent on the findings being rich enough to permit empirical measurement of one of the relevant properties, so the analyst in constructing the model must keep in mind the range of data that are available. The *validity* of the inference about time sequence from such an approach is dependent on whether the assumptions about the properties of the phenomenon are strongly grounded in past theory and evidence and developed logically. Durkheim was forced to use

---

52. Italics ours.

such an approach frequently because it was a secondary analysis, and we shall use the *Suicide* as our first example.

We have already alluded to Durkheim's dilemma in deciding whether the immunity from suicide of married people is a product of experience subsequent to marriage or of recruitment into marriage of those *not* predisposed to suicide and the rejection of those who for reasons such as pathology are predisposed. To decide which sequence is at work, he elaborates various models of the way the phenomenon should behave under each of these alternative conditions. Thus, for example, he argues that if selection were operative, the influence of marriage on the suicide rate should be the *same for both sexes, across many countries* "for wives are recruited in the same manner as husbands," i.e., at least insofar as the rejection of the unfit. However, if it is the experience *after* marriage that is the cause of the phenomenon, the rate should change differentially for men and women and different countries, because the domestic environments of the sexes are different. He then examines the data for congruence with the model and finds support for the second time sequence. (pp. 183-184)

A variety of other properties of the phenomenon under the two conditions, selection vs. experience, are derived by speculation and the corresponding empirical data are examined. All of these tests provide support for Durkheim's interpretation in favor of the second time sequence.

Lipset presents another instance of this approximation in a recent inquiry.[53] He conducted a survey among students at the University of California as to their *general* attitude toward the employment of Communists on the Faculty and their *specific* attitude toward the plan of the Regents to institute a "loyalty oath" as the means of controlling the employment of Communist teachers. While all the newspapers in the area were opposed in their editorial policies to the employment of Communists as teachers, they varied in their editorial position on the desirability of the oath. In the course of the study, Lipset obtained a relationship between student attitudes and the newspapers they read, and he then poses the problem of time sequence: "One could not conclude . . . that the newspapers of the Bay area played an important factor in the *development of opinion on the oath* and the hiring issues. It is possible that the readers of the different papers differentiated on other factors, such as class in school or political sympathies. One would have expected that liberals *would have been more prone to read a liberal newspaper*."

Lipset employs an elaborate and complex approximation to decide which time sequence is operative. While the entire procedure is most deserving of the student's careful attention, we shall limit ourselves to only

---

53. S. M. Lipset, "Opinion Formation in a Crisis Situation," *Publ. Opinion. Quart.*, 17, 1953, 20-46. Quoted by permission of the publishers. Reprinted in D. Katz, *et al, Public Opinion and Propaganda* (New York: Dryden, 1954), 584-598.

one aspect. Central to the procedure is a logical derivation such as we are now discussing, and one which has *general application* to the problem of time sequence for relations involving exposure and attitudes. Let us first state the logic in most general terms. If one conceives of attitude *not as unitary,* but as a constellation of component views, one would normally expect that self-selection of media would be predicated on relatively *undifferentiated* or non-specific attitudes. A man does not pick his daily newspaper on the basis of some specific, transient, segmental attitude but on the basis of a general orientation, radical-conservative, isolationist-internationalist, etc. By contrast, the effects of media content, if any, ought to be reflected in particular component attitudes which correspond to the specific character of the editorial material to which he is exposed. Consequently, if one examines the series of relations between exposure and a variety of responses within some attitudinal domain, he should be able to appraise which time sequence is operative. Now, Lipset observed "that readers of the more conservative papers tended to be more conservative on the *policy issue* of Communist employment than . . . the readers of the liberal papers. This was at least in part a result of selective purchasing of newspapers" (p. 29), for as Lipset comments this might represent the general ideology of the respondent, on the basis of which he might well pick his daily newspaper and also have a view on the employment of Communists as teachers. In the particular inquiry, the conclusion is, of course, not only plausible but exceedingly likely, because of the accidental fact that *all* newspapers in the area were *against* the employment of Communists as teachers. One would be hard pressed to account for *differences* in attitude as the result of exposure to a particular paper, when no matter what paper the person read, the position taken was substantially the *same.* Yet, this last point, while central in Lipset's study, is only incidental to our abstract discussion. Lipset then also observed a relation between the papers read, which varied in their editorial position on the oath, and the attitude specific to the imposition of the oath. He then notes "it is significant . . . that the relationship between newspaper read and attitude toward the oath was *greater* than the one between the paper and attitude toward the policy, suggesting . . . *the influence of the newspaper* on students' attitudes toward the oath." (p. 31) [54]

If merely selectivity on the basis of a general predisposition toward the issue of Communist teachers were operative, there should have been no increment of difference on the oath issue specifically. However, if the experience of reading the specific and varying treatment of the oath issues had an additional effect, one would expect the difference to widen. This latter phenomenon is the very one observed, and strengthens Lipset's conclusion.

We shall present one more particularly interesting illustration of this approach from a survey, which we shall have occasion to examine again later

---

54. Italics ours.

in the text. In 1946 and 1947, the American Military Agency in Occupied Germany conducted surveys and asked the question "Have you read *Mein Kampf?*" About one-fifth of the sample had read all or part of the book. The analysts examined the extent of readership in various population groups but also determined the relation between having read Hitler's work and the possession of certain attitudes or ideology. Before presenting the actual finding, the reader can anticipate the formal problem the analyst will face. Did the reading of the book produce such attitudes, or did people with particular attitudes selectively expose themselves to the book?

It will become self-evident shortly that the finding is of such a nature that the analyst can make a reasonable decision without any special devices of the types earlier described, and that this decision is predicated on a logical analysis of the phenomenon. We have previously argued that if an attitude is a product of exposure, it should exhibit certain *specificities* that correspond to the contents to which one is exposed. It so happens that the actual finding obtained is that those who have read *Mein Kampf* are *considerably more likely to be opposed to absolutism* as manifested in the proposition: "All personal rights of the people can be taken away by the state, if it is for the good of the whole people." It would seem absurd to argue that the time sequence involved is that the reading determines ideology, because the attitude observed is so contrary to the message in the book. Unless one hypothesizes a kind of "boomerang" in which the very effect of Hitler's polemic is to persuade the reader in reverse, the finding is so patently an absurdity that one of the time sequences must be rejected as a possibility.

But let us consider the alternative time sequence: that the more *liberal* are predisposed to select certain kinds of reading matter, namely, *Mein Kampf.* That selective exposure occurs is well known, but that individuals are so *perverse* as to expose themselves to reading matter that is *not* congenial to their attitudes also appears to be an absurdity and contrary to past literature on self-selection. Thus, the analyst confronts here a situation in which logical analysis suggests that neither time sequence is congruent with the particular character of the findings. We shall leave the solution of this mystery to a later page in the text, and hope that the reader will anticipate our discussion.

We have now illustrated a series of devices for treating the problem of time sequence. In the absence of a definitive solution for the problem of time sequence the analyst may choose from among these for treating the problem. However, the student should realize that these do not exhaust the possibilities and that many ingenious variations on these procedures can and must be *invented* to suit the particular research problem he faces. Moreover, since these are generally only approximations to the ideal, it is wise to employ a number of them simultaneously. As an illustration of this over all strategy and of research ingenuity, we shall present a recent inquiry by Deutsch and Collins in which *no less than eight* different types of approximate solutions are employed.[55] In addition, it should be noted that a variety of specific tests are devised within these general classes of solutions. Thus, *no less* than 20 actual tests are made.

Deutsch and Collins' "Interracial Housing"—A Case Study of Multiple Approximations for the Solution of the Time Order of Variables: We first give a very brief outline of the inquiry and the problem faced by the analysts. Deutsch and Collins were concerned with evaluating the *effects* of alternative race relations policies in public housing on the behavior, attitudes and social relations of the occupants. More specifically, they inquired as to whether whites living in *integrated* interracial housing projects in which *apartments* are assigned without regard to race, *become* more favorable in their race relations than whites living in bi-racial projects, where the apartments within the project are assigned on a *segregated* basis. Two projects exhibiting each of these contrasted occupancy patterns but matched in a number of other major respects were selected, and interviews covering a variety of aspects of race relations were conducted with the occupants. The white occupants of the integrated projects were found to have more intimate contacts with Negroes, more frequently to have norms and expectations that Negro-white relations were proper, and to have less prejudiced attitudes towards Negroes than the white occupants of the bi-racial projects. The analysts interpret these differences as support for the hypothesis that the *experience* of living in an integrated project *produces a change* in the race relations of whites towards Negroes. However, they were thoroughly aware of an alternative explanation of the empirical findings obtained. The critic might well argue that those white individuals who *initially* were more favorable towards Negroes were the ones who would select to move into the integrated project. Since there were no surveys taken prior to residency in the project to establish initial attitudes, the differences obtained conceivably reflect this reverse time ordering of the variables, and constitute no support whatsoever for the original hypothesis. Deutsch and Collins, therefore, present a variety of solutions of this analytic dilemma and much data which taken all together permit great confidence in their interpretation. We shall outline some of the explicit solutions and some of the inferences as to time order that grow out of bodies of data incidentally presented in the study.

1. *Comparisons by Length of Experience in the Project:* When residents in one integrated project were sub-divided into sub-groups varying in length of residence in the housing project, it was found that those older in residence showed less prejudice. Consequently, the original relationship could not have been *solely* a function of self-selection on the basis of initial atti-

---

55. *Op. cit.*, all the subsequent quotations are reprinted by permission of the publishers.

tudes of non-prejudice. If it were, increased length of experience should have resulted in no further reduction in prejudice.

This same analysis illustrates the methodological problem associated with such "interseniority comparisons" to which we have previously alluded. In the second integrated housing project, the recent residents as contrasted with the old residents moved following World War II mainly as a result of preference given to veterans. They constitute therefore a younger group who are better educated, more liberal, and less prejudiced and this vitiates the use of the procedure in this particular project. (102-103)

2. *Measures of Initial Level of Prejudice at the Time of Occupancy and of the Occurrence of Change in Attitude Were Obtained by Retrospective Questions:* a. Evidence that attitude had changed as a function of the experience rather than self-selection having occurred was provided by retrospective questions which asked: "How much have your ideas about colored people changed since you have lived in the project?" (If some change) "In what ways have they changed?" The results of these questions indicate a much greater reported change in attitude towards non-prejudice among the residents of the integrated projects. (96-97)

b. An inferential measure of initial level of prejudice is obtained by retrospective questions on associations with Negroes prior to occupancy either as friends, fellow workers, or neighbors. These data establish that the occupants of both types of projects had equivalent amounts of past intimate, equal-status experiences. Deutsch and Collins raise the question of the limitation of such data about behavior as an index of prejudice, but note that a number of research studies have demonstrated the relation of such contacts to prejudice. Consequently the inference seems warranted that the initial levels of prejudice were the same and that the original results represent the effect of experience. (48-49)

c. Measures of the initial attitudes of the tenants of the respective types of projects were inferred from the retrospective question: "Can you remember what you thought colored people were like before you moved into the project?" In the aggregate, these data establish that the initial levels of attitude in the different types of projects were equivalent and that the original findings must therefore represent changes following residence. (96) [56]

d. Deutsch and Collins by additional analysis of these data confirm their point beyond any doubt. The tenants of the respective projects are subdivided on the basis of the retrospective measure of initial attitude and their present attitudes are examined. Thus, among those tenants of integrated projects who reported initially unfavorable attitudes, approximately 50% had favorable attitudes at the time of the inquiry, whereas among the equiv-

---

56. In point of fact, there is an additional complexity involved in this particular analysis arising out of certain demographic differences between the two *integrated* projects. We shall not discuss this finer point of the analysis. The reader is referred to p. 96 if he is interested.

alent group in the segregated projects only 8% had favorable attitudes at the time of inquiry. In other words, when the two groups are matched on initial attitude, the differences still obtain. (96-98)

3. *The Use of Previous Research Gives Additional Weight to the Interpretation in Favor of One Time Order:* Deutsch and Collins note that six previous studies support the hypothesis that "equal-status contacts with Negroes are likely to reduce prejudice." They therefore suggest that the same inference in their study, rather than the alternative explanation in terms of self-selection, has greater credibility. (123)

4. *Qualitative Data Give Plausibility to the Interpretation by the Elaborateness and Apparent Veracity with Which a Process of Change is Reported:* Deutsch and Collins remark: "The interview material provides dramatic illustration of the nature of the attitudinal changes which occurred among many of the housewives in the integrated projects. Thus, one woman when asked to tell how she felt about living in the project, said, 'I started to cry when my husband told me we were coming to live here. I cried for three weeks. I didn't want to come and live here where there were so many colored people. I didn't want to bring my children up with colored people, but *we had to come; there was no place else to go.*[57] Well, all that's changed. I've really come to like it. I see they're just as human as we are . . . I've come to like them a great deal. I'm no longer scared of them.' " Deutsch and Collins quote other respondents as well and note that these particular data are not atypical. (98-99)

5. *Checks Upon the Volitional Base Required for the Phenomenon of Self-Selection:* It was noted in our earlier formal discussion of approximate solutions to the problem of time order that self-selection on the basis of prior attitude can be conceptualized in terms of two factors; motivation plus the conditions insuring that the individual engage in the particular act of self-selection.

Deutsch and Collins present a variety of evidence based on a number of different sources that the necessary conditions for self-selection are not operative.

a. With respect to the *strength of motives to engage in self-selection* they note that the "housing need in low-income groups . . . was desperate. . . . To be eligible for admission into a public housing project, the need had to be particularly desperate, since only a small percentage of those in need could be admitted." (46) Consequently, any tendency to self-select the integrated projects only by those with non-prejudiced attitudes was likely to be overridden by other stronger needs for housing.

b. With respect to external restraints upon voluntary self-selection, Deutsch and Collins note that the two integrated projects were in New York

---

57. Italics ours to underscore the point made below on the basis of quantitative data about the non-volitional character of the behavior.

City and "at the time of tenanting . . . a prospective tenant could only move into an integrated project. No segregated projects existed and no vacancies existed in the few older all-white projects. All other available projects were integrated; none were segregated bi-racial." (46) Consequently, any motives towards self-selection could not become operative in the integrated projects because of the external restraints in the situation.

By contrast, the two segregated projects were in Newark where there were alternatives of all-white projects. Thus, a person who chose the segregated but interracial project might well have been initially less prejudiced than the occupant of the integrated project for whom there was no other choice. Deutsch and Collins thus argue that initial self-selection on a voluntary basis might well have worked to minimize any differences in the direction of non-prejudice emerging from the experience in the integrated project. (151)

c. More direct evidence on the lack of self-selective behavior in such a motivational setting was available from an analysis of *refusals to rent among prospective tenants.* "The rate of refusals was low—estimated as less than 5% (for all reasons, only a few of which are relevant to race) . . . " (150)

d. *The cognitive basis for initial self-selection was examined by the retrospective questions:* "Did you know that there would be colored and white families here?"; (if yes) "Did you think that colored and white families would be living in the same building?" The analysis of these data was quite involved and revealed a number of significant findings. Thus, it is interesting that while all the projects—segregated or integrated—were interracial, between 19% and 36% of the samples in the various projects believed that the projects were to be *all* white. However, among the remaining majorities, the data established that the tenants of the respective types of projects were *aware* of the different occupancy patterns at the time they became tenants. Consequently, for the majority there was a cognitive *basis* for self-selection.

Deutsch and Collins, therefore, cannot use these latter data in support of their inference about the effect of experience and are forced into a more refined analysis. The tenants in each type of project were subdivided on the basis of their initial awareness of the occupancy pattern and their attitudes then examined. If the cognitive basis for self-selection *actually* did result in self-selection which in turn accounted for the original aggregate differences between projects, one could make certain predictions about the sub-groups. For example, one would expect those tenants in the integrated projects who initially self-selected it on the *false* ground that it was segregated to have levels of prejudice equivalent to tenants in segregated projects with the same initial expectations. The results of such analyses showed, on the contrary "that regardless of pre-application expectation the frequencies of unprejudiced response are much higher in the integrated than in the segregated projects." (152-155)

e. *With respect to self-selection on the cognitive basis of subsequent knowledge rather than foreknowledge,* Deutsch and Collins present statistical records from the projects to indicate that "voluntary move-outs, for all reasons, have been infrequent . . . at an average annual rate of about 3% in Koaltown and of about 6% in Sacktown." (150) [58]

6. *Parallel Comparisons for Related Exposed Individuals Other Than the Original Decision Makers:* It was previously noted that self-selection usually involves a particular *individual* engaging in some *voluntary act* on the basis of a prior predisposition. Consequently, if one obtains similar results from individuals who by virtue of some accidental association with the original respondents are also exposed, one can argue that they had no opportunity to indulge their own choices and that the results are therefore the product of the experience. This design may seem sound but academic as a procedure. Yet, it is relatively easily employed, since individuals in surveys are usually sampled within a family context. The analyst may with little additional difficulty or expense draw a sample of related family members. Deutsch and Collins followed such a design. They used housewives in the projects as their major subjects. However, a small number of the children were also interviewed and it was found that both attitudes and behavior involving friendly race relations were more characteristic of children in integrated projects. In comparison with the adult data, these findings seem even less vulnerable to the criticism of self-selection on the basis of initial attitude. Self-selection as voluntary individual behavior would conceivably characterize the adults who made the decision to become tenants, but the children have no such option—they simply go with their parents. True it is that positive relations between the attitudes of parents and children have been generally established in the literature, but these coefficients are only moderate in magnitude.[59] Consequently, while the child of a self-selecting parent in the integrated project might be initially a little less prejudiced, it seems more likely that the sizable differences demonstrated at the level of children, where attitudes are still in the process of growth and only moderately predetermined by parents, support the original inference. (61-62, 88) [60]

---

58. These are the pseudonyms for the two integrated projects.

59. For example in Newcomb and Svehla's study, the coefficients ranged between .4 and .6 depending on the attitude studied. See Murphy, Murphy and Newcomb, *op. cit.,* p. 1036.

60. Klineberg, in a sense, also makes use of this test for time sequence. His data are based on the higher intelligence of Northern *children,* and as he notes the argument of selective migration, strictly speaking, applies to the *parents* or families of the children. "These children were not in any sense the originators of the migration; they went *passively* with their parents. May it not be that even though the adult migrants constituted a superior, selected group, their children would not reflect any such superiority?" He thus points out that implicitly "the hypothesis of selective migration involves the further hypothesis that superiority is inherited" and remarks, "There is probably a certain amount of mental similarity between various members of

7. *A Logical Model of the Functioning of Attitude in Relation to Experience or Self-selection is Derived and the Findings Examined for Congruence with the Model:* One may argue that attitudes of prejudice towards Negroes prior to residence which might operate as a basis for self-selection would be relatively *undifferentiated,* or *non-specific.* The respondent who would desire to enter the integrated project, for example, might be more liberal and non-prejudiced than a respondent who would be hostile to residence, but his attitudes would probably not incorporate any particular contents that are specific to the character of the actual integrated project in which he subsequently lived. By contrast, attitudinal change following experience would be expected to exhibit *certain specificities* of content corresponding to the nature of experience. Similarly, one would expect these initially unprejudiced who selected the integrated project on that basis to show lack of prejudice over a wide variety of ethnic groups, for generality of prejudice has been well established by past research. By contrast, attitudes of non-prejudice emerging out of residency would be expected to exist more *discretely* in relation to Negroes rather than to other ethnic groups, for this was the essence of the experience for the respondent and the lesson might well not carry over to other objects of prejudice. A whole series of such models of the different ways in which attitudes might function, given these alternative processes, can be elaborated and compared with the data. In all such instances, Deutsch and Collins' findings confirm their hypothesis inferentially.

a. Thus, both the respondent's attitudes towards the Negro people in the project and his attitudes towards Negro people in general were obtained. The differences between integrated and segregated projects were greater with respect to attitude toward Negroes in the project which is the expected pattern if experience is the explanatory variable. (90)

b. The respondents were asked what traits they attribute to Negro people in the project. Among "positive attributes," one in which differences between integrated and segregated projects was very marked was "helpfulness" or "neighborliness," an element clearly related to the context of experience in the project rather than to the usual cognitive structure of non-prejudice in a person who would have a predisposition initially to become a resident. Similarly, a "negative attribute" which was very frequently mentioned in the integrated project and very rarely mentioned in the segregated project was that Negroes have an "inferiority complex about prejudice." Here again one has an element of the cognitive structure of prejudice that would be exceedingly rare in non-prejudice solely on the basis of initial predisposition to residence, and clearly to be expected on the basis of close contact

---

the same family, but the extent of this similarity is still an open question. It is *not* likely that the resemblance between parents and children is so close as the hypothesis of selective migration would demand." (Pp. 15-16), *op. cit.,* italics ours.

with Negroes and a growing awareness of their sensitivity to injury and hurt from whites. (80-81)

c. Social Distance towards various ethnic groups other than Negroes was determined. With respect to Puerto Ricans, residents of both types of projects had about the same attitudes. With respect to Chinese, attitudes of the respondents in the integrated project were somewhat more favorable, but the differences were considerably smaller than for the Negro social distance items. Again, such a model of relatively specific change is what one would expect as a product of experience, whereas self-selection on the basis of initial attitude would call for a more generalized anti-prejudice position. (105-106)

d. Individuals with initial prejudice towards Negroes would be expected to have a generalized hostility to living in *any* inter-racial project, whether the occupancy pattern was integrated or not. Consequently, by the choice of contrasted types, both exhibiting an inter-racial character, one would expect that self-selection would have operated as a constant in the comparison and could not account for any differences. Deutsch and Collins further note that all four projects were located in predominantly Negro neighborhoods making it likely that any initially prejudiced person would self-select against residence in any of the projects. (151)

8. *The Use of Stable Characteristics Correlative with Prejudice for Inferential Evidence on Self-Selection:* While Deutsch and Collins do not have any measures of level of prejudice prior to occupancy, other than retrospective ones, they know from accumulated research findings that prejudice tends to be correlated with a variety of personal characteristics. Since these latter characteristics are, by definition, *stable or persistent entities* in the life history of the adult, there is no problem of retrospection as in the case of such changeable factors, for example, as past contacts with Negroes.[61] Consequently, by comparing the residents in the two types of housing projects in these respects, they can infer whether or not there was self-selection on the basis of initial differences in prejudice. As they remark: "if selectivity . . . was at work during the tenanting of the various projects one would expect it to be reflected in differences among these characteristics of the housewives. That is, it is not unreasonable to assume that if the housewives moving into the New York projects were less prejudiced before their moving, this lesser degree of prejudice would be associated with the amount of their education, their type of political belief, their religion, or some combination of these factors." (47)

Examination of these data shows that the residents of the integrated

---

61. This is not to deny that there are response errors in the measurement of stable demographic characteristics. There is considerable evidence to this effect. However, such errors do not relate to the problem of memory, for these characteristics are indicative of the *current status* of the individual. For evidence on unreliability or response error in the measurement of such characteristics, see, P. Kendall, *Conflict and Mood, op. cit.*

projects are more frequently Jewish, politically liberal, and at least in one instance better educated. Thus, it is *possible,* although not established, that they were also initially less prejudiced and in turn, self-selected the particular projects because the past research studies establish relations between non-prejudice and these factors. Given these suggestive data, Deutsch and Collins cannot terminate the particular analysis. Just as in the instance of the retrospective measures of cognition, the analysis had to be pursued in order to establish whether self-selection did or did not actually account for the findings, given the possibility. The mode of analysis employed follows the general pattern described in (2d, 7d) above.

a. The comparisons of respondents in integrated and segregated projects on a variety of measures of prejudice are made separately for sub-groups matched with respect to demographic characteristics. In all these sub-group comparisons, the original differences persist. Consequently, Deutsch and Collins argue that occupancy changes prejudice. Since whatever self-selection could have occurred in the *aggregate* groups on the basis of prior attitude is controlled in these refined tests and still the differences obtain, occupancy must have an independent effect. Since the procedure or logic is quite complex, a few concrete examples may clarify it for the reader. For example, Deutsch and Collins compare liberals in both projects. The liberals in the integrated project conceivably had initial attitudes of non-prejudice and engaged in self-selection. However, there exist a smaller proportion of liberals presumably initially non-prejudiced also, who by some accident ended up in the wrong project, a segregated one. The liberals in the integrated projects, however, turn out to be much less prejudiced. Similarly, Deutsch and Collins compare conservatives in both types of projects. The conservatives in the segregated project conceivably had initial attitudes of prejudice and engaged in self-selection. A smaller proportion of conservatives, presumably initially prejudiced also, by accident ended up in the wrong project, an integrated one. The conservatives in the integrated project turn out to be less prejudiced. (58-61, 117-119)

b. A *more powerful* test of this general type is also employed. The reader may well have entertained legitimate doubts as to the validity of the procedure and argued that any such demographic characteristic is only *moderately* correlated with prejudice and that the matching procedure therefore may reduce variations in initial level of prejudice, but certainly does not exclude all such variation. Therefore, Deutsch and Collins, no doubt thinking in this same vein, match residents in both types of projects *simultaneously on all three characteristics.* Such a matching is naturally more likely to reduce initial variations in prejudice. Yet, the original differences still persist. (60, 118)

c. The reader might still argue that some residual variations in initial level of prejudice persist despite such an elaborate matching. Consequently

Deutsch and Collins employ still another approach which is ingenious and even more powerful in its impact on and support for their hypothesis. They compare those individuals in *integrated* projects whose demographic characteristics are such that their initial attitudes would be likely to be *prejudiced* with individuals in *segregated* projects whose demographic characteristics are such that they would be likely to be *non-prejudiced*. In other words, granted that the *magnitude* of these correlations is far from unity, their *direction* is indisputable. Despite this "unfair" matching, which handicaps the original hypothesis in the way it allocates any initial differences in attitude, the differences persist. For example, Deutsch and Collins note that "whereas almost all of the liberals in the segregated projects are entirely devoid of neighborly relations with Negro tenants, this can be said of only a considerably smaller percentage of the conservatives in the integrated projects." (60) [62]

The Distinction Between the Search for an Explanation and the Demonstration of a Relationship

The analyst is always searching for the explanation of the phenomenon under study. His search is successful when he obtains reliable evidence of the influence of one or more independent variables on the phenomenon. A detailed discussion has been presented already of certain of the empirical procedures that the analyst employs in this search. These procedures *always* involve the examination of the relationship of the phenomenon to *particular* independent variables, and from the findings conclusions are then drawn as to the determinants of the phenomenon. Frequently, the variables that are initially hypothesized as the determinants are the subject of *direct* examination. In such instances, it is most disappointing when *no* relationships can be demonstrated, for it means that the analyst has been unsuccessful in supporting the hypothesis. Consequently, analysts are usually very happy to demonstrate empirical relationships between variables. This pat-

---

62. The reader may have noted a formal resemblance between these matching procedures employed as solutions for interpreting time sequence and the matching instituted in survey analysis as a control on spuriousness. While the *technical procedures* are the same, the purpose is clearly different. In the instance of such matching for control on spuriousness, the analyst would have in mind the possibility that some third variable, education *per se* or liberalism *per se* were correlated with the independent variable, occupancy experience, and by matching control the effect of such a variable. In the present discussion, however, these characteristics are not manipulated in order to separate their particular influence on the phenomenon. Rather they are used as indicators of a *totally different variable, initial attitude*, for purposes of evaluating the time order of the original two variables. Admittedly, the procedure employed could also be used by Deutsch and Collins for purposes of control of spuriousness, i.e., for asking whether the findings are due to education or liberalism originally uncontrolled in the analysis. However, in the present discussion it serves only the one purpose.

tern of direct demonstrations is so common in the explanatory survey that it has come to be identified with *all* explanatory analyses. The analyst tends to regard success as identical with positive demonstrations of a relationship. He tends to glorify the findings of differences in the phenomenon between individuals or groups contrasted with respect to some independent variable, and to search exclusively for such differences. There is great danger in this pattern of analysis. When the analyst concentrates solely on such differences, he loses a great deal.

This is most obvious in the instance of experimental surveys whose value lies in the *disconfirmation* of previously reported findings. We have already alluded in the previous chapters to the possibility that positive findings as to an explanation may be due to some error introduced during the earlier survey process; or that the findings may be real but limited in scope because of the partial and inadequate conceptualization of the phenomenon or because of the particular point in time and human universe that was sampled. Quite often the analyst may or should undertake a new survey, under new conditions of sampling or conceptualization or measurement and the *lack* of a relationship rather than the demonstration of one in the second survey will be of great importance in qualifying the meaning of earlier explanations.[63]

We shall see that there are many other types of explanatory analyses in which success requires that *no* empirical relationship be demonstrated between *particular* variables. All of these analyses are predicated on one central point. The empirical demonstration of the nature of the relationship between particular variables is not the same as the conclusion that is to be drawn about the correlates or cause of the phenomenon. The empirical demonstration often bears on the goal of explaining the phenomenon only in an *indirect* way, for it may well be that the hypothesized explanation is never put to a direct test. The test that is actually made—the demonstration of a relationship between particular variables—may *refer inferentially* to an independent variable which cannot be or deliberately was not examined directly. The analyst for a variety of reasons may be interested in variable or Cause #1 but will actually test the influence of Cause #2 on the phenomenon. He will by some process of inference then argue as to the significance of Cause #1 from the findings observed for Cause #2. We shall see that only through such a pattern of analysis which approaches the problem of explanation in a roundabout or indirect manner have we a *unique* key to certain survey problems, and an improved mode of analysis for other survey problems. And the analyst is barred from such gains when he neg-

---

63. The significance of such disconfirmation is well demonstrated by one of our later case studies, Sewell's inquiry into the effect of infant training on adult personality patterns where the negative findings are most relevant to psychoanalytic theorizing about character types. See Part IV, p. 357.

lects the distinction between the conclusion or *inference* which ends the search for an explanation and the *empirical demonstration* of a relationship between particular variables. Not only is he barred from functioning effectively, but he is discouraged when he should not be and he ignores the meaning and value of empirical findings that are negative. We shall first illustrate in detail this indirect approach to explanation from one of the case studies we have used earlier, Durkheim's *Suicide*.

Durkheim's "Suicide"—A Case Study of Indirect Explanation Through the Demonstration of No Relationship Between Particular Variables and the Phenomenon: The reader will recall our discussion in Part II of Durkheim's analytic approach. Following the model of a descriptive survey analysis, Durkheim initially examines data on suicide rates computed for nations over long periods of time. He observes a regularity in the phenomenon. He notes a distinctive and persistent rate for different nations and is therefore led to or strengthened in the view that the phenomenon is dependent on *causes of "broad generality."* He reasons that the explanation of a phenomenon that has a widespread distribution must lie in one or more causes sufficiently widespread to comprehend the phenomenon. Durkheim does not dispute, of course, the possibility of idiosyncratic factors in accounting for the origin of *individual* suicides, but his concern is with suicide rates for large *aggregates* of people and his train of reasoning is simply that "individual conditions are *not general enough* to affect the relation between the total number of voluntary deaths and the population. They may perhaps cause this or that separate individual to kill himself, but not give society as a whole a greater or lesser tendency to suicide." The causes must be "capable of affecting not separate individuals but the group . . . society as a whole." [64] Durkheim therefore seeks the explanation in variables that are "expressly social," and tries to test his hypothesis by demonstrating differences in the suicide rate of groups contrasted in certain social respects. In these tests, he hopes to find *positive evidence* of a relationship. Yet prior to all such tests or demonstrations, a whole series of other empirical tests are conducted in which his purpose and hope is to find *no* evidence whatsoever of a relationship, and some *150 pages of text* and analysis are devoted to such procedures. In no instance in these 150 pages are any "expressly social" factors examined directly. Yet, all of these tests provide evidence *inferentially* in support of the influence of social factors on suicide. They do not constitute a mere digression and are essential to the strengthening of the total work, for Durkheim recognizes the clear distinction between evidence relevant to the search for an explanation and the empirical demonstration that there is a relationship. What is involved?

While Durkheim reasoned from his descriptive data on suicide rates that the regularity and widespread distribution of the phenomenon im-

---

64. *Op. cit.*, 51-52, italics ours.

plied a cause of broad generality, he recognized that there are *two* classes of independent variables that would satisfy this requirement of broad generality, ones that are widespread but *extra-social* and others that are widespread and *social* in character. To Durkheim, the extra-social causes were either "organic-psychic dispositions" in which are included psycho-pathology, racial and hereditary factors or factors of the "physical environment" such as climate or temperature. Insofar as nations or groups varied in these extra-social respects, for example, differed in their geographical location and mean temperature, the explanation of the suicide rate might be of an extra-social nature. Consequently, Durkheim could support his theory *indirectly* by a demonstration that the first class of factors shows *no* relationship. By this elimination or exclusion, evidence in support for the *only* other class of factors, the expressly social, would be provided without any recourse to the direct test of the relationship of suicide to social factors. The editor and co-translator of the English edition of the work presents in his preface the design of the procedure: "The early chapters in Durkheim's work are devoted to the *negation* of doctrines which ascribe suicide to extra-social factors. . . . Here in these early chapters Durkheim is involved in a process of *elimination:* all these which require resort to individual or other extra-social causes for suicide are dispatched, leaving only social causes to be considered. This is used as a foundation for *reaffirming* his thesis." [65] We shall abstract Durkheim's discussion to emphasize the approach:

First, Durkheim examines by a variety of tests the relationship between psychopathology and the suicide rate. For example, the relation between the rate and proportion of insane and idiots in the population of given countries is examined. The relation between suicide and alcoholic psychoses and total consumption is examined for given large groups. Durkheim remarks, "no psychopathic state bears a regular and indisputable relation to suicide."

Secondly, Durkheim examines by a variety of tests the relationship between "normal psychological states," i.e., racial and hereditary predispositions, and suicide and concludes that the evidence is negative.

Thirdly, he examines by a variety of tests the relationship between suicide rate and "cosmic factors." For example, the climate and suicide rates for given latitudes of Europe are examined. Finally, the influence of individual psychological processes of imitation on the suicide rate is examined, and Durkheim concludes that "imitation . . . does not contribute to the unequal tendency in different societies to self-destruction, or to that of smaller social groups within each society. . . . Imitation all by itself has no effect on suicide." [66]

On the basis of this total analysis, which led to the demonstration of *no*

65. *Ibid.*, 13-14, italics ours.
66. *Ibid.*, p. 140.

relationships, which *denied* all the initial hypotheses advanced, Durkheim then remarks: "The results of the preceding book are *not wholly negative*. We have in fact shown that for each social group there is a specific tendency to suicide explained *neither* by the organic-psychic constitution of individuals *nor* the nature of the physical environment. Consequently, *by elimination* it must *necessarily* depend on social causes and be in itself a collective phenomenon." [67]

There are, of course, *methodological* problems associated with such an approach. There are questions of *error* in the analyses, measurements, and tests of the influence of the variables. There are questions of the *sampling* basis of the data that are used in the tests. However, all of these problems are *methodological* problems of a general nature which apply equally to demonstrations of relationships of a positive kind and tests of an indirect or negative kind. They have been treated in detail earlier and will be discussed again in later sections.

We shall also see shortly that there are special *analytic* problems in such an approach. For example, the question may well arise as to whether the *choice* of specific variables which are examined and which presumably *exhaust* the class of factors whose influence is to be *rejected* does in fact exhaust the class. Thus, it might be that Durkheim neglected an extra-social factor of significance, even though he considered this question carefully and implies that this is not the case. He remarks on this question: "There are two sorts of extra-social causes to which one may, *a priori,* attribute an influence on the suicide rate." [68]

In addition, there is the analytic problem of avoiding *arbitrariness* by the setting of different standards for the rejection of the evidence of a series of such tests and the acceptance of the evidence of other tests. Another one of our cases which also employs negative evidence as inferential support for its central hypothesis provides an illustration of the seriousness of these analytic problems. For the moment we wish merely to emphasize the basic distinction between the empirical demonstration of a relationship and evidence in support of a given explanation. We wish to show the logic of the approach which makes use of indirect evidence and thereby provide the student with additional resources in doing explanatory surveys.[69]

The student may have noted one strange feature in the design followed by Durkheim. After he completed all these *indirect* tests whose sole purpose was the negation of all possible explanations other than social causes, he

---

67. *Ibid.,* p. 145, italics ours.

68. *Ibid.,* p. 57.

69. The reader may recognize that this approach to survey analysis is but an application of general principles from the field of the logic of science having to do with the logical relations between propositions. For a systematic treatment see: M. Cohen and E. Nagel, *An Introduction to Logic and Scientific Method* (New York: Harcourt, 1934), Chap. III. For a rare example of the discussion of such indirect methods in social research, see H. Zetterberg, *On Theory and Verification in Sociology* (New York: The Tressler Press, 1954), p. 21, ff.

then proceeded to make direct tests of the influence of social factors. One ponders this fact. If the logical analysis originally made was correct—if suicide can only be due to A or to B—and if Durkheim is able to reject hypotheses other than B—the social, why does he then bother to make direct tests of the social factors? Or one might reverse the question and ask why does Durkheim bother initially with all the indirect tests which are used inferentially to support an hypothesis when he obviously has at his disposal resources for a direct test of his hypotheses and actually conducts such direct tests. While we can, of course, only speculate as to why *Durkheim* as an analyst followed this design, we can present a rational argument as to the relative advantages of the indirect vs. the direct test or the advantages of the combined approach of indirect and direct tests.

1. Unique Use of the Indirect Test

There are unusual instances in explanatory survey analysis where *in practice* no direct test is possible. Under such conditions, the indirect test provides the only avenue of support for an hypothesis, and the distinction we have been making between explanation and the demonstration of a relationship is crucial for the analyst. It is difficult to find a specific example of such a situation in published survey analyses for one obvious reason. The lack of general awareness of the indirect approach has led analysts to conduct survey research on problems that were manageable or solvable through the use of direct tests. They have rarely exploited indirect tests and the range of findings has unfortunately been restricted. However, Durkheim's own study provides the clue to one type of problem that would be amenable to study mainly via such an approach. We note that Durkheim was interested in independent variables or causes of an *extreme macroscopic* type, the influence of societal factors. As in all survey analysis, *direct* evidence as to the influence of a given variable requires that individuals or groups be *contrasted* with respect to that variable. Durkheim was able to do this directly through the use of *existing records* on suicide rates available for very large aggregates such as nations. Thus he could range over the universe and examine the influence on the suicide rate of the diverse social systems of Denmark and Spain, of the political climate of 1830 and 1849, of military vs. civilian life. But much survey analysis deals with phenomena which are not represented in existing archives and records, and yet the analyst might well wish to examine the relevance of global social determinants. Generally, he can do little in the way of huge comparative research; his surveys cannot cover the universe or the centuries or even a decade. Yet, following the logic of the indirect test, perhaps these types of explanations can be put to test. For example, to support the notion of a cultural or societal factor in the formation of an opinion, and yet not be able to compare societies directly, one might well examine whether sub-groups in a society

show different values of the phenomenon. Such groups vary in many respects and are the same only in having some common overarching membership, e.g., in the society. If *all* the tests made demonstrate *no* effect of the
sub-group factors, one would infer that the determinant lies at the global,
transcendent level.[70] The analyst under such conditions seeks not to find
differences, but to find *uniformities* between groups. Our only illustration
of such a survey finding constitutes an approximation to this type of indirect test. The British Social Survey conducted an inquiry into the causes
of rural depopulation in Scotland.[71] For a period of over 50 years the population had been declining and the Dept. of Health for Scotland desired
guidance. In the course of this survey, residents of a series of regions in
Scotland were asked whether they planned to migrate.

Alternative hypotheses as to the explanations of migration might involve either a theory of *specific* factors impinging on particular individuals
or a theory of some constellation of factors which characterize rural Scottish life *generally.* Consequently, the relation between the phenomenon of
plans to migrate and region *within* rural Scotland was examined. It was
found that the proportion "does not differ significantly between the regions," suggesting that the specific features of the local environment are not
the major explanation, but that there is a global social movement related
to rural Scottish life as such.

A somewhat parallel analytic approach can be used where one wishes
support for a theory of *extreme microscopic* psychological factors, without
being able to identify or measure such factors directly and examine their
effect on the phenomenon. If one is able to demonstrate that the phenomenon is not frequent, shows marked *variation* within a given society or population and yet is unrelated to any sub-group or social factor, by inference,
one draws the conclusion that the determinants must lie at a more idiosyncratic psychological level. Here one seeks to find differences, rather than
uniformities, but differences that are inexplicable at a certain gross level.

Many illustrations of such an indirect approach to explanation are available. For example, we can refer to a study we cited earlier of popular surfeit with war news over the radio.[72] Depending on the definition of surfeit
and the corresponding index used, a minority of the sample ranging between 15% and 35% were classified as "surfeited." The obvious hypothesis
about the explanation of why certain individuals are surfeited, while the
majority are not, involves some notion of ideological and emotional or

---

70. The methodological problem to which we alluded above, the *exhaustiveness* of the tests
of the factors whose influence is to be rejected, is crucial to this conclusion. However, we shall
neglect this problem and all we wish to do is emphasize at this point by various illustrations
the great usefulness of the indirect approach.

71. B. Hutchinson, Depopulation and Rural Life in Scotland, Central Office of Information,
The Social Survey, NS 120 (d), 1949.

72. Surfeit with War on the Radio, *op. cit.*

psychological factors which determine the tolerance of the individual to stimulation about war. And while some direct tests were actually made of the relationship of surfeit to ideology, no direct tests were made of the influence of factors within the personality. However, inferential support for such an hypothesis is available by use of indirect tests. In three independent studies of the problem it was found that "being fed up with the amount of war talk on the radio is not closely related to any particular personal characteristics. It does not vary much for different ages or educational levels, by sex, or economic level." [73] Consequently, it strengthens the view that the explanation must lie at a more idiosyncratic psychological level.

A specialized type of such indirect analyses is particularly useful in explanatory surveys of a *programmatic* nature, i.e., those concerned with the amelioration of phenomena involving criticism, dissatisfaction, disruptive or maladaptive behavior. In such surveys, among the group who are found to show the unsatisfactory side of the phenomenon, the explanation may lie either in exposure to stimuli and experiences which would legitimately create dissatisfaction or in more idiosyncratic psychological processes that do not derive directly from the bad features of the environment. The former explanation, if supported by evidence, leads to programs of reform. If the latter explanation is correct, amelioration is of a different order. Now it is often quite difficult to make direct tests of the influence of such psychological processes. However, if the phenomenon is examined for groups varying in their exposure to the unsatisfactory environment, and *no* relationships are demonstrated, it provides indirect support for the latter theory.

An illustration of this use of the indirect test is available in the study previously cited of Rural Depopulation in Scotland. As the analysts remark: "it might have been expected that the desire to migrate would have been noticeably more frequent amongst people living in lonely and isolated dwellings, on whom the full force of the disadvantages of rural life is turned." Yet, there is the alternative hypothesis which involves so-to-speak the notion that loneliness is a state of mind rather than a reaction to specific features of reality. The analysts examine the former hypothesis and find little evidence in support of it. Thus, 84% of those actually living in isolated houses as compared with 84% of those living in social contact in villages wished to remain.

Similarly, for other objective inadequacies in the environment no relationships to desire to migrate can be demonstrated. Partial data bearing on these analyses as summarized from the original report are presented below.[74]

---

73. *Ibid.*, p. 12.
74. The data are taken from pp. 27-28, Tables 21, 22, 23 of Depopulation and Rural Life.

TABLE VIII—The Relationship of Desire to Migrate Among Rural Scottish People and Various Physical Amenities

(An illustration of indirect support for a theory deriving from negative findings.)

	Percent who have particular characteristics among those who plan	
	To Remain	To Move
Percent who have indoor water supply	66%	69%
Percent who have plumbing involving main drainage	61	66
Percent having gas supply	29	36
Percent having electricity supply	52	59
Percent having refuse collection service	54	62
Percent connected to telephone	15	17
Percent having none of above 4 services	27	20

Another one of the case studies discussed earlier illustrates the same mode of analysis. In the study by Hyman and Sheatsley, the phenomenon of being uninformed was shown to be of a generalized character. This finding of a "chronic know-nothing" group led the analysts to conclude that the explanation of lack of information must be sought at a *general* level rather than in some specific factor. But as was pointed out earlier, there were two classes of factors both having a general character which might be relevant— the chronic know-nothings might live in an *environment which was lacking in sources of information,* or they might be individuals with a generalized *personality* pattern to reject information. Hyman and Sheatsley initially test the theory that a general feature of the objective environment is responsible and find little evidence of a relationship. This indirectly strengthens their theory that the explanation must lie in some general intra-psychic process. As the writers remark: "It is possible, of course, that the existence of this group may be related to external factors of accessibility to information media, and that if the information were somehow channeled into their vicinity, they would soon become exposed." They then make some empirical tests of this theory, using size of community as a crude index of the richness and availability of media in the environment. They find very little relationship, and remark, "the next section discusses the effect of certain psychological factors on level of knowledge." [75]

Supplementary Use of the Direct Test

Thus far, we have tried to illustrate the way in which the analyst could make use of evidence that there is no relationship of particular variables to the phenomenon to support, by inference, the influence of other determinants. We have suggested that particular types of problems, in practice, may *only* be amenable to this approach. Notable among such problems are ones where the explanation is believed to lie either at a macroscopic social or microscopic psychological level, which cannot be tested directly either be-

---

75. H. Hyman and P. B. Sheatsley, Some Reasons Why Information Campaigns Fail, *op. cit.*

cause of a lack of resources for comparative study or because the psychological processes are too elusive and subtle. In such instances the indirect approach is crucial.

Now let us consider other uses of the indirect approach. In the Durkheim case after the extra-social factors were rejected, the social factors were put to direct test. In the Hyman and Sheatsley case, after the objective environmental factors were rejected, the psychological factors were put to direct test. In the Scottish study a variety of psychological correlates were explored after the negative findings on amenities. In these instances, the direct test was supplementary. It was *apparently* unnecessary. Yet it was employed. What seems to be involved here? One thing is immediately clear in all of these studies. The logical examination of possible explanatory factors is rather *formal* in character. It merely identifies alternative *classes* of causes. Consequently, when one class of causes is rejected, it permits the inference that the other class is operative but does not identify in any concrete or detailed way what *specific* variables within the remaining class of factors are important. Consequently, the direct tests that are then employed serve the *function of locating*, within the operative class of factors, those that are of importance. Durkheim's study provides an ideal example of this fact, and all that is necessary is to enumerate the great variety of specific social factors whose relationship to suicide is examined in order to demonstrate that the indirect test by itself could not locate the determinants. Among the variables that Durkheim examines are formal religion, educational level, occupational class, marital status, sex, presence of children, size of household, presence of political crisis, membership in the military, and presence of economic crisis.[76] Obviously, without recourse to these many direct tests, the prior negative evidence on the influence of extra-social factors could not provide any guidance as to the significance of particular social factors.

Put in another way, Durkheim's well-known finding of three different types of social processes which lead to suicide, then termed *egoistic, altruistic* and *anomic* suicide, would otherwise never have been established, for this classification was dependent on the analysis of the specific factors which correlated with suicide.

Supplementary Use of the Indirect Test

We have suggested that in certain instances negative evidence from a test would be sufficient to confirm indirectly an alternative general hypothesis, but that supplementary analyses would still serve a function of locat-

---

76. As the reader of Durkheim will, of course, note these variables are merely the indices of or antecedent conditions for some particular underlying process, e.g., integration of the individual into the collectivity. However, this does not deny the point we are making of the host of specific factors which may be operative within a class of factors which by earlier indirect tests was found to be important.

ing the specific explanation. However, the reader might well raise the question as to why it would be necessary or desirable to undertake analyses whose purpose was to reject a given hypothesis. For example, granted that it was wise for Durkheim to make supplementary use of *direct* tests of social factors after the negative findings on extra-social factors, it would seem that the analytic process could still have been simplified. Why not undertake *initially* the direct tests of the social factors. This establishes the merits of the general hypothesis and also locates the specific explanation. Then there would have been no apparent need for conducting the other tests whose purpose was to reject extra-social factors. This might well be true if the logical analysis which is the preliminary basis for setting up the alternative hypotheses in Durkheim's work were sound. In the Durkheim and other examples posed the alternative hypotheses are posed as if they were *exclusive* in character. Suicide must either be due to extra-social *or* social factors. The chronic "know-nothing" must either be due to external factors *or* to psychological factors. Desire to migrate must either be due to external objective conditions *or* to more subtle psychological processes. But is it not perfectly possible that a phenomenon might be due to *several* sets of factors? If this assumption is correct, then it is clear why positive evidence on behalf of a given hypothesis *initially* would still call for supplementary use of indirect tests whose purpose is to reject another hypothesis. If there are only a limited number of explanations involved, and one is excluded initially, then the second is indirectly supported. But if several explanations may be involved, and one is confirmed, it provides no evidence that the other one is not also operative. One must undertake an empirical demonstration in order to reject the possibility that the other explanations are also involved. Thus, one comes to the simultaneous use of a series of tests, some of which are intended to yield positive, and some of which negative evidence, for it appears to be the analyst's desire usually to show not merely that his explanation is of *some* importance, but is of *primary* importance. Thus, in all these examples the simultaneous use of both kinds of tests has a special—almost polemic—value. It establishes the merits of a theory and it also establishes the *superiority* of that theory to other possible theories. The negative evidence thus serves the function of supporting by inference the superiority or primacy of a given explanation.

In a number of other case studies we have previously cited, we note this pattern of analysis. A series of possible determinants of the phenomenon is advanced and the analyst seeks to provide evidence for some of these explanations *but* against others. Thus in the studies of industrial morale and absenteeism, Katz and Hyman remark that their "aim was to establish some of the explanation of . . . absenteeism by correlation with over-all *plant and community* conditions. . . . The *relative significance* of these sets of factors needed to be demonstrated. Also the question of the effect of *objective* conditions of work *vs.* deeper *psychological* factors needed to be evaluated." [77]

We may recall that this inquiry was what we have labelled *programmatic*. The findings were intended to lead to action which would ameliorate the situation. In such instances, it is especially valuable to be able to order a variety of determinants in terms of their relative or exclusive importance. Resources may be so limited that it is essential to concentrate effort in the most fruitful direction. One may be unable to deal with all the possible significant factors and one wants to pick wisely. Thus, the findings that inplant conditions were more important determinants of absenteeism than out-plant or community conditions was helpful in focussing action.

Similarly, in the inquiry into class consciousness, despite considerable evidence in support of his original hypothesis, Centers is not content to terminate the analysis. He somehow wishes to establish the *exclusive* importance or superiority of his explanation. Thus following the major analysis he remarks that:

> class affiliations and politico-economic orientations are both to a very large extent direct consequences of the differing socio-economic positions of people in our system of production and exchange of goods and services. The objective status and role of persons is accompanied by such distinctive psychological manifestations that an inescapable suggestion of a cause and effect relation arises. . . . It would be most hasty and rash to be content with this impression without a more thorough appraisal of the nature of these relations, however. There are too many correlates of social class identification and conservatism-radicalism for one not to suspect many of them of having significant bearing of their own in shaping the complex of psychological manifestations that have been described.[78]

He therefore examines the *independent* influence of other determinants of ideology, formal education, age, church membership, factors of residence. His purpose here is distinct from the treatment of the special problem yet to be discussed of the confounding of variables and possible spuriousness in the original evidence in support of his theory. His purpose is to show the *superiority* of one set of determinants over another, for we note such scattered remarks in the text as "Age is to a minor degree related to class identification and attitude, but the differences 'due' to it are much *smaller* than those 'due' to occupation." "There is no consistent trend shown for the relationship of nativity to class identification. . . . The large differences that are found linked to the difference in occupational station are again clearly *more important*." "The differences in class identification and attitude that are linked to differences in religion are of definitely *lesser consequence* than those occasioned by occupational stratification." Following the examination

---

77. *Op. cit.*, p. 17, italics ours.
78. *Op. cit.*, p. 160, by permission of the publishers.

of the relation of ideology to size of town, he remarks, "the trends are both of only *minor importance* in comparison with the variations in attitude and class identification due to occupational differences." Following the series of such analyses, Centers remarks: "The above extended series of comparisons of the influence of occupational stratification with that of each of several other factors has indicated clearly that occupational stratification is a distinctly *more important* index to class identification and conservatism-radicalism than any of those that have been considered." [79]

Similarly, another one of our cases *The Authoritarian Personality* is not content merely to provide evidence in support of one explanation. The analysts wish to demonstrate the exclusive or prior importance of this explanation as compared with other possible determinants of the phenomenon. Thus they wish to show that "the political, economic and social convictions of an individual often form a broad and coherent pattern . . . and that this pattern is an expression of deep lying trends in his personality" but they also wish to show that this pattern "could *not* be derived solely from external factors, such as economic status, group membership or religion." [80]

Consequently apart from the direct demonstrations of the relation of ideology to personality factors, the analysts also test for the influence on ideology of such group membership characteristics as income, religion, parental occupation, organizational membership, etc. Their hope here is to find *little or no* relationship, and to use the negative evidence in two ways: —for the inferential argument that since social determinants are not significant, by elimination, personality determinants must be significant, and second, to prove by the relative magnitudes of the correlations the superiority or primacy of their explanation.

The reader may wonder why it is that the analyst is not satisfied with finding *an* explanation—why he seeks to find the *best* explanation, the *sole* explanation. Only when his search has this goal, is it understandable why simultaneous findings of both a negative and positive sort are sought. We cannot provide any principle as to why it is that analysts impose this special feature on their search. However, it is clear from the variety of surveys we have just described that this is not a rare practice of an occasional analyst.

Our last example, that of *The Authoritarian Personality*, illustrates some of the analytic difficulties that may be present in the use of the indirect test exclusively or in conjunction with the direct test. We previously alluded to three special problems: the soundness of the *logical argument* as to the number of possible determinants and their exclusive importance, the degree to which the empirical tests whose goal is *rejection* of one class of determinants *exhaust* the influence of the class, and the question of *arbitrariness in standards* for the rejection and acceptance of evidence from the

79. All of the above quotations are from Chapters X and XI, *ibid.*, italics ours.
80. *Op. cit.*, p. 1, 603, italics ours.

two classes of tests. Hyman and Sheatsley in a critique of this work treat these three problems. We quote them at length to show the formidable difficulties.[81] On the problem of the logical structure underlying the exclusive use of the indirect test, they remark:

> In general, the argument is advanced that insofar as objective group membership correlates are not significant, it then follows that emotional or personality factors are the determinants. But does this necessarily follow? Are there not other possibilities besides personality factors which could account for the attitude? Consider the argument advanced in the treatment of class differences in political ideology: "In view of the intergroup as well as the intra-group variability, it seems safe to conclude that over-all class differences in political ideology are not extremely large, and that individual and group differences within each class are so great that they become the primary problem requiring explanation. . . . Why does one middle-class individual join a service club while another becomes a supporter of Henry Wallace? . . . These may be not so much questions of actual class or group *membership* as questions of class or group *identification*—and 'identification' is a psychological variable. . . . We shall have occasion to consider further, in the chapters that follow, the deeper emotional trends that help to determine the individual's group memberships and identifications." [82]

Hyman and Sheatsley then comment:

> The authors are correct in pointing to the phenomenon of group identification as a factor attenuating the relation between objective membership and ideology, but to interpret this, in turn, as indicative of deeper emotional trends is quite a jump. One need only examine Merton and Kitt's discussion of reference group theory to note a whole host of factors that may account for the selection of a reference group. The fact that a person's social class does not determine whether he joins a service club or supports Henry Wallace does not prove that the choice is determined by deeper emotional trends. He may join for social or financial reasons, mere proximity to the group may lead him to identify with it, any one of a hundred accidental factors may be responsible. And even apart from questions of group identification and reference groups, there are a host of what we might call "situational factors" which operate in the individual's contemporary environment and which influence his ideology, he falls in love, loses his job, suffers a sickness, reads a particular magazine article, etc., etc. It is a vast oversimplification to argue that everything that is not determined by formal group membership must by default be due to deeper emotional trends. This is to make personality theory identical with all of psychology, which it is not, and to reduce all of the complexity of social structure to a few group memberships.[83]

On the exhaustiveness of the tests which lead to the rejection of a certain class of determinants they remark:

---

81. *Op. cit.*
82. *Ibid.*, pp. 114-115.
83. *Ibid.*, p. 115.

It should be noted . . . that the authors did not exhaust the universe of group memberships available to the individual. Out of the richness of possible affiliations, only a few were chosen and examined and these not necessarily the central ones. . . . The analysis hardly permits, therefore, after the examination of one rudimentary relationship—political party affiliation —the immoderate statement that "these intra- and intergroup variations suggest that group membership is not in itself the major determinant of ideology in the individual." . . . Moreover, the analysis was not only limited to a small number of group membership characteristics, but it studied these individually, each in isolation from the others, whereas virtually all current work emphasizes the influence of *multiple* overlapping or contradictory group memberships. Thus, it is noted in the analysis that "No broad grouping in this study showed anything approaching ideological homogeneity," and from the variations in attitude within each group, the inference is drawn that individual personality factors account for the attitude. But is it not equally possible that intra-group variability in attitude is due to the fact that individuals sharing one group membership in common often differ with respect to other group memberships? Lazarsfeld, in his classic study of political behavior in Erie County in 1940, showed that among Catholics, a predominantly Democratic group, almost one-fourth expressed Republican preferences. Under the principles of the present study, this intra-group variability would be accepted as evidence to deny the effect of group membership and to emphasize the importance of personality factors. But if we look only at those Catholics in the lowest economic level we find only one in seven expressing a Republican preference, and among Catholics who are laborers, the incidence of Republican preference is but one in ten. Thus, the intra-group variability is progressively lessened as other memberships of the individual are taken into account, and in the absence of any higher order cross-tabulations to observe the effect of *multiple* group memberships on prejudice, the inference drawn from the variability within single groups is unwarranted.[84]

On the question of arbitrariness in the treatment of the negative and positive findings Hyman and Sheatsley suggest that there is the:

application of a double standard of statistical treatment for the personality variables as determined by the interviews and for the study of group membership factors on the basis of the scale scores. In the interview study, two extreme groups are compared on a series of personality factors. Intermediate groups are not examined and the fact that all the individuals in one extreme are not homogeneous is ignored. Further, if there is *some group trend,* it is accepted as evidence. In the case of the group membership data, on the other hand, a whole series of small groups are compared and any minor inversions of the findings are noted. In addition, the procedure is carried out separately for each of the small groups: e.g., the relation of income to ethnocentrism is studied on the basis of six income groups, and this is done separately for college students, working class men, middle class women, etc. It is then noted that prejudice does not vary consistently by income over the entire range of values, and that the relation between prejudice and in-

84. *Ibid.,* pp. 113-114.

come is not the same among the different groups studied. It is also pointed out generally in this discussion that no grouping shows homogeneity. This procedure is admirable in its detail. . . . We object not to the thoroughness and precision of this analysis, but to the use to which its findings are put, in contrast to the statistical analysis of the interview data. Had a single standard been applied, and the latter materials subjected to the same microscopic scrutiny, it is possible that similar irregularities would have turned up in the functional relations between prejudice and personality.[85]

85. *Ibid.*, pp. 116-117.

CHAPTER VI

The Introduction of

Additional Variables and the

Problem of Spuriousness

IN THE problems of the explanatory survey thus far presented, a variety of procedures are used in conjunction with the analyst's examination of the simple relationship between *two* variables. In the problem we are to present now, the original simple relationship between two variables is elaborated through the *systematic introduction of additional variables*. The analytic procedures now involve the manipulation and examination of the relations between *three* or more variables. The analysis of such complex relationships provides a solution to the problem we shall call, *Spuriousness*, and permits the analyst to infer that the original relationship involves cause and effect. This is not to deny the relevance of the previous problems for the inference of cause and effect, but there still remains the crucial problem of spuriousness. Before presenting the procedures, we shall discuss the logic of the classic experiment for it illuminates the nature of spuriousness and implies the direction of the solution.[1]

---

1. The design of the experiment we present should be regarded only as a convenient model and constitutes a deliberate oversimplification. For example, the earlier discussion of the "refinement of values" in survey analysis would obviously imply even to the unsophisticated reader the fact that most experimentation involves more than *one* experimental group. Similarly, the problem that is solved by the application of "control group design" sometimes necessitates *not one* but a number of control groups. For a schematic representation of multiple control groups in experimental design, see Jahoda, Deutsch and Cook, *op. cit.*, pp. 66-67. Yet, we oversimplify our presentation and present only two groups, an experimental and a control

The Controlled Experiment as a Model

The scientific model for the study of cause-and-effect relationships is the *controlled experiment*, in which the responses of an experimental group, exposed to the crucial stimulus, are compared with those of an equivalent control group, from which the stimulus has been withheld.

Diagrammatically, the controlled experiment can be represented by the following scheme:

	Experimental group	Control group
Time 1	x_1	y_1
	Exposure to stimulus	No exposure to stimulus
Time 2	x_2	y_2

Let us suppose, for the sake of illustration, that our experiment is concerned with the effect of televised proceedings of political conventions on interest in political affairs. At Time 1, before the conventions started, we would divide our total sample into two equivalent, matched groups. One of these would be chosen to serve as the experimental group, and the other to serve as the control. At Time 1 we would also record the level of political interest exhibited by the two groups at that time, and would designate these measures x_1 and y_1. If the two groups are correctly matched, they should have the same degree of interest initially; in other words, x_1 should equal y_1. As the conventions get under way, the experimental group will be shown the telecast proceedings, while the control group will somehow be prevented from seeing them. At the close of the conventions, both groups will be

---

group. There are in current research practice an endless variety of experimental designs each created for the solution of some special problem, often not that of spuriousness, and there has been in classic experimental fields a great many different designs, some of which do not correspond to our model. The reader is referred to R. A. Fisher, *The Design of Experiments* (London: Oliver and Boyd, 4th ed., 1947); W. G. Cochran and G. Cox, *Experimental Designs* (New York: Wiley, 1950), who provide thorough treatments of modern methods of experimentation and convey the endless variety that is normally subsumed under the label "experiment." Such a classic work as R. S. Woodworth, *Experimental Psychology* (New York: Holt, 1938), written almost 20 years ago which systematically treats the accumulated literature in a traditional laboratory experimental field also conveys the wide variety of procedures, all of which are legitimately entitled to be called "controlled experiments." One need only read pp. 2-3 of his introduction to see that the "controlled experiment" does not necessarily involve any special "control group," and that control is achieved in many ways. However, the model we present while only suited to one special type of problem is sufficiently common to be useful, and is appropriate to the problem we are discussing.

tested once more with regard to their interest in political matters, and new measures, x_2 and y_2, will be recorded.

How does one go about determining, from this scheme, whether the TV programs had any effect? One might be tempted to answer that a comparison of the level of interest manifested by the experimental group before and after the conventions will provide the necessary information; in other words,, one might say that the comparison $(x_2 - x_1)$ is the crucial one. But this may not be entirely correct. At the time of the conventions, political matters are of great public interest. The mass media other than television give great prominence to the course of events at the conventions and to speculations about the course of events following the conventions. Informal discussion of the candidates, their chances, their merits become favorite topics of conversation. Unless it is kept completely isolated, then, the experimental group is likely to be exposed to these "extraneous" influences, and the difference $(x_2 - x_1)$ will reflect the effect of these factors as well as of the experimental stimulus. In other words, it is impossible to separate out what part of the difference $(x_2 - x_1)$ is due to the telecasts of the conventions and what part to other "irrelevant" stimuli.

This is where the control group enters. It presumably has been exposed to all the same stimuli as has the experimental group, *except* the single one in which the experimentor is vitally interested, in this case, television.[2] Thus, the difference between the pre- and post-convention level of interest exhibited by the control group reflects the influence of those other stimuli. That is, $(y_2 - y_1)$ measures the effect of the non-experimental stimuli, those that are not controlled by the experimenter. These two differences, when considered together, provide a measure of the effect of the experimental stimulus. In words:

Effect of television = (Effect of television + effect of other stimuli) — (effect of other stimuli)

Or, symbolically:

Effect of television = $(x_2 - x_1) - (y_2 - y_1)$

If the two groups were properly matched to start with, so that they manifested identical degrees of political interest initially, this measure of effect becomes simplified. For under these conditions, $x_1 = y_1$, and the effect of the stimulus reduces to the following:

Effect of television = $(x_2 - y_2)$

The logic of controlled experimentation, and the specific experimental designs called for under different conditions, have been well systematized.

2. The experimenter must assume that the control group has been exposed to these other stimuli with the same intensity and with the same effect as the experimental group. If the two groups were well matched to start with, this assumption is probably correct.

But the student will find that very little attention has been given to spelling out the problems which lie in the way of effective experimentation in the social sciences. The experimenter, for example, finds it difficult to manipulate social groups and social institutions as he would like to for his experimental purposes. Nor is the social science experimenter able usually to maintain the controls over his subjects which are required for adequate experimentation. The result is, then, that experimentation has become the rarely realized ideal in the social sciences. It remains the model against which other research designs are judged and in terms of which research results are evaluated. But actual social science studies are generally carried out through some kind of approximation procedure.

There are various ways in which the logic of experimentation can be approximated, but the type most often used in survey analysis is that of *subgroup comparisons*. This involves a comparison of the frequency with which groups *characterized in different ways* express a certain attitude or exhibit a particular characteristic. For example in Havemann and West's study of college graduates it was found that men who attended the so-called Ivy League colleges received higher salaries in their later careers than did the graduates of other institutions. In such comparisons, the analyst assumes that the subgroups which he has formed approximate the experimental and control groups of an actual experiment, and that the characteristic which distinguishes the different groups approximates the experimental stimulus.

The difficulty in equating the simple cross-tabulations of a survey to real experimentation, is the danger that the relationship obtained is a spurious one. In order to introduce the notion of a spurious relationship, let us consider how these sub-groups comparisons might be represented schematically.[3]

	"Experimental" group	"Control" group
	Exposed to "stimulus"	Not exposed to "stimulus"
Time 2	x_2	y_2

The "stimuli" in these comparisons are, to use our previous illustration, such variables as the kind of college from which one graduated. The critical attitudes or behavior, recorded in the measures x_2 and y_2, are such variables as yearly income. Although the "effect" of these stimuli might be gauged in a variety of ways, the measure which is simplest and most appropriate for our purposes is the difference, $(x_2 - y_2)$.

---

3. The schematic representation of different approximation procedures follows closely an article by Samuel A. Stouffer, entitled "Some observations on study design," *Amer. Jour. Sociol.*, LV, 1949–50, 355–361.

This diagram, which is comparable to the one representing controlled experimentation, points up clearly some of the essential differences between true experimentation and the approximating procedure of sub-group comparisons. The scheme suggests that these comparisons are a form of truncated experimentation, in which one decisive step is missing. One of the essential features of experimentation, we may recall, is that, through matching and/or randomization procedures, the experimenter makes sure that his two groups are initially identical in all important respects. The survey analyst, on the other hand, comes upon his groups when they are already constituted—when they have already had a chance or not had one to choose their Army jobs, when they have already graduated from college, or when they have been residents of a housing community for varying lengths of time. In other words, he has no opportunity to control the composition of his "experimental" and "control" groups in advance, so as to be certain that they are initially identical.[4] Then, there is always the danger that the relationships which the analyst finds in his survey data are spurious, that they arise out of initial differences between the groups being compared. The so-called "stimulus" may erroneously appear to have an "effect" only because of initial variations between the groups. Since they destroy what otherwise seem to be meaningful relationships, the factors making for initial differences between the sub-groups under study will be called "invalidating factors."

Let us consider this problem more concretely. In West's study of college graduates, for example, there is immediate cause for suspicion that the relationship she reports between the type of college attended and later income is a spurious one. We may ask immediately whether the students at Ivy League colleges were not wealthier to start with than was generally the case with the graduates of other colleges. The high costs at Ivy League institutions, coupled perhaps with the admission policies of those colleges, may favor the sons of well-to-do families. And those well-to-do families may be able, in turn, to provide their sons with the social and professional contacts through which they can more easily obtain well-paying jobs. In other words, there may appear to be a relationship between graduation from an Ivy League college and financial success only because the Ivy Leaguer comes from a well-to-do family which, in turn, helps him to become financially well off.

Another instance of the problem of spuriousness is provided by our ear-

---

4. This statement is, of course, not appropriate to explanatory surveys which followed the principle presented in Chapter II of the *restriction of the universe*. Under such conditions, the universe from which all sub-groups come is relatively homogeneous and therefore the sub-groups are, by definition, matched in certain major respects. However, in Chapter II, we also discussed the many instances in which this principle of a restricted universe is not or cannot be followed, and the need for after-the-fact attempts at control. The discussion in this entire section is appropriate to the explanatory survey of this latter type.

lier example, the survey with the paradoxical finding that Germans who had read *Mein Kampf* exhibited more liberal attitudes. In discussing the possible time sequences involved in this empirical relationship, it appeared that either sequence presented us with an apparent absurdity. But, it can now be seen that the finding makes perfect sense. It is well known from Communication research that reading *per se* is a generalized pattern which is strongly dependent on formal education.[5] Consequently, those individuals who read *Mein Kampf* were very likely to be more educated than those who had not read it—not because there is any inherent interest in *Mein Kampf* among the educated, but simply because there is an inherent tendency to read more. Education, or, rather, *Bookishness*, was an uncontrolled factor in the comparison of *Mein Kampf* readers vs. non-readers. Given the fact that these people were also more likely to exhibit this particular liberal attitude, it thus turned out empirically that the apparent effect of *Mein Kampf* was to produce liberalism.

Thus, in order to minimize the danger that such spurious relationships remain undetected, we employ analytical procedures which enable us to examine the relationship between the assumed cause and the assumed effect *when the influence of the possible invalidating factor is eliminated.* That is, we try to eradicate initial differences between the sub-groups which might produce spurious relationships. The analytical procedures for achieving this involve some manner of "holding constant" or "controlling" the possible invalidating factors.

Problems and Methods of Control in the Survey

One of the case studies we have used frequently, Durkheim's *Suicide,* provides many examples of the danger of spuriousness, and treats in a very clear and explicit way the technical solution of the problem in survey research. It also illustrates certain special new features of the treatment of spuriousness. The very nature of the inquiry was such that the danger of spuriousness was *magnified.* It was a *secondary* analysis—the data available to Durkheim were records of past suicides, sometimes so tabulated that he could examine variations in rates for a variety of sub-groups, e.g., region, time period. Obviously, these sub-groups varied in a great many respects, but often the records were of such a nature that Durkheim could *not* find a statistical series for very refined sub-groups who were alike in many re-

---

5. See, for example, B. Berelson, *The Library's Public* (New York: Columbia University Press, 1949), Chaps. I, II.

spects. Consequently, he coped with the problem by a variety of ingenious approximations.

Durkheim's Suicide—A Case Study in Problems of Control: Let us illustrate the problem using his very words because of their clarity of presentation.

> If one consults only the absolute figures, unmarried persons seem to commit suicide less than married ones. Thus in France, during the period 1873–78, there were 16,264 suicides of married persons while unmarried persons had only 11,709. The former number is to the second as 132 to 100. As the same proportion appears at the other periods and in other countries, certain authors had once taught that marriage and family life multiply the chances of suicide. Certainly, if in accordance with current opinion one regards suicide primarily as an act of despair caused by the difficulties of existence, this opinion has all the appearance of probability. An unmarried person has in fact an easier life than a married one. Does not marriage entail all sorts of burdens and responsibilities? To assure the present and future of a family, are not more privations and sufferings required than to meet the needs of a single person? *Nevertheless, clear as it seems, this a priori reasoning is quite false and the facts only seem to support it because of being poorly analyzed.* . . . Really to appreciate the figures given above, we must remember that a very large number of unmarried persons are less than 16 years old, while all married persons are older. Up to 16 years the tendency to suicide is very slight, due to age, without considering other factors. In France only one or two suicides per million inhabitants are found at this time of life; at the following period there are twenty times as many. The inclusion of many children below 16 among unmarried persons thus unduly reduces the average aptitude of the latter, since the reduction is due to age, not celibacy. If they seem to contribute fewer suicides, it is not because they are unmarried but because many of them are yet immature. *So, if one tries to compare the two populations to determine the influence of marital status and that alone, one must rid oneself of this disturbing element and compare with married persons only the unmarried above 16.* When this subtraction is made, it appears that between 1863–68 there were on the average 173 suicides in a million unmarried persons above 16 years and 154.5 for a million married persons. The ratio of the first to the second number is that of 112 to 100.[6]

But Durkheim now continues and shows us that while the *formal* solution to the problem of spuriousness was sound, there was a technical difficulty still not solved, which applies generally to all survey procedures of control or matching in order to eliminate the influence of invalidating factors. It is simply the problem of the *crudity of the measurements* which sets limits on the precision of the control:

> There is thus a certain accretion due to celibacy. But it is much greater than the preceding figures show. Actually, we have assumed that all unmarried persons above 16 years and all married persons were of the same

6. *Op. cit.,* pp. 171-172, italics ours.

average age. This is not true. The majority of unmarried men in France, exactly 58 per cent, are between 15 and 20 years; the majority of unmarried women, exactly 57 per cent, are less than 25 years. The average age of all unmarried men is 26.8, of all unmarried women 28.4. The average age of married persons, on the contrary, is between 40 and 45 years. For both sexes combined, suicide develops according to age as follows:

From 16 to 21 years	45.9 suicides per million inhabitants
From 21 to 30 years	97.9 suicides per million inhabitants
From 31 to 40 years	114.5 suicides per million inhabitants
From 41 to 50 years	164.4 suicides per million inhabitants

These figures refer to the years 1848–57. If age were the only influence, the aptitude of unmarried persons for suicide could not be above 97.9 and that of married persons would be between 114.5 and 164.4, or about 140 suicides per million inhabitants. Suicides of married persons would be to those of unmarried as 100 to 69. The latter would be only two-thirds of the former whereas we know that they are actually more numerous. The effect of family life is thus to reverse the relation. Whereas without the effect of family life married persons should kill themselves half again as often as unmarried by virtue of their age, they do so perceptibly less. Thus marriage may be said to reduce the danger of suicide by about half or, more exactly, non-marriage produces an increase expressed by the proportion 112/69, or 1.6. Thus, if we represent the suicidal tendency of married persons by unity, that of unmarried persons of the same average age must be estimated as 1.6.[7]

As Durkheim notes, the differences that are found following the institution of controls may still represent the influence of the invalidating factor, if the matching of groups was only crude. The influence of age has been reduced, but not excluded. In this particular instance, the crudity of control fortunately does not obscure the general relationship because following the institution of control, the initial finding is *reversed*. Despite the fact that the unmarried group is still somewhat younger and thus *less* predisposed to suicide on grounds of the residual uncontrolled factor of age, the comparison now reveals a *greater* rate of suicide among them. Thus, the finding is a determinate one and quite compelling because it is demonstrated despite the handicap of the crudity of control over age. But there are many instances where the problem of crudity of control leaves the relationship truly *indeterminate*. Such an instance would occur where following the control procedure, the initial relationship is somewhat reduced.[8] The analyst would then confront the dilemma: Does the new finding represent the valid explanation, or would the finding be further reduced and *ultimately* reversed

---

7. *Ibid.*, pp. 172-173.

8. It can be readily seen that one other pattern of findings would be determinate. If, when the control were instituted, there were *no change* from the original finding, this would permit the analyst to draw an inference despite the crudity of the matching. If the factor that is being controlled had any relevance, its effect should be removed in part when some control, no matter how crude, is instituted. Therefore, the analyst argues that it cannot have operated initially.

if the controls could be made more and more refined. If there is no empirical method for instituting such additional control, and since there is no logical method for resolving the dilemma, the finding is truly indeterminate. Luckily, in *primary* analyses, the investigator has the opportunity to measure any variable to a refined degree and thus can *theoretically* solve the problem. In practice, however, the measurements and correspondingly the controls may be crude, and the example cited reminds us of the general technical problem. Where the investigator is limited to *secondary* analysis, however, the problem is a serious one. Despite the best of intentions, an ideal degree of control may be impossible. Thus Durkheim remarks:

> . . . with the data available, this method of calculation is the only one applicable in almost all cases. . . . If consequently it must be used to establish the general situation, its results can be only roughly approximate. Of course, it suffices to show that non-marriage increases the tendency to suicide; but it gives only a very inexact idea of the extent of this increase. . . . The only way to avoid these difficulties is to determine the rate of each group separately, at each age. Under such conditions one may, for example, compare unmarried persons of from 25 to 30 years with married and widowed persons of the same age and similarly for other periods; the influence of marital status will thus be isolated from all the other influences and all its possible variations will appear. Besides, this is the method which Bertillon first applied to mortality and the marriage rate. *Unfortunately, official publications do not contain the necessary data for this comparison. Actually, they show the age of suicides independently of their marital status.* The only publication which to our knowledge has followed a different practice is that of the grand-duchy of Oldenburg (including the principalities of Lubeck and Birkenfeld). For the years 1871–85 this publication gives us the distribution of suicides by age for each category of marital status considered separately. But this little State had only 1,369 suicides during these fifteen years. As nothing certain can be concluded from so few cases, we undertook to do the work ourselves for France with the aid of unpublished documents in the possession of the Ministry of Justice. We studied the years 1889, 1890 and 1891. We classified about 25,000 suicides in this way.

These troubles of the analyst of secondary sources incidentally cause Durkheim to end this passage with the remark:

> Yet the labor of assembling these data, considerable if undertaken by an individual, might easily be accomplished by the official bureaus of statistics. All sorts of valueless information is given and only that omitted which, as will be seen below, might show the state of family life in the different European societies.[9]

In this example of Durkheim's, and in the prior examples, *empirical* procedures of control were achieved through the *matching* of sub-groups in certain respects. Durkheim's procedure, while only a crude control or match-

9. *Ibid.*, pp. 171-175, italics ours.

ing, was nevertheless an orthodox analysis. The solution was straightforward and Durkheim merely followed the analytic model prescribed.

But we earlier remarked that Durkheim, because of the limitations of his sources, had to engage in other approximations to the treatment of spuriousness. Examination of such approximations is most rewarding for the survey analyst. Where he works on secondary analyses, *necessity* may force him into Durkheim's position. And even where he is engaged in a primary analysis, he may through lack of foresight, which is only too common, find that he would have liked to control a certain factor in a comparison, but, alas, he did not have the ideal data for the actual matching of groups in a subsequent refined comparison. How then shall the analyst treat of the problem of spuriousness in the absence of procedures of matching of subgroups? The answer in *principle* is simple. We substitute for *direct empirical* methods, a variety of *indirect* methods.

The most frequent type of indirect method still involves empirical procedures of matching of control groups, but *on a variable that is presumed to be related* to the variable which the analyst would have liked to control. The method is indirect in that there is the assumption that the one variable can be substituted for the other. If this assumption is warranted, the subsequent procedure of comparisons between matched sub-groups is sound. An illustration of such an indirect procedure is available in Havemann and West's study.

West was aware that the relationship she reported between type of college attended and annual salary was possibly a spurious one because of differences in the family backgrounds of students whom she compared. She therefore made an effort to control this factor which might have invalidated the reported relationship. She could not do this directly, since the schedule used in the survey did not include any direct measure of the student's family background at the time he went to college. However, she had an indirect measure—the student's need to earn part or all of his college expenses. West reasoned in the following way: A student who was forced to earn all or part of his college expenses will have come, on the average, from a less well-to-do family than a student who was entirely supported by his parents while in college.

Of course, this is not an infallible index of family wealth. Some quite poor families may make great sacrifices in order to support their children in college; in other instances, wealthy families may consider it "honorable" or "good training" for their children to have to earn part of their college expenses.[10]

___

10. In addition, the variable "earning one's college expenses" is one of those ambiguous variables which can assume different meanings in different contexts. In the present case, it is used as a measure of *need*, and therefore indirectly as a measure of family background. It could also be taken as an index of the kinds of experiences which the student acquired during his college days, *op. cit.*, Chap. VI, Chart 3.

While she should not assume a one-to-one correspondence between family background and the need to earn at least part of one's college expenses,
West felt that the latter was a sufficiently good index of the former for her
purposes. What she did, then, was to select two extreme groups from the
total group of men 40 years of age and older: those who had earned *over
half* of their own college expenses, and those who had earned *none* of their
expenses. Within each of these groups, she then studied the relationship
between the type of institution attended and annual earnings.

She found that the relationship which she originally observed still persisted when the possible invalidating factor was held constant. That is,
when she was able to equate the sub-groups on their family backgrounds
prior to their student days (as measured by need to earn college expenses),
she still found that the kind of college attended had an "effect" on later
earning powers. She can thus be confident that the original relationship
which she reported is not invalidated by this factor.

There are other methods which involve even more indirect treatment of
the problem of control and the danger of spuriousness. In these procedures,
control through matching of sub-groups is, in fact, not instituted. Some
process of speculation, and logical analysis substitutes for the empirical
procedure of control. So to speak, the controls are instituted *symbolically*
—in the mind of the analyst. He can inspect the concrete research situation
and infer that the possible invalidating factor could not have been operative. He can construct mentally a variety of derivative consequences that he
would expect to find if the invalidating factor were or were not operative.
There is no limit to the approximations of empirical control one can invent
by such indirect methods. Durkheim, perhaps out of necessity, manifests
great ingenuity. The references will be postponed to a subsequent section
because they also illustrate other analytic principles. The reader is referred
to p. 264.

In the examples we have cited thus far, the findings are subject to question on the grounds of some *single* uncontrolled factor. But often there are
relationships which are suspect on the ground that a *series* of other variables might be operating simultaneously and responsible for the finding.
In such instances, more than one control has to be introduced as a protection against spuriousness. However, the quality of any analysis is dependent
not so much on the *sheer number* of controls that are instituted in a purely
mechanical fashion, but rather on the *relevance* of the particular controls
that are applied. Now, of course, the criterion of relevance is somewhat
arbitrary. What is one man's relevance, is another's irrelevance: One is re-
minded of R. A. Fisher's remarks in the introduction to his classic work on
experimentation. He talks somewhat sarcastically of the criticisms that are
made by a "heavy weight authority."

Prolonged experience, at least the long possession of a scientific reputation, is almost a prerequisite for developing successfully this line of attack. Technical details are seldom in evidence. The authoritative assertion 'his *controls* are *totally* inadequate' must have temporarily discredited many a promising line of work; and such an authoritarian method of judgment must surely continue, human nature being what it is, so long as theoretical notions of the principles of experimental design are lacking.[11]

Perhaps there is some ground, neither that of heavy weight authority nor that of ultimate explicit principle, but of *reason* on which the investigator can pick his controls wisely. Let us illustrate the kind of criterion of relevance that might be considered, taking as an example, one of our major case studies, *The Authoritarian Personality*. In the analysis, differences in level of ethnocentrism were traced to explanatory factors within the personalities of the subjects. But, there was the danger that other factors associated with the personality differences were operative and that the original findings were spurious. Consequently, the investigators matched the ethnocentric and non-ethnocentric "in terms of age, sex, political and religious affiliation, as well as national and regional background." Certainly, the institution of *six* controls is as *elaborate* a procedure as one can demand, and these controls do seem relevant. Yet Hyman and Sheatsley in their critique of this study take strong objection to the findings on the ground that another factor which was uncontrolled might plausibly account for the original findings. We quote their remarks at length to show the logical basis for the criticism:

> . . . the controls exercised do not by any means exhaust the possibilities. . . . Now obviously we cannot expect the analyst to control every possible factor which could remotely account for the correlations. . . . All we can ask is that the analyst take account of the more obvious variables . . . and either control for those in his analysis or qualify his conclusions in the light of the omission. . . . Despite the authors' concern in matching their groups on such demographic characteristics as sex and age, they completely overlook a quite obvious factor which could easily account for the correlations they report. That factor is formal education, or years of schooling completed. Neither in the original choice of the groups nor through higher order cross-tabulation in the subsequent analysis was there any control of possible education differences among the ethnocentric and non-ethnocentric respondents. Although there is never any detailed description of the educational level of the two groups, it is clear from a number of sources in the text that the non-ethnocentric have had considerably more formal schooling. . . . We do not feel that we are being academic in raising the issue. . . . As one examines the interview excerpts in the text, one is continually and vividly struck by the fact that some of the differences obtained, which are treated as determinants of ethnocentrism, seem actually mere reflections of formal education. For example, one of the factors found to differentiate the ethnocentric

---

11. R. A. Fisher, *The Design of Experiments*, 4th ed., 1947, published by Oliver and Boyd Ltd., Edinburgh, p. 3, by permission of the author and publishers.

most significantly is a conventionality with respect to sex. . . . The authors state: "In contrast with the stereotyped and conventional description of their desired or real mates given by the high-scoring subjects, the typical low-scoring subject takes a much more individualized attitude, as shown in the following quotations." One of the quotations then goes as follows (italics ours): "She has to be intelligent, mature, emotionally stable, have *adequate physiological characteristics,* as well as have *culture and personality* that goes with this. . . . She should have a maximum of *femininity,* since we're all *bisexual.* You can think of it in terms of a polyfactorial setup (subject then quotes *Rosanoff's theory* of four factors in sex)." As one reads this case, the thought occurs that this is not at all an individualized attitude. This is the language of a pseudo-intellectual student.

The high scorers, on the other hand, say "It was love at first sight. He has brown hair, brown eyes, white teeth, not handsome, but good clean-cut looking" and "A very good wife, good mother, and darned good cook."

These are far from isolated examples; they occur throughout the analysis. . . . All of the differences referred to could well be artifacts of an uncontrolled educational difference. That these "personality traits" do vary with education has been demonstrated in many representative samples of the adult population. It is surprising indeed that in the kind of detailed inspection and analysis which the interviews received there was never any concern expressed regarding this factor of education . . . we contend that the significance of these personality variables to the problem of ethnocentrism seems dubious in the light of the known correlation with education of many of the *indices* employed, and the failure to take account of this factor in the analysis of the two groups.[12]

The Distinction Between Developmental Sequences or Configurations and Problems of Spuriousness

We have thus far suggested that the analyst must guard any obtained explanation of a phenomenon against the danger that the relationship observed was *spurious.* The particular independent variable that at first is demonstrated to be related to the phenomenon may merely be the *apparent* explanation. There may be some other prior condition or variable which is actually the hidden cause of the phenomenon since it was associated with the independent variable that was examined. To solve the difficulty, we have discussed *procedures* by which the analyst can *control* or exclude the influence of such other variables in order to test whether the original relationship persists. If it persists, the claim of spuriousness cannot be levelled against the explanation the analyst has given.

The principle appears simple. But what if an original relationship disappears—if it is found to be dependent on some other hidden independent

---

12. *Op. cit.,* pp. 90-94.

variable. *Is it always the case that the claim of spuriousness should be levelled at the original explanation?* We shall argue *NO!* The analyst must be careful not to *accept* an original explanation too quickly and too easily—generally he must invoke the logic of spuriousness and the corresponding empirical tests. But he also must be careful not to *reject* too quickly all explanations which have been found to depend on the operation of other related variables.

Following the principle presented earlier to its logical extreme, we shall see that *there remains not a single instance in all of survey research where an explanation can remain invulnerable.* But this must be an absurdity. Obviously, findings cannot be rejected so quickly or we shall do away with all possibilities of explanatory surveys. The principle is not so simple as it might have appeared! But if it is not simple, it certainly is confusing to the reader, or perhaps he may even regard it as confused. Under what conditions following procedures of control, shall the operation of another independent variable *not* be taken as evidence that an original relationship was spurious? The reader will intuitively grasp one condition immediately by reference to a quotation in Krech and Crutchfield.

> Explanations may frequently deteriorate into an endless search for the "ultimate" or "first" cause. If it be said that Mr. Arbuthnot seeks membership in the country club because he sees it as a goal of social approval, it is then asked why he seeks that goal. If it is answered that this goal has arisen because of a need for personal security, it is then asked why that feeling of insecurity arose. If it is answered that the feeling of personal insecurity has arisen because of a socially embarrassing speech defect that Mr. Arbuthnot has acquired, it is then asked why that speech defect. The answer may be that the speech defect was a defense against a precocious younger brother. Thus, at this stage, we are to understand that Mr. Arbuthnot seeks membership in the country club because his younger brother was precocious! *But why stop here? The analysis can go as far as the ingenuity of the theorist will carry him, without ever really reaching the ultimate, or first, cause.*[13]

The point should be clear. Any independent variable that is examined as cause of a phenomenon has, in turn, its own causes. Unless one reached the *most primitive* original cause that initiated the sequence that led to the independent variable under study, one would always be able to find at least in principle an antecedent condition that really was responsible for the effect. In this sense, all demonstrations of relations—all explanations are spurious. Now in practice one can never reach the original cause in the developmental sequence and for this reason alone such an unrestricted usage of the procedures of control and the logic of spuriousness becomes an absurdity. But, in addition, the concept of spuriousness cannot *logically* be intended to apply to antecedent conditions which are associated with the

13. By permission from *Theory and Problems of Social Psychology*, by D. Krech and R. Crutchfield, 1948, McGraw-Hill Book Company, Inc., p. 34, italics ours.

particular independent variable as part of a developmental sequence. Implicitly, the notion of an uncontrolled factor which was operating so as to produce a spurious finding involves the image of something *extrinsic* to the original independent variable, something apart or separate *in nature* from the apparent cause, but which through empirical accident got intertwined with the apparent cause. Developmental sequences, by contrast, involve the image of a series of entities which are *intrinsically* united or substitutes for one another. All of them constitute a unity and merely involve different ways of stating the same variable as it changes over time. The entities are empirically associated not through accident, but because they have to be. Consequently, to institute procedures of control is to remove so-to-speak some of the very cause that one wishes to study. Thus, the demonstration that an apparent explanation is no longer tenable following controls of this type should not lead to the assertion of "spuriousness." By implication, it leads one to assert with even greater confidence that the original explanation was real. For it says in effect "first you introduced the cause and observed an effect—now you remove part of the cause and you reduce the effect. The very *procedures* of "control" of earlier stages of a developmental sequence may well be used by the analyst, but we shall see shortly that they lead to inferences other than spuriousness.

The principle having to do with procedures of analysis involving control of variables can now be restated as follows: *Spuriousness applies to situations where a variable other than the apparent explanation was found to have produced the observed effect, providing the other variable is not an intrinsic part of the developmental sequence which produced the apparent explanation.* Now while the logic of this more refined principle is clear and it protects the analyst from confusing pseudo-spuriousness with spuriousness, it can lead in practice to arbitrariness. How shall the analyst know what antedent conditions are intrinsic parts of a developmental sequence? Every time a finding is found to be dependent on some prior factor, the emotionally committed analyst can defend and maintain his original explanation. He can argue that the variable that was "controlled" was an earlier stage of the sequence, and thereby obstruct the argument of spuriousness. Unfortunately, we can provide no simple rules or formulas for deciding what antecedent conditions are intrinsic or extrinsic to the original developmental sequence. However, in practice it should not be difficult for the *reasonable* analyst to make a sound judgment. One guide, for example, can be noted: instances where the "control" factor and the apparent explanation involve *levels of description from two different systems* are likely to be developmental sequences. For instance, an explanatory factor that was a personality trait and a control factor that was biological such as physique or glandular function can be conceived as levels of description from different systems. Similarly, an explanatory factor that is *psychological* and a control factor that is *sociologi-*

cal can be conceived as two different levels of description, i.e., one might regard an attitude as a derivative of objective position or status or an objective position in society as leading to psychological processes such as attitude. Thus, the concept of spuriousness would not be appropriate.[14]

It is on this ground that Allport questions some of the analytic procedures and the inferences drawn in *The American Soldier*. With reference to the attribution of causality, he first cites certain examples:

> *Units* with the lowest morale before entering combat (as determined by a relevant set of questions) had appreciably higher non-battle casualty rates when plunged into combat (II, 19). Also *individuals* whose attitudes were unfavorable toward combat while they were in training actually are rated as relatively poor in combat performance over a year later after having had their baptism of fire (II, 33). To my mind we have clear evidence here that attitudes are dynamic forces; they *cause* behavior. But the authors are super-cautious about making this obvious interpretation. They seem to fear that there may be some uncontrolled variable (in the second illustration, perhaps ill health) that might be the determinant of *both* the attitude and the performance.

Their caution leads them throughout their exposition to hold constant all available variables so that only a simon-pure relationship between attitude and performance can appear. They call this the conservative way of portraying the relationship. Conservative, it surely is—and to my mind, theoretically questionable. Thus, in the case just cited, they report the relationship between individual attitudes and later combat performance only after holding constant 'background factors,' such as age, marital condition, education, AGCT scores. The authors realize that if these factors were not held constant the demonstrated relationship between attitude and performance would be greater (II, 35). One reason, for example, is that men with higher education have much more favorable attitudes toward combat and also higher combat ratings. By comparing only men of *equal* education they rule out a large part of the potential correspondence.

The reasoning involved in this procedure is, to my mind, false. It says in effect: whenever you are attempting to account for behavior, ascribe as much of the influence as you can to class, status, or ecological determinants—and the remainder you may ascribe to "attitude." Here we clearly encounter a sociologistic bias. Let me state the opposite (and to me preferable) interpretation. Nothing ever causes behavior excepting mental sets (including habits, attitudes, motives). To hold education or any other background factor constant is to imply that it alone may directly determine behavior. It is illegitimate to by-pass in this way the personal nexus wherein all background influences must be integrated. Background factors never directly

---

14. We shall see shortly that there is a mode of elaboration of an analysis known as "interpretation" in which an original relationship between an initial condition and some consequence is demonstrated to be dependent on some *linking* variable which mediates the sequence. The intervening variable *follows* rather than precedes the explanation. But suppose one had started the analysis with the intervening variable, and had left out the initial condition. One would not think of this as an uncontrolled factor, but merely as an earlier form of the intervening variable.

cause behavior; they cause attitudes; and attitudes in turn determine behavior.

I am not, of course, arguing against the use of breakdowns or matched
groups. They should, however, be used to show where attitudes come from,
and not to imply that social causation acts automatically apart from attitudes.[15]

We can illustrate the problem even more vividly by the example of a well
known inquiry involving procedures of control. Chapin in his discussion of
experimentation in Sociology discusses a study by Christiansen as a classic instance of what he labels the *ex post facto experiment*.[16] Greenwood in his trea-
tise on *Experimental Sociology* discusses the study at considerable length.[17]
Neither writer notes a special feature. This was an inquiry into economic adjustment and its relation to progress in high school. The phenomenon of
adjustment was measured by reference to the job record of the individual and
the independent variable, progress in high school, was measured by the
amount of high school attendance the subject had completed. Now, it is
obvious that any relationship initially found between better adjustment and
more high school might be spurious. For example, a youth from a wealthier
home might be better able to afford to complete high school and also more
likely to get better employment simply because of his father's greater economic influence in the community.

Such reasoning led Christiansen to control *six* variables in the comparisons of the economic adjustment of subjects with varying lengths of high
school residence: age, sex, nationality of parents, father's occupation, residential neighborhood, and mental ability in the narrow sense of academic
grades. Chapin, in addition, suggested that it would have been desirable to
control the additional factors of physical health, the presence of a broken
home, and the trait of persistence. Upon examining this list of nine controls,
the reader should be able to distinguish *one* control factor which, by reference to our discussion appears different in kind from the other eight control
factors. Thus sex or age or nationality does *not* appear to be an *intrinsic*
part of the developmental sequence essential to completing high school. But
mental ability or its index, academic performance certainly is an intrinsic
pre-requisite for completion of high school. If one could conceivably find
subjects *extremely low* in mental ability who managed to complete high
school, one would be dealing with the variable of high school attendance in
a form that rendered it completely meaningless. The student would be
physically present in high school, yes! But, he would be unresponsive to the
didactic work and stimulation that is the essential element of the high

---

15. G. W. Allport, Review of The American Soldier, *J. Abnorm. Soc. Psychol.*, 45, 1950,
p. 172. Reprinted by permission of The American Psychological Association.
16. *Op. cit.*
17. *Op. cit.*

school experience.[18] Under such conditions of "control," one would naturally find the influence of the original independent variable to be negligible, but it would be perverse to conclude that the original relationship was spurious. Christiansen's own data strike home the point in a rather odd way. At first, she only controlled the five factors other than mental ability. At a subsequent stage, she attempted to introduce controls over this latter factor by sub-dividing the groups in terms of academic performance. Ideally, then her design should have had the following formal pattern.[19]

1. Graduates with *high* mental ability, i.e., *good* academic grades
2. Non-Graduates with *high* mental ability, i.e., *good* academic grades
3. Graduates with *low* mental ability, i.e., *poor* academic grades
4. Non-Graduates with *low* mental ability, i.e., *poor* academic grades.

The complete test for spuriousness would have involved a comparison of group 1 and 2 in economic adjustment, and group 3 and 4 in economic adjustment. Then depending on whether the differences persisted or disappeared, a corresponding conclusion would be reached as to the problem of spuriousness. In Chapin's and other summary accounts of this study, the reader is informed that such controls were instituted and the original relationship re-examined. But this statement glosses over one strange fact. Examination of the original research report will reveal that while groups 1 and 2 above were compared, *no comparison was made* of groups 3 and 4 above. In other words, the effect of school attendance on economic adjustment was made under the condition of equally *good* grades, but *not* under the condition of equally *bad* grades.[20] Why? This was certainly not arbitrariness. Christiansen had no alternative! Inspection of the distribution of grades for the various experimental groups shows that there was *no single* graduate with academic marks below 75. By contrast, among non-graduates, 17% of the group had grades below 75. Given these respective distributions of the control factor among the groups to be contrasted, it was impossible to in-

---

18. The correlation between mental ability and performance in school or college is not high, as demonstrated in a variety of studies using established tests of intelligence. However, these coefficients generally approximate to a value of between .4-.6 and there are also studies showing that a given *minimum* level of mental ability is required to complete certain types of academic work. See T. L. Kelley, *Interpretation of Educational Measurement* (New York: World Book Co., 1927).

19. In actuality, she had many more groups. On the experimental variable there were four groups ranging from 1 year of attendance to completion of high school, and each of these was sub-divided on the control variable, academic grades, not merely into good and poor, but into five classes ranging from excellent to very bad grades. However, the logic will be conveyed by our abbreviated design.

20. H. F. Christiansen, The Relation of School Progress, Measured in Terms of the Total Amount of School Attendance or Course Completion, to subsequent Adjustment, M. A. Thesis, University of Minnesota Library, June, 1938. What Christiansen actually did then was to have a whole series of comparisons between graduates and non-graduates, first under conditions of excellent grades, then very good grades, then good, etc. But the number of such comparisons simply gives the *appearance* that groups 3 and 4 in our schema were compared. One can sub-divide the "good students" again and again, and still one will never have the comparisons of the "really bad" students.

stitute the proper comparisons for spuriousness. The connection between grades and length of high school attendance was so *organic,* involved, in our terms, such a developmental sequence, that the conditions for the complete test of spuriousness simply do not exist! The concept of spuriousness seems an absurdity given this patterning of reality.

This is not to say that such *procedures* of "control" of earlier developmental factors should not be applied where possible. They illuminate the process that led to the formation of the independent variable and to its significance as a cause. It is to say, however, that this should not be confused with the specific *test* of a hypothesized cause. In the context of a treatment of psychological theory, Krech and Crutchfield clarify the distinction for us:

> It is essential to make a clear distinction between the *immediate dynamic* problem—how the needs and goals of a given individual at a given time in a given situation determine his behavior—and the *genetic* problem—how these needs and goals and this situation have come into being in the course of the individual's development. . . . A comprehensive explanation of the "causation" of the individual's behavior will, of course, require a consideration of both the immediate dynamic and the genetic problems; but for most efficient analysis and to avoid conceptual confusion, the two should be kept separated.[21]

Thus far our discussion has clarified one instance in which the control of a variable shall not be regarded as a test for spuriousness, the instance we have labelled a developmental sequence where the control variable represents an earlier stage of a larger temporal process. There are however, other instances in which the control of a variable shall not be regarded as a test for spuriousness. These involve the notion that the control factor and the original independent variable form a unity, but the unity does not involve a sequence in time, but rather a *configuration* in space. Such unities and their operation must be distinguished from problems of control for spuriousness in exactly the same way as was done for the developmental sequence. We shall merely note that such configurations can be of two types, the *psychological* configuration and the *social* configuration.

The clearest case of a psychological configuration is a *general attitude.* We have in such instances a series of component attitudes inextricably related one to the other to form some general attitude or configuration. The case studies we have cited earlier provide many examples of such configurations. Thus, in the Absenteeism Inquiry, a whole series of components, satisfaction with the job, the plant, the promotional policy, the health conditions, the safety conditions, etc. combined to form a generalized level of morale which was related to absenteeism. In *The American Soldier,* we have many such configurations. For example, a general conformity to the army

---

21. By permission from *Theory and Problems of Social Psychology,* by D. Krech and R. Crutchfield, 1948, McGraw-Hill Book Company, Inc., pp. 33-34.

as evidenced by such component beliefs as AWOL was a serious offense, the army discipline was not too strict, the army is run well, etc., was related to the phenomenon of mobility or promotion. In both these examples, the analysts did examine the influence of isolated components on the phenomenon, but it will be seen shortly that the *logic* was other than control for spuriousness. While the *procedure* apparently involves the "control of another variable," the more general configuration from which the component derives, we do not conceive of this as evidence on spuriousness. The explanatory factor, the component, is an intrinsic part of the larger configuration and excluding the configuration so-to-speak removes some of the very dynamic force of the component. The kind of inference to be drawn, and the purpose behind such refined analyses is yet to be presented.

We can suggest in a *conservative* way how the introduction of control over part of a generalized attitude can reduce the effect observed by reference to some data in *The American Soldier*. In a study of the effect of conformity with army norms on subsequent promotion, two sets of data are presented. In one, the influence on promotion of differences in score on a *scale measuring the configuration, general conformity*, is observed to be 14%, 14%, and 25% depending on which ranks are examined. In the other set of data, the influence on promotion of a *component* item of conformity, drawn from the scale, is demonstrated to be 17%, 6%, 7%, 14%, 8%, 0% depending on which particular ranks and attitude items are examined. When the problem is studied in terms of the configuration, the influence of the hypothesized cause is much *greater*.[22] It should be noted that this is a conservative demonstration, since the comparisons involving discrete items do not actually engage in matching of the groups on the other items from the scale. Only *some* of those individuals who demonstrate conformity on the given item have *not* endorsed the other items in the total configuration and it is only for this portion of cases that the comparison implicitly relates to the control of the configuration. Nevertheless, the reduction in effect observed is sizable.

We may also conceive of configurations of a *social* nature. As distinct from the psychological configuration, these involve an inextricable combination of *environmental* conditions. A certain feature of the operation of society is always found in the context of certain other features. If the reader wishes, he may conceive of the psychological configuration as the product of such social configurations, but we are not concerned with this problem at the moment. One classic example of such configurations in survey research is a variable of a demographic sort from the *face sheet*. Thus "residence in the South" is an index of a highly complex social environment, involving a whole series of stimuli, treatments, and experiences. The classification on the face sheet, "Negro," is short-hand not for color alone, but for certain

---

22. *Op. cit.,* pp. 262-265, Table 11 and Chart XI.

economic, educational, and social experiences. When we compare Negroes and whites in an explanatory survey with respect to some phenomenon, and control, for example, economic and educational level, it is not in terms of the logic of spuriousness. Such a procedure of control will eliminate some of the initial difference that was observed, but this is not to say that the original finding was spurious. The assumption is that such economic and educational experiences are a part of the social unity that is labelled "Negro," and not merely an accidental accompaniment of the empirical classification by color in this survey.

If we pursue this example to a logical—if fantastic—extreme, the point will be even more dramatic. Let us assume that we wished to examine the influence of the attribute, "Negro-white," on some phenomenon such as "apathy-involvement" in politics. For this purpose we elaborated the analysis as described earlier, and then compared sub-groups of Negroes and whites *matched* in the following respects: well educated, high income, professional occupation, and resident in the same neighborhood—i.e., Park Avenue in New York City. We then found that any initial differences between Negroes and whites had disappeared following the institution of such "controls." Consequently, the analyst following the usual rules concludes that the original relationship was spurious. Being a Negro has no explanatory power for understanding apathy; it does not cause apathy. The original finding was misleading. The critic, on the contrary, might well cry out that the *analyst* is being misleading. After destroying the very *social* reality of the determinant "Negro," the tests no longer constitute a test of the determinant. Of course, they do constitute a test of the biological entity of "color," but not of the social attribute "Negro," for all the essential social accompaniments have been stripped away.[23] This is not to suggest that the *procedure* might not be employed, but merely that the inference of "spuriousness" should not be made. The procedures may be employed in conjunction with a different logic and type of inference to be presented shortly.

The other common instance of such social configurations in surveys occurs in the programmatic inquiry, where given variables deliberately created by some agency are applied as part of some larger program and occur only in that context.

Earlier we noted that an element of arbitrariness can be introduced by the analyst. Where he is emotionally committed to a given explanation which is found to depend on a spurious relationship, he can then argue

---

23. The concept of a configuration, and correspondingly the application of controls for spuriousness depends on the implicit plans and type of conclusions the analyst has in mind. Obviously, if his inquiry into the influence of "Negro" was in terms of the biological category, the control of the social factors would be appropriate. However, if his intent was to examine the influence of the attribute "Negro" in all its social implications, then he would have in mind the total configuration, and the concept of control would not be appropriate. A given entity can be conceived of in many ways, and our discussion is keyed to the intended use of the entity.

that the uncontrolled factor is an intrinsic part of the developmental history of the variable. So, too, the arbitrary analyst can argue that some uncontrolled factor is an intrinsic part of a configurational variable and thereby escapes rejecting an explanation to which he is attached. Again, the general solution for this is reasonableness.

We have discussed in sufficient detail the instances in which the procedures of control shall not be employed as tests for spuriousness.[24] However, we have suggested that these very procedures may well be used for *other* purposes, without clarifying such purposes. We turn to this now. Thus far, we have argued that the explanation of a phenomenon can be in terms of independent variables that have *complexity*, either historically or in configurational terms. To test the *explanatory* power of such factors means to test them at whatever level of complexity is involved. Otherwise the test is simply not what it purports to be. However, once such an explanation is demonstrated, then the analyst may wish to understand it better. He may wish to *refine* the complexity—to *analyze* it—to *separate* the configuration into its components—to *trace* out the emergence of the factor—so as to understand the way in which the explanation works. This latter purpose should not be confused with that earlier part of the analysis that involved the empirical test of the explanation. For this latter purpose, the procedures of control of other factors constitute the *empirical means* by which the analyst observes what component parts of the totality are crucial to its effectiveness. Since such refinement of an original complexity is a common practice we shall devote considerable discussion to it.[25]

---

24. Certain discussions in the literature are relevant to our treatment of controls and the proper application of the concept of spuriousness. Thus, Doob in his work on Public Opinion implicitly treats the problem in distinguishing the association between attributes as an *artifact of some bias in the sampling procedure* vs. association between attributes *in the population itself*. He clearly notes that controls should be introduced in the *former* instance. Otherwise a truly causal relationship may be confused with an apparent causal relation that is purely the accident of sampling. See, L. Doob, *Public Opinion and Propaganda* (New York: Holt, 1948), pp. 108-110. R. A. Fisher predicates much of his objection to the classical experiment on the ground that controls of all but the single experimental factor make it impossible for the investigator to observe the *interactions* between component factors, a central problem of investigation. "The modifications possible to any complicated apparatus, machine or industrial process must always be considered as potentially interacting with one another, and must be judged by the probable effects of such interactions. If they have to be tested one at a time this is not because to do so is an ideal scientific procedure." R. A. Fisher, *The Design of Experiments*, 4th Edition, 1947, p. 89, published by Oliver and Boyd, Ltd., Edinburgh, by permission of the author and publishers. Similarly, Egon Brunswik adopts the same general position with respect to the application of classical notions of control to psychological research. He remarks: "What remains to be done is to see as a virtue what was considered the calamity of imperfect control" (p. 41). See his *Systematic and Representative Design of Psychological Experiments* (Berkeley: University of California Press, 1949).

25. The reader may feel somewhat uneasy because of the dilemma, noted several times in this discussion, that there are no systematic criteria for differentiating developmental sequences or configurations from instances of spuriousness. We have been unable to establish formal criteria up to this time. The writer and Dr. Hans Zetterberg are working on one approach which if ultimately fruitful will be reported in the literature.

1. The Refinement of a Complex

We present two detailed examples from Durkheim's *Suicide* of the introduction of controls for purely *analytic* purposes rather than as tests of spuriousness. These incidentally constitute the illustrations of the point alluded to earlier that logical and inferential procedures often must be substituted for the actual empirical procedures of matching groups on the control factor.

Durkheim's Suicide—A Case Study in the Refinement of A Complex by Indirect Methods of Control: In our first example, Durkheim is concerned with the influence on suicide of the general class of factors he labels "cosmic." In the course of this discussion he notes a finding so *universal,* so *regular* that it has the rare status of a *law. Suicide generally has its highest incidence in the month of June.* The explanation of suicide inheres in something having to do with the entity "June." Now June has somewhat the status we have called a "configuration." It is an astronomical pattern, it is a certain temperature level, it connotes a certain pattern of human activity, etc. Obviously, Durkheim is concerned to analyze what in June is responsible for suicide, and therefore must try to separate by methods approximating to controls the *component* that is significant. The reader recalling our earlier discussion of Durkheim will, of course, realize that the intention will be to dispute the fact that this explanatory principle is the temperature level and to locate the principle in some social aspect of the month of "June." We shall elaborate the procedures of quasi-control shortly, but in connection with our general argument, it should be noted that nowhere does Durkheim argue that the original explanation is spurious. He does not reject the fact that June is responsible, because some component within the June configuration is essential. The aim of the control procedure is simply analytic! Durkheim proceeds by a variety of means, only a few of which we shall discuss.

He finds an ingenious way of *actually* instituting a control over temperature. He compares different months having the *same* temperature, and finds that the original differences in suicide persist. Thus, the initial difference cannot have been due to temperature. "In one and the same country, months with an essentially similar temperature produce a very different proportion of suicides (for instance, May and September, April and October in France, June and September in Italy)."

His other procedures, however, are indirect. They do not involve actual controls but simply logical elaborations of the way certain bodies of data must arrange themselves, if a particular component factor were at work. Thus, if the temperature were the significant component behind June's effect, Durkheim reasons suicide should show some orderly increase with heat. Instead "Far more suicides occur in Spring than in Autumn, although it is a little colder in Spring."

He reasons by the same token, that if temperature were significant, suicide should show some more orderly *decrease* with cold. Instead, "In Italy the winter temperature is much lower than that of Autumn . . . and yet suicide-mortality is about the same in both seasons."

Similarly, he reasons that if temperature were significant, seasons differing markedly in temperature, should differ markedly in suicide rate. Instead, "Everywhere the difference between spring and summer is very slight for suicides but very high for temperature." The parallel argument should hold for months. Yet: "January and October, February and August in France have a like number of suicides in spite of great differences in temperature."

Another argument is slightly different in character and perhaps a little more tenuous, since it involves an assumption about the function for suicide and temperature being *continuous*. Durkheim reasons that if temperature is responsible for June's pre-eminence in the production of suicides, it should be the case that suicides should be maximum at the time of maximum heat. Instead "Suicide . . . does not reach its height in the hottest months which are August or July." By extension, suicides should reach their lowest point at the time of lowest temperature. Instead "It reaches its lowest point not in January, the coldest month, but in December."

The argument becomes more inferential yet. If temperature were significant, not only should the arrays for periods of the year behave in certain ways, but by extension countries characterized by given temperature levels should array themselves in certain ways. "The hottest countries should be those most stricken." Instead the evidence refutes the theory. Suicide "is least developed in the southern countries of Europe."

Ultimately, by many such logical devices and corresponding inspection of the data, Durkheim concludes that "the direct action of cosmic factors could not explain the monthly or seasonal variations of suicide. . . . If voluntary deaths increase from January to July, it is not because heat disturbs the organism but because social life is more intense." [26]

Our other example from the *Suicide* again involves Durkheim's examination of the influence of marital status as an independent variable. It will be recalled that Durkheim was concerned to isolate and control the influence of age which is associated with marital status, since this obscured the original relationship. He regarded age as a possible source of *spuriousness*. However, marital status itself is a configuration of many other components besides age, and Durkheim is concerned to isolate which of these remaining components is the essential element in reducing the vulnerability of the married to suicide. By contrast with the treatment of age, it should be noted that Durkheim does *not* regard these different components as sources of spuriousness. The separation of them is purely for analytic purposes, rather

26. *Op. cit.* All the above quotations are taken from pp. 109-122.

than for purposes of rejecting the initial findings. As Durkheim remarks, the initial result "must be further defined; for the family environment consists of different elements. For husband and wife alike the family includes: 1. the wife or husband; 2. the children. Is the salutary effect of the family on the suicidal tendency due to the former or the latter? . . . We must investigate whether both take part, and, if so, the share of each." [27] Again his procedure for separating and isolating the effects of these components is a combination of straightforward controls plus more indirect and logical methods.

The direct method, as Durkheim notes, involves a "way of measuring exactly the real influence of *conjugal* association upon suicide; that of observing it when reduced to its own isolated strength, or in families without children." Thus Durkheim compares the rates of married individuals without children. and unmarried individuals, controlling in what is already a refined analysis the sources of spuriousness, age and sex. Then comparisons are made between these rates and the rate for married individuals with children, again controlling sex. On the basis of such analysis involving procedures of matching and control, Durkheim is able to establish that the major component in the marital configuration is the presence of children.

Durkheim also employs methods of a more indirect sort. Thus, for example, he argues that if the conjugal component were the major one, there should be little change in the suicide rate over time, since marriage rates have been fairly stable. Instead "the marriage rate has changed very little since the first of the century (19th), while suicide has tripled." [28]

But Durkheim employs still another approximation to estimate the influence of the conjugal component. Instead of *matching* married vs. single groups in respect of children, he does something bizarre and yet ingenious. He, contrary to all orthodoxy, lets *two factors vary simultaneously* and compares the suicide rates. How then shall he estimate which of these factors is operative? It is in the ingenious combinations of the two factors that the key lies, and its logic is immediately patent. *Widowed with children* are compared with *married without children* matching them for age and sex. The first group has not the benefit of conjugal association but the benefit of family, whereas the second group has the benefit of conjugal association but not the benefit of family. Since he finds that widowed have *greater immunity*, despite the lack of conjugal association, his inference is that the family component is the major one.[29]

The starting point for refinement of some complex factor that was used

---

27. *Ibid.,* pp. 185, 186.
28. *Ibid.,* p. 185.
29. *Ibid.,* p. 187. It should be noted that in this particular analysis Durkheim again has to cope with the problem of *crudity* in the control of age. Again the crudity luckily does not jeopardize the comparison but makes it more compelling.

as an explanation is the analyst's implicit and commonsense understanding that a particular configuration involves a whole cluster of specific attitudes, past experiences, and characteristics. When we make educational comparisons, for example, we "understand" that, in contrast to those with little formal schooling, college trained persons have high level occupations, are wealthy, have articulated opinions on a wide range of issues, are capable of expressing themselves, and so forth. Similarly, when we carry out age comparisons, we implicitly introduce our "knowledge" that young people have different interests than do their elders, that they have greater physical energy and less varied background of experience to guide them. Nor does this implicit knowledge enter in only in connection with the more familiar demographic variables. If we compare the attitudes of combat veterans and green troops, we would call forth a whole range of associations about the different experiences of the two groups, what kinds of fears they had, their convictions regarding their personal contribtutions to the war, and the like.

The analyst in examining an explanatory finding marshals such thoughts. But often his usual background knowledge will not serve him sufficiently well. The range of associations called forth will be limited in instances where the variable used is strange or new to him. For example, if we come across a comparison of Jordanian and Indonesian Moslems, it is unlikely that many of us would try to anticipate, in terms of common-sense expectations, what such a comparison might reveal. But even in the instance of familiar categories, where the analyst can readily make assumptions, such an intuitive approach is generally not adequate. The configuration may involve a great many components and which of these is significant is the question. So, too, his assumptions about the presence of other components may be in error. Consequently, it is important to provide an empirical basis for such refinement by the introduction of questions which check on the components. Then, rather than remaining dependent on our assumptions, we have measures which will tell us whether, in fact, well-educated persons are more articulate than uneducated persons, whether the young have greater vitality than their elders, whether combat veterans are more likely than green troops to feel that they have done their personal share in the war. And once such refinements are at hand, critical relationships emerge more clearly.

Our first example of such a mode of analysis is taken from a survey of residential mobility carried out in Philadelphia during the fall and winter of 1950.[30] This study was not only concerned with actual experiences of mobility, but also with the desires and attitudes of the householders sampled. It was discovered during the analysis of the data that there was a strong relationship between desires to move and status as an owner or a renter. This relationship is recorded in Table IX.

---

30. P. Rossi, *Why Families Move.* (Glencoe: The Free Press, 1955).

TABLE IX—Desires to Move According to Status as Renter or Owner

	Renters	Owners
Anxious to stay	24%	52%
Want to stay, but not anxious	15	15
Want to move, but not anxious	25	20
Anxious to move	36	13
Total cases	477	429

There were more than twice as many owners as renters who expressed a strong desire to remain in their present homes, and, at the other extreme, nearly three times as many renters as owners who expressed an equally strong desire to move.

Now this finding makes good common sense, and it does so largely because we endow the statuses of renter and owner with a variety of implicit meanings. Home ownership, we feel, denotes a certain kind of stability which is likely to reflect itself in a desire not to move. But renters have more the character of "rolling stones," and are more likely, therefore, to want to change their place of residence.

It was not possible in the present instance to make direct checks of these assumptions: The survey did not include any "personality" questions which would have differentiated those of stable character from the "rolling stones." But it was possible to refine the broad categories of renter and owner. Each of the sample householders had been asked whether his family preferred to own or rent their home. This question permitted the analysts to distinguish between those who occupied their owning or renting status voluntarily and those who did so apparently against their will. By making use of this question, they are in a better position to talk about the stable householders (the owners who want to own) as distinct from those householders who seem particularly unstable (the renters who want to rent).

It turns out, upon analysis, that almost all of the then-owners were satisfied with their status—there were only a handful who said that they would prefer to rent their homes. But the level of satisfaction is not nearly so high among the renters. Indeed, less than half of this latter group—206 householders out of a total of 477 renters—said that they actually prefer renting a home to owning one. The remaining 271 renters would have preferred, according to their own reports, to own their homes. That they could not do so was undoubtedly due to a variety of factors: Lack of money, the tight housing market, the uncertainty of job opportunities in the area, and so on.

When this new and more refined system of categories is put into use, unexpected findings are disclosed. Table X examines the attitudes of owners, voluntary renters and involuntary renters toward remaining in their present dwellings:

TABLE X—Desires to Move According to Status as Owner, Voluntary Renter, or Involuntary Renter

Attitude toward moving	Owners	Renters who prefer to rent	Renters who prefer to own
Anxious to stay	52%	36%	15%
Want to stay, but not anxious	15	21	11
Want to move, but not anxious	20	22	27
Anxious to move	13	21	47
Total cases	429	206	271

Because there were so few owners who wanted to rent their homes, they have not been distinguished here from the owners who are satisfied with their status. But the two groups of renters are considered separately, and it is apparent that they differ considerably in their desires to move. If we consider the first two answer categories as favorable replies, then the voluntary renters seem to be almost as favorable in their attitudes toward their present residences as are the owners: 57 percent of the former, as compared with 67 percent of the latter, want to remain where they were at the time they were interviewed. It is true that the owners more frequently express a strong desire to stay in their present dwellings, but the difference is not as large as it originally appeared to be.

It is the involuntary renters who are really dissatisfied with their present dwellings. Nearly half of them—47 percent—report that they are anxious to move; this is a much larger proportion than is found in either of the other groups. At the other extreme, only about one in every seven involuntary renters said that he was anxious to stay in his present home, and only a total of about one in every four gave what we have considered to be "favorable" replies.

This new finding forces us to revise our original assumptions regarding the relative stability of renters and owners. A renter who prefers that status is apparently not especially anxious to move, not for the time being, at least. The renter who would prefer to own his home, on the other hand, is especially anxious to move. In other words, it is the householder whose desires are frustrated who is most unstable potentially. He is in a transitional status, so to speak. But, very probably, once he has succeeded in purchasing a house of his own, he will settle down quite permanently.

A second example is essentially similar, although the meaning attached to the initial broad categories is not as immediately obvious as in the case of renters and owners. Merton's study of housing communities focusses at many points on the contrast between two very different communities— Craftown and Hilltown.[31] But until we know something more about the backgrounds of these communities, we are in somewhat the same position

31. R. K. Merton, P. West, M. Jahoda, *Patterns of Social Life: Explorations in the Sociology of Housing* (in press).

as when we contrast the behavior and attitudes of Jordanian and Indonesian Moslems—we do not know what to expect from the comparisons.

Merton describes the contrasts between Craftown and Hilltown as quite conspicuous. Craftown is a separate community, in a suburban setting and with a township government of its own; Hilltown, on the other hand, is part of a large urban community, and, while it is architecturally distinct from the rest of the city, it is neither isolated nor independent nor self-sufficient. Although in the context of the example which we shall give these differences between the two communities are the most significant ones, there are other important contrasts between them. Most of the residents of Craftown are skilled workers, although there are some white collar workers as well living in the community; all of them are white; most are young married couples. The residents of Hilltown are much less homogeneous. In the first place, the community is a bi-racial one, with almost equal numbers of Negro and white families. Occupationally, too, the community is lacking in the homogeneity characteristic of Craftown—in addition to numbering among its residents skilled workers and white collar workers, it includes, especially among its Negroes, a large number of service workers. Finally, there is a greater range in the age distribution of the Hilltown residents than is the case in Craftown. One would expect, from this description of the two communities, that the patterns of friendship within the community would be quite different. The figures reported in Table XI demonstrate that this is the case.

TABLE XI—Friendship Ties Within the Community in Craftown and Hilltown

Pattern of Friendship	Craftown	Hilltown
Spend more time with project friends	52%	34%
Spend more time with non-project friends	39	54
No discernible difference	9	12
Total cases	313	707

There is indeed a difference between the two communities. In Craftown, the relatively more isolated and self-contained settlement, somewhat more than half of the residents report that they spend more time with their project friends than with those living outside the community. This contrasts with about a third of the Hilltowners who indicate similar friendship patterns. Conversely, more than half of the Hilltowners, compared with about 40 percent of the Craftown residents, state that their friendship ties are predominantly with persons living outside the community. As Merton puts it, "This appears to confirm the widespread impression that the location of housing projects materially affects the ensuing patterns of interpersonal relations. When projects are built in the midst of an established residential area (and particularly one in which some of the project residents have lived), prior friendships are more likely to be retained." [32]

But this is still a relatively unrefined relationship, based on our knowledge of the way in which the two communities differ in their gross aspects. There is as yet no confirmation of our assumption that it is the isolation and self-containment of Craftown which produce an inward orientation in friendship patterns. Let us study how Merton refined the broad categories with which he started. How can he demonstrate more convincingly that it is the self-containment of Craftown which produces an inward orientation in friendship patterns, and the dependence of Hilltown on its environing area which leads to an outward orientation in these friendship patterns? How can he show that it is these features of the communities, and not some others, which are crucial in determining interpersonal ties? The device which he used was an indirect and ingenious one. By showing that it was the group most highly integrated into the area surrounding the community which at the same time was most outward oriented in its friendship patterns, he was able to give further support to his original contention.

The area surrounding the Hilltown community is largely Negro in composition, and, further, 12 percent of the Hilltown Negroes (as contrasted with 4 percent of the whites) formerly lived in that area. It is highly probable, then that Hilltown Negroes will have some ties in the surrounding area—they are not as likely as whites to consider Hilltown an isolated community. By showing, then, that more of them maintain strong interpersonal relations outside the community, he lent strength to his original assumption about the features of community life which are relevant in the formation of personal ties within the community. The finding is shown in Table XII.

TABLE XII—Friendship Ties Within the Community in Craftown and Hilltown When Race Is Held Constant

Pattern of Friendship	Craftown	Hilltown Whites	Hilltown Negroes
Spend more time with project friends	52%	38%	31%
Spend more time with non-project friends	39	51	57
No discernible difference	9	11	12
Total cases	313	351	356

2. The Deliberate Creation of a Configuration

We have noted that independent variables which are used as explanations of a phenomenon may occur at different levels of complexity. While there are relatively unitary variables, we also find more complex ones that we have labelled configurations. In both instances, the direction that the analysis *ultimately* takes is towards *refinement*. The unitary variable is examined

---

32. *Ibid.*

in its purity through the introduction of controls over other factors. The configuration is examined in its full complexity *at first,* but it may then be analyzed and fragmented for purposes of *understanding* how the different parts interact or operate to produce the effect. What we wish to discuss at this point is a procedure of analysis that goes in an opposite direction—the independent variables initially are at some level of relative purity and are manipulated to a stage of greater complexity. Oftentimes, the analyst may be concerned to test the explanatory power of some configuration which is not necessarily natural, or frequent. The actual independent variables that he has measured are simpler. Consequently, he then *pools* information from several of these variables and forms an index which represents the more complex and *synthetic* configuration whose explanatory power he then examines.[33] Our early discussion had suggested that the elaboration of the analysis goes in the direction of refinement and control of factors, and this seems a strange procedure. However, the fact that configurations are *deliberately* created often in analyses strengthens our recent point that the analyst should often treat natural configurations as explanatory factors.

Perhaps the best known example of this new procedure is from *The People's Choice.*[34] In this instance, an *index of political predisposition* was compounded of three less complex variables, socio-economic status, religious affiliation, and residence. The influence of these three factors combined and interacting in various ways—contradictory or complementary, on voting behavior was then examined. We have here a configuration that is artificial—certain combinations that were examined are neither frequent nor natural, as in the instance of individuals under cross-pressures. Yet the analysts heap complexity on complexity. Starting from three separate, *relatively* unitary factors they do not then examine each of these by controlling the other factors as tests of spuriousness. They put them all together in various complicated ways and examine the effects of such configurations. We present below illustrative data to convey the analytic procedure.

The analysis has one special feature worthy of emphasis in this context. It can be noted that the independent variable that is used as an explanatory factor is itself a compound of several variables. However, the analysis subsequently involved the introduction of *still another* factor, level of interest, which was controlled in the comparisons of groups varying in the susceptibility to cross-pressures. In other words, whether a configuration or a unitary variable is used as the initial independent variable, controls can be introduced subsequently. The procedure is shown in Chart VI below which deals with time of vote decision rather than voting preference.

We have now treated the variety of problems in explanatory analysis hav-

---

33. We shall not discuss actual methods of index construction which are the subject of a forthcoming monograph in this series.

34. P. Lazarsfeld, B. Berelson, and H. Gaudet, *The People's Choice* (New York: Columbia University Press, 2nd edition, 1948). The figures are reproduced by permission of the publishers.

Chart V

The Use of a Configuration in an Explanatory Analysis

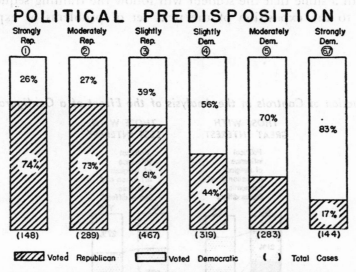

POLITICAL PREDISPOSITION

High SES level, affiliation with the Protestant religion, and rural residence predispose a voter for the Republican party; the opposites of these factors make for Democratic predisposition. Summarized in an index of political predisposition (IPP), their effect is illustrated by the high correlation with vote intention.

ing to do with the testing of an obtained relationship for spuriousness. The discussion, however, has been in terms of the *logical principles,* rather than the *technical procedures* involved. It should be clear to the student that the simultaneous study of three or more variables presupposes considerable skill in machine processing of data. While, the student has already learned the *fundamental* features of machine processing in the *descriptive* survey, he must now extend his skills to a new and more refined level. He must now learn to manipulate the cards so that the three variables or even more than three can be examined simultaneously.

Problem Exercise IV, in Appendix C, is intended to provide the student practice in machine processing of explanatory surveys and should be undertaken at this point.

After the student has learned the methods of machine processing, he must have skill in treating the complex data that express the numerical relationships that obtain among many variables.

To provide practice in these respects, Practice Exercise I, Appendix D, should now be undertaken. In this exercise, a series of tables has been adapted from research reported in *The American Soldier.* The tables are ordered in a series of increasing complexity which shows the student in detail how the numerical relationships obtained following machine processing are presented, examined and evaluated.

We shall assume that the student will follow the training sequence and now turn to the exposition of the next set of problems of explanatory analyses.

Chart VI

The Introduction of Controls in the Analysis of the Effect of a Configuration

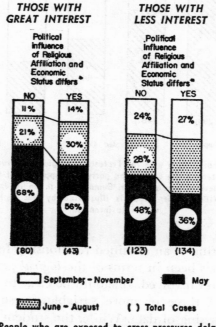

THOSE WITH GREAT INTEREST

Political influence of Religious Affiliation and Economic Status differs*

	NO	YES
	11%	14%
	21%	30%
	68%	56%
	(80)	(43)

THOSE WITH LESS INTEREST

Political influence of Religious Affiliation and Economic Status differs*

	NO	YES
	24%	27%
	28%	
	48%	36%
	(123)	(134)

☐ September – November   ■ May

▨ June – August   ( ) Total Cases

People who are exposed to cross-pressures delay their final vote decision. This is true separately for people with great interest and those with less interest. The effect of the cross-pressure is illustrated in each pair of bars.

* Poor Protestants or rich Catholics.

CHAPTER VII

The Introduction
of Additional Variables
and the Elaboration of the Analysis

THUS far we have described two series of procedures in the analysis of explanatory surveys. First in Chapter V we dealt with the problems in treating simple relationships between two variables. Then in Chapter VI we dealt with the introduction of additional variables as a solution to the problems of spuriousness. We now turn to a final stage of the analysis. When the analyst has satisfied himself that these prior problems have been solved, he raises a different set of questions. He explores the relationship that has been established, elaborating and clarifying it further by the introduction of additional variables.

This mode of analysis, which we shall call the process of *Elaboration*, always treats variables which are ordered in time. And, although it involves a series of apparently specific and discrete procedures these can all be represented in one generalized formal scheme. However, as we shall see, certain

---

* The major sections of this chapter have been written by Patricia Kendall and represent an enlargement of an earlier analytic schema. That schema constituted a formalization of the analytic procedures used in the research reported in *The American Soldier*. It has now been re-examined in the light of other empirical data reported in other surveys. However, the schema has not yet been extended in the light of a wide enough range of survey analyses to constitute a generalized model. Nevertheless, it is presented at this time because it constitutes the best approximation to our ultimate goal and it does order the *major* features of explanatory analyses. For the original formulation, the reader is referred to P. F. Lazarsfeld and P. Kendall, *Survey Analysis, op. cit.*

of the prior analytic procedures relevant to the problems of spuriousness can also be subsumed under the same formal schema. The formal schema we shall present shortly is only a model and still needs to be extended. Ultimately it will represent in *generalized formal* terms the total sequence of features of an explanatory analysis. At the present time, however, it is incomplete, and the student must make continuing reference to certain details and qualifications which we have presented in *narrative* terms in the previous chapters.

Interpretation and Its Place in a General Schema of Elaboration

We shall first describe the general features of one type of elaboration which we shall call *Interpretation*. When the analyst interprets a relationship, he determines the process through which the assumed cause is related to what we take to be its effect. How did the result come about? What are the "links" between the two variables? Answers to these questions are provided in the interpretation of the result. Described in formal terms, the interpretation of a statistical relationship between two variables involves the introduction of further variables and an examination of the resulting interrelationships between all of the factors.

Let us see concretely what this means in the light of an actual example. To illustrate the steps which one goes through in interpreting a result, and to indicate the kinds of material wihch are required, we shall start with one relationship in *The American Soldier* for which an interpretation was suggested. On one index of personal commitment, "At the time you came into the Army did you think you should have been deferred?", the analysts found a position correlation between education and positive responses: The higher the education of the soldier, the more likely he was to say that he had volunteered or that he should not have been deferred.[1] This finding was somewhat surprising in view of the general tendency of better educated soldiers to be more critical of the Army. The authors interpret the results in terms of the concept of "relative deprivation," which they define in the following way:

> Becoming a soldier meant to many men a very real deprivation. But the felt sacrifice was greater for some than for others, *depending on their standards of comparison.*[2]

The analysts suggest that the lower educated soldiers, coming mainly from skilled labor occupations which accounted for many exemptions from

---

1. *Op. cit.*, Vol. I, p. 124, Table 3.
2. *Ibid.*, Vol. I, p. 125, authors' italics.

service in the Army, compared their lot with that of their friends, many of
whom had been deferred because of the importance of their jobs. On the
other hand, "The great mass of professional, trade, and white-collar occupations were not deferable. . . . The average high school graduate or college
man was a clear-cut candidate for induction . . ." [3] In other words, lower
educated soldiers, coming from an environment in which deferments were
relatively frequent, were more likely to experience their inductions as a personal sacrifice than were the better educated soldiers, fewer of whose friends
had received deferments.[4]

How would one go about studying this interpretation? To simplify our
discussion of the actual procedure, we should perhaps first restate the interpretative statement, so as to see the statistical relationships which it implies.
It might read as follows:

> Better educated soldiers are more likely to accept their inductions, because
> better educated soldiers come from an environment in which deferments
> are infrequent, and coming from an environment in which deferments are
> infrequent leads to more willing acceptance of induction.

When we rephrase the statement in this way, we note that one characteristic
of any "complete" interpretation is that the interpretative variable, the "test
factor" as it might be called, is related to each of the original variables. The
Research Branch interpretation implies (a) that the test factor, relative frequency of deferment in the environment from which the individual soldier
comes, is negatively related to education (the higher the level of education,
the lower the rate of deferment in the individual's social environment), and
(b) that the same factor is also negatively related to the dependent variable
in the original relationship, the soldier's acceptance of his induction into
the Army (the higher the rate of deferment in the social environment of the
soldier the less likely he is to accept his induction willingly).

But this feature is not the only one. If we extend our reformulation of
the interpretive statement, we note another aspect of "complete" interpretations.

> If it is true that the relationship between education and attitudes toward
> one's own induction can be explained entirely by the frequency of defer-
> ments in one's civilian environment, then when soldiers are classified accord-
> ing to this test factor, when they are separated into different groups accord-
> ing to the frequency of deferments in the environments from which they
> come, there should no longer be any relationship between education and
> attitude toward induction.

Stated in somewhat more technical terms, we expect that when the population is stratified according to different values of the test factor, the partial

---

3. *Ibid.*, Vol. I, p. 127.

4. Interestingly enough, however, out of a cross-section of soldiers, only about one-fifth of
those who said they should have been deferred mentioned the importance of their jobs as the
reason. (See *Ibid.*, Vol. I, p. 123, Table 2.)

relationships between the two original variables will vanish.[5] If we can classify men according to whether or not they came from an environment in which deferments were frequent, we shall find, within any of the homogeneous groups thus obtained, that there is no relationship between education and acceptance of induction. The well-educated soldiers who come from an environment in which deferments were common will be just as disgruntled about their inductions as are poorly educated men from similar backgrounds; conversely, the less well educated soldier from an environment in which there were few deferments will be as likely to accept his own induction as is the better educated man in the same kind of situation. In other words, if the partial relationships between education and attitudes toward induction disappeared when soldiers were classified according to the frequency of deferment in their civilian environments, we would conclude that one's previous environment completely interpreted the original relationship.

This line of reasoning prescribes the kind of information we must obtain and the kinds of relationships we must examine if we are to test the interpretation. First of all, we would need to know something about the rate of deferment in the civilian environment of each man. This information, apparently not available in the Research Branch study, might have been obtained from answers to a question like "Have some of your friends or acquaintances been deferred because they are in indispensable civilian occupations?" [6] Let us assume, for the sake of illustration, that such a question actually had been asked, and that about half of the soldiers answered in the affirmative.

The next step would be to see whether this test factor actually is related to the original characteristics, education and attitude toward induction. Again we must invent the two relationships if we want to end up with the full scheme for testing interpretations. We shall assume, finally, that, had information on this test factor been available, it would have provided a complete interpretation of the original result. Then we would have found a set of tables like the synthetic ones presented below.

Table XIII is actually less complicated than it may appear to be. It is made up of three four-fold tables connected by equals and plus signs. In each of the three tables the relation between education and attitude toward induction is examined.

From where did these three tables come? The first one, that to the left

<hr />

5. Partial relationships are those observed within particular sub-groups of the total sample. They are obtained when other variables, in this case what we have called the test factor or factors, are held constant.

6. It might be preferable to have some objective measure of the deferment rate since answers to a question like the one suggested are sometimes colored by present attitudes. We disregard this difficulty at the moment, however, since we are interested only in outlining the steps involved in an interpretation.

TABLE XIII—Hypothetical Figures Interpreting Relationship Between Education and Attitude Toward Induction

	Total Sample			Friends or Acquaintances Deferred			No Friends or Acquaintances Deferred		
	High Educ.	Low Educ.		High Educ.	Low Educ.		High Educ.	Low Educ.	
Volunteered or should not have been deferred	1556	1310	2866	210	939	1149	1346	371	1717
			=			+			
Should have been deferred	205	566	771	125	545	670	80	21	101
	1761	1876	3637	335	1484	1819	1426	392	1818

of the equals sign, is a simplified version of the findings actually reported in *The American Soldier*.[7] We shall call it the "original relationship."

The two tables to the right of the equals sign show the partial relationships between education and attitude toward induction when rate of deferment is held constant. The reader will note that these two tables are obtained by a "decomposition" of the original relationship. That is, the original sample is divided into two groups by the test factor, rate of deferment, and then within each of these groups the two original variables are cross-tabulated. Because of this decomposition, equivalent cells in the two partial tables add to the corresponding cell in the original table. The reader can verify this for himself. These two partial tables might have been observed empirically. As we have already indicated, however, the Research Branch apparently did not have any measure of deferment rate. Consequently, the figures presented here are hypothetical, and to indicate this we have italicized them. While the figures are hypothetical, they were not invented haphazardly. We worked out the partial tables so that they meet the conditions which we said were required in a complete interpretation.

Now that the construction of the three tables has received some clarification, we can analyze more specifically what they reveal. In the original table we observe a fairly high relationship between education and attitude toward induction. This can be seen most easily by noting that, among the highly educated soldiers, the ratio of favorable to unfavorable attitudes regarding induction is more than 7 to 1; among the soldiers with lower levels of education, however, this ratio is less than 3 to 1. The original relationship, then, is a relatively strong one.

But what happens in the two partial tables? Brief inspection would seem to indicate that in neither of these tables is the relationship between education and attitude toward induction as close as it was in the original table. And closer analysis reveals that there is actually *no* relationship between the two original variables in either of the partial tables:

_____

7. *Op. cit.*, Vol. I, p. 124, Table 3.

TABLE XIV—Hypothetical Partial Relationships Between Education and Attitude Toward Induction With Rate of Deferment Held Constant

	Percent who say they volunteered or should not have been deferred	
Deferment rate	High education	Low education
Friends or acquaintances deferred	63%	63%
No friends or acquaintances deferred	95	95

What we have done here is percentage the figures of the partial relation, ships in Table XIII, and presented them as a three-dimensional table of the kind in Appendix D. Each row now represents the partial relationship between education and atttitude toward induction. In each case it can be seen that the original relationship has vanished entirely. Although those coming from different civilian environments have quite different levels of favorableness to their own inductions, it now turns out, according to the figures which we invented, that such attitudes are not at all related to education once rate of deferment is held constant.

There are other aspects of Table XIV which might be commented on, but we shall reserve discussion of these until later when we present the process of interpretation in more technical terms. Here we have simply outlined, in somewhat systematic fashion, the steps involved in interpreting a statistical relationship. We can now summarize the lesson of the present example. If a particular test factor actually does interpret the relationship between two variables, we shall find that the relations between all three are characterized in the following ways:

I. The test factor is related to the assumed causal variable in the original relationship.

II. The test factor is also related to the assumed effect.

III. When the sample is stratified according to the test factor, the partial relationships between the original variables are smaller than the original relationship.

Interpretation will receive an even more formal definition if we relate it to other elaboration procedures. Let us summarize three sets of results which illustrate the processes of elaboration.

1. Havemann and West found that there was a relationship between the type of college from which her subjects graduated and their subsequent salaries. In order to make sure that this relationship was not a spurious one, she examined it after holding constant the family background of the students, as measured by their need to earn part or all of their expenses while in college.

2. Stouffer and his associates found that better educated men accepted their induction more willingly than did less well educated soldiers. They suggested that this might be interpreted in terms of the lower rate of defer-

ment among white collar workers, which made the induction of the better educated man less of a personal sacrifice when he compared his lot with that of his friends and acquaintances.

3. Mills and his associates found that Puerto Rican migrants to New York City who had been there for a relatively long period of time had been able to achieve a greater degree of upward occupational mobility than was the case among migrants who had arrived only recently. In exploring this relationship further, they found that it held only for men migrants. Among the women, time of arrival made no difference in the direction of their occupational mobility.

The reader may feel that there is little similarity between these three results, that the objectives and the accomplishments of the analysts are so different in each case that there can be little which they have in common. In the first example, the analysis succeeded in "saving" the original relationship from disqualification as *spurious;* the second case is one in which the analysis provided *"links"* between the original variables; in the third example, the analysis specified the *conditions* under which the original relationship held true. With the functions of the analysis so varied, there may seem to be little which could tie the several results to each other.

However different these three results may appear to be, they have one important characteristic in common. In all three we started with the relationship between two variables, and sought to clarify this by the introduction of a third variable. In the first example, starting with type of college and later salary, the relationship between these was elaborated by consideration of the need of the student at the time that he went to college. In the second example, education and attitudes toward induction were our starting variables; rate of deferment in the civilian environment of the soldiers was the third factor introduced into the analysis. In the final example, starting with time of arrival in New York City and the direction of occupational mobility among Puerto Rican migrants we introduced into the relationship between these two variables a third factor—sex.

It turns out that the examination of the relationship between two variables in the light of a third is a very general mode of analysis. And, as we shall be able to demonstrate, the three examples which we presented are closely related to each other, despite our initial feeling that they represent very different kinds of analysis.

In order to formalize this general mode of analysis, let us consider systematically what happens when a third factor is introduced into the relationship between two variables. Essentially the introduction of a third variable results in a number of new relationships. These can be represented by returning to the hypothetical example on p. 279. We find, by examining these figures, that we have the following relationships:

(1) *Original relationship* [xy]

We have the original relationship between the two starting variables. .This is found, in our example, in the table on the left of the equals sign. We have symbolized it with the expression, [xy]

(2) *Partial relationships* [xy; t+] and [xy; t−]

We have the two (or more) partial relationships, that is, the relationships between the original variables in the homogeneous sub-classes obtained by stratifying the total sample according to the test factor. In our example, these partial relationships are found in the two four-fold tables to the right of the equals sign. (How the different partial relationships are labelled—which is [xy; t+] and which is [xy; t−]—depends on how the test variable has been defined.)

(3) *Marginal relationships* [xt] and [ty]

Finally, we have what might be called the marginal relationships, a fact already alluded to but not explicitly discussed. There are two of these, the relationship between the original *x* variable and the test factor, and the relationship between the original *y* variable and the test factor. These too can be found in Table XIII, although it may not be immediately obvious how or where.

(a) *Relationship between "independent variable" and test factor* [xt]

This, are we know, is the relationship between education and deferment rate. The figures indicating this relationship are found in the *totals rows* of the two partial tables. Thus

	High educ.	*Low educ.*	*Total*
Friends or acquaintances deferred	335	1484	1819
No friends or acquaintances deferred	1426	392	1818
Total	1761	1876	3637

Even the briefest inspection of this table reveals that, in the present hypothetical example, the [xt] relationship is a strong one.

(b) *Relationship between test factor and "dependent variable,"* [ty]

This is the relationship between deferment rate and attitude toward induction. It, too, is found in the marginal figures of the partial tables, only now it is found in the *totals columns* of these tables. Thus

	Friends or acquaintances deferred		
	Yes	*No*	*Total*
Volunteered or should not have been deferred	1149	1717	2866
Should have been deferred	670	101	771
Total	1819	1818	3637

We start with one relationship, [xy]. The introduction of a third factor results in a minimum of four new relationships, the partial relationships and the marginal relationships. (If the test factor is divided into more than two classes, there are more than two partial relationships, and therefore a total of more than four new relationships.) [8] Once these new relationships have been obtained, there is a rather startling development. When arranged in appropriate combinations, these new relationships can be equated to the result with which we started. The equation by which this is achieved is as follows: [9]

$$[xy] = [xy; t^+] \oplus [xy; t^-] \oplus [xt][ty] \quad \dots\dots\dots\dots\dots\dots\dots(1)$$

Let us restate this equation verbally. It says that the original relationship between two variables, designated here as "x" and "y," is equal to the sum of the partial relationships between x and y when the sample is stratified according to the $+$ and $-$ values [10] of the test factor, t, plus a term which is the product of the relationship between x and t, on the one hand, and between t and y, on the other.[11] (The plus signs in Equation (1) have been circled to indicate that the summation is not quite so simple as we suggest here; in order to work out the equation arithmetically, one must take into consideration certain weighting factors which we have ignored.)

1. Two Types of Elaboration: The M and P Types

Equation (1) is not a computing equation in the more familiar sense of the word. That is, we do not need Equation (1) in order to determine the original relationship, or, for that matter, any of the other relationships. The value of the equation, then, is that it makes explicit the varied relationships which develop when a third variable is introduced into the relationship between two others, and it shows how these several relationships are connected with each other. It is, in other words, what might be called a "formalizing" equation, since it formalized the interconnections between several relationships.

One of the first things one does with such a formalizing equation is to consider how its several terms can vary, to determine what values they can

---

8. Rearrangement of the figures in Table XIII would result in still other new relationships. For example, we could obtain the partial relationships between t and y with x held constant, or the partial relationships between x and t with y held constant. As we shall see presently, these relationships have no special meaning for the mode of analysis which we are developing, even though they may be interesting in themselves.

9. The full equation for the three-attribute case can be found in Yule and Kendall, *An Introduction to the Theory of Statistics* (London: J. B. Lippincott Co., 12th ed., 1940) Chapter 4. The equation can vary according to what coefficient is used to express the various interrelationships. It is important to keep in mind that the distinctions which will be made in the course of the present section are, in general, not affected by the choice of any specific coefficient. The application of the formula to an analysis of interpretation as a research operation was first presented by Paul F. Lazarsfeld at the 1946 meetings of the American Sociological Society. If more than one test factor enters into the analysis, the basic formula becomes more complicated, but the mode of analysis is not essentially altered.

10. For the sake of simplicity, we shall confine ourselves to dichotomous items, recognizing that the same logic which applies to them also applies to continuous variables.

11. The similarity of Equation (1) to standard formulae for partial correlation is obvious. The main difference is that here, instead of having only one overall measure of the partial relationship, we have two (or more) partial terms, one associated with the positive and the other with the negative value of the factor being partialled out.

take, and to match these variations to corresponding empirical situations. In the present section, then, we shall examine Equation (1) in some more detail, and shall introduce some of the different forms which it takes.

An important feature of Equation (1) is that, because its terms are joined by summation signs rather than by multiplication or division, these terms can vary independently. Thus a specified magnitude of $[xy]$ ($[xy] \neq 0$) can come about in a variety of ways.

There are two situations which interest us especially. The first of these occurs when the test factor is unrelated to one or both of the original variables. Then the last term in Equation (1), the "marginal" term, reduces to 0. The original relationship between x and y is then shown to be the weighted average of the two partial relationships. Stated symbolically,

$$[xy] = [xy; t^+] \oplus [xy; t^-] + (0)\,[ty]$$
$$\text{or, } [xy] = [xy; t^+] \oplus [xy; t^-] + [xt]\,(0) \dots\dots\dots\dots\dots\dots\dots\dots (1a)$$

We shall designate the situation represented in Equation (1a) the "partial" or *P type*, since the original relationship depends on the values of the partial relationships.

The second situation in which we are particularly interested comes about in the reverse fashion. In this case it is the partial relationships which disappear. Then the original relationship is seen to be the result of the marginal terms—the product of the relationships between the test factor and each of the original variables. Symbolically,

$$[xy] = 0 + 0 + [xt]\,[ty] \dots\dots\dots\dots\dots\dots\dots\dots\dots\dots\dots\dots\dots (1b)$$

This case will be called the "marginal" or *M type* of elaboration, depending as it does on the marginal relationships betwen the three variables.

In actual practice it is rare to find pure P or M types. Usually we find that the terms which should be 0 according to Equations (1a) and (1b) have values which are not precisely 0. Our interest in the two cases, then, is not that they represent common empirical situations, but rather that *they represent, in schematized form, certain familiar research procedures and types of analysis.* They translate into symbolic terms those mental processes which are involved in the elaboration of an analysis.

When we approach the distinction between the P and M types of elaboration from the point of view of the different mental processes which they represent, rather than the different mathematical relationships which they assume, we note that the primary distinction is one of emphasis. In the P type of analysis, we are essentially interested in the *relative size* of the partial relationships. And even if the marginal relationships are not 0, as the ideal case assumes they will be, we disregard them as irrelevant for the particular purpose of our analysis. We want to see whether the relation between length of time in this country and upward occupational mobility is different for Puerto Rican migrants characterized in different ways. Under what conditions is this relationship high, and under what contrasting conditions is it not so high? In other words, we look for test factors which lead to partial relationships differing significantly in size. Mills and his associates found that one such factor was sex.

In the M type of analysis, on the other hand, our main interest is to see whether, after the introduction of a test factor, the partial relationships between the variables with which we started are smaller, on the average, than the original relationship. Thus, we examine whether, after men are classified according to the rates of deferment among their civilian friends and acquaintances, the partial relationships between formal educational level and attitudes toward induction are as large as was the original relationship between these two variables. If they are not, if they are smaller, then we say that the test factor, rate of deferment, interprets the original correlation. Or, we study whether, when college graduates are stratified according to the wealth of their families just before they went to college, the partial relationships between the type of institution they attended and their later salaries are smaller than the original relationship had been. If they are, then we say that family background operated as an invalidating factor to make the relationship between type of college and income a spurious one.

In the terms of our equation, these last two examples are exactly alike; in both we observe what happens to the average value of the partial relationships once the test factor is introduced. Nonetheless, we experience them psychologically as different. Had the partials been reduced in our example of interpretation (as they were in our hypothetical figures), we would have experienced it as a positive contribution to our knowledge. We would have felt that it added something to our understanding of the way in which attitudes are formed. If, on the other hand, the partial relationships are reduced when we are exploring the possibility that invalidating factors operate to make a relationship spurious, then our reaction is quite a different one. We no longer experience the analysis as a positive contribution; rather we think of it as the clarification of a misleading result.[12] It tells us what is *not* the case, and thereby leaves us where we started.

Why do we react differently to the two types of M elaboration? In order to find the answer we must introduce still another distinction. This concerns the time sequence of the *x* and *t* factors. In interpretation, the test factor lies *between* *x* and *y* in time, or, in other words, it follows *after* *x*. This

---

12. In some cases, this type of elaboration not only clarifies misleading results but, "explains away" absurd findings. For example, one can show statistically that there is a positive correlation between the number of storks in a given area and the birthrate in that area. Does this mean that storks bring babies? No, because the result is a spurious one. If one separates the different areas according to their degree of urbanization, and then examines the original relationship within the rural and within the urban areas, one finds that the partials have vanished. In all of this discussion, we assume that *x* precedes *y* in time. This emphasizes once more the importance of being able to distinguish the time order of the variables with which we deal.

is what we mean when we say that the interpretive factor provides a "link" between x and y. Only those factors which *precede* x in time, however, can be invalidating factors. This is so because only factors which precede x can "account" for it in the way we have shown to be the case in a spurious relationship. For the sake of convenience, we shall label these two time orders. A test factor which follows after x will be referred to as an *intervening variable,* while one which precedes x will be called an *antecedent variable.*[13]

This difference is an important one, for, when it is not kept clear in mind, we are apt to confuse the two types of elaboration, despite their very different objectives.[14] In the example of interpretation which we considered, the time relation of x and t is clear: There can be little doubt that an individual's formal education precedes in time the number of deferments among his friends and acquaintances. In other words, the test factor is an intervening variable. If the rate of deferment is a relevant test factor, its relevance is as an interpretive variable, providing a *link* between education

---

13. The statement requires two exceptions. First there is one class of factors which may be *subsequent* to X, but which produce spuriousness. These are factors which arbitrarily occur during the survey and which attach themselves to one sub-group rather than another. They are quite common in surveys. Thus, for example, a finding might be due to the fact that sub-group A was subsequently interviewed by a certain type of interviewer, or interviewed on a day when some accidental event occurred. These arbitrary variables which remain uncontrolled in the comparison are sources of spuriousness even though they occur subsequent to X. However, they can be logically distinguished from intervening variables, which are variables that are subsequent to X *and also emerge in some organic way from X.* Second, there is one class of factors which precede X, but which do *not* produce spuriousness. These are factors which form developmental sequences or configurations with X. However, these logically can be distinguished from antecedent variables which create spuriousness, since they *merge organically with X.* The nature of the distinction has already been treated at length in our Section on "Developmental Sequences, Configurations and Spuriousness." Ultimately these two exceptions must be given formal logical representation and incorporated into the present model of analysis. However, as we have indicated, the model under discussion does not represent the ultimate formalization of analysis which is our goal.

14. In one of our case studies, Centers' *Psychology of Social Classes,* this distinction is not always borne in mind and as a consequence, different modes of analysis are obscured. In discussing this basic thesis, Centers makes the following comment. (In order to facilitate our later discussion of this passage, we have numbered the test factors.) "Perhaps it would be nearer the truth to think of objective socio-economic status and role, not as causes or determinants in themselves but simply as variables which incorporate in themselves, so to speak, something still more basic. These more basic causes could be [1] the factors which got the person into a given socio-economic position in the first place, [2] the stresses and strains inherent in occupancy of the position once there, and [3] the whole complex of forces and circumstances which surround the individual's life as a consequence of his occupancy of the status and role . . ." (p. 160). Centers is saying essentially, that his original relationship between objective status and attitudes might be elaborated in terms of a number of other factors. This, he feels, would provide a "more basic" relationship. And he suggests what some of these other factors might be. However, these new variables do not all bear the same time relationship to his x factor, objective status. The first one which he mentions, "the factors which got the person into a given socio-economic position," is an antecedent variable—by definition it precedes x. But the other two factors which Centers suggests are in his own words *consequences* of a particular status, and, as such, they can only intervene between x and y.

Translated into our terminology, then, Centers seems to be talking about two different kinds of analysis. The first test factor which he suggests is one which might show the relationship between objective status and class affiliations to be "spurious"; the other factors are ones which might provide the links between these two original variables.

and acceptance or rejection of one's induction. In contrast, when Research Branch analysts sought to make sure that the relationship between contact with Negroes and willingness to serve with them in mixed companies was not a spurious one, the factor which they introduced as a check—various measures of initially favorable attitude—was one which was clearly *antecedent* to the assumed cause.

We have thus distinguished three different types of elaboration.[15]

I. *The M type* in which one is interested in noting whether the partial relationships become smaller than the original relationship. This can be further sub-divided according to the time relation of x and t.

A. *Interpretation* in which the test factor is an intervening variable.
B. *Explanation (and/or control for invalidating factors)* in which the test factor is an antecedent variable.

The distinction between interpretation and explanation can be represented schematically in the following way:

Interpretation   *Explanation*

$$t$$
$$\swarrow \searrow$$
$$x \to t \to y \qquad\qquad\qquad x \qquad y$$

II. *The P type* in which interest is focused on the relative size of the partial relationships in order to specify the circumstances under which the original relation is more or less pronounced. This type of elaboration will be called *specification.*

We are now in a position to review much of this discussion. In an earlier chapter we talked of the way in which we control for invalidating factors. This, as we now see, is one type of a more general system of elaboration, that type which we now call "explanation." In our earlier discussion we talked somewhat loosely about invalidating factors. A more precise definition is now possible. The definition which we have arrived at in the course of our discussion is as follows: An invalidating factor is an antecedent variable which, in the M type of elaboration, reduces the average of the partial relationships.[16]

---

15. We want to stress the irrelevance of the particular labels which are attached to each type of elaboration. In the literature, every one of these words has been used in every sense. Similarly, in earlier portions of the text the term "Explanation" has been used loosely to cover all such modes of analysis. The objective of our formalization is to distinguish and describe the different analytical processes without regard to what they have been called in the past or what they will be called in the future.

16. The notion of explanation provides an analytic basis for defining clearly a causal relationship between two variables. *If the partial relationships never disappear, even when every conceivable antecedent test factor is introduced, then the original relationship is a causal one.* This definition reproduces in statistical form the situation existing in ideal controlled experiments. Through matching procedures, one automatically eliminates the relationship between the antecedent test factor and the stimulus, or x variable. That is, the experimenter creates a situation in which $[xt] = 0$ for every antecedent t. Thus, if $[xy]$ exists, the partials must also exist.

We then turned to a kind of analysis which we have called interpretation. We based our discussion on an example suggested in *The American Soldier* and, using hypothetical figures, indicated the conditions to be met if the interpretation were to be a complete one. These conditions received more formal statement when the general process of elaboration was dealt with systematically.

It may be advisable now to present some further examples of this mode of elaboration with which we already have some familiarity—interpretation. We shall try to indicate, through examples taken from actual surveys, how these different types of analysis are actually worked out. Interpretation, like the other modes of analysis which we are considering here, starts with the relationship between two variables. For example, we might find, as did Lazarsfeld, Berelson and Gaudet that there is a relationship between education and intention to vote.[17] While this relationship was not a particularly strong one, it could not be dismissed. Those on the higher educational level were more likely to say that they intended to vote in the fall elections.

TABLE XV—Relationship Between Educational Level and Intention to Vote

Educational level	Percent who said during summer that they intended to vote in fall	
Have had at least some high school	92	(1613)
Have not gone as far as high school	86	(1199)

When we start out to interpret such a result, we raise a distinctive set of questions. Basically we ask, "Why is there a relationship between these variables? What links them together?" We look for consequences of the *x* factor which might lead to the *y* variable. In the present instance, the link which suggested itself to the analysts was *political interest*. Their reasoning might have been as follows. The better educated individual is more likely to have had training in civics and to have been taught the responsibilities of all citizens. At the same time, because of his better socio-economic status, he can afford to have broader interests than does the person who must expend all of his energies on economic worries. Further, he probably enjoys a relatively greater degree of power within his community, and therefore may be less inclined to feel that political participation is futile. All of these elements predispose the better educated citizens to higher levels of political interest. And, in turn, one immediate expression of this interest is the intention to vote in important elections.

Having developed their reasons for believing that political interest might interpret the relationship between education and vote intention, the analysts are then in a position to test whether, in reality, this is a correct interpretation. It is certainly plausible when stated verbally. But the crucial question is whether the data meet the conditions which, as we have seen,

---

17. *The People's Choice.*

they must if the logic of the interpretation is to be supported by the empirical findings.

The chief condition, we recall, is that the partial relationships between education and vote intention must be smaller when the total sample is stratified according to different levels of political interest than it was originally.[18] Consequently, the next step is to separate the total group into subgroups which are homogeneous in degree of political interest. And, once this is achieved, then the final—and crucial—step is to see what happens to the original relationship within each of these homogeneous sub-groups. These two steps are combined in Table XVI.

TABLE XVI—Relationship Between Education and Intention to Vote When Political Interest Is Held Constant

	Percent who say in the summer that they intend to vote in the Fall	
Political interest	At least some high school	No high school
Great interest	99 (495)	98 (285)
Moderate or mild interest	93 (986)	90 (669)
No interest at all	56 (132)	59 (245)

Before turning to the crucial question as to whether interest interprets the relationship between education and vote intention, let us review once more what a table like this one shows. This is a typical three-dimensional table: the percentages indicate the proportion of persons in each education-interest group who intend to vote, and the bracketed numbers indicate the size of each sub-group.

What relationships can be found in a table of this sort? First of all, reading across the rows of Table XVI gives us the partial relationships between education and vote intention when political interest is held constant. Reading down the columns of the table shows the partial relationship between interest and vote intention with education held constant. (The marginal relationship between interest and vote intention is not shown here. It could be found by working out the appropriate marginal figures, disregarding education.) Table XVI also contains the marginal relationship between interest and education—this is to be found in the bracketed base figures.

Now let us turn to the main question. What has the introduction of political interest done to the original relationship between education and intention to vote? Because there are three different interest levels, we have to examine three different partial relationships in order to answer this question. We recall that 92 percent of the well educated and 86 percent of the

18. Reference to Equation (1b) indicates that another condition of interpretation is that the marginal relationships—those between the test factor and each of the original variables—must exist. But this condition is automatically met if the data conform with the requirement about the partial relationships. For, if these latter are smaller than the original relationship, then, it is an arithmetic necessity that the marginal relationships exist.

less educated intended to vote. (See Table XV.) In the three partial tables obtained through the introduction of political interest, the relationship between the two starting variables is less strong. Among those with great interest there is now only a difference of 1 percentage point between the two educational levels; among those with a moderate degree of political interest there is now only a 3 percent difference; and, finally, among those with no interest at all, there is also a difference of 3 percent, but in the opposite direction of that originally observed. Because all of these partial relationships are smaller than the original relationship, and, indeed, have virtually disappeared, we conclude that political interest does interpret the relationship with which we started.

A second example from Merton's study of housing communities may make the process of interpretation still clearer.[19] One of the questions asked in the bi-racial community which he investigated was a retrospective one asking the residents to recall their expectations regarding bi-racial living before they had moved into the community. On the basis of their answers, Merton was able to distinguish residents who anticipated that the two races would be well integrated, those who expected that they would be able to accommodate to each other, and those who expected open conflict of one kind or another. It turned out, further, that these various anticipations were related to the race of the individual expressing them. This relationship is shown in Table XVII.

TABLE XVII—Expectations About Bi-Racial Living According to Race

Expectations	Negro	White
Integration of races	10%	7%
Accommodation of races	68	58
Conflict between races	22	35
Total cases	211	205

Few residents of either race expected complete integration in the community to which they were moving, and most of both races recalled that they anticipated some form of accommodation between the races. But Table XVII shows that there was, at the same time, a relationship between race and expectations. Considerably more of the white residents reported that they had originally anticipated that there would be overt conflict in the community.

There are a number of questions one might raise about this relationship. One might wonder about the foundation of the answers, for example. Perhaps the more favorable expectations of the Negro residents represent some form of wishful thinking, while the less optimistic anticipations of the whites represent a fearful expression of their prejudice or dislike of the idea of bi-racial living arrangements.

19. *Op. cit.*

But one might also wonder whether differing experiences of whites and Negroes might not provide a link between race and original expectations about bi-racial living. It is generally true that Negroes are more likely to have lived in mixed Negro-white communities than are whites, and perhaps these previous experiences in bi-racial living lead to more optimistic expectations about the situation in a new community. Accordingly, if we can separate out those who have and those who have not had previous experience in living in a mixed area, we can test the correctness of this interpretation. Table XVIII shows the relevant figures:

TABLE XVIII—Relationship Between Race and Expectations of Bi-Racial Living According to Previous Experience

Expectations	Have previously lived in bi-racial area		Have not previously lived in bi-racial area	
	Negro	White	Negro	White
Integration of races	11%	9%	5%	5%
Accommodation of races	69	72	50	39
Conflict between races	20	19	45	56
Total cases	193	115	18	90

Because the dependent variable in this example has three classes instead of two, we cannot present the result in a three-dimensional table. Nonetheless, the information provided here is exactly the same as that given in earlier cases.[20]

Examination of the two partial relationships—one of these is found in the first and second columns of the table, and the other in the third and fourth columns—indicates that both are smaller than the original relationship, although the reduction is not uniform in the two cases. Among those who have previously lived in a bi-racial area, all relationship between race and expectations has disappeared. But among those without previous experience there is still some relationship, although it is not as strong as originally.

In our formal terms, then, this is an example of the M type of elaboration. But how do we know that it is an example of interpretation, rather than one of what we have called explanation? The answer to this question lies in the time order, we remember, of the x and t factors, in this case race and previous experience respectively. In this case it is not difficult to determine the time sequence of these variables. Clearly, the individual's race precedes in time the areas of a community which are open to him, and therefore the kinds of residential experiences which he is likely to have acquired. Thus previous experience is a link between race and anticipations about the conditions one will find in a new community; it is an interpretive variable.

---

20. The reader might determine for himself the relationship between race and previous experience in bi-racial living, and he might see how to go about finding the relationship between such previous experiences and expected relations in the new community.

The same study provides an example in which the suggested interpretation did not prove to be correct. Merton found, in this same community, that there was a definite relationship between race and type of occupation, with the white residents of the community working at more prestigeful and better paying jobs than did the Negro residents.

TABLE XIX—Occupation According to Race

Occupation	White	Negro
White collar job	38%	10%
Skilled work	12	6
Semi-skilled work	30	18
Unskilled work	15	46
Service jobs	5	20
	—	—
Total cases	287	318

The kinds of jobs held by the Negro residents of the community are quite different from those held by the whites. Nearly 40 percent of the latter, but only 10 percent of the Negroes, held white collar jobs. At the other end of the prestige scale, nearly half of the Negroes, but only 15 percent of the whites, worked as unskilled laborers, and 20 percent of the Negroes, contrasted with only 5 percent of the whites, worked in service jobs as porters, cleaning men and women, and the like.

Before concluding that this finding was evidence of racial discrimination on the part of employers in the community in which Hilltown is located, Merton attempted to find some more "pleasant" interpretation of the relationship. One possibility which occurred to him was that the Negroes of Hilltown were not as well qualified as the whites educationally, and that this might account for the infrequency with which they held white collar or skilled labor jobs. Educational opportunities—in the sense both of facilities open to them and economic ability to continue schooling—are generally less good for Negroes than they are for whites; and, indeed, Merton did find that the Negroes in his sample had a lower educational level, on the average, than did the whites. And their lower level of education may have prevented them from obtaining the more desirable jobs.

In order to test this interpretation, Merton divided his total group into different educational levels—those who had only completed grade school; those who had some high school training, but had not completed that training; and, finally, those who had graduated from high school and had perhaps had some college training. Within each of these educational groups he then examined the relationship between race and occupation (Table XX).

Here again, because the test factor has three values instead of two, there are three partial relationships to be examined. Furthermore, these are more complicated than those dealt with previously. In this example, the dependent variable—occupation—has five different categories. Therefore, in order

TABLE XX—Occupation According to Race With Education Held Constant

Occupation	Grade School		Some High School		Completed High School	
	White	Negro	White	Negro	White	Negro
White collar job	31%	4%	37%	10%	49%	24%
Skilled work	14	6	14	6	9	3
Semi-skilled work	28	13	31	21	32	23
Unskilled work	20	60	13	36	8	36
Service jobs	7	17	5	27	2	14
Total cases	124	146	78	113	85	59

to draw any conclusions about the partial relationships, one must make five comparisons within each of the educational groups.

Once these complications are recognized, however, they do not make for any special difficulties. When the required comparisons are made, we find that the original relationship between race and occupation is not in any way reduced. For example, before the test factor was introduced, we found that 38 percent of the white residents and 10 percent of the Negro residents—a difference of 28 percent—worked at white collar jobs. The introduction of education leaves this difference pretty much intact. Thus in the group with only grade school education, there is a difference of 27 percent between the races in regard to holding white collar positions; in the intermediate educational group, this difference is also 27 percent; and in the best educated group the difference is 25 percent. Similarly for the other occupational categories. In none of them does the introduction of education appreciably lower the racial differences originally observed. We are forced to conclude, therefore, that it is not the possession of appropriate qualifications which permits the white residents of Hilltown to occupy the more desirable positions; even when they have comparable educational qualifications, the Negro residents are found to be working at lower status jobs.

One final example may illustrate the weaving back and forth between speculation and examination of the data which is always involved in the interpretation of an empirical result. In their study of residential mobility, Rossi and his associates found a relationship among renters between the size of family and the desire to move into new homes.[21] This is shown in two ways in Table XXI. Whether one considers the number of children in the family, or the number of adults, one finds a consistent, and strong, relationship between family size and desire to move.

The analysts' next step is to interpret this relationship. Their first hypothesis is that it is perhaps the objective amount of space in the rented home which provides the link between family size and desire to move. Large families undoubtedly have more difficulty than small families in renting a home which satisfies their space needs. And, of course, a family living in cramped quarters is more likely to want to move.

21. *Op. cit.*

TABLE XXI—Relationship Between Family Size (Among Renters) and Desires to Move

Number of children under 18	Percent Desiring to Move	Total cases
None	51	321
One	72	74
Two	82	49
Three and more	95	39
Number of adults over 18		
One	37	118
Two	68	321
Three and more	70	44

To test this interpretation, the analysts studied the relationship between family size and desire to move after the total sample had been divided into those with adequate and those with inadequate space.[22] The relevant data are shown in Table XXII.

TABLE XXII—Relationship Between Family Size (Among Renters) and Desire to Move With Adequacy of Space Held Constant

Adequacy of space	One Person	Two Persons	Three Persons	Four or more Persons
		Percent who want to move		
Adequate	33% (24)	61% (121)	74% (58)	81% (42)
Inadequate	28 (65)	52 (59)	80 (10)	83 (34)

The two partial relationships are found in the rows of Table XXII. We observe that, even when the total sample is sub-divided into those having an adequate amount of space and those living in cramped conditions, the relationship between family size and desire to move remains a very close one. The analysts are therefore forced to conclude that their initial hypothesis is not confirmed, and that the objective size of the dwelling unit does not provide a link between the original variables.

The failure of this first test factor to interpret their original relationship led the analysts to look for other possibilities: "Perhaps it is not so much the objectively available amount of space which produces the desire to move but the subjective evaluation of that space as fulfilling household requirements." Here is another test factor; its relevance as an interpretive variable must also be considered.

As a measure of the householders' subjective evaluation of the space available to them, the analysts made use of complaints registered by the re-

---

22. For the purposes of this example we have introduced a somewhat arbitrary modification of the table reported by Rossi and his associates. We have assumed that 3 rooms or more represents adequate space for families which have no more than 3 persons in them, and that any dwelling smaller than this is inadequate in size. We have also assumed that adequate space for a family which includes four or more persons is a minimum of 5 rooms. The table which we present here is not exactly comparable to Table XXI, because it considers the total family size, rather than the number of children under 18 or the number of adults over 18. This difference, however, is not of major consequence.

spondents about the amount of space in the dwelling unit. Those who made no complaints on this score were considered to have a favorable evaluation of this feature of their homes; those who raised one or more complaints were considered dissatisfied. Within each of these groups, then, the original relationship between family size and desire to move was examined once more.

TABLE XXIII—Relationship Between Family Size (Among Renters) and Desire to Move With Subjective Evaluations of Space Held Constant

| | Percent who want to move | | | |
Subjective evaluation	One Person	Two Persons	Three Persons	Four or more Persons
No space complaints	19% (70)	45% (103)	67% (40)	66% (35)
One or more space complaints	57 (33)	71 (99)	86 (43)	93 (72)

The partial relationships are again found in the two rows of Table XXIII. Despite the small number of cases in some of the sub-groups, the original relationship between family size and the desire to move persists with remarkable consistency. Whether or not the householder expressed any complaints about the spaciousness of his home, the larger the family the more the desire to move. The analysts are therefore forced to the conclusion once more that the test factor which they introduced does not satisfactorily interpret the relationship with which they started.

The analysts might have continued this process of testing possible interpretations for their original finding. As a matter of fact, they did suggest what some other interpretive variables might be: "It is apparently the case that only one of the household needs created by numerical size is for greater space. Numerical size probably creates additional needs; perhaps for particular types of conveniences, for particular kinds of dwelling unit layouts, etc." But since they did not have adequate measures of these additional needs, they were not able to investigate the correctness of these further interpretations.

2. The Specification of a Result—the P Type of Elaboration

Specification differs from both interpretation and explanation not only in its formal aspects, in the kind of statistical interrelationships which it presupposes, but also in its objectives. There is no attempt to "explain away" absurd results or to spell out the process linking two variables. Instead, specification involves the discovery of conditions under which the original result is more or less pronounced. This means, as we have already suggested, that we focus our attention on the relative size of the partial relationships.

Because the P type of elaboration is so different from the M type, it may be instructive to illustrate it with several numerical examples. As we present these we shall, at the same time, try to indicate the different kinds of substantive findings made possible by the introduction of different kinds of specifying variables. We make no claim that our classification is an exhaustive one, or that important types of specification have not been omitted. It is our feeling, however, that this important mode of analysis will be more easily appreciated if its substantive contributions as well as its formal character are clarified.

Specification in Terms of Interest and Concern: In recent years, increasing attention has been paid to the role of interest and concern in the formation and persistence of attitudes. We have learned that persons interested in a particular topic are more likely to acquire information on that topic, that they have more stable opinions on the issue, and so on. It is also becoming clear, as research on the question accumulates, that interest—in its broadest sense—specifies one condition under which the effectiveness of a stimulus is more or less pronounced.

Harold Gosnell, for example, carried out an experiment designed to test whether certain propaganda materials which he prepared could be effective in persuading Chicago voters who might not otherwise have done so to register.[23] The answer, he then discovered, was that they could. Persons who received the material registered in greater proportions than did those who had not been exposed to his stimuli. This is shown in Table XXIV.

TABLE XXIV—Effect of Propaganda on Registration

	Percent who registered	Total cases
Experimental group which was exposed to material	74	2612
Control group which was not exposed to material	64	2204

Ten percent more of the experimental group than of the control group registered to vote.

One of the specifying variables which Gosnell introduced in his efforts to find out under what conditions the materials were particularly effective was political interest. As his measure of interest he employed previous voting experience, assuming that those who had voted in 3 or less of the previous 7 elections were uninterested, while those who had voted in at least 4 of the last 7 elections were interested. Classifying both the experimental and the control groups according to these two levels of interest, Gosnell found that his materials were particularly effective among those whose previous voting behavior had indicated little interest in politics.

TABLE XXV—Effect of Propaganda on Registration According to Level of Political Interest

Level of Interest	Percent who registered Experimental Group	Control Group
Low interest (voted in less than 4 of the last 7 elections)	61 (1383)	44 (1090)
High interest (voted in at least 4 of the last 7 elections)	89 (1229)	82 (1114)

23. H. Gosnell, *Getting Out the Vote, An Experiment in the Stimulation of Voting.* (Chicago: University of Chicago Press, 1927.)

The partial relationships between exposure to the materials and registration behavior are found in the two rows of Table XXV. If we compare the relative size of the partials we find that Gosnell's experimental stimulation had little effect on the prospective voters who were highly interested in politics. The large majority of them, regardless of their exposure, registered. But the materials did stimulate those with little interest—there was almost a 50 percent increase in registration among those who saw the handouts distributed by Gosnell.

Another example, from another study of voting behavior, uncovered similar findings, although the "stimulus" in this case could not be simply identified as a leaflet or handbill. Lazarsfeld, Berelson and Gaudet found in their investigation of voting decisions that women were less likely than men to say that they intended to vote in the coming election.[24] This initial relationship was as follows:

TABLE XXVI—Vote Intention According to Sex

	Percent who said that they intended to vote	Total cases
Men	98	1294
Women	82	1418

They concluded from this finding that the social role played by women in our American society demands less active political participation.

But they sought to specify this relationship further, again in terms of the political interest manifested by the respondents. Unlike Gosnell, however, who used the behavior of his subjects as an index of their interest, the respondents in this second study were asked to classify themselves according to their interest. They were asked whether they had "a great deal of interest in the coming election, or a moderate or mild interest, or no interest at all." When this three-way classification was introduced, and the relationship between sex and vote intention was studied on each interest level, it was found again that the "stimulus" had most effect upon those with least interest. That is, the influence of the varying social roles—and social responsibilities —of men and women was most pronounced among those who expressed least interest in the coming election.

TABLE XXVII—Vote Intention and Sex Specified by Political Interest

Level of interest	Percent who say that they intend to vote Men		Women	
Great	99%	(449)	98%	(328)
Moderate or mild	98	(789)	87	(852)
No interest at all	83	(56)	44	(238)

24. *Op. cit.*, pp. 48-49.

Once more, each of the rows contains a partial relationship. If we examine these we see that, among those with great interest, all of the men and also all of the women expressed an intention to vote. In other words, on this interest level, there was no relationship between sex and voting intention. Within the group which claimed a moderate degree of political interest, there was some relationship, although still not an especially marked one. But among those who had expressed no interest at all, sex seems to play an important part in determining whether or not one intends to vote. Even in this group almost all of the men say that they plan to vote. But the women with no political interest apparently do not feel compelled to vote, and nearly half of them do not intend to do so. In sum, just as Gosnell's experimental propaganda was most effective among those who displayed little interest, so the influence of different sex roles is most pronounced among those who express a lack of interest in political affairs.

On the basis of these two results, we might attempt to make some generalizations about the role of interest in attitude formation and change. Individuals who have developed interest in a particular topic are likely, at the same time, to have formed relatively strong and stable attitudes or behavior patterns. They are not likely, therefore, to respond to stimuli, whether these stimuli be relevant events, documentary materials or culturally defined social roles. Receptivity to such stimuli is most probable among those who have little interest in the matter, and who therefore have not already developed strong attitudes or stable patterns of behavior.

Specification of Time and Place: It is quite clear that the relationship between two variables can vary according to the time at which that relationship is studied, or the place in which it is investigated. For example, we would expect a pro-Soviet film to be considerably less effective with an American audience in 1952 than it might have been in 1945. Again, we can assume that the relationship between profession of the Catholic religion and political radicalism or conservatism would be different in Europe than it is in the United States.[25]

An example of this kind of specification is provided by a study by Mills and his associates. It was found that Puerto Rican male migrants had a better chance of achieving upward occupational mobility than did Puerto Rican women migrants to New York City.[26] (See Table XXVIII.)

Among both men and women migrants, occupational stability is the most characteristic situation. That is, among both, a majority of the migrants neither moved upward nor downward in the occupational scale. But there are nonetheless differences between the sexes in this regard. The most con-

---

25. Another example is provided by our earlier discussion of the relationship between suicide and war as it was dependent on modern vs. ancient wars. See p. 115.

26. *Op. cit.,* p. 70. This discussion is based on a rearrangement of the table presented by the authors. The index of mobility was based on a retrospective question to which we have alluded in our earlier treatment of time sequence.

TABLE XXVIII—Occupational Mobility Among Puerto Rican Migrants to New York City According to Sex

Occupational mobility [27]	Men	Women
Upward	28%	14%
Stable	55	67
Downward	17	19
Total cases	266	310

spicuous of these is that the proportion of men achieving upward mobility is precisely twice as great as the corresponding proportion for women. Apparently there are fewer occupational opportunities for women than for men.

But the analysts went on to inquire whether this situation was different for migrants arriving in the United States at different times. Perhaps time of arrival is one condition for the relationship between sex and occupational mobility. In order to explore this, they classified the migrants into two groups. One was composed of those who were considered "early arrivals;" the other was made up of those who had migrated relatively later. This led to the following results:

TABLE XXIX—Relationship Between Sex and Occupational Mobility According to Time of Arrival

Occupational mobility	Early arrivals		Late arrivals	
	Men	Women	Men	Women
Upward	42%	11%	15%	12%
Stable	38	75	63	73
Downward	20	14	22	15
Total cases	144	122	167	143

Time of arrival does indeed provide a condition for the relationship between sex and occupational mobility. The original occupational advantage which men seemed to have over women migrants disappears entirely when one considers the late arrivals. Indeed a somewhat larger proportion of the recently arrived men have experienced downward mobility in their job status. It is only among those who arrived in New York City at a relatively early date that men have been able to achieve substantially greater upward mobility than women.

Another example of the same kind of specification comes from *The American Soldier*. Stouffer and his associates found, during the course of a study of social mobility within the Army, that there was a positive relationship between formal educational level and rank among enlisted men: The

---

27. The index of mobility was based on a comparison of the first job held by the migrant after his arrival in New York City with that held at the time of the interview.

better educated the soldier, the more likely he was to have higher rank.[28] This relationship is presented in the following four-fold table:

TABLE XXX—Relationship Between Rank Among Enlisted Men and Educational Level

Rank	High school graduate or better	Less than high school graduate
Non-commissioned officer	61%	43%
Private or private-first-class	39	57
Total cases	3222	3152

It occurred to the analysts that the time at which one entered the Army might affect the correlation. It might be that not even the better educated men had much chance to be promoted if they came into the Army at a late date, when tables of organization were pretty well fixed. Accordingly, length of time in the Army, indicating the time at which one had been inducted or had volunteered, was introduced as a test factor.[29] The partial relationships thus obtained were then examined:

TABLE XXXI—Relationship Between Rank and Educational Level According to Length of Service

| Length of service | Percent who have been promoted to non-coms | |
	High school graduate or better	Less than high school graduate
Have served for less than 2 years	23% (842)	17% (823)
Have served for 2 years or more	74 (2380)	53 (2329)

As in the previous example, the partial relationships are found in the rows of Table XXXI. Examination of these indicates that the relationship between educational level and promotion to non-com status is, indeed, conditional on the time at which one entered the Army. Among late entrants, the better educated men had only slightly greater chances for promotion than did less well educated soldiers. Among those who had come into the Army at an earlier stage of the war, however, the better educated had considerably greater chances of being promoted.

Specification of the place at which the relationship is observed also can uncover conditions under which a correlation between two variables is more or less pronounced. Merton investigated the circumstances through which the residents of housing communities met their close friends in the com-

---

28. *Op. cit.*, Vol. I, p. 249, Table 7. As with many other numerical examples taken from *The American Soldier*, this four-fold table and the ones which follow are great simplifications of the tables in the text. We have "collapsed" the original table so that we can deal with dichotomies.

29. Length of service, as we have already mentioned in an earlier connection, is an ambiguous variable. It can indicate, as it was intended to here, the date on which one entered the Army. But it might also be taken as an indication of the length of time which one has had to be observed by one's officers, and therefore, perhaps to be selected for promotion.

munity.[30] He found that "propinquity in general conduces to the formation of friendships," in the sense that most of the residents reported that they met their close friends as neighbors in the project. He also found, however, that the influence of propinquity was different for different groups among the residents. Members of community organizations were less likely than non-members to report that they had met their friends as neighbors, and more likely to report that they had made friends at community affairs. This relationship, for the moment combining the data obtained in the two major communities, was as follows:

TABLE XXXII—Organizational Roles as a Factor in the Forming of Friendships

Close friends met	Organization Members	Organization Non-members
As neighbors	53%	71%
At community affairs	21	3
Elsewhere	26	26
Total cases	483	849

A majority of both the members and non-members met their close friends as neighbors. But the role of such propinquity is not as great for those who participate in local organizations as it is for those who do not take part in such activities. A fifth of the members, contrasted with an insignificant 3 percent of the non-members, report that they met their friends through community affairs.

But it turns out, upon further specification, that this result depends very much on the nature of the community in which it is studied. Merton, it will be recalled, collected his material in two quite distinct communities —Craftown and Hilltown. The important differences between the two localities make for a varying degree of relationship between organizational activity and the circumstances under which friendships are formed:

TABLE XXXIII—Organizational Roles as a Factor in the Forming of Friendships According to Community

| | Craftown | | Hilltown | |
Close friends met	Organization members	Organization non-members	Organization members	Organization non-members
As neighbors	47%	63%	66%	77%
At community affairs	25	4	11	2
Elsewhere	28	33	22	21
Total cases	334	343	149	506

In Craftown, there are many organizations and these are active. This is evidenced, if in no other way, by the fact that nearly half of the Craftown population belongs to one or more organizations. Hilltown, in contrast, has

---

30. *Op. cit.*

few organizations, and these play only a minor role in the community. This is indicated by the relatively small proportion of Hilltowners who can be considered organization members.

This difference in the nature of the two communities provides a condition for the relationship between organizational affiliation and the way in which friendships are formed. Inspection of Table XXXIII indicates that, in the community where organizational activities are at a minimum, membership does little to lessen the role of propinquity in the formation of friendships. In Craftown, on the other hand, 25 percent of the members have made friends through attending community affairs, while this is true of only 4 percent of the non-members who occasionally attend these activities.

Specification of Qualifications: Still another type of specification is provided by the discovery of special qualifications which make the original relationship more or less marked. Not every individual is in a position—objectively or psychologically—to manifest the particular behavior or attitude which constitutes the *y* variable. Not every individual will be equally responsive, therefore, to the *x* variable.

Two concrete cases, which may appear to be very different, will exemplify this type of specification. The first of these is a finding taken from *The American Soldier.* In one of their studies the Research Branch analysts found that there was a relationship between theater of service and willingness for further service in the Army. The relationship, after simplification for our present purposes, appears as follows: [31]

TABLE XXXIV—*Relationship Between Theater of Service and Willingness for Further Service*

Theater of service	Percent who are willing to serve further	Total cases
Overseas	51%	1462
Not yet overseas	68	253

Half of those stationed overseas, compared with more than two-thirds of those not yet in overseas theaters, expressed a willingness to serve further in the Army.

But the analysts wondered whether this relationship between theater of service and attitudes toward remaining in the Army might not be different for those with different qualifications. And the major qualification which occurred to them was length of time in the Army.[32] They felt that those who had been in the Army for varying lengths of time might respond differ-

---

31. *Op. cit.,* Vol. I, p. 159.

32. The many meanings which can be attached to a variable like "length of time in the Army" should be clear by now. We have already used it as an index of time at which the soldier entered service. We have also suggested that it might stand as a measure of the length of time which the soldier has been under observation by his officers. Here we use it as an index of qualifications, or the "justification" for holding a particular attitude.

ently to the fact of overseas service. Their analysis, when carried out, justified this expectation:

TABLE XXXV—Relationship Between Theater and Willingness for Further Service According to Length of Service

	Percent who are willing to serve further	
Length of service	Overseas	Not yet overseas
3 plus	33% (465)	66% (57)
2–3	60 (997)	68 (196)

Once more the partial relationships are found in the two rows of Table XXXV. It is immediately obvious that they differ markedly. Among those who have served in the Army for only a relatively short period of time, the place where one is stationed makes relatively little difference so far as willingness for further service is concerned—those in overseas theaters are only slightly more likely than those in the United States to express the feeling that they should be discharged. But theater of service makes a great difference among those who have been in the Army a relatively long time. Only one-third of the overseas soldiers, contrasted with two-thirds of those not yet overseas, express a willingness to continue their service. Apparently, then, the length of time one has spent in the Army operates as a psychological qualification or justification for the development of specific attitudes. There seems to be some sort of belief that one does not merit a discharge, no matter where one has served, until one has been in the Army a certain length of time.

The second example is taken from a very different kind of study, and introduces the notion of "objective" qualifications, in contrast to the "subjective" ones just considered. This result is taken from a small-scale investigation of communications behavior among special samples in four Arabic countries—Syria, Lebanon, Jordan and Egypt.[33] In considering the movie-going behavior of the persons interviewed, the analysts felt it likely that they would find religious objections or resistances to motion pictures among the devout. In this predominantly Moslem sample, they believed, traditional religious proscriptions against the pictorial portrayal of human beings would constitute a barrier to movie-going, particularly among those who felt their religion to be of great importance.[34] When the respondents were classified according to their devoutness,[35] this expectation was indeed borne out:

---

33. P. Kendall and E. Katz, *Communications Behavior and Political Attitudes in Four Arabic Countries: a Quantitative Comparison* (Bureau of Applied Social Research, 1952).

34. It was only in Lebanon that there was a sizeable number of Christians. In the other countries, the samples were made up almost entirely of Moslems.

35. The question used for this purpose asked, "In guiding your actions every day, do you personally find that your religious beliefs are very important, fairly important, a little important, or not important at all?" Those who answered "very important" were classified as devout.

TABLE XXXVI—*Relationship Between Religious Devoutness and Movie-Going Behavior*

Frequency of movie attendance	Devout	Less devout
Sees at least one film a week	31%	49%
Sees films occasionally	42	36
Never sees films	27	15
Total cases	520	334

What interests us, is the comparative behavior of those expressing differing degrees of religious devoutness. A larger number of the devout report that they never see any films, and a substantially smaller number of this group report that they attend movie theaters at least once a week.

But the analysts believed, further, that the relationships between religious fervor and movie-going behavior might depend on the abilities or qualifications of the respondents to express their religious objections. It is not easy to manifest one's disapproval if an occasion for the expression of that disapproval never arises. Nor is it easy to make it clear that failure to behave in a particular way signifies objections to that behavior if other circumstances prevent one from carrying out the objectionable acts. To explore this possible condition for the original relationship, the analysts attempted to separate out those who were and those who *were not in a position to give expression* to their religious objections to movies. It was their hypothesis that well-to-do persons living in urban areas, who therefore had both geographical and economic access to movies, could better express their objections than could poor people who lived far from a movie theater, and who could not afford to attend one even if one were near. As the best single index of these socio-economic factors, the analysts employed educational level, which is known to be highly correlated, in the Arabic countries, with wealth and place of residence. The results which they then obtained were as follows:

TABLE XXXVII—*Relationship Between Religious Devoutness and Movie-Going Behavior According to Educational Level*

	Low education		High education	
Frequency of movie attendance	Very devout	Less devout	Very devout	Less devout
Sees at least one film a week	21%	29%	43%	58%
Sees films occasionally	41	36	43	35
Never sees films	38	35	14	7
Total cases	280	101	240	233

This division of the total sample into those who do and those who do not have the objective qualifications—or opportunities—to express their religious objections to motion pictures does indeed specify an important condition for the relationship between religious devoutness and movie-going behavior. It is only among those who had the choice of acting or not acting with regard to movies that the original relationship persists. Among those with little education, who are, at the same time, the poor and rural residents, the economic and geographical barriers to movie-going preclude the expression of religious objections.

Specification of Conditions and Contingencies: One aspect of the examples discussed in previous pages has not been considered thus far. This concerns the time relationship of the x and t variables.

If one reexamines these several cases and kinds of specification, one will find that in some of them the t factor preceded the x factor, while in others exactly the reverse time relationship prevailed. Let us review the various cases in order to appreciate this distinction more fully. In the example taken from Gosnell, the relationship between exposure to his experimental materials and registration was specified by previous voting behavior, clearly antecedent to membership in either the control or the experimental group. The next example, from *The People's Choice,* related sex and voting intention, and this relationship was then specified by political interest; but this variable quite clearly follows after, rather than preceding, sex. The next example, from the study of Puerto Rican migrants, was also one in which the specifying factor intervened between the x and y variables. The next case which we considered was one in which the relationship between educational level and rank was specified by the length of time the soldier had served in the Army; this too is an example in which the test factor intervenes between the x and y variables. But the situation is somewhat different in the next case which was presented, that relating organizational members and the place where residents of a housing community had met their friends; this relationship, we recall, was specified by the type of community in which the residents lived, and is a case, therefore, in which the specifying factor preceded both the x and y variables. Similarly, the next example, in which the relationship between theater of service and willingness for further duty was specified by length of service, is a case in which the specifying variable was antecedent to x. Finally, the last example which we considered, that in which the relationship between religious devoutness and movie-going behavior was specified by socio-economic level, was also an instance in which the specifying factor preceded the x variable.

In the M type of elaboration the time order of the x and t factors made for a very important distinction, that between explanation and interpretation. We felt this distinction necessary partly because of our very different reactions to the two types of cases. A test factor preceding the x variable in the M type of elaboration, we felt, "accounted for" an absurd or misleading result. An intervening test factor in the same type of elaboration, however, increased our information, we believed.

Similar distinctions with regard to the P type of elaboration do not seem so necessary, mainly because we do not experience any difference in reaction to the two types of cases. We can slip back and forth between them easily, feeling that both represent equally valuable contributions to the analysis, and contributions which are of the same order.

Nonetheless, there is a difference between the two types. We may try to summarize this briefly. In both cases, we attempt to identify factors which make the original relationship more or less pronounced. In some instances, however, this factor may refer to a situation existing prior to the operation of the *x* variable, while in other cases it may refer to a development following after the *x* factor. We shall speak of the former situation as the *conditions* for the relationship; the latter as the *contingencies* of the relationship. Thus we might say that the effectiveness of Gosnell's propaganda was conditioned by the previous voting experience of the persons to whom he showed it, while the relationship between sex and voting intention is contingent on the amount of interest in political affairs developed by men and women.

In actual research practice it is more common to find examples in which the conditions, rather than the contingencies, of a particular relationship have been specified. We are more likely, in other words, to find cases in which the starting relationship has been specified according to the prior characteristics of the respondents, the time or place of the observations, or the like. Since the specification of contingencies is also an important research operation, however, opportunities for carrying out this kind of analysis should be carefully noted and exploited. One final example may make still clearer the value of specifying contingencies. In general, the Elmira voting study found a tendency to maintain the voting tradition of one's father.[36] This is shown in Table XXXVIII.

TABLE XXXVIII—Relationship Between Father's Vote and Own Vote in Elmira

Father's vote	Percent who plan to vote Republican [37]	Total cases
Republican	87%	331
Democrat	51	216

The tendency to maintain the tradition of one's family vote is quite strong. But it undoubtedly depends on a number of factors. One of these, the analysts supposed, might be the amount of counter pressure to which the subjects were exposed. It is difficult to maintain a tradition in the face of pressures to break that tradition. To test this possibility, the analysts introduced as the specifying factor the length of time the subjects had lived

36. This example is taken from an analysis prepared by Norman Kaplan.
37. This table includes only the voters who had a definite intention at the time of the interview.

in Elmira. This is a community with a long-standing and solid Republican background. It can be expected, therefore, that residents will be subjected to more and more Republican influence the longer they live in the community. For voters with a Republican family background these community pressures will only serve as reinforcing agents on family tradition. But, for voters with Democratic background, these pressures will strain the family tradition. In other words, we can expect that the maintenance of a family tradition in voting will be contingent on the presence or absence of counter-forces. This actually turns out to be the case:

TABLE XXXIX—Relationship Between Father's Vote and Own Vote According to Length of Residence in Elmira

	Percent who plan to vote Republican [38]	
Length of residence in Elmira	Republican father	Democratic father
Old-timer	87% (284)	53% (189)
Newcomer	85 (47)	37 (27)

Regardless of the length of time they have resided in Elmira, the voters of that community tend to carry on their father's tradition of voting. But this tendency is considerably more pronounced among the newcomers to the community, who, presumably, have not been subjected to Republican influences for as long as have the so-called old-timers. The maintenance of a voting tradition, thus, is contingent on the absence of counter-influences.[39]

The specification of zero-relationships: A particularly discouraging kind of discovery is that no relationship exists between variables which one had expected to be correlated. Quite often this means that the relationship is regretfully dismissed, and attention turned to other problems. But sometimes it is possible, by pursuing the analysis of this seemingly negative result, to uncover factors which show that, although the original relationship is not significantly different from zero, the partial relationships are. Since the original relationship is a weighted average of the partials, this almost inevitably means the discovery of factors which reveal one of the partials to be positive and the other negative.

We shall present a number of examples of this kind of specification. Merton, for instance, expected to find a relationship between job satisfaction and participation in community activities in Craftown. But it turned out that no such relationship existed.

---

38. As in the previous table, only voters with a definite vote intention at the time of the interview are included here.

39. To test the meaning of this specification adequately, it would be necessary to carry out a similar study in a predominantly Democratic community, and to see, whether in such a place, those with a Republican family tradition were affected in the same way as were residents of Elmira who came from Democratic backgrounds.

TABLE XL—Relationship Between Job Satisfaction and Participation in Community Activities

Job satisfaction	Percent who belong to organizations	Total cases
Satisfied	41%	160
Dissatisfied	38	117

While Merton was forced to conclude that there was no significant relationship, he did not leave the matter there. He wondered whether it was not possible to specify conditions under which that relationship did exist. One of the variables which he considered, and which did accomplish what he had hoped it would, was the resident's own class identification—his feelings of belonging either to the working class or to the white collar class. When he introduced this specifying factor, he found that the partial relationships were indeed different from zero, *and* in opposite directions.

TABLE XLI—Relationship Between Job Satisfaction and Participation in Community Activities According to Class Identification

Class identification	Percent who belong to organizations Satisfied		Dissatisfied	
White collar	33%	(42)	44%	(18)
Working class	44	(118)	36	(99)

Among those who identified themselves with the white collar class, community participation is negatively related to job satisfaction; that is, the satisfied persons are less likely to take part in community activities than are the dissatisfied. Among those who considered themselves members of the working class, however, exactly the opposite is true. Within this group, it is the satisfied workers who are more likely to participate.

The full meaning of this result needs further clarification. We might conclude tentatively, however, that it is the deviant members of the white collar class—those who are dissatisfied with their jobs—who seek compensatory gratifications by participating in the activities of this predominantly working class community. Among the dominant group, however, it is exactly the reverse type of person who is most likely to be an active participant. But, even though any conclusions about the meaning of the relationship must be tentative, we have nonetheless succeeded in establishing formally one condition under which the original absence of relationship was specified.

We can present two further examples of the same kind. Both illustrate the way in which an initial finding of the absence of relationship between two variables can be specified to show the existence of a relationship. Lazarsfeld reports a number of studies in which it was possible to correlate age with the amount of listening to serious programs on the radio.[40] "The

40. Paul F. Lazarsfeld, *Radio and the Printed Page* (New York: Duell, Sloan and Pearce, 1940), pp. 96 ff.

focus of these studies," he comments, "was to learn whether biological maturity went with closer attention to serious broadcasts." One kind of serious program type investigated was classical music. But, as Lazarsfeld points out, the investigators were disappointed to learn that the relationship between age and amount of such listening was rather inconclusive. As Table XLII reveals, there was almost no relationship at all between age and listening to classical music.

TABLE XLII—Relationship Between Age and Listening to Classical Music

Age	Percent who listen to classical music	Total cases
Below 40	65%	603
40 and older	64	506

Formally, this is very similar to the Craftown result. There is no relationship between the starting variables. "But," Lazarsfeld continues, "then another consideration was introduced. If interest in serious broadcasts depends mainly upon the background against which they are received, the influence of age should be different on different cultural levels. On a high level, where the general background provides continuous intellectual stimulation, there should be an increase of serious listening as people grow older, while on a low level the contrary should be true. The stimulation which people on the lower level get in school and during the more excitable period of adolescence is not maintained afterward as their background in later life is poor. Hence they might be expected to listen to fewer and fewer serious broadcasts as they grow older." These expectations were borne out although the relationships are still not particularly strong ones.

TABLE XLIII—Relationship Between Age and Listening to Classical Music Specified by Cultural Level

Cultural level	Percent who listen to classical music	
	Below 40	40 and older
High level	73% (224)	76% (251)
Low level	60 (379)	52 (255)

The newly discovered partial relationships are not large. But they are larger than the original relationship was. Furthermore, they are of opposite sign. On the high cultural level the partial relationship between age and serious listening is a positive one—the older people listen to classical music more than do younger listeners. On the lower cultural level, however, exactly the opposite is true—the younger listen more than do their elders.

The final example comes from one study reported in *The American Soldier*. Again it is a case on which we cannot base too many speculations. The differences, when they exist, are small; and, unlike the example taken from Lazarsfeld's study of radio listening, there is no ready theory to explain why the result turns out as it did. But it is worth reporting to illustrate the type of analysis being considered here. The original zero relationship is presented in Table XLIV.

TABLE XLIV—Relationship Between Length of Service in Army and Incidence of Anxiety Symptoms

Length of service	Percent who have critical anxiety score	Total cases
Over 1 year	27%	3033
1 year and under	26	1551

Rather surprisingly, there is no relationship between length of service in the Army and the incidence of anxiety symptoms. In their efforts to clarify this apparent lack of relationship, the analysts discovered that the age of the soldier seemed to determine the way in which the two starting variables were related:

TABLE XLV—Relationship Between Length of Service and Incidence of Anxiety Symptoms Specified by Age

Age of soldier	Percent who have critical anxiety score			
	Have served over 1 year		Have served 1 year and under	
Under 25	24%	(1659)	21%	(1024)
25 and over	30	(1374)	36	(527)

Among the younger soldiers we find the expected relationship between length of service and the incidence of anxiety symptoms, with those who had served for a longer period showing a greater degree of anxiety. Among the older soldiers, however, exactly the opposite is found. Within this group, those who had served for less than one year manifest greater anxiety than those who have longer records of service. In neither case is the difference large, but in view of the size of sample there is little doubt that the relationships, particularly that observed among the older men, is statistically significant. We may conjecture on the basis of this result that, as the war progressed, physical and psychological qualifications for induction were gradually lowered, so that the older men with psychoneurotic symptoms were accepted.

Having outlined the major types of specification, a final comment on the relationship of specification and interpretation may help to round out this discussion. The reader may have noted in our discussion of specification that we almost invariably introduced what might be considered a fourth variable.

After specifying the relationship between sex and vote intention in terms of political interest, we brought forward the notion that social roles are particularly compelling when there is no inner motivation to behave in a particular fashion.

We saw that the relationship between organizational membership and the way in which one made friends depended on the level of organizational activity in the community; we then suggested that an active community provided more opportunities and occasions to meet other project residents in places and situations not determined by propinquity.

We found that the relationship between the theater where one was stationed and willingness for further service depended on the length of time one had been in the Army; this, we suggested, might indicate that the soldiers had interiorized a feeling of a "personal tour of duty," and, before this was completed, they did not feel justified in believing that they deserved to be discharged.

We saw that family traditions of voting were more likely to be maintained if one had lived for only a short time in a community with a strong political tradition of its own; this, we suggested, means that biographical influences can be modified by those present in one's immediate environment.

We see in each of these examples that what started out in each case as the specification of the relationship between two variables in the light of a third became, by the end of our discussion, a consideration of four variables. But how and why were these fourth variables introduced? Generally, it will be seen, they were introduced to *interpret* the relationship between the x and y variables. If one reexamines the list once more, it will be noted that the newly introduced variable is intended to clarify the link between the original variables. We may ask, then, why is such interpretation injected into the specification of a result? The answer seems to be that it is almost the natural outcome of specification. By showing in what situations the relationship is particularly pronounced, the specification of a result makes it easier to see how that result may be interpreted. By clearing away the confusing aspects of the relationship, by revealing the situation which prevails when the starting variables are most intimately related, such analysis quite naturally leads to questions about why the relationship exists and what the links between the original variables are. Thus, specification may almost always be considered a prelude to interpretation, rather than an analytic operation which is sufficient in itself.

General Principles for the Elaboration of Explanatory Analyses

We have discussed a variety of modes by which the analysis of an explanatory survey can be elaborated. But should all of these modes be employed in every survey, or employed to equal extent in an explanatory survey? The question of the appropriateness of a specific mode of elaboration arises—the order in which different elaborations are employed—the extent to which a particular formal type of elaboration is pursued—also arise. The reader might answer the basic question by remarking that *all* modes of elaboration shall be applied to their *fullest* extent because quality and *comprehensiveness* of explanation is the ultimate goal. But while this answer might be true academically, it cannot be true in practice. Few analysts are blessed with a maximum of resources of time or energy or money, and they must allocate these resources most wisely. Moreover, even where practical exigencies do not operate, research comes to an end. The analyst must stop at some point simply because he cannot see continuing indefinitely! Thus, it is far better to plan the process of elaboration and to define an end to it—even if it be somewhat arbitrary—than to have the analysis expire in some shapeless way because of boredom or exhaustion. Every survey analyst can recall with discomfort from his early experience the surfeit that comes from having too many tabulations and cross-tabulations, from having too many findings rather than too few, and being unable to encompass the richness of the available materials in the final rushed treatment of the inquiry. What principles can be given as to the degree and types of elaboration that are employed?

Our starting principle is that the analyst will or ought to have some definite purpose in mind, and a guide to this purpose is available in the classification of explanatory surveys we originally presented in Chapter II. That classification itself implied that explanatory surveys differ in their purposes, and the analyst attunes his procedures to the type of survey involved, the *theoretical* or experimental, the *evaluative* or programmatic, and the *diagnostic*. In all of these types of surveys, the starting point for the explanatory analysis is the same. *The first step is one or more attempts at explanation by the demonstration of the relationship of the phenomenon to some initiating factor or independent variable.* The *number* of such attempts at finding explanations, however, would vary with the type of inquiry. Usually, the *theoretical* inquiry is undertaken as a test of some relatively specific hypothesis, and consequently the number of attempts at explanation are few and predetermined in content. One is, by definition, not seeking to explore the universe of all possible determinants, but merely to test the validity of some one or few hypotheses. Negative findings might legitimately constitute an end to the analysis. In the evaluative inquiry, the range of attempts at explanation is also usually fairly well defined in advance and limited in number, although somewhat *wider* than in the theoretical inquiry. The emphasis is upon factors manipulable by some action agency. There will usually be a variety of such factors, but they are not unlimited. In the diagnostic inquiry, where the aim is upon the search into the unknown, the content and range of explanations that are examined is undefined in advance and generally very many in number.

These initial attempts at explanation are then followed in all explanatory surveys by tests of the validity of the explanation that has been demonstrated. We wish to establish whether or not the results are spurious. Here again, the question arises as to how far such elaborations are pursued. How many attempts are made to invalidate or substantiate the original findings, and what direction do these attempts take. In part, the dilemma may already be resolved to some extent for the analyst. Obviously, his resources may be limited and it may not be feasible to make many tests. So, too, these attempts are limited in number and direction by the original research design in that no antecedent variable can be controlled unless at least some *rudimentary* source of data was available as a result of provisions made in the original inquiry.[41]

The prior research design in the theoretical or evaluative survey may have been of such a nature that the imputation of spuriousness because of particular extraneous factors is not legitimate. Thus, we noted early that explanatory surveys often exclude certain sources of variation in the phenomenon by the restriction of the universe. In such instances, particular factors are controlled, by definition, and do not have to be considered in the subsequent analysis.

The amount of such elaboration—the number of tests for spuriousness—will vary with the type of explanatory survey. In diagnostic surveys, emphasis is less upon trustworthiness of specific explanations than upon exploring the range of possible explanations. Rigorous tests in a *new* survey are, so to speak, an outgrowth of such surveys but rarely would elaborate provisions have been made for this in the initial inquiry. For reasons already discussed, the amount of such elaboration would be less in the evaluative inquiry than in the theoretical inquiry. The evaluative inquiry often deals not with refined and *unitary* variables and their *intrinsic* effects but with manipulable *constellations* or compounds of unitary variables, for example, with programs. The notion of spuriousness, of other independent variables that are operative, is in a sense a product of *logical reduction or analysis.* If other variables are regarded as part of a corporate entity, rather than as external and separate factors, the notion of spuriousness would not be involved. There is only so to speak one variable. It is only as we see these other variables as not an intrinsic part of the original explanatory variable

---

41. The principle should be clarified, perhaps. Analysts gain insight into possible determinants often as a result of the on-going research process. They may then seek to introduce this factor as a "control" in the subsequent analysis, and obtain a measure for it by such devices as the re-reading of the original interviews and the rating of implicit cues or comments or answers to open-ended question or by the re-coding of some original datum. But the general principle holds in that no such re-processing of data can provide any measure of the new variables unless some source is rich enough to yield at least rudimentary data.

that they begin to concern us as sources of spuriousness in the original finding.

Granted these guides, we engage in various elaborations to test the spuriousness of the original findings as to an explanation. We introduce the antecedent test factors which are related to both of the starting variables, and we watch to see whether the partial relationships become substantially smaller after these are introduced. There are two alternative outcomes, and the consequences of each are quite different. On the one hand, our analysis can uncover invalidating factors which reveal the original relationship to be a spurious one. Then we proceed in a new direction. Or, on the other hand, such attempts may fail and it may turn out that the relationship with which we started does not appear from our analysis to be spurious. Then we proceed in another direction.

Let us assume that the original relationship turns out to be a spurious one. What happens then? There is no hard and fast rule. Where the survey was not limited to *one* specific hypothesis, the analyst will generally turn to other independent variables whose influence on the phenomenon he wishes to examine. He then repeats the original sequence of elaborations already described. Where the inquiry was of a theoretical nature, and interest was focussed on only one specific independent variable, a common experience is that the analyst turns his attention to other relationships made explicit during the course of his explanatory analysis, namely to the [xt] and/or the [ty] relationships. True, he could terminate his analysis at this point. He has the answer to the problem he originally posed, albeit a negative answer. But since this is a somewhat abortive end or is often experienced as such he frequently pursues interesting problems that have emerged. Let us consider this in the light of concrete examples. We may refer to a study in which it was found that there was a relationship between soundness of sleep and the kind of mood one was in the following day. Now let us suppose that closer analysis showed that this result is a spurious one, that ease of sleep is *determined* by the kind of mood one is in when he goes to bed, and that a bad mood persists from one day to the next. Under these conditions, the analyst can no longer pay very serious attention to the possibility that sleep is the prime determinant of mood. But he does not abandon the findings entirely. Instead, he is likely to turn to other questions about the same general problem. He might ask, for example, how a bad mood disturbs sleep. What are the mechanisms relating a psychological state and a physiological process? In raising this kind of question, the analyst would be focussing on the relationship between the test factor and the *x* variable in the original relationship.[42] Or, he might raise a different series of questions.

---

42. It could be, of course, that this relationship is also spurious, that bad mood does not of itself lead to uneasy sleep, but that both are the result of some kind of physiological disturbance. This possibility must be explored, just as the spurious character of the original relationship was examined.

He might explore a fact turned up in his analysis, namely that bad—or good—moods seem to persist. This is implied in the relationship which we assume he has discovered between the test factor and the original y variable. Focussing on this relationship, he might attempt to learn for how long a time period moods persist, under which conditions they change, and so on.

In this first example, both marginal relationships seemed to call for further elaboration. But there are other cases in which only one of them is likely to command attention. For example, in particular instances it may be only the [ty] relationship which seems to demand examination. Recall the somewhat absurd finding that there is a positive relationship between the number of storks counted in an area and the birthrate of that area. This result was "explained away" by consideration of the rural-urban dimension: Rural areas harbor a larger number of storks, and, at the same time, they are characterized by a high birthrate. But we do not consider this result uninteresting just because the original relationship turned out to be spurious. Our interest, however, is likely to focus on the relationship between the test factor and the y variable. The [xt] relationship seems obvious. It is not difficult to understand why rural areas shelter a larger number of storks than do urban areas, and we are not likely to think, therefore, that this relationship needs further elaboration. But such is not the case with the relationship between the rural nature of a particular area and its high birthrate. Understanding of relationships such as this has been one of the prime concerns of demographers and of rural sociologists. We therefore find it is very worthwhile enterprise to try to interpret this relationship.

To summarize the process thus far, there is the attempt to find antecedent test factors which might demonstrate the result to be spurious. If one locates such factors, then the original result is put aside, and attention turns to new factors or other relationships. In the latter instance, the effort may be to interpret either or both the [xt] and the [ty] relationships. The direction which these efforts take depends largely on the nature of the problem and of the relationships under consideration. If the relationship is not an obvious one, in the sense that one can understand the links between the two variables which are involved, then one usually feels compelled to provide these links through the analytic process of interpretation.

However, if after appropriate tests have been made, the original result does not seem to be a spurious one, further elaboration takes a somewhat different form than that just considered. *Where the original result appears valid, efforts are then made to interpret and to specify it.* Here again questions arise as to which of these two modes of elaboration shall be employed, how far shall each be pursued, and what particular variables shall be employed. Again, the type of explanatory inquiry provides, in part, answers to these questions.

As we noted in Chapter II, the *evaluative* or programmatic inquiry generally emphasizes *specification* as a mode of elaboration rather than inter-pretation. One naturally seeks to specify the conditions under which the independent variables have an effect, so that action can be more focussed and efficient. The content of the variables that are used for specifying the relationship also are given ready definition, in that the most meaningful specifications are *those differentiations in the environment for which cor-respondingly there are differentiations possible in the action agency's op-erations.* One may raise the question as to why interpretation as a procedure is less employed. The reason is that such surveys are concerned with *change in some end product.* Success does not call for analysis—it is gratefully ac-cepted. The goal is pragmatic. One is less concerned with *why* something produces an effect, than with demonstrating that it has or can work. This is not to say that the problem of understanding the process by which the effect occurred is never at issue, but that it is merely of lesser interest to the practitioner.

Moreover, the independent variable that was originally examined as the explanation of the phenomenon was itself the product of some apparently rational decision. Usually therefore the positive finding is not problemati-cal; it was expected and there appears to be no difficulty in interpreting it by *a priori* methods. If anything, there is a somewhat perverse situation in the evaluative survey in that *negative* findings about some original explan-atory factor seem to the client or researcher to call for interpretation.

This may appear strange. We have thus far suggested that the mode of elaboration called interpretation is not applied unless the original explana-tion of the phenomenon is found to hold. Under those conditions, one seeks to interpret the connection in terms of some intervening process which links the initiating factor and the end product. We had also suggested when an original explanation is found initially to have no significance one usually does not dwell on that variable but turns to other analytic problems. Yet, we are here extending the use of the concept of interpretation to just such relationships in evaluative surveys and suggesting that they too be elaborated. The fact, in these instances, is that the independent variable was presumably one that rationally should have produced some effect. Yet it did not and this seems to demand interpretation. What then occurs to the an-alyst is the possibility that, in some manner, the variable generated some untoward psychological process which in turn hindered or barred or de-railed the effect on the phenomenon. The analyst then seeks to uncover this intervening variable—to test such an interpretation—with the ultimate goal of manipulating the independent variable in such a way as to lessen these untoward psychological consequences. By way of illustration of this un-usual use of interpretation we can refer to one of our original case studies, the inquiry into Absenteeism.

In one phase of this inquiry, an evaluation was made of the effectiveness of various remedial programs that were already in operation in particular plants for the reduction of absenteeism. The analysts examined whether or not absenteeism was controlled or reduced by the presence of such programs and, if so, by which particular types of programs. Plants were classified by reference to the independent variable, program type, and compared in overall rate of absenteeism. The data are presented in Table XLVI below reproduced from the original report.[43]

TABLE XLVI—Mean Plant Rates of Absenteeism as Related to Type of Program

Type of Program	Rate
Preventive Programs	3.3%
Educative Programs	6.3
Punitive Programs	6.1
No Programs at all	8.4

Statistical tests established the fact that the differences between educative or punitive programs and no programs at all were not significant. The preventive programs, however, were established as effective. No interpretation of this latter finding seems necessary. It is plausible, and the reason for the effectiveness is obvious. The greatest portion of absences were explained by non-voluntary factors such as illness and accident, and programs which prevented such causes from occurring through medical and related measures were bound to reduce the rate. Obviously, the program had in the first place been predicated on such rational considerations and perhaps even on an empirical basis.

What does, however, seem to call for interpretation is the fact that the other types of programs do *not* explain the plant level of absenteeism. After all, these too had been predicated on a rational basis. Some of the causes of absenteeism were voluntary, such as, low morale. Why is it therefore that punishment or the discussion of the need for regular attendance at work did not reduce the plant rate? What peculiar psychological processes were generated such that educational and punitive measures did not work toward their normal and expected course of reducing absence. A series of attempts at interpretation, at demonstration of such hidden intervening processes were made, and the paradox was finally resolved. For punitive programs to be effective in *preventing* the absence of a worker, there had to be knowledge that punishment would be invoked. Otherwise punishment only comes *after* the fact and cannot constrain the worker. It is like the old absurdity which is used in testing the intelligence of children. The psychologist quotes to the child the story: "The judge said to the prisoner, 'You are to be hanged, and I hope it will be a warning to you.' "[44] The average eleven-year-old appreciates the absurdity and the same dynamics

43. Katz and Hyman, *op. cit.*, p. 26.
44. L. Terman and M. Merrill, *Measuring Intelligence* (Boston: Houghton Mifflin, 1937), p. 108.

are here involved. The punishment to be a deterrent to absence must operate *prior* to the act. Data on cognition were obtained in the survey and provided a demonstration that: "about one-quarter of all workers did not know whether their company was doing anything"; "an additional 20% . . . described the program in grossly inaccurate terms"; "women and recent employees (those very groups found most prone to absence) were more uninformed of the plant program." Thus a necessary psychological link was missing.

But punishment to be effective must not only be represented psychologically; the threat, if perceived, must *not* produce psychological consequences of hostility, resentment, etc. which might produce lowered morale and in turn foster the very causes of voluntary absence. In point of fact, it was established that where awareness of punishment was present it did produce these very processes and thereby increased the causes leading to absence.

Similarly, the ineffectiveness of educational programs was traced to psychological variables of such a nature that the very messages disseminated were rejected or disbelieved and therefore their hortatory implications for changing the worker's conduct were not realized.

Let us turn to the other types of explanatory surveys and the question of the appropriateness of specification and interpretation as modes of elaboration of the analysis. As with other modes of analysis, the *diagnostic* survey engages in these procedures in only rudimentary or exploratory fashion. Emphasis would be placed more on the *range of suggestive* interpretations and specifications of the original explanations than on their definitive treatment. The content of the variables chosen for these analyses would be more a matter of taste and hunch or imagination than a function of any basic research decision.

In the instance of the theoretical inquiry, the need for specification is in part dependent on the original formulation of the problem. The particular specifications that should be examined, if any, may have been formulated as explicit parts of the original hypothesis and the direction the analyst follows is therefore pre-determined. Of course, why any formulation is made initially in terms of particular variables is itself a question which might be posed. Here again this may be a sheer matter of taste, or due to the general systematic orientation of the scientist. In some instances, the formulation represents some continuity in research and grows directly out of prior research by other investigators. Often the amount of specification that occurs in practice in theoretical surveys is too little. Investigators may seek generalizations, universals, and therefore are not favorably disposed to showing that their explanation of a particular phenomenon is limited, is contingent upon some special set of conditions. We are not advocating this practice, but merely reporting it. There should be considerable specification of the conditions under which an original hypothesis holds for this constitutes the empirical test of its generality.

What about interpretation as a mode of elaboration of relationships in a theoretical inquiry? Again, the extent and content of such elaboration is, in part, dependent on the original formulation. The original hypothesis may have been explicitly limited in character and the actual analysis may therefore require little in the way of interpretive links. Or the interpretive links to be examined may have been explicitly formulated initially. In general, however, interpretation is a crucial requirement in theoretical surveys for the ultimate purpose of all such inquiries is to increase our fundamental *understanding* of phenomena. We wish to determine not only the initiating factors but also the process by which their effects are mediated. Particularly, where the independent variable is *abstract* in character or *remote in time* from the effect or *approximate* in its impact upon the person, one finds it difficult to see how it produces some ultimate end-effect. Consequently, one elaborates the interpretive links which make plausible the original nexus. Of course, whether an explanation is regarded as plausible, as self-evident, or conversely as demanding further interpretation is dependent on the background of the investigator. Thus, for example, relations between traditional sociological categories as independent variables and psychological phenomena as dependent variables may appear natural, perhaps inevitable, to a sociologist. Why shouldn't the individual be the product of a milieu? To a particular psychologist, by contrast, who emphasized individual variations, non-passivity in relation to experience, idiosyncratic definitions of experience, the same relationship might appear far from self-evident, perhaps even bizarre. It would therefore call for interpretation through the introduction in the analysis of intervening variables which link the initial social conditions with the end-product. For example, note the way in which Krech and Crutchfield—social *psychologists*—formulate the problem. They fully acknowledge the role of social factors as *initiating* conditions in producing such psychological phenomena as beliefs and attitudes, "fundamental psychological processes . . . do not operate in a vacuum. The nature of the psychological field . . . is dependent upon the nature of man's 'real' environment . . . in a systematic, even if not simple, manner." But they then remark that "exposure to a characteristic and defined range of stimulation does not, in itself, result in the growth of a uniform set of beliefs. . . . Beliefs and attitudes . . . develop selectively. . . . This selective nature of the formation of beliefs and attitudes acts as a limiting factor on the effectiveness of the cultural pattern. . . . It is because of these limitations that the effect of cultural influences upon the formation of beliefs and attitudes is not a simple and direct one." Consequently, they emphasize the need for interpretation in connection with empirical studies of such relationships. They "are difficult to interpret for purposes of shedding any light on the basic processes involved in belief and attitude formation. . . . To evaluate the significance of these studies and to understand the role and limitations of cultural determinants requires a closer analysis of the fundamental psychological processes involved . . . the study of such correlations taken by themselves, can give us but little scientific understanding of the development of beliefs and attitudes in people." [45]

The same position is demonstrated frequently in the psychological literature. Thus, Asch expresses a strong psychological position on the problem:

> Many of the data upon which social psychology today relies are of the order described. They take the form of stating a relation between a sociological variable (membership in an economic group or residence in a given region) and an end-result of action or judgment (a voting decision, or expressed antipathy toward foreign groups). . . . But our concern is not only to "control and predict"; we want also to understand the psychological sources of action, the processes that intervene between conditions and consequences. . . . A sociology that would predict with accuracy the relations between social circumstances and actions would be of value; it would also be blind. . . . Economic and political regularities persist only as long as individuals act to produce them. Viewed in this light statistical regularities are essentially recordings of facts and external relations at a given time. The keeping of records is necessary in science, but it does not supplant the need for principles.
>
> What the study of sociological uniformities fails to supply is precisely the functional relations between conditions and consequences. Between these stands nothing less than the individual himself, his tendencies, capacities, and group relations. Unless we take into account what he understands and feels about his situation, we do not understand the sense of the given relation in a single instance. In fact, the most optimistic students of social regularities do not rely upon them alone; they never fail to introduce psychological assumptions. The very selection of questions for quantitative investigation presupposes some assumptions about what is psychologically relevant. This holds also for the interpretation of quantitative results. The data examined above come to life only when we inquire into their meaning. As soon as we do so we move into psychological ground. The sociologist cannot dispense with the attempt to establish a meaningful nexus between his variables. In fact, he does introduce assumptions about psychological processes that produce a given relation between economic interest and political action or between group membership and group standards. Usually, however, these are quite general; they represent little more than commonsense ideas, which themselves need study and revision. Often we do not realize sufficiently how dependent quantitative data are on qualitative distinctions and assumptions. Unless we clarify and test the qualitative factors we may delude ourselves with the conviction that we are in possession of knowledge about massive group trends, although in fact we lack clear understanding of the psychological situation of any individual in the group. [46]

45. By permission from *Theory and Problems of Social Psychology,* by D. Krech and R. Crutchfield, 1948, McGraw-Hill Book Company, Inc., pp. 176-178.

46. S. Asch, *Social Psychology* (New York: Prentice Hall, 1952), pp. 531-533. Reprinted by permission of the publisher.

Asch and Krech and Crutchfield are supported by other psychologists. G. W. Allport in his review of *The American Soldier,* presented earlier, praises the work in the most laudatory fashion. Yet, in connection with a discussion of the controls introduced for spuriousness to which we have alluded, he states the same position. We repeat a portion of the earlier quotation:

> Nothing ever causes behavior excepting mental sets (including habits, attitudes, motives). . . . Background factors never directly cause behavior; they cause attitudes; and attitudes in turn determine behavior. I am not, of course, arguing against the use of breakdowns or matched groups. They should, however, be used to show where attitudes come from, and not to imply that social causation acts automatically apart from attitudes.[47]

Even within a discipline, particular orientations would affect whether or not some initial explanation is regarded as self-evident. Thus, one sociologist might see "class" as inevitably producing given consequences. Another might not find this obvious. Among psychologists, some might see political attitudes as naturally growing out of the background of childhood experience; others would feel surprised and would ask for further interpretation of such a finding. Such differences in point of view creating different felt needs for interpretation of relationships hardly demand further illustration.

The demand for interpretive links is not confined, however, to instances where the explanation involved a *mixture* of variables from different realms, as in the relationship of a sociological category and a psychological product. These are merely examples where clearly the connection does not seem direct and self-evident, and thus an interpretive link is elaborated. We might say that the felt need and the relief derived from the elaboration of an intervening process is directly proportional to the experienced "distance" between x and y. When we are told that women vote proportionately less frequently than do men, we feel that we must interpret this relationship, for we feel that there is great "psychological distance" between the fact of being born a man or woman and adult voting behavior. When, on the other hand, we are told that there is a relationship between marital status and the amount of time spent in housework, we feel a less urgent need to spell out the interpretive process. The connection seems to us clear, and we do not experience a need to introduce intervening variables.

The need for interpretive links might even arise where both independent and dependent variables are from the same general realm, e.g., both being psychological entities. Thus Hyman and Sheatsley, in their critique of *The Authoritarian Personality,* argue that the interpretation of the original explanations was inadequate. Yet, in this instance the independent variables were of a very strict *psychological* character, and might thus appear linked to the *psychological* phenomena which were studied. Nevertheless,

---

47. *Op. cit.,* Reprinted by permission of the American Psychological Association.

these critics feel that the respective psychological realms involved are so-to-speak *functionally far apart.*

Let us assume that the contrasted groups were found to differ significantly with respect to ninety variables of personality. Such would be the findings, but a meaning must still be read into them. How, for instance, does one relate a variable of early childhood to an ideology in adult life? . . . *All such correlations must be interpreted through some logic by which the two entities are bound together. It is not always readily apparent how certain variables, separated by many years in time and experience, ultimately become converted into prejudice, and in any analysis of such relationships, one wishes to safeguard the interpretations of these processes and, if possible, to illumine them directly.* So, in the clinically oriented method, one observes the growth in time, following the process longitudinally and noting directly the logic of the relationship. In more experimental work, one attempts to measure directly some of the factors which intervene between the two variables, and so highlight the process. Or taking a cue from phenomenological work in social psychology, we might seek to understand such relationships as the authors demonstrate through detailed cognitive material which would help us understand, for example, how a respondent sees a Negro in the image of some more prototypical problem of his own. Such analyses . . . put a constraint upon the analyst of the data and caution him against imputing his own dynamic theory to the bare statistical finding. . . .

In the interview procedures here used, while the content of the variables is the quintessence of dynamic psychology, the formal mode of analysis is as statistical as can be. All the dynamics are simply imputed by the analyst, without benefit of any of the direct types of data that we have referred to above. For example: "The assumption behind this question, later proved correct, was that the pattern developed in the relationship to the father tends to be transferred to other authorities and thus becomes crucial in forming social and political beliefs in men." But the transference is never demonstrated, the process never explained. Prejudice and childhood relationship to father merely correlate. Again: "Where there is no readiness to admit that one's parents have any weakness in them it is not surprising to find later an indication of repressed hostility and revengeful fantasies behind the mask of compliance." It occurs to us to wonder *why* this is not surprising, or why this repressed hostility necessarily related to the person's attitude toward Jews. . . .

We present a number of similar quotations: . . . Indignation about people considered as inferior "seems to serve the double purpose of externalizing what is unacceptable in oneself, and of displacing one's hostility which otherwise might turn against powerful 'ingroups,' e.g., the parents." The low scorer, as a child, "seems to have enjoyed the benefit of the help of adults in working out his problems of sex and aggression. He thus can more easily withstand propaganda which defames minorities or glorifies war." To this latter "conclusion," as well as to the others, it is fair to ask, "How come?" We have presented, we hope, enough quotations of this type to show that the dynamic processes are simply imputed to the statistical findings or juxtaposed against them. Armed variously with such concepts as "projection," "displacement," "generalization," "repression" and the like, the analyst "explains" the data. But nowhere are the processes illuminated directly nor is it clearly demonstrated how they actually work out in the particular forms of attitude described.[48]

The general desirability of interpretation, and the particular situations calling for its application, have now been discussed in considerable detail. But there are two further problems in interpretation, not entirely solved by formal principles. These concern the content of the variables employed in the interpretation, and the point at which the interpretation may be considered as adequate. Let us consider these problems one by one.

With respect to the *content* of the variables, there are no generally accepted principles. Apart from variables which are explicit in the original formulation, the investigator usually chooses in the light of his own systematic orientation. However, the correctness of an interpretation does not depend only on persuasive powers of the person offering that interpretation. As we know, there is an empirical test of an interpretation, and therefore a formal way of deciding whether an interpretive variable is or is not appropriate. It is possible in this way to eliminate many interpretive arguments which might be advanced initially. However, since it is rare to find "complete" interpretations in actual nature, that is, factors which make the partial relationships vanish entirely rather than just becoming smaller than the original relationship, it is usually possible to find two or more interpretive variables, if the appropriate data are available. In that event, the analyst must resist whatever temptations he has to claim superiority for one of the interpretations over all the others.

In deciding what specific interpretive factors to introduce, investigators naturally show partiality to that *general order* of variables which corresponds to their backgrounds. In broadest terms, we may distinguish two types of interpretive variables. There are, on the one hand, *external or behavioral characteristics* which *emerge from the original independent variables* such as, for example, amount of book-reading, church attendance, education, and the like. In contrast to these are such *internal psychological states* as level of interest or involvement, good or bad mood, optimism-pessimism, feelings of security, level of information or knowledge, etc. Thus, in the earlier quotations from Asch and other psychologists, the directive is not merely to engage in interpretation but to make use of strictly psychological variables. Such intervening variables appear to these writers as more basic or meaningful or revealing for interpretation of some originally obtained relationship. However, it should be noted that the *formal logic* of an interpretation of a relationship is independent of the general type of variable used. Whether or not *a particular* interpretation is meaningful depends only on the formal and statistical conditions described earlier. The choice of a

---

48. *Op. cit.,* italics ours, pp. 96-98.

variable for such analyses is essentially a theoretical problem, and often-times a matter of taste. It is not a matter which can be decided through any process of empirical analysis; rather, it is prior to analysis.

However, in one special sense the choice is not as arbitrary as might appear. Thus far we have touched only the question of the content of variables used for *an* interpretation, for providing *a* link between some initial condition and some consequence.

For *any single* interpretation, there is no formal criterion available for deciding which is a better type of variable to choose. However, the process that connects such initial and end factors may conceivably involve *a long chain* of interdependent intervening variables, and the problem that therefore arises now is what *amount* of interpretation is needed in order to make the original relationship understandable. If a whole chain of intervening variables can be inserted into the sequence, how many do we insert and study? When is the interpretation complete?

We shall see that there is no simple answer to this new question. Logical analysis and conceptual refinements of a process can go on almost indefinitely. But one partial answer can at least be given. Interpretive variables that involve external factors, such as exposure to an event, are intervening only in the formal temporal sense that they emerge from some earlier independent variable. If they are to produce some alteration in the behavior of the subjects who are studied, they must operate by, in turn, changing some psychological system within the individual. They cannot work in a mechanical or direct manner. An *organism,* a *person,* is the ultimate link and his internal processes are undergoing change. Thus reading a book changes knowledge or belief or involvement; attendance at a church may provide some new purpose, education provides new ideas, etc. Consequently, the use of one intervening variable of a psychological order is not a complete elaboration of any relationship. It only provides one link. Links involving external factors may also be present. But any link of an external nature, if it is to operate to produce some effect, can in turn be reduced to an intervening variable of a psychological nature. In this sense, if one must limit himself, psychological variables provide closer approximations to ultimate understanding of an original relationship, even though they may be incomplete interpretations.

Such psychological processes may themselves be subjected to further refinements. Here the degree of refinement is arbitrary and depends essentially on the background and taste of the analyst. One case from the literature will illustrate this pattern of successive interpretations by the introduction of more and more refined psychological variables. In a study of reactions to cartoons which contained an anti-bias theme it was found that prejudiced readers misunderstood the cartoons more frequently than did those with little or no signs of anti-Semitic and anti-Negro feelings.[49] Furthermore, it was established that this relationship was not a spurious one, at least so far as factors such as education, familiarity with the cartoon medium, race, and so on were concerned. Diagrammatically, this result can be represented in the following way:

$$\text{Prejudice} \qquad\qquad \overset{\text{Misunderstanding}}{\text{of cartoon theme}}$$
$$(x)\longrightarrow(y)$$

Of course, this diagram truncates the entire analytic sequence originally involved. The original independent variable (x) was exposure to the cartoon and the ultimate dependent variable (y) is some attitudinal or behavioral change. Originally, the analysis involved the specification that prejudiced individuals were not affected by the cartoon in the intended manner. The basic interpretive link then introduced was a process of misunderstanding. The need for interpretation in this instance constitutes another demonstration of the point we made earlier, that in evaluative inquiries, interpretation is introduced often to clarify why a given independent variable produces *no* effect. However, for our immediate purpose we need diagram only that part of the analysis relevant to our discussion, and label these initial and end products x and y.

Now the links between these two variables are not immediately obvious, and we therefore feel called upon to find some further interpretation for the result. The first link suggested by the analysts was contained in the notion of "resistance"; according to their hypothesis, prejudiced men did not want, and actively resisted, understanding the message of the cartoons which ridiculed prejudice. This new link in the overall process can also be represented in the diagram:

$$\text{Prejudice} \xrightarrow{\overset{\text{Resist understanding}}{\text{cartoon message}}} \underset{(t_1)}{} \xrightarrow{\qquad} \overset{\text{Misunderstanding}}{\underset{(y)}{\text{of cartoon theme}}}$$

But there are few people probably who would be satisfied that this interpretation is sufficient. Most would probably want to find a link between x and t_1, on the one hand, and between t_1 and y on the other. They would ask, Why do prejudiced men resist understanding, and how can resistance lead to misunderstanding? The answers given by the analysts were that prejudiced men resisted understanding the message of the cartoons because of the threat which such understanding implied for their egos, and that, once their resistance had taken hold, they were "derailed" from an under-

49. P. Kendall and K. Wolf, "The Analysis of Deviant Cases in Communications Research," in P. Lazarsfeld and F. Stanton, eds, *Communications Research, 1948–1949* (New York: Harpers, 1949), pp. 152-179.

standing of cartoons by their efforts to ridicule the central character. These new links too can be inserted into the diagram:

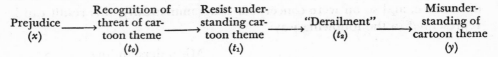

Prejudice (x) → Recognition of threat of cartoon theme (t_0) → Resist understanding cartoon theme (t_1) → "Derailment" (t_2) → Misunderstanding of cartoon theme (y)

Thus, what started out as a simple relationship between two variables ends up with a long chain of intervening variables. We stop inserting new links into this chain only when we feel psychologically satisfied that the underlying process has been clarified.

It is clear from the discussion thus far that the elaboration of an explanatory analysis can become exceedingly involved. Independent variables are first introduced as hypothesized explanatory factors. But this creates the new problems of interpretation. And once any interpretive sequence is elaborated, it seems to generate further interpretations which then require additional analysis. The process appears endless, and the reader may well have despaired. As a solution to his difficulties, he may have seen an apparent shortcut. The independent variables are reduced so-to-speak to the operation of intervening variables. The intervening variables of an external sort then generate some psychological process. If this be the end of the analytic sequence, why not slough off the beginning? Start the explanatory sequence with independent variables that are more proximate to the phenomenon, and thereby avoid the excess burden of the other procedures. Start with the most fundamental psychological process which directly precedes the end-product and examine this as an independent variable, an antecedent, which explains the phenomenon. Granted there are instances where this is inappropriate because the original formulation explicitly specified other types of independent variables. But these apart, this would appear a most legitimate and efficient procedure.

Now while one cannot object to such an approach on formal grounds, it has certain limitations. We may well illustrate these by taking some liberty with a passage in Cohen and Nagel.[50] In the context of a discussion of causation, they cite the fact that a house burns down:

> What is the cause of this event? Perhaps the house was destroyed because of an overturned kerosene lamp, or because of defective electric wiring, or because of a faulty chimney. The reader may be tempted to retort . . . "if the alleged causes of the fire were examined more carefully . . . a circumstance common to all of them would be found. . . . The occurrence of a rapid oxidation in some part of the house is such a common circumstance. And that common feature of the many alleged causes is *the* cause of the event." Such

50. M. R. Cohen and E. Nagel, *An Introduction to Logic and Scientific Method* (New York: Harcourt, Brace, 1934), p. 269. By permission of the publishers. Cohen and Nagel expand on this particular passage for purposes of criticizing the doctrine of "plurality of causes" but this does not concern us here.

an analysis is not very satisfactory. If the reader were investigating that fire for an insurance company and submitted such an analysis, he would not retain his post for long. "The occurrence of a rapid oxidation," the company would doubtless declare, "is an explanation of all fires. It was not your job to discover the most general conditions under which fires occur, for we knew that all the time; it was your job to find the special conditions under which this one occurred."

One moral we may read from the story is quite clear. It may well be that the analyst concentrates on and identifies a fundamental intervening variable which might be regarded as the most proximate cause of a phenomenon. In so doing the special conditions or independent variables that initiate the process would be lost to sight, and it might be very desirable for the analyst to illuminate these variables as well. Otherwise the explanatory sequence may be stated too generally and the phenomenon remains disembodied or isolated from the environmental circumstances in which it rests. Certainly, the psychological links in the process are worthy of fundamental study, but not to the exclusion of their anchorage in some initial conditions. Thus, if the reader re-examines the earlier quotations from Asch and Allport and Krech and Crutchfield, one notes that all of these writers emphasize interpretation *not* to the exclusion of the study of initial external causes, but as modes of illumination of processes following from these causes.

Similarly, in their critique of the Authoritarian Personality, Hyman and Sheatsley react to the analysis with a sense of its incompleteness. This is not because the interpretation is not elaborated, but because the explanatory sequence omits the initial environmental circumstances. They note that certain of the phenomena which are described and then derived from "psycho-dynamic processes, can be shown to have a wide distribution in American society, and, quite regularly, to show a clear correlation with such objective factors as formal education." Consequently they argue: "If these dynamics are involved, they should at least be given some social location. They may define the *process* of such attitude formation, but the location of this process within some part of the social order would seem to require that adequate reference be made to the fact." [51]

PROBLEM EXERCISE V

Selected Modes of Elaboration Employed in the Industrial Absenteeism Inquiry

To give the student practice in the variety of elaborations which may be employed, we present below in tabular form some selected findings, not discussed in the published account, of the absenteeism inquiry. Reconstruct the logical development that led to each of the analyses presented. Label

51. *Op. cit.*, pp. 106-107.

each table in terms of the type of elaboration that was involved, and draw one or more conclusions from each table.

TABLE V-1—Absenteeism as Related to Sex

	Percent Showing No Absence Within Past Three Months
Male	44%
Female	37

TABLE V-2—Absenteeism as Related to Marital Status and Sex

	Percent Showing No Absence Within Past Three Months
Married: Males	49%
Females	31
Unmarried: Males	43
Females	43

TABLE V-3—Absenteeism as Related to Length of Employment in Plant

	Percent Showing No Absence Within Past Three Months
Under three months	55%
3 Months—2 years	36
Over two years	49

TABLE V-4—Absenteeism as Related to Inclination to Quit

	Percent Showing No Absence Within Past Three Months
Inclined to quit	36%
Not inclined to quit	45

TABLE V-5—Absenteeism as Related to Spouse Working

	Percent Showing No Absence Within Past Three Months
Married Respondents (both sexes)	
Both husband and wife working	38%
Only one spouse working	45

TABLE V-6—Absenteeism as Related to Marital Status and Inclination to Quit

	Percent Showing No Absence Within Past Three Months
Inclined to quit	
Married: Males	43%
Females	29
Unmarried: Males	43
Females	35
Not Inclined to Quit	
Married: Males	52%
Females	32
Unmarried: Males	44
Females	44

TABLE V-7—The Relation Between Sex and Absenteeism in Different Plants

	Correlation Between Female Sex and Absenteeism
Southern Ordnance	.70
Ohio Machinery	.35
Midwestern Machinery	.38
Illinois Machinery	.31
Northwestern Ordnance	.20
New England Electrical	.35
Western Aircraft	.25
Eastern Electric	.35

In the ten other plants studied the correlation was less than .20

THE UTILIZATION OF SURVEY FINDINGS
AND THE FUNCTIONS OF THE ANALYST:
SOME EXAMPLES

Introduction

Part IV

WE HAVE TRIED thus far to present principles which will improve the analyst's ability in conducting effective surveys. We have described the setting within which he works and the effects this setting has on the formulation and conduct of the research. We have presented theoretical and technical principles for achieving a sound description of some phenomenon or for establishing accurately the relationship between a phenomenon and one or more determinants. On this basis, the analyst should be able to arrive at sound conclusions as to the problem under study.

But the analyst's role usually extends beyond the realm of the *immediate* findings and the *specific* conclusions drawn from the data. A survey is rarely undertaken for the mere purpose of reporting some *limited* conclusion. Where the survey has an applied function as in the case of many descriptive surveys and in the case of explanatory surveys of an evaluative, programmatic or diagnostic type, the purpose of the research is to extend the conclusions into the realm of a policy decision or an action program. Where the survey is not of an applied character, the purpose is nevertheless to go beyond the limited, immediate findings and conclusions. Here the aim is to increase systematic knowledge —to give strength to some larger body of theory or some systematic formulation upon which the specific empirical test presumably bears.

The analyst faces many difficulties in the extension of the specific findings either into the realm of application or of theory. A survey can be analyzed impeccably and the conclusions can be accurate and yet, have little value for action or theory. Worse yet, the analysis may be effective, and the implications drawn for action or theory may even be misleading. There are consequently special requirements which the analyst must be familiar with in order to insure that his specific findings are extended properly.

Some of the skills that lead to more effective *application* of findings are strictly speaking *not* analytic or scientific skills. The analyst's ability to write persuasively, to communicate findings to a larger audience, to present things clearly, to manipulate practical situations, to gauge other considerations in an action situation—all these increase the likelihood that survey findings will be acted upon in a proper fashion. Even the pedestrian factor of his efficiency in expediting the survey is crucial often to its application, for action must be taken in time and the survey must keep pace with the decision or be wasted.[1] Other

---

1. In this connection, a valuable procedure for the survey analyst is that of *trial tabulations,* in which ideally a random sample of the total sample is processed first. This reduces the magnitude of the processing that must be done and yields quick and generally reliable estimates

conditions that affect application are even completely beyond the control of the analyst as in the case of surveys which relate to policies around which there are powerful and conflicting interest groups.[2]

Some of the factors that lead to survey findings being brought properly to bear on larger problems of *theory* are also strictly speaking *not* the analytic skills of survey research. For example, effective communication is important. Here too, some of the considerations are beyond the control of the analyst. For example, the sheer accident of continuity or discontinuity in the work of other professionals affects the value of any specific survey finding for larger bodies of theory.

Such non-analytic considerations are outside of our discussion although they are exceedingly important for the analyst.[3] However, on the basis of Part I, the setting of social research, the analyst should have an increased sensitivity to the social forces which affect the likelihood of findings being acted upon. Only those aspects of the early and terminal stages of a survey wherein *analytic* functions can make a difference in the utilization of findings will be treated. Implicit in earlier chapters were certain procedures which aid in this connection, and while we shall refer to the procedures the technical discussion will not be repeated.

Unfortunately, the presentation will be deficient for there has been no systematic treatment of the problem in terms of principles derived from comprehensive study of many surveys. At least, we shall emphasize the need for special analytic procedures which maximize the utilization of survey findings. And through selected examples so chosen as to illustrate each of the major instances of the problem, the utilization either for theory or for application of either descriptive or explanatory survey findings, we shall suggest the direction for ultimate development of systematic principles.

---

of the larger findings. Quite often, however, the completed questionnaires are returned to the office in no particular order. Under such conditions, trial tabulations of the *first* returns may not be representative of the larger sample. Nevertheless, they can be used with caution and give some immediate guidance. For an example of such trial tabulations and their value for immediate policy decision, see: H. Alpert, "The Invalidation of Food Ration Currency, December, 1944," *J. Soc. Issues*, 3, #4, 1947, 40-48.

2. In this connection, it is interesting to note the comment made by one General Officer in the U.S. Army after reading the results of an attitude survey having to do with the integration of Negro Troops: "The study is quite general in its treatment of fundamental concepts and basic facts. Some conclusions appear supported by information obtained specifically for preconceived results, or by opinion and impression of the researcher. Information from which the deductions are drawn is from anonymous sources, without authentication, on some important issues 'volunteered'". Quoted by R. Davenport, "The Negro in the Army—A subject of Research," *J. Soc. Issues*, 3, #4, 1947, 32-39.

3. For a most interesting series of case studies of the relation of survey findings to political decisions, plus some inductive principles as to the factors increasing the likelihood of application, see: "Social Research in Political Decision," *J. Soc. Issues*, 3, 1947, Number 4.

For a general treatment of application of findings see Jahoda, Deutsch and Cook, *op. cit.*, Chaps. 10, 11; H. Zeisel, *Say it With Figures* (New York: Harpers, 1947), *passim;* or M. Parten, *op. cit.*, Chap. XVII.

CHAPTER VIII

Utilization of Descriptive Survey Findings and the Functions of the Analyst

WE SHALL present two problems in the application of descriptive survey findings for which special analytic procedures provide some solution.

The Application of Public Opinion Surveys to the Determination of Public Policy

Descriptive surveys cover a great many different phenomena and serve a variety of applied purposes. Often, the conclusions from such surveys are applied *without complication* to the action or policy requirements of particular sponsors. There is no problem, generally, in drawing the proper larger inferences from a descriptive survey on public information conducted for some agency, assuming the data have been effectively analyzed. A low level of information may provide evidence that a past educational campaign has been ineffective, or that a new campaign must be undertaken. An inquiry into the attitudes of a particular public on a specific governmental program of action already adopted may indicate the sources of opposition which act as hindrances to the smooth operations of the program, and may suggest a variety of measures to ameliorate such opposition. A similar type of inquiry may reveal that a contemplated administrative action should be modified if it is to receive a cordial reception. Inquiries of fact-finding nature as to level of employment, state of savings, medical needs, and the like provide clear guidance for the action agency. All such descriptive inquiries involve technical complexities, but these have been treated in Part II, and, granted their solution, there is little difficulty in making proper broader inferences from the specific conclusions.[1]

In all of these instances, either the directive for policy has already been established or is to be established on the basis of other considerations, and the survey results merely serve the *instrumental* function of aiding the action agency or administrator in achieving his general goals. This is not to disparage this function, because it is of great value, but to indicate its circumscribed character.

However, there is one type of descriptive survey in which the larger implications for action of the results must be examined very carefully, since great complication attends the extension of findings. In certain surveys high policy itself is to be guided by the results. As an illustration we shall treat descriptive surveys of *"public opinion,"* in which some defined population, generally, the *total adult population* or citizenry of the country, is queried and their *attitudes* on a variety of *political issues* are determined. Insofar as these results are to be extended or applied in some way, the actions to which they pertain are *political decisions or policies at a high level.* Either the issues relate to legislation which is already being considered, or presumably ought to be considered, or which possibly should be re-considered, or they relate to policy decisions to be taken by some administrative agency of government. Apart from the pure *theoretical* value of such data for those interested in problems of opinion formation and change, and their *journalistic* value, this is the only meaning of the great range of questions put in many national surveys which deal with such global matters as the public's feelings about American participation in the UN, the public's satisfaction with American policy toward Russia, what should be done about the atom bomb, etc. It is important for the analyst of such surveys to examine exactly how pertinent the results are to the political decision-making process, so that any extended conclusions he draws are appropriate. Moreover, insofar as he wishes to increase the pertinence of surveys to high policy he must design and conduct his analysis in a way that has political significance. We shall take up both these matters and seek an understanding of the complexity by turning

---

1. For a brief review of various governmental applications of survey research, see: A. Campbell, "The Uses of Interview Surveys in Federal Administration," *J. Soc. Issues*, 2, #2, 14-22; M. Kriesberg, "Opinion Research and Public Policy," *Int. J. Opin. Attit. Res.*, 3, 1949, 372-384; D. Truman, "Public Opinion Research as a Tool of Public Administration," *Publ. Admin. Rev.*, 5, 1945, 62-72.

our attention to the criticisms of opinion surveys by political scientists. These criticisms implicitly incorporate a view of the political process which involves first, an appraisal of the *realities* of decision making, and second, a normative conception of the way in which democracy should *ideally* function. To the degree that the opinion survey is not analyzed in relation to political realities, the results will be irrelevant to the decision maker; to the degree that the sheer surveying of public opinion and the *usual analysis of data* violate an ideal conception of democratic functioning, it might be regarded as not merely irrelevant, but pernicious.

From the examination of these criticisms we can then develop a set of tentative principles for the modes of analysis of descriptive opinion surveys which will make such results more relevant to decision makers, *if that be our goal*,[2] plus some modes of analysis which will serve better the ideal political process, and finally a sense of the proper limits to be put upon opinion survey findings. It may appear that we impute too much validity to these criticisms, some of which may be polemic in character. Moreover, the analysis of the decision-making process that we use as a guide may itself be fallible. However, since we will examine a considerable number of such views, both from friends and enemies of the institution of survey research, and appraise the views cautiously, the danger is not great.

1. Political Realities and Modes of Analysis

Most obvious as a starting point for our discussion is the fact that politics involves the operation of pressures or influences or power to which decision makers may accommodate willingly or at least must consider in some degree in deciding on the probable opposition to a given decision.

For example, Schlesinger remarks in the context of a review of Strunk and Cantril's *Public Opinion* that a decision by a statesman "is generally the result of an accommodation between his own views of what is wise and the felt pressures upon him as to what is possible." Similarly, Binkley in the context of a review of Bruner's *Mandate from the People,* a book based on public opinion data, quotes as a definition of politics "the translation of social pressures into public policies." So too, Rogers in a treatment of public opinion surveys and their relation to politics quotes such remarks as typifying political reality as "most legislation . . . represents the insistence of a

---

2. We qualify this suggestion, for it may well be that accommodating survey research to these realities only makes more efficient an *undesirable* feature of current political decision-making. Thus, we shall shortly see that one criticism of survey research is that it ignores the political *power* behind the opinions of each respondent, the very element that may make a legislator responsive to an expression of opinion. By designing surveys to differentiate results in such terms makes them more relevant but perpetuates this state of affairs. One argument in behalf of surveys has always been that it gives expression to the inarticulate and the impotent, thus serving a desirable goal, if perhaps one that is somewhat academic in terms of power conflicts as they affect politics.

compact and formidable minority."[3] Elsewhere he remarks "constitutional governments not infrequently take action when conscious, informed, and vigorous minorities demand it and are able to have their way because the majority, although not in favor of the action, is confused or indifferent." Later he quotes Bryce "ten men who care are a match for a hundred who do not."

Rogers reminds us that this feature of politics does not merely represent an ugly reality. Pressures *should be* considered because "the task of government . . . is . . . to effect adjustments among the various special wills and purposes which at any given time are pressing for realization. Decisions that are reached have to be accepted, and without a broad basis of consent, democracy does not work."

Given this as the reality, these same writers criticize public opinion surveys for their neglect of these considerations. And it should be noted that these criticisms are not exercised indiscriminately, for praise is given the polls where it is due. Thus, Binkley praises Bruner's book in many ways, and nowhere criticizes its technical features. Binkley remarks on the "pioneering venture"; how "skillfully" the data are treated; the "imposing appearance" of the body of data; the provision of a technical appendix covering the research procedures underlying the data which provides "precisely what one wants to know"; on "how fascinating" certain findings are; on the evidence of "emerging methods of testing the strength of public conviction." Yet he expresses some misgivings in the light of his knowledge of the *historical and political context in which policy must be formulated.*

With respect to data that Bruner presents showing preponderant support for the Spanish Republic rather than for Franco, he remarks in appraising Roosevelt's policy of nevertheless withholding military supplies from the Loyalists that this popular support did not matter, and that the minority:

> was mainly Catholic—an integrated, organized dynamic pressure group, holding balances of power in plenty of congressional districts. The pro-Republic Americans, though three-times as numerous, were dispersed among many Protestants and other elements who doubtless "meant well feebly." . . . Moreover, only one voter in six favored lifting the embargo by changing the Neutrality Act so as to send aid to the Spanish Loyalists. The policy carried out then represented not so much a "mandate from the people" as an *absence* of one.[4]

Binkley summarizes his position: "opinion polls consist of no more than a counting of heads in utter disregard of the 'social pressures' they may or may not represent. Such counts are inevitably heavily weighted with the masses of the politically uninfluential. Moreover, the effortless response to the inter-

---

3. A. Schlesinger, Jr., Review of M. Strunk and H. Cantril, *loc. cit.*; W. E. Binkley, "Mandate by Polls," *Publ. Opin. Quart.*, 8, 1944, 425-429; L. Rogers, *The Pollsters* (New York: Knopf, 1949), pp. 32-33, 46-47.

4. *Op. cit.*, Reprinted by permission of the publishers.

viewer's question provides no measure of the will to do anything about the matter, even as much as going to the polls and casting a ballot."

This same notion of political reality and the corresponding limitation of opinion surveys for policy-making is expressed by Kriesberg, a survey research specialist himself. Moreover, his position on the limitation of surveys is taken despite full awareness of sophisticated research techniques which we shall see provide some *approximate* solution to these political problems:

> Polls do not reflect the weight of political power within the nation, and power is basic to governance. Polls may measure relative intensity of feeling on specific issues, but there is no necessary relation between expressed attitudes and political action. . . . Another reason to question the validity of poll findings as a mandate is the great difference in political power among individuals. While each person can cast but a single ballot and therefore the opinion of each is of equal political importance in the election booth, most issues are not decided by referendum. In the absence of a popular referendum on a given issue, the opinion of a newspaper editor or radio commentator, a big ranch owner, manufacturer or trade union leader, is far more important politically than that of an average worker or farm hand. Politicians guide themselves by the balance of political power in their constituency; the public opinion polls are not designed to gauge that balance. The politicians weigh the complex forces involved in an issue and act in accordance with the public will, the *weight of opinion* rather than the majority of individual views. While the democratic ideal of political equality is advanced by polls, suggestions that it might be attained through polling fail to take into account the realities and requirements of organized political society.[5]

In a more extreme form, Blumer, in a well known paper on public opinion polling, makes this general argument one of his central criticisms of current survey research. He remarks on the "differences in prestige, position, and influence that characterize groups and individuals" and contends that polls do not and even *cannot* describe a respondent in terms of the "significance of him or of his opinion in the public opinion that is being built up or which is expressing itself functionally in the operation of society." [6]

So, too, Cottrell and Eberhart, the analysts of one of the major surveys we have discussed throughout the text, concerned with a matter of overpowering political importance, the atom bomb, indicate that while opinion surveys have many uses, they also have certain limitations. They note that "indifference, disparities in education, and variations in sense of social responsibility are facts of our political life that exercise their own influences. Certainly each person's opinions or preferences do not exercise the same force. Nor is any given individual or group as influential for some issues or circumstances as for others." In this connection, their implicit

---

5. M. Kriesberg, *op. cit.*, pp. 376, italics ours.
6. H. Blumer, "Public Opinion and Public Opinion Polling," *Amer. Soc. Rev.*, 13, 1948, 542-549.

recommendation for the researcher is an awareness of the separation between certain spheres of politics and public opinion. "The opinion surveys have taken as their province the study of the public as a whole, not the study of 'pressures' or special influences, which manifest themselves directly and are in themselves major areas of investigation." Elsewhere they remark with respect to opinion survey data, "the error . . . is not in attaching significance to public opinion; it is rather in assuming that public opinion must function as a directive." [7]

Granted the legitimacy of this view of politics and admitting certain limitations on the political function that opinion surveys can have, it might be asked whether this inadequacy is irremediable. Perhaps, opinion surveys can be so designed and so analyzed that the *opinions expressed can be weighed in terms of some "coefficient of power"* behind the individual or group opinion. In this connection it is interesting to note that while Blumer, one of the critics cited earlier, suggests that the difficulty is insuperable, the discussants of that original paper disagree. Both Newcomb and Woodward remark on a number of obvious ways of manipulating opinion data so as to express the variations in the weight of opinions. We shall indicate some approximate solutions.[8]

In a rudimentary sense, all public opinion research conducted by the major research organizations takes this problem into account, by decision *to exclude certain groups from the definition of the population* to be covered or sampled. None of the research agencies samples children, and many public opinion surveys limit themselves to voters or to citizens. In effect, the weight given to the excluded groups is *zero* on the assumption that these groups carry no influence whatsoever or ought not to carry any influence and therefore that their opinions should not be incorporated into the survey. We have already treated in Chapter III of the problems of the relevant population for an inquiry and shall not pursue the discussion further. It provides a first approximation for bringing surveys into accord with political realities.

For groups that have zero weight, the analyst's problem is relatively simple. However, included within the survey data are a variety of opinions from individuals and groups, all having *some* political weight, but each differing in the amount of weight behind the opinion. The analyst *can differentiate his results in such a way as to convey the variations within this remaining group.* Within the descriptive survey, *cross-tabulation of the data by various factual characteristics* provides some evidence on this problem. The usual sub-group characterizations do have some political significance,

7. Cottrell and Eberhart, *op. cit.,* pp. 3, 4, 10. All quotations are reprinted by permission of the publishers.

8. T. M. Newcomb and J. Woodward, Discussion of the Blumer paper, *Amer. Soc. Rev.,* 13, 1948, 549-554.

and differentiated descriptions by sex, age, region, size of place, race or economic level give some clue to the weight of the opinions politically.
Membership in one of these *categories* is some index of the political significance of the person and his opinions. More important, measuring *membership in some functioning group* provides an even better clue to the weight
to be given to certain opinions in survey data. Thus it is that the factual
data may often include the person's affiliation with a given political party,
or his membership in a union or church or in some voluntary association.
Differentiation of the data for sub-groups representing such memberships
is a desirable practice in opinion surveys intended for policy determination.
We have already treated in Chapter III the general technique of differentiation of the aggregate description, and raised problems as to what characteristics are meaningful to use for such purposes. We shall not pursue this discussion and merely indicate its relevance for providing a second approximation for bringing surveys into accord with political realities.

However, there are still other grounds upon which a person's opinion
can or should have especial weight in influencing political decisions. These
grounds are more subtle and not represented by any standard operating
procedures for the choice of population and sub-group descriptions. Within
the mass of opinions are expressions by individuals who are apathetic, who
do not bother to vote, who will never write to a Congressman, whose hostilities to a contemplated course of action are weak and easily dissipated,
whose opinions are easily swayed. The pressures of such opinions on the political process will never be felt, and the analysis must provide some clue to
these factors underlying some of the collected opinions. Now while the
usual demographic clues provide some clue to such psychological aspects of
the individual, they are only crude indicators. As a third approximation for
bringing surveys into accord with such realities, direct measures of *a variety
of dimensions of opinions and attitudes must be incorporated into the design and analysis of the survey.* Here again we have treated the problem in
Chapter III and have discussed such dimensions of attitude as intensity,
strength, stability. The measurement of such aspects at the individual level
will permit the analyst to accompany his description of the *content* findings
with data on their political import.

2. Political Ideals and Modes of Analysis

Apart from questions of the *power* behind the opinions that are enumerated in surveys, and the relevance of such considerations for practical
matters of politics, many writers note that not all opinions constitute wise
directives for political decisions. For example, opinions ought to be differentiated, if democracy is to function effectively, in terms of opinion that is
informed, that is derived after mature *reflection* about the consequences,
that is *not predicated merely on narrow, selfish interest,* that *following in-*

teraction leads to moderation and accommodation to the viewpoints of others.

Critics of the use of opinion polls as guides to political decision-making argue that such factors are not carefully enough considered in analyzing and reporting data from surveys. Thus with respect to *informed* opinion, Rogers remarks: "The public's lack of information on certain important issues suggests that in many cases the pollsters should have viewed their percentages with suspicion and should have boldly declared that there was no opinion for them to try to measure." [9] Cartwright, a survey research expert, makes the same general point: "Public opinion polls which go to the people and ask them to choose among specific proposals for the solution of these detailed problems actually force many people to make pronouncements upon matters about which they know little." Cartwright notes that this problem not only has political implications, but should concern the technician as well since "when information is meager, minor variations in the wording of the question can produce widely different answers. Surely, an administrator can be seriously misled if he follows uncritically the majority opinion registered in a poll without knowing the level of information . . . associated with that opinion." [10]

On this particular problem, *the knowledge behind the preferences,* the implications for the analyst and designer of surveys are clear, and the technical solutions straightforward. First, a limited class of *issues involving technical or esoteric knowledge might better never be the subject of survey research.*

Leaving aside such issues, the principles advanced in Chapters II and III about the restriction of the universe, differentiation of the description, and conceptualizing a phenomenon as involving cognitive structures as well as attitudinal structures provide a general solution for the analyst. For the issues that should be posed in surveys, the opinion findings should be *differentiated in terms of the knowledgeability* of the respondents. This can be accomplished in a variety of ways. A crude approximation is provided by *cross-tabulation of the replies by formal education,* a routine item in the factual sheet of most surveys. Finer approximations are provided by the incorporation of special *questions* on awareness of the issue, specific knowledge of it, concern about it, discussion of it, etc. In such instances, either the opinion questions are *only* put to the sub-group who have some familiarity (a technique known as filtering), or the opinions can be differentiated in terms of level of information of the respondents by cross-tabulation of the knowledge and opinion questions.

A procedure that is used all too rarely, but one that often provides a so-

9. L. Rogers, *op. cit.,* p. 141.

10. D. Cartwright, "Public Opinion Polls and Democratic Leadership," *J. Soc. Issues,* 2, #2, 1946, 23-32. Reprinted by permission of the publishers.

lution to the problem, is to *limit the population* sampled to a more restricted group which has some basis of knowledge or experience. The results then uniformly apply to a level of at least minimally informed opinion.

So much for the strictly informational basis of opinions. But there are other requirements for appraising what opinions are worthy of political consideration. Arbuthnot in a critique of opinion research as it relates to British politics, titles her paper *"Democracy by Snap Judgment"* to convey the fact that . . . "the snap judgment of the public on isolated questions or part-questions will obtrude itself uneasily and perhaps disproportionately in the minds of legislators considering long-term or main policies." Later she elaborates the point by noting that the *timing* of a public controversy by leadership is a matter of great importance. "It must not be done until *sufficient inside information has been made public to enable the public to form a reasoned opinion.* . . . The organizers of polls, however, may be quite irresponsible in timing such questions. They decide whether to put questions on the powers and composition of the House of Lords, before or after debate in the House has clarified the various arguments; how long to wait after nationalization of an industry before asking the public whether they think it is a success." [11] If we ignore the fundamental criticism of the entire *institution* of opinion surveys on matters of politics, we realize that, thus far, Arbuthnot is arguing that the expression of opinion that has significance is one based on reflection, and consideration of the relevant context. But elsewhere she suggests yet another condition underlying expressions of opinion that would have some validity for public policy:

> Policy making is a complicated process of weighing a series of interlocking problems. To take the simplest sort of example, it may be clear to a Chancellor of the Exchequer that a particular and apparently desirable policy—say an increase in old age pensions—may involve an increase in the rate of taxation. He will put this view to the Cabinet and decisions will be taken in the light of it. Meanwhile the public without being unduly stupid might, on two separate polls, have expressed a desire for an increase in the old age pension and for a reduction in taxation. There is no way of making policy by *ad hoc voting on specific questions.* . . . It will never be possible to replace the representational system of modern democracy by direct voting because obviously you must have a small group to make policy, to supply the thread of consistency and to sort out the main from the subsidiary issues.

Again, if we ignore the radical criticism of the institution of surveys, we see that Arbuthnot is suggesting that the opinion on any specific issue must be weighed in the light of the interlocking issues that are related, and that issues in a survey must not be posed in such a manner that they are isolated from their proper context.

What principles can the analyst consider in design and analysis of his

---

11. H. Arbuthnot, "Democracy by Snap Judgment," *The Listener,* March 4, 1948, 367-368, italics ours. Reprinted by permission of the author.

survey that will help approximate to the requirements that Arbuthnot states? We note first of all that the principle we raised in Chapter III of the *temporal location* of the phenomenon is most relevant. There, however, we did not stress the political implications and merely noted that for theoretical reasons the timing of a survey was important for the analyst to consider. Obviously, where the analyst has some special purpose in studying opinion *formation,* he may well decide to conduct a survey prior to an issue being widely discussed. However, he would then qualify his findings in the light of the timing of the inquiry. Where he has no special interest in problems of opinion formation, he would follow the implications of Arbuthnot's remarks and conduct the survey at a much later point in time.

The timing of the survey, however, only provides a crude approximation for solving the problem posed. It merely defines in a gross way the fact that *all* respondents have had the *possibility* of predicating their opinions on the basis of some reflection and information.

A procedure that has been too rarely employed is one that has been labelled "Deliberative Technique," and it provides some approximate solution to the problem. In this procedure, the interviewer leaves a printed form of the questionnaire with the respondent, and returns only after some period of time to conduct the actual interview. Presumably the passage of time has permitted the respondent to reflect on the issues presented in the questionnaire.[12]

There is also some possibility of treating the same problem by manipulation of the questionnaire.[13] It is quite common, for example, to present respondents with a short statement of facts upon which they are, in turn, to express an opinion. Conceiving of the questionnaire not merely as an avenue for the solicitation of the respondent's views, but as an experimental instrument for the presentation of various stimuli opens up many possibilities for approximating conditions which will meet Arbuthnot's objections.

Nevertheless, there may still be many respondents who have not carefully considered the information that was *objectively* available on the issue that was posed, and the analyst should be able to differentiate opinions within the aggregate data that are reflective or deliberative from those that

---

12. We attribute this procedure to Helen Verner Huth who conducted, under a grant-in-aid from NORC and with the direction of Don Cahalan, a methodological study of the effect of opportunities to deliberate vs. no such opportunity on the results obtained in an opinion survey. *The Effect of a Deliberative Interviewing Technique on a Public Opinion Survey,* Unpublished Master's Essay, University of Denver, 1949. The procedure is clearly to be distinguished from the usual *mail* questionnaire or *self-administered* questionnaire. The mail questionnaire provides opportunities for deliberation but is subject to well known difficulties of bias due to non-response and has other limitations, use among illiterates, etc. The self-administered questionnaire has no properties of deliberation in the way that it is *usually* employed, and eliminates the gain of procedures of probing, etc., which the interviewer can contribute.

13. For an example of such manipulation to test the effect of experimentally presented information, see: H. Hyman and P. B. Sheatsley, "Some Reasons Why Informations Campaigns Fail," *op. cit.*

are not. Consequently, the analyst incorporates into the study, questions covering such matters as whether or not the respondent has discussed the issue, considered it, read or heard about it, how certain he feels in his judgment, etc. By simple cross-tabulation, descriptive data can be differentiated for sub-groups varying in these respects.

Arbuthnot's other objection—that opinions on specific issues are obtained in isolation from the context of related policy questions—is not difficult to deal with *in principle*, but, in practice, has created many problems. We have commented frequently in earlier portions of this manuscript on the institutionalization of given procedures in survey research, and on the conflict in goals that the analyst experiences. Traditionally, the concern of the analyst has been with the measurement of attitudes; the measurement being as *purified* as is possible from pressures of a social and psychological sort. Witness the concern for studying hot and explosive social issues with questions that are not loaded or biased, for measuring opinions under conditions where the respondent is anonymous and free of any fear of punishment for expressing a deviant opinion, for obtaining an opinion uncontaminated by conflicting issues. A question is never double-barreled—the context of questions in the interview is such that other issues are not raised. All these procedures were developed historically for good reason, but they may be inappropriate for survey research with other objectives. Yet because they are historically rooted, they are applied as standard operating procedure. One can in principle manipulate the questionnaire or even a few questions so that a series of other issues are treated prior to the discussion of a specific issue.[14] Then the opinion that is expressed by the respondent is in its proper political setting.

This procedure would provide all respondents with *objective* opportunities to express a more meaningful opinion from Arbuthnot's point of view. However, one could also deal with the same problem for sub-classes of respondents by technique of open-ended questions in which the broader considerations that the respondent might *naturally* include in forming his opinion would be elicited. On the basis of such data, differentiated descriptions could be obtained for sub-groups of respondents varying in the degree to which their opinions were rooted in a larger political context.

But in the judgment of various writers, still another condition attaches to opinions which would have some validity for the political process. We noted in another context in Chapter III Schlesinger's distinction between *responsible* and *irresponsible* opinion. He remarked that the polls collect expressions of opinion that are "irresponsible because no action is intended to follow. The expression of opinion is not burdened, in other words, by a

---

14. For a discussion of survey procedures as they bear on such problems plus empirical evidence on the influence of related issues in changing results on specific questions, see: H. Hyman, "Inconsistencies," *op. cit.*

sense of accountability for consequences; when that sense of accountability enters; then the expression may very likely be different." [15] But Schlesinger is not alone in this position. The identical point is made by Arbuthnot. In discussing various poll questions, she remarks that the respondent "had not expected to assume *responsibility* on the question." And Rogers implies the same basic point when he refers to the apathetic groups in the population who do not vote: "What weight should be given opinions about which men and women care so little that they do not bother to take a small amount of trouble in order to express them?" [16] We noted earlier that policy makers weigh popular opinions in relation to the degree of influence or power or pressure accompanying the opinion, but this concept of *responsible* opinion should be clearly distinguished from the naked power behind an opinion.

What these writers are alluding to is not the exercising of a *selfish* opinion or the willingness to take strong action to implement some *private* goal. True, they refer to willingness to take action for and to bear the many and varied consequences arising from a decision, but implicit here is also the notion that the popular support for the decision is not merely on narrow, selfish grounds.

Similarly, we have already discussed the degree to which opinions are informed. Obviously there is a relationship between informed and responsible opinion. By definition, a man cannot have been willing to bear certain consequences when he expressed himself if he were unaware of the events that might flow from the decision. But while knowledge increases the likelihood that the opinion is responsible, there is more to it than that, for a person can be aware of the consequences of a decision without being willing to bear some responsibility.

Now while the concept involved is quite particular, the technical *procedures* the analyst might employ to treat the problem are in general the same as we have already discussed. The measurement of such dimensions as intensity and the like provide some approximate solution in that the analyst could estimate the willingness to take action in behalf of some policy. The measurement of opinions in a questionnaire containing a context of related issues would approximate the requirement that the varied consequences of a decision be known by the respondent and that the specific opinion be predicated on this ground.

A great deal can also be done via manipulation of the *specific question* so as to measure opinions in particular contexts. The question can be couched in terms of the narrow frame of reference of the respondent or in terms of the frame of reference of others in the society.[17]

---

15. A. Schlesinger, Jr., *op. cit.*
16. L. Rogers, *op. cit.*, p. 83.
17. For an experimental demonstration of the effect of varying the frame of reference from a personalized to a more altruistic one and its effects on results, see: S. Payne, "Some Opinion Research Principles," *op. cit.*

A specific question can contain a statement of facts or probable contingencies so as to obtain an opinion based on awareness of at least *hypothetical* consequences. Of course, here one must recognize that technical difficulties accompany such question formulations and that mere phrases about a consequence may have little reality for the respondent. Arbuthnot presents us with an example of such a question formulation in Britain and argues that it is but a poor approximation of the real thing. The question was: "If the tax on U.S.A. films means that we get no more American films after a few months should the tax remain or be removed?" And she remarks: "How many people have any idea how many British films can be made or how much the loss of American films will restrict their cinema-going or what effect paying for American films will have on food-queues." [18]

However, none of these procedures meets the problem of measurement of opinions that are *responsible* in the sense that they are not exclusively private and selfish views. Here, it might well be that one solution would be in the *selection* of issues to be posed in a survey. Rogers suggests that "when the pressing problems are where, which, and how much services shall be provided, the populace is not the proper deciding organ. The matters to be passed on are . . . too close to the selfish interests of local or economic groupings." [19]

Cartwright notes that while certain issues are not reacted to in terms of selfish interest, policies may even be supported *contrary to the best interests* of the individual or the society. Such is the case when the question *"engages"* some extraneous value or psychological process and the person is enticed into support for the decision on so-to-speak irrational grounds. Here again the opinion would not be responsible in that it is certain that the individual would not want to bear unforeseen consequences which jeopardized him. He cites the example of the sales tax. "Economists agree that it is regressive, placing a heavier burden on those least able to pay. That the little man does not recognize this fact and is for some reason enticed into supporting the tax in a poll seems poor reason to impose it upon him." [20]

All this is not to suggest that the analyst should never study opinions rooted in private interest or opinions that rest on irrational grounds. He may have good reasons for inquiries of this type. However, where surveys are to be instrumental for *policy-making*, he might either exclude such issues from study, or in treating the results in such areas, he would analyze the basis of the opinions in order to convey their real meaning for the policy-maker.

There is one final condition which these various writers argue is appro-

---

18. *Op. cit.*
19. *Op. cit.*, p. 69.
20. D. Cartwright, *op. cit.*, p. 26.

priate to policy-making in relation to the popular will. All emphasize that the proper role of political leadership is not merely the direct implementation of the popular will. Yes, Public Opinion must be considered, but leadership must be consistent, wise, inventive, and creative. In the instance of some of these writers, it is felt that the very institution of the publication of opinion surveys constitutes a pressure preventing leadership from fulfilling its proper role. Arbuthnot presents this point of view:

> What will happen if upon this existing system we superimpose a system of public opinion sampling on *ad hoc* questions? I submit that, first of all, it will become increasingly difficult for any government to plan and carry out any consistent policy at all and that, apart from the chaos which this will create at home, it will make it virtually impossible for Britain to play any important part in international politics. . . . The only question therefore is what influence the publication of the results of public opinion polls may have on the elected policy-makers. Surely in the long run it can only be an influence towards vacillation, timidity and lack of policy. The snap judgment of the public on isolated questions or part-questions will obtrude itself uneasily and perhaps disproportionately in the minds of legislators considering long-term or main policies. There is a risk that they will become the straws that flutter in every breeze. . . . We should ask ourselves what the value of the answers is, what is the effect on our elected representatives and their policy, and above all whether in the name of democracy, any non-elected organization should wield power of such potential force. It is at least arguable that opinion and political polls should only be sponsored, or should at least be supervised by a body responsible to the House of Commons, so that we may have some democratic control over this powerful new instrument which has been hailed as the new voice of democracy.[21]

With respect to this problem, there are no technical procedures which the analyst can employ. The criticism is fundamental to the very process of opinion research as it bears on public policy. All that the analyst can do is present his general findings as a factual description rather than as a directive to be followed automatically.

The detailed treatment of modes of analysis appropriate to public opinion surveys which are designed for the determination of public policy constitutes but one illustration of the general need for special analytic procedures which maximize the application of descriptive surveys. On the basis of comprehensive study, analogous principles will have to be developed for effective analysis of descriptive surveys designed for private policy determination, e.g., market research surveys, studies of consumer wants, or industrial surveys. Perforce, we must omit such a comprehensive treatment for

---

21. Arbuthnot, *op. cit.* While the rejection of the institution of opinion surveys for policy-making is not categorical among the other writers we have discussed, all agree that there is a problem in the proper relationship between leadership and the popular will as expressed in surveys. See comments by Binkley, Cartwright, Kriesberg, Rogers, and Schlesinger. In the paper by Barkin, cited earlier, the same general problem is raised in the context of the relationship between labor leadership and the opinions expressed by rank-and-file in opinion surveys.

the present. However, we shall present one example of a rather general problem of application in descriptive surveys from these other fields. The problem is solved by the development of a very simple but, nevertheless, frequently neglected analytic procedure.

Distinguishing Repetitive Instances of Behavioral Phenomena in Descriptive Surveys Intended for Application

In descriptive surveys concerned with phenomena of a *behavioral or objective* nature, a problem which affects the proper application of the findings is that of *repetitive tendencies within a given individual*. The problem is relatively simple in nature and easily dealt with technically, but neglect of it is frequent and can produce misleading conclusions for action or policy. Many descriptive surveys are concerned with the determination of the magnitude of some entity in a population. Take, for example, such undesirable conditions as unemployment, illness, absenteeism, apathy, or ignorance on which surveys might be conducted. If the phenomenon is widespread, some remedial action is suggested. Or consider some desirable condition such as extensive health insurance coverage in the population, or large financial assets, or widespread book reading. If the phenomenon is widespread, the action agency is happy and merely pursues its former course. The analyst in conducting descriptive surveys on such phenomena, however, could pose the question to be answered in one of two ways. *What is the extent of such a phenomenon in the total population under study? What is the number or proportion of people in that population who exhibit the phenomenon?* For certain types of surveys, both questions lead to the identical result and the problem is academic. These are surveys where the phenomenon is conceived of in a unitary way and there is only one possible occurrence of it per respondent. All public opinion or attitude surveys are of this type. True a man may be more or less radical on some scale of measurement— more or less informed or apathetic, but the measurement of his characteristic only enters once into the total. Consequently, whether one adds up the number of people who exhibit the phenomenon or adds up the occurrences of the phenomenon ignoring the question of specific people, one comes to the same sum or end-result. However, there are other types of surveys where the end result is different depending on which of the two questions about magnitude is posed. These are surveys where *each* individual can exhibit *repetitive* instances of the phenomenon. For example, one wealthy respondent may have four health insurance policies and his behavior could enter into a survey description of coverage against illness four times, with quite misleading implications for the problem of the nation's health. The total extent of a phenomenon in the population may therefore be very large in particular surveys, but the total number of people exhibiting the phenomenon may be very small if a particular group of individuals is involved in most of the occurrences. In such instances the policy maker may be seriously misled if the analyst does not clearly distinguish the two results.[22]

One of our cases illustrates a phenomenon of such a repetitive nature. In the inquiry into industrial absenteeism, it is clear that the severity of the problem and the type of action to be taken in relation to the problem is best gauged by presenting *both* the total extent of absenteeism, e.g., number of man-days lost, and the distribution of incidence of multiple absences on the part of the same workers for these two statements are quite different in their implications. Katz and Hyman report that repetitive absences among a small group of workers was very characteristic. Thus "When one examined the total amount of absenteeism in the samples of workers drawn, one found that 40% of the rank and file respondents contributed *none* of the absences, and the worst 10% of the sample contributed 54% of the total amount of time lost." [23]

Incidental data in one of our other cases, the radio inquiry, provides many illustrations of the distinction between these two approaches to the magnitude of some phenomenon. In that inquiry, for example, 91% of the sample owned at least one radio. However, if one examines the distribution of number of radios per home, one notes that 10% of the sample had three or more radios in their homes.[24]

None of our other cases provides any illustration of the problem but dramatic examples can be cited from many other surveys. Communications Research often shows repetitive phenomena of exposure being located in a very narrow group within the population. For example, in one survey of book reading, approximately one-third of the national sample accounted for 94% of all the books read in the country.[25] In another such survey one-tenth of the population accounted for more than two-thirds of all book reading.[26]

---

22. For a general treatment of the problem of statistical devices for its solution see, H. Zeisel, *Say it with Figures, op. cit.*, chap. II.

23. Katz and Hyman, *op. cit.*, p. 18.

24. Lazarsfeld and Field, *op. cit.*, p. 96.

25. H. C. Link and H. A. Hopf, *People and Books*, A Study of Reading and Book Buying Habits (New York: Book Industry Committee, 1946).

26. A. Campbell and C. Metzner, Books, Libraries, and other Media of Communication, in D. Katz, *et al* (ed.) *Public Opinion and Propaganda* (New York: Dryden Press, 1954), 235-242. The findings are also reported in B. Berelson, *The Library's Public* (New York: Columbia University Press, 1949), Chap. I.

CHAPTER IX

Utilization of Explanatory
Survey Findings and the
Functions of the Analyst

IN MANY places in our earlier discussion, distinctions have been made among explanatory surveys. The explanatory survey designed to verify some hypothesis relevant to some larger body of theory has been distinguished from the diagnostic survey designed to explore some novel problem or the evaluative survey designed as a test of the practical value of some action program or the programmatic survey designed to guide the most effective application of a future action program. Correspondingly, the analytic principles thus far presented were qualified in terms of relevance to explanatory surveys which aim at the utilization of the data for one rather than another of these purposes.[1] However, the analytic procedures that were treated were relatively general in character. Consequently, we shall present three detailed examples of more special problems of utilization of explanatory survey findings for application or theory and particular analytic procedures that are helpful.

---

1. See the section of Part III, General Principles for the Elaboration of Explanatory Analyses.

Gauging the Practical Significance of Cross-Tabulations in Explanatory Surveys Conducted for Applied Purposes

In Part III, we emphasized strongly that the basic element of all explanatory survey analysis is the cross tabulation. In employing cross tabulations, however, the analyst must always keep in mind the central distinction in the goals of different types of explanatory surveys for depending on the purpose, the same exact cross-tabulation must be evaluated differently. Where the explanatory survey is intended to lead to action, to deliberate change in some situation, the *practical* significance of the cross-tabulation must be treated. Where the survey is theoretical, such considerations can be ignored. The point appears platitudinous, but it is too often neglected. The heavy historical emphasis on cross-tabulation procedures in explanatory surveys and the search for factors that correlate highly with some phenomenon generally leads the analyst to value cross-tabulations in proportion to the size of the differences that is demonstrated. But the size of the difference may be a very misleading guide to the *practical* importance of the finding.

The problem can be illustrated by an example from one of our case studies, Centers' inquiry into class consciousness. Here the goal of the explanatory part of his survey was to demonstrate the relationship between politico-economic orientation and various measures of class position. We reproduce below a portion of one of the cross-tabulations that was conducted.

Class Identification	Percent who are "ultra-conservative"
Upper Class	42%
Middle Class	35
Working Class	12
Lower Class	0

Such a cross-tabulation is most unusual in social research, for the relation of the phenomenon of ideology to the respondent's class identification is striking. The difference in percentage points between contrasted groups, in this instance between the magnitude of ultra-conservatism in the upper as compared with the lower classes, is far greater than is usually obtained in the run of social surveys. The student need only look at some of the tables presented earlier in this text to confirm this fact. Consequently, the analyst in a survey intended for *theoretical purposes* would be exceedingly happy and he would draw the conclusion that his hypothesis is confirmed and that he has one of the central keys to a man's ideology. Apart from technical statistical procedures of testing whether or not the difference could be accounted for on grounds of sampling variance, or reporting some measure of the association between the characteristics, or examining the finding to make sure that it was not an artifact, the conclusion would be legitimate. But this particular cross-tabulation takes on a totally different meaning in an *applied* survey. We present below the distribution of class identification in Centers' total sample to illustrate a consideration that the analyst might otherwise overlook.

	Percent of Total Sample
Upper Class	3%
Middle Class	44
Working Class	52
Lower Class	1
N =	1073

It is clear from the juxtaposition of the two tables that while an identification with the upper or lower class has powerful consequences on a man's ideology, such identifications are *so rare* that they have little significance at a practical level. The finding is so-to-speak striking, but academic! Centers' own comment is appropriate to the problem. He remarks that since the middle and working classes "are *numerically the two principal classes in the class system,* this . . . makes it seem reasonable to regard the *difference between them as constituting the principal line of cleavage* in the social body." [2]

The principle is simple, although often neglected. As a first approximation we might state it as follows: In explanatory surveys which have practical implications, the cross-tabulation must be assessed by reference *both to the relationship demonstrated with an independent variable and the numerical size of the groups* exhibiting given values of the independent variable.[3] The point becomes even clearer if we construct a hypothetical and extreme case. Let us suppose in a given survey that the presence of attribute A changed opinions by 70 percentage points, but that there was only one such individual in the entire population. The difference is tremendous but *effectively* is zero because a minority of one person counts for so little and it is not likely that this attribute will increase in frequency in the population.[4]

We present below some examples from our other case studies. In each of the three instances, we have a relationship that is unusually dramatic for survey research. The variation in the phenomenon with a change in the value of the independent variable is striking and large. However, in each of these instances the finding, although of significance at a

2. R. Centers, *op. cit.,* p. 120, italics ours.

3. The student should distinguish between such an appraisal of the numerical size of the sub-groups, and the consideration of the number of cases in a test of significance. In the latter instance, it is true the size of the group enters into the statistical calculation, but once the test has been performed, the analyst ignores whether given sub-groups were small or large.

4. We, of course, are making some assumption about the relation between mutability and rarity, but it does not seem too far fetched to argue that anything that occurs so rarely in the society under natural conditions is going to be difficult to propagate.

THE RADIO INQUIRY [5]

Among Rural People	Percent who show an evening program preference for "classical music"
College educated	49%
High school educated	24
Grammar school educated	12

ATOM BOMB INQUIRY [6]

	Percent who believe that secret of manufacturing atomic bomb is known to other countries
Highly informed	75%
Highly uninformed	34

	Percent who believe we should try to work out system of international control of bomb
Highly informed	62%
Highly uninformed	30

theoretical level as revealing a determinant, is somewhat academic. In the atom bomb inquiry, the highly informed only constitute 8% of the total sample, and in the radio inquiry, the proportion of college educated only constitute about 15% of the total rural group.

Thus far we have oversimplified the problem. It is clear that the numerical strength of a group is one index of its practical relevance for social change, but it is obviously a crude index. A factor that is found to be a determinant of some phenomenon might be of practical importance even if the subgroup exhibiting it was small, *providing that the group had some other strategic significance.* Strength or importance can be predicated on numbers, but it can also be predicated on other grounds. For example, under certain conditions, a small group might have great *political power* in which case any finding about the variation in the phenomenon in this group would not be academic. Consequently, the analyst must appraise the practical implications of a cross-tabulation in terms of whatever other criteria besides numbers seem appropriate. It is difficult to define such criteria in any formal way. The analyst must simply be alerted to the special importance of examining the subgroups who exhibit given values of an independent variable for their relevance to action or policy.

This same problem of assessing cross-tabulations for their practical significance takes on a number of different forms. The social consequences of a given determinant are dependent not only on the *numerical strength* or *strategic importance* of given sub-groups, but also on the *manipulability* of

5. Lazarsfeld and Field, *op. cit.,* p. 140.
6. Cottrell and Eberhart, *op. cit.,* pp. 102, 115.

an independent variable.[7] Our case study of opinions on the atom bomb implicitly reveals the application of such a principle in the analysis. The independent variable that organizes the entire analysis is *"level of information."* A series of attitudes towards international control of the atom bombs are examined systematically in relation to the respondent's awareness or knowledge of a variety of facts. One searches in vain through the book to find examples of the routine cross-tabulations usually performed in survey analysis. Such independent variables as the demographic factors of sex or age or region or psychodynamic factors about the individual's personality, are hardly, if ever, examined. Moreover, the research design involved the comparison of attitudes before and after the event of the Bikini test of the atom bomb, implicitly a test of the effect of an informational variable, exposure to the knowledge of the Bikini test. Obviously, the analysts emphasize such a determinant because it is a *stimulus condition* subject to some manipulation through all the organs of communication. It is true, of course, that information is not *that* easily absorbed and a variety of psychological barriers and resistances to being informed have been demonstrated in experimental studies.[8] However, such considerations do not alter the fact that a contemporary, stimulus variable is at least manipulable in principle whereas an historical determinant or a demographic characteristic has no such manipulable feature whatsoever.

The principle for the analyst is clear. Where he is concerned with practical matters, a *non-manipulable determinant demonstrated to have a high correlation with a phenomenon is generally of less significance than a manipulable determinant demonstrated to have only a moderate correlation.* The value of the former type of cross-tabulation is purely the negative one of making the action agency more realistic and pessimistic about changing the situation, whereas the latter type of cross-tabulation has the positive value of leading to action and amelioration of the situation.

This same problem takes on still another form. An independent variable that is manipulable, that occurs frequently, or refers to a sub-group in the population that is strategic is of practical importance. Such considerations modify the appraisal of the size of the correlation with the phenomenon. In addition, there are special instances of cross-tabulations where the effect on a phenomenon may be small but of practical importance because *the change in the phenomenon occurs at some crucial cutting point.* McNemar

---

7. The same point is emphasized by Catherine Bauer in a discussion of social research as it bears on problems of Housing. She remarks with respect to such research that the planner wants to know "the specific effect of a particular factor in environment *over which he has some bona fide control."* Later she remarks that the planner "needs to know what to do, *not merely what to avoid"* and that the planner is interested in "the social effect of the kind of environment produced, or *capable of being produced today."* See, "Social Questions in Housing and Community Planning," *J. Soc. Issues,* 7, 1951, p. 7, italics ours.

8. For a general treatment of such barriers, see: H. Hyman and P. B. Sheatsley, "Some Reasons Why Information Campaigns Fail," *op. cit.*

provides us with a hypothetical example. It is couched specifically in terms of time as the variable, but the student can easily see the more general principle. He remarks:

> Suppose that the number of cases in two samples taken at different times were such that the shift from 38% to 42% for issue A and the shift from 48% to 52% for issue B were both statistically significant. The former shift might be judged of little social significance whereas the latter, *being a shift to the majority,* might be regarded as of great importance . . .[9]

The practical importance of an independent variable is dependent not only on the magnitude of its effect, but also on the location of the effect at some crucial cutting point for social change.

Gauging Side Effects
in the Evaluative or Programmatic Survey

There is one problem peculiar to the evaluative or programmatic survey which illustrates the need for analytic attention to the utilization of findings. If it is neglected, the findings can be accurate but exceedingly misleading. The goal of an evaluative survey is rarely what it appears to be! It appears to be simply a variety of explanatory survey in which some agency is interested in determining the effect of some one or more manipulable factors *on some specific phenomenon.* And while this is *one* goal, it is not the only goal. If the analyst finds that a given factor will lead to a change in a particular phenomenon, it may still be unwise to manipulate this factor. Most action agencies are concerned with a *wide array of social consequences,* and it is often the case that a given programmatic factor will be effective in changing the phenomenon under study in a favorable way, but will also produce other undesirable consequences. In essence the wiser formulation of the evaluative survey is to *test both the effects of some manipulable factor on a given phenomenon and its effect on a range of other social phenomena which might concern the action agency.* Once the analyst rephrases the problem this way, success in application is greatly increased. The original conceptualization includes other dependent variables, and parallel analyses of the influence of each given factor on the range of phenomena are made.

The problem can be illustrated by one of our case studies, the Japanese Bombing Survey. Strictly speaking the inquiry involved the evaluation of the effect of strategic bombing on the war morale of the Japanese people,

---

9. Q. McNemar, Opinion-Attitude Methodology, *Psychol. Bull.*, 43, 1946, p. 344, italics ours. Reprinted by permission of The American Psychological Association.

i.e., their willingness and ability to wage war. The findings of the inquiry were that morale indeed could be reduced by bombing, and on this basis a military establishment might be encouraged to endorse a policy of emphasis on bombing in its future planning. But such a policy decision might be unwise. For example, if ability to wage war is reduced but at the same time those exposed to bombing develop and harbor long run resentments against the victorious power, the evaluation of the desirability of strategic bombing might be quite different. No amount of care in conceptualization of the phenomenon under study—war morale—will lead the analyst to include such other variables in his planning. Such a consequence or side effect is not any part of the domain of morale. What the analyst must do in the evaluative survey is to start at the other end now—with the independent variable or factor that is likely to be introduced or manipulated and consider what are the multiplicity of effects it is likely to generate. In this way, he insures that he will measure the many consequences which should be weighed before a given program is instituted.

If we examine the narrative account of the Japanese Bombing Survey we note that the analysts conceptualized the problem in these broader terms. Thus, prior to the inquiry, the Study Director in an official report states:

> The objective of the Morale Division of the United States Strategic Bombing Survey is *two-fold:* The *primary* objective is to determine the direct and indirect effects of air attack, including the atomic bomb, upon the morale of the Japanese civilian. Here we are interested in discovering the effects of such bombing upon the attitudes and behavior of both the Japanese people and their leaders with particular reference to their willingness and capacity to give effective and continued support to the war effort. . . . The *secondary purpose* is to determine the socio-economic and political attitudes and expectations of the Japanese people today. This "secondary" purpose is an attempt to discover what *long-range* effects resulted from the bombing attacks on the Japanese homeland. *Data of this latter sort are necessary for a well-rounded analysis of the effect of strategic bombing on morale since it is important to know not only the immediately effective consequence of bombing but also how deeply the Japanese people were influenced by bombing and what ultimate significantly-rooted and long-term attitudinal consequences result from bombing attacks and the use of atomic bombs.*[10]

Consequently a series of possible side effects were anticipated in the planning and incorporated into the survey. Thus:

> The question was raised explicitly as to what the *post-war attitude of Japanese* was to each of the allies and the relation of such attitudes to bombing. For example, do they resent the U.S. for having dropped atomic bomb? (p. 6)
>
> A problem on which a solution was sought was whether the *long-run political repercussions* of bombing, especially atomic bombing, would be to strengthen groups such as the military and the Imperial System as against

---

10. Krech and Ballachey, *op. cit.,* p. 98, italics ours.

more liberal and democratic groups? (p. 6) In this connection questions irrelevant to the effects of bombing on wartime morale were asked of each respondent. These questions, however, provided data on postwar attitudes which could be related to past bombing experiences. For example, open questions on "how the respondent and his family will fare in the post war period, on what changes he would like to see occur in the society, on his current feelings about the emperor" were asked.

Other problems for study were whether the bombings altered post-war ability of the society to recover, and if so, how great was the set-back. (p. 7) What effect did the bombing of various shrines have on the virility of Shintoism and religious and mystical influences in the society? (p. 7)

Comprehending a Discursive System in an Explanatory Survey Utilized for Verification of Theory

We have thus far treated some of the problems that affect the use of explanatory survey findings for *applied* purposes. We now turn to a general problem that besets the analyst when he tries to extend the findings of an explanatory survey into the broader realm of theory. Obviously the relevance of any empirical investigation *of any type* to some larger body of theory is limited by a variety of methodological considerations such as—the accuracy of the findings, the choice of the population investigated, the size of the sample, the time period that is sampled, etc. All of these matters have been dealt with in earlier chapters. However, one problem that the survey analyst must consider carefully in the planning stage is whether his conceptualization parallels the original system or theory. Many of the theories which explanatory surveys treat of are elaborated in *very discursive form,* and involve a whole series of *component hypotheses.* Often the *relations are not articulated* and the *concepts are ambiguously stated.* Consequently, the survey that is conducted may be methodologically sound and may involve ingenious hypotheses, but its significance as *evidence* for or against some theory may be dubious. Admittedly, the fault lies with the theory or the original theorist rather than with the survey analyst. But since the analyst must take the theory as a given, he has only the alternatives of deciding that the theory is so stated that no survey would carry any weight or planning the investigation so that it comprehends the theory as well as possible.

Unfortunately, the major case studies we have used in earlier chapters provide no illustrations of the problem. However, an inquiry alluded to in passing constitutes a compelling illustration.

Sewell's Inquiry into the Effect of Infant Training on Personality—A Case Study of the Difficulties of Verifying a Discursive Theory: Sewell conducted a field inquiry to test the validity of psychoanalytic theorizing about the relation of infantile experience to personality formation. Our concern here is not with the technical features of the research design, but merely with the nature of the conceptualization and the tests that were made.[11] Sewell realized that such theorizing cannot be formulated *merely in terms of a restricted hypothesis* involving one or a limited number of indicators or variables of infantile experience and of personality patterns. The theory is too discursive and such a limited test would provide no crucial evidence. Thus in describing the general theoretical position of psychoanalysis on this problem he elaborates a *series* of independent variables—"breast feeding, a prolonged period of nursing, gradual weaning, a self-demand nursing schedule, easy and late bowel and bladder training, frequent mothering, freedom from restraint, freedom from punishment, sleeping with the child, and so on. They (those endorsing psychoanalytic theorizing) have assumed that these practices will promote the growth of secure and un-neurotic personalities." But the dependent variable, personality pattern is also a manifold entity. Again, Sewell elaborated a series of measures of personality, which finally number *46 specific indicators*. These are reproduced below in Chart VII taken from the original study.

Chart VII

Sewell's Measures of Personality Patterns

(An Illustration of Elaboration of Variables
To Comprehend a Complex Phenomenon)

GENERAL ADJUSTMENT MEASURES

Total adjustment score	Personality adjustment rating (Wisconsin Test of Personality)
Social adjustment score	Teachers' rating of child's adjustment
Self-adjustment score	General adjustment index

COMPONENTS

Self-reliance	Social skills
Sense of personal worth	Antisocial tendencies
Sense of personal freedom	Family relations
Feeling of belonging	School relations
Withdrawing tendencies	Community relations
Nervous symptoms *	Nervous symptoms *
Social standards	Emotional adjustment

---

11. W. H. Sewell, Infant Training, *op. cit.* The reader is referred to the original study for information on the technical aspects of the inquiry. All subsequent quotations are reprinted by permission of the publishers.

BEHAVIOR MANIFESTATIONS

Aggression (total)	Eating troubles
Arguing	Penuriousness
Fighting	Acceptance of authority
Temper (extent)	Self-assertiveness
Temper (demonstration)	Reaction to frustration
Biting nails	Emotional responses
Sucking fingers—now	School behavior
Sucking fingers—baby	Crying
Stuttering	Sleep disturbances
Fears	Cautiousness
Learning to talk	Cuddling
Bashfulness	Jealousy
Feelings hurt	Happiness

* These refer to two different indices based on different instruments.

Then to test the more general theory, Sewell computed the relationship between each of *seven* specific infant training practices and each of the *forty-six* personality indicators. In other words, a *total of 322 specific empirical tests* were regarded as necessary by Sewell to evaluate the *general* theory. We shall examine a little more closely exactly how Sewell proceeded to evaluate the theory in order to emphasize certain problems in the use of field inquiries for evidence on discursive bodies of theory.

Sewell regarded the general theory initially as a sort of *additive* theory based on a series of more specific hypotheses. Consequently, he stated seven specific hypotheses, each involving one *specific aspect* of infant training which was hypothesized to have some *broad* effect on personality patterns. The relationship of each of these aspects *by itself* to each of the 46 measures of personality was determined, and the validity of each hypothesis was regarded as denied on the basis of the *generalized lack of effect* of the specific independent variable on the 46 traits of personality. The findings were almost uniformly negative. We quote from Sewell to show the logic of the ultimate *general* test of the theory.

> Because it was not possible on the basis of the analysis to reject any of the specific null hypotheses concerning the association between training experiences and personality adjustments and traits, the general null hypothesis that the personality adjustments and traits of the children who have undergone varying infant-training experiences do not differ significantly cannot be rejected.

Sewell implicitly thus far has developed a method for coping with *the problem of the articulation of component parts* of a more general theory, and thus far he has regarded the articulation as a kind of additive process. But the tests made thus far do not fully represent the adding together of the aspects of infant experience in the *actual lives of these respondents*. Only the *results* of separate tests had been put together and the joint or compound effects of these specific practices on given individuals had not been examined. Consequently,

> it was decided that some attempt should be made to determine the joint effects of the several infancy experiences on personality adjustment. Consequently, a crude index was developed to indicate degree of infantile security. This index was based on the simple assumption that the combined effects of the various training experiences which are believed to be favorable would produce a more favorable infancy than would the combined effects of those training experiences which are assumed to be unfavorable. In arriving at the index scores, one point was given for each of the supposedly favorable infant-training experiences, and a total was computed.

A second *general* test of the theory then involved the determination of the relation of this general measure of infant training to each of the 46 aspects of personality. Here, again the evidence was negative. However, it should be noted for purposes of our later discussion that in the original 322 tests and in these 46 new tests, occasional relationships to particular aspects of personality were found to be significant. These were regarded as having no evidential value on grounds of accepted statistical logic as to the chance occurrence of occasional significant values in a large number of statistical tests, and *implicitly on the ground that the theory had not given any special weight or priority or place to any one particular aspect of personality* among the 46 aspects used.

Thus far, we have noted that Sewell in the absence of any statement in the general theory to the contrary had regarded each of the seven aspects of infant training as being additive, each deserving equal weight in the measure of total infant-training practices. However, he realized that this was an *a priori* treatment of the components. Consequently, on the basis of a factor analysis of child-training practices he derived factor scores for given aspects of infant training and determined the relationship between these new scores and the 46 personality indicators. In other words, the weight of given aspects of training was no longer arbitrary but in terms of empirically demonstrated relationships. On this basis, the evidence with respect to the general theory was again found to be negative.

We have elaborated Sewell's study at considerable length since it demonstrates so vividly for the survey analyst the complexity of testing a theory that is *general*, but *discursive*, and one in which the *component hypotheses* are not *explicitly articulated* and the initial *concepts vague or non-unitary* in character. We see that a large number of specific tests are needed to comprehend the theory, but that the analyst is faced in turn with the dilemma of how to combine the evidence from the many specific tests, in the absence of a clear directive from the theory. We shall shortly see that difficulty enters even earlier in the choice of the specific empirical indicators of the concepts included in the original theory.

The results of all of Sewell's analyses were unequivocal in character. In the original inquiry, methodological factors that might possibly have obscured positive evidence were also examined. For example, sign tests were used in addition to parametric tests. Consideration of whether the hypotheses in the theory involve a statement of the direction of the effect and therefore involve one-tail or two-tail tests was taken. Consideration was taken of whether the theory implied that only extremeness with respect to a given aspect of infant training would have consequences for personality patterns. We shall not refer to these matters but merely summarize that all such considerations did not change the original unequivocal negative findings. These additional considerations and the consequent procedures do, however, underscore our point about the laboriousness of testing a discursive theory.

We have noted thus far that certain assumptions had to be made by Sewell as to the relative significance of given independent variables of infant training and given dependent variables within the total personality. The theory was insufficient guide for Sewell and he consequently formulated the theory in *a number of different ways* and then made his tests. Thus he treated the theory in one instance as a kind of additive theory with all the components taking on equal weights. But he also inspected the discrete relationships for given variables in the light of the general theory. He examined the joint effects based on a factor analytic solution to the problem of the components and their weights. Despite all this laborious process, the evidence of the study was still disputed! Certainly a polemic element enters into the dispute, but the existence of the controversy over the results and the contents of the argument do establish our general point that tests of discursive theories despite maximum care, permit of considerable disagreement as to the weight of the evidence. In this particular instance, LaBarre argues, among other things, that the evidence is not appropriate to the theory because Sewell used as one of his measures of type of infant-training, whether or not the child slept with the mother during infancy, and regarded the occurrence of this fact as leading to greater security. We quote LaBarre:

> Sewell dreams up an ignorant and silly hypothesis, that of "High Sleep Security," which he then imputes to the Freudians, only to find it roundly disproved. No person oriented in psychoanalysis has ever stated that sleeping with the mother, Sewell's "High Sleep Security," is conducive to later personality adjustment. On the contrary, all would agree that this is an index of maternal overprotection that bodes ill for later personality adequacy and adjustment. Who can be surprised, then, that chi-square negates his absurd hypothesis; and what informed person can see it as other than

establishing the actual position of psychoanalysis? Sewell is manifestly ignorant of the real position of his opponents.[12]

Our concern with LaBarre's argument for the moment is only to point out that the concepts in the general theory are ambiguous and that he, therefore, can claim that Sewell misunderstands the theory when he uses this specific indicator as a basis for one of the sets of 46 empirical tests. Sewell in a reply acknowledges the fact that the choice of this indicator and the hypothesized direction of effect were subject to some doubt. He remarks that among the independent variables used, "all but one of these, that cited by LaBarre, were based directly on the feeding and toilet training so much emphasized in psychoanalytic theory." He also indicates the dilemma in advancing an hypothesis about this factor: [13]

> my favorable classification of the experience "slept with mother during first year of life" was based on the widely held view that extensive physical contact with the mother during early infancy is security-inducing. This practice, if prolonged, may also be taken as an indication of maternal over-protection. There was only one instance of the practice being prolonged beyond six months, and in most cases it was terminated after a few days or weeks; consequently, I decided to classify it as favorable to later adjustment.

Sewell points out, in addition that the test of this specific hypothesis found that there was *no* significant effect of the variable of "sleep with mother" on general personality patterns, so that irrespective of which direction of effect is implied by the theory, the evidence is negative. However, this fortunate resolution of the controversy does not change the intrinsic fact we are emphasizing of the ambiguity of given bodies of theory and the consequent difficulties of empirical verification.

More generally, Sewell emphasized, in answer to LaBarre, a principle to be commended to the analyst dealing with such situations in survey research. It might be labelled the principle of *distribution of risk*. Granted that the relevance of any given empirical test to an ambiguous or discursive theory is difficult to state and is therefore disputed as evidence, one must make a sufficient number of tests of different aspects of the theory, so that the *total* weight of evidence on the theory has some stature. The risk from ambiguity is too great to warrant exclusive reliance on tests of a small number of component parts of the theory. As Sewell points out:

> I attempted to test a general hypothesis by means of ten null hypotheses dealing with the relationship between specifically defined infant-training practices and various indicators of personality adjustment. . . . The statistical analysis indicated that none of these experiences was significantly related to personality adjustment as assessed in the study. Consequently, the evidence

———
12. W. LaBarre, Sewell's Infant Training and the Personality of the Child, *Amer. J. Sociol.,* Letters to the Editor, 58, 1952, p. 419. Reprinted by permission of the publishers.
13. W. Sewell, Letter to the Editor, *Amer. J. Sociol.,* 58, 1952, 419-420.

did not permit the rejection of any of the specific null hypotheses or of the general null hypothesis.

However, this distribution of risk principle in turn creates a problem for the analyst in terms of how to combine the evidence from the many specific hypotheses. In the absence of a statement of the hierarchy of importance of specific hypotheses in the larger theory or a statement of the way the component hypotheses are interrelated and articulated, the analyst must combine the evidence the best way he knows how. Thus, Sewell gave central emphasis to the realm of "toilet and feeding training in testing the psychoanalytic position rather than to sleep security" in elaborating the original hypotheses and gave the tests of specific variables equal weight as evidence. Here again, disputation over the evidence could enter.

We have picked a relatively extreme example of the difficulty of using survey research as evidence with respect to some larger theory, but it illustrates the problem and modes of dealing with it.[14]

_____

14. At least two other controversies in the literature attend empirical studies of psychoanalytic theory, suggesting the considerable problem in this particular realm. See: J. P. Seward, "Psychoanalysis, Deductive Method, and the Blacky Test" and G. Blum, "A Reply to Seward's 'Psychoanalysis, Deductive Method and the Blacky Test', *J. Abnorm. Soc. Psychol.*, 45, 1950, 529-537; R. F. Winch, "Further Data and Observations on the Oedipus Complex," *Amer. Soc. Rev.*, 1951. Claude Bowman, "A Sour Note on Questionnaires," R. F. Winch, "Rejoinder: A Plea for Sweet Reasonableness," *Amer. Sociol. Rev.* in Communications and Opinion, 1952, 17, 362-364. For more general summaries of empirical studies in the psychoanalytic realm and critical discussion of these, see: R. Sears, *Survey of Objective Studies of Psychoanalytic Concepts* (Social Science Research Council Bull. #51, 1943), or H. Orlansky, "Infant Care and Personality," *Psychol. Bull.*, 1949, 1-48. For a general treatment of the problem of empirical verification of one part of psychoanalytic theory see, W. Seeman, "The Freudian Theory of Daydreams: An Operational Analysis," *Psychol. Bull.*, 48, 1951, 369-381.

A Concluding Note for the Reader

BY NOW the reader may have learned the basic principles
of survey analysis, developed some of the technical skills, and sensed the
requirements of his professional role. He now has the *makings* of the experienced survey analyst. But training is never-ending and these final remarks
are directed to the future training of the analyst. It will take time for the
beginner to exploit the material he has learned. What has been learned
may appear abstract and academic for the moment. Not until some pressing
analytic problem is confronted in a future survey will the lesson strike roots.
The usefulness of many procedures may become clearer in the course of
actual research undertakings. The reader should therefore use this work
as a handy reference book, re-reading portions of it in conjunction with
his on-going research activities. Thereby he may see the principles in their
most convincing context. The Table of Contents has been designed with
these needs of easy reference in mind, and the range of alternative solutions
presented for the same formal problem is intended to give the prospective
analyst much choice to suit the peculiar requirements of different surveys.

But the reader must also go far beyond the book if he is to become an
effective analyst. Methodology is an on-going endeavor. New principles are
developed and old ones modified to cope with the novel features of each
new survey. We have tried to convey this spirit of analysis in our earlier
discussion. We hope that the reader will himself be inspired not only to
the use of present-day methods but to the invention or creation of new
analytic procedures and principles.

The Questionnaires from the Major Surveys Discussed in the Text

THE QUESTIONNAIRES from certain of the major case studies used in the text are not presented for the following reasons. For the inquiry into *The Authoritarian Personality*, the questionnaires were so many in number that space limitations preclude their reproduction. However, they are presented in entirety in the original work. As the student will recall, Kinsey did not make use of any formal questionnaire. The questionnaire from the study of War Bond Redemption is not yet readily available, but will be obtainable in the future when Cartwright's work is published. The Questionnaire from the survey of opinions on radio is presented in Appendix C since it is the basis for the Problem Exercises on Machine Tabulation.

Questionnaires Used in a Study of American Attitudes Toward the Atomic Bomb

The General Plan of the Intensive Interview

After the original objectives of this study were decided upon, a questionnaire was designed to meet these objectives. In formulating the questions an important consideration, aside from stating them in such a way that they would be easily understood, was to phrase them in such a way as to encourage discussion of the issue rather than to present a categorical choice to the respondent. This was also accomplished by the method of interviewing whch was used. The interviewers were instructed to ask the questions exactly as they were stated, but to use additional "non-directive" probes, such as "Why is that?", "Why do you feel that way?", etc. wherever necessary in order to obtain as clear a picture as possible of the individual's reasoning. Each answer was recorded as nearly verbatim as possible.

The interview opened with several broad appraisal questions which, because they were rather easily answered, served the purpose of getting the interview started and also provided information about the individual's general outlook on world affairs. Following these, a number of questions were asked about each of the major topics covered by the study. As will be seen from examination of the questionnaire, these groups of questions were arranged in the following order:

	Questions numbered:
Role of the United States in world affairs	2-6
England	7-10
Russia	11-14
United Nations	15-22
Hypothetical world organization	23-25
Atomic bomb	26-32
Effect of development of atomic bomb on size of armed forces in the United States	33-35
Bikini test	36-38
Sources of information about the atomic bomb	39-43

The questionnaire reproduced here is the one used in June. The questions asked in August were identical with these with two exceptions:

(1) The question about the British loan was rephrased as the loan had been approved by Congress in July:

9. You probably know that Congress recently voted to lend a large amount of money to England. How do you feel about that? Why?

(2) The questions about Bikini had to be changed because the tests had taken place. In June the questions about the test were asked of everyone; if an individual had not heard of the plans for Bikini, a brief description of the projected test was given him and the questions asked. In August, however, the questions about Bikini could be asked only if the people had heard of the tests. The questions used in August were the following:

36. Have you heard anything about the atomic bomb tests the Navy made last month in the Pacific?
If no, skip to Question 42
37. (If yes to 36) Do you happen to know how many bombs were exploded?
38. Did you expect the bomb (or bombs) to destroy most of the ships or just a few of them?
39. Did you expect the bomb (or bombs) to be as destructive against these ships as it was against the Japanese cities?
40. (If R knows two bombs were exploded) Which of the two explosions did you think was most destructive? Why did that one seem more destructive?
41. Did the bomb do as much damage as you thought it would?

QUESTIONNAIRE

1. Now that the war is over, how do you feel about the way the countries of the world are getting along together these days?

2. How satisfied are you with the way the United States has been getting along with other countries since the war ended?

3. Do you think the United States has made any mistakes in dealing with other countries since the end of the war?

3a. (If yes) What?

4. What do you think is the best thing that the United States could do to help keep peace in the world? Why?

5. Some people would like to see Government keep to itself and not have anything to do with the rest of the world. How do you feel about that?

6. Some people say we should use our Army and Navy to make other countries do what we think they should. How would you feel about that?

7. How about some of the other countries. Do you think the English Government is trying to cooperate with the rest of the world as much as it can?

7a. In what ways?

8. How about the United States? Do you think we can count on the English Government being friendly with us? Why?

9. There's talk now about the United States lending a large amount of money to England. How do you feel about that? Why?

10. Do you think we have anything to gain from making the loan? Why?

11. How about Russia? Do you think the Russian Government is trying to cooperate with the rest of the world as much as it can?

11a. In what ways?

12. How about the United States? Do you think we can count on the Russian Government being friendly with us? Why do you feel that way?

13. There's talk now about the United States lending a large amount of money to Russia. How do you feel about that? Why?

14. Do you think we have anything to gain from making the loan? Why?

15. Have you been following the news about the United Nations organization during the last few months?

16. As you see it, what is the main thing the UNO * is set up to do?

If familiar with UNO

17. How do you feel about the general idea of having an organization like the UNO? Why?

18. How satisfied are you with the way the UNO has worked out so far? Why so?

19. Do you think the United States has given in too much or has had its own way too much in the UNO?

20. Do you think the United States ought to have more say than the other big countries or should they all have the same? Why?

21. How successful do you think the UNO will be in keeping peace among the countries? Why?

22. Suppose the United States and another country had a disagreement which they couldn't settle; do you think the UNO should have the power to tell both of them what ought to be done? Why?

23. Do you think it would be possible to organize the nations of the world in the same way the states in this country are organized, with a government over them all to make laws that they would all have to obey? Why?

24. How would you feel about this country belonging to a world organization where we would have to follow the decisions of the majority of the nations? Why?

25. (If Yes or uncertain to 24) Do you think this world organization should have armed forces to carry out its decision if necessary? Why?

26. Do you think the discovery of the atomic bomb has made it easier or harder to keep peace in the world? Why?

27. How worried do you think people in this country are about the atomic bomb? Why?

28. How about yourself? Why so?

29. How long do you think it will be before the other countries are able to make atomic bombs? Why?

30. Do you think the secret of the bomb should be turned over to the UNO or

---

* The initials UNO were used during the interview rather than the correct UN, as the former seemed to be more widely understood.

should the United States try to keep the secret itself? Why?

31. Do you think we will be able to work out a defense against the bomb before other countries learn how to make it? Why?

32. Do you think there is real danger that atomic bombs will ever be used against the United States? Why do you feel that way?

33. Do you think the discovery of the atomic bomb makes any difference in the size of the Army we need? Why?

34. How about the Navy? Does it make any difference in the size of Navy we will need?

35. What about the Air Force? Does it make any difference in the size of Air Force we will need?

36. Have you heard of the test the Navy plans to make of the atomic bomb?

(Read to everyone)
The Navy has collected about a hundred old ships in the South Pacific and is going to explode an atomic bomb over them.

37. Do you expect the bomb will destroy most of these ships or just a few of them?

38. Do you expect the bomb to be as destructive against these ships as it was against Japanese cities? Why?

39. We're interested in knowing how people keep up with the news on the atomic bomb. Where would you say you've gotten most of your information on the atomic bomb?

39a. Have you heard anything about the bomb over the radio?

39b. Have you read anything about the bomb in the newspapers?

39c. Have you read anything about the bomb in magazines?

39d. Which of these three (radio, newspapers, or magazines) do you trust the most for information about the atomic bomb? Why?

40. Have you seen any movies or newsreels about the atomic bomb?

41. Have you talked it over with other people?

41a. (If Yes) Would you say you do that rather often or just now and then?

42. In general, which of these ways of getting information has given you the best idea of how destructive the atomic bomb is?

43. Which of all these ways has been most important in helping you make up your mind about who should have the secret of the bomb?

OPINION SURVEY

1. Would you agree that everybody would be happier, more secure and more prosperous if working people were given more power and influence in government, or would you say we would all be better off if the working people had no more power than they have now?

☐ **More**   ☐ **Same**   ☐ **Less**   ☐ **No Opinion**

2. Which of these statements do you most agree with? (HAND RESPONDENT CARD)
   ☐ 1. The most important job for the government is to make certain that there are good opportunities for each person to get ahead on his own.
   ☐ 2. The most important job for the government is to guarantee every person a decent and steady job and standard of living.
   ☐ No Opinion

3a. Which of these four statements comes closest to your own ideas? (HAND RESPONDENT CARD)
   ☐ 1. I think there is bound to be another world war within the next 25 years.
   ☐ 2. Things certainly are bad now, and it looks as though they will get worse, so there may be another world war within 25 years.
   ☐ 3. Things don't look too good now, but the nations will work out ways of getting along better, so that there may not be another world war within 25 years.
   ☐ 4. I do not think there will be another world war within 25 years.
   ☐ No Opinion

b. How sure are you of this opinion, very sure, fairly sure, or aren't you at all sure one way or the other?

☐ **Very sure**   ☐ **Fairly sure**   ☐ **Not sure**   ☐ **Don't know**

4. With which one of these four statements do you come closest to agreeing? (HAND RESPONDENT CARD)
   ☐ 1. It is very important to keep on friendly terms with Russia, and we should make every effort to do so.
   ☐ 2. It is important for the U. S. to be on friendly terms with Russia, but not so important that we should make too many concessions to her.
   ☐ 3. If Russia wants to keep on friendly terms with us, we shouldn't discourage her, but there is no reason why we should make any special effort to be friendly.
   ☐ 4. We shall be better off if we have just as little as possible to do with Russia.
   ☐ No Opinion

5. Now I'd like to ask you a few questions like those you hear on radio programs.
   a. Do you happen to know who is the U. S. Secretary of State at the present time?

   ☐ **Yes**   ☐ **No**

   If "YES," ask:

   b. What is his name?.....................................
   ASK EVERYONE:

   c. The name of General Leslie R. Groves has been mentioned occasionally in the newspapers and over the radio in recent months. Can you tell me in what connection?
   ....☐ **Don't know**

   d. Do you happen to remember what country was recently charged before the United Nations Organization with keeping her troops in Iran longer than she was supposed to?

   ☐ **Yes**   ☐ **No**

   If "YES," ask:

   e. Which country?..................................

6. Do you think the secret of making atomic bombs should be put under the control of the United Nations Organization, or should the U. S. keep the secret to itself?

   ☐ **UNO Control**   ☐ **U.S. should keep**   ☐ **No Opinion**

   ☐ **Other**.................

7. Which of these three statements comes closest to what you think the U. S. should do? (HAND RESPONDENT CARD)
   ☐ 1. The U. S. should go on making atomic bombs and not depend on systems of international control of the bombs.
   ☐ 2. We should go on making atomic bombs for the time being, but try to work out a system of international control to prevent any nation, including our own, from using atomic bombs.
   ☐ 3. We should stop making atomic bombs right now and try to work out a system of international control to keep other nations from making them too.
   ☐ No Opinion

Now I am going to read you four statements. In each case will you tell me whether you agree or disagree?

8a. The atomic bomb has shown that all we need is an air force; we can cut down on most of our Navy now.

☐ **Agree**   ☐ **Disagree**   ☐ **Don't know**

b. How do you feel about this—very strongly or not very strongly?

☐ **Very strongly**   ☐ **Not very strongly**   ☐ **Don't know**

9a. The atomic bomb does not change the fact that we should keep our Navy at least as large as it was when Japan surrendered.

☐ **Agree**   ☐ **Disagree**   ☐ **Don't know**

b. How do you feel about this—very strongly or not very strongly?

☐ **Very strongly**   ☐ **Not very strongly**   ☐ **Don't know**

10a. Even though we have the atomic bomb, the United States needs a large Navy in order to help keep peace in the world.

☐ **Agree**   ☐ **Disagree**   ☐ **Don't know**

b. How do you feel about this—very strongly or not very strongly?

☐ **Very strongly**   ☐ **Not very strongly**   ☐ **Don't know**

11a. We need a big Navy as well as the atomic bomb in order to make sure we can defend ourselves in case we are attacked by some enemy country.

☐ **Agree**   ☐ **Disagree**   ☐ **Don't know**

b. How do you feel about this—very strongly or not very strongly?

☐ **Very strongly**   ☐ **Not very strongly**   ☐ **Don't know**

12a. Do you think there is a real danger that atomic bombs will ever be used against the United States?

☐ **Yes**   ☐ **No**   ☐ **No Opinion**

If "YES," ask:

b. Do you think the danger that you or any members of your immediate family will ever be killed by an atomic bomb is very great, fairly great, or only very slight?

☐ **Very great**   ☐ **Fairly great**   ☐ **Only slight**
                   ☐ **No danger**   ☐ **No Opinion**

13a. Can you name the materials from which atomic energy is being made now?

☐ **Yes**   ☐ **No**

If "YES," ask:

b. What materials?.................................
....

(OVER)

14a. Do you happen to know whether there is any plan to test the atomic bomb in the near future?

☐ Yes   ☐ No   ☐ Don't know

If "YES," ask b and c:

b. Will you tell me what the targets are going to be in testing the bomb?

_____ ☐ Don't know

c. Do you think the bomb test will show that the Navy will need more or fewer men in the future than you have said the Navy should have now?

☐ More   ☐ Fewer   ☐ Same   ☐ No Opinion

d. Why? ....

15. Do you think the U. S. will be able to work out an effective defense against the atomic bomb before other nations could use it against us?

☐ Yes   ☐ No   ☐ Don't know

16. What is your occupation? (Record *SPECIFIC* occupation, not just industry or name of organization worked for).

Write in description of occupation:. ....

....

(If housewife, widow or student, record occupation of head of family. If retired or unemployed, give former occupation).

17a. Do you remember FOR CERTAIN whether or not you voted in the 1944 presidential election?

¹☐ Yes, voted   ²☐ No, didn't vote
³☐ No, too young to vote   ⁷☐ Don't remember

If "YES, VOTED," ask:

b. Did you vote for Dewey, Roosevelt or Thomas?

⁴☐ Dewey   ⁵☐ Roosevelt   ⁶☐ Thomas   ⁷☐ Other

18. What is the last grade or class you completed in school?

¹☐ No schooling
²☐ Grammar school (grades 1 through 8)
³☐ High school, incomplete (9th, 10th or 11th grade)
⁴☐ High school, graduated (12th grade)
⁵☐ College, incomplete   } What type of college?
⁶☐ College, graduated   } _____

19a. Are you (or is your husband), a member of a labor union?

☐ Yes   ☐ No

If "YES," ask:

b. Which one?

☐ C.I.O.   ☐ A.F. of L.   ☐ Other_____

20. Please tell me in which of these groups the average weekly income of your immediate family belongs? Please call by letter. HAND RESPONDENT CARD.

¹☐ A. Under $10
²☐ B. Between $10 and $14.99
³☐ C. Between $15 and $19.99
⁴☐ D. Between $20 and $29.99
⁵☐ E. Between $30 and $39.99
⁶☐ F. Between $40 and $59.99
⁷☐ G. Between $60 and $99.99
⁸☐ H. $100 and over

21a. Are you a member of a church?

☐ Yes   ☐ No

If "YES," ask:

b. Which denomination?. ....
                        (Please get specific denomination)

If "NO" on a, ask:

c. What is your religious preference?. ....
                        (Please get specific denomination if possible)

22a. Is there a telephone in your home?

☐ Yes   ☐ No

If "YES," ask:

b. Is the telephone listed either under your name or the name of a member of your immediate family?

☐ Yes   ☐ No

ASK ONLY OF MEN:

23. Did you serve in any branch of the armed forces in World War II?

☐ Yes   ☐ No

PLEASE COMPLETE ALL VITAL INFORMATION BEFORE LEAVING RESPONDENT

Classify respondent as: Check whether:

☐ W   ☐ AV   ☐ OAA   ☐ Farm Resident   ☐ On Farm   ☐ Man   ☐ Wh.
☐ AV+   ☐ P   ☐ OR   Interviewed: ☐ In Town   ☐ Woman   ☐ Cl.

RESPONDENT'S AGE ............STREET...CITY...................
                                     Street and number

INTERVIEWER...Date this interview was made.................

№ 4015

QUESTIONNAIRE FROM CENTERS'
STUDY OF CLASS CONSCIOUSNESS

THE RESEARCH COUNCIL, Inc.
Box 429, Princeton, New Jersey

1. Do you agree or disagree that America is truly a land of opportunity and that people get pretty much what's coming to them here?

   ¹☐ Agree   ²☐ Disagree   ³☐ Don't know

   ☐ Other..............

2. Do you think that all the modern scientific inventions of new machines and materials will result in a better standard of living -for all of us, or do you think that these things have been overrated?

   ¹☐ Better standard of living   ²☐ Overrated   ³☐ Don't know

3. Would you say that on the whole people take religion too seriously, or that they don't take it seriously enough?

   ¹☐ Too seriously   ²☐ Not seriously enough   ³☐ Don't know

   ☐ Other..............

4. Would you agree that everybody would be be happier, more secure and more prosperous if the working people were given more power and influence in government, or would you say we would all be better off if the working people had no more power than they have now?

   ¹☐ Agree   ²☐ No more power   ³☐ Don't know

   ☐ Other..............

5. As you know, during this war, many private businesses and industries have been taken over by the government. Do you think wages and salaries would be fairer, jobs more steady, and that we would have fewer people out of work if the government took over and ran our mines, factories and industries in the future, or do you think things would be better under private ownership?

   ¹☐ Better under government   ²☐ Better under private owners

   ³☐ Other..............   ⁴☐ Don't know

6. Which one of these statements do you most agree with?

   ¹☐ (1) The most important job for the government is to make it certain that there are good opportunities for each person to get ahead on his own.

   ²☐ (2) The most important job for the government is to guarantee every person a decent and steady job and standard of living.

7. In strikes and disputes between working people and employers do you usually side with the workers or with the employers?

   ¹☐ Workers   ²☐ Employers   ³☐ Neither   ⁴☐ Won't say   ⁵☐ Don't know

   ☐ Qualified answer..............

8a. If you had a choice of one of these kinds of jobs which one would you choose? (HAND CARD TO RESPONDENT). Just call out the letter.

   ¹☐ A   ²☐ B   ³☐ C   ⁴☐ D   ⁵☐ E   ⁶☐ F   ⁷☐ G   ⁸☐ H   ⁹☐ I   ˣ☐ J

b. What is your second choice?

   ¹☐ A   ²☐ B   ³☐ C   ⁴☐ D   ⁵☐ E   ⁶☐ F   ⁷☐ G   ⁸☐ H   ⁹☐ I   ˣ☐ J

c. Would you like to make a third choice?

   ¹☐ A   ²☐ B   ³☐ C   ⁴☐ D   ⁵☐ E   ⁶☐ F   ⁷☐ G   ⁸☐ H   ⁹☐ I   ˣ☐ J

9a. What do you do for a living?..............
   (If farmer, does he own or rent farm?)

ASK EMPLOYERS:
   b. About how many people do you employ?..............

ASK SUPERVISORS, MANAGERS, ETC.:
   c. About how many people do you have working under your direction? ....

ASK ONLY EMPLOYED PEOPLE:
10a. Do you sometime hope or expect to own your own business?

   ¹☐ Yes   ²☐ No   ³☐ Don't know

If NO, ask:
   b. Do you ever hope or expect to be a manager or executive of some kind?

   ¹☐ Yes   ²☐ No   ³☐ Don't know   ⁴☐ Doesn't apply

ASK EVERYONE:
.11. About what was the longest time you were ever out of work?..............

(OVER)

12a. Are you satisfied or dissatisfied with your present job?
   ¹☐ Satisfied   ²☐ Dissatisfied   ³☐ Other

If SATISFIED on a, ask:
   b. What is it that you like about your job?...
If DISSATISFIED on a, ask:
   c. What is it that you don't like about your job?...

ASK EVERYONE:
13. Do you think your pay or salary is as high as it should be, or do you think you deserve more?
   ¹☐ High as should be   ²☐ Deserve more   ³☐ Don't know

14a. Do you think working people are usually fairly and squarely treated by their employers, or that employers sometimes take advantage of them?
   ¹☐ Fair treatment   ²☐ Employers take advantage   ³☐ Don't know

ASK EMPLOYEES ONLY:
   b. What about your own treatment by your employer?
   ¹☐ Fair treatment   ²☐ Employer takes advantage   ³☐ Don't know

ASK EVERYONE:
15. Do you think you have a good chance to get ahead in your present line of work?
   ¹☐ Yes   ²☐ No   ³☐ Don't know

16a. Do you belong to a union?
   ¹☐ Yes   ²☐ No

   b. Do you think belonging to a union usually hurts people's chances for advancement in their jobs, makes no difference, or helps their chances for advancement?
   ¹☐ Hurts chances   ²☐ Makes no difference   ³☐ Helps   ⁴☐ Don't know
   ☐ Other_____

17. Would you say that your children had just as good a chance, a poorer, or a better chance to rise in the world as anybody else's?
   ¹☐ Just as good   ²☐ Poorer   ³☐ Better   ⁴☐ Don't know

18. Do you think you have as good a chance to enjoy life as you should have?
   ¹☐ Yes   ²☐ No   ³☐ Don't know

19. Do you think woman's place should be in the home or do you think women should be free to take jobs outside the home if they want them?
   ¹☐ In the home   ²☐ Outside   ³☐ Don't know
   ☐ Other_____

20. Here's a list of several groups of people: (HAND CARD TO RESPONDENT)
   a. Are there any on that list that you think get too much pay? Just call out the letters...................................
   b. Are there any of those who don't get enough pay?...

21a. Do you think most people who are successful are successful because of ability, luck, pull, or the better opportunities they have had?
   ¹☐ Ability   ²☐ Luck   ³☐ Pull   ⁴☐ Better opportunities   ⁵☐ Don't know
   b. Is this the way you think it ought to be?
   ¹☐ Yes   ²☐ No   ³☐ Don't know
If NO on b, ask:
   c. What should success depend on then?...

22a. Why do you think some people have been able to get rich, because of ability, luck, pull, their better opportunities, or something else? (If something else, ask what).
   ¹☐ Ability   ²☐ Luck   ³☐ Pull   ⁴☐ Better opportunities   ⁵☐ Don't know
   ☐ Other_____

   b. Why do you think some of the people are always poor?..
   ....

23a. If you were asked to use one of these four names for your social class, which would you say you belonged in; the middle class, lower class, working class, or upper class?
   ¹☐ Middle   ²☐ Lower   ³☐ Working   ⁴☐ Upper   ⁵☐ Don't know

   b. Which of those in this list would you say belonged in the..................class (whichever respondent has chosen) (HAND CARD TO RESPONDENT). Just call out the letters.
   ¹☐ A   ²☐ B   ³☐ C   ⁴☐ D   ⁵☐ E   ⁶☐ F   ⁷☐ G   ⁸☐ H   ⁹☐ I   ˣ☐ J   ʸ☐ K

c. In deciding whether a person belongs to your class or not, which of these other things do you think is most important to know: who his family is, how much money he has, what sort of education he has, or how he believes and feels about certain things?

¹☐ Family   ²☐ Money   ³☐ Education   ⁴☐ Beliefs   ⁵☐ Don't know   ☐ Other..............

24a. What would you say puts a person in the upper social class?..

....

b. What would you say puts a person in the lower social class?...

....

25a. Now, I'd like you to pick out from the statements on this card the one that best describes the way you feel about negroes? (HAND CARD TO RESPONDENT).

¹☐ A   ²☐ B   ³☐ C   ⁴☐ D   ⁵☐ Don't know

b. How strongly do you hold this opinion, very strongly, fairly strongly, or don't you care one way or the other?

¹☐ Very strongly   ²☐ Fairly strongly   ³☐ Don't care

26. Do you think that the Jews have too much power and influence in this country?

¹☐ Yes   ²☐ No   ☐ Don't know

FACTUAL

27a. Are you a member of a church?   ¹☐ Yes   ²☐ No

b. Which denomination?...

28a. Whom did you vote for in the last presidential election?

¹☐ Dewey   ²☐ Roosevelt   ³☐ Other   ⁴☐ Didn't vote

b. What political party did your father usually support?

¹☐ Republican   ²☐ Democratic   ³☐ Other

c. What party did your mother support?

¹☐ Republican   ²☐ Democratic   ³☐ Other

29a. Do you remember the name of the school you last attended?...

b. What was the last grade you completed in that school?

¹☐ No school   ⁵☐ Completed high school

²☐ Grades 1-6   ⁶☐ Had some college

³☐ Grades 7-8   ⁷☐ College graduated

⁴☐ Grades 9-11   ⁸☐ College post graduate

☐ Other..........................

30a. Could you tell me how far your father went in school?...

b. If you have a son or had one, how far would you expect him to go in school?.................................

c. How about a daughter?...

31a. In what country were you born?...

b. In what country was your father born?...

c. In what country was your mother born?...

32a. What was or is your father's occupation?...

b. What was or is your father-in-law's occupation?..

33. May I ask your age?...

Economic Status: ¹☐ Wealthy   ³☐ Average   ⁵☐ Poor

     ²☐ Average plus   ⁴☐ Poor plus   ⁶☐ On relief

Date of interview.......................... City and State...

Interviewer ....

HAVE YOU CHECKED ANSWERS ON EACH QUESTION AND ALL VITAL INFORMATION?   N⁰ 7080

INTERVIEW SCHEDULE

FOR STUDY OF INDUSTRIAL ABSENTEEISM

1. Would you say it is easy or hard for people to get a good place to live in around here?

2. On the whole, do you like the place you are living in now?

A. (If "No" or "Qualified answer") Why is that?

3. Do you usually have trouble getting to and from work?

4. On the whole, do you feel that this town is a good place to live in?

5. How is this town as a place to have a good time? Is it good, fair, or poor?

A. (If "Fair" or "Poor") What don't you like about it?

6. About how long have you been working where you are now?

7. How do you feel about the type of work you are doing now? Would you say you like it a whole lot, just about so-so, or that you dislike it?

(ASK IN EVERY CASE) What makes you feel that way?

8. How many hours a week do you usually work?

9. As far as you are concerned, is that too long for you, or just about right?

10. About how many hours a day do you usually work?

11. Is that too long for you, or just about right?

12. What shift are you on now?

13. Do you like or dislike that shift?

(ASK IN EVERY CASE) Why is that?

14. Does your job give you enough time to do the things you want to do after work?

A. (If "No" or "Qualified answer") What sort of things don't you have time for?

15. Do you feel you're being paid enough for the job you're doing?

16. How does it compare with what other plants around here pay for the same job? Is it more, less, or about the same?

17. What chance does a worker have to be upgraded or promoted at your plant? Are the chances good, fair, or poor?

(ASK IN EVERY CASE) What makes you feel that way?

18. Aside from hours and wages, is your plant a good place to work in?

(ASK IN EVERY CASE) What makes you feel that way?

19. How are the safety conditions where you work? Would you say they're good, about fair, or poor?

A. (If "Fair" or "Poor") How could they be better?

20. Is your plant a healthy place to work at?

(ASK IN EVERY CASE) Why?

21. Do you usually bring your lunch to work with you?

A. (If "Yes") Are you satisfied with that arrangement?

B. (If "No") Are you usually able to get the kind of meals you need, in or near your plant?

(1) (If "No" to B) Why not?

22. Is there enough work in your shop to keep you busy all the time?

A. (If "No") Why do you suppose that is?

23. Has production in your plant ever been held up because of shortage of materials?

A. (If "Yes") Would you say that happens often or only occasionally?

24. Can you depend on things at your plant, or do they seem to change their minds a good deal about what should be done?

A. (If "Can't depend") What makes you feel that way?

25. How good a job is management doing in turning out the stuff at your plant—very good, just fair, or poor?

26. Have you ever felt like quitting the job you have now?

(If "Yes" ask both A and B)

A. Why was that?

B. What made you stay?

27. Why do you think some of the workers at the plant take days off without notice?

28. How about yourself—have you stayed away from the job anytime in the last couple of months?

A. (If "Yes") Why was that?

29. What happens to a person at your plant when he's late?

(ASK IN EVERY CASE) How do you think it should be handled?

30. What does the company do when a man just stays away from work without notice?

(ASK IN EVERY CASE) What do you think the company should do?

31. Is it easy to arrange in advance with the office to get a day off if you need it?

32. What do you feel could be done in your plant to cut down the number of days workers stay off the job?

FACTUAL DATA

Occupation:

About how long have you been on that particular job?

(If less than 2 years, ask A, B and C)

A. What sort of work did you do before?

B. How long were you on that job?

C. And what was the weekly pay on that job?

How many days a week do you usually work?

Do you work the same shift every week?

(If "No") How often do you change shifts?

What is your average weekly wage?

Do you do any of your work at piece-rate?

Are you a member of any union?

(If "Yes") Is that CIO or AFL?

About how long does it take to get to and from your job (round trip?)

Are you married, or single?

A. (If "Married" ask 1, 2 and 3)

(1) Do you have any children under 14?

(2) Is your family with you now?

(3) Is your (husband, wife) working too?

(a) (If "Yes") Does (he, she) work on the same shift you do?

B. (If "Single") Do you help support anybody?

(1) (If "Yes") How many?

Would you mind telling me your approximate age?

How long have you lived in this city?

(If less than 2 years) Did you come from a city, a small town or a farm?

What was the last grade you finished at school?

Do you have any close friends or relatives in the armed forces?

Sex:

(If "Male") What is your draft classification?

Type of residence (specify)

Race:

Questionnaire and Design Used in the United States Strategic Bombing Survey of Germany

Experimental Design of Study

The experimental design of the study called for two forms of interview schedule. Form A was given to every third respondent who had been bombed. Schedule B, given to all unbombed people and to two out of three bombed individuals, did not inquire into bombing experience until the very end of the interview. There was an opportunity for spontaneous report about bombing to appear early in the schedule. But the indirection was devised to compare morale of unbombed and bombed people when they themselves did not know the purpose of the interview. This procedure had the advantage, moreover, of vitiating inaccuracies in the report of respondents. The analysis is not concerned with the absolute level of morale but with relative morale as it corresponds to degrees of bombing exposure. It may be, for example, that the absolute morale level of people who now report war weariness is too high since they would like Americans to believe that they were not highly identified with the war effort. But the important point is that there are significant differences between the bombed and unbombed areas, in the number of people who say they did not want to go on with the war. These relative differences in morale are thus a function of bombing, since the respondents in schedule B did not know why they were being questioned.

The Interview Schedules

The English translations of the two forms of the interview schedules follow. Schedule A was given to every third respondent who had been bombed. It asks information about bombing more directly than does schedule B, which was given to two out of three bombed respondents and to all unbombed respondents.

Schedule A

1. How is it going with you now under the occupation?
2. Is it better or worse than you had expected?
3. What did you really expect?
4. How do you think you and your family will fare in the next 3 or 4 years?
5. How do you think you and your family would have fared in the next 3 or 4 years if Germany had in the end won the war?
6. When was your city bombed for the very first time?
7. Did the first air raid surprise you, or had you expected it?
8. Did you believe at that time that there would be more raids on your town after this first raid, or did you think that your town would now be left alone?
9. (If further raids expected) What did you think *then that the future raids would be like?*
10. When did you first experience a *big* raid?
11. How did you fare at that time? What were your experiences?
12. (If not covered) What did you do?
13. What were your feelings then, and did you react to it?
14. How many big raids did you experience?
15. Altogether, how many air raids did you experience?
16. Were you more and more afraid as the raids continued, or did you get used to them?
17. Did these repeated raids have any other effect on your state of mind?
18. Which of the following bombs did you find most terrible: Incendiaries, explosives, phosphorous, air mines?
19. Which were more terrible, day or night raids?

20. Did you blame the Allies for the air raids?
21. In your opinion, what do you think the Allies wanted to accomplish by these raids?
22. Do you think that this city was bombed more than was necessary for military purposes?
23. Do you think that the people here suffered more than those in other cities in Germany?
24. Did the newspapers and the radio correctly describe the general state of mind in the city after each air raid? (If no, then): Give me an example?
25. In what way was your normal way of life most upset by the air raids?
26. How were your family relationships affected by the raids?
27. Was your work affected in any way by the air raids?
28. How many workdays were you absent from your work in 1944?
29. Why were you absent?
30. How much free time did you take on your own?
31. Did you ever have to use any kind of subterfuge in order to get some free time?
32. (If subterfuge used) How many free days did you get by such subterfuge?

If respondent took no time off either on his own or through subterfuge ask 33 and 34:

33. How does it happen that you didn't take more free time for yourself?
34. Did you ever want to?
35. In your opinion, how well was your home town protected against air raids?
36. Was everything possible done?
37. (If dissatisfaction expressed) Who was to blame for it?
38. How good were the special meas-

ures and welfare services after the raids?

39. Was everything possible done?

40. (If dissatisfaction expressed) Who was to blame for it?

41. Did you people here in .... help each other after the raids, or did they only help themselves?

42. Did your opinions on the war change when the air raids didn't stop?

43. Did you ever come to a point because of the air raids where you simply didn't want to go on with the war?

44. What did you think at the time of "unconditional surrender?"

45. What in your opinion was the chief cause of the war?

Additional Questions: Evacuation

If respondent falls into A, B, or C, ask the appropriate questions:

A. Respondent evacuated from one community to another because of bombing or the threat of it.

B. Respondent's *family* evacuated because of bombing or the threat of it, but respondent remained behind.

C. Respondent and family did not evacuate, but lived in community to which evacuees came.

GROUP A

51. Did you leave .... voluntarily, or were you forced to go away? Please explain further.

52. Were official arrangements made for your trip and living facilities, or did you have to arrange them yourself?

53. Did your whole family that lived with you go with you, or did some of your family stay behind?

54. (If some stayed behind) Who? Why?

55. (If some stayed behind) Were you able to keep in touch regularly with the members of your family that were left behind?

56. In the main, how were you housed in the place to which you went?

57. Could you explain to me in a few words how you reacted to the evacuation?

GROUP B

61. Did your family leave .... voluntarily, or were they forced to go away? Please explain further.

62. Were official arrangements made for the trip and living facilities, or did you have to arrange them yourself?

63. Were you able to keep in touch regularly with the members of your family?

64. In the main, how were they housed in the place to which they went?

65. Could you explain to me in a few words how your family reacted to the evacuation?

GROUP C

71. Were there many evacuees or only a few?

72. Did you lodge any evacuated people?

73. (If *yes* to 72) Why did they live with you particularly?

74. (If *yes* to 72) How did it work out?

75. In general, what kind of people came to this community?

76. How well did the newcomers fit into their new surroundings?

Schedule B

1. How is it going with you now under the occupation?

2. Is it better or worse than you had expected?

3. What did you really expect?

4. How do you think you and your family will fare in the next 3 or 4 years?

5. How do you think you and your family would have fared in the next 3 or 4 years, if Germany had in the end won the war?

6. What do you think will happen to prices in the next few years?

7. If Germany had won the war, what do you think would have happened to prices?

8. What, in your opinion, is the chief reason that Germany lost the war?

9. What first brought you to the belief that Germany would lose the war?

10. As the war continued, what other influences strengthened your belief that Germany would lose the war?

11. Was your war leadership as good as you had expected?

12. Is that your opinion for both the political and military leadership?

13. How did you think about this shortly after the beginning of the war?

14. (If changed) Why did you change your opinion about it?

15. During the war, did you believe that your war leaders wanted what was best for you or not?

16. How well handled were the problems which the war brought here at home?

17. Do you think that you, personally, got along worse during the war than other people?

18. How did people of your circumstances get along in comparison with other people?

19. At the beginning of the war, did you expect that your life would be completely upset, or did you think that you yourself would not be affected by the war?

20. What was it that was hardest for the German civilian population during the war?

21. During the last year did you reflect much on the state of the war, or didn't you have time for that?

22. (If reflected) What did you think about?

23. Did you at any time during the war come to a point where you simply did not want to go on with the war?

24. What brought you to this point?

25. What did you think at that time of "unconditional surrender?"

26. How many workdays were you absent from your work in 1944?

27. Why were you absent?

28. How much free time did you take on your own?

29. Did you ever have to use any kind of subterfuge in order to get some free time?

30. (If subterfuge used) How many free days did you get by such subterfuge?

If respondent took no time off either on his own or through subterfuge, ask 31 and 32:

31. How does it happen that you didn't take more free time for yourself?

32. Did you ever want to?

33. What were your experiences with air raids?

34. During the war did you expect that you in this immediate vicinity would be exposed to air raids, or did you think that you would be spared?

35. Did the news of air-raid damage in other cities strengthen or weaken your will to see the war through?

36. Did you blame the Allies for the air raids?

37. In your opinion, what did the Allies want to accomplish with these raids?

38. During the war were you uneasy that the German armament industry would be critically damaged by the air raids or did you think that the armament industry was safe?

39. What did you think of the V-weapons when they were first used?

40. Did you ever listen to Allied broadcasts?

41. When did you first begin to listen?

42. What programs did you listen to?

Additional Questions: Evacuation

Some additional questions on evacuation as under schedule A.

Illustrative Examples of Procedural Materials Used to Guide Staff Members During the Processing Phases of Survey Research

National Opinion Research Center, New York Office

Basic Coding Instructions

A. *General Instructions*

Coding of survey results is a process of classifying into a limited number of categories the unique responses each person makes. It's purpose is to summarize the original data so that they may be transferred to punch cards and tabulated mechanically. A key number or code is assigned to each major response category, and these numbers are later punched onto a card to represent an individual's response. A punch card has eighty columns, each of which is used for a question or part of a question; the complete card represents one respondent's answers to the entire survey.

This brief description by itself should tell you that the fundamental rule in coding is: BE ACCURATE. If you assign the wrong code to an answer or write your figures so illegibly that the puncher misinterprets them, or puts them in the wrong column, the results of the survey are distorted. So we give you these general rules to follow:

1. Use red pencil.

2. Write your figures clearly.

3. Do not erase. Cross out incorrect material.

4. Enter your codes just to the right of the column number.

In surveys, two types of questions are generally used: PRECODED and FREE-ANSWER. A precoded question is one for which the answer categories were supplied in advance. These categories are printed in the questionnaire with the code numbers already assigned to them. Free-answer questions, on the other hand, are not worked out in advance. The interviewer simply writes down exactly what the respondent says. In general, the following rule applies: On precoded questions, you edit the interviewer's work to see that an appropriate code number has been circled; in free-answer questions, you enter the appropriate code number yourself.

B. *Instructions for Precoded Questions*

These questions are for the most part already coded by the interviewer who has circled a code number to stand for the respondent's answer. *You are to check and edit the interviewer's coding.*

1. Make sure that a code has been circled for each question which should have been asked of the particular respondent.

2. Make sure that nothing has been circled if the question *should not* have been asked of the particular respondent.

3. If the interviewer has placed his circle badly—so that the puncher might misinterpret the number he is to punch— recircle accurately in red.

4. If the interviewer has skipped a question which should have been asked, code the question "Y" (answer not ascertainable).

5. If the interviewer has left the question uncoded but has written in what the respondent said—as he will sometimes do if he is not sure how to classify the respondent's answer—read the comments and circle the code which seems to you to come closest to the respondent's opinion. If the written answer is too qualified to fit any of the major categories, it will have to be edited to the "Don't Know" category.

6. If the interviewer has circled two contradictory codes on the same question —for most of these questions only one code can logically be circled—you are also to edit by reference to the comments as in No. 5 above. If there are no comments, edit to "Don't Know."

7. If an answer has been circled but the accompanying comment suggests that a different answer should have been circled consult your supervisor.

8. A *sub-question* should have been asked only when it is applicable. Its applicability is usually dictated by the answer to the original question itself. If the sub-question is answered and the original question is blank, or if applicable and inapplicable code numbers have been circled in the original question, the sub-question is to be considered applicable. In case of contradiction, consult your supervisor.

9. In some cases you will have to code an "other" or "qualified" category on precoded questions. Here you supply the proper code from your code sheets.

C. *Instructions for Free-answer Questions*

Codes have been developed for these questions by reading a sample of responses. These codes appear on the code sheets which have been given you.

1. Whenever the question is applicable, at least one code must be entered. If a code sheet states "multiple coding permitted," this means that more than one code may be used for the question. In all other cases, only one code is to be used. As before, if the question should have been asked but was left blank, enter Code Y.

2. Familiarize yourself with the codes and make sure you understand the distinctions between codes for a given question. Read all the examples. The title on the code category is merely a guide, *not a complete statement* of what is contained in the category.

3. Read each verbatim response and assign a code or codes to it. You are coding *ideas* not words, so you may not find the exact phrase before you on your code sheet. Most of the time you will find the idea behind it in the code, however.

4. *One idea should receive only one code.* If you use two codes you should be able to point to *separate* words, phrases or clauses in the answer corresponding to them. If you have to point to the same set of words for both codes, only one code should have been used. This difficulty usually arises when a coder thinks an answer could be *either* Code 1 or Code 2, and then codes both to save making the decision. *Double-coding of an "either-or" type of problem is always incorrect.*

5. *Where multiple codes are permitted, every idea in the answer should be coded.*

6. When more than one code is used they are usually to be listed alongside of each other with a dash between each number as: 2–5.

7. A *"miscellaneous"* code is provided for *all genuine ideas* which are not contained in the code proper. Do not put

unintelligible, vague, irrelevant responses in the "miscellaneous" category; separate provision is made in the codes for this sort of response. *A "miscellaneous" answer must be one for which a separate code could be provided if it arose with sufficient frequency.*

8. Write in on your code sheet all answers which you have coded "miscellaneous." Unanticipated answers may come up with a frequency which dictates that they be reported separately. Writing in all miscellaneous responses enables us to know what is contained in the "miscellaneous" category.

9. "Vague, irrelevant," "Don't know" and "No answer" codes always apply to the entire answer and are, therefore, *not to be coded in combination with any other code.* If anything else can be coded, these codes are not used.

D. *Checking Procedure*

During the course of your coding you will frequently be asked to check a certain percentage of the work of other coders. The colored "check-sheet" on top of each pack is used for checking. When a pack is given to you to be checked on a particular page, the supervisor will tell you what percentage of the questionnaires are to be checked—1/3, 1/2, 100%, or whatever. You will then apply the correct ratio in your checking. For example, if the ratio is one-third you will check the first, skip two, check the next one, etc., checking every third questionnaire.

Make an entry on a separate line of the check-sheet each time you disagree with the coder, or each time you discover an error or omission by the original coder —either on a precoded question or on a free-answer question. Do not make entries when you agree. In each instance of a disagreement, enter in the first column the page number, in the second column the number of the question, in the third column the number of the interview (questionnaire), and in the fourth column the name of the interviewer.

In the next column labeled "by coder," write in whatever the coder has coded, and in the column labeled "by checker," write in what you think *should* be coded. Enter here the *complete code* you believe should be used, not merely any additions you feel should be made. Thus, in a ques-

tion permitting multiple coding, if the coder has coded a 1 and you feel it should be 1 *and* 2, write down "1–2." Leave the final column blank for the supervisor to resolve the differences between you.

In checking try your best to *make an independent judgment.* Coders sometimes make the mistake of too readily agreeing with another coder, and often are too easily impressed by the fact that a particular code number has been judged correct by someone else. If you are thoroughly familiar with the code, you should be able to make correct independent judgments in most cases.

A certain percentage of all coders' work is checked, and all coders are asked to do some checking.

E. *Administrative Procedures*

Questionnaires are numbered as they are received and grouped in packs of one hundred. A pack (or one hundred questionnaires) is the unit with which you will usually be working at any given time. As a general rule, coders are asked to code *only one page at a time* on a given pack. In this way they become familiar with the codes for the questions on that page more quickly than if they were to code the entire questionnaire at once. Thus at any given time you will be working on "Pack X, Page X." When you complete the page assigned for the entire pack, return it to the supervisor to be entered on the control sheet, and you will then receive a new assignment.

We have established several rules concerning coding operations, which we ask you to observe:

1. *If you are in doubt about what code number to place on a questionnaire,* consult your supervisor, *not your fellow coders.* Since we maintain a record of the reliability of our coding operations, we want the independent judgment of the coder on a question, rather than group judgments. The individual whom you consult might later be asked to check your work, and would of course find himself in agreement with you, thereby spuriously inflating the reliability of our operations.

2. *If you wish to consult the supervisor on a coding problem, wait until you have finished a pack on a given page.* Bring up all the questions you have on that

pack at that time. This procedure saves time for the supervisor who is usually engaged in other work.

3. *Please keep discussion at a minimum during working periods.* Due to crowded conditions it is difficult for a coder to work accurately while conversation is going on, and errors inevitably result when a coder is trying to code and listen to an interesting conversation at the same time. Whenever you need a break from the work—take it. But don't get involved in any discussions *while* working, or in the same place others are working.

4. It is the responsibility of coders coding *page 1*, to make sure that the questionnaire has been properly processed. The following check should be made by those coding page 1:

(1) See that the questionnaire is adequately stapled.

(2) See that each questionnaire has been assigned a number, and that there are no numbers omitted or duplicated. Any numbering deficiencies should be reported at once to the supervisor.

(3) Rewrite any questionnaire number which is illegible.

5. Coders in general should watch out for duplicate pages, or omitted pages in the questionnaire. Tear out any duplicate pages. Report to the supervisor as soon as discovered.

6. *All material is to be considered confidential.* This includes questions, codes, responses and any names or addresses that come to your attention during coding. NORC surveys are done entirely for nonprofit organizations and institutions and we have committed ourselves to both our clients and our respondents not to reveal anything about the survey to unauthorized persons. We ask you to aid us in keeping our pledges. Please do not discuss any aspect of the survey with anyone except NORC personnel.

F. *Coding Factual Data*

On NORC surveys we regularly secure factual information about the respondents. As in the case of opinion material, some of the factual questions are precoded and some free-answer. The same coding rules which apply to opinion material also apply to factual material.

Since a good many factual items have been standardized and are repeated in almost all surveys, instructions are given below for coding those items which usually appear on NORC surveys. Instructions for coding factual items not included here will be supplied to coders along with code sheets for specific surveys.

The following items are usually precoded. Instructions covering pre-coded questions are applicable in general. In addition the specific instructions for particular items are to be followed.

Education. One and only one code number must be circled in each case. Where more than one code has been circled, edit to the *lowest* amount of schooling (the highest code number). The "name of last school attended" should be used to decide cases in which the interviewer circled no code.

Political Preference. One and only one code number must be circled in each case. If two or more are circled or if the respondent refused to answer, edit to "Don't Know." Note however, that as usual with pre-coded questions, if the interviewer failed to ask the question, Code Y should be entered.

Religion. One and only one should be circled. "Catholic" refers to Roman Catholic only. Greek Orthodox respondents should be coded as "Other." All Protestant denominations should be coded Protestant. If "Other" has been circled in the case of a Protestant denomination, the code for "Other" should be crossed out and Protestant circled by the coder. "Latter-Day Saints," "Christian Scientists," "Holy Rollers," "Amish," "Mennonites," "Jehovah's Witnesses" and other more or less unusual denominations are "Protestant." In case of doubt consult your supervisor.

The following items are pre-coded, and should be treated the same as other precoded items with one exception. *In the case of the following items, an omission or contradiction should not be coded before consulting with the supervisor.* These items are characteristics by which the sample is selected, so frequently an error can be remedied by consulting the quota or check-in sheets.

Sex, Race, Economic Level, Size of Town. One code only should be circled in each case. In case of doubt consult supervisor.

The following items are not pre-coded, and *must be coded according to the codes herein given, unless you are otherwise instructed:*

MAIN EARNERS OCCUPATION

AGE

PLACE AND STATE

The last two of these are also characteristics by which the sample is selected so the rule cited above concerning doubtful cases is again applicable: *In case of doubt, consult before coding.*

To sum up then, in coding the following items you will *not* follow the regular rules for omission and contradiction on pre-coded questions, but will consult the supervisor for the correct information: *Sex, Race, Economic Level, Size of town, Age and Place and State.*

Codes for Free-answer Factual Items

The following code is to be used for occupation of the main earner.

1. *Professional, Business, White-collar, Clerical, Sales.* This includes all proprietors and owners, entertainers, administrators, supervisors, army officers. In general, people who do not do manual work, or whose manual work is confined to their own business.

2. *Manual workers.* This includes skilled, semi-skilled and unskilled workers who are in non-service industries (see below). All these who are *directly* engaged in industrial production in manual occupations.

3. *Service workers.* These engaged in personal or domestic services. Those who receive tips and those who are in protective service occupations. Included are occupations such as waiter, barber, beautician, taxi driver, usher, maid, household cook, laundress, policeman, fireman, watchman, guard, mail carrier, milkman, motorman, hearse driver, bartender, army enlisted personnel.

4. *Farm workers and owners.* All people who work on farms as their principal occupation.

5. *No main earner.* Retired, unemployed, living on a pension, students, living on income.

Y. *Not ascertainable.* Occupation omitted or indeterminable.

In case two or more occupations have been listed by the interviewer and neither has been designated as the principal oc-

cupation, consult your supervisor before coding.

The following code is to be used for age:

2. 21–29

3. 30–39

4. 40–49

5. 50–59

6. 60–69

7. 70 and over

Y. Not ascertainable

Respondents under 21 should not have been interviewed. Please report any such cases to the supervisor.

The following code is to be used for place and state:

1. East. New England, Middle Atlantic: (Maine, Vermont, Connecticut, Massachusetts, Rhode Island, New Hampshire, New York, New Jersey, Pennsylvania)

2. Midwest. East North Central, West North Central: (Ohio, Indiana, Illinois, Michigan, Wisconsin, Minnesota, North Dakota, South Dakota, Iowa, Nebraska, Kansas, Missouri)

3. South. South Atlantic, East South Central, West South Central: (District of Columbia, Virginia, West Virginia, Delaware, Maryland, North Carolina, South Carolina, Georgia, Florida, Kentucky, Alabama, Tennessee, Mississippi, Louisiana, Arkansas, Oklahoma, Texas)

4. Far West. Mountain, Pacific: (Montana, Idaho, Washington, Oregon, Wyoming, Colorado, Utah, Nevada, New Mexico, Arizona, California)

Codes for other free-answer factual items which are included from time to time will be distributed with the code sheets.

The following items which usually appear among the factual data *are not to be coded* unless instructions are issued to the contrary.

NAME OF LAST SCHOOL ATTENDED

RESPONDENTS HOME ADDRESS

Interviewer's name is sometimes coded and sometimes not. When it is to be coded, you will receive a code sheet listing the number of each interviewer.

G. *Special Instructions for Miscellaneous Responses to Free-Answer Questions*

1. *Coding.*

Whenever you code a free answer in the miscellaneous category on any question, in addition to marking the ballot, do the following:

Record page number, question number, and interview number on the back of the code sheet designated for miscellaneous responses. (In addition to the regular Code Check Sheet(s) for each pack of ballots there will be one or more check sheets for miscellaneous responses only.)

2. *Checking.*

Whenever checking a pack of questionnaires, follow the usual checking procedure, doing a one-third or one hundred percent check as instructed.

AT THE SAME TIME check ALL the miscellaneous responses that the coder has indicated on the back of the code sheet for miscellaneous answers.

(a) If you *agree* with the coder—that the answer belongs in the miscellaneous category—place a check-mark to the right of the coder's entry on back of sheet.

(b) If you *disagree* with the coder and feel that the answer should not have been coded "miscellaneous," make a disagreement entry on the front of the miscellaneous code sheet in the usual way, indicating what you think should be coded.

CODE CHECK SHEET

MAKE ENTRIES FOR EACH DISAGREEMENT

NC--Not Coded
E--Editing Error

Survey No._____
Ballot Nos._____to_____

Page No.	Ques No.	Ballot No.	By Coder	By Checker	Final Code	Page No.	Ques No.	Ballot No.	By Coder	By Checker	FiNal Code

1	10	19	28	37	46	55	64	73
2	11	20	29	38	47	56	65	74
3	12	21	30	39	48	57	66	75
4	13	22	31	40	49	58	67	76
5	14	23	32	41	50	59	68	77
6	15	24	33	42	51	60	69	78
7	16	25	34	43	52	61	70	79
		35	44	53	62	71	80	
		36	45	54	63	72		

In the *code sheet* above, each numbered box represents a column. The *coder* enters the appropriate code in the proper box. Then independently, the *checker* performs the same operations on a sub-sample of answers using another code sheet. The two code sheets are then compared by a third person, the *resolver*, who notes the disagreements on the *code check sheet* shown above, and decides which of the two original codes shall be the final code. In this manner, the coding is checked, errors are spotted and corrected, and an estimate of the magnitude and type of error present is made available to the analyst.

MISCELLANEOUS RESPONSES

✓ - Coder Correct

Ballot Nos._____ to _____   Survey No. _____

Page No.	Ques. No.	Ballot No.	Enter Verbatim All Miscellaneous Responses	By Checker	Final

Subject: Sex x Source of Book Obtainment

Study: NAB (all)

NO. SHEET / ANAL. / TAB. / TOTAL CARDS / CARDS USED / TOTAL

No Duplicates — COL. 54 / COL. 65

COL. NO.		1	%	2	%
1	public library	67	16%	107	21%
2	rental library	26	6	43	8
3	borough public library	70	17	143	28
4	bought	174	42	126	25
5	home collection	35	8	42	8
6	gift	22	5	18	4
7	"don't remember"	6	2	11	2
8	other	16	4	20	4
9					
0					
x					
y					
r					
	TOTAL	421		510	

Problem Exercises

Problem Exercise I: Routine Punch Card Processing for Descriptive Surveys

The following exercise is designed to acquaint the student with the *rudiments* of punch-card processing and to enable him to develop facility with the fundamental techniques. It is designed for use with the IBM Card Counting Sorter, Type 75, the equipment which has been common in most social research organizations and therefore most probably what the student will have at his disposal.[1] It provides an introduction to the basic equipment and skills needed.

The survey from which the exercise was built was that of *American Opinion on Commercial Radio*, previously discussed in the text. The student will, therefore, have some familiarity with the content of the study, but he should reacquaint himself with the questionnaire on p. 400. The student should also familiarize himself with Figure I, p. 22, since reference will be made not only to the research process elaborated therein, but also to the specific mechanical parts of the SORTER shown in the diagram.

The processes with which we will be dealing come under the heading of *sorting* and counting. We will be working with cards *already* punched and verified. The cards included in the practice deck are only for those respondents who possessed radios in working order at the time the survey was administered. In other words, they would have had to answer YES to question 1A in order to be included in the practice deck.

---

1. A new and more complex machine is now coming into use for the same research operations as are discussed in the Exercise. The IBM Electronic Statistical Machine, Type 101, offers many advantages in speed and efficiency.

Materials needed:

Deck of punch cards punched for Survey 238 (Special deck) [2]
Blank tabulation sheets
IBM Card-Counting Sorter, Type 75 [3]
Code book for the Radio Survey, #238, and questionnaire

IA. Counting of Straight Runs for Aggregate Description [4]

Illustrative Example

Question 2 of Survey 238 reads:

Taking everything into consideration, which one of these do you think did the best job of serving the public during the war: Magazines, newspapers, moving pictures, or radio broadcasting?

Problem

Each respondent picked one of these categories as his choice, and now we want to know how many respondents picked each of the four categories, in other words, the *distribution of choices.*

Step 1

Look up in the questionnaire and code book the column into which the responses to Question 2 were coded and punched. In this case, it will be Column 6.

Note:

Each column may be punched in 12 positions, designated as 1, 2, 3, 4, 5, 6, 7, 8, 9, 0, x, y. In practice, however, not more than two or three of these positions are normally utilized on each column. In the case of Question 2, the column contains only one punch per respondent and is said to be *single punched.* When two or more positions are punched for each respondent the column is said to be *multiple punched.*

In the questionnaire and code book we notice that each category of Question 2, magazines, newspapers, etc., has been assigned a different code number, each of which corresponds to the numbered position punched into the column of the IBM card. For example, if the respondent selects *magazines* in answer to the question, his choice is coded 1, and a hole is punched into the "one" position of Column 6.

Step 2

Prepare the tabulation sheet. In the sorting and counting operation, the sorter automatically classifies and counts the cards according to the number punched into the specified column, in this case, Col. 6. In order to record the results, we prepare a *tabulation sheet* as follows:

COL. 6

	Code	Number of Respondents Answering
Magazines	1	
Newspapers	2	
Moving pictures	3	
Radio broadcasting	4	
No opinion	5	
Total N		

After the cards are "run," the number of cards falling into each code category will be read off the counting board and

---

2. In order for the student to complete the Exercises in reasonable time, only a portion of the total sample from the original survey is used.

3. Other types of sorters are not equipped with counting boards. Figure I shows the Card Counting Sorter, the type needed for the Exercises. The Counting Board contains 15 dials: twelve of these are numbered to correspond to the twelve positions that can be punched in a column and count the occurrence of the corresponding *punches.* The student should note that dials numbered "11" and "12" are the equivalent of the punches on the card labelled "x" and "y". The thirteenth dial counts the cards which have *no* punch in the particular column, cards which are "rejected." The 14th and 15th dials count the sub-total and grand-total of all cards. As will be explained later, the counting and sorting operations are essentially independent, so that *under certain conditions,* the number of cards in a given *pocket* cannot be determined from the counting dials, although the number of cards with that particular *punch* will be accurately recorded.

4. A discussion of the application of aggregate descriptions is contained in Part II of the text.

entered in the proper spaces on the tabulation sheet.

Step 3

Set the column pointer so that the pointer is opposite the number "6" on the column indicator guide. The close-up Figure presented below conveys the location of the column pointer, indicator guide, and the crank handle and thumb lever used in setting the machine for the correct column. Normally, the setting is done by rotating the small crank handle located at the front of the feed hopper. Each rotation of the handle moves the pointer one column on the guide. The pointer may be moved more quickly across a number of columns by raising the crank handle to the upper position and moving the pointer to the desired column by pressing down on the thumb lever on the top of the assembly.

Step 4

Carefully place the cards in the hopper. If the card deck's edges are not *even,* they may jam in the machine. The student can insure that they are even by the following procedure of *tamping.* Hold the cards loosely in one hand, on the glass joggle plate, with the back of the cards toward you, and one end of the cards against the end of the joggle plate. The cards

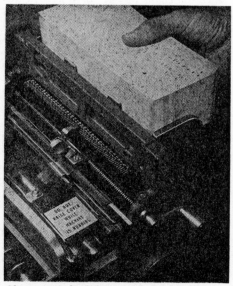

Close-up of the Hopper and Column Pointer

are then tapped at the top and other end of the cards until all four sides are even. Ideally, the edges should be about as even as the pages of a closed book. Next the cards are placed *face down* (printed side down) in the hopper so that the *lower edge* (the 9 position) will feed into the machine *first.* In the Figure below, the operator has his fingers and thumb arranged around the deck in such a way that it will be fed into the machine properly. The card weight should always be placed on top of the cards.

Step 5

Clear the counting board so that any previous totals are eliminated. All counters can be cleared in a single operation by pushing the bottom clutch lever that juts out from the lower right hand corner of the counting board and rotating the clearing crank.

Step 6

Arrange the SORTING and COUNTING switches. These switches are usually on the front of the machine near the Hopper and are clearly marked. When both switches are ON, the machine will simultaneously sort all cards passing through into the pockets, and will count the punch holes appearing in the column being sorted. When only the sort switch is ON, the machine sorts the cards into pockets but will not count. When only the count switch is on, the machine will count the punched holes, but all cards will be deposited into the "R" or *reject* pocket. In the illustrative problem, *all* we wish to know is the distribution of replies, i.e., the *number of cards* having each of the punches in the code. There is no need for us to have the actual cards *separated* or sorted into piles depending on their answers since we do not plan any subsequent tabulation of these separate groups. The student should therefore place the Count switch ON, and the Sort switch OFF.

The student who has read the text can surmise that *aggregate description of a discrete dependent variable* or description of a *discrete characteristic of the aggregate sample* only involves Counting. In descriptive analyses, the only phases where one needs to *sort* or separate cards into sub-groups for some subsequent counting would be for *differentiated* descriptions of a discrete dependent variable, *inter-correlations* to establish the generality or specificity of a phenomenon, or *index-construction* involving the pooling of information from a number of discrete variables.

Caution

Before starting the machine, check with your instructor to insure that all adjustments have been properly made. Faulty procedure can jam the machine and possibly ruin an expensive deck of cards.

Step 7

Press the start button. Once started, the machine will continue to operate automatically. It is equipped with several *safety devices* which are activated under certain conditions and which automatically stop all operations. Some of the "safety devices" do not indicate any mishap: A. The machine will stop automatically when the *Hopper runs out of cards* to feed. B. Each pocket of the sorter is equipped with an automatic pocket stop. When any one of the thirteen *pockets becomes filled to capacity* with cards (approximately 550 cards), the machine automatically stops. When this occurs, the student should remove the cards from the loaded pocket, placing them on a convenient shelf or in the racks common in machine rooms, being sure to note the number of the pocket involved. After the pocket has been cleared, the machine can be re-started by pressing the start button. C. *When a card is damaged, it may fail to feed* into the machine. In such instances, the machine automatically stops. The student should then call the instructor, since the card may have to be duplicated before the machine run can be continued.

With practice, a machine operator can keep a machine in continuous operation by adding cards to the hopper while the original batch is being fed. Sometimes, during uninterrupted sorting, cards may not fall smoothly into their pockets. If not, the student should press the *stop button,* rearrange the cards in that pocket into a smooth pile and then re-start the machine.

If the student checks on all of these above conditions which govern the activation of the safety devices and still cannot account for the stoppings, he should consult his instructor.

While the cards are being "run," observe how the machine operates. All cards with a "1" punched into Col. 6 are being registered on dial 1 of the counting board; dial 2 is registering the cards punched "2," etc. The dials numbered 11 and 12 correspond to the punches "x" and "y" on the card. As you probably have surmised, this operation is known as "counting" and we frequently talk of "runs." As explained above when the sort switch is OFF, all the cards will be dropped into the "R" pocket.

Occasionally, it is the case that one or more respondents are not assigned any code at all and have no punch entered in a given column. For example, the question may not have been asked of them, in which case, the column may contain no punch. The "13" Dial on the counting board corresponds to this "R" or reject category. It so happens that in the questionnaire for Survey 238, Question 2 was asked of all respondents. However, a quick glance through the ballot will show that not all the questions were asked of every respondent. This is important to remember in recording future "runs" since the *count* on "R" or rejected cards will often explain a discrepancy between the total count of other punches and the total number of cards, to be expected for the entire sample. Since one is only engaging in Counting, such rejected cards will be mixed in with all other cards in the reject pocket, but this is of no consequence for our tabulation.[5]

Step 8

Record the information contained on the counting board dials onto the tabulation sheets. Your own results should coincide with the following distribution: (the number of respondents answering each category of Question 2 is called the *distribution of responses* to Question 2.)

If any errors have occurred, carefully review the initial procedure. In the event that a discrepancy still exists, consult your instructor.

---

5. It will be clear to the student shortly how these cards could be separated if desirable.

Q. 2, COL. 6

Category	Code	Number of Respondents Answering
Magazines	1	28
Newspapers	2	71
Moving pictures	3	14
Radio broadcasting	4	462
No opinion	5	40
Total N		615

Step 9

Carefully remove the cards from the pockets and prepare them for the next run. That is, straighten the edges of the deck.

In practice, a whole series of such distributions of responses may be obtained, one for each question. This is the basis for any aggregate description.

Simple Sorting

To illustrate the simplest aspects of *sorting* for the student, we shall now repeat the same illustrative problem and *sort* in addition to counting. We repeat the necessary steps of clearing the counting board, tamping the cards and putting them properly into the hopper. However, now in what was Step *six*, we shall also turn the *Sort Switch to ON*. There is also one additional step necessary in doing sorting, in contrast with counting.

Step 7

Set the Selection Switches. These can be identified from the close-up Figure presented below. There are 12 small black switches and one large red switch around the rim of a metal circle. These can be moved in or out, towards the rim or towards the center of the circle. The selector device is on the front of the machine below the crank for the column pointer. For special types of problems to be presented below, these switches are very important and each must be set in a rather complicated way. For all of the problems you will deal with, the *red* switch must always be set *OUT*, i.e., pushed to the *edge or rim* of the circle. For *regular sorting on single punched columns,* as in our illustrative problem, *all the black switches with the same numbers as the punches in that column,* in

this case, 1-5, must be set OUT, i.e., pushed toward the rim of the circle.

Press the start button, and observe how the cards are automatically sorted. Each pocket has a number corresponding to the numbered position on the card. All cards with a 1 punched into Col. 6 will fall into pocket 1, cards with a 2 punch will fall in pocket 2, etc. Meanwhile the counting dials are registering. The results of the count naturally should agree with the first run you made.

PROBLEMS IN COUNTING

1. Tabulate the distribution of responses to Question 7. In other words, find out how many respondents select each category.

2. Tabulate the distribution of responses to Question 5.

Note: There are several things that must be taken into account in performing this exercise. First of all, it is apparent that unlike Question 1, this is not a *pre-coded* question. The respondent is not restricted by the question structure to choosing a response from a limited set of pre-designated alternatives, but is permitted to offer any answer that occurs to him. Such questions are frequently referred to as *open-ended,* and the answers called *free-answers.* The categories into which such responses fall are constructed *after* the questionnaires are returned. Each category is then assigned a code number. Frequently, in answer to a question such as this, a given respondent will offer several responses, and, it may turn out that each of these responses falls into a different category. In this case each of them receives a code. There then appears on the card as many punches as there are codes; a column with several punches is known as a multiple punched column, as distinct from a *single punched* column. Because each respondent is permitted to offer several responses, each one of which is coded and punched, the total number of responses will *exceed* the total number of respondents.[6] It is important to remember this when performing computations such as percentaging, on such data.

The *counting* dials work in exactly the

---

6. For an excellent discussion of different modes of analytic treatment of such problems, see Hans Zeisel, *Say It With Figures* (New York: Harpers 1947), Chapter 2 and 4.

same fashion whether there is single punching or multiple punching. They will register the existence of punched holes in *any* of the numbered positions in the column even where other punches also exist on that column of that card. The *sorting*, however, is complicated by the presence of multiple punching. (Multiple punching can, of course, occur in many situations other than open-ended questions.) It is obvious that the machine can only *sort* a card on the basis of *one* of its punches at a time. Usually, the machine will sort on the *highest* numbered punch to touch the sorting brush, and ignore the others.[7] Consequently, if a respondent answered the question in terms of several categories, say codes 2, 4, and 7, the machine would sort the card into pocket seven. This means that the cards for many of the respondents (those who offered multiple responses) would be deposited into the *highest* numbered pockets. However, since the *counting* operation of the SORTER is essentially *independent* of the *sorting* operation, the counting dials will still record accurately *all* the punches in the column. Consequently, it is obvious that in the case of *multiple punching*, when the counting dials are recording *all* the punches, but the cards are being sorted only into the highest numbered pockets, the dials cannot give an accurate representation of the number of cards in *each pocket*. This is extremely important to remember. If one had engaged in *sorting* for purposes of separating a given subgroup which would subsequently be tabulated on some other variable, some of the cards which one would want in that subgroup might be present in another pocket, if they had been multiply punched with a higher numbered position. This problem is solved by the special use of the *selection* switches, and will be dealt with at the proper time.

3. Tabulate the distribu-

tion of responses to Question 4-A.

Note: When the student has completed the problem, he will see that not only does he have the distribution of answers to Question 4A (the number of cards punched 1, 2, and 3) but that all the other counting dials have entries. While *Question 4A* was single punched, this is because Questions 4b, 4c, and 4d were also coded onto this same column by the use of multiple punching. Thus, by *one single* machine operation or count, descriptions on *four* different variables have been obtained. The student can see that this represents a real gain in efficiency. Particularly, where the questions are *dependent* variables, for which *no future sorting* is likely to be required, such a procedure of coding is especially useful. However, let us suppose we had wished to sort the cards by reference to the answers to question 4A for some subsequent analysis. The student can see that the multiple punching would create difficulties. The cards would be sorted into the *higher numbered* positions, and one could not engage in the necessary separation. This is where the use of the selection switches is required.

USE OF SELECTION SWITCHES

Despite the fact that Column 10 is multiply punched, there is a simple way

Close-up of the Selector Switches

---

7. This follows from the way the card is fed into the machine. Since the lower edge, punch 9, is fed first, the machine will drop a card that is multiply punched into the 9 pocket first. The 8 pocket would take precedence over 7, 7 over 6, etc., in instances where such pairs of punches exist on the card.

to sort the cards into groups that have been punched 1, 2, or 3. In regular sorting as previously noted, *all* the switches for which there were corresponding punches are pushed *out* to the rim. When only the cards punched in certain positions are to be selected, or sorted into a given pocket, it is necessary to pull toward the *center* all the selection switches except those corresponding to the positions to be selected.

When a particular switch is *"out,"* cards punched in the numbered position corresponding to the number on the switch will be sorted, i.e., *"selected"* into the pocket bearing the same number.

When a particular switch is *IN,* the card will not sort into that pocket.

For example, if a 5 is punched into a particular column, and we are sorting on that column with the selector switch out, the card will be deposited into pocket five. However, if the switch corresponding to pocket five is pushed in, *away from the rim,* a card with a punch in position five will not be deposited into pocket five, but instead will be placed into the *reject or R pocket,* if the column is *single punched.* However, when a column is *multiply punched,* the machine will sort on the highest other punch whose selector switch has *not been pushed in.* It will then deposit the card into the pocket corresponding to that numbered position. Should it turn out that *all* of the switches corresponding to the punches in a particular column for that card are pushed in, the card will then be deposited in the reject or R pocket.

Thus, to sort on question 4A, the student would set the selection switches 1, 2, and 3 *OUT* to the rim, and would push *all* the remaining *black* switches in towards the center. The bigger *red* switch should be left *out* towards the rim. The student should now select and sort on Q. 4A. He will see that the cards sort into pockets 1, 2, and 3. After doing this, put all the cards together and prepare for the next exercise.

We shall now turn to a new stage of machine operation appropriate to other types of analytic problems in descriptive survey analysis.

IB. Simple Cross Tabulation of Two Variables for Purposes of Differential Description, Explanation or Illustrating Interrelationships.[8]

ILLUSTRATIVE EXAMPLE

Problem

Do men differ from women in the source from which each receives daily news? In other words, does the variable of sex differentiate respondents in terms of their source of news? Or putting the question in another way, what is the distribution of responses to Question 4A *separately* for men and for women?

Step 1

Look up the code book and determine the column for sex and the column for Question 4A. *Prepare the tabulation Sheet.* A convenient model appears below.

		COL. 67		
		Men 1	Women 2	Total
Col. 10	Code			
Newspapers	1			
Radio	2			
Don't know	3			
Total		___	___	___

This operation involves three runs. The respondents will first be *sorted* according to sex (run 1). Then, the distribution of each sex's responses to Question 4A will be *counted.* (run 2, run 3).

Step 2

Set the column indicator to the proper number, in this case column 67. Place the cards in the hopper, clear the board, make sure that *both* the sorting and counting switches are in the *ON* position, push the selector switches 1 and 2 out to the rim, and finally press the start button.

When the machine has stopped, all male respondents should be in pocket one, and all female respondents should be in pocket two.

Step 3

Record the number of men and women as registered on dials one and two of the

---

8. For further discussion, see p. 121 of the text.

counting board. Enter these on the tab sheet on the "total" line under the appropriate category.

Step 4

Clear the counting board.

Step 5

Remove the cards from pockets one and two, being careful *not to mix up the two piles.*

Step 6

From the code book we know that the responses to Question 4A are contained in Column 10, so we set the column indicator to 10.

Step 7

Take only the cards belonging to the male respondents (those from pocket one), and place them in the hopper. Turn the sorting switch *OFF,* since we only need to count on column 10.

Step 8

Start the machine. When the cards have been run, record the results from the counting board onto the tab sheet. This provides the distribution of news sources for male respondents. Then clear the counting board.

Step 9

Repeat steps 7 and 8, only this time for *female* respondents. Take the cards that were in pocket two and run them. Record the results in the same fashion as for males. Notice that we made two runs on the *same* column. This is done because we have two categories on the independent variable and we wish to determine how the distribution of responses to a particular question varies for each category of the independent variable. Thus, we now have the distribution of

responses for men separately, and for women separately. Your results should coincide with those just presented.

Note: The totals for men and women, 270 and 345, are obtained automatically from the counting board. However, the other set of totals, 184, 408, and 23, must be obtained *manually* by adding across the rows of the tabulation sheet. This is because they derive from two *separate* machine runs (the count based on the men and the count based on women). Thus, they will not be totalled by the machine.

These totals illustrate one type of *check the operator can make on accuracy* of his runs. These totals happen to correspond to the marginals or straight run on Col. 10, Question 4-A, which was obtained previously in Problem 3 above. The present totals should therefore be cross-checked against the earlier results. If they do not agree, an error has occurred in *one* of the runs, for example, in the operator's addition, in "posting" the numbers from the counting dials on to the tabulation sheet, in running the wrong column by accident, etc. A variety of cross checks are possible between separate runs, or between a run and independent figures on the size of the sample or of given cells, or against the code book to see whether multiple punching or a given code category could legitimately have occurred. All such cross-checks are desirable in insuring accuracy.

The student will note that the dials for punches other than 1, 2, and 3 have also registered. This is because column 10 was multiply punched to contain the answers to questions 4 b, c, and d. Thus, the one machine procedure netted 4 cross-tabulations. Again, one can see the gain in efficiency for cross-tabulation, when *dependent* variables have been multiply punched.

Problems—B

1. How does *education* influence the source from which a respondent gets most of his daily news? [9] Do people with different educational backgrounds choose different news sources?

2. How is magnitude of *evening* listen-

COL. 67

Col. 10		Men 1	Women 2	Total
Newspapers	1	109	75	184
Radio	2	154	254	408
Don't know	3	7	16	23
Total		270	345	615

9. It will be noted that two cards are coded Y, meaning that *education* for these respondents was unascertainable. In performing future cross tabulations it is important to keep this in mind. Usually, such cases are discarded in any educational breakdown.

ing differentiated by educational background? In what way does it vary with education?

Note: Generally, for reasons discussed in the text, it is desirable to have the independent variable (e.g. education) originally coded into many fine subdivisions. However, for certain analyses such refinements will not be used. For example, instead of using education divided in seven levels, analysis is simplified or aided by the use of only three gross levels: college, high school, and grammar school or less. The seven levels are collapsed into three in the following manner:

Code

1. completed college
2. some college } college

3. completed high school } high
4. some high school } school

5. completed grammar
   school
6. 4-7 yrs. grammar school } grammar
7. No school to 4 years } school

This combination of categories can be accomplished in two ways. The distribution of the dependent variable can be tabulated for *each* of the refined subdivisions (all seven levels) of the independent variable, and the final results combined *manually* by adding cell frequencies. Two major disadvantages are inherent in this method: it takes much more time to run the cards on seven levels than on three, and, the process of adding cell frequencies can easily result in computational errors.

There is another method which is easier and more efficient. The cards are sorted in terms of the independent variable as before, so that, for example, education would be sorted into seven categories. Then, simply combine the cards in pocket 1 with those in pocket 2, combine the cards in pocket 3 with those in pocket 4,

and combine the cards in pockets 5, 6, and 7. In this way the seven refined subdivisions of the independent variable have been combined to produce three gross subdivisions. Now the distribution of the dependent variable (e.g., amount of evening listening) can be tabulated for each of the three educational levels, requiring three runs instead of seven, and no additional computations.[10]

In this manner, the categories of many independent variables are frequently collapsed.

Note: The juxtaposition of problems 1 and 2 illustrates another feature of efficient machine operations. It suggests the general problem of *sequences of sorting for maximum reduction of running.* When a series of tabulations are to be made which *have in common one column or variable,* one can arrange the sequence of runs so as to exploit previous sorting in reducing the sorting otherwise involved in a subsequent tabulation. Thus, in problem 1, the same exact results would be obtained whether one sorted on source of news and counted on education or sorted on education and counted on source of news. It would be a total of two machine operations either way. Similarly, in problem 2, independent of which variable is sorted and which one counted, the same result would be obtained and the number of machine runs would be the same. However, since education was *common* to both cross-tabulations, it would be more efficient to sort initially on education. Then one counts on source of news for problem 1, and immediately thereafter uses the same educational groups for counting magnitude of evening listening for problem 2. Thus, one sorting is obviated. Here, the net gain is small. However, for a large number of cross-tabulations, proper scheduling of the sequence of runs can result in great savings of time.

In this discussion, we have ignored the considerations of efficiency involved in picking for the *sorting* variable in a cross-tabulation the variable with the *smallest* number of sub-divisions, since each sub-

10. Of course, one disadvantage of this method is that the analyst does not have the distribution of responses for very fine divisions of the independent variable. If, in *an after thought,* he desires these particular distributions, the runs must be repeated. However, if foresight is employed, and the analyst knows what he wants, the method recommended above is obviously superior.

division naturally requires a "counting run." Thus in the illustrative problem for cross-tabulation, sex only has 2 sub-divisions, whereas source of news has 3 sub-divisions. Thus sorting by sex only involves 2 counts, whereas sorting by source of news involves 3 counts. The experi-enced machine operator plans his sequence of runs in such a way as to gain the maximum reduction in tedious work to be derived from both of these considerations.

3. How does the distribution of responses to Question 21 vary with sex?

Problem Exercise II: Punch Card Processing for Explanatory Surveys

As noted in the text, the skills of descriptive survey analysis are a necessary prelude to the analytical skills required in explanatory surveys. Similarly, the machine procedures covered in Problem Exercise I are essential to an understanding of the material now to be presented. Just as explanatory surveys have new analytical requirements, so too the corresponding machine operations are more elaborate. The actual techniques still involve the same basic procedures of cross-tabulation, sorting on one variable and counting on another. But now the cross-tabulation is moved to a higher level of complexity; three or more variables are treated simultaneously for the purposes of control of spuriousness and specification or interpretation of relationships.[11]

ILLUSTRATIVE EXAMPLE

Problem

In previous examples, the student was asked to determine how the distribution of evening listening varied with sex and then with education. While both of these distributions are useful, neither one enables the analyst to answer such questions as: is the distribution of news sources for *college* men different from that of *college* women? Is there a greater difference between news sources preferred by *college* men and news sources preferred by *high-school* men? Was any original difference between men and women due to the amounts of education they possessed?

In other words, we are now dealing with *three* variables, holding one constant (sex) and describing the relation between the other two (education and news source). Put in another way, how does the distribution of news source vary with education when sex is held *constant?*

The many modes of analyses involving more than two variables have been discussed systematically in the text. However, the *machine operations for manipulating three variables are always the same no matter what the analytic purpose.*

Procedure

The steps to be followed are very similar to those followed in problem 1 in part B above. There, the problem was to treat only *two* variables to find the way in which news source varied with education for *all* the respondents, *irrespective* of sex. Now, we want to describe the same distribution, but for each sex *separately*. That is, we treat 3 variables simultaneously in order to describe the way news source varies with education *but for males and females* separately.

Step 1

The tabulation sheet is set up as follows:

SEX—COL. 67

	MEN (1)			WOMEN (2)		
	Education—Col. 60			Education—Col. 60		
Col.10	Coll.	H.S.	Gmr.	Coll.	H.S.	Gmr.
1 Newspaper						
2 Radio						
3 No prefer-ence: or Don't know						
Total N						

Step 2

Sort the cards according to sex by following the steps learned in previous examples.

Step 3

After sorting, the males should be in pocket 1 and the females in pocket two.

---

11. For further discussion, see Part III of the text.

Remove the cards from the pockets being careful to keep the two piles separate. Place the women aside for the time being.

Step 4

Take the cards representing *male* respondents and sort them according to educational level. The result should be seven piles in pockets 1-7.

Step 5

Since the tabulation sheet calls for only three educational sub-divisions, it is necessary to combine the seven into three as was done in problem 2, part B.

Note: A helpful way of keeping the piles separate is to identify each with a slip of paper. In many machine rooms, large trays are provided with convenient slots so that the individual card piles may be kept separate.

Step 6

Turn the Sorter Switch *OFF*. Count the pile marked *college* according to *source of daily news*. This is done by setting the column indicator to column 10.

Step 7

Record the results from the counting board onto the tab sheet under the heading of college men.

Step 8

Clear the board and repeat steps 6 and 7, only for *high school men*.

Step 9

Clear the board. Repeat steps 6 and 7 for *grammar school men*.

In this way, male respondents were first categorized according to *educational level* and then, each of the educational levels was run against *source of most daily news*.

To tabulate the same information for female respondents, repeat steps 4-9, only with the cards representing *female* respondents. Your results should conform to the figures below:

SEX COL. 67

Col. 10 Code		MEN Education [12]—Col. 60			WOMEN Education—Col. 60		
		Coll.	*H.S.*	*Gmr.*	*Coll.*	*H.S.*	*Gmr.*
1		31	46	31	29	31	15
2		21	61	72	45	132	76
3		1	3	3	3	10	3
	Total N	53	110	106	77	173	94
				269			344

Problems

1. How does the average amount of evening radio listening vary with *education* when *sex* is held constant? When *age* is held constant? (Combine age groups in such a way that only two are used: 40 or over, under 40 years of age.)

2. How does the distribution of responses to Question 21 vary with economic level when *education* is held constant. Combine economic levels A and B before proceeding with the cross tabulation.

Summary

The operations involved in these problems may seem complicated and drawn out, but as the student repeats these exercises several times or invents new ones from other questions, he will soon see that these processes become very simple and routine. The long series of steps for any particular problem are actually accomplished in very short order.

The exercises cover the *basic* operations with the Sorter that are employed in processing surveys.

---

12. There is one card in the *male* group and one card in the *female* group which was coded Y because education was not ascertainable. These cards have not been included in the cross tabulations which explains why the two sub-totals, 269 and 344, do not add up to 615. In the sorting operation both cards will be deposited in the Y pocket.

Questionnaire and Selected Portions of the Code Book for Survey 238, The Radio Survey

№ ~~1234~~ 2858   NATIONAL OPINION RESEARCH CENTER   **CONFIDENTIAL**
                                        UNIVERSITY OF DENVER   Survey 238
                                                                                            . 10-31-45

5

		Yes	No
1.	A. Do you have a radio in working order?	1	2
	B. Do you usually read a daily newspaper?	3	4
	C. Do you usually read a weekly newspaper?	5	6
	D. Do you read any magazine regularly?	7	8

2. Taking everything into consideration, which one of these do you think did the best job of serving the public during the war—magazines, newspapers, moving pictures, or radio broadcasting?

6

Magazines	1
Newspapers	2
Moving pictures	3
Radio broadcasting	4
No opinion	5

3. In every community, the schools, the newspapers, the local government, each has a different job to do. Around here, would you say that the schools are doing an excellent, good, fair or poor job? How about the newspapers? The radio stations? The local government? The churches?

		Excellent	Good	Fair	Poor	Don't Know
A.	Schools	1	2	3	4	5	7
B.	Newspapers	6	7	8	9	0
C.	Radio stations	1	2	3	4	5	8
D.	Local government	6	7	8	9	0
E.	Churches	1	2	3	4	5	9

IF "NO" TO Q. 1-A (NO RADIO IN WORKING ORDER), SKIP TO FACTUAL DATA

		Newspapers	Radio	Don't Know
4.	A. From which one source do you get most of your daily news about what is going on — the newspapers or the radio?	1	2	3	10
	B. Which one gives you the latest news most quickly—the newspapers or the radio?	4	5	6
	C. Which one gives you the most complete news — the newspapers or the radio?	7	8	9
	D. And which one gives you the fairest, most unbiased news—the newspapers or the radio?	0	X	Y

5. In what ways do you think radio news could be improved?

NOTE   11

As an aid to the student, the appropriate column numbers have been written in beside each question. For example, the answers to question 2 are punched in Column 6, the answers to question 4 are in Column 10.

6. As far as your own listening is concerned, is the radio giving too much time, about the right amount, or not' enough time to . . .

	Too Much	About Right	Not Enough	Don't Know
A. News about other countries?	1	2	3	4
B. News about this country?	5	6	7	8	12
C. News about things around here?	9	0	X	Y

7. If you had to give up either going to the movies or listening to the radio, which one would you give up?

Movies	1
Radio	2	13
Don't Know	3

8. If you had to give up either reading the newspapers or listening to the radio, which one would you give up?

Newspapers	1
Radio	2	14
Don't Know	3

9. On an average weekday, about how many hours do you listen to the radio during the daytime—that is, before 6 o'clock in the evening?

15

10. And on an average weekday, about how many hours do you listen to the radio after 6 o'clock in the evening?

16

11. A. Here's a set of cards listing different kinds of radio programs. (HAND RESPONDENT SMALL CARDS) Would you mind looking through those cards, and telling me the types of programs you like to listen to in the daytime?
   B. Now which types of programs there do you like to listen to in the evening?

	17 Daytime	18 Evening
Children's programs	1	1
Classical music	2	2
Comedy programs	3	3
Home-making programs	4	4
Live stock and grain reports	5	5
News broadcasts	6	6
Old familiar music	7	7
Popular and dance music	8	8
Quiz programs	9	9
Radio plays	0	0
Religious broadcasts	X	X
Serial dramas	Y	Y
Sports events	1	1
Talks on farming	2	2
Talks or discussions about public issues	3	3	19 20
NONE	4	4
DON'T KNOW	5	5
DON'T LISTEN	6	6

12. Are there any *kinds* of radio programs that aren't on when you'd like to listen to them?

No 1

21

IF "YES", ASK BOTH "A" AND "B"

A. What kinds?

B. Around what time would you like it to be on?

A. Kinds of Programs	B. Hour
	22
	23

13. Are there any *kinds* of programs you'd like to hear *more* of?

No 1

24

IF "YES", ASK BOTH "A" AND "B"

A. What kinds?

B. Around what time would you like it to be on?

A. Kinds of Programs	B. Hour
	25
	26

14. Are there any kinds of programs you'd like to hear *fewer* of?

No 1

27

A. IF "YES": What kinds?

28

15. Aside from news, in what other fields does the radio add to your information or knowledge?

29

30

16. As far as you know, is the radio broadcasting in England run any differently from the way it is here?

Yes 1*
No, no difference 2
Don't know 3

31

*A. IF "YES": What is the main difference?

17. Do you ever feel like criticizing when you listen to the radio?

32   Yes 1*
      No 2

*A. IF "YES": What are some of your main criticisms? Any others?

33

18. As far as you know, where do radio stations get the money to run them?

34

19. As you know, every radio station broadcasts many different programs each day. About how many of these programs would you say are sold to advertisers—all of them, about three-quarters of them, about half of them, about one-quarter, or less than that?

35

All are sold 1
Three-quarters 2*
Half are sold 3*
One-quarter 4*
Less than one-quarter 5*
Don't know 6

A. UNLESS "ALL" OR "DON'T KNOW": Who pays for the programs broadcast during the rest of the time?

36

	Yes	No	Don't Know
20. A. If your newspaper could be produced without advertising, would you prefer it that way?	1	2	3
B. If your radio programs could be produced without advertising, would you prefer it that way?	4	5	6

37

C. (If reply is not the same for both, probe informally to find out why his answers are different)

38

21. Which one of these four statements comes closest to what you yourself think about advertising on the radio? (HAND RESPONDENT WHITE CARD)

40.

A. I'm in favor of advertising on the radio, because it tells me about the things I want to buy 1

B. I don't particularly mind advertising on the radio. It doesn't interfere too much with my enjoyment of the programs. 2

C. I don't like the advertising on radio, but I'll put up with it 3

D. I think all advertising should be taken off the radio 4

Don't know 5

---

22. Would it be worth it to you to pay a tax of $5 a year to get radio programs without any advertising in them?

*A. IF "YES": Would it be worth a tax of $10 a year?

*B. IF "YES" TO "A": Would it be worth a tax of $25 a year?

	$5	$10	$25
Yes	R*	R*	5
No	1	3	6
Don't know	2	4	7

41

---

23. Can you give an example of what you think is the best advertising you've heard on the radio? (Get all possible details on name of program, sponsor, station, etc., so we can identify it)

No 1

42

A. IF "YES": What did you like about it?

---

24. Can you give me an example of what you think is the worst advertising you've heard on the radio? (Get all possible details on name of program, sponsor, station, etc., so we can identify it)

No 1

43

A. IF "YES": What didn't you like about it?

---

25. Here are some criticisms of radio advertising or commercials. (HAND RESPONDENT YELLOW CARD) Would you tell me which ones, if any, you feel strongly about?

Too long 1	Too many jingles 8
Bad taste 2	Claim too much for
Too detailed 3	product 9
Too much singing 4	Too many of them 0
Too repetitious 5	DON'T FEEL STRONGLY
Interrupt programs 6	ABOUT ANY .... Y
Silly 7	

44

---

26. (ASK RESPONDENT TO TURN OVER YELLOW CARD) Are there any products listed there which you think should *not* be advertised over the radio?

Gasoline 1	Tooth paste 9
Laxatives 2	Headache remedies 0
Cigarettes 3	Bread X
Automobiles 4	Beer .... Y
Whiskey 5	ALL SHOULD BE
Ice cream 6	ALLOWED TO
Liver remedies 7	ADVERTISE .... R
Deodorants 8	

45

---

27. Do you think that radio stations should sell time for the following things, or should they give the time free, or shouldn't they be on the air at all? How about . . .

	Sell	Give	Not on air	Don't Know
A. To solicit Red Cross memberships?	1	2	3	4
B. To solicit labor union memberships?	5	6	7	8	**46**
C. To solicit Community Chest donations?	9	0	X	Y
D. To solicit correspondence school registrations?	1	2	3	4
E. To solicit members for business men's organizations?	5	6	7	8	**47**
F. To solicit funds for churches?	9	0	X	Y
G. Political broadcasts?	1	2	3	4

48

---

28. As far as you know, does the government have anything to do with the operation of radio stations?

49

Yes 1*

No 2

Don't know 3

IF "YES", ASK BOTH "A" AND "B"

*A. As far as you know, which of these powers does the Federal government have over radio stations? (HAND RESPONDENT REVERSE SIDE OF WHITE CARD)

*B. Which of those powers do you think the Federal government *should* have over radio stations?

	A. Does	B. Should
(1) Give each station a regular place on the dial	1	1
(2) See to it that news broadcasts are truthful	2	2
(3) Decide how much advertising can be broadcast	3	3
(4) Approve of changes in the ownership of radio stations	4	4
(5) Decide what kinds of programs are to be broadcast	5	5
(6) Tell each station exactly how much power it can use to broadcast its programs	6	6
(7) Limit the profits of radio stations	7	7
NONE	X	X
DON'T KNOW	Y	Y

50 51

29. As far as you know, does the government require radio stations to broadcast a certain number of religious and educational programs, or do the stations broadcast these voluntarily?

52

Government requires 1
Do it voluntarily 2
Don't know 3

30. I'd like to ask you how *fair* you think radio stations, newspapers and magazines generally are. For example, do you think *radio stations* are generally fair in giving both sides of an argument? How about newspapers in general? Magazines?

61

		Yes	No	Don't Know
A.	Radio stations	1	2	3
B.	Newspapers	4	5	6
C.	Magazines	7	8	9

FACTUAL DATA

1. About how many times did you go to the movies during the last month?

53

2. RADIO OWNERSHIP DATA:
   A. Number of radios in home *54*
   B. UNLESS "NONE" Age of one most frequently used: *55*

		Yes	No
C.	Is there a car radio?	1	2
D.	Is there an FM radio?	3	4

3. Is there a telephone where you live?

Yes .... R*
No 1

57 A. IF "YES": Is it listed either in your name or your family's name?

Yes 2
No 3

4. RESPONDENT'S OCCUPATION OR STATUS:

Job:

58

Industry:

(If respondent is not the main earner in the family, specify occupation of breadwinner below)

Job:

Industry: *59*

5. EDUCATION:

What was the name of the last school you attended?

What was the last grade (or year) you completed in that school?

Completed college 1   Completed grammar school 5
Some college 2   Some grammar school   6
Completed high school 3   No schooling 7
Some high school 4

60

6. MARITAL STATUS:

62

Single 1
Married 2
Widowed, divorced, separated 3

7. NUMBER IN FAMILY LIVING AT HOME (*including respondent*):   *63*

8. NUMBER OF CHILDREN UNDER TWELVE: *64*

9. POLITICAL PREFERENCE:
   Did you favor Roosevelt or Dewey in the last Presidential election?

65

Roosevelt 1
Dewey 2
Neither 3
Don't know 4

10. AGE: What is your approximate age?

66

11. RENT: (*Do not record for farm respondents*)
    Contract rent (*if renter*) ....
    Estimated rent (*if owner*) ....

12. SEX: *67*

Male 1
Female 2

13. ECONOMIC LEVEL: *68*

A 1
B 2
C 3
D 4

14. RACE: *69*

White 1
Colored 2

15. RESPONDENT'S HOME ADDRESS:
    Size of town — 70

16. PLACE AND STATE:
    Region — 71

17. INTERVIEWER'S SIGNATURE:
    Time Zone - 72

18. DATE:

Portions of the Code Book

QUESTION 1

	Yes	No	Col. 5
A. Do you have a radio in working order?	1	2	
B. Do you usually read a daily newspaper?	3	4	
C. Do you usually read a weekly newspaper?	5	6	
D. Do you read any magazine regularly?	7	8	

One of the two code numbers should be circled for each of the four parts of this question.

If both "Yes" and "No" are circled, or if neither is circled, they should be coded as not ascertainable, unless a written-in comment enables you to determine the proper answer.

If the answer to "A" is not ascertainable, write in *Code 9 on line A.* (The proper answer to "A" can usually be determined on the basis of whether or not Qs. 4-30 are filled in.)

If the answer to "B" is not ascertainable, write in Code 0 on line B.

If the answer to "C" is not ascertainable, write in Code X on line C.

If the answer to "D" is not ascertainable, write in Code Y on line D.

The number of codes circled or entered on the whole question should add to four in every case.

If code 2 is circled, edit questions 2 and 3, and then check to see that the remainder of the interview is blank except for the factual data on the last page.

QUESTION 2

Col. 6

Taking everything into consideration, which one of these do you think did the best job of serving the public during the war—magazines, newspapers, moving pictures or radio broadcasting?

One code number only should be circled in every case.

If more than one code is circled, or if no code is circled, edit to Code 5 (No opinion), unless written-in comment indicates otherwise.

QUESTION 4

Col. 10

A. From which one source do you get most of your daily news about what is going on —the newspapers or the radio?

B. Which one gives you the latest news most quickly—the newspapers or the radio?

C. Which one gives you the most complete news—the newspapers or the radio?

D. And which one gives you the fairest, most unbiased news— the newspapers or the radio?

One of the three code numbers should be circled for each of the four parts of this question.

If more than one code is circled, or if no code is circled, edit to "Don't know" unless written-in comment indicates otherwise.

QUESTION 5

Col. 11

In what ways do you think radio news could be improved?

Multiple answers permitted

1. *Less advertising*—Cut down on commercials, Don't interrupt programs with advertising.

2. *More complete news, more details, longer broadcasts*—Take more time, Explain more fully, More interpretation, More commentators, More of it.

3. *Less restriction on news presentation*—Tell the public more about what goes on, They don't tell everything, Be more frank, Let commentators say what they want.

4. *More accurate news*—Check facts, Less rumors, premature stories.

5. *More frequent news, shorter programs*—More 5-minute broadcasts, Give it more often, Have it better spaced during day.

6. *Less repetition, less frequent news, more concise news*—Don't announce same

news so often, Say it in fewer words, Don't repeat news already published in papers.

7. *Less opinion, more facts*—Cut out commentators' opinions, Fewer commentators, More straight news, Less prejudice, politics, propaganda, contradictions, exaggeration, Give both sides.

8. *Requests for more of specific types of news*—More foreign news, More local news, More stock reports.

9. *Better presentation*—Make it more adult, Cut out the dramatics, Have better announcers, Don't talk down to public, Give it more slowly, They talk too fast.

0. *Miscellaneous suggestions and criticisms*—Too much news now, have less news, In every way.

X. *No criticisms, good as is*—OK now, doing splendid job, Seems all right to me, I'm satisfied.

Y. *Don't know, No answer*—Never listen, Don't care, Couldn't say.

QUESTIONS 7-8

Cols. 13-14

If you had to give up either going to the movies or listening to the radio, which one would you give up?

If you had to give up either reading the newspapers or listening to the radio, which one would you give up?

One code number only should be circled in every case.

If more than one code is circled, or if no code is circled, edit to Code 3 unless comment indicates otherwise.

QUESTIONS 9-10

Cols. 15-16

On an average weekday, about how many hours do you listen to the radio during the daytime—that is, before 6 o'clock in the evening?

And on an average weekday, about how many hours do you listen to the radio after 6 o'clock in the evening?

One code only must be entered on each of the two questions in every case

Answers under 10 ("One," "Eight," etc.) should be interpreted as hours. Answers of more than 10 ("20," "30," etc.) should be interpreted as minutes.

1. *None, don't listen*—Never.

2. *Up to 15 minutes*—

3. *16-30 minutes*—Half an hour, 15 minutes or half hour, 20 minutes.

4. *31-60 minutes*—One hour.

5. *Over 1 hour to 2 hours*—Two hours.

6. *Over 2 hours to 3 hours*—Three hours, 2½ hours.

7. *Over 3 hours to 4 hours*—Four hours, 3 or 4 hours.

8. *Over 4 hours to 5 hours*—Five hours, 4 or 5 hours, 4½ hours.

9. *Over 5 hours to 6 hours*—Six hours.

0. *Over 6 hours*—7 hours, 8 hours, 6 or 7 hours.

Y. *Not ascertainable*—Don't know; vague, irrelevant, unclassifiable replies.

QUESTION 16

Col. 31

As far as you know, is the radio broadcasting in England run any differently from the way it is here?

A. *"IF YES"*: What is the main difference?

Multiple answers permitted, subject to conditions listed below:

If the question is blank, edit to "Don't know" by circling Code 3.

In all cases where the respondent has given a positive answer to the sub-question, it will be necessary to *cross out the circled Code 1 and insert the proper code.*

1. *Yes, there is a difference but don't know what*—This applies where interviewer has circled Code 1 and recorded a "DK" answer to "A." It also applies where the interviewer has circled Code 1, but has left "A" blank. In such cases, no code need be entered; the circled "1" is sufficient.

Code 1 must always stand alone. You cannot have Code 1 and any other.

2. *No, no difference*—This will usually be circled by the interviewer. No code need be entered.

Code 2 must always stand alone.

3. *Don't know whether there is any difference or not*—This will usually be circled by the interviewer. No code need be entered.

Code 3 must always stand alone.

4. *Yes, the main difference is this: No advertising* (no mention of government control)—They have no sponsors, They don't allow commercials, They leave off the advertising, No advertisements, Programs not paid for by advertisers.

Code 4 can be combined only with Codes 9, 0, X or Y.

5. *Government owned* (no mention of advertising)—All done by govt, Controlled entirely by govt, Run by govt, State owned, Heard something about govt in radio over there.

Code 5 can be combined only with Codes 8, 9, 0, X or Y.

6. *Government owned and no advertising* (both mentioned)—Programs don't have private sponsors; government controls. It's run by govt. no paid announcements.

Code 6 can be combined only with Codes 9, 0, X or Y.

7. *Paid for by tax,* or *Paid for by tax and no advertising*—They tax every radio and have no commercials. Radio service is paid for by the people; no advertising over there. They don't have commercials; it's a tax proposition. No advertising and they pay a tax to listen. It's government owned and you pay a tax to listen. You pay for the use of the radio and there are no commercials.

Code 7 can be combined only with Codes 9, 0, X or Y. Any mention of "tax" or method of financing British radio goes here, regardless of whether advertising or government control are also mentioned.

8. *Less advertising*—They don't allow as many commercials, They aren't allowed to interrupt the programs with ads, They don't have as many sponsors, They censor their commercial talks, Their commercials aren't as long.

Code 8 can be combined only with Codes 5, 9, 0, X or Y.

9. *Programs or techniques are inferior*—Programs not as good as ours, We have better programs, We are far ahead of them in methods, technology, They don't have as much variety, We have more interesting programs, Their schedules are less exact, Announcers are bad.

Code 9 can be combined with any other code except 1, 2 or 3.

0. *English programs or techniques are superior*—They have more good music, They don't have so many silly programs, They have more educational programs.

Code 0 can be combined with any other code except 1, 2 or 3.

X. *More censorship, politics*—They only get what the govt wants them to hear, Theirs isn't as free as ours, Ours is more democratic, Over there a poor singer can get on the air if her uncle is a lord.

Code X can be combined with any other code except 1, 2 or 3.

Y. *Miscellaneous and irrelevant answers*—They're set up differently, You can't understand it (obviously thinking of short-wave reception), They have fewer stations, The time is different.

Code Y can be combined with any other code except 1, 2 or 3.

QUESTION 18

Col. 34

As far as you know, where do radio stations get the money to run them?

Multiple answers permitted

1. *Advertising or sponsors*—The people who broadcast, who put the programs on, The big manufacturers, From soap companies mostly, From the commercials, They sell the time, What they charge each one, The stuff they advertise, Sponsored by different companies, Business men.

2. *Networks or investments*—Private investments in the stations themselves, From the big networks they get some, It's run on a stock basis.

3. *Government or taxes*—The city pays for it through taxes, From tax money, Income tax probably, Public pays in taxes, I don't know maybe the county, From the government I imagine, Taxpayers.

4. *Political parties*—Politicians buy time so they can speak, I wonder if the political parties don't pay some, Political organizations.

5. *Religious, charitable, civic organizations*—Churches donate for time, Donations from civic organizations, groups.

6. *Newspapers.*

7. *The public, individuals*—The general public, The people, Private subscriptions, People who give it to them.

8. *Radio manufacturers*—Royalties from radios, Selling radios.

X. *Miscellaneous or vague*—They form a corporation, It's monopolized, Labor unions.

Y. *Don't know or no answer.*

QUESTION 21

Col. 40

Which one of these four statements comes closest to what you yourself think about advertising on the radio?

One of the five code numbers must be circled in every case.

If more than one code is circled, or if no code is circled, edit to Code 5 unless written-in comment indicates otherwise.

QUESTION 25

Col. 44

Here are some criticisms of radio advertising or commercials. Would you tell me which ones, if any, you feel strongly about?

Multiple answers are permitted. Any, all or none of Codes 1-0 may be circled.

But an answer of "Don't feel strongly about any" *excludes any other code.* If Code Y is circled, no other code may be circled.

Thus, either *Code Y* must be circled *alone,* or one or more other codes must be circled.

If one or more other codes are circled and Code Y is also circled, *edit out the Code Y,* unless comment indicates otherwise.

If the question is blank, code X.

QUESTION 26

Col. 45

Are there any products listed there which you think should *not* be advertised over the radio?

Multiple answers are permitted. Any, all or none of Codes 1-Y may be circled.

But an answer of "All should be allowed to advertise" *excludes any other code.*

Thus, either *Code R* must be circled

alone, or one or more other codes must be circled.

If one or more other codes are circled and Code R is also circled, *edit out the Code R,* unless comment indicates otherwise.

If the question is blank, circle Code R.

FACTUAL DATA—1

Col. 53

About how many times did you go to the movies during the last month?

Code once only in every case.

1. *One*—Once or twice.
2. *Two or three times*—Three or four.
3. *Four or five times, Once a week.*
4. *More than five times*—Once or twice a week, Twice a week, Almost every day.
0. *None*—Once a year.
Y. *No answer, Don't know.*

FACTUAL DATA—2-A

Col. 54

Number of radios in home.
Code once only in every case.

Count only those sets in working order. Thus, "Three, but one is broken" should be coded "2."

Code the same number mentioned: 0 for none, 1 for One, 2 for Two, etc.

Code X for Ten or more, in the rare event that anyone should have that many radios.

Code Y for No answer.

FACTUAL DATA—5

Col. 60

What was the name of the last school you attended?

What was the last grade (or year) you completed in that school?

Don't code the name of the school.

One code only should be circled in every case.

If more than one code is circled, edit to *highest schooling* indicated.

If no code is circled, code 1, 3 or 5 on basis of last school attended. If this information is lacking, code "Y."

FACTUAL DATA—10

Col. 66

What is your approximate age?
Code once only in every case.

Code the first digit of the person's age:
2 for persons 21-29, 3 for persons 30-39,
etc.
Code "Over 40" as 4, etc.
Code omissions as Y.

FACTUAL DATA—12-14

Cols. 67-69

Sex	67
Economic level	68
Race	69

One code only should be circled in
every case on each of these three questions.
If more than one code is circled, or if
no code is circled, edit to Code Y.

FACTUAL DATA—15-18

Cols. 70-72

Respondent's home address: (Col. 70)

SIZE OF TOWN

Enter one of the following codes in
the "Respondent's Home Address" space
in every case:

1. *Metropolitan Districts over 1,000,000*
—New York, Philadelphia, Pittsburgh,
Boston, Chicago, Cleveland, Detroit, St.
Louis, Baltimore, San Francisco, Los
Angeles—and suburbs.
2. *Metropolitan Districts under 1,000,-
000.*
3. *Towns 2,500 to 50,000.*

4. *Rural non-farm.*
5. *Farm.*

Place and state: (Col. 71)

REGION

Enter one of the following codes in the
"Place and State" space in every case:

1. *New England*—Maine, New Hampshire, Vermont, Massachusetts, Connecticut, Rhode Island.
2. *Middle Atlantic*—New York, New
Jersey, Pennsylvania.
3. *East North Central*—Ohio, Indiana,
Illinois, Michigan, Wisconsin.
4. *West North Central*—Minnesota,
North Dakota, South Dakota, Iowa, Nebraska, Kansas, Missouri.
5. *South Atlantic*—Delaware, Maryland,
District of Columbia, West Virginia, Virginia, North Carolina, South Carolina,
Georgia, Florida.
6. *East South Central*—Kentucky, Tennessee, Alabama, Mississippi.
7. *West South Central*—Louisiana, Arkansas, Oklahoma, Texas.
8. *Mountain*—Montana, Idaho, Wyoming, Colorado, Utah, Nevada, New
Mexico, Arizona.
9. *Pacific*—Washington, Oregon, California.

Interviewers signature: (Col.
72)

TIME ZONE

Enter one of the following codes in the
"Interviewer's Signature" space in every
case.
See map for boundaries of each zone.

1. *Eastern*
2. *Central*
3. *Mountain*
4. *Pacific*

Practice Exercise 1

Manipulation and Evaluation of Complex Numerical Relationships in Tabular Form

The *principles* of explanatory analyses have already been treated in detail in the text. The reader should now have an understanding of the way in which explanations are inferred from the empirical relationships demonstrated between two variables, and the way in which such inferences are refined and safeguarded through the introduction of additional variables. In practice, however, there are further demands on the successful analyst than the sheer application of the logic and principles previously presented.

The analyst must also have skill in the *manipulation and evaluation* of large amounts of data exhibiting numerical relationships of considerable complexity. The *mechanics* of obtaining these data is no problem. The use of machine equipment reduces the data quickly and efficiently into numbers, series, tabulations and cross-tabulations. Still there is an intermediate step between the machine results and the application of the analytic principles which lead to ultimate conclusions. The results must be arranged, presented, inspected and manipulated. Skill in this intermediate step requires practice, and in the hope that the student will develop facility at these intermediate operations, we present an exercise in the manipulation and evaluation of tabular data. We shall use as our illustration material from a series of studies reported in *The American Soldier*.[1]

---

1. *Op. cit.*, Chap. 9, Vol. II, pp. 411-455.

During their studies of soldiers during World War II, the Research Branch of the Army investigated the incidence of anxiety symptoms, such as nightmares, sweating, trembling, vomiting and so on, and tried to find out how these symptoms were related to particular experiences and characteristics of the soldiers. One of their findings was that the incidence of such anxiety symptoms was positively related to the soldiers' nearness to actual combat. This relationship is most simply expressed in Table I.

TABLE I—Nearness of Combat and Anxiety Symptoms

Anxiety Symptoms	Men never under enemy fire	Men under long range fire only	Men under close-range fire	Men in actual combat	Total
Show critical score	34%	38%	42%	48%	42%
Do not show critical score	66	62	58	52	58
Total Cases	917	793	615	1897	4222

Let us inspect this table carefully. Across the top of the table, the 4,222 soldiers considered in this survey have been divided into four groups, according to their nearness to combat. If one examines the four categories, one discovers that they are arranged consecutively. Starting at the left, the first group includes those 900-odd men who have never been under enemy fire, while the final group contains the nearly 2,000 who have been in actual combat.

Each of the four groups has then been classified into those who did and those who did not receive critical scores on the anxiety symptoms test.[2] (A critical score is one believed to reveal a high level of anxiety.)

If we examine the last column of this table, we discover that 42 per cent of the soldiers received critical scores. Does this fact have any *absolute* meaning? For example, would we be justified in saying that approximately two out of every five soldiers were anxious? The answer is "no." It was an *arbitrary* decision of the Research Branch analysts as to which test scores would be considered critical, i.e. indicative of anxiety and which not. Had they dichotomized the test some other way, it might have appeared that almost all of the soldiers, or almost none, revealed anxiety symptoms. While the magnitude of the "critical score" therefore has no absolute meaning in terms of the incidence of anxiety, nevertheless, such a rsponse can be legitimately used to examine the *differential occurrence* of anxiety among different groups of subjects, as a basis for inferring the cause of the phenomenon. Whatever arbitrariness attends the particular index chosen applies equally to all four groups and should therefore not impair the comparison.

Returning now to the table with which we started, we may ask on what basis we decide that the incidence of anxiety symptoms is related to nearness to combat. How do we know that there is a relationship between these two variables? In its simplest terms, the answer is that we observe that the proportion of men receiving critical scores on the anxiety symptoms test increases progressively as one moves from the group who had never been under enemy fire to the group which had been in actual combat.[3] To put it somewhat more

---

2. It is customary to use the different categories of the so-called independent variable as the base on which to compute the percentages. For a fuller treatment of the direction in which percentages should be computed, see Hans Zeisel, *Say It With Figures, op. cit.*

3. We are, of course, over-simplifying the actual operations that would occur in practice. We must introduce various considerations having to do with the fact that these inferences are predicated on sample data, and test whether the findings should be rejected as due to variations of a sampling nature rather than to any real relationship. Such tests of signifi-

formally, if, as one moves from the lower to the higher categories of one variable, the proportion of subjects characterized in a particular way increases (or decreases) progressively, we conclude that there is a positive (or negative) relationship between the two variables.

The two key words in this definition of a relationship are *increases* (or *decreases*) and *progressively*. They provide the clues to the situations in which we would conclude that there is *no* relationship between the variables. Essentially, there are two such situations. The first, and most clearcut, is that in which there is no progressive change in one variable as one moves from the lower to the higher categories of a second. In terms of our example, had we found that the incidence of anxiety symptoms—i.e., the proportion of men receiving a critical score on the test—was the same in all four classes of nearness to combat, we would have concluded that there was no relationship between the variables.

The second situation in which we are likely to conclude that there is no relationship between the two variables is that in which there is no consistent pattern of change in one variable as one moves from the lower to the higher categories of the second. Thus, had the cross-tabulation of nearness to combat and incidence of anxiety symptoms come out in the following way, we would have concluded that there is no relationship between the two:

Anxiety symptoms	Men never under enemy fire	Men under long range fire only	Men under close range fire	Men in actual combat
Show critical score	38%	34%	48%	42%
Do not show critical score	62	66	52	58
Total cases	917	793	615	1897

The incidence of anxiety symptoms shows no regular pattern of variation in relation to nearness to combat, and we conclude, therefore, that the two variables are unrelated. (Clearly, however, this kind of unrelatedness is considerably more complex and ambiguous than is the kind considered previously, where there is no variation at all. Whether or not we conclude that there is a regular pattern of variation depends partly on our subjective evaluation, on what we read into the data. Thus, some might see in the previous table a complex pattern of curvilinear form. For the sake of simplicity, however, we shall deal in this exercise only with the more easily recognized linear relationships, those in which there is regular increase or decrease.)

Now that we have some notion of what happens when two variables are cross-tabulated and their relationship inspected we may consider the complexities brought about by the introduction of a third variable.

In the example adapted from the work of Stouffer and his associates, we can introduce age as a third variable. We then obtain the following table:

cance, however, are omitted from our discussion, and we shall rely here only on common-sense inspection of the actual data. We omit such discussion with the full realization that the skilled analyst must have training in problems of Statistical Inference. However, we have adopted the view that training in that area is a major task in its own right. Attempts to cover both survey analytic principles and the principles of statistical inference would be too huge a task and doom us to failure. We shall merely try to formulate and demonstrate the basic analytic procedures, and hope that the student will obtain the necessary statistical sophistication from other works and didactic courses.

TABLE II—Nearness of Combat and Anxiety Symptoms According to Age

Percentages who have critical score

Age	Men never under enemy fire	Men under long range fire only	Men under close range fire	Men in actual combat
30 years of age and over	49(204)	39(224)	54(153)	54(293)
25–29	34(234)	42(214)	45(173)	52(540)
Under 25	28(479)	35(355)	36(289)	44(1064)

The figures which are not bracketed are percentages; those in parentheses are so-called base figures. One fact which is immediately apparent is that none of the percentages in either the rows or the columns add to 100 per cent. This is different from the tables which we have reported previously, and may seem quite strange at first. It is explained by the fact, as the labelling of the table indicates, that only the proportions of men receiving critical scores on the anxiety symptoms test are recorded here. The complements of these figures are understood implicitly. Thus, the figure 49 in the upper left-hand corner of the table indicates that 49 per cent of the men 30 years of age and over who have never been under enemy fire receive critical scores; although it is not reported explicitly in the table, we know that 51 per cent of this group did not receive critical scores. Similarly, the figure 52, the second row in the last column, signifies that 52 per cent of the men between 25 and 29 years of age who had been in actual combat received critical scores; 48 per cent of the same group, then, had lower scores. And so on for each cell in the table. It is important to recognize that, whereas particular cells in previous tables were defined in terms of one dimension only—nearness to combat—the cells in this table are defined in terms of two dimensions—nearness to combat *and* age.

Tables of this kind have been called "three-dimensional tables." Implicitly, each percentage figure is a portion of a unit bar rising out of the page. And, indeed, if one were to try to represent this table graphically, one would discover that it is necessary to add a third dimension to the plane of the page.[4] They provide a very useful tabular device for the presentation of complex results.[5]

Now that we have clarified the form of such three-dimensional tables, let us see what Table II reveals about the relationship of anxiety symptoms to nearness to combat and age. By reading across the rows of the table, we can find out the relation of anxiety symptoms to nearness to combat, with age held constant.[6] By reading down the columns of Table II, we can determine the relationship of anxiety symptoms to age, with nearness to combat held constant. What do we find? We saw previously (in Table I) that the incidence of anxiety symptoms is related to nearness to combat. Table II reveals that this remains the case, by and large, even when age is held constant. In two of the three age groups, the proportions of men receiving critical scores on the anxiety symptoms test increases steadily as one moves from the group never under enemy

---

4. For further and more detailed discussion of three-dimensional tables, see Hans Zeisel, *op. cit.*, Chapter VI. Zeisel indicates various ways in which different types of dependent variables can be manipulated so that they lend themselves to such three-dimensional presentations. He also discusses the *cautions that the analyst must employ* in such manipulation so that the picture of the dependent variable will not be falsified.

5. The reader can verify for himself how much more complicated and cumbersome the table would be if it were presented in more usual form, with the proportions of men not receiving critical scores also indicated.

6. The notion of holding variables constant has been discussed in considerable detail in the text. All that we need indicate here is that we examine the relationship between nearness to combat and anxiety symptoms *separately in different age groups.*

fire to the group which had seen actual combat. Thus among the soldiers 25-29 years of age, the relevant proportions are 34-42-45-52; and among those under 25, the corresponding figures are 28-35-36-44. The one exception is the oldest of the three age groups, those 30 years of age and older, where the proportions are 49-39-54-54; in this age group, in other words, there is no clearcut relationship between anxiety symptoms and nearness to combat.

The columns of Table II tell a new story, for we have not previously had any information on the relationship of anxiety symptoms to age. Reading down the four columns of the table we find that, generally, there is a positive relationship between the incidence of anxiety symptoms and age when nearness to combat is held constant. That is, among those with roughly equivalent combat experience, the older the soldier the more likely he is to receive a critical score on the anxiety symptoms test. The one exception to this general statement is found in the group of men who had been under long range enemy fire. There we see that the oldest group was somewhat less likely than the 25-29 year old group to receive critical scores; the difference is not a large one, however.

We can summarize the basic findings of Table II in the following way: The closer the soldier is to actual combat, the more likely it is that he will receive a critical score, and the older he is, the more likely he is to exhibit a high level of anxiety. Combining these two pieces of information, we are led to expect that the group showing the smallest proportion of critical scores will be the young men who have never been under enemy fire. This is indeed the case: When we look for this group, in the lower left-hand corner of Table II, we find that only 28 per cent of them received critical scores. This is a smaller figure than can be found anywhere else in the table. Conversely, we expect that the highest rate of critical scores will be found among the oldest soldiers who have been in actual combat. Again these expectations are borne out by the data. Looking in the upper right-hand corner of the table, we find that 54 per cent of these men received critical scores; there is no larger proportion in the table.

Table II contains one further piece of information. So far we have examined the relationship of anxiety symptoms to nearness to combat, on the one hand, and to age, on the other. How are these last two variables related to each other? That is, what is the relationship between age and nearness to combat? The answer can be found in Table II, although it may not be immediately obvious. The figures in parentheses beside each percentage figure indicate how many men there are in each age-combat experience group. Thus, there are 204 men who have never been under enemy fire who are 30 years of age and over, 234 in the same combat experience group who are between 25 and 29, and 479 in the same combat experience group who are under 25. Comparable age distributions will be found in the other columns as well. This is just the information we need to determine the relationship between age and nearness to combat. These

TABLE III—Nearness to Combat According to Age

Nearness to combat	Men 30 years of age and over	Men 25–29	Men under 25
Never under enemy fire	24%	20%	22%
Under long range fire only	26	18	16
Under close range fire	17	15	13
In actual combat	33	47	49
Total cases	874	1161	2187

figures have been percentaged in Table III, considering age the independent variable, and nearness to combat the dependent variable.

The reader is invited to interpret for himself what Table III reveals about the relationship between age and nearness to combat.

In actual research practice, particularly when one is dealing with a survey which includes several thousand cases, it is not uncommon to find still more complex tables showing the interrelationships between four or more variables. As a matter of fact, the example which we have been using here was presented in *The American Soldier* as a four variable table. We condensed it for the purposes of the present exposition. Originally, however, it was as follows:

TABLE IV—Nearness of Combat and Anxiety Symptoms According to Age and Educational Level

Age and Educational Level	Percentages who have critical score			
	Men never under enemy fire	Men under long range fire only	Men under close range fire	Men in actual combat
High School Graduate and Over				
30 years of age and over	38(79)	33(101)	38(61)	47(88)
25–29	23(109)	29(119)	35(79)	47(207)
Under 25	20(246)	30(205)	27(150)	36(500)
Some High School But Not Graduation				
30 years of age and over	54(63)	41(69)	58(50)	48(83)
25–29	42(69)	48(65)	51(53)	52(180)
Under 25	34(152)	40(97)	43(81)	47(351)
Grade School Only				
30 years of age and over	57(62)	50(54)	60(42)	63(122)
25–29	43(56)	77(30)	56(41)	57(153)
Under 25	40(81)	45(53)	48(58)	57(213)

Complex as this table may seem, it does not differ in its form from Table II. It too is a three-dimensional table, in the sense that only the percentages of those receiving critical scores are reported. The complements of these figures indicate how many men in each sub-group did not receive critical scores.

The only basically new feature of Table IV is the large number of partial relationships which it contains. This necessitates making a large number of comparisons when examining the relationship between any two variables. This as we have already seen is the essence of the complicated analysis of an explanatory survey. In Table I, which presented the simple relationship between the incidence of anxiety symptoms and nearness to combat, it was necessary to make only one comparison in order to determine how the two variables were associated. In Table II, where age was introduced as a third variable, it was necessary to make three comparisons—one for each age group—in order to determine how anxiety symptoms were related to nearness to combat. (In order to find out how age was related to anxiety symptoms, it was necessary to make four comparisons—one for each of the nearness-to-combat categories.) Now that educational level is introduced as a fourth variable, it is necessary to make *nine* comparisons—one for each of the nine rows of Table IV. In a similar fashion, it is now necessary to make *twelve* comparisons in order to determine the relationship between the incidence of anxiety symptoms and either age or educational level.

One new complication might be pointed to. In previous tables, the relevant comparisons have been found either by reading straight across the rows of the table or straight down its columns. When there are four variables, however, it is not possible to make all of the comparisons this simply. Consider the relationship of education and incidence of anxiety symptoms. The twelve partial relationships indicating the association of these two variables must be searched for to some extent. Within each column, they can be found by comparing the first, fourth and seventh rows of the table (the relationship between anxiety symptoms and educational level for those with a given degree of combat experience who are 30 years of age and older); the second, fifth and eighth rows (the comparable relationship for those with a given degree of combat experience who are between 25 and 29); and, finally, the third, sixth, and ninth rows (the relationship between education and anxiety symptoms for those with a given amount of combat experience who are under 25 years of age). These three comparisons carried out for each of the four categories of nearness to combat, yield the twelve partial relationships between education and incidence of anxiety symptoms. The reader can determine for himself, that, by summing the appropriate base figures in Table IV (those in parentheses), he can obtain the figures showing the relationship between education and nearness to combat. These figures are as follows:

Nearness to combat	High school graduate and over	Some high school but not graduation	Grade school only
Never under enemy fire	434	284	199
Under long range fire only	425	231	137
Under close range fire	290	184	614
In actual combat	795	614	488
Total cases	1944	1313	965

It is possible, through similar operations, to determine from Table IV the relationship between age and educational level. It is as follows:

Age	High school graduate and over	Some high school but not graduation	Grade school only
30 years and over	329	265	280
25–29	514	367	280
Under 25	1101	681	405
Total cases	1944	1313	965

APPENDIX E

Answers to Problem Exercises

Answers to Problem Exercise I

Routine Punch Card Processing for Descriptive Surveys

(Radio Survey—Special Deck)

Problem A–1

Col.	
13–1	545
2	46
3	24
N	615

Problem A–2

Col.	
11–1	76
2	64
3	19
4	33
5	15
6	36
7	51
8	20
9	24
0	18
X	142
Y	182
N	615

Problem A–3

Col.	
10–1	184
2	408
3	23
N	615

Problem B–1

Col. 60

Col.	1	2	3	4	5	6	7	y	N
10–1	30	30	44	33	32	13	1	1	184
2	15	51	105	88	75	70	3	1	408
3	3	1	9	4	3	2	1	0	23
									615
N	48	82	158	125	110	85	5	2	

Problem B-2

Col.	Col. 60 College	High School	Grammar
16-1	1	8	6
2	3	3	2
3	4	6	13
4	18	28	31
5	36	62	56
6	30	66	45
7	26	81	31
8	3	20	7
9	3	6	6
0	3	2	3
x	0	0	0
y	3	1	0
N	130	283	200	⌐ 613 [1]

Problem B-3

	Col. 67 1	2
Col. 40-1	70	96
2	100	145
3	69	84
4	24	13
5	7	7
N	270	345	⌐ 615

Answers to Problem Exercise II

Durkheim's "Suicide" as an Exercise in the Evaluation of Findings in Relation to Artifacts

"Suicide"—Page No.[2]

p. 134. In relation to the influence of imitation as a factor in the production of suicide.

Artifact in the independent variable.

No arbitrariness in the argument.

Empirical procedure to control the error factor.

p. 146. In relation to the general problem of a typology of suicide based on different causative factors.

Artifact in the independent variable.

No arbitrariness in the argument.

Logical procedure developed to treat the problem.

p. 148. In relation to the general discussion of causes of suicide.

Artifact in the independent variable.

No apparent objective basis for the decision as to the presence of error.

Argument is simply rhetorical and analogical and by reference to past authorities.

p. 363. In relation to a universal generalization about suicide.

Artifact in the dependent variable.

No arbitrariness in the initial argument.

But development of problem is essentially by analogy.

p. 178. In relation to the conclusion as to the relation between age of marriage and suicide within the male group.

Artifact in the dependent variable and in the independent variable due to a confounding of age and marital status.

In the case of the independent variable, the argument is objective and a logical and empirical procedure is developed to test whether or not the finding is purely due to this artifact.

pp. 191-192. In relation to the hypothesis as to the influence of widowhood on suicide and its differential impact on the two sexes.

Artifact is essentially a function of the method of index construction.

Logical and empirical procedure developed to allow for past inaccuracies in the method of index construction.

p. 198. In relation to the hypothesis as to the influence of family size on suicide.

Artifact in the independent variable.

Logical and empirical procedure developed to treat this artifact.

---

1. Two cards coded "y", education not ascertainable.

2. The page numbers are taken from the English translation, *Suicide,* by Emile Durkheim (Glencoe: The Free Press, 1951), first printing.

p. 228–229. In relation to the hypothesis as to the relation between suicide and military status.

Artifact in the dependent variable.

No arbitrariness in the argument.

p. 229–230. In relation to the same general hypothesis, but the test is for noncommissioned officers vs. civilians.

Artifact in the dependent variable, i.e., in the lack of comparability of the suicide data for the two contrasted groups.

Logical procedure for evaluating the possible effect such an artifact would have on the direction of the difference.

p. 235 footnote. In relation to the finding of a difference between military and civilians in the incidence of suicide for Austria.

Artifact in the dependent variable.

No apparent arbitrariness, but no procedure elaborated for treatment of problem.

p. 237. In relation to a finding on differences in rates of suicide between elite troops and ordinary troops.

Artifact lies in method of index construction.

Logical procedure elaborated for evaluating what effect such an artifact would have on the observed finding.

p. 338. In relation to the hypothesis as to the relation between time series for suicide and other forms of crime.

Artifact in the reporting of given types of crimes.

No apparent arbitrariness in the treatment of the problem, but problem is left unresolved.

p. 342. Also in relation to the hypothesis as to the relation between suicide and other forms of crime.

Artifact in the reporting of given types of crimes.

A certain arbitrariness in the assumptions made to treat the artifact.

Answers to Problem Exercise III

Presentation of Procedure and Error Factors

"These statistics are based on a mail canvass"

2 (a). Type of canvass

"supplemented by a field enumeration"

2 (a). Type of canvass

"conducted by the U.S. Forest Service and the Tennessee Valley Authority"

4. Auspices

"In the field enumerations Forest Service and TVA representatives"

3. Interviewer

"interviewed mills that did not respond to the mail canvass, and, in addition, conducted an intensive search for mills"

7. Nonresponse or

11. Sampling biases

"Among the smaller mills, bookkeeping is generally inadequate. Even the total cut for the mill may be an estimate, and the species breakdown for such a mill, particularly in areas of diversified growth, must frequently be estimated by the mill operator or by the enumerator. . . . Difficulties in enumeration because of lack of adequate mill records were overcome in many cases where the mill disposed of its total cut through a concentration yard. In such instances enumerators were able to obtain information for individual mills from the yard operator, particularly in the South and Southeast where concentration yards are an important factor in the distribution of lumber. This approach was not satisfactory, however, when an operator sold his lumber to several different yards in the course of the year, and where the records at the concentration yard did not indicate clearly whether the cut was for 1942 or 1941"

Possibly 1, also 5, also factor not explicitly denoted in original listing, i.e., "response error"

"Mills engaged solely in remanufacturing, finishing, or otherwise processing lumber were excluded"

Implicitly 11, Sampling Bias, more clearly "definition of population"

"In a number of cases, the mill reports were in terms of dressed or processed lumber, since many integrated mills, i.e., those both sawing and dressing, were able to report only on a finished basis. The discrepancy, which is of unknown magnitude, is equivalent to the amount of waste in processing. In canvassing integrated mills, however, the cut was counted at only one point in the processing operation, so that no duplication occurred"

5 (a). Ambiguity

"An ever-present complicating factor in the canvass was the extreme mobility of the smaller mills"

implicitly 7, Non-Response or omission or 11, Sampling Bias

Answers to Problem Exercise IV

Punch Card Processing for Explanatory Surveys

		Men				Women		
	Coll.	H.S.	Gmr.		Coll.	H.S.	Gmr.	
Col. 16–1	0	3	3		1	5	3	
2	3	2	2		0	1	0	
3	4	6	9		0	0	4	
4	6	15	15		12	13	16	
5	20	35	35		16	27	21	
6	13	18	24		17	48	21	
7	4	27	12		22	54	19	
8	2	2	3		1	18	4	
9	0	2	2		3	4	4	
0	0	0	1		3	2	2	
x	0	0	0		0	0	0	
y	1	0	0		2	1	0	
N	53	110	106	269 [3]	77	173	94	344 [3]

		College			High School			Grammar	
	A&B	C	D	A&B	C	D	A&B	C	D
Col. 40–1	7	15	2	8	45	19	12	37	21
2	13	40	3	16	78	20	5	37	31
3	10	25	3	11	51	19	3	20	11
4	5	5	0	0	9	2	4	3	9
5	1	1	0	0	4	1	0	4	3
N	36	86	8 130	35	187	61 283	24	101	75 200

Answers to Problem Exercise V

Selected Modes of Elaboration Employed in the Industrial Absenteeism Survey

Table I reflects an early analytic stage of the inquiry. It was part of the attempt to locate those groups within the work force who were more prone to absence and from the simple relationships observed to draw some inferences as to the causes of the phenomenon. In Table I it can be seen that women are more prone to absence than men, although the difference is only moderate in magnitude. Thus far the relationship has not been elaborated at all, and the analyst can only conjecture as to the validity of the finding and the processes that might underly such a relationship.

Table II grows out of such conjectures. Recalling the situation in wartime industry, the analysts consider a number of possibilities. Women were suddenly recruited in considerable numbers into the labor force during World War II. Perhaps, the apparent sex difference only reflects certain peculiarities of this historical pattern of recruitment. For example, women might constitute the *most recent* employees; the higher rate of absence might simply reflect the novelty of their situation and the consequent problems of adjustment. The women who were recruited into the labor force, under conditions of wartime emergency, came mainly from the ranks of the *married*, traditional housewives, and perhaps the higher rate of absence is a function of their role as house-

---

3. Total N's do not add up to 615 because one card in both male and female groups was coded y: education not ascertainable.

wives rather than characteristic of all women. Consequently, the analysts introduce in Table II a *third variable, marital status,* and re-examine the former relationship between absenteeism and sex. The elaboration at this point may either result in a *specification of the original relationship or a control for spuriousness.* The table can be inspected in either of two ways. We shall first examine the differences in proneness to absence between males and females when their status with respect to marriage is the same. We then observe that the sex difference persists *only among the married.* Single men and single women are equally prone, but married women are much more likely to be absent than married men, or for that matter than any of the three other groups in the table. The mode of elaboration is clearly that of *specification;* the condition under which the sex difference occurs is now specified. Incidentally, we observe that the original sex difference was not spurious. It cannot be completely obliterated by controlling marital status.

Table II may also be inspected in another way, although this does not follow the trend of the analysis we are now developing. We may, if we wish, examine the influence of marital status on absenteeism, and control for sex. This is done by comparing line 1 with line 3, and line 2 with line 4 in the table. We then observe that, among males, marital status has the effect of *reducing* the likelihood of absence; among females the effect is the opposite, marital status *increases* the likelihood of absence. Again the elaboration involves specification of the conditions under which marital status operates to affect rate of absence.

The findings of Table II lead to further conjectures and attempts at *interpretation* of the observed relationships. Why is it that married women are prone to absence? However, the analysts must also continue to direct their attention to questions of *spuriousness* and correspondingly the control of variables. All that Table II did was to examine *one particular* third variable, marital status. The analysts recall their earlier conjectures that still other factors, recency of employment and the like, might account for the original sex differences.

At this point the analysts do *not* engage in any higher order cross-tabulations involving *three* variables. They decide to examine the relation between the phenomenon of absenteeism and some of these other variables, using simple cross-tabulation procedures. These simple procedures are pre-sented in Tables 3 and 4. In this way, they will see whether their conjectures as to the role of these other factors in affecting absence have any validity. Depending on the outcome of these analyses, they will or will not engage in the complexities of elaborating relationships involving three variables.

Thus, they examine the relation between absenteeism and recency of employment. They observe a most interesting *curvilinear* relationship.[4] Those individuals who have been employed either for very long periods or very short periods in the plant are less prone to absence. It is the intermediate group in recency of employment which is most prone. This suggests, although it does not prove, that the original sex difference is probably not a function of recency of employment. Married women would be likely to be *very recent* employees, and if recency is not a factor in itself, there may be no need to control it in examining the relationship between sex and absenteeism. In itself, the table forces the analysts to conjecture as to what process would interpret such a relationship. Why should the "sophomores" in the plant be most prone to absence? Why should the newcomers be less prone to absence?

In Table IV, a Simple relationship is observed between the phenomenon of absenteeism and an index of general involvement or morale, the inclination to quit. Such a psychological variable is properly speaking an *intervening* variable, normally introduced by the analyst as an interpretive link between some antecedent condition and some consequence. However, within the confines of the table, it functions as an independent variable. The analysts are concerned with the hypothesis as to whether absence is a product of a more general orientation towards work. When this turns out to be the case, the analysts are encouraged to introduce this as a probable link to account for the relationships observed in Tables I and II. The proneness of women, more particularly married women, may reflect their lower general morale, which manifests itself in turn in absence.

The direction the analysis should be elaborated is certainly clear. There does not seem to be any *requirement* to re-examine the original relationship in the light of recency of employment, although that might be done. There certainly seems to be good reason to test the interpretation of the original relationships in terms of intervening variables of a morale nature.

Before the analysts pursue these elabora-

---

4. The reader will recall our earlier discussion in the text of the problems of curvilinear relationships and the need for examining relationships in terms of many groups varying in *refined degrees* on the independent variable. The table provides additional support for this analytic principle.

tions, however, they conjecture as to other interpretations of the original relationship. Perhaps, the proneness of married women to absence is not dependent on such psychological processes as lack of or loss of involvement in the work. Perhaps it is dependent on processes of a more objective nature. The married woman has heavy responsibilities. Perhaps when pressures occur and she has conflicts between such responsibilities and plans or desires to be present at work, she is forced into absence. Again before introducing such variables as links in the analysis between the original two variables, the analysts engaged in some simple cross-tabulations to provide some suggestive evidence as to whether such conjectures are warranted, and in turn, whether the higher order cross-tabulations shall be undertaken.

Table V represents a fragment of such analyses. As an approximate approach to such variables of responsibility and pressure, the analysts examine the relation between absence and the fact that in the family structure, both spouses are at work. Implicitly, such families will have difficult responsibilities which may force their members into absence. Such is seen to be the case.

In Table VI, we turn to an elaboration intended to *interpret* the original relationship between absence and marital status. The analysts re-examine the original finding of proneness to absence among married women in the light of the intervening variable of inclination to quit. It is observed that married women are more prone to absence than married men, even when they are matched in this morale index. Such women are prone to absence even when

their morale is good; and they are much more prone to absence than men who are equally demoralized. Clearly, the interpretive link to account for the behavior of *married women* lies in *another* direction, perhaps in the direction of other more objectified factors consonant with their role.

The last table presented in the exercise is again a prelude to refined elaborations. It is presented in correlational terms for purposes of compactness, but it is the equivalent of a series of higher order cross-tabulations. The relation between sex and absence is examined in the light of a third variable, the nature of the plant within which the respondent works. It is observed that the influence of sex on absence is dependent on the type of plant. The original relationship has now been further *specified*. Of course, it is specified only in terms of a *crude complex of factors* rather than a unitary and refined variable since the plants differ in a variety of ways. Nevertheless, it is highly informative, and the analysts intended it as a useful prelude to further tests of interpretation. The analysts turning from the negative evidence of Table VI sought the process underlying the proneness of married women in such objective conditions as pressures and hardships. The plants were known to differ in the circumstances of work, their transportation facilities, their provisions for various auxiliary measures and services which might ease the burden of the employee. The findings of Table VII suggest that indeed the key to the original relationship may lie in structural factors in the plant setting that mediate the likelihood that married women will be absent.

Index of Names and Studies

BOOKS PUBLISHED BY
The Free Press

LORD ACTON: *Essays on Freedom and Power* $6.00
ARISTIDES: *To Rome*   1.00
ARISTOTLE: *The Constitution of the Athenians*   temporarily out of print
MIKHAIL BAKUNIN: *The Political Philosophy of Bakunin*   6.00
EDWARD C. BANFIELD: *Government Project*   3.50
BERNARD BARBER: *Science and the Social Order*   4.50
SALO W. BARON: *Freedom and Reason*   5.00
REINHARD BENDIX AND SEYMOUR MARTIN LIPSET:
     Class, Status and Power: A Reader in Social Stratification   7.50
BERNARD BERELSON: *Content Analysis*
     in Communications Research   4.00
BERNARD BERELSON AND MORRIS JANOWITZ:
     Reader in Public Opinion and Communication   5.50
BRUNO BETTELHEIM: *Love Is Not Enough*   4.50
BRUNO BETTELHEIM: *Symbolic Wounds*   4.75
BRUNO BETTELHEIM: *Truants from Life: The Rehabilitation of*
     Emotionally Disturbed Children   5.00
HERBERT BUTTERFIELD: *The History of Science*   2.50
RICHARD CHRISTIE AND MARIE JAHODA: *Studies in the Scope*
     and Method of "The Authoritarian Personality"   4.50
ALBERT K. COHEN: *Delinquent Boys: The Culture of the Gang*   3.50
MORRIS R. COHEN: *American Thought*   5.00
MORRIS R. COHEN: *A Dreamer's Journey*   4.50
MORRIS R. COHEN: *King Saul's Daughter*   3.00
MORRIS R. COHEN: *Reason and Law*   4.00
MORRIS R. COHEN: *Reason and Nature*   6.00
MORRIS R. COHEN: *Reflections of a Wondering Jew*   2.75
DONALD R. CRESSEY: *Other People's Money*   3.00
HERBERT DINERSTEIN AND LEON GOURE: *Two Studies in*
     Soviet Controls   4.50
EMILE DURKHEIM: *The Division of Labor in Society*   5.00
EMILE DURKHEIM: *Elementary Forms of the Religious Life*   5.00